Edith Wharton

By R.W.B. Lewis

The American Adam

The Picaresque Saint

Trials of the Word

The Poetry of Hart Crane

Edith Wharton: A Biography

Editor:

Malraux: A Collection of Critical Essays

Herman Melville: A Reader

The Presence of Walt Whitman

*The Collected Short Stories of Edith
    Wharton*

*American Literature: The Makers and the
    Making* (with Cleanth Brooks and Robert
    Penn Warren)

Edith Wharton

A BIOGRAPHY

R.W. B. Lewis

HARPER & ROW, PUBLISHERS
New York, Evanston
San Francisco, London

Illustration Credits

Pictures 1, 2, 3, 4, 7, 14, 15, 16, 17, 20, 22, 24, 25, 26, 27, 29, 30 are from the William Royall Tyler Collection.

Pictures 5, 8, 9, 10, 11, 12, 13, 28 are from the Beinecke Library.

Pictures 6 is used courtesy of Mary Pitlick.

Picture 23 is from the Berenson Archives, Villa I Tatti.

Picture 18 is from the Smith College Archives.

Pictures 19 and 21 are used courtesy of Marion Mainwaring.

FIRST EDITION

Designed by C. Linda Dingler

Library of Congress Cataloging in Publication Data

Lewis, Richard Warrington Baldwin.
    Edith Wharton: a biography.
    Bibliography: p.
    Includes index.
    1. Wharton, Edith Newbold Jones, 1862–1937.
PS3545.H16Z696   813'.5'2   [B]   74–1833
ISBN 0–06–012603–5

75 76 77 78 79 10 9 8 7 6 5 4 3 2 1

For Nancy
and for N.L.L., S.B.L., and E.K.L.

Contents

x   *Contents*

V.   *The War Years: 1913–1918*

VI.   *The Possessive Years: 1919–1937*

Appendixes

Preface

When Edith Wharton—at the time, the early 1920s, the most renowned writer of fiction in America—broached to her publisher the idea of writing her autobiography, she explained that she thought she should do it "to avoid it being done inaccurately by someone else after my death, should it turn out that my books survive long enough to make it worth while to write my biography." A decade later, in 1934, after she had completed her memoirs, *A Backward Glance*, she observed to a friend that she had hesitated before writing them, "but one sees nowadays so many post-mortems attempted by biographers on a basis of guesswork and gossip, that I thought I would rather tell my uneventful story myself!" Even so, when Edith Wharton's papers were delivered to the Yale University Library a year after her death, they included a packet labeled, in her own hand, "For My Biographer." (The packet consisted mostly of letters relating to her husband's various illnesses and her divorce from him in 1913.) She obviously expected to be the subject of a biography, and she has proven an uncommonly cooperative one.

The point may be stressed: if Edith Wharton did look forward rather fearfully to being given biographical treatment, she also took pains to see that the biographer would have at his disposal as complete a record as possible. In this regard she differed markedly from, say, Emily Dickinson, Henry James, or Willa Cather, writers who carefully destroyed a great many personal documents and who left strict instructions about the eventual burning or long inaccessibility of other papers. Edith Wharton destroyed relatively little and destroyed selectively—most notably, the letters she had written Walter Van Renssellaer Berry and the majority of letters Berry had written to her over the years. She left behind, meanwhile, a number of extraordinarily revealing documents: diaries, unpublished poems, fragments of autobiography, unfinished stories, which, to speak personally, shook to pieces most of the preconceptions with which I came to this work.

My understanding of Edith Wharton, some eight years ago, had been established by the graceful and adroit *Portrait of Edith Wharton* by her English friend Percy Lubbock, published in 1947. I took her to be an undoubtedly fascinating woman and, as the author of *Ethan Frome*, *The Age of Innocence*, and *The House of Mirth*, a person of high literary accomplishment. But she struck me, in

Lubbock's account, as rather too much of the *grande dame*, the aloof and fashionable woman of the world who, in the old-fashioned phrase, really did "draw herself up" when expressing disapproval. She was an individual, I had gathered, whose private life was a narrow one, who was cool and even abrasive in her outward relationships, and puritanically repressed within. She even seemed to take her art more casually than she should, between her duties as a busy hostess.

But early and late, in Europe and in this country, I came upon unsettling evidence that Edith Wharton had preserved (as it turned out) for my illumination. She was one of the most intelligent American women who ever lived, and there is no doubt that she was looking forward with customary shrewdness. She foresaw the stiffly conventional image of herself that would be perpetuated by Percy Lubbock and others, and she wanted to have her posthumous say about the realities of her life and character.

In a diary she kept spasmodically between 1924 and 1934, she remarked: "If I ever have a biographer, it is in these notes that he will find the gist of me." This particular diary is, in fact, disappointingly sparse, but it reflects her increasing concern over the figure she would cut in years to come. Her aim, she told herself, was to

gather together the floating scraps of experience that have lurked for years in corners of my mind. . . . I may even be able to jot down a sketch of myself—my own growth and history. When I get a glimpse, in books and reviews, of the things people are going to assert about me after I am dead, I feel I must have the courage and perseverance, some day, to forestall them.

She wanted, in short, to outflank her observers and to be known in her entirety, as she truly was. She came to see herself, I think, as a creature of impulses, experiences, and reaches of the imagination that a well-bred woman was not supposed capable of in an age of delimiting propriety, of imposed disguises. Edith Wharton made no real attempt to depict such a creature in her own autobiography—though she did begin to do so in a fifty-page fragment called "Life and I," which she apparently, and rightly, decided it was not yet timely to publish. She looked beyond her lifetime toward an age, like ours, of greater freedom and candor.

But in addition to the more startling evidential findings, there are many hundreds of letters by her, and comments by her ever-watchful friends, in which one comes upon feelings, attitudes, and habits of conduct that accumulate into a picture of a woman hardly recognizable alongside the Edith Wharton of legend. There was, after all, a fund of passion and of laughter in her, and almost unbelievable energy. There was genuine daring of both a personal and a literary variety. She was as materially generous as, for the most part, she was spiritually kind, and she had a lifelong capacity (upon which almost everyone who knew her well has remarked) for deep and abiding friendship.

As the years went by, she also developed a knack for occasionally infuriating some of the most devoted among her friends; more than one of them oscillated between adoration and fits of seething impatience. No account of her should fail to say that she could be excessively demanding of those close to her, especially in her later years, and humiliatingly curt or embarrassingly icy with strangers. She entertained prejudices that, however one explains them by reference to her background and to the times, one can only find regrettable. She was too large a person, one feels, for these clichés of bigotry.

At the same time, for all her strength of character, she was vulnerable in the extreme, particularly when it came to human relationships. She was not spared a series of blows under which a person of less strength might well have staggered and fallen. But neither was she denied her long moment of emotional gratification. What she called her "uneventful life" was in certain periods so eventful—in both an exhilarating and a wounding manner—that she could barely keep pace.

On the literary side, Edith Wharton was almost without peer in her American generation as a judge of achievement in fiction and poetry. She was decades ahead of critical opinion in her high assessment and appreciation of poets as remote from each other as John Donne and Walt Whitman; and her most unfashionable pronouncements in the 1920s on new literary idols like Joyce and Eliot seem, in certain special perspectives, to have more cogency with every passing year.

Her dedication to her own creative task, meanwhile, was complete, and no one worked more strenuously or revised more thoroughly. It was her habit of deprecating her talent—when measured against that of the great masters of fiction—that could be construed by the unperceptive as indicating a less than wholehearted involvement. It is the conviction behind this biography, after the statutory observation that her work was decidedly "uneven," that a good many of her books have survived (to pick up her word) and will continue to survive. They have an elegant shapeliness of form: Thomas Traherne's "Order the beauty even of Beauty is" was one of her favorite quotations. With their muted subtleties, their preciseness of allusion, and above all the compassion for the wounded or thwarted life that flows through them, they are among the handsomest achievements in our literature. I have wondered, with other admirers of Edith Wharton, whether her reputation might today stand even higher if she had been a man.

Her writings find their larger human implications out of a vast imaginative report on one segment of American social history and on Americans glimpsed over more than forty years amid the international community. They are also quiet, continuing testimony to the female experience under modern historical and social conditions, to the modes of entrapment, betrayal, and exclusion devised for women in the first decades of the American and European twentieth century.

In view of the steady vein of satire and irony with which even the most poignant moments are sometimes tinged, her writings may likewise be taken as Edith Wharton's *comédie humaine*, in the phrase employed about his own *oeuvre* by one of her favorite novelists, Honoré de Balzac. As such, they accurately reflect Edith Wharton's life, which itself appears in retrospect as a *comédie humaine*, with all the vicissitudes and varieties of experience the phrase implies.

The question of the relation between the life and the work, always a central one for the literary biographer, has an engrossing complexity in Edith Wharton's case. Like most other writers, she drew upon her life for her fiction; *Ethan Frome*, for example, is one of the most autobiographical stories ever written. But like fewer other writers—among them Henry James—she also drew upon her fiction for her life. She turned back to her work at times to interpret and appraise particular situations she found herself caught up in. The final twist occurred in her later years. In her fifties and sixties, her deepest feelings were reserved for her work; it was there, in her novels and stories, that they had their real existence. As a consequence, she took to drawing upon her writings *for* her writings, creating new novels in part out of the emotional and psychological ingredients of old novels or unfinished fragments of novels. This phenomenon will need further exploration. But whatever else the pattern may suggest, it demonstrates that Edith Wharton was a literary personality to her fingertips.

The scores of individuals who have been of indispensable help to me in the writing of this book are gratefully acknowledged in the back. One can also find there a list of the correspondences, memoirs, and other sources I have made use of, and their locations. My major acknowledgment, not for the first time, is at the head of my dedicatees.

R. W. B. LEWIS

Florence, Italy, 1969
Bethany, Connecticut, 1974

Old New York: 1862-1890

1. The Span of Time

On Tuesday, January 24, 1922, Edith Wharton wrote in her diary *"Aet. 60!"* The weather was rainy and windy, she noted with precision; the temperature was 45 degrees Fahrenheit. She was spending the winter at Ste. Claire, a château above Hyères on the southern coast of France which she had leased and remodeled two years before, and the possession of which was one of the joys of her life. "I am thrilled to the spine," she wrote a friend as negotiations were concluding. *"Il y va de mon avenir,* and I feel as if I were going to get married—to the right man at last!"

Edith Wharton's literary fortunes were at their peak. Her novel *The Age of Innocence,* after immense critical and commercial success, had won the Pulitzer Prize the previous year. She was preparing an introduction to a handsome special edition of *Ethan Frome,* first published a decade earlier and now well established as the most widely admired of her books—though not, she had observed dryly, the most widely bought. It would still be almost two decades before the story became a perennial seller. The work in progress was *New Year's Day,* a tale about a muted scandal in the society Edith Wharton had known in her youth, and the last of the four novellas which (under the collective title *Old New York*) would further heighten her reputation. The second of them, *The Old Maid,* had been written in the last months of 1921, and had been rejected by several magazines because of what one editor called "its powerful but unpleasant subject"—illegitimacy, a subject in which Edith Wharton was alleged by some to have a personal interest. (On the question of Edith Wharton's own rumored illegitimacy, see Appendix A.)

Appleton and Company, her chief publishers since 1912, were about to pay Mrs. Wharton a tribute by bringing out a pamphlet—timed to coincide with the publication of her next novel, *The Glimpses of the Moon* (it too a huge and instant success)—in which she would be credited with the "unique achievement . . . of possessing a distinguished style and a sophisticated point of view, and at the same time, of producing, whenever she feels like it, a best-seller."

Her novels, the pamphlet would claim, were marked by a "clear perception of vital and universal things," along with a "magnificent gift of story-telling, pure and simple." Edith Wharton tended to undervalue her work—her friends felt that she measured it against excessively high standards—and she was generally indifferent to praise, especially of so platitudinous a kind. She was pleased, however, by this particular eulogy. The author of it, Katharine Fullerton Gerould, was at once a novelist of some real competence and the cousin of a man who at one time had played a central role in Edith Wharton's life.

The morning of her sixtieth birthday was devoted to writing. She awoke early, and after discussing the plans and menus for the day with Gross, her Alsatian housekeeper, and Elise, her French personal maid, Edith Wharton set to work. She did so sitting up in bed with a loose silk cap covering her abundant auburn hair, a writing board on her knees, scribbling steadily in pen on foolscap. Books, magazines, and correspondence were strewn across the foot of the bed, and a small Pekinese lay asleep under her left elbow. Through the bedroom window she could see the thin strip of land that curved out into the Mediterranean to the Giens peninsula. As the pages of *New Year's Day* were finished, they were allowed to drift to the floor, thence to be rescued by her secretary, Jeanne Duprat, and carried away to be typed. Around noon, dressed and buckled, combed and manicured, she went downstairs to the library. There her houseguest of the moment, Robert Norton, was awaiting her.

Most days, this was the time for a stroll through the elaborate gardens she had created on the several levels of Ste. Claire, followed by a meticulously arranged picnic on the beach of a nearby cove or in the hills toward Toulon. The weather this day prevented any such excursion; the southeast gales that began to blow in the afternoon, with bursts of rain, also ruled out the customary drive through the local countryside. Two days before, Edith Wharton and her guest had motored to the top of Mont des Oiseaux and then had walked down to Les Plantiers in Costebelle to call on her old friends Paul Bourget and his ethereal wife, Minnie. The day before that they had explored the slopes above St. Bernard, the adjoining villa recently purchased for the young Vicomte de Noailles.

Housebound on her birthday, Edith Wharton spent the afternoon sorting books in her library and drawing room. She had learned from Bernhard Berenson, the great art critic, to take a professional librarian's attitude toward her own private library, and the disposition of books—which flowed in daily by mail and hand—was a severe and necessary exercise in imposing order on impending disarray. At teatime there arrived the Comtesse Philomène de Lévis-Mirepoix, a younger friend who both fascinated and puzzled her.

Other guests were expected in the days to come, and she listed them carefully in the back of her diary. They constituted her "regulars," an inner circle bereft now of Henry James and one or two others particularly dear to her over many years. She had counted the more on this community of friends ever since she had largely withdrawn from Paris *salon* life.

On February 1, Percy Lubbock, the adroit English biographer and editor and inordinately graceful stylist, would appear. Ten days later Margaret (Mrs. Winthrop) Chanler, whom Edith had known since 1867, was to be met at 7:40 P.M. at the Toulon station. Elisina Tyler, indispensable aide-de-camp and friend since the first days of the war, was due on the twenty-second, bringing with her Gioia Grant Richards, her daughter by a former marriage. It might even be that William Tyler, Gioia's eleven-year-old half brother and Edith Wharton's favorite among small boys, would come down from his school in England. Mary Cadwalader Jones, Edith's beloved and sometimes exasperating sister-in-law, was expected on March 14. And on March 9 there would be Walter Berry, that evasive figure (then head of the American Chamber of Commerce in Paris) whom "Daisy" Chanler once described as "the dominant seventh chord" in Edith Wharton's life.

Gaillard Lapsley, the American don teaching at Cambridge in England, had come and gone. Neither Berenson nor John Hugh Smith, most cultivated and tough-minded of English bankers, would be present this season. But otherwise, almost every member of the inner circle could be looked forward to. Meanwhile, there was *New Year's Day* to get on with writing, and immediately after it *False Dawn*, another of the *Old New York* novellas. Contemplating this latter tale, Edith Wharton was carried back in memory to stories her parents had told her of certain romantic events that had occurred some years before her own birth, and that had eventually led to it.

2

A little less than sixty years earlier, on April 20, 1862, after a brief ceremony in Grace Church, on the corner of Broadway and Eleventh Street in Manhattan, the baptism of Edith Newbold Jones was recorded in the parish register. The name "Jones" at the extreme left commanded the entries running across the page. The date of the child's birth was given as January 24, 1862. Her sponsors were Mrs. Thomas H. Newbold and Mr. Frederick J. Rhinelander, Edith's aunt and uncle on her mother's side, and a Miss C. King. In the column where the parents' names were to be listed, there was inscribed "George F. & ———." At a later date the blank was filled in with the penciled notation "Lucretia Rhinelander."

The absence of Lucretia Rhinelander Jones's name from the original record is a puzzle that is only heightened by the fact that it is equally missing from the baptismal register of Edith's two older brothers, Frederic in January 1846 and Harry in May 1850. Such maternal reticence over so long a period is without parallel in the Grace Church records; and although Lucretia was nominally a member of Calvary Church in Gramercy Park, her name was well enough known to the Rector and the upper-middle-class congregation of Grace Church, where it was more fashionable to have one's child baptized.

The society to which Lucretia Jones belonged held firmly to the principle that a lady's name should appear publicly on only three occasions: birth, marriage, and death. Did Lucretia adhere so literally to this rule that she refused to lend her name even to a modest public statement of her children's christenings? If so, she was virtually the only woman in New York society who did. Other possible explanations rise and wither; the true one no doubt lies buried in some unfathomable eccentricity on the part of the always somewhat baffling Mrs. Jones.

The infant girl who was born in January 1862 during a critical moment of the American Civil War would live to see the storm clouds gathering over Europe on the eve of the Second World War, and would somberly recognize them. During the long years between, she saw several of her friends depart for the Spanish-American conflict and spent the whole of the First World War in France, working endlessly for the hordes of Belgian refugees who came flooding into Paris and making frequent visits to the forward areas and the actual battle scenes.

The span of Edith Wharton's lifetime—1862 to 1937—can be measured in other ways, and the enormous changes that were wrought in it go far to account for one of her major literary themes: significant historical change and its impact upon the individual. Abraham Lincoln was President of the United States when Edith was born. It seems likely that she attended a reception at Newport for President Chester Arthur in the 1880s. In 1905 she had lunch at the White House, the guest of her ebullient friend and fellow book lover Theodore Roosevelt. Roosevelt was for her the model American statesman, and she had only harsh words for Woodrow Wilson, especially since he seemed so laggard about leading his country into the war. She lived to be dismayed by the second election of Franklin Delano Roosevelt, a man she regarded as no better than a socialist.

She also lived to see Germany, the country she had explored so extensively and affectionately before the First World War, fall into the hands of Adolf Hitler, to whose "angry screams and accusations of cowardice" she listened, appalled, on her wireless set. And she looked on with mounting revulsion while Italy—always to some extent the country of her heart, and one that she had known intimately since she was five—succumbed to Fascism and the dictatorship of Benito Mussolini. But long before those quasi-apocalyptic developments, she had enjoyed from within the varied enchantments of what the French came to call nostalgically *la belle époque*, that time of seemingly permanent grandeur between the turn of the century and the outbreak of war in 1914. She had experienced the slow, profound transformation of the England she knew, as the Victorian age gave way to the Edwardian, and that in turn to the Georgian.

There were other sizable changes during her life that she not only adjusted to but rejoiced in. These included technological innovations, in her response to which Edith Wharton proved herself very much a woman of the twentieth century. In her childhood she drove a dogcart in the summer at Newport, and in the winter went about New York in her parents' elegant horse-drawn carriage. But she was one of the first American women to own and make great use of what she always called a "motor-car." She had in succession a Panhard, a Mercedes, a Peugeot, and a Lincoln, and by the end there were few roads on the European continent or in Great Britain or New England along which she had not been driven by one or another of her series of chauffeurs.

"The motor-car has restored the romance of travel," she once remarked, and there you have one of the quintessential aspects of her nature. The new technology was welcomed because it brought back the old romance. Motoring was by all odds her favorite form of travel. She made some sixty trips back and forth across the Atlantic, on many of the greatest steamers of her day; but though her accommodations were almost always luxurious, with ample space for housekeeper and maid, she declared that sea voyages made her nervous. She quite reveled in the new deluxe trains after the war, and from Paris took the Blue Train to the Riviera, the Golden Arrow on the ferry to England, the Arlberg–Orient Express to Salzburg.

She was on hand to witness one of the first significant tests of a French airplane (it climbed to some nine hundred feet) in the spring of 1908, and a year later, from the Place de la Concorde, she watched the first plane to fly over the city of Paris. She herself never traveled by air, but in later years she regularly met guests or saw them off at Le Bourget airport, and of a summer afternoon saw the daily plane to London roaring over her suburban villa at St. Brice.

Edith Jones began to peck at the new typewriting machine soon after it was invented in the early 1870s—though as Edith Wharton, she long used the word "typewriter" to refer to the young lady who typed her stories. She grew so dependent upon the telephone that she was shocked when she discovered that the country house she had rented for the summer of 1914 was lacking in that indispensable instrument. By the time the first motion pictures were being experimented with, she was solidly established as a leading American novelist, and a six-reeler was made of *The House of Mirth* some years after its publication in 1905. In the 1920s a successful film, starring Bebe Daniels and Nita Naldi, was made of *The Glimpses of the Moon*. There were dickerings about film versions of others of her novels, and at the time of her death an excellent screening of *The Old Maid* was in the making. Edith Wharton herself appears never to have entered a movie theater.

The literary age of Edith Wharton may be said to have begun with Henry Wadsworth Longfellow, whose friendly words about some of her adolescent verses led to one of them being published in the *Atlantic Monthly*. Later she was on terms of varying intimacy with three of the most eminent American writers before the First World War: William Dean Howells; even more, Henry Adams; most of all, Henry James. After that generation passed, she was surprised and touched by the warm admiration, almost the reverence, expressed to her by

Sinclair Lewis and F. Scott Fitzgerald. In her final years she was much in the company of Aldous Huxley, a winter neighbor on the Riviera. She shared a friendship, greatly valued on both sides, with Kenneth Clark, and became godmother to his second son. She met up several times with the young Italian novelist Alberto Moravia.

A writer whose literary relationships embraced Longfellow and Moravia is not an easy one to take sights on. Yet it is another measure of Edith Wharton and the range of her literary world that the British novelist whose output she came most to respect was Anthony Trollope, while she struggled for years against what she regarded as the exaggerated claims made for James Joyce's *Ulysses*—retaining a peculiarly skeptical eye about the psychological authenticity of Molly Bloom's long concluding erotic monologue.

3

If these various tides of history flowed forward over the years of Edith Wharton's life, in her own vision—when she was writing her autobiography *A Backward Glance* in the early 1930s—the history that had a personal meaning for her could also be seen receding backward in time, at least as far as the Boston Tea Party and the American Revolution. She was slow to take an interest in ancestry; when she did it was not in genealogical charts but in human realities with which she could feel some personal connection, in personalities remembered and anecdotes handed down. Of all her more remote ancestors, the one who appealed to her most was Ebenezer Stevens, who performed valiantly as an artillery officer throughout the Revolutionary War.

Stevens, who could in turn trace his ancestry in the New World back to the 1630s and one of the most disputatious of the New England divines, was the grandfather of Edith Wharton's mother: "our great progenitor," Edith Wharton called him. At the age of seventeen, in 1768, he joined a Boston artillery company, and it was this company that late in 1773 was ordered by Samuel Adams to patrol the fleet of English ships that had entered the Boston Harbor and to prevent their shipments of tea from being landed. "I went from the South Meeting House just after dark," Stevens would recall, telling his sons about the Boston Tea Party.

The party was about seventy or eighty. At the head of the wharf we met the detachment of our company on guard, who joined us. . . . We commenced handling the boxes of tea on deck, and first commenced breaking them with axes, but found much difficulty, owing to the boxes being covered with canvas—the mode that this article was then imported in. I think that all the tea was discharged in about two hours. We were careful to prevent any being taken away; *none of the party were painted as Indians*, nor, that I know of, disguised, except that some of them had stopped at a paint shop on the way and daubed their faces with paint.

Stevens was appointed first lieutenant in a company of artillery he helped organize, took part in the Battle of Bunker Hill, and in June 1776 was attached to the headquarters of Major General Horatio Gates at Ticonderoga. It was Stevens who deployed the artillery battalion that played a central role in the defeat of General Burgoyne at Saratoga; one American eyewitness to this turning point in American military history described "the commanding officer of artillery, Major Stevens" as "gallant, vigilant and ready to improve every advantage."

In 1778 Stevens, now a lieutenant colonel, came under the command of the young Marquis de Lafayette. The two became close friends and soldiered together during the last stages of the war.

Many years later, Lafayette, after meeting one of Stevens' sons in Paris, wrote his old comrade in the following warm terms:

> Paris, July 13, 1822
>
> I seldom have felt so great a gratification as when I discovered it was your son whom I took by the hand, and with whom I could talk of our old times and your actual situation. Those American times have been the happiest period of my public life; the remembrance of my brotherly friends in the army do more lively vibrate in my heart. I was therefore highly pleased to hear of you and very affectionately interested by the particulars I received from your worthy son. What I have seen of him has appeared to me an object of sincere congratulations to you. Receive them, my dear sir, as heartily as they are offered and believe me
>
> your faithful friend
> Lafayette.

Stevens, who entered New York with his regiment the very day the British departed, decided to remain in that city. He proved as zestful and as "ready to improve every advantage" in business as in war, and before long had his own fleet of ships to carry on trade around the world. Nor did his public career abate: he became, among other things, agent of the War Department, a member of the New York assembly, and a major general of the Artillery of the State of New York.

A number of Ebenezer Stevens' eleven children—most of them by Lucretia Ledyard, the daughter of a Hartford judge and according to Edith Wharton a "dusky and handsome lady"—enhanced the clan's prestige by marrying into families of weight and distinction on the New York scene. Rebecca married John Peter Schermerhorn of the rock-solid mercantile family. Byam Kerby Stevens brought into the family Frances Gallatin, the daughter of Jefferson's Secretary of the Treasury and minister to England and France. It was the youngest of the general's children, Mary Lucretia Lucy Ann (born in 1798), who made the alliance with the Rhinelanders by marrying Frederic William of that name. Their first child, Lucretia Stevens, Edith Wharton's mother, was born in 1824.

When she was fifteen Edith Jones was taken by her parents to the Capitol in Washington to see John Trumbull's famous Revolutionary War canvases in the Rotunda, and the figure of her great-grandfather was pointed out to her in the two surrender scenes at Saratoga and Yorktown. What drew her to her great progenitor, then and later, was his tremendous energy, his "swift adaptability," his appetite for adventurous experience whether in war or commerce. It must have been from Stevens too—one looks elsewhere in vain—that she inherited her zest for the crowded and the far-flung life. It is even possible to see a physical resemblance in her erect head, her keen sidelong glance, her strong, almost masculine jawline. During the war, when she was running a massive organization to house and feed refugees, she was known to her fellow workers as "our commander in chief."

4

The Rhinelanders could claim no single figure as impressive as Ebenezer Stevens, but a number of them showed themselves even more astute—perhaps one should add more ruthless—than Stevens in matters financial. The first of them, a Huguenot émigré, came to America in 1686 and acquired considerable property in New Rochelle, New York. But the family fortune was effectively begun by William and Frederick Rhinelander, two enterprising young men who moved onward from a little bakery shop on William Street in Manhattan during the Revolution to canny dealings in sugar and then to shipbuilding and foreign trade.

The revenue from these ventures was used to purchase land in Manhattan. Accusations have not been lacking against the Rhinelanders, any more than they have against other wealth-accumulating families, of acquiring land and water grants in New York by shady maneuverings. Like the Astors and others, the Rhinelanders did a thriving rental business from a number of overcrowded and totally neglected tenement houses. Although no precise figure is possible for the holdings of such millionaires, the estate of William Rhinelander was estimated around 1900 as upwards of fifty million dollars.

Soon after the Revolution the original William had married Mary Robart, a singularly lovely young woman if her portrait is to be trusted, a descendant herself of a Huguenot family which, like the first Rhinelander, had come to America in 1686. She also appears to have been a rather lordly creature, and may have been the source of the imperious side, which sometimes showed, of her great-granddaughter. The William Rhinelanders had seven children, the sixth of whom, Frederick William (born in 1796), married Mary Lucretia Lucy Ann Stevens.

It was the misfortune of their first-born, Lucretia, having passed her childhood in a sort of dwindling affluence, to spend the psychologically critical years of her adolescence in something like poverty. Her father, a handsome and intelligent man, was one of the few forebears of Edith Wharton to be traceably addicted to the reading of books; by the same token, he lacked the customary Rhinelander drive in business affairs. When he died in 1836, at the age of forty, his widow turned his already diminished fortune over to his older brother. The latter, who had grown rich by marrying the land-owning Miss Rutgers, grew richer still—Edith Wharton would say—by manipulating his late brother's finances to his own benefit, unworried that Mary Stevens Rhinelander and her children "remained poor."

Lucretia was twelve when her father died. A notebook she was given in her thirteenth year, and in which she made sparse and intermittent entries, reveals a starved, cramped, touching little life. There are bits of poetry about "woman" (including Wordsworth's "A perfect creature nobly planned . . .") and sadly conventional passages about home and mother, death and eternal repose. There is an occasional touch of wan humor, the source of which would dry up with the years. The high points were a few visits to West Point in her sixteenth year, and from such moments two or three leaves were plucked and pressed forlornly among the pages.

At her social debut Lucretia wore a white tarlatan gown pieced together at home and her mother's decrepit and ill-fitting white slippers. She would speak about the indignity and physical suffering of that evening with never-failing resentment. One probably need seek no further for an explanation of Lucretia Jones's all-consuming passion in later years for fashionable costumes and the impatience with which she awaited the annual new wardrobe from Paris.

But "poor" is a relative word when the Rhinelanders are in question. Lucretia Rhinelander, along with her two younger sisters and her brother, was educated by English governesses and tutors, and was taught needlework, drawing, and the chief European languages; a deep respect for correctness (though not at all stiffness) of English speech was early instilled in her. Each child had her or his own horse and riding habit. The family home at Hell Gate, just north of the city, was not lacking in servants and comfort.

Each of the children, moreover, grew up to "marry well." Lucretia's sister Mary, who was a beauty, married the well-established Thomas Newbold. Frederick married Frances Skinner, and Eliza was wed to the young and dashing Commodore Edgar. Around 1842 Lucretia herself met George Frederic Jones, a young man of splendid expectations.

5

George Jones was twenty-one years old, the youngest of the three surviving children of Edward Renshaw and Elizabeth Schermerhorn Jones. The year before he met Lucretia he had graduated from Columbia College, where he had pursued an awkwardly constructed and short-lived program of studies known as "The

Literature and Scientific Course" (a combination of intellectual interests which would also appeal to his daughter). He seems to have been an amiable if rather sober youth, yet with a streak of the romantic in him and a shy taste for poetry. He had been mostly confined to the family homes on Mercer Street in Manhattan and on Long Island Sound; but at the age of seventeen he had made the prescribed tour of Europe with his father, and another time had traveled across the United States at least as far as the mouth of the Mississippi.

He was undoubtedly good-looking: six feet tall, with black hair and dark blue eyes; a high forehead, straight nose, rounded chin, and fair complexion; and an erect bearing. He had grown up amid sumptuous conditions. George Frederic would recall for his daughter Edith—and she in turn would linger over it in the novella *False Dawn*, based in part upon her father's courtship—the extravagant meals sometimes laid out on the tables assembled on the lawn of the country home which swept down from the classically styled house to the water. There would be platters piled high with raspberries, strawberries, and Delaware peaches; a Virginia ham surrounded by cookies, strawberry shortcake, and hot cornbread; scrambled eggs on toast and broiled bluefish; side dishes of deviled turkey legs and creamed chicken hash; endless heaps of waffles and silver jugs of maple syrup.

The youth's manly appearance, the glamour of his surroundings, and the small fortune he had inherited after his father's death in 1839 were more than enough to attract the youngest of the "poor Rhinelander girls." There was some opposition to the match from George Frederic's family—though probably not from his kindly and cautiously liberal older brother Edward. It came most likely from his widowed mother and perhaps even more from his much older unmarried sister, a severe and repressive woman.

George Frederic in love proved himself both persistent and resourceful. He took to stealing down at dawn to a cove where he kept a large rowboat. He improvised a mast—all this can be found in *False Dawn*, as well as in *A Backward Glance*—by lashing the oars together end to end and fixing them upright in the boat, attached the quilt from his bed as a sail, and guided his little craft a few miles along the Sound to a beach near Hell Gate. Here the lovers met. The secret courtship went forward, and eventually such family disapproval as there was evaporated. George Frederic and Lucretia were married on October 17, 1844, at Hell Gate. The groom was not quite twenty-three. The bride was nineteen.

They took a long honeymoon in Cuba, where they drove about in *volantes* and paid visits to the fashionable plantations. Back in New York, they moved into a house of their own at 80 East Twenty-first Street, in Gramercy Park. In January 1846 their first child, Frederic Rhinelander, was born.

When Lucretia Jones was asked which Mrs. Jones she happened to be, she would reply firmly—so it has been said—"I am *the* Mrs. Jones." Not many members of New York society would have conceded her that honor: there were simply too many rivals for it. One looks, indeed, with a certain consternation through the intricate genealogies of the proliferating Jones clan, even if one stays within hailing distance of George Frederic and does not go back as far as the John Jones who came to America from Cornwall in the early eighteenth century and was buried in the Trinity Church cemetery, or his descendant of the same name who acquired the 132-acre farm, part of it later known as Jones's Wood, extending north from East Sixty-sixth Street in Manhattan to Seventy-fifth and from Third Avenue to the East River.

What the expanding network of family relationships gave Edith Wharton was a heightened awareness of *kinship* in the old New York she had known: the society she belonged to was, as someone has put it, one vast community of cousins. There were, for example, a number of marriages, perhaps as many as five, between Joneses and Schermerhorns (the latter name, incidentally, being pronounced something like "Skairmern" in the nineteenth century, as Rhinelander was pronounced "Ryelanner"). George Frederic's father, as has been mentioned, was married to Elizabeth Schermerhorn. His aunt Sarah was the wife of Peter Schermerhorn—"Peter the Younger"—who crowned the family's financial triumphs by becoming a director of the Bank of New York.

Abraham Schermerhorn, the brother of Peter and Elizabeth, became the father of the Caroline Schermerhorn who, after marrying William Backhouse Astor, succeeded in establishing herself as *the* Mrs. Astor. This regal creature, leader and part founder of the social elite known as "The 400," was thus a first cousin of George Frederic Jones and a first cousin once removed of Edith Wharton, who would draw a somewhat harrowing picture of her in the tale "After Holbein."

Then there were the many marriages between the Joneses and the Masons, and it is in this branch of the family that we locate the most arresting of Edith Wharton's Jones relations: Mary Mason (Mrs. Isaac) Jones, one of the great ladies of the still older New York, and a magnificent wreck of a survival in Edith's youth. Aunt Mary Mason, after living for some years in downtown Waverley Place, startled society by moving almost beyond visibility to build a majestic Parisian mansion on Fifth Avenue between Fifty-seventh and Fifty-eighth Streets: a structure of pale cream stone with balustraded pavilions looming up amid the debris, the rocks, and the makeshift shanties that otherwise characterized the area. Here, with advancing years and increasing obesity, she lived in a suite off the entry hall from which she would be carried in to dominate a reception (as it might be) for a great-granddaughter. Edith Wharton, after drawing Aunt Mary into more than one of her short stories, would have her preside over a good part of *The Age of Innocence* in the guise of the redoubtable Mrs. Manson Mingott —shrewd, overwhelming, profoundly benevolent.

Of Edith Wharton's more immediate family, she had relatively little to say about her grandfather Edward Renshaw Jones, a shadowy figure who improved the family fortunes both by his business activities and by his marriage to Miss Schermerhorn. Two of his five children, Margaret and Joshua, contracted tuberculosis and, following the curious Anglo-American habit, went to Rome to seek the cure. Like a number of others, they died there and were buried in the Protestant cemetery. When their sister fell victim to the same disease, her parents simply shut her up in her bedroom, sealed the windows and lit the fire, and kept her there for nine months. She emerged in robust health and lived into stiff-backed old age. For her niece, she was a Gothic terror inhabiting a Gothic mansion at Rhinebeck-on-Hudson whose ugly turrets and harsh exterior quite resembled (so Edith thought) her own grimly crenelated features.

It is perhaps a pity that Edith Wharton scarcely had the opportunity to know her uncle Edward Jones, who died in 1869 when Edith was seven and living abroad. Edward Jones, nine years older than his brother George Frederic, was a physician by profession, a dryly engaging human being, and for two decades (from 1849 onward) an influential member of Columbia University's board of trustees. With the astronomer Lewis Rutherford and the great diarist George Templeton Strong, he formed the liberal bloc which helped select a new uptown site for Columbia and introduced graduate study in law and mining. He also helped liberate the board from its traditional control by the clerical representatives. A usually staunch and congenial colleague, Strong reported; a man of high character and good judgment, Columbia said upon his death.

6

George Frederic and Lucretia—or "Lu," as he called her—were in Paris with their two-year-old son Freddie when revolution broke out in February 1848. They had spent the previous year in a long slow tour of Europe, traveling as far east as Prague and gathering attractive memories for family conversation. At Waterloo they had been guided over the battlefield by a British veteran of the great encounter; in the Volksgarten in Vienna they had listened to Johann Strauss the Elder playing his own waltzes with "a very fine band"; in Florence they had enjoyed the annual grape festival. They had attended an early performance of Verdi's *Macbeth* in Rome, and in the course of his wanderings through the city George Frederic had struck up a friendship with Luther Terry, an artist expatriated from Connecticut, addicted to large, solemn, neoclassical paintings. Many years later Terry's daughter Margaret (eventually Mrs. Chanler) and George Frederic's daughter Edith would become the closest of friends.

The Joneses had been in Paris six weeks when the uproar started with the resignation under pressure of Louis Philippe's minister François Guizot, a torch-light victory parade, and the onslaught of the Municipal Guard which killed a number of the celebrants. Agitated Americans rushed in to the Jones suite in the

Hotel Windsor, on the Rue de Rivoli, with each latest dispatch—finally, with the news that the seventy-four-year-old king had been forced to abdicate and, with Queen Marie Amélie, had fled to St. Cloud. A republic was declared with Alphonse de Lamartine as its provisional head. Staring out of the *salon* windows, George Frederic and the others could see furniture and clothing being hurled from the upper floors of the Tuileries and burned in the garden.

George Frederic, though he loved Paris above any other city, was anything but happy with the new regime. There was a serious problem of getting money from home. More than that, the whole of revolutionary Europe in 1848 alarmed him as the totalitarian trends in the 1930s would alarm his daughter. "Streets detestable on account of the noise and the crowds," he wrote in his diary on April 8. "Not at all pleased with a republic at Paris, decidedly too much equality.— Took an ice at Tortoni's."

It was a rare interlude of violence in a generally placid and unadventurous life. The Joneses took a summer home in Newport in the 1850s; that still quiet resort offered sea fishing, boat racing, and wild-fowl hunting during the holiday months. In the New York winter, the main diversion was supper parties, of which there was no end. George Frederic and his wife forgathered mainly with other young married couples of their clans: the Newbolds, the Edgars, the Rhinelanders, the Schermerhorn-Joneses. It was a well-to-do, well-ordered, unimaginative little world, devoted to the inculcation of good manners and to kindness and decency. Any violation of the accepted rules of conduct set up vibrations through the whole enclosed society.

On May 29, 1850, Lucretia Jones gave birth to a second son, Henry Edward. Twelve years then elapsed before the Joneses' third and last child, Edith, was born in January 1862. Her father had just turned forty, her mother was thirty-seven.

Edith Jones's first recorded memory was familial. In it, her father towered above her with his ruddy complexion and intensely blue eyes as they walked along Fifth Avenue—in 1865, probably—her small hand in his. Walking with Papa was always an event for the child, but hardly less significant that morning was a new white satin bonnet and a fine wool veil hanging over her cheeks. They made their way up the avenue with its leisurely traffic, its landaus and broughams and victorias, going past the rows of indistinguishable and uninspiring brownstone houses and past the fenced-in yard where the Misses Kennedy's cow was pastured. Here they ran into George Frederic's cousin by marriage, Henry Fearing, and his small boy Daniel. The lad gazed earnestly at Edith for some time, then lifted her veil and kissed her on the cheek.

Other memories of those first years included the gift of a white Spitz puppy, the first of a long series of little dogs that Edith would yearn over and fancy she could converse with. There was a day in the woods near Mamaroneck, and the discovery of flowers, of grass, of still, leafless branches and the mysterious appeal of physical nature. And always, close by, there was Doyley—Hannah Doyle, the ever-protective Irish nurse.

Edith, who was barely three when Lee surrendered to Grant at the Appomattox Courthouse, retained no infant memories of the Civil War that played itself out in these same years. The war, indeed, wrought curiously little change in the Jones family's routine of life. One hears of Lucretia Jones—like Mrs. Astor and Mrs. Peter Schermerhorn—keeping open house as punctiliously as ever on New Year's Day and of George Frederic entertaining old friends and former college mates at Newport. Edith's brothers were too young for military service, and her closest male cousins were younger yet.

The war could hardly be expected to reverberate, in any obvious way, in Edith Wharton's fiction. It figures only as the background of an early story, "The Lamp of Psyche," and as the setting for the *Old New York* novella *The Spark*, in which Walt Whitman is seen tending to the wounded in the military hospitals in Washington. Yet it does provide an undercurrent, faint but palpable, in Edith Wharton's sketches of the society of her youth. If that society had acquired a certain nostalgic charm with the passage of years, it also appeared to some extent as a fallen world—a postwar world. In it, manners were giving way, moral distinctions were blurring. Some strong, cohesive component of a dimly perceived and idealized prewar community was slowly eroding.

2. Miss E. N. Jones

Real estate values in New York declined sharply after the end of the Civil War, and George Frederic Jones, whose income derived mostly from city land, made the decision to lease the two homes in Manhattan and Newport and take the family to Europe for what turned into a stay of six years. Freddy Jones alone remained behind when the family sailed for England in late November 1866. Edith's other brother, the sixteen-year-old Harry, was scheduled to enter Trinity Hall College at Cambridge. The nurse Doyley was on hand to look after her four-year-old charge.

Having settled Harry in one of the smallest and most gracious of the Cambridge colleges, where he would make a desultory study of civil law, the others moved on through France to Rome. What clung to Edith's memory of the year spent there was less the ancient monuments and ruins than walking in the gardens of the Roman villas, the fountains of Frascati, the tulips and dandelions on the Spanish Steps. Best of all was romping on Monte Pincio with Daisy Terry. The Joneses renewed their friendship with the American expatriate painter Luther Terry, who in the intervening years had married the sister of Julia Ward Howe, Mrs. Thomas Crawford. His stepson, F. Marion Crawford, developed into a craftsmanlike novelist, the author of some two-score historical romances, among them *The White Sister.*

There followed a trip across Spain by diligence, an experience that remained for Edith a jumble of images—steep and ragged hills, bad roads, squalid inns, jabbering beggars, a procession of churches, and the "fantastic visions" of Cordova, the Alhambra, the Escorial. By the winter of 1868 the family was established in Paris for two years.

Edith did not at this time share her parents' fondness for the French capital. She was too young for the opera and the ballet, or for her mother's tours of the dressmaking shops. She found little excitement in Mlle. Michelet's dancing class, where she dutifully learned the minuet and the shawl dance. She would, nonetheless, associate Paris with the first faint stirrings of her inward life. As she passed her sixth birthday, she began to be seized with a passion for storytelling, what she called "making up." Walking up and down the living room of their suite, holding a book in her hand and pretending to read it—her favorite was *The Alhambra* by her father's friend Washington Irving—she would invent her own tales. These were always stories about "real people," that is, grown-up people.

She was never much drawn to fairy tales, though despite her old-age disclaimer she reveled as a child in the *Contes de Perrault*, mainly because of the romantic and terrifying illustrations by Gustav Doré. What intrigued her more was humanized mythology—of the sort supplied her by an amiable visitor from Newport who acted out a number of mythological tales in a way to make the gods and goddesses of Olympus seem very like the ladies and gentlemen Edith saw driving about in the Bois de Boulogne. Her short stories "The Lamp of Psyche" in 1894 and "Pomegranate Seed" in 1929 suggest how long this taste persisted.

It was early in the Paris stay that her father, observing Edith's affection for turning the pages of books, taught her how to read. She appears to have acquired the skill with remarkable speed and, wasting no time on easier materials, to have begun almost at once the reading of serious literature. She would always recall shouting the recently discovered *Idylls of the King* through the japanned ear trumpet of her ninety-year-old grandmother, Mary Stevens Rhinelander, who had come over to join the Paris household for many months.

The Joneses were in the Black Forest, at a watering place where Lucretia was "taking the cure," when the Franco-Prussian War broke out in the summer of 1870. Edith's parents thus missed the opportunity to be in Paris during another major upheaval in French history, and heard safely from afar the news of Bismarck's devastating victory and the collapse of the Second Empire. As for Edith, she could hardly take it in that the Empress Eugénie—whom she had seen the previous autumn in the Champs Elysées, flashing by in her open carriage—had fled to England.

In Bad Wildbad, meanwhile, Edith began the study of German, reading aloud from the New Testament with the help of a German *Fraülein*. She rambled among the pines of the Black Forest and climbed the woodland paths. On such an outing one morning, she was suddenly seized with an excruciating pain; it was typhoid fever, that most dangerous and unconquerable of European illnesses. All local doctors had been called up, but a Russian physician who happened to be on the scene prescribed the treatment—still used today—of plunging the young patient into ice-cold baths. This Lucretia shrank from doing; but she did wrap the child in wet sheets, and Edith slowly recovered. It had been a close call.

Late in the same year the family went to Florence, which had temporarily recovered some of its former bustle and importance as the capital (since 1865) of the newly created kingdom of Italy. But even as the Joneses were moving into a suite of rooms overlooking the Arno, Italian forces were wresting Rome from the French and King Victor Emmanuel and his parliament were preparing to transfer down to the city on the Tiber. Only indistinctly aware of this historical drama, Edith took happily to her Italian lessons and played with a new puppy, a *lupetto* known as Florentine Foxy. Partly in order to keep warm in the chilly high-ceilinged rooms, she went into a frenzy of "making up," whirling across the cold stone floors, imagining a rush of stories about people like her parents and their friends.

The Joneses returned to America in the summer of 1872. Edith was ten years old, and had become well acquainted with portions of Italy, France, Germany, and Spain.

Some thirty years later, as she was about to leave America for Paris and England, Edith wrote a friend about "the curse of having been brought up there" —in Europe—"and having it ineradicably in one's blood." Edith in fact passed the larger part of her childhood and adolescence in New York and Newport. Yet it remains true that between her fifth and her twenty-first birthday, she had spent almost eight years abroad, most of that time, moreover, not amid the hurry and rapid changes of travel but living months or years at a stretch in one or another European city.

What "Europe" meant to the child was first of all languages and literature. Coming back to America, Edith could already move about with some ease in French, German, and Italian. Europe was also a variety of styles of living, dressing, eating, talking. It was the experience of a great variety of manners; as a result, Edith would look with a particularly acute and probing eye at the manners of her own American society. It was above all the almost painful discovery of unfamiliar physical beauty, beauty of landscape and garden, of forest and country road, of village and cathedral. Ugliness, she said, always rather frightened her. But the so diversely beautiful vistas of Europe were now, indeed, ineradicably in her blood.

2

Edith's newfound sense of beauty received a shock when the Joneses' ship docked in New York and she stared down at the squalor and confusion of the waterfront. She once asked an old New Yorker why he had never been to Europe; when he replied "Because I can't bear to cross Murray Street," naming the street closest to the piers, she knew exactly what he meant. But the Joneses swiftly left that ugly scene behind and went directly to Newport. Edith was soon enjoying again the pleasure of summer days at Pencraig, the Joneses' island home.

Pencraig was a roomy, bulgy affair, a cluster of gables and chimneys, with honeysuckle and clematis swarming over the verandah that ran around the house. It stood on Harrison Avenue, on the opposite side of the island from the long, undulating cliffs overlooking the Atlantic to the east. Along those cliffs, two decades later, the Vanderbilts, Astors, Goelets, and others had built (often by that architect of uncertain genius, Richard Morris Hunt) their enormous and flamboyant "cottages"—The Breakers, Marble House, Ochre Court, Belcourt.

Edith would detest the Newport of those later days. She knew it as a still rustic resort, as a community rather than a stage; the Newport of *The Age of Innocence.*

After six years of impersonal and confining hotel rooms and suites, Edith loved dashing up and down the stairs in her own home, picking strawberries in the kitchen garden, playing in the meadow below the lawn, riding on her pony through the unspoiled countryside. Looking down through the trees from Pencraig, one could see the Newport harbor and the little lighthouse, and beyond it the queerly shaped Goat Island and Narragansett Bay. The Joneses had a private dock and bathing beach in the harbor. Though Edith did not care much to go out into the bay in her father's or brothers' catboats, she liked swimming in the cove and fishing off the dock for "scuppers" and "porgies."

Newport offered a variety of sports. Tennis did not come in until the later 1870s. But in addition to swimming and sailing and fishing, there were croquet and cricket, bicycling, roller skating and skeet shooting. Edith, who restricted herself mainly to swimming and riding, can also be imagined digging for clams. She must, more than once, have attended a clambake, a periodic island ritual at which one tasted a savory combination of clams, fish, lobsters, sweet potatoes, and corn, all cooked together on hot stones and smothered with rockweed.

The most picturesque of the sporting events were the archery contests. Edith Wharton left a glowing account of these in *A Backward Glance:* the parents seated on the turf in a semicircle, the children permitted to roam about (the three Jones children, in the early days, on the back of a donkey), "the lovely archeresses in floating silk or muslins, with their wide leghorn hats, and heavy veils flung back only at the moment of aiming."

Edgerston, the property adjoining Pencraig, belonged to Lewis Rutherford, the large and stately professor of astronomy at Columbia. On Sundays, Professor Rutherford took Edith with his own children for a walk over the Rocks, a rugged country path that led around from the bay to the Atlantic. Edith also went over to Edgerston of a morning to continue her German lessons with young Anna Bahlmann, the governess of the Rutherford children, later Edith's own *Fraülein* and then her secretary. It was she who introduced Edith to a range of German poetry from the medieval minnesingers to the Romantics. In the course of these visits, Edith formed an adolescent attachment to the somewhat sophisticated Winthrop Rutherford and wrote him letters which she never sent. She was drawn as well to the older Rutherford girls—Margaret, most skillful and queenly of archeresses, who in 1879 married the young diplomat Henry White and went abroad to live; and the romantically inclined Louisa, or "Poodle," as her family called her.

An exciting event had seemed in the offing in the fall of 1873. Edith's brother Harry, whom she adored, became engaged to Caroline Hunter, a charming girl who lived with her parents and her two sisters on K Street in Newport. On November 15 the entire Hunter family sailed for France on the *Ville de Havre,* one of the largest and best-equipped passenger ships afloat. On the night of the twenty-second, it was run into on its port side by a small sailing vessel, the *Lock Earn*, which appears to have had an inadequate lookout system. The seas were heavy, but it was a clear night. The collision must have been frightful. Amid scenes of horror, indescribable confusion, and great bravery, the *Ville de Havre* went to the bottom. Two hundred lives were lost, among them Caroline Hunter and both her parents. Her two sisters were flung into the sea but managed to cling to a floating timber until picked up by an English boat.

Greatly compounding the shock and grief the entire family felt for Harry's loss was the fact that also among those drowned was Lucretia's sister Eliza Edgar and one of her daughters.

The earliest of Edith's extant letters—to Mrs. "Pauley" Du Pont in London, on September 3, 1874—gives a faint flavor of Newport life, and of its twelve-year-old author. It was dictated to a young woman named Anna, a neighbor who was also about to enter the family by marrying Dr. Beverley Robinson, Edward Jones's brother-in-law. Edith began by remarking how flustered Anna had been by a recent house visit from Dr. Robinson.

Can't you imagine how that wretched infant Harry teased her? She is so sweet about it all, and everybody was so delighted to have seen Doctor Robinson that although we still declare that there is no man *quite* good enough for her, she is left in peace otherwise.

Harry was usually away anyhow, Edith added, working in his brother Freddy's warehouse in New York—for the first and apparently the only time in their lives, the Jones brothers were engaged in trade. She went on to describe throwing "torpedoes" at Colonel Du Pont's hat on the Fourth of July, and Anna and a friend taking a walk around the cliffs and returning "in perfect raptures." The other excitement was Edith's dog Crumpet being delivered of four puppies. Harry "measures their noses every day to see which has the shortest."

Those stretched-out sentences with their archness of tone are recognizably the product of a young girl, but also of an uncommonly articulate one. Lucretia Jones's insistence on learning proper, if also allowably colloquial, English speech had served its purpose. Edith was ready to try her hand at other modes of writing.

3

The New York that Edith came to know between 1872, when the Joneses returned from Europe, and 1880, when they again went abroad, was, she would admit, only that tiny fraction of the city that "came within the survey of a much governessed and guarded little girl."

Geographically, it extended along Fifth Avenue from Washington Square to "the" Central Park. It only reached that still remote site because Aunt Mary Mason had persuaded her cousin Mr. Colford Jones to build a home next to her own, just before the park gates. New York society wondered whether party guests would manage to travel all the way downtown at the end of a late evening without risk. But then Edith's Aunt Mary Newbold, that beautiful if humorless woman, put up a white marble home nearby, with smaller dwellings for Tommy and his wife and the other Newbold children. "The Jones blocks" were established, and so, temporarily, were the boundaries of decent and sensible society.

Socially, Edith's New York in the 1870s was limited to the small, intricately interrelated and ritualistic world of what George William Curtis, an editor of *Harper's Weekly*, identified as "the good old families"—virtue and age being the chief qualities of perhaps the only real aristocracy New York would ever know. The New York that struck the fancy of Edith's future friend William Dean Howells when he and his wife moved down from Boston in the 1880s—the New York of cablecars and Italian grocers, German immigrants and Russian refugees, Mott Street, Chatham Square, and the picturesque litter of Third Avenue: all this was invisible and inaudible to the world in which Edith Jones was decorously growing up. It was scarcely guessed at by that world, though Edith, to judge from a couple of her early stories, must somehow have caught a fleeting glimpse.

The Joneses' narrow-fronted, three-story brownstone was on West Twenty-third Street near Fifth Avenue. Passing up the inevitable Dutch stoop, one entered a vestibule painted in Pompeian red, and beyond it the first of several cramped sitting rooms. The white-and-gold drawing room on the second floor was rigorously protected from the world outside by two layers of curtains: sashes, lace draperies, and damask hangings. Heavy pieces of Dutch marquetry adorned it, and a cabinet displayed a number of old painted fans and exquisite and never-used pieces of old lace brought back from Venice and Paris. A Mary Magdalene, etched in copper, was on the Louis Philippe table: in the dining room, adjoining, there was an imitation Domenichino; both were nearly invisible in the well-bred gloom.

Edith Wharton, who would develop a remarkable knowledge of architecture and house decoration, thought in retrospect that it was a rather cheerless house. The overcrowded rooms, like those of most other New York town houses of the period, were so designed as to lack any clear identity and to make privacy impossible. Each seemed somehow to be part of the room next to it—the drawing room was part of the hall, the library part of the drawing room. In the latter, inflammable draperies above the mantelpiece made it dangerous to light the fire in the hearth. The ground-floor sitting rooms were like the waiting rooms in a dentist's office. The house was expensively but unharmoniously furnished, though among the heavy upholstery were some fine and undervalued colonial pieces.

George Frederic Jones was a man of leisure, his income fluctuating with the rise and fall of real estate prices. Any increased affluence was more than matched by Lucretia's increased expenditures on clothes. One of the sights most familiar to his daughter was George Frederic seated at his desk worriedly going over his accounts. He did his social duty by serving as a director of the Blind Asylum of New York and the Bloomingdale Insane Asylum. During Lent, Lucretia held sewing classes to make garments for the poor.

When they were not, as often, quietly at home, George Frederic and Lucretia passed their time going to the theater and opera (George Frederic was unusual in regarding opera-going as a musical rather than a social experience); in paying and receiving calls; and in giving or attending lunch and dinner parties, intimate or ceremonious.

Hanging over the stair rail, Edith would watch, fascinated, as her mother swept out to her carriage, dazzling in her train and opera cloak, a spray of gems covering her hair. At other times she could observe the guests as they entered the drawing room: rosy and white-whiskered gentlemen, as she would remember them, and ladies with bare sloping shoulders, low-cut bodices, and voluminous skirts.

The Joneses entertained well, even lavishly, and the guests sat long and contentedly at table. In this leisurely life, hurry was unknown; and besides, a good meal was to be taken with all due seriousness. The Jones cooks were famous in New York: Mary Johnson, a towering black woman with golden hoops in her ears, and Susan Minneman, a small soft-spoken mulatto. For daily fare, they served up corned beef, boiled turkey with oyster sauce, fried chicken and stewed tomatoes; for dinner parties, they provided terrapin and canvasback ducks, soft-shelled crab and Virginia ham cooked in champagne, lima beans in cream and corn soufflé.

After dinner the ladies repaired to the drawing room, where after an interval the gentlemen, having partaken of their claret and Madeira (the Jones Madeira was also famous), drunk their coffee, and smoked their cigars, came to join them. Frequently, additional guests would arrive, the gentlemen carrying their white gloves and top hats, and ten o'clock tea would be poured. Edith was sometimes allowed to stay after her normal bedtime, and so it was that her youthful mind could record the habitual conversation.

It was safe, monotonous, and rigidly circumscribed, with scarcely a word about literature or music or art. There was soft talk about the dinner just completed, about planned changes in the Newport homes and itineraries for European travel. Discreet gossip was permitted about a handful of families that counted socially but were not too close kin to those present. At its most adventurous, conversation might touch on Uncle Fred Rhinelander's queer dream of an art museum in Central Park or Cousin John King's efforts to store in the New-York Historical Society a collection of peculiar pictures someone had given him. (These pictures were identified many years later by Bernhard Berenson as comprising a treasure of early French and Italian paintings.)

If this manner of spending an evening, endlessly repeated, perfectly suited the former Lucretia Rhinelander, it is much less clear that it represented an ideal of life for George Frederic Jones. There was about him, his daughter always felt, something repressed, an air of some larger opportunity lost. In the world where he played his carefully prescribed part, there was no way to nourish the slender romantic streak of his young manhood. He had, as has been said, a kind of baffled love of poetry; he could recite Macaulay and was moved by the rhythms of Tennyson.

I imagine there was a time when his rather rudimentary love might have been developed had he any one with whom to share it. But my mother's matter-of-factness must have shrivelled up any such buds of fancy. . . . I have wondered what stifled cravings had once germinated in him, and what manner of man he was really meant to be. That he was a lonely one, haunted by something always unexpressed and unattained, I am sure.

Those words, needless to say, reveal Edith Wharton's attitude to her mother as much as to her father. What one comes to feel about Lucretia Jones, indeed, is a sort of absence, an emptiness, gaps of character filled in by artifice and trivia. In her earlier years she was close to being beautiful; in middle age she was obviously the model for Mrs. Welland in *The Age of Innocence,* with her "firm placid features, to which a lifelong mastery over trifles had given an air of factitious authority." The relationship between George Frederic and Lucretia, in their daughter's version of it, provided Edith Wharton with the first and most compelling instance of what would become one of her central themes: the larger spirit subdued and defeated by the smaller one.

4

As Edith Jones entered into her adolescence, in the mid-1870s, she was evolving into a decidedly complex, indeed a contradictory young person. She was not very robust; there were no traces of the typhoid fever, but occasionally there were smudges under her eyes. She was, however, a pretty girl: prettier than she would be as a grown woman, when the adjective habitually used about her was "handsome." Her best features were her red hair, which the sunlight tinted with gold, and her large, worried brown eyes. Her family never praised her for good looks. Her brothers in fact told her teasingly that her hands and feet were too big, and her sense of being the least physically attractive member of the family was one of the reasons for a growing shyness and self-consciousness. Edith was undemonstrative by nature, which led her mother—who also looked askance at her use of "long words"—to rebuke her for having "less heart" than her brothers.

At the same time, unknown to anyone else, Edith was possessed of a terror of certain nameless horrors which she was convinced were lying in wait for her. This haunting fear had its origins during her convalescence after the attack of typhoid fever in Germany, when someone put in her hands a tale of mystery and violence that frightened her so much she had a serious relapse. Five years later she still was having an acute, recurring apprehension, as she put it, of "some dark undefinable menace forever dogging my steps, lurking and threatening." It was worst when she came back at the end of her daily walk through the afternoon dusk; there, on the threshold of the house, she was sure, the horror was preparing to spring upon her, and no one, not even her father, could protect her. She could not sleep at night unless a light was on and a nursemaid in the room with her.

Her conscious mind seems never to have grasped the cause of what she would describe as a "choking agony of terror." Yet who was waiting, ominously, inside the house—ready perhaps to scold, humiliate, frighten, and increase the anxiety in the child's eyes—but her own mother? Against that force, young Edith had already realized, not even her father could always defend her.

Despite her mother's repressive influence, two other strands in Edith's character were emerging: the first was a vital eroticism. She referred to this with reminiscent euphemism as "real Life," and said that in her teens it

was singing in my ears, humming in my blood, flushing my cheeks and waving in my hair —sending me messages and signals from every beautiful face and musical voice, and running over me in vague tremors when I rode my pony, or swam through the short bright ripples of the bay, or raced and danced and tumbled with "the boys."

Lucretia Jones, when Edith shyly asked her what this might mean, told her that she was too young to understand or that "It's not nice to ask about such things." Once an older cousin informed her that babies came from people and not from flowers, but when she went to her mother for confirmation, Lucretia gave her a scolding lecture about not being nice. Edith worked out the theory that married people had children because God, looking down through the roof of the church, saw the clergyman marrying them and took appropriate if unfathomable steps.

God was much in her thoughts at this time. In her childhood she had come to believe that there were two inscrutable beings whom she was obliged to try to please—"God and my mother"; but in her adolescence, her religious preoccupations took a more illuminated turn. She began to read widely and indiscriminately in religious literature, particularly sermons of every kind of doctrinal persuasion. Here, as in most other aspects of her education, Edith was entirely on her own. Though her parents went to church socially every Sunday, religious matters were never touched on, even in passing, in the household conversation, any more than they were in that of the Joneses' neighbors.

On the moral side, George Frederic and Lucretia stood for what was known as "worldly probity," a code of behavior which took no account whatever of Christian moral doctrine but which regarded ill-breeding (a failure of politeness, for example, or a tendency to grab) as the only wrongdoing. Not that Edith— though she was becoming, in her own words, "passionately interested in Christianity"—mulled very long over the subtler teachings of the church. The exception was the doctrine of the Atonement, which perplexed her mightily. By what logic had God sacrificed his only son to atone for the sinful conduct of *humans?* She told herself in the idiom of her surroundings: "But if the servants did anything to annoy Mamma, it would be no satisfaction to her to kill Harry or me." Not even Mamma would go so far.

She took the existence of God for granted. He appeared to her a dreadful kind of being, but she assumed that God was simply one of the "dark fatalities" with which mortal existence was burdened. Human life, indeed, sometimes struck her as a burdensome affair. In a gloomy moment she wrote in her notebook: "If I ever have children I shall deprive them of *every pleasure*, in order to prepare them for the inevitable unhappiness of life."

Her adolescent nature contained a set of contradictions by no means uncommon with young persons of intelligence, imagination, and incipient talent. Externally, she was a creature of gaiety, given to bursts of enthusiasm, to harmless vanities and constant physical activity. She also experienced chills of embarrassment and self-doubt. But all the time her inner life was burgeoning; beautiful objects made her senses race, and great poetry set her aglow. Almost by the same token, she was overcome at times by the mysterious and romantic sadness of life. She took nothing calmly.

5

Edith's several qualities were recognized in the variety of names by which she was addressed. It was her mother who coined the name "Puss" or "Pussy," and it was by this that she was most widely known. To Doyley she was "Sweet," and to the Rutherfords "Lily." Her brother Harry, detecting the streak of virile toughness that lay behind her enjoyment of pretty dresses and of inspecting herself in the mirror, amusedly called her "John."

It is not recorded what her brother Freddy called her, and in fact for Edith her older brother might not have existed. The sixteen years' difference between their ages was partially responsible, but it was obvious that they had nothing in common. If she saw Freddy at all, it was because she had quickly grown fond of the delightful twenty-year-old girl he had married in Philadelphia in 1870. Mary Cadwalader Rawle came from a line which had resided in or near Philadelphia for almost two hundred years (the first American Rawle had been a friend of William Penn's). She spoke French as well as she did English, had traveled abroad somewhat, and was accustomed to the presence of the great. Thackeray had been a visitor at the big old house on Walnut Street, and James Buchanan; at the age of eleven Mary had gone to the White House and met President Lincoln, to whom her father, an able and influential lawyer, was reporting on English attitudes toward the United States during the war.

The Frederic Joneses lived in a comfortable home on East Eleventh Street.

They were quite glittering members of society, though Mary (or "Minnie") Jones soon came to prefer lively conversation in her own drawing room to the banalities of formal social intercourse. A daughter, Beatrix, was born in 1872—the only close relative, as it would turn out, of Edith Wharton's in the younger generation. It was not a happy marriage, and would be dissolved before many more years passed. But by that time Minnie and Edith Jones had formed a strong attachment. Minnie had been struck at once by the "clever child with a mane of red-gold hair" who could always be seen "scribbling stories on any paper that came handy," and in the course of time they became closer than blood sisters.

For the moment, however, Edith, while treasuring her solitude, had reached the age where she was conscious of the acute loneliness of her life in the dark little house on West Twenty-third Street. To be sure, there was the comfortable Doyley, and there was Anna Bahlmann; Anna came around each day to give Edith language lessons while Doyley slowly and thoroughly combed the young girl's hair. Then, in 1875, Edith met Emelyn Washburn, the only child of the rector of Calvary Church, and there began the most valuable friendship Edith would have with another girl.

On Ash Wednesday, 1875, Mrs. Washburn, Emelyn's mother, spoke to a meeting of the Calvary Missionary Society about the child of an impoverished couple at a mission in the Far West; a few days later there arrived a box containing a complete child's outfit, exquisitely made, with a card signed Miss E. N. Jones. At her mother's request Emelyn went around to call and asked for Miss E. N. Jones, only to be told by the footman that Mrs. Jones was not at home. She repeated her desire to see *Miss* Jones, and—apparently in obedience to another of Lucretia's inexplicable whims—received the same firm answer. As Emelyn departed, she heard Edith running down the stairs and saying with anguish: "But Mamma, she asked for *me*—twice!" The two girls met at last that summer in Newport.

Emelyn Washburn was six years older than Edith: a rather poised young woman, quick-minded, and with an affectionate nature. Looking back, Edith Wharton suspected her of a streak of "degeneracy"—that is, lesbianism—but no such suspicion disturbed the growing friendship. Emelyn, for her part, always regretted that Edith knew so small a portion of New York, and was ignorant of the Manhattan she herself so enjoyed: the colorful Italian life on Mulberry Street, South Street with its tall ships, the gulls over the East River, the midwinter icefields being carried up and down the harbor by the tides. She suffered from severe eye trouble, and part of her attempted cure was to spend several hours a day on the ferries, watching the passing show and talking with the deck hands.

Edith gave up the afternoon drives with her mother in favor of going over to the Washburn house in Gramercy Park, escorted by Doyley. Here she might trim a bonnet with a blue "riband" (recalling the scarlet riband of Thackeray's Beatrix Esmond) or make use of the new contraption, a typewriter, that Dr.

Washburn had bought to type out letters to the Rutherford boys or friends of her brother Harry, each a mass of mistakes and crossings-out. Best of all were the hours she spent in Dr. Washburn's extensive library, where she joined Emelyn in the study of such abstruse subjects as Anglo-Saxon, Icelandic, Old Norse, and Old and Middle High German. In the warm weather, the girls climbed through Emelyn's bedroom window onto the library roof and read Dante aloud together.

As for Emelyn, though she found these afternoons stimulating, she could not help wish that they were not so confined to languages and literature. She preferred listening to music, but music at this time interested Edith hardly at all. More than that, Emelyn wanted to talk about the pressing political and social problems both in New York and in the country at large. Her father was a cousin of Ellen Tucker, the first wife of Ralph Waldo Emerson, and had met with the members of the far-seeing, reform-spirited Concord group. Before the war he had organized a school for Negro slaves in Savannah, Georgia, and later studied at first hand the sorry conditions of the Chippewa Indians. In New York he worked energetically to alleviate the lot of the poor, and besought his parishioners to join him in doing so.

Edith would recognize these qualities in a poem she wrote a few years later, after Dr. Washburn's death:

> He fought and suffered in one cause sublime,
> Strong-armed to strike at ignorance and crime,
> With gentle hands to help the maimed and bound.

But for the time being, she seemed immune to the issues that beset the American world just outside her world.

6

Those issues, of course, had never on any occasion disturbed the gentle atmosphere of the Jones household, with its flow of guests. What the family home offered Edith was not an opening onto contemporary history—it was rather an escape from it, in her father's library.

It was a small room on the ground floor, with green damask curtains and a massive oak mantelpiece supported by two visored knights (the influence of Sir Walter Scott lay heavy on New York upper-class culture), four more of whom served as legs for the huge writing table. There were probably not more than six hundred volumes behind the glass doors of the bookcases, but for Edith they constituted an almost unbearably exciting treasure for mind and imagination. She spent hours squatting on the "Turkey rug" in the library, pulling out book after book and glancing inside it. She rarely read a book through. Emelyn Washburn observed with pain her friend's habit of putting a book down unfinished, and blamed it on her governess's lack of discipline.

George Frederic's collection included the chief historians from Plutarch to Parkman and the most illustrious poets from Homer to Dante, Milton and Pope and the English Romantics. There were the English and French dramatists, the great diarists, and assorted works of philosophy and art history. Of classical fiction there was little: the works of Scott and Irving stood in lonely dignity on the shelves, there to be joined by Thackeray. As to more recent fiction, Lucretia Jones, feeling required to control her daughter's reading, took the easy path of forbidding her to read any new fiction at all. This, Edith Wharton would think, was probably all to the good. Bereft of the popular and trashier contemporary novelists, she could lose herself in the Old Testament and the Book of Revelation, in the Elizabethan and Jacobean playwrights, in Keats and Shelley.

Apart from the American names already mentioned, and Longfellow, American writing was sparsely represented. Even Herman Melville, though related to the Van Rensselaers, was excluded because of his alleged bohemianism. Edith would come to the leading native writers of the generations preceding hers—Poe, Hawthorne, and Melville, and Emerson and Whitman, whom she would admire passionately—on her own. The American literary idiom, accordingly, contributed only slightly to her adolescent self-education.

Those afternoons in the library provided her, in her own phrase, with "a secret ecstasy of communion." It was secret almost of necessity. The elders who surrounded her, she was becoming aware, had "an awe-struck dread of . . . intellectual effort," and were distinctly ill at ease in the presence of anyone who openly enjoyed serious reading, even more so of a recognized person of letters. Not that New York in the 1870s had many of the latter. Boston was still the citadel of literary culture: if its power was weakening, it was, for the moment, being challenged rather from the Middle West than from New York. It would not be until around 1890, with the arrival of Howells and the emergence of Stephen Crane, that New York could begin to claim anything like literary dominance. In the 1870s the writers most lionized were such members of the establishment, of the twenty-five-year-old Century Association, as Edmund Clarence Stedman, Henry Harland, and Richard Henry Stoddard, for whose names today one has to grope in encyclopedias.

Edith, anxious not to disturb her parents and their friends, hugged her treasures to herself in secret. But an act of "ecstatic communion" was undoubtedly taking place. The words and rhythms of poetry and the play of philosophic ideas stirred her enormously, though even to herself she could not say quite how or why. The closest she got at this time to explaining the urgency of her response to poetry was to declare that no one who was not instantly aroused by the Miltonic line "Yet once more, ye laurels, and once more" would ever understand the beauty of English verse.

In 1873, during her twelfth year, Edith decided to write a story: she would, that is, set down one of her inventions on paper. She would "make up." Like her earlier imaginings, this would have to do with something resembling the everyday life of her parents. She made a start:

> "Oh, how do you do, Mrs. Brown?" said Mrs. Tomkins. "If only I had known you were going to call I should have tidied up the drawing-room."

Edith thus began her fictional career on the decidedly realistic note of the unexpected social call. But when she shyly brought the page to her mother, Lucretia Jones gave it only a swift glance before handing it back with the chilling observation that "drawing rooms are always tidy."

In the Jones house, they undoubtedly were: tidy and cluttered. But Edith was so stricken by the criticism that she abandoned fiction for the time being and turned instead to poetry. Three years later, however, between the autumn of 1876 and early January 1877, she made another and larger effort, and this time brought to conclusion—keeping the matter a secret from everyone except Emelyn Washburn and perhaps one other girl—a thirty-thousand-word novella called *Fast and Loose*.

It is in some ways a sentimental and ineptly melodramatic performance; but in other ways it is an astonishing achievement for a much governessed and guarded New York society girl not yet fifteen. The cast is largely English, and the narrative moves between England and the continent. Georgie Rivers, a spirited girl with an intense desire for material comfort (she is not so remote, really, from Lily Bart in *The House of Mirth*), throws over her impoverished fiancé Guy Hastings to marry the aging, gouty Lord Breton and become the queen of the London season. Guy, much embittered, goes off to Rome, where he shares a studio with a misogynist friend.

Later, in Switzerland, he meets and becomes engaged to the beautiful, blushing, frail Madeline Graham, the daughter of a wealthy middle-class couple. Lord Breton then dies of his various ailments, and Georgie herself, who has caught pneumonia at a ball, comes to Nice to die. She summons Guy to a deathbed reconciliation. After her death Guy marries Madeline; as a husband and father, he is the soul of courtesy and kindness, but his heart (so the story ends) "is under the violets on Georgie's grave." (In one of her first published stories, "April Showers," Edith Wharton gently spoofed her adolescent novella by quoting its last lines as the conclusion of what is presented as an insipid short story by a rather silly young girl. "Fast and Loose" is also the title she slyly chose for a scandalous and successful novel in the excellent little satire of 1904, "Expiation.")

Despite such goings on and such rhetoric, the tale is promising. It is impressively literate, perhaps ostentatiously so; the language is clean and supple, and there are traces of the cool-eyed satire which would be a hallmark of Edith Wharton's best work. Mrs. Rivers, with her sallow face framed in a widow's cap, is seen as "one of those weak, shrinking women who seem always overwhelmed by her clothes." There are some finely detailed descriptions, particularly of the studio in Rome, presumably based on that of Luther Terry. Most of all, there is the incipient vision of human affairs at work in the novella, something that would not change fundamentally but would only expand and thicken in Edith's maturing imagination. This is the vision, based primarily upon her observation of her parents' life together, of human aspiration doomed to defeat almost by its very nature.

But though *Fast and Loose* has much to commend it, Edith began at once to deprecate the work. She wrote a number of mock reviews, attributed to various New York and London periodicals, each denouncing it in uncompromising terms. In the wittily harshest, adopting the authoritative voice of *The Nation,* she declared, "It is a false charity to reader and writer to mince matters. The English of it is that every character is a failure, the plot a vacuum, the style spiritless, the dialogue vague, the sentiment weak and the whole thing a fiasco." At so early an age did Edith adopt the habit of critically, and perhaps defensively, downgrading her own writing.

Edith was also writing a great deal of verse, kneeling on the library rug and scribbling on paper that had been used to wrap parcels. She had moved on from quantities of dramatic and historical poetry ("Scene: A Venetian Palace") to lyric poems, which she composed with "a lamentable facility." In the fall of 1878, Lucretia Jones, who kept a notebook of her daughter's poetic writings, made a selection from those written over the previous two years and had them privately printed in Newport by C. E. Hammett, Jr.

The twenty-nine items in *Verses* compare with *Fast and Loose* much as Edith Wharton's later poetry would compare with her incomparably superior fiction. They reveal technical competence and verbal assurance, a fairly wide range of reading in English and German poetry, and an occasional vivid detail; but there is not much vitality or originality. The best, "Some Woman to Some Man," is based vaguely on Browning's "Any Wife to Any Husband" and has a dash of Browning's conversational manner:

> We might have loved each other after all,
> Have lived and learned together! Yet I doubt it.

Elsewhere, *Verses* reflects Edith's sensitivity to physical nature, her interest in history (including ancient history), considerable reading in Browning, Swinburne, Tennyson, and Rossetti, and her limited religious feeling. She wrote a number of other poems in these years on religious subjects, including a lugubrious effort about a dead maiden near whose bed Christ appears, saying, "She is not dead but liveth." It would take a much later and soul-shaking experience truly to awaken her religious consciousness (as distinguished from wayward interest) and stir such authentic poetic talent as she did possess.

Edith's own copy of *Verses* carried the inscription:

> Who wrote these verses, she this volume owns.
> Her unpoetic name is Edith Jones.

It is the only instance in the little book of Edith in a frivolous vein—as she so often was. Absent from *Verses*, perhaps regretfully, was a racy mock-tragic poem she composed at this time, called "Ye Romantic Ballad of Ye Portuguese Plum," about a Spanish maid named Elvira, her poor but honest lover Don Luis Hava-payne, and her wicked uncle who insists she marry a lustful Moor, thereby causing her to reel, faint, and sink to the floor.

The summer after *Verses* was published, Allen Thorndike Rice, a Newport neighbor and later editor of the *North American Review*, sent some of the poems to Henry Wadsworth Longfellow, commenting that they were quite remarkable for a girl of sixteen who belonged "to a most estimable New York family" and who had been "brought up in fashionable surroundings little calculated to feed her taste for the Muses." Longfellow passed them on with a friendly word to William Dean Howells at the *Atlantic Monthly*, and that great editor, always ready to encourage the literary young, chose one of them to publish. Two other occasional poems—one about the suicide of a child—appeared in the New York *World* the following year. It was a hopeful start, but Edith would publish nothing more for a decade.

3. A Young Man of Property

Before her social debut in 1879, Edith's chief diversions outside her home and that of the Washburns were going to church and the theater, experiences that were sources of comparable pleasure for her—the pleasure of listening to great language. At one of the Sunday evening lessons in Calvary Church, she was so absorbed by the majestic cadences of the King James Bible, beautifully rendered by Dr. Washburn, that she unconsciously pulled off, one by one, the long white hairs from the camel's-hair coat of Emelyn Washburn sitting next to her. At the theater she allowed the soaring lines of Shakespeare to leap and swim in her imagination (she especially relished the speech of King Henry V: "And gentlemen of England now abed . . .") and at Wallack's she responded to the sterner rhythms of Goethe as intoned by visiting players.

Until about 1870 the social emergence of a young New York lady had consisted in assembling in her own home assorted relatives and family friends and solemnly introducing the girl to them. But in 1870, Archibald Gracie King had the idea of hiring the largest room in the fashionable Delmonico's—then situated on Fifth Avenue where Broadway and Twenty-sixth Street transected it—for a ball and supper in honor of his daughter's entrance into society. Thereafter the first appearance of debutantes became increasingly a public affair.

When it came time for Edith's debut, however, Lucretia refused to countenance so vulgar a display. The affair took place late in 1879 in the private ballroom —one of the few in the city—of Mrs. Levi Morton, wife of the well-known millionaire, on Fifth Avenue near Forty-second Street. Edith apprehensively accompanied her parents there, clad in a low-necked bodice of pale green brocade and a white muslin skirt, carrying a bouquet of lilies of the valley. The event was not as terrible for Edith as her mother's coming-out had been for Lucretia, but Edith would recall it as "a long cold agony of shyness"; nothing paralyzed her more than to be the object of attention by scores of people. She huddled next to Lucretia, unable to accept the many invitations to dance, and scarcely able to exchange greetings with the young men who had so often dined in her home. It was a memorably painful initiation for one whose social life in later years on two continents would be so full and not infrequently so extravagant, but for whom shyness, variously caused and variously disguised, would be a permanent feature in her character.

At the time Edith Jones was edging into it, New York society was contradictory in nature, and it had upon her a contradictory but lasting effect. Much of that social world was subject to incessant change and movement, as fortunes sprang up and ever larger mansions were built. The Joneses and their kin, however, belonged to the narrowest and stablest portion of society: an enclave of sorts within—in their view, *above*—the broader, looser, and much more conspicuous element. The latter was made up of exceedingly wealthy and often recently arrived commercial folk, with homes on Fifth Avenue; and it was their children, in a phrase of the 1880s, who filled the ranks of "the ultra-fashionable dancing people," and who indeed constituted society for the outsider or the visitor. There was of course considerable mingling between the two sets and a partial sharing of mores. But they tended to look askance at each other, to measure breeding against wealth and tradition against display. We shall shortly see a characteristic episode of social war between them—one of enduring importance for Edith Wharton.

She was acutely watchful of the entire social spectrum, from aristocrat to *arriviste*, but it was the narrowest segment that went into the early shaping of her. Looking back upon it, she was to think that its ideals were small, cautious, and essentially middle class. Yet they struck her in retrospect as "singularly coherent and respectable as contrasted with the chaos of indiscriminate appetites which made up [New York society's] modern tendencies." Moral coherence, restraint, dignity, integrity, and fidelity to the domestic pieties: these were among the values to be prized.

Life within the enclave was quiet and leisurely, almost as much so as it had been for young George Frederic and Lucretia Jones. There were little dinner parties of ritualistic solemnity, beginning at seven and offering as fare oyster soup, shad, canvasback or terrapin or broiled turkey, with vintage wines (if the host or hostess were knowledgeable enough) and port or Madeira. The early hour made possible after-dinner calls, at which the ladies who received the company usually wore long dresses of whaleboned silk, open at the neck, with lace ruffles and tight sleeves down to the wrists, on one of which an Etruscan bracelet might be observed. The young men, who invariably sported full mustaches, curled at the ends, showed up in evening dress, with a white waistcoat and a gardenia. Edith may be imagined clad from throat to ankles in a close-fitting dark dress with a flounce around the middle, white gloves, and a gardenia in her hair.

It was not a world that encouraged literary leanings. Edith Wharton retained the impression that the intellectuals and artists who might be encountered amid the wholly masculine company at the Century Club were on the whole a boring lot. Most persons in her own set were interested mainly in elegant dining, clothes from Paris, and money, though a few, like Edith's father, enjoyed traveling and the occasional book. No young girls in Edith's community of cousins attended a school, though their brothers went to Harvard or Columbia, and some to

English universities. The Reverend Morgan Dix, rector of Trinity, spoke for the community regarding the education of women when he declared that it should be solely for womanly purposes—"in order to be to the man all that he needs." A woman should be a "moral lever," and her role in life was "to keep her home pure and sweet, to rule and govern it prudently."

It was amid such circumstances and attitudes that Edith Jones completed her adolescence and entered womanhood. Beneath her quietly watchful exterior, she was absorbing and combining, rejecting and no doubt mentally reaching beyond the assorted qualities of the life around her. She could not, anywhere in her old New York, have been the easiest of company. She was clothes-conscious and money-conscious, but she was also addicted to books and ideas and the world of the imagination. There was, indeed, no one quite like her in her New York generation. A growing awareness of the fact deepened her sense of loneliness and gave her an air of unpredictability. She was everything that was right and regular, someone was to say about her, but the young hawk looked out of her eyes.

In the phrase Edith Wharton used about it, it was an age of innocence. The word applied in particular to the young girl, the debutante, whose single-minded purpose, her elders constantly reminded her, was to make a suitable marriage. To this end her mother's function was to supply her with elegant clothes and make every arrangement to launch her upon a proper worldly career. It was not her mother's function, Edith Jones had to learn, to supply any hints about the real relationship between married men and women. About all that, the maternal contribution was an elaborate pattern of mystification, something which the mature Edith Wharton regarded with rancorous regret.

But the age was innocent in larger and more appreciable ways. If social engagements were all-absorbing, the pace was leisurely and the atmosphere decorous. One associated social life with the arrival of winter—the "season" began around the first of December—and one saw it, in retrospect, through a haze of snow. It seemed to snow more often in those New York winters, and the snow seemed to lie in cleaner heaps on the sidewalks than in later years. One of the regular diversions was to walk along Fifth Avenue or Broadway, well muffled, while snow swept down silently onto the roofs of the horsecars and the steps of the basement entryways. Snow could also provide difficulties. Edith Jones seems to have been the girl she herself referred to in a memoir who turned up at the wrong brownstone front door one evening in a driving snowstorm. Informed of her mistake and turned back, she stood amid the swirling snow uncertain which of the other indistinguishable brownstones was her correct destination.

When the ultrafashionable young were not dancing, they could be found tobogganing, sleigh riding, and ice skating in Central Park. But of dancing there was no end. At the series of great balls between December and April, all of them held at Delmonico's, there was dancing—waltzes, quadrilles, "germans," square dances—sometimes until three in the morning, with time out for a midnight supper and champagne. Under the yellow light that shone in soothing dimness at the Family Circle Dancing Class, some two hundred people followed the steps of the two leaders of the cotillion. There was holly on the mirrors and evergreen on the walls at the First Cotillion, just before New Year's, and the ballroom was lit by candles and gaslight. Dance orchestras also played evening after evening in the ballrooms of private homes; fancy-dress balls were revived, and the guests wore their elaborate costumes to dinners before the event.

It was discovered that the number of people who could be fitted comfortably into Mrs. Astor's ballroom at Fifth Avenue and Thirty-fourth Street was about four hundred; Ward McAllister, Mrs. Astor's social entrepreneur, declared that number to represent the maximum size of the whole of genuine New York society. "The 400" turned out pretty much en masse for the three Patriarchs' Balls, the first of which took place a week before Christmas. Delmonico's was more than usually festive for these occasions (also organized by McAllister), the most prestigious ones of the New York season. The music balcony was hidden behind thick hemlock boughs; poinsettia leaves and evergreen adorned the walls, and floral bells made of red and white carnations hung from the chandeliers.

Members of the far-reaching Jones clan, and many of their present and future friends, were in regular attendance at these gatherings. Edith and her brother Harry appeared occasionally, though Lucretia never. Relatives abounded: Rhinelanders and Schermerhorns, Ledyards, Van Rensselaers, and Gallatins. The familiar names of the wealthy and sophisticated recur on the lists compiled by society reporters: Astors and Vanderbilts, Goelets and Yznagas, Lorillards and Belmonts. The imposing Mrs. Paran Stevens, about to play so curious a role in Edith Jones's personal life, rarely failed to show up. There were also such friends-to-be of Edith Wharton as the middle-aged Egerton Winthrop and Mr. and Mrs. Theodore Roosevelt; and conspicuous figures at the ball in December 1882 were Theodore's cousin James Roosevelt and his bride of two years, Sara Delano, the mother almost a year before of an infant boy, Franklin.

While the young women were being feted and courted—the "dancing people" also met one another at almost daily lunch parties, receptions, or picnics—the men had their own independent gratifications. There were beginning to be enough men's clubs in New York to satisfy the different kinds of masculine leisure. Preeminent among them was the Union Club, founded in 1836 and demonstrating its exclusiveness by a ten-year waiting list. A Jones and a Stevens were among the early presidents of the Union, Goelets and Schermerhorns among its members. The Knickerbocker, at Fifth Avenue and Thirty-second Street, was formed in 1871 by younger men like John Jacob Astor and William Cutting who were impatient with the delay in getting into the Union. In 1873 the exceedingly clubbable William R. Travers helped launch what became the very popular Racquet Club. The Metropolitan came into being a good deal later.

The physical contours of Edith Jones's New York were slowly shifting and expanding. The most fashionable quarter of the city was still the Murray Hill district from Thirty-second Street to Forty-fifth between Third and Sixth Avenues; but the socially influential were visibly moving further uptown, though the George Frederic Joneses, on West Twenty-third Street, showed no disposition to follow suit. Up beyond the big homes of Mary Mason Jones and her cousin lay the great nine-hundred-acre Central Park, a creation of genius by Frederick Law Olmsted. Here, after dashing across it on sleighs in the winter, Edith in the summer could join her friends in less strenuous boating parties. Adjacent to the park, on Fifth Avenue opposite Eighty-third Street (where Uncle Fred Rhinelander had wanted it to be), was the enormous Metropolitan Museum, twice displaced uptown from Fourteenth Street and Fifty-third Street and formally opened in its permanent site by President Arthur in March 1880.

Toward the other end of town, below Delmonico's, was the Society Library, from which Edith periodically borrowed books and where several members of her father's family served on the board. Nearby was the Academy of Music at Irving Place on Fourteenth Street: a red brick building with a handsomely appointed interior which held 2,400 seats. It was the musical shrine of the old families, and evening dress was de rigeur at the monthly concerts of classical music by the Philharmonic Orchestra and the Monday and Wednesday evening performances of the opera. Grand Central Station, from which trains ran north and west, loomed bulkily at Forty-second Street and Fourth Avenue; but to get to the big reverberating station of the Pennsylvania Railroad for trains to Philadelphia, Washington, and the South, one had to take the ferry at the foot of Cortlandt Street over to the depot in Jersey City.

2

Soon after her coming-out party at Mrs. Levi Morton's, Edith made the acquaintance of a young man named Henry Leyden Stevens. He was a popular member of New York society, and with his glamorous sister Minnie—there is no other adjective for the tall, lovely Mary Fisk Stevens, with her graceful carriage and her rather hard green eyes—he had been coming to Newport for many summers. Their mother, Mrs. Paran Stevens, belonged to what the Joneses and their circle regarded as the pushy and ostentatious new element of society with whom Lucretia Jones did not encourage her children to mix. One imagines that if Lucretia and Marietta Stevens passed one another in their carriages on Bellevue Avenue in Newport, they would exchange only the barest of nods.

Harry Stevens was born in Boston in 1859. He entered St. Mark's School, but left there in 1873 before graduating, probably because of illness. It was at this time, apparently, that he contracted the disease which we have come to recognize as tuberculosis. He went on to Oxford for a stint, less to pursue academic study than (as a newspaper story would put it) to "learn the manly arts and elegances," and thence to Switzerland, the most healthful country in Europe for anyone suffering an affliction of throat or lungs. He made what seemed a complete recovery, and back in Newport he rapidly became known as a leader in sporting events and an expert organizer of games and social outings. It was said to be Harry Stevens who, after visiting his sister in England, brought back sufficient equipment to lay out, on the grounds of his mother's big cottage at Bellevue and Jones Avenues, the first lawn-tennis court in Newport.

Harry must have pursued Edith most assiduously during the winter and spring (1880) after they met. It was certainly the New York season that Edith Wharton would most enjoy remembering. Thanks in particular to her amiable brother Harry's great popularity, she received a swarm of invitations to dinner parties with the young married set and to informal Sunday lunches. Harry Stevens, one supposes, managed to penetrate this tightly knit little group, perhaps to escort Edith to the opera and to meet her in those houses where the drawing rooms were large enough for impromptu dances.

In Newport in June and July, Edith could watch Harry among the other young gentlemen in tail coats playing tennis with the young ladies in tight whaleboned dresses—tennis had replaced archery as Newport's favorite pastime —and no doubt he joined her at bathing parties and took her for an excursion up Narragansett Bay in his mother's white steam yacht. Society's habits were loosening a little, and the old requirement of ladies spending most of their time calling on other ladies had pretty much been given up by Edith's generation. She was free to be driven by her brother or her suitor along the newly built Ocean Drive, which circled down from the bay around to the Atlantic.

One surmises these things with some confidence since before the summer of 1880 was half over, Newporters were beginning to wonder whether Pussy Jones and Harry Stevens might not already be engaged. In fact, they were not. But Harry was probably the young man observed one evening that summer by Daisy Terry holding "animated conversation" with Edith in what looked like a "possibly important tête-à-tête." Daisy had come over from Rome with her father on her first visit to America, and Luther Terry urged her to have a word with her sometime companion, the daughter of his old friend. But seeing Edith withdrawn from the others in so intense and seemingly intimate a dialogue, Daisy hung back.

She had the impression that Edith had "plenty of admirers." This, surprisingly enough, was for the moment the case, though it had been anything but so until recently. Edith tended to alternate between frozen shyness, which could be taken as youthful hauteur—Maude Howe Elliott saw her as "icy cold," with an aristocratic bearing and a taste only for the ultrafashionable—and bursts of somewhat intellectualized conversation. Such was not calculated to attract the young sports of Newport and New York. Harry Stevens was attracted, though; he was a fairly intelligent as well as an affable person, and in the interests of courtship he was willing to be exposed to Edith's private world of books and ideas. By a familiar law of human attraction, the attentions of a man as good-looking and of such fine expectations as Harry Stevens drew still others to Edith's side. The summer of 1880 was the summer of Edith's greatest success with eligible young males.

In late July, Edith, with her parents and with Harry Stevens in close attendance, turned up at Bar Harbor, that burgeoning resort on the northeast shore of Mount Desert Island, just off the coast of Maine. Mary Cadwalader Jones was already there, in a cottage next to that of the Lewis Rutherfords. Young Poodle (Louisa) Rutherford, writing to her sister Margaret White in Paris, expressed astonishment that Lily Jones was willing to leave Newport at the height of the season. The reason, she learned, was that Lily had not been well; and indeed, Poodle thought, she did look wretched, very pale and drawn and with such a worried expression. A lurking anxiety or apprehensiveness—due apparently to generally well concealed and even unnamed inner fears and uncertainties—did appear not infrequently in Edith's eyes, though few were as observant as Poodle Rutherford in detecting it.

The Jones contingent rented one of the many cottages which had been built in the previous few years and took their meals—they "mealed," in the island jargon—at the Hotel des Isles. Life at Bar Harbor, where the mountains reared up in spectacular fashion above a rocky coastline, was more invigorating than that in Newport, and more in keeping with Edith's inclinations. The young went canoeing and rowing on the enchanting mountain lakes; they went fishing and bicycling and looking for odd-shaped rocks along the shore. The air was superbly fresh and clear, and one could exhilarate in it while racing along Bar Harbor's own wildly beautiful Ocean Drive. The innumerable mountain trails that ran obliquely across the island were an invitation to constant long walks.

Talk was better at Bar Harbor than at Newport. The conversational tone was set not by the New Yorkers but by the more intellectually minded Boston and Philadelphia families, and the discussions were intelligent, lively, and entertainingly serious. This gratified a part of Edith's nature, but at this stage it was almost as important for her that the young Bar Harborites excelled at the art of flirtation. The essayist and novelist Charles Dudley Warner, after due consideration, pronounced Bar Harbor to be "the finest sanitarium on the continent for flirtation." Parents and chaperones seemed to absent themselves more than elsewhere, and it was not thought improper for a young lady to go on buckboard parties or to take moonlight drives with the young gentleman of the moment. For these occasions Edith Jones had her own young man very definitely in tow.

Poodle Rutherford, watching intently, wondered if Lily would actually marry Mr. Stevens. "*I* don't think so," she told her sister, "but appearances are against me, as they are together perpetually when they walk or drive, and Stevens is her shadow." Poodle was put out by Lily's unprecedented success with the attractive young males, and passed on to her sister the rumor that Lily "let men take liberties with her."

All unconscious of such insinuations, Edith flourished. The crisp air, the strenuous walking, the good talk, and the flirtatious life quite restored her to health. The Joneses and Harry went back to Newport, and soon afterward Poodle Rutherford quoted a visitor from the island as saying that everyone there was now positive that Lily Jones was engaged to Mr. Stevens. Poodle remained unconvinced. "Pussy still smiles on the attentions of Mr. S.," she commented at the end of September, "but I can't believe she means to marry him."

3

One of the advantages of Bar Harbor over Newport for Harry and Edith was that it removed them from the sphere of Mrs. Paran Stevens. That somewhat overwhelming woman was not eyeing the courtship with much approval, and given her strength of character she would have the determining voice as to its outcome.

Mrs. Stevens was in the midst of one of the most remarkable and telling social careers in the New York history of the time. The former Marietta Reed was the daughter of a well-to-do grocer of Lowell, Massachusetts. While still in school she attracted the attention of the father of one of her friends, Paran Stevens of Boston, a wealthy widower in his late forties. Stevens fell immediately in love with the gray-eyed, spirited, and rather voluptuous young woman of nineteen, and they were married in 1846.

Stevens had begun his own impressive career by working in a Boston "cook house." Showing a certain genius at hotel management, he built or purchased a string of hotels in several cities and a row of shops and other property. The most luxurious and successful of his ventures was the Fifth Avenue Hotel, of which he had been a part owner since its construction in 1858, on Madison Square, where Broadway and Fifth Avenue divided. Here the Prince of Wales came to indulge in youthful misbehavior; Brazilian, French, and Siamese royalty appeared; and the leaders of New York's Republican party came to discuss, over excellent meals, how to enlarge their share in the city's political and financial future.

Paran Stevens was far more interested in buying fine race horses than in the social life of the day, and it was not until after his death in 1872 that Marietta Stevens felt free to launch her attack upon New York society. The first step took her, with her daughter Minnie, to England, where she met up again with the Prince of Wales and elicited invitations to Sandringham and Marlborough House. The Stevens ladies made a very handsome pair and were the best of company; they were warmly received on all sides. Before the season was over,

Minnie Stevens, after rejecting the proposal of a duke, became engaged to Lord Arthur Paget, a captain in the Guards and the second son of Lord Clarence Paget.

The Duchess of Argyll, wife of the Secretary for India under Gladstone, could echo the resentful rumor that the Paget boy was marrying an American innkeeper's daughter, and express her patrician understanding that all Americans were innkeepers or tradesmen. But by overseeing the match, Mrs. Paran Stevens moved at a stroke close to the forefront of the New York social scene. For this was the social epoch characterized by the marriage of American girls into the British aristocracy; social eminence in New York was partly measured by the distinction of one's noble in-law in London. Minnie Stevens had grown up with Consuelo Yznaga, who became the Duchess of Manchester, and she would later use her wiles to promote the marriage between the reluctant Consuelo Vanderbilt and the Duke of Marlborough. She also knew the Jerome sisters, one of whom, Jennie, made the seemingly brilliant marriage with Lord Randolph Churchill, while another, Leonie, was more happily wed to an Irish baronet, Sir John Leslie. With all these women, and especially Leonie Leslie, Edith Wharton would be on terms of friendship; and to the cluster of comely transatlantic invaders in the 1870s, she would devote her last and remarkable, though unfinished, novel, *The Buccaneers.*

A main sign of society's surrender to the former grocer's daughter was the moment in the late 1870s when Mrs. August Belmont drove up all conspicuously one morning to pay a call at 244 Fifth Avenue. Part of Mrs. Stevens' success was due to her combative character, which landed her in court on a number of occasions, but it was due also to the increasing and confusing fluidity of the New York social world, at a time when wealth was becoming as powerful an entrée as birth. The constituency of the old guard, the good old families, could be detected easily enough by the knowing. They were characterized by a long American ancestry, a cautious evasion of publicity, imperturbable social assurance, and a slowly diminishing energy. But the members of the new breed seemed to spring up out of nowhere.

"How many of the swellest of the swell today were anything at all twenty years ago—fifteen years ago even?" asked an editorial in the gossipy *Town Topics* in 1877. "Where were the Vanderbilts, socially, even five years ago? The Astors had just fifteen years the social start." One recognized these phenomena by their display of wealth, their hearty enjoyment of publicity, and the number of dinners and balls they attended and concerts they gave. The struggle between the two social elements came to something of a climax on an evening in late October 1883, at the opening of the Metropolitan Opera House.

The new breed had attempted to buy into the old Academy of Music, offering as much as thirty thousand dollars for a box. The old guard indignantly resisted, and the younger millionaires decided to build a house of their own, on Broadway between Thirty-ninth and Fortieth Streets. At the opening—with the Swedish soprano Christine Nilsson singing the role of Marguerite in *Faust* (as she would be heard doing in *The Age of Innocence*)—"all the nouveau riche were on hand," as one reporter wrote with some contempt. "The Goulds and Vanderbilts and people of that ilk perfumed the air with the odor of crisp greenbacks." Downtown that same evening, the writer continued, the people who truly represented New York society, and who were "distinguished by their brilliant social altitude and by the identification of their names with Manhattan's history," crowded the Academy of Music "to show their willingness to support an opera season backed by something more than the money bags of indiscreet speculation." Mrs. Paran Stevens, who owned boxes in both places, sized up the situation perfectly and divided her evening between them.

She had, meanwhile, inaugurated a series of Sunday evening musical teas, where talented American and foreign musicians performed and tea was served from one of the only two samovars in New York. The genial William Travers, who was encouraged to say such things, was heard to remark to Mrs. Stevens that the music must indeed be good, since certainly no one would come to eat the food she served. She entertained foreign nobility; she arranged dazzling international marriages; her stately figure was photographed in the costume of Queen Elizabeth at the Vanderbilts' enormous fancy-dress ball. "Everybody goes to Mrs. Stevens'," said a social columnist, "and she is acknowledged to be one of the cleverest and most accomplished women in society."

The word "everybody" was an exaggeration. Many in the old guard continued to look at her with uneasy resentment, one of them voicing his displeasure at even having been invited to dine at the Washburns in order to meet her. Unfortunately for Edith Jones and Marietta Stevens' son Harry, a number of those hostile to Mrs. Stevens belonged to the Joneses' social contingent. Emelyn Washburn noticed the Rhinelanders, among others, coming to pay their New Year's Day call and behaving with studied rudeness to Mrs. Paran Stevens, who had arrived, full of vitality and charm, on the same formal errand.

4

In November 1880 the Joneses prepared to go abroad once more. As Edith's father approached his fifty-ninth birthday, his health was failing badly. He had been declining for more than a year, and he appears to have remained in New York against his doctor's wishes only so that Edith could make her social debut there. But by the fall of 1880 he was seriously unwell: his kindly nature was succumbing to nervousness and irritability; his cheeks were sunken, his face looked aged. His doctor was adamantly opposed to his spending another winter in the city and felt that the warmer climate of southern France might prolong his life for several years.

Distressed as she was by the reason for their journey, Edith could not help being excited at the prospect of returning to Europe after eight years of what suddenly seemed to her complete, if enjoyable, frivolity. In London she braved the fogs and biting cold to roam the streets, stare at the old houses, and wander through the National Gallery. The family moved on to the Riviera and rooms in a little hotel in Cannes. That still quite rustic resort consisted largely of a quiet colony of villas with leafy gardens, and Lucretia Jones discovered there old American friends who had married into the European aristocracy. With the Princess Jeanne de Polignac, the daughter of one of them, Edith formed a lasting friendship.

She passed a winter and spring of harmless amusement: picnics on the shore, walks through the pine woods, tennis parties and informal dinners on the lawn, and in the company of agreeable people who would, she felt, no more understand her literary dreams than her friends had back in New York. But those dreams were fading; she continued to read everything she could lay her hands on, but she was writing almost nothing at all.

One literary effort was occasioned by the appearance of Harry Stevens, who caught up with the family in Venice in September 1881. Edith's father had given her Ruskin's *The Stones of Venice* and Pater's *Renaissance Studies,* and the combination of her eagerly attentive suitor and those two very different discourses upon beauty led Edith to compose a poem called "Intense Love's Utterance."

It is an elegant hoax, in which the male lover, after softly sighing the intensity of his desire for his "heart's lady," is forced to admit that he simply does not have the money to give her the kind of artistic gifts she is used to.

> How far would a poor fellow's income
> Extend to your dadoes and friezes,
> Your Chippendale table, your ceiling
> From a study of Paul Veronese's?

The inventory continues ruefully, in a cascade of Swinburnian rhythms, to conclude in gloomy rumination:

> No, no—what is life? A succession
> Of fleeting pulsations (as Pater
> Has told us in *Renaissance Studies*),
> Which must cease for us sooner or later,
> And Art can alone make them precious,
> And lovely and dear as old plate—
> Go back to your dadoes and friezes,
> For love is a thing out of date!

George Frederic was growing steadily worse, and in early 1882 the family went back to Cannes. Harry Stevens stayed with them throughout the last illness, and his courteous, even-natured presence, along with his open devotion to Edith —so Lucretia wrote Emelyn Washburn—was a comfort to them all. In early March, Edith's father was stricken by paralysis, and he died ten days later. "I am still haunted by the look in his dear blue eyes," Edith would write in her memoirs, "which had followed me so tenderly for nineteen years, and now tried to convey the goodbye message. Twice in my life I have been at the death-bed of some one I dearly loved, who has vainly tried to say a last word to me; and I doubt if life holds a subtler anguish." (The other occasion was the death of Walter Berry in 1927.)

Lucretia and Edith returned to Newport, Harry Stevens either accompanying them or arriving shortly afterward. The courtship went forward amid walks and drives, tennis parties, and dancing till late hours at the Newport Casino. That capacious assembly of entertainments had been recently built by James Gordon Bennett of the New York *Herald* and equipped with club quarters, dance floor, restaurant, theater, and what quickly became the most famous tennis courts in the country.

This time, the persistent rumors about Harry Stevens and Pussy Jones were approaching truth. On a stiflingly hot Sunday in August, Edith appeared at the home on Redwood Street of her Uncle Fred Rhinelander, bearing a note from her mother.

My dear Fred—

I had hoped to go to you today with Pussie to announce her engagement to Mr. Stevens, but the heat has made me feel so wretchedly for the last day or two that I was afraid even to venture to Church today. So she must tell her own story—as I wished you and Fanny to know before it is announced to her friends tomorrow.

I shall hope soon to be able to tell you how pleased we all are, notwithstanding this other loss to me within these last months, which naturally is hard for she has always been so very, very dear to me in all the years we have had together, friend and loving child in one. Love to all—

Affectionately yours,

L.S.J.

The incoherence of the second paragraph and the faintness of the handwriting can probably be attributed to heat, as well as to the "other loss" Lucretia had suffered with the death of her husband. One is skeptical at the description of Edith as a "friend and loving child in one," but it is easy to imagine that Lucretia was genuinely pleased to have her oddly difficult daughter off her hands, and in so excellent a match.

On August 19, *Town Topics* in Newport told its readers that "Mr. Henry Stevens, only son of Mrs. Paran Stevens, is reported to be engaged to Miss Edith Jones, daughter of the late George F. Jones, Esq." Despite such revelations, Harry's mother was ominously withholding her approval. She could almost be said not to have acknowledged that an engagement had taken place. Mrs. Paran Stevens appeared regularly at the Monday evening dances at the Casino: she made one of a small dinner party given by Julia Ward Howe for Oscar Wilde, who had booked in at Ocean House in Newport on his well-publicized tour of the United States; in early September she gave a huge reception for President Chester Arthur. It is not recorded that she arranged a single event in honor of her son's forthcoming nuptials and of her prospective daughter-in-law.

The marriage, according to *Town Topics*, was scheduled to be held at All Saints Church in New York in the middle of October. Then on October 28 the same paper reported, with an air of quietly rubbing its hands, "The marriage of Mr. Henry Stevens, Mrs. Paran Stevens's son, to Miss Edith Jones, which was announced for the latter part of this month, has been postponed, it is said, indefinitely."

Rumors and counterrumors flew across the island. As Emelyn Washburn would remember it in her old age, Lucretia Jones told her that Mrs. Stevens was intensely resentful of the coldness shown her by members of the Joneses' set and had refused, as it were, to allow her son to marry into the enemy camp. The fifteen-year-old Helen Rhinelander, Edith's first cousin, gave a rather different story in a letter to her brother Tom:

> Is it not sad about Pussy's engagement being broken? I have only seen her once and then she did not appear particularly sad. It is evidently Mrs. S's fault, or rather she is the cause. We have not heard much about it, only Mrs. S behaved insultingly to Aunt Lu! Don't repeat this for the world. Aunt Lu told this to Mamma! I doubt Pussy and H have changed in their feeling for one another, but that Mrs. S is at the bottom of it all.

The Newport *Daily News* provided still another speculation:

> The only reason assigned for the breaking of the engagement hitherto existing between Harry Stevens and Miss Edith Jones is an alleged preponderance of intellectuality on the part of the intended bride. Miss Jones is an ambitious authoress, and it is said that, in the eyes of Mr. Stevens, ambition is a grievous fault.

What is not to be doubted is that Marietta Stevens was the one to bring the engagement to an end; her son, however gallant a courtier, did not have the strength of character, and perhaps not the will, to stand up to her. Yet from all that one knows of her, it seems unlikely that Mrs. Stevens was moved primarily by a spirit of social revenge, though that probably played some part. For all her forcefulness and flashes of temper, Mrs. Stevens was essentially a kind woman, and one more apt to abet than to oppose the marital desires of the young. A more serious consideration had to do with property.

Paran Stevens' will had declared that his son would come into direct possession of his property either upon his twenty-fifth birthday or upon the occasion of his marriage. Harry's share of his father's estate amounted to more than a million and a quarter dollars. In order to maintain the very social display which had aroused the ill will of the Rhinelanders and others, Mrs. Stevens needed to retain control over her son's trust fund and to divert some of it into her own hands; it was in fact her constant litigation about the fund that got her into court so frequently. Harry was twenty-three in the summer of 1882. By forbidding his marriage to Edith Jones, Mrs. Stevens could at least hold the financial reins for two more years, and she might even win out in the long struggle with her stubborn co-executor.

Edith wrote Emelyn Washburn a short flat note, saying only that she had *had* to break the engagement; Marietta Stevens evidently allowed Edith to make the formal gesture. Four weeks later, toward the end of November, Edith was in Paris with her mother and her brother Harry. She called on Margaret Rutherford White, whose husband was attached to the American Embassy, and wrote young Lewis Rutherford cheerfully enough that his sister looked lovely and that the new baby was delightful.

She was probably less in love with Harry Stevens than he was with her. But the experience, while highly educational for the future social historian of New York in the 1870s and 1880s, was for the moment a deeply wounding one. Early in 1883 she was back in New York, and went to the second Patriarchs' Ball of the season on the arm of Julian White, Henry White's younger brother. As they entered Delmonico's, Julian could feel her begin to tremble, and he confided to his family how brave and shaken Pussy Jones had seemed under the watchful and knowing eyes of the other guests.

4. The Inconceivable Thing

In *A Backward Glance*, Edith Wharton remarked that after she came back to America with her mother in the wake of her father's death, "there followed two gay but uneventful New York winters." Thus silently and understandably did she pass over the entire episode with Harry Stevens.

Whether the winter and spring of 1883 were gay or not, they seem certainly to have been uneventful; not until the summer of that year did there occur another critical event in her life. She was taken up, meanwhile, by the somewhat older married women, the true rulers of society, and her calendar was a crowded one. The humiliation of the broken engagement was gradually forgotten, and Edith inspired expressions of devotion from several eligible young men. But though she was capable of a kind of innocent ardor, she could feel no more than a modest liking for any of her new suitors.

She felt, indeed, that her existence was somehow a partial one. None of the companions she lunched, dined, and attended dances with showed any interest in her own world of hidden beauty—of language, of thought, of sensation. She had an unfocused sense of inner strength unused and, by others, unvalued. Yet in her sensitiveness to such matters, her young women friends struck her as cleverer than she was and quicker at light repartee. She also thought they were for the most part better-looking than she—though at twenty-one, Edith Jones was undeniably attractive: her figure was well developed and her carriage graceful; a slightly turned-up nose added piquancy to her otherwise regular features; she had a rather sweet shy smile, and her eyes were alternately watchful and tender. Her swept-up russet hair clustered tightly about her well-shaped head.

Edith had also at this stage achieved a degree of financial independence. By the terms of George Frederic's will, his widow inherited books, pictures, and furniture, an amount not to exceed thirty thousand dollars for the purchase of a new home, and an annuity of six hundred dollars. Her husband explained in the will that Lucretia had already "a considerable income in her own right"; in the late 1870s she had come into a sizable legacy from a Rhinelander relative. Edith and her two brothers each inherited twenty thousand dollars outright and an equal share of the estate remaining after the other bequests.

Edith's share was held in trust for her by her brothers and a third person. In support of this clause, her father observed that in all probability she would before long "possess much other property in her own right"—presumably by inheritance from other sources. The trust fund grew steadily, as any investment in New York property was almost certain to do in the late 1880s. By mid-decade it amounted perhaps to eight or nine thousand dollars a year: not the income of a Vanderbilt, obviously, but a healthy sum when multiplied nearly ten times to give it modern meaning.

It was at Bar Harbor in July 1883 that Edith had her first encounter with a young man named Walter Van Rensselaer Berry. He was the second child of Nathaniel Berry and Catharine Van Rensselaer, and in the old New York way was distantly related to everybody, including Lucretia Jones. He was three years older than Edith, having been born in 1859 in Paris, where his parents had come with their infant daughter for the season. Nathaniel had himself been born in Connecticut, but after his marriage he had moved to Albany to take up residence in his wife's family property there. It was in Albany that Walter grew up. He graduated from Harvard in the class of 1881, taking an "Honorable Mention" in French, and set off at once for a grand tour of Europe which lasted eighteen months. Upon his return near the end of 1882 he settled in Washington to begin an extensive private reading in law. By the time he met Edith Jones he was almost ready to present himself for admission to the bar.

Walter Berry was strikingly tall, six feet three, and strikingly thin, with probing blue eyes set in an oval face (his left eyelid tended to droop a little in concentration), a modest brown mustache, and an aristocratically prominent nose.

Though committed to a legal career, and by personal inclination to international law, Berry had a cultivated and discriminating literary mind. Unlike any of her current New York friends, whose social equal he so manifestly was, he was willing to talk at length about great literature and was able to point out to Edith fresh beauties in poems and novels that she loved and had thought to understand perfectly. He seemed to talk to her from a great height, and yet to draw her up level with him to share his somewhat austere vision of artistic beauty.

He was given to periodic apothegms, in which Edith found nothing didactic. On one occasion during the few weeks he spent at Bar Harbor that summer, Berry remarked with decision: "It is easy to see superficial resemblances between things. It takes a first-rate mind to perceive the differences underneath." Edith felt that the words gave her, on the spot, the critical orientation she had been looking for, and for the first time in her life she had the sense of a genuine communion of intelligence and literary appreciation. She pressed Berry to continue in the same vein—more so, as it turned out, than Berry congenitally wanted to.

Since Edith had last been at Bar Harbor, there had been added a resplendent hotel called Rodick's, which would gain national prestige during its twenty-year life. It had five hundred rooms, but since many visitors—like Berry, and Edith and Lucretia Jones—rented cottages and only "mealed" at the hotel, eight hundred guests might be served at mealtime. One can imagine Edith and Walter Berry, engrossed in conversation, strolling the long twenty-foot-wide piazza that ran partway around the building, or meeting by arrangement in the famous main lobby (known by the young as "The Fish Pond"), where the Bar Harbor talent for flirtation reached its finest and fullest expression. They went bicycling together, tramped along the mountain trails, and canoed on the lakes.

Before Berry's brief stay was over, both he and Edith realized that their rapidly developing relationship had become a serious one, though not an explicit word had been voiced by either. Each was dreaming of the possibility of marriage, yet something held both of them back. In a letter written to Edith Wharton four decades later, Walter Berry gave the following account of his view of what happened.

Two days before he was due to depart for Washington, and after a particularly intimate afternoon on the lake, matters between them were obviously approaching a climax. Berry lay awake that night in his cottage, wondering should he marry this remarkable and so well suited girl, who, he was sure, was ready to accept his proposal. In the light of day, it astonished him that he had even considered proposing marriage. He told himself that he was nothing but a penniless lawyer, and not even that yet, no more than a student, with hardly enough money to pay the canoe rental and his bill at Rodick's. He said nothing during another day of walking and canoeing, and that night he felt intuitively that the moment had passed. Next morning he took his leave, and it was fourteen years before the friendship would be renewed.

Such was Walter Berry's reminiscence of 1923. The truth appears to be otherwise. There is no reason to doubt that Berry was greatly taken with Edith Jones and that he did meditate marriage, though probably not as earnestly as he would suggest. For one thing, Berry (who was anything but penniless) maintained a careful lack of final seriousness in his relations with women. His tastes, then and later, drew him betimes to women more frivolous and fluttery than Edith, not to say more beautiful and rich. Even while discoursing on literature and criticism, his eye did not fail to notice some ravishing debutante passing by. He wearied a little of Edith's persistent intellectuality, but when he tried to steer the conversation toward the personal and even the lightly amorous, Edith, with a kind of alarm, hurried on to a new literary topic.

For her part, Edith thought sadly in retrospect that she had behaved ineptly, and in too reserved and "unwomanly" a manner. She still had a romantic vision of some great love that would harness the dormant power within her and harmonize her inner and outer worlds. In Berry she thought for a fleeting moment that she had found it. But in addition to the distracting excitement of his talk, something prevented her from offering him at just the right instant the encouraging look, the responsive smile. It was not puritanism, though she may have heard her mother's voice saying that such conduct was "not nice." It was certainly not the stiff control of her feelings that would later characterize her. More than anything, it was a shy ignorance of the arts of love making.

This time, after Berry made his courteous departure, the humiliation was a hidden one; no one close to her realized what she had gone through. Only from seeming echoes in her fiction can one guess at the depth of her disappointment at the word not spoken.

2

Edith, in the phrase she employed in a very similar context, was "still quivering with pain and bewilderment" when there appeared at Newport in August yet another suitor for her affections. This was a thirty-three-year-old gentleman from Boston named Edward Robbins Wharton—"Teddy" to his intimates. He had been friendly over the years with Harry Jones—they were of nearly the same age—and had visited Pencraig a number of times. Now he began to be drawn further into the Jones family circle.

Teddy's father, William Craig Wharton, had belonged to the Virginia branch of the proliferating and always socially impressive Wharton clan, but after he married Nancy Spring of Boston he settled in that city, and Teddy was born in the suburb of Brookline. He was admitted to the sophomore class at Harvard in 1870, and during the next two years he distinguished himself by being "publicly and privately admonished" more than fifty times for absences from class and chapel. His intellectual and theological enthusiasms were indeed scanty; he was always happier when he could be away camping, or on horseback, or fishing for salmon in Canada or perch and sunfish in New England.

He was said to have been the best-looking man in his Harvard class of 1873, and his graduation picture reveals a dignity of feature and expression, an attractive combination of gentleness and maturity which seemed to augur a career of useful and influential activity beyond anything he ever made the slightest pretense of attempting. He left all that to his older brother William Fisher Wharton, who went on from Harvard College to the Harvard Law School and thereafter entered a period of public service which culminated in his appointment as Assistant Secretary of State by President Benjamin Harrison in 1889.

In 1883 Teddy was living on Beacon Street in Boston, in a household presided over by his capable mother. Teddy called her "Duck," and regarded her (as he told an aunt) as "the most attractive woman I know, apart entirely from the fact of being my mother." His wants were also catered to by his younger sister Nancy, a somewhat rattlebrained spinster, inclined to stoutness. Teddy had no money of his own, but his parents gave him an allowance of two thousand dollars a year, and under the circumstances his needs were few. He had no vocation, nor any intention of seeking one. He was popular and gregarious, and something of a gourmet and connoisseur of good wines; he was as welcome as a handsome, well-born bachelor might be expected to be at Boston social gatherings. He made the customary gesture of helping out in several of the city's charitable institutions.

Late in August, Lucretia Jones gave a dinner party in Teddy's honor, the only dinner of her social life so elaborate that it earned mention in *Town Topics*. But if it was her aim to rouse her easygoing guest to a more ardent courtship, the effort was not visibly successful. Teddy had been too comfortable a bachelor for too many years to invite any sudden and radical change in his life.

The months drifted by. In February 1884, Teddy came to New York to escort Edith to the second Patriarchs' Ball, an affair attended also by Mrs. Paran Stevens and her daughter and son-in-law, though not by Harry; by the Freddy Joneses and a variety of Schermerhorns and Van Rensselaers; not to mention Mrs. Astor and Ward McAllister, the Lorillards, the Cornelius Vanderbilts, and hordes of others. Following it, Edith and Teddy went their own ways.

It was not until the end of March a year later (1885) that *Town Topics* could announce the engagement of Miss Edith Jones to Mr. Edward Wharton of Boston. According to the paper's Boston correspondent, the news was a chief topic of conversation in the city: "The lady," he said, "is not generally known here," but Mr. Wharton's great popularity made his "good fortune" a matter for rejoicing. To an abbreviated list of relatives and friends, Lucretia Jones sent an engraved wedding invitation which failed to mention Edith's name: "Mrs. George Frederic Jones requests the honour of your presence at the marriage of her daughter to Mr. Edward R. Wharton, at Trinity Chapel, on Wednesday April Twenty-ninth at twelve o'clock."

The ceremony was performed by the Reverend Morgan Dix, the rector of Trinity. "The wedding was a quiet one," *The New York Times* reported, in a column which also detailed the lavish arrangements and vast attendance at a marriage of two other socialites the same day. *Town Topics* raised its eyebrows at the absence of any bridesmaids—"which many people," it murmured, "expected there would have been." There were four ushers, including one of Edith's Rhinelander cousins; Teddy's best man was Percival Lowell.

Edith appeared in a white satin dress, with a court train covered with puffs of white silk mull; there was more drapery of mull and lace at her throat, and a cluster of lilies of the valley. Her veil, which was of tulle, was fastened by a glittering diamond tiara: some of the diamonds had been worn by Lucretia when she married George Frederic Jones more than forty years before; the rest were a gift from Teddy. Instead of the usual bouquet, Edith carried a gilt-bound prayer book. After the wedding, breakfast was served for an even more select group in Lucretia's new home at 28 West Twenty-fifth Street.

The bride and groom went directly to Pencraig ("Mr. and Mrs. Alfred Wharton have arrived in Newport," *Town Topics* observed conscientiously). They began at once to take part in social activities rather more energetically than

Edith was accustomed to. On Memorial Day the Whartons were noticed among the fashionable crowd around the clubhouse in Jerome Park—it was the opening day of the spring races—in company with the Perry Belmonts, the Goelets, the Marquis of Queensbury, and James and Sara Roosevelt.

Six weeks later Edith heard that Harry Stevens had died in Newport Hospital. Since the breaking of his engagement to Edith Jones, Harry had been as visible as ever in New York and Newport society. But he fell ill in the midst of the season, and the doctors were unable to diagnose the cause. There was some talk of an abdominal tumor; one member of the Rutherford household put it about that Harry had gone insane after being jilted by Edith. In the Stevens family memory, it was an unexpected eruption of his youthful illness, tuberculosis. Harry died on July 18, just twenty-six years old.

3

A quarter of a century later Henry James would say that in marrying Teddy Wharton, Edith had done "an almost—or rather an utterly—inconceivable thing." By that time most of Edith's friends felt much the same way; and yet, considering her situation in 1885, her acceptance of Teddy is understandable enough. There had been the bruising termination of her engagement to Harry Stevens, followed all too quickly by the damage to her emotions and her self-confidence by the bewildering silence of Walter Berry. As 1884 gave way to 1885, moreover, Edith found herself entering her twenty-fourth year, dangerously close to the age beyond which the young women of her set became steadily less marriageable. And whatever her innermost opinion of the ways of New York social life, it had been drilled into her that marriage was the only real goal of the debutante.

If Emelyn Washburn's old-age memory is to be trusted, Edith felt herself during the brief engagement to be really in love for the first time; and in a memoir of her own in the 1930s, Edith repeated much the same thing. Teddy's attractions, it should also be remembered, were genuine ones.

He was extremely good-looking, he had the best of dispositions, he was a man of taste, and he was thoroughly devoted in a winningly subservient way. There was no suggestion, for example, that the married couple should settle in Boston and create their social world out of Teddy's family and friends. Their different financial situations may have affected the decision; in any event they took up their married life in Edith's New York and Newport. Teddy, like Edith, was fond of the out-of-doors and of horses; and if his literary sophistication lagged far behind his gourmet habits, there was some recompense, from his wife's point of view, in his affectionate and intimate manner with small dogs.

Boston-bred though he was, Teddy Wharton had something of the social ease Edith was used to in the old New York families; he was half a Virginian and seemed to her largely liberated from the stammering self-consciousness she had observed in the proper Bostonians. Newporters took to him from the day of his brief exchange with a wealthy *arriviste* from the Middle West. Hurrying up Bellevue Avenue, overdue for a lunch engagement, Teddy had thumbed a ride in a butcher's cart to the cottage where he was expected. Hearing of this, the Midwesterner took Teddy aside and said: "Wharton, I hear you rode up the Avenue in a butcher's cart. I wouldn't do that if I were you." Teddy gazed at him blandly and said: "No, if I were you, I wouldn't do that either." The anecdote must have delighted and comforted Edith, as representing the perfect distinction between snobbery and the aristocratic temper.

In considering Edith's motives, finally, we must take into account the role of Lucretia Jones. It is possible to make too much of the several oddities: the bride's name missing from the invitation, the hastily prepared wedding (barely a month between the engagement and the ceremony), the absence of bridesmaids, and so on. Still, Lucretia does seem to have been more determined than ever to have her daughter's marital destiny settled. And Edith herself may be imagined as longing to escape from her mother's supervision. It would not, immediately, be much of an escape. For the next few years the Whartons, when not abroad, lived in a cottage on Lucretia's Newport estate, and on their visits to New York they invariably stayed in the house on West Twenty-fifth Street.

There is no question that the sexual side of the marriage was a disaster. Edith entered into it in almost complete ignorance of sex and a blind dread of what was in store for her. Lucretia adamantly refused to enlighten her. A few days before the wedding, Edith plucked up her courage and went to her mother, her heart beating wildly, to ask "what marriage was really like." Lucretia's face instantly took on the look of icy disapproval which Edith most feared, and she answered with impatience: "I never heard such a ridiculous question!"

Edith's tormented anxiety spurred her to continue. "I'm afraid, Mamma— I want to know what will happen to me." After an awful silence, during which Lucretia's expression changed to disgust, she said with a distinct effort: "You've seen enough pictures and statues in your life. Haven't you noticed that men are . . . made differently from women?" Edith faltered out an uncomprehending "Yes." "Well, then—?" Edith stood staring blankly at her mother, quite unable to grasp her meaning, until Lucretia brought the conversation to an abrupt end: "Then for heaven's sake don't ask me any more silly questions. You can't be as stupid as you pretend."

The marriage was not consummated for three weeks. Whatever happened on those first occasions, it had the effect of sealing off Edith's vibrant but untutored erotic, nature for an indefinite period, with far-reaching consequences for her psychological makeup and her very practice of life. She would in fact say that the failure of her mother to supply her with even the rudiments of sexual education

—a failure Lucretia shared, of course, with most other New York society mothers of the day—"did more than anything else to falsify and misdirect my whole life." The falsity and misdirection were in fact overcome in time, but she always felt that the wilfully obtuse parental treatment of young women like herself with regard to sex contained the seeds of tragedy.

4

During the first three or four years of her marriage, Edith Wharton led a life which, if not misdirected, seemed to lack any clear direction at all. Not that it was incoherent. On the contrary, it adhered to a strict pattern: the Whartons spent the period of June to February each year in Pencraig Cottage, just across Harrison Avenue from Pencraig itself, and from February to June they traveled in Europe, mostly in Italy. It is no doubt too facile to say that her suppressed sexual energy went into the work of creating a home and a social ambience, and planning complicated European journeys; but it remains true that she went about these tasks with remarkable vigor and resolution, of a sort she would display ever after in a series of homes and an endless succession of travels.

The household gradually took shape. Central to it was the housekeeper, Catharine Gross, a buxom, round-faced, placidly competent Alsatian woman in her early thirties (she had apparently been deserted by her husband, and had a teen-age son living in Europe) who had been taken on the year before the marriage as Edith's attendant. They seem to have communicated largely in French; Edith, who invariably called the other woman Gross or Grossie, would grow fonder of her than of almost anyone else in her life. The other key figure was the butler, Arthur White, an Englishman in his late twenties who joined the Whartons in 1888. He had a marked Cockney speech, remarking once to a visitor who admitted to feeling poorly: "I thought you 'ad an 'ectic flush, sir"; but his bearing was benignly authoritative. There were, in addition, several housemaids, a cook, and a small staff of gardeners.

Pencraig Cottage—which really was a cottage, unlike the grand mansions called "cottages" beginning to arise along the cliffs—was a compact frame building of no particular style. But a broad pleasant lawn ran back behind it, with tall trees that provided shade on the warm summer days, and Edith could busy herself with her staff laying out a garden. In this, she took an increasingly professional interest. It was a happy distraction, for Newport as a whole was losing its charm for her as the old rustic atmosphere of her youth gave way before the bustling show of enormous wealth. The island life was much to Teddy Wharton's taste, however; both the opportunities it offered for fishing and riding, and the often ingenious social activities that filled the days and evenings during the five months of the season. Edith now regarded these affairs as "mundanities," but she played her social role with determined skill, aided invaluably by the imperturbable Gross.

Nor should it be said, for all her expressed disdain, that her matronly obligations were truly abhorrent to her: early and late Edith Wharton retained the social zest and aptitude inherited from her New York background.

The relation between husband and wife appears to have settled into an amicable one. There was neither a shared literary interest nor passion between them; but on Edith's part there was a companionable fondness, and on Teddy's an admiring if wary devotion. There is no indication how Teddy felt at this time about the virtual—more likely, the total—cessation of their sexual life together; he seems simply to have accepted it, however it may have perplexed him. He was a cheerful soul: "Teddy is like sunshine in the house," Lucretia Jones told Emelyn Washburn, who could believe it—she had warmed to Teddy, who never failed to call upon her, accompanied by a swarm of Edith's little dogs.

It was Edith, obviously, who dominated the Wharton household. As time passed, she may almost be said to have assumed a parental relation to her husband, thirteen years older though he was. In her memoirs she would stress his "natural boyishness"; but if she developed a maternal attitude toward him, there was also something of the affectionately impatient father in her posture. Teddy acknowledged this, and her strength of character, by sometimes calling her "John," following Harry Jones's habit. Edith called him "Old Man," but rather with the air of one who addresses a big man as "Tiny."

Her entire situation seemed to her static and obscurely frustrating, and she was restlessly on the lookout for persons of greater mental vitality than she could find in Newport or in her own home, and with a greater interest in books and painting, a keener awareness of history. She found a few such persons in a slowly accumulating group of New Yorkers, some of whom she had known since adolescence, and others whom she had met in her first married years and particularly after she and Teddy made a home for themselves in New York in 1889. Among them was Robert Minturn, whose family had provided the city with social and intellectual leaders for several generations: a man of exquisite artistic taste and a fine linguist, but whose chronic ill-health limited him to a life of appreciation and collecting. Ogden Codman, a younger architect of considerable promise, sometimes made part of the group, and John Cadwalader, Princeton graduate and lawyer, the son of a former Assistant Secretary of State.

And there was Bayard Cutting, Sr., one of the most prodigiously successful of the post–Civil War railroad tycoons, a sworn enemy of the "robber barons," and an enthusiastic and fairly discerning purchaser of European art treasures for his New York home at Seventy-second Street and Madison Avenue and his charming country estate, Westbrook, on Long Island. Cutting and his wife, Olivia, were close friends of the Freddy Joneses, and regular fellow attendants at the Patriarchs' Balls.

Thinking back to these men and two or three others, Edith Wharton said that they "had at last stirred the stagnant air of old New York, and in their particular circle" (a circle, she added, that "had happily always been mine") "it was full of the dust of new ideas." But she also came to feel, as she once told Bernard Berenson, that with one or two exceptions these individuals had led "starved existences . . . compared to what they might have been in England and France," and reading over their memoirs and their published correspondence in her old age, she found in them a "withered wistfulness" and a "loneliness that wrings the heart of those who have escaped it."

In the 1880s and 1890s, Edith Wharton was too grateful for the chance to talk seriously about literature and ideas to be more than indistinctly conscious of the wistfulness and loneliness. But she was aware of how little connection there was between the cultivated side of her friends' personalities and the rest of their lives. Theirs was a passive and restricted intelligence. A genuine interest in the arts did not bestir them to seek out those few in New York who were actively engaged in them. If they did not positively frown on well-born persons dedicating themselves to creativity, as the friends of Edith's parents had done, they did nothing to encourage Edith's subdued literary aspirations. When she returned to writing, the best of them worried that her work might interfere with her worldly responsibilities.

Among the latter was Egerton Winthrop, to whom of all the group Edith gave her strongest and most long-lasting affections. He was a man twice her age (his son Egerton was born the same year as Edith). He was cosmopolitan by nature, and had lived for many years in Paris, but after his wife's death he came back to New York in 1885 and settled in a nicely adorned little house on East Thirty-ninth Street. Like Edith, he could trace his ancestry back to colonial America: he was directly descended from John Winthrop, the far-seeing early governor of Massachusetts Bay. Even more than Minturn and the others, Egerton Winthrop combined a passionate interest in high society with a widely ranging love of literature, the arts, and scientific thought. All in all, he was the most rewarding and admirable person that Edith Wharton's segment of New York could provide her with.

Edith felt that she was one of the very few ever to understand him, for while others observed his fussy concern over the details of a dinner party or his rather pompous appearance in the ballrooms, she was almost alone in being exposed to his deep personal kindness and thoughtfulness (if Edith talked to anyone in these days about her own dissatisfactions, it was to Winthrop) and to his intellectual side. Taking up where Walter Berry had left off, Winthrop directed Edith to the French novelists, historians, and critics. This was of major importance, but perhaps even more so was his introducing her to the extraordinary world of Darwin and Spencer, Huxley and Haeckel. It was to Winthrop that she owed such understanding as she reached not only of the theory of evolution, but of the naturalist theory of the implacable power of the environment. Those fictional figures of hers who struggle pathetically and unsuccessfully against their stifling surroundings are belated offsprings of the tutelage of Egerton Winthrop—a combination, as it were, of Flaubert's *Madame Bovary* and the teachings of Herbert Spencer.

Married men were not missing from Edith Wharton's early New York group, though they never appear as such in her recollections of them; but there was a notable proportion of bachelors and widowers. It is our first occasion for seeing Edith's tendency to surround herself with unmarried males. There were to be several sets of this species, and probably a somewhat different reason may be assigned for Edith Wharton's enjoyment of each in turn. But it was a basic fact that she drew more substance from the company of men than of women, and the more so if the men in question could give her their undivided attention.

5

Italy was the first European love of Edith Wharton's maturity, and the annual tour of it was the happiest period of the year for her. It was a form of escape—from her mother and more largely from Newport—and it was a recurring act of discovery. What satisfied her most was to explore, exhaustively, little-known places, to inspect villages, churches, paintings unmentioned in the standard guidebooks. A chance remark by Julian Story—the youngest child of the sculptor and essayist William Wetmore Story, and a portrait painter of greater reputation than genius—put her on the track of the Italian eighteenth century, a chapter of cultural history which, like most people, she had hardly known existed. She had assumed that what was interesting about the Italy of former days had come to an end around 1600; now she began to travel in search of the painting and architecture, the beautifully carved and painted Venetian furniture of the *settecento*, supplementing her findings with broad reading in the social and political history of the epoch.

Teddy Wharton fell in easily with his wife's desire to travel as often and for as long as possible. He had made the prescribed European tour after graduation and had been abroad once or twice since; now he joined in the excursions into northern Italy with every sign of relish. Egerton Winthrop regularly accompanied the Whartons on these trips, and while he and Edith proceeded in a more leisurely manner, Teddy hurried on ahead in another carriage to reserve rooms at the next inn and arrange for meals. Since Gross and probably Edith Wharton's personal maid were also along to cater to the three travelers, the entourage, as it moved on from village to village, resembled that of some eagerly awaited visiting dignitary.

Under Winthrop's skillful guidance and learned commentary, Edith gradually took imaginative possession of the *settecento* world. From her American point of view, it seemed to her almost an ideal world: a world of vital interconnections, one in which the arts, the play of intellect, the graces of life, and a concern, however laggard, for the betterment of the social order went hand in hand. For the moment, that was enough for her: an alternative vision of the possibilities of life that she could look back on from the limited horizon of Newport. No intention had yet formed in her mind of converting her European experiences into literature. She was simply expanding on the knowledge and cultivating the taste acquired in her childhood and her premarital years. But given the intensity and the grasping power of her curiosity, she was also, almost without knowing it, collecting materials for fiction—in particular, and in northern Italy, for her first full-length novel, *The Valley of Decision.*

Winthrop was valuable in other ways. Pouring so much of her otherwise unused energy into the strenuous activity of travel, Edith allowed herself to grow querulous if the accommodations were not perfectly to her liking. When she complained about the relative uncleanliness of some Italian hotel, Winthrop could bring her down to earth by reminding her gently that the Princess of Wales might equally find Edith's "toilet appointments" inadequate. He was judicious, too, in helping her choose those items of Venetian furniture which, in the course of time and after many trips, made the décor of her Newport home as beautiful in its small way as that of any house on the island.

One day in the winter of 1888, Edith exclaimed to a friend that she would give everything she owned to make a cruise through the Aegean islands. The friend, James Van Alen (scion of one of the *very* good old New York families), replied that such a cruise need not cost as much as all that, and that he would be happy to charter a yacht if the Whartons would come as his guests. Edith and Teddy, appreciative as they were, decided it would be a better arrangement if they divided the expenses with Van Alen, and so feel free to make suggestions about some of the ports of call. Upon calculation, it turned out that their share of the four-month trip would almost exactly equal their total income for an entire year: about ten thousand dollars. Edith's brothers, the co-executors of her trust fund, remonstrated strongly; the entire Wharton clan protested that a cruise of this kind was unheard of and preposterous. Edith wavered, but when Teddy asked her if she seriously wanted to go and she made it clear that she did, he simply said "Come along, then."

It was an unforgettable experience. Edith brought with her Andrew Lang's translation of the *Odyssey,* and with Lang's elegantly archaic language and rolling prose rhythms in her ear, the adventure rose to epic proportions. In Piraeus, they picked up "Mind" Fearn, the American minister to Greece, and under Van Alen's leadership (he had known Greece well in his youth) the foursome steamed slowly through the islands, Edith as usual wanting especially to see the smallest and the least visited. In some places they were the first outsiders, so Edith understood, to enter the harbor. At Astypalaia the priest and head man led all the inhabitants out onto the ramparts to greet them, as though they were mysterious deities to be placated.

The Aegean cruise, Edith was to feel, was the crown of her youth. But heading back to Athens at the end of it, the Whartons had to face up to the awkward question of how they could manage for the remaining six months of the year. In Athens, however, a letter awaited Edith informing her that she had just come into a substantial legacy.

Her benefactor was Joshua Jones, who had died on March 14, 1888, at the age of eighty-two. He was a cousin of Edith's grandfather Edward Renshaw Jones, and Edith had barely heard his name mentioned. He was also one of those splendid eccentrics that had given spice to old New York. For the past two decades he had lived at the New York Hotel, a nearly total recluse and utterly parsimonious. He refused to indulge in the expense of a wood fire in his apartment during the winter, and when he ventured forth he eschewed both a private carriage and public transportation and went on foot to whatever point in the city he wanted to reach, however distant. It was in fact after such a walk one freezing night in the previous winter that he had caught pneumonia and died. But the size of his estate when he died proved, so Minnie Jones remarked to Edith, that he had all along merely been practicing a wise economy.

The estate consisted largely of shares in the Chemical Bank of New York and a number of properties on the West Side purchased with the annual yield from them. For more than half a century the Chemical Bank had been the private possession of the Jones and Mason families, whose intermarrying was extensive even in a period of multiplying cousinships. Control of the bank had passed intact between the generations from Mason to Mason and Jones to Jones; but when the bachelor John Quereau Jones died, he broke the chain by leaving his whole estate to his vocationless brother Joshua. The latter survived his other brother and his two sisters as well, inheriting from each in turn. Hoarding his increasing money over many years, he left a fortune well in excess of seven million dollars.

The balance, after a million dollars went to charities and special bequests, was divided between nephews, nieces, and cousins. As Joshua's second cousin, George Frederic Jones had been willed half of a one-ninth share of the remaining estate. A clause in the will provided that if George Frederic were deceased, the legacy would be divided equally among his surviving children. Edith Wharton and her two brothers each received outright real and personal estate amounting to upwards of $120,000 (equal today to at least half a million dollars after taxes). With this goodly sum, plus the rising income from Edith's trust fund and the amounts paid to Teddy, the Whartons' financial position was firmly established once and for all.

6

The coincidence of the Aegean adventure—the climax of several years of free-dom-finding European travel—and the inheritance from Joshua Jones marked a distinct stage in Edith Wharton's development. To an important degree, she was coming into her own. Until recently the elements in her life—even her husband —had been, so to speak, pressed upon her by her family and their friends. Now she was, within limits, pursuing her own interests and choosing her own associ-ates. She was storing up experiences of her own making, and she had at last an independent income. At twenty-six Edith Wharton was very nearly a person in her own right.

The next step was to find a home of her own, and to this end, in the winter of 1889, she and Teddy rented a small house on Madison Avenue and made their first independent trial of New York. A more significant sign of newly acquired freedom and identity was a sudden return to writing after a curiously inactive decade. Edith went back to the lyric poetry she had abandoned after 1878 and within a few months produced a number of new verses, several of them dealing with subjects drawn from her investigations of the Italian *settecento*. At the same time, partly under the worried prodding of Egerton Winthrop, she continued her life as a busy lady of the best society. A vague confusion of roles is suggested by the fact that, when she had selected three poems for possible publication and copied them out by hand, she sent them off to *Scribner's, Harper's,* and the *Century* accompanied only by her formal calling card.

One morning two weeks later, coming down into the narrow hall and looking into the letter box, she found three letters of acceptance. Dazed with excitement, she ran wildly up and down the stairs several times until she was calm enough to report the news to Teddy. In the perspective of her later career, the most important of the three poems was "The Last Giustiniani," which Edward L. Burlingame took for *Scribner's* and published in the October issue of the maga-zine.

The poem is a slender portion of historical romance set in eighteenth-century Venice and apparently based remotely on an actual incident (the same incident would provide Henry James a few years later with the kernel of his ill-fated play *Guy Domville*). The twelve stanzas are addressed by the last surviving member of the Giustiniani family to his bride, reminding her how he had been released from the monkish vows he had sworn many years before and been brought back to Venice to marry and perpetuate his race after all other Giustiniani males had died fighting valorously for their native city. Until now, he says, all women had been concentrated for him in the figure of the Virgin, and before a woman of flesh and blood he stands abashed (sacred as against earthly love was a theme Edith Wharton would come back to under different circumstances). "And yet," he tells his bride in the one stanza that hovers toward poetry:

And yet, stand back, and let your cloth of gold
Straighten its sumptuous lines from waist to knee,
And, flowing firmly outwards, fold on fold,
Invest your slim young form with majesty
As when, in those calm bridal clothes arrayed,
You stood before me, and I was afraid.

If her sense of history was stylized and Italianate, Edith Wharton's knowledge of dress could yet summon language to its aid.

In late August, Edith sent Burlingame another poem, and in her euphoria even asked him about the possibility of a volume of her verses. Burlingame told her gently that "we cannot like this poem quite as well for our purposes as 'The Last Giustiniani,' " and that the volume she suggested was not quite practical at the moment. But he added his hope that she would show him more of her work, and in September he selected "Happiness" from among a batch of longer poems.

While continuing to write poetry, Edith Wharton was also gearing herself to try her hand at fiction again. The following spring she presented Burlingame with "Mrs. Manstey's View," a nice little tale about an elderly widow living out her days in the third-floor back room of a New York boardinghouse, and her efforts to preserve her view of the cluttered gardens below—the one consolation of her life—against a construction going up on the house next door. Like several others of Edith Wharton's earliest stories, this one has no obvious bearing on the life she was actually leading; it was, rather, an imaginative escape from that life, even if toward penury and solitude.

On May 26, 1890, to his own mild surprise ("We cannot often use a sketch as slight as that which you have kindly sent us"), Burlingame took the story for *Scribner's,* and Edith Wharton's first avowed work of fiction went to press.

The Writing of Fiction: 1891-1905

PART TWO

5. Breakdown

Edith Wharton was twenty-nine before her first short story was published, and she appeared in no hurry to follow up on that small success (which was reprinted in a slim volume of the year's best stories). She had no clear sense, evidently, of having embarked upon a literary career: the few extant letters of the time make no mention of literary interests; domestic and social duties and travel were still her main preoccupations. We must remember as well her creative solitude; her associates in Newport and New York were unlikely to spur her on by inquiries about her "work." And she was beginning to suffer intermittently from mysterious spells of illness that interrupted such creative activity as she was inclined to attempt.

It was more than a year after she dispatched "Mrs. Manstey's View" before Edith Wharton had anything further to show. In the summer of 1891, after she and Teddy returned from their annual European trip—this one taking them to Paris and the French Riviera, and to Florence and Venice—she completed and sent to Burlingame a whimsical little allegory called "The Fullness of Life." The *Scribner's* editor thought it "a capital conception," but suggested revisions; part of the dialogue struck him as overly "soulful." When Mrs. Wharton unaccountably proved unable to make the changes, Burlingame offered to do them himself; to this proposal there was no answer. Burlingame finally begged his mutely mulish young author simply to return the story as it was, and in August 1893 Edith sent it back "with sincere regret that it is not better suited to your purposes."

Edith's recalcitrance during this small episode may have been due to the fact that "The Fullness of Life," dreamlike though it is, was a fairly direct literary transcription of her married life which she had no heart to tinker with further. The story begins with a nameless woman sinking through a peaceful stupor to her death. She awakes in the next world, on the threshold of eternity, and here she is interrogated by the Spirit of Life about her earthly experience. She complains to him that she has never known "the fullness of life." "You were married," says the Spirit; "yet you did not find the fullness of life in your marriage?" "Oh, dear no," she answers with some scorn; "my marriage was a very incomplete affair."

At this point Edith Wharton launched one of her most elaborate images, drawn typically from the interior design of a house, to provide an almost nakedly revealing summary of her psychological and sexual relationship with her husband.

I have sometimes thought that a woman's nature is like a great house full of rooms: there is the hall, through which everyone passes in going in and out; the drawing room, where one receives formal visits; the sitting room, where the members of the family come and go as they list; but beyond that, far beyond, are other rooms, the handles of whose doors are never turned; no one knows the way to them, no one knows whither they lead; and in the innermost room, the holy of holies, the soul sits alone and waits for a footstep that never comes.

Her husband had never gotten beyond the sitting room of her nature; in addition, his boots creaked, he never read anything but "railway novels," and he was stolidly unresponsive to artistic beauty (in all this, we recognize the first faint influence of *Madame Bovary*). Even so, when the Spirit of Life proposes matching her up with an ideal escort through eternity, she decides after all to wait for her husband. She has not loved him, but she was fond of him and would not feel at home without him. Besides, she adds with sad affection: "He is so helpless. His inkstand would never be filled, and he would always be out of stamps and visiting cards."

No clearer expression could be asked for of Edith Wharton's mixture of feelings about Teddy, six and seven years after their marriage: irritation at his shortcomings, wistful regret at the lack of full intimacy, a lingering maternal fondness. Teddy, from all that can be gathered, took this and other public dissections of their marital situation in good part, if indeed he read his wife's stories with any care. He was admiring and humble. "You know," he remarked to Sara Norton a number of years later, "I am no good on Puss's high plain of thought"; and he showed an astonished pride that anyone so vibrant socially, not to say so slim-waisted, was possessed of creative talent.

The early phase of Edith Wharton's literary life was characterized by spurts and pauses like those which held for "The Fullness of Life." Over a number of months in 1892 she worked on a novella called *Bunner Sisters*. When he received it in late December, Burlingame was warily complimentary: "I liked and admired much of it quite unreservedly," but "the motif and the admirable detail and color of the story fail to carry its great length"—it ran to about thirty thousand words. He concluded that he could not accept it for *Scribner's;* it was too long to print in a single issue, and it would be fatal to divide it—the effect of each half on the other would be one of "dreariness." A year later there was another occasion for Edith to suggest publishing it; but *Bunner Sisters* did not in fact see print until it was included in the collection called *Xingu* in 1916.

Bunner Sisters represents an effort much more ambitious than "Mrs. Manstey's View" to get imaginatively as far away as possible from the New York of the brownstone houses and Mrs. William Backhouse Astor that Edith Wharton felt pressing in on her. The story begins, indeed, with a contrast between that world and the inconspicuous shop near Stuyvesant Square run by Ann Eliza and

Evelina Bunner. The Bunner sisters live marginally, in their tiny shop and the one room in the back that serves as kitchen, bedroom, and sitting room; they are as poor as people can be without actually starving, and the main event of the opening pages is Ann Eliza's reckless purchase of a clock costing a dollar and seventy-five cents for her sister's birthday. Yet the motif of the tale is the stripping away from the penniless Ann Eliza of everything that she does possess or hold dear, every physical object and emotional tie, every dream of the future and link with the past.

As Edith Wharton's vision of human life steadied and clarified, it was, thus from the outset, one of experience as suffering: a mature version of her occasional childhood gloom. The question, meanwhile, of how Mrs. Edward Wharton of Madison Avenue and Newport could know anything about such lower-class misery is probably answered by a figure in the story known as "the lady with puffed sleeves." This mysterious and romantic personage appears from time to time, wearing a sweet sad smile, to buy black thread and silk or to order a bonnet made for her; then, the New York season over, she disappears for unknown places. One visualizes Edith Wharton paying occasional visits to a shop like that of the Bunner sisters, where her observant eye would record the details of the scene: the pavement outside littered with the lids of tomato cans, old shoes, and cigar stumps; the display window with its artificial flowers, wire hat frames, and jars of home-made preserves; and within, the orderly counters and the cramped living space beyond.

2

Edith Wharton was making practical, if still limited, gestures toward distancing herself from Lucretia Jones and her circle. In November 1891, after a somewhat obscure two-year legal wrangle, Edith had purchased for $19,670, from one Sarah Joseph, a small house described at the time as being located on Fourth Avenue near the corner of Seventy-eighth Street. Its address eventually became 884 Park Avenue, and it was nearly as far removed from Lucretia's home on West Twenty-fifth Street as social decency permitted. As late as 1901, Edith felt that she was " 'far from today' up in this suburb."

It was a tiny house, so tiny in fact (only fifteen feet across the front) that Edith and Teddy did not attempt to live in it at first, but rented it out at $1,300 a year, payable quarterly. But the furnishing of its rooms gave Edith Wharton another opportunity for one of the undertakings she came most to enjoy and to excel at: the creation of a new home. A few years later she managed to acquire the equally toylike house next door at 882, with the help of a twelve-thousand-dollar mortgage. It was just large enough to shelter the other members of the Wharton household. Edith and Teddy moved into 884 Park Avenue, and for the better part of a decade this would be their New York residence.

By that time Edith had already come into possession of the first real home of her own. In March 1893 she had paid the whopping sum of eighty-thousand dollars for a property on Ledge Road in Newport known as Land's End. This, similarly, was at the furthest possible distance from her mother's Pencraig, lying, as its name may suggest, at the far opposite end of the island, at the foot of the cliff walk, its windows looking directly across the Atlantic toward Ireland.

Edith, evidently, was willing to pay heavily for the privilege of putting several miles between herself and Lucretia Jones; in 1898 she took a fifty-thousand-dollar mortgage on the property to complete payment on it and to make improvements. The estate consisted of some two hundred thousand square feet, and contained a stable for the Wharton horses and another frame building in addition to the main house. Not much could be done with the ugly exterior of the house, but Edith lent grace and dignity to the grounds by laying out a circular court with high hedges and trelliswork niches. The interior was more susceptible to Edith Wharton's energetic creativity. She and Teddy—who was showing unexpected acumen and extremely good taste in the details of house design—held long consultations with the Boston architect and interior decorator Ogden Codman. Between them they arranged and discreetly related the rooms (sometimes combining two into one to gain an atmosphere of greater spaciousness) in the simple and functional way all three preferred, and in prominent places Edith set the Venetian pieces she had brought back from her journeys.

The total effect was civilized, and every attention was given to the comfort of guests; yet more than one of the latter felt that, aesthetically beautiful though it undoubtedly was, Land's End lacked warmth and was more of a showpiece than a home. The expression of high regard, in *A Backward Glance*, for Land's End —"with its windows framing the endlessly changing moods of the misty Atlantic, and the night-long sound of the surges against the cliffs"—perhaps reflected Edith's remembered relief at her newly won independence. Berkeley Updike, the stylish craftsman who printed several of Edith Wharton's early books and who was a frequent visitor, recorded the impression that she never cared a great deal for Land's End and that high rocks and breaking seas comprised a setting rather too elemental and untamed for her nature.

Among the first guests to be entertained at Land's End were Paul Bourget, the internationally famous French novelist and essayist, and his wife, the former Minnie David. Their visit in the early autumn of 1893 was a momentous one for Edith Wharton. She had been perfecting her role of hostess and had at dinner a procession of Astors and Van Alens, Belmonts and Goelets; but she was growing more depressed than ever by her Newport neighbors. They seemed to her, in her own phrase, hermetically sealed off from those cultural movements which in Europe, as she understood, touched and affected even the socially frivolous. With the Bourgets, literature and thought entered her living room almost for the first time, and on an imposing scale.

Paul Bourget, who was ten years older than Edith, had by 1893 produced more than half a dozen novels, a certain amount of verse, and a number of exceedingly well turned literary essays; he was on the verge of being elected to the French Academy. Edith was rather repelled by his fiction—though not for the reason given by the editor of *Town Topics*, who a few years before, assuming his customary air of moral pain, had denounced Bourget's novel *Cruelle Enigme* as "the worst book that ever found its way under a woman's pillow," and by way of showing its scabrous nature quoted several of its most erotic sentences. Then as later Edith Wharton was left coolly unconvinced by the masculine analysis of feminine sensuality.

But she admired Bourget's essays, particularly *Sensations d'Italie* of 1891, and she shared his immense fondness for Stendhal. Most of all, she liked the man, with his beautiful head, his grave and sometimes troubled features, his quick gay smile, his searching glance. She was perhaps even more taken with the Madonna-like Minnie Bourget, with her large gray eyes which always seemed lost in some faraway reverie, and her deep yet curiously accessible inwardness.

Bourget had come to America to write a series of articles about the country for the New York *Herald* (they were later collected in a volume called *Outre-Mer*). In Paris he was friendly with a cousin of Teddy Wharton's mother, and before he sailed was given a letter of introduction to the Whartons. During his three weeks' stay in Newport he came regularly to Land's End. Edith was at first a trifle intimidated. But Teddy, an invariably gracious host, no doubt eased matters by his friendly interest in their guests' comfort and by showing them around the property; and Bourget flattered Mme. Wharton by identifying many of her furnishings as deriving from the Italian *settecento*, and by carefully inspecting her crowded bookshelves and piles of literary magazines.

He drew her into talk about books and ideas; and more exciting yet for an uncertain apprentice, he exchanged with her—no one in her life had done this before—notions about fictional technique. His presence aroused in Edith Wharton a swirl of confused feelings about her own creative intentions, and at the same time it unloosed a flood of highly intellectualized conversation—to the point where Bourget seems to have been rather taken aback. It is obvious that Edith Wharton was the model for Bourget's portrait of the "intellectual tomboy" that he encountered in Newport. His initial response to her was at best ambivalent.

The intellectual tomboy, Bourget wrote, was one who

has read everything, understood everything, not superficially, but really, with an energy of culture that could put to shame the whole Parisian fraternity of letters. . . . Though like the others she gets her gowns from the best houses of the Rue de la Paix, there is not a book of Darwin, Huxley, Spencer, Renan, Taine, which she has not studied, not a painter or sculptor of whose works she could not compile a catalogue, not a school of poetry or romance of which she does not know the principles.

Then, moving in for the sword thrust:

> She has not an idea that is not exact, yet she gives you a strange impression as if she had none. One would say that she has ordered her intellect somewhere, as we would order a piece of furniture, to measure, and with as many compartments as there are branches of human knowledge. . . . Before the intellectual girl one longs to cry— "Oh, for one ignorance, one error, just a single one. May she make a blunder, may she prove not to know!" In vain. A mind may be mistaken, a mind may be ignorant, but never a thinking machine!

The description is a robust statement of Gallic masculine vanity, something almost harder to cope with, in its way, than the suave male indifference to intellectual matters that Edith Wharton was so often afflicted by in her native land. Not that the portrait lacks relevance. The phrase "energy of culture" is a happy one to identify a quality in Edith's nature and in those few others of her sparsely populated type; and described with a less severe irony, there has always been something moving about the American intellectual's need to compose the whole of his culture by himself.

Unaware, in any event, of Bourget's mixed reactions, and conscious only of their exhilarating conversations, Edith felt sure, when the visit came to an end, that a long friendship had opened between them, one that would play a large role in her life. Less than two months later the Whartons met up again with the Bourgets in Paris, where the latter were still occupying Bourget's old bachelor apartment in the Rue Vaneau, in the Faubourg St. Germain.

3

Bourget's visit aroused Edith Wharton to a little flurry of creative activity, the first of its kind, and before the end of October she had written two new and quite substantial stories. Burlingame took them both for *Scribner's*, declaring the first of them, "That Good May Come," to be "capital," and adding that he would take "everything else of the same quality you are willing to give me." His praise of the second, "The Lamp of Psyche," was more guarded; only later could he realize that it was not only the best of her works to date, but the first one in what would become her characteristic vein of somewhat astringent social comedy, with a turn of verbal wit and a strain of pathos.

Burlingame took the occasion on November 24 to issue a formal invitation:

> What should you think of letting the firm publish a volume of collected stories and sketches when these three ["The Fullness of Life" was also about to come out] have appeared in the magazine? I make the proposal officially and formally—they would be very glad to do it. There must be enough now, with some I have seen in manuscript.

Edith's reply revealed a stir of self-confidence mingled with hesitancy about her capacities; and it marked the beginning of a precarious sense of herself, less as a social matron who experimented cautiously with short stories from time to time than as, just possibly, a developing writer of fiction. After acknowledging how gratified she was by "Messrs Scribners' proposition," she informed Burlingame that she had several more stories he had not seen and spoke in an incipiently professional manner about

the longer one called "Bunner Sisters" which you may remember my sending you a year or two ago. You then pronounced it too long for one number of the magazine and unsuited to serial publication, but you spoke otherwise very kindly of it, and though I am not a good judge of what I write, it seems to me, after several careful readings, up to the average of my writing.

After closing up Land's End for the season, Edith and Teddy went up to Boston for a fortnight with Teddy's mother at 127 Beacon Street. Edith never enjoyed these visits very much, though the city itself, as she once said, refreshingly shook up her New Yorker's sense of life. Back in New York, in the second week in December, she had an inspiriting conference with Burlingame in the Scribners office before she and her husband sailed for Europe. They reached Paris just after Christmas and called at once upon the Bourgets. Paul Bourget endeared himself even more by suggesting that a poem Edith had recently written— "Life," a "sonnet after Carducci"—should appear in *Scribner's* in the same issue with a comparable poem of his own.

From Cannes in early March, Edith sent Burlingame a story which she then called "Something Exquisite." Burlingame rejected it almost with severity (he had turned down only one of her fictional offerings to date, the trifling item called "April Showers" in July 1893). Returning "Something Exquisite," he remarked that "I don't like the story as well as any of your others . . . in spite of the excellence (as always) of the execution." He thought that the narrative tone was forced and that the heroine's plight and her "aromatic pain" verged on caricature.

Edith's fragile self-confidence crumbled at once, and though she made a valiant effort to assure Burlingame how much she welcomed and needed his criticism, her letter of reply trembled with uncertainty about her ability and even about her literary identity.

Pray . . . have no tender-hearted compunction about criticizing my stories. Your criticism is most helpful to me, and I always recognize its justice. . . . I should like to bring out the book without adding many more stories, for I seem to have fallen into a period of groping, and perhaps, after publishing this volume, I might see better what direction I ought to take and acquire more assurance (the quality I feel I most lack). You were kind enough to give me so much encouragement when I saw you, and I feel myself so much complimented by the Messrs Scribners' request that I should publish a volume of stories, that I am very ambitious to do better, and perhaps I could get a better view of what I have done and ought to do after the stories have been published. I have lost confidence in myself at present. . . . Pray don't regard this as the wail of the rejected authoress—it is only a cry for help and counsel to you who have been so kind in giving me both.

The cry for help and understanding was written from Florence on March 26, 1894; but there were, luckily, several attractions on the Tuscan scene to ease Edith's spirit, if only temporarily. In Paris, Paul Bourget had given her a letter to a Florentine resident, Violet Paget, the brilliant and scholarly Englishwoman who, under the name of Vernon Lee, had written *Studies of the Eighteenth Century in Italy* and other superior works of the kind—volumes Edith Wharton had long treasured and had carried with her on the excursions into the remoter parts of Italy with Teddy and Egerton Winthrop. Now, in Florence once again, she drove out to Vernon Lee's villa, Il Palmerino, in Maiano (near Fiesole) and, after leaving Bourget's letter with the maid, she was soon invited to call.

Bourget had explained that Miss Paget rarely saw visitors, her time being taken up with her invalided half-brother, Eugene Lee-Hamilton, whose health had been broken by working overtime in the British Embassy in Paris during the Prussian siege of 1870. But as it happened, Lee-Hamilton, whose tenuous hold on life consisted mainly in having poetry read to him for a few moments each day (he was himself a poet of minor talent), had been much impressed by one of Edith Wharton's sonnets in *Scribner's*, and he urged his sister to invite Mrs. Wharton to call.

Edith found her brief glimpse of Lee-Hamilton, lying exhaustedly on his bed in a darkened room, surprisingly refreshing. It quickly became evident, however, that Vernon Lee was restive and resentful under the strain of tending for her half-brother (not to mention her two elderly ailing parents), and relations between brother and sister were edgy. By way of compensation, Miss Paget subjected her guest to a spate of almost overpowering talk.

Vernon Lee was slight in stature, with a long oval face and gleaming, bespectacled gray-green eyes. She dressed in a mannish style with collar and tie, and she was indeed lesbian in her inclinations. Edith, who was probably unaware of this, took to the older woman at once, as she would to other women over the years who, like Vernon Lee, combined gifts of mind and imagination with a somewhat unorthodox private character. Vernon Lee was, besides, one of the great talkers of her time. She was voluble, forceful, wide-ranging, and mercilessly clever, and she exuded such a knowledge of historical Italian life that more than once during these first visits Edith Wharton was reduced to humble silence.

All the more could Edith preen herself on a small but significant adventure in artistic discovery that befell her at this time. She had heard vaguely of a monastery, somewhere in the Tuscan hills southwest of Florence, that was said to contain a series of terra-cotta groups representing the scenes of the Passion. They were attributed to one Giovanni Gonnelli, known as the Blind Man of Gambassi, a seventeenth-century artist of no surviving reputation. Edith resolved to have a look at them. After some inquiry she learned that the monastery was thought to be near an obscure village named San Vivaldo, and on an April morning she and Teddy set off in search.

The monastery lay in a large opening within a hushed woodland area; monks could be seen (as they still can) working the vegetable gardens nearby. The terra cottas were housed, one by one, in the twenty-odd little chapels dotted amid the woods and on the slopes. One of the monks escorted Edith and Teddy through the chapels, gravely rehearsing the life and miracles of San Vivaldo (he was born in San Gemignano in the thirteenth century, and spent most of his life in a hollow chestnut tree on what is now the site of the monastery).

Expecting to find nothing more than crude imitations of better-known seventeenth-century terra cottas, Edith was instantly alerted by much finer and, she was rapidly convinced, much earlier work. In half a dozen cases, the life-size figures, set in a depressed arch at the far end of each chapel, had a severe simplicity, an absence of agitation, and sometimes a look of wondering ecstasy that Edith Wharton associated rather with the late fifteenth and early sixteenth centuries than with the stylized period of the Blind Man of Gambassi. In "Lo Spasimo" (the swoon of the Virgin at the sight of Christ bearing the cross), for example, she detected "an extremity of speechless anguish which is subtly contrasted with the awed but temperate grief of the woman who bends above her"; and she was reminded of a superb terra cotta in the Bargello museum in Florence which was confidently attributed to Giovanni della Robbia, of that most famous and prolific family of terra-cotta workers.

On her return to Florence she persuaded Signor Alinari, the distinguished photographer, to take pictures of six of the San Vivaldo group, and when she showed the results to Professor Enrico Rodolfi, director of the Royal Museum, that hitherto skeptical gentleman was persuaded. He declared in an orotund official statement that the terra cottas photographed had definitely been done around the turn of the sixteenth century and by "an artist of the school of the Robbias." They are now attributed to Giovanni della Robbia, and Edith Wharton could claim credit for identifying, in her words, "a remarkable example of late *quattro-cento* art [that] has remained undiscovered, within a few hours' journey from Florence, for nearly four hundred years."

At the end of July she sent off an account of the adventure to Burlingame. It was her initial effort in the genre in which she would become one of the most accomplished practitioners in American literary history—the genre unsatisfactorily known as "travel writing." Her talent is already evident here in the delicately precise evocation of the changing Tuscan landscape. She could not restrain a little crow of triumph in her accompanying letter: "The terra-cottas are *entirely unknown*, even Miss Paget (Vernon Lee) who has lived so long in Italy and devoted so much time to the study of Tuscan art, never having heard of them or of San Vivaldo."

In the same letter she turned to the proposed book of stories, and again struck a note of forlorn lack of assurance. She thanked Burlingame for the "long and helpful criticism" of another story he had rejected (though he urged including it in the book) and said, "If Messrs Scribners still want to publish a volume of my stories . . . I should rather have another six months in which to prepare it, for I haven't a sufficient number ready now for the autumn."

Then a total silence descended on Edith Wharton's side of the correspondence. Burlingame wrote in September to assure her that Scribners would publish the volume the moment it was ready. But Edith did not address him again for more than sixteen months.

4

For the previous four years, Edith Wharton had been afflicted on and off, and occasionally for several weeks at a time, with an apparently undiagnosable illness. The symptoms, as she described them long afterward to Sara Norton and Bernhard Berenson, were constant nausea (an "occult and unget-at-able nausea") and fatigue such that, when she was not actually bedridden, she often had to lie down and rest half a dozen times a day. To these we may confidently add: loss of weight, frequent headaches, and worst of all a recurring and desolating mental depression. It was a "form of neurasthenia," she told Sara Norton. "My 'seasickness' defied all cures, diets, and everything that the medical arts could devise (they mostly made me worse)."

Since she was almost always better when traveling abroad, she was inclined later to blame her condition on the soft, warm seashore climate of Newport: hence her name for it, "seasickness." But she also admitted that weariness and anxiety could bring on the malady wherever she happened to be, and it is obvious that a cluster of other factors contributed, in the late summer of 1894, to a total nervous collapse that endured, all told, for more than two years. It is risky indeed for a layman to attempt to diagnose an illness that occurred some eight decades ago and about which there are no extant medical records. But putting together several varieties of evidence along with certain of the more persuasive of recent psychiatric findings, one can perhaps make some reasonably educated guesses.

There was, to begin with, Edith's relationship with Teddy after nine years of marriage. It is suggestive that the only piece of writing she produced in the year 1895 was an untitled sonnet in which the speaker, a woman, bitterly laments the fact that she has never experienced the full fire of sexual love. She had been stirred by erotic desire (as Edith had been) "at the first springing of youth's upward ways," but thereafter she had been consigned to stand guard outside love's temple: peering in she could see "the altar's awful blaze," but she was never herself admitted to know the grandeur and the grief of love.

Two fictional works written not long before the worst onset of the illness bear further testimony to her sense of the marriage. One of these, the title story in a collection of ten brief fables called *The Valley of Childish Things and Other Emblems,* tells of a little girl who lives in a valley populated entirely by children, and who determines to go out and see the great world. In the course of observing cities and men, she grows into womanhood. On her way back to the valley, she encounters a former boy-playmate who had also visited the world and achieved manhood. They return full of schemes for transforming their old homeland, but once inside, while the woman retains her maturity and ambition, the man reverts to childhood and falls to making pretend gardens for another child. The years of European travel, the tale says rather flatly, have had their emancipating effect upon Edith but they have not helped Teddy outgrow the infantilisms of Newport life or his own boyishness.

"The Lamp of Psyche" is much more subtle and telling. Delia Corbett is introduced as the extraordinarily happy wife of the elegant, urbane, and cultivated Laurence Corbett. But on a visit to her aunt, Mrs. Mary Mason Hayne (Edith playfully drew upon the name of her kinswoman), it is revealed more or less by accident that Laurence, though of age, had not taken part in the Civil War. When asked why not, Laurence answers, smiling, "I don't think I know," and Delia, losing control, accuses him of cowardice. She later apologizes and is forgiven, but she knows that, though she will go on loving him, "her love had undergone a modification which the years were not to efface." Like Psyche in the fable of Apuleius, she had made the fatal mistake of gazing upon her loved one bare.

Unbroken proximity with Teddy was a source of great and growing distress, especially since, though the relationship was a sexless one, she had to share a bedroom with him in their small New York and Newport homes (one of the attractions of travel, presumably, was the possibility of separate rooms in inns and hotels). Edith Wharton was grimly fond of the comment by Dorothea Brooke in George Eliot's *Middlemarch,* always high on the list of her favorite English novels: "Marriage is so unlike anything else—there is something even awful in the nearness it brings." (In "Souls Belated" [1899], Lydia Tillotson would give different expression to this same thought.)

Such emotional and sexual deprivations might have been borne were there not other disturbing elements. Within the space of six months, Edith Wharton had been invited to bring out a volume of her stories; she had come to know Paul Bourget, one of the most celebrated living practitioners of the art of fiction; and she had spent hours in the company of Vernon Lee, the first truly cultivated *woman* she had yet encountered. If these experiences were blood-quickening for her, it may be supposed that they were also frightening. Burlingame's invitation had the effect upon Edith of asking her to commit herself at last to a career of writing. At the same time, Bourget and Vernon Lee, however dazzling it might

be to think of them as future colleagues, could also take the guise of overpowering
rivals. The coincidence—if it was a coincidence—of writing several stories which
Burlingame was forced to reject immediately after he had proposed the collection
could only have added to her unsettled state.

These various factors came together in the challenging question that could
no longer be postponed. What, at the age of thirty-two, was her fundamental role
in life: wife, social hostess, observer of foreign parts—or, drawing on all of these,
a writer of fiction? There is evidence that she had absorbed into a guilt-ridden
corner of her being her society's and her mother's distrust of a person of good
family who took seriously to writing. One can only employ the phrase "severe
identity crisis" to describe the terrible and long-drawn-out period Edith Wharton
was passing through: a period of paralyzing melancholy, extreme exhaustion,
constant fits of nausea, and no capacity whatever to make choices or decisions.
Those more knowing in these matters tell us that such a condition may itself be
a decision of sorts—a deliberate, if unconscious, putting off of commitment.

This is the place to dispel two of the minor legends that have clung to the
story of Edith Wharton's life. The first is that her physician during the breakdown of 1894–95 was Dr. S. Weir Mitchell, the distinguished Philadelphia nerve
specialist and novelist; and the second is that she began to write fiction under
Dr. Mitchell's direction as a mode of therapy. In fact, as we shall see, Dr. Mitchell
did not appear on Edith Wharton's medical scene until 1898, and then only
marginally; she once made a point of saying that she knew him only slightly. As
to her writing, Edith Wharton had of course been publishing fiction for several
years before the collapse, and the suggestion that she had produced enough for
a volume actually helped precipitate the crisis.

5

Edith broke the silence on December 14, 1895. "Since I last wrote you over a
year ago," she said to Burlingame, "I have been very ill, and I am not yet allowed
to do any real work." She sent him a few pages written some time earlier, though
she apologized for offering "such a waif instead of the volume that Messrs
Scribners were once kind enough to ask for." She ended on a note of frail
gallantry: "I still hope to get well and have the volume ready next year."

The waif in question was "The Valley of Childish Things," and Burlingame
promptly turned it down on the grounds that it was too esoteric (as it may have
been). He hastened to express his regret over Mrs. Wharton's illness, and added
that he had "thought very often" about the volume but had not wanted to pester
her. But this was the third time in succession that he had rejected her work, and
the apparent dwindling of his confidence, perhaps even of his interest, in her
writing appears to have brought about a relapse. Ten more silent months passed
before Edith ventured to try again, this time (in November 1896) with what she

referred to as "a little dialogue," called "The Twilight of the God."

After a number of weeks Burlingame returned the manuscript with a somewhat impatient comment. "For the first time," he wrote, "I do not catch your point"; and he urged her, by implication, to abandon the fantastic and the obscure and to go back to the kind of writing she did best. "The magazine has long been without anything from you." "The Twilight of the God" is not altogether coherent; it is more than a mere dialogue, although rather less than a short play; but there is nothing obscure about its theme. Like "The Fullness of Life," "The Lamp of Psyche," and "The Valley of Childish Things," it has to do with a woman's disillusionment with the man she has loved: the theme that obsessed Edith Wharton's imagination in these years.

She made no reply to Burlingame's letter of rejection, and on his side he must have gradually realized that his editorial manner was not well suited to induce good work from so complex and vulnerable a woman as Edith Wharton. In July 1896, happily taking two of three sonnets she had given him, he seized the moment to insist that he had not been scoffing but had been quite serious in saying he had not understood "The Twilight of the God." But by this time Edith had recovered much of her health and most of her good humor. "You are entirely too tender-hearted to be an editor," she wrote. "I saw no undue flippancy in your manner of refusing my little dialogue, and was only sorry that I couldn't think of just the right way of changing it."

She could have added that she was feeling vivified by a very different literary enterprise. This was the book, eventually called *The Decoration of Houses*, which she was writing with the cultivated, congenial, and somewhat effeminate architect Ogden Codman, who had worked with the Whartons on the refurbishing of Land's End. They had begun their collaboration on the book toward the end of winter, and in the early summer Edith Wharton took an incomplete manuscript and some photographs to New York and left them with Burlingame. The latter turned the package over to William Crary Brownell, a senior "literary consultant" in the Scribners publishing firm, and after a good deal of deliberation Brownell agreed to publish it—if a royalty of ten percent (presumably to be divided between the two authors) after the sale of the first one thousand copies was acceptable. Charles Scribner privately confessed his lack of enthusiasm for the book. Brownell was careful to say that it would appeal "to the intelligent and educated rather than to the most numerous public," and that Mrs. Wharton and Mr. Codman had better be prepared to be disappointed in the sales.

For the moment Edith Wharton was less concerned with earnings than with the quality of the book. The authors' memories are at odds as to which of them wrote the first draft, but in any case Edith found much of it congested and clumsy. It was Walter Berry who came to the rescue. He arrived at Land's End in late July for a stay of a month—by far the longest period he and Edith had been in each other's company since the summer of 1883, fourteen years earlier;

during the interval she had caught only a few fleeting glimpses of him. She showed him the manuscript and, according to her later account, Berry, after looking at a few pages, gave a shout of laughter. He then said, "Come, let's see what can be done," and began to suggest widespread changes of style and organization. Codman was down with sunstroke, and under Berry's close supervision Edith did all the rewriting herself.

She was working under pressure, for Brownell had set a deadline of September 1 for delivery of the manuscript, and she had to draw daily on energy she had not possessed for a long time. But she summoned up all the stamina she needed, and more—the surplus going into a series of notations to the publisher. From the moment she signed the contract for *The Decoration of Houses*, she began showering Brownell with suggestions about its manufacture. She regularly apologized for interfering, hoped she was not being a bore, begged to be forgiven for her inexperience and ignorance—and proceeded to some new and insistent proposal. She argued about the binding and the lettering of the front cover, the design and the exact style of print for the title page, the number and size of the illustrations. Brownell had cautiously estimated that Scribners could afford thirty-two plates; shocked, Edith Wharton went round to his Newport summer home to remonstrate with him. Retreating inch by inch, Brownell at last consented to fifty pages of illustrations; the published volume has fifty-six half-tones. When the whole matter was settled, Brownell wrote with weary courtesy that the publishers "had a comfortable feeling of how ship-shape and business-like your end of the task has been."

The Decoration of Houses, which appeared on December 3, 1897, moves learnedly and knowingly from one feature to another of an upper-class private city home: doors, walls, fireplace, ceiling; from drawing room to ballroom, from library to dining room, from bedroom to bath to schoolroom and nursery (with those latter two items the authors sound only dimly acquainted). In each instance a lucid little history is given of the traditional method of arrangement; thereafter the authors suggest ways of achieving harmony and proportion between the elements, and between the overall décor and the living habits of the residents of the house.

Codman obviously contributed from his architectural experience, and Edith Wharton from her close looks into a variety of European houses—though her nearly professional competence, then and later, regarding architectural design and interior decoration is another not entirely explicable quality in this offspring of old New York and descendant of Joneses and Rhinelanders. The book may even be seen as an indictment of that background as represented by its habitual living conditions, and this is what gives it at times an unexpected vitality. On a certain level, *The Decoration of Houses* is a paying off of scores against the physical surroundings Edith had grown up in and perhaps against her mother as their creator.

Lucretia Jones, it should be said here, was no longer on Edith's horizon. Sometime after the fall of 1893 (the date of Edith's last reference to her mother as being in Newport), Lucretia, now around seventy years old, had removed herself to Paris, where she was living in close proximity with both her sons. She had not, evidently, been among the elements Edith had had to contend with during her troubled time, but in *The Decoration of Houses* Edith went back with a kind of zestful scorn to the period when her mother had dominated her life.

The cramped, crowded house of West Twenty-third Street which she would linger over nostalgically in her last years here becomes the model of the cold, ugly, uncomfortable, cluttered habitation the book was written to oppose. "Who cannot call to mind," she wrote, "the dreary drawing-room in small town-houses," with their "exquisite discomfort" and their two sets of curtains so draped as to cut off light by day and impossible to be dropped at night. Space that might have been used for a writing desk "is generally taken up by a cabinet or console, surmounted by a picture made invisible by the dark shadow of the hangings." In so chilling and repellent a place, Edith Wharton concluded, neither an individual nor a family could in any sense be said to *live*.

Contrasted with all that were the tasteful arrangements of the grand palaces of France and the ducal homes of Italy. The book was certainly addressed to a wealthy audience, Berry observed wryly; and so it deliberately was, as one or two reviewers noted disapprovingly. But its elegant snobbery proved attractive. *The Decoration of Houses* was not quite the long-range best seller that Edith Wharton would claim it to be in her memoirs, but it did surprisingly and steadily well. The initial one thousand copies were sold in a few months, and, the sales continuing, Edith Wharton received the first royalty check of her life—for $39.60—in the late summer of 1898. The book continued to pay small but regular dividends for a great many years.

6. Oscillations

Walter Berry was thirty-seven years old when he reentered Edith Wharton's life in the summer of 1897: a tall, slender man with a well-trimmed mustache, owning a reputation for urbanity, a range of humanistic learning, and a habit of mildly lewd facetiousness; a persistent gallant and a confirmed bachelor who was much in demand in Washington society. He had been admitted to the Washington bar in 1885, two years after his first meeting with Edith Jones, and set himself up as an attorney-at-law with Benjamin Minor and Malcolm Bruce in an office in the Federal Building at 344 D Street, Northwest (the office, according to the letterhead, boasting of a "long distance telephone"). During the intervening years he had traveled a great deal, generally to places far distant from those portions of Italy and France where he might have run into the Whartons—to Finland and Russia, to Greece and Turkey, to Morocco and Algiers. In his legal practice he had begun to specialize in international law, performing such valued services for the Italian monarchy that King Victor Emmanuel made him Knight of the Order of the Crown of Italy.

In the spring of 1898 Berry persuaded Edith to come down with Teddy to Washington for her first view of the national capital since her adolescence. Edith had again been ill—"really ill," as she put it to Burlingame—through the damp New York winter at 884 Park Avenue, and she welcomed the change.

The most interesting of the persons she met through Berry's wide acquaintanceship in the city was George Cabot Lodge—called "Bay" ever since his sister, in his infancy, addressed him as "*Ba*-by"—a twenty-five-year-old aspiring poet who made a living as secretary to his father Henry Cabot Lodge, then completing his first term as the already formidable senator from Massachusetts. Young Bay was descended from the Cabots of Boston through both his parents; but if there was a Lodge family tradition of public service, Bay also inherited from his father a concern with literature and a sense of kinship with the Brahmin writers of New England. After graduating from Harvard in 1895, Bay had spent two years in Paris and Berlin dutifully studying languages and literature. He developed an almost singleminded passion for poetry, and when Berry brought him around to Edith at the Gordon Hotel, he had virtually completed his first volume of verse, *The Song of the Wave*, a collection of eighty-five poems, some of which his father's friend Theodore Roosevelt had browbeaten various editors into publishing.

Edith Wharton found Bay Lodge's poetry earnest and even forceful, but, except for the occasional significant line, falling short of genuine beauty. The man, however, made an immediate impression on her: one of "joyous physical life"—Lodge was over six feet tall, and at this time in exuberant good health; of "deep eyes full of laughter and visions"; of a personality in which "the natural man was so wholesomely blent with the reflecting intelligence." They could share, among other things, a profound hatred of what Lodge called "the philistine-plutocrat atmosphere" of Newport and a reverential love for the poetry of Walt Whitman. The friendship formed quickly, and would renew and enlarge itself in years to come. But in April the Spanish-American War erupted; by June, Bay Lodge, following the example of Roosevelt and others, was on his way to Cuba as a cadet on his uncle's naval vessel.

Edith's illness during the first months of 1898 had not kept her from writing. She told Burlingame with a touch of gaiety that "my *matière grise* is so soft and sloppy that I can't do much work," but by the end of March she had translated three Italian short stories for *Scribner's* and had completed and sent on one of her most pleasing tales, "The Pelican." Burlingame was delighted with this gently ironic account of a rattlebrained woman who lectures, incoherently but success-fully, to pay for her son's schooling, and then continues to do so for the same alleged motive long after the boy has grown up, repaid his mother every cent, and branched out on his own. The *Scribner's* editor tentatively suggested toning down the last section, but, probably recalling the two years' delay with "The Fullness of Life," he hastily added that his opinion was "very debatable." Edith cheerfully made the revisions along the lines "indicated by your criticism (in which I agree)," and passed the manuscript back.

She continued to produce at a pace and on a level of excellence she had never before reached. From Land's End in June she dispatched "The Muse's Tragedy," a deft study of the contradictions of literary genius. She went on to compose "Souls Belated," one of her three or four finest stories; "The Coward," an anecdote alive with comical tonalities; and "The House of the Dead Hand," her only inept effort in this period. She also managed to rework "The Twilight of the God" and a long story, "A Cup of Cold Water," which Burlingame had rejected in 1894 as "wildly improbable."

The beginning of Edith Wharton's sustained literary career can accordingly be dated with some precision as the stretch of months between March and July 1898. Eight years had passed since Burlingame took "Mrs. Manstey's View" for the magazine, and almost five since the notion of a volume had first been broached. She was in her thirty-seventh year—an age by which Stephen Crane had long been dead, his several masterpieces permanent fixtures in American literature; Henry James had a decade of rich productivity behind him; and Sarah Orne Jewett was at the midpoint of her own brilliant if less conspicuous career.

This first genuinely creative period, however, soon unsettled her, and during the late summer and early fall, in her relations with Scribners, she put on one of her strangest performances. She informed Burlingame that she should have a volume of stories ready for publication in the autumn; Burlingame urged a few months' delay, in order to revive her name by bringing out two of the new tales in the magazine. Mrs. Wharton accepted his argument as "irrefutable," then followed this with a letter asking, on several grounds, that the book be brought out as quickly as possible. She appealed to other members of the firm, and in early September again wrote Burlingame with "another suggestion" (as though a new one), which repeated almost word for word what she had said before. It was with a sort of recovered sanity that, on September 18, she told Brownell: "I am only sorry to have bored you with the request, since I see now that it would have been impossible for you to comply with it."

She had in fact been going through another bad time. In August she had fled the debilitating dampness of Newport for Minnie Jones's home at Reef Point in Bar Harbor, only to find that normally brisk climate no less fogbound and muggy; for a number of weeks she seems not to have been entirely in her proper mind. The intense creative commitment, which had produced seven stories in four months, suddenly dissolved. She was seized with the old paralyzing depression, and more desperately uncertain than ever about the quality of her work and the possibility of a literary career. As she would voice it a little later to Walter Berry when the book was at last in proof: "With all my trying I can't *write* yet. . . . There isn't a single sentence in the book with natural magic in it—not an inevitable phrase."

To this Berry answered by quoting shrewdly from Gustave Flaubert after the publication of *Madame Bovary:* "The sight of my printed work has ended by stupefying me. It seems to me utterly flat." Edith made a brief and partial recovery in mid-September, but there followed another relapse which reduced her to silence for a month. Finally, on October 19, she announced to Brownell in a strained little note her intention of going down to Philadelphia for a long rest cure.

2

The "rest treatment" for cases of nervous exhaustion was largely the invention of S. Weir Mitchell, by 1898 the country's best-known neurologist, to whose Philadelphia office patients came from all over the world. He had first come upon instances of acute exhaustion during the Civil War, when, in his thirties, he was serving as a battlefield surgeon. Rest and proper diet restored these individuals to health; but after the war Mitchell became interested in cases where extreme weariness was complicated by nervous depression.

He began to publish his findings, most importantly perhaps in *Lectures on the Diseases of the Nervous System, Especially in Women*, in 1881, and gave a long series of "conversational clinics" in a Philadelphia hospital. Mitchell traced the origins of the rest cure to the treatment he devised in 1874 for a certain Mrs. G—— of Maine. Mrs. G——'s symptoms were similar to those of Edith Wharton later: fatigue so extreme that she could do no more than take a few feeble steps about her room each day; loss of weight; inability to read or write; frequent headaches and constant nausea; profound melancholy. This condition was customarily diagnosed at the time as hysteria; but Mitchell felt that hysteria was simply a convenient label to relieve the doctor of responsibility, and scarcely of any help to the patient.

When Edith Wharton came to Philadelphia in October 1898 she was subjected to the same treatment, now fully perfected, that Mitchell had so successfully worked out for Mrs. G——. As an outpatient, she was given rooms at the Stenton Hotel, on the corner of Broad and Spruce Streets. Dr. Mitchell personally supervised the cases of all patients in the Orthopedic Hospital, but outpatients were overseen by other physicians trained under him. It must be supposed that Dr. Mitchell looked in on Mrs. Wharton once or twice—he would have taken a special interest in the younger literary colleague and fellow Newporter —but Edith's chief physician during her three months at the Stenton Hotel was a Dr. McClellan.

The first principle of the rest cure was total separation from the patient's normal surroundings, her family and friends, her physical home. Mitchell wanted no suggestion of the sick-room-at-home, with its inducement to selfishness and its solicitations of sympathy. Unlike some patients, Edith was allowed to receive mail. Teddy and Berry wrote almost daily, but not a single visitor entered her room from October through January.

Next came the requirement of total rest in bed, along with massage. It was only when he hit upon the simple but crucial notion of massage for Mrs. G—— that Mitchell finally saw the pattern of the rest treatment. Absolute rest, though clearly imperative, seemed to rule out the kind of exercise needed to rehabilitate the body. It occurred to Mitchell that skillful body rubbing of the sort he had once or twice observed might do for the muscles and the circulation of the body what voluntary exercise would otherwise do; it would be "exercise without exertion," and so it proved to be. Massage, it may be added, was virtually unheard of in America till Mitchell began to employ it; it had been practiced a little in Europe (and had been a staple treatment in the Far East for ages), but it was Mitchell and his rest cure which gave it international vogue.

Electric treatment was then added to tone up the muscles. And Edith was forced to eat abundantly—three big meals a day and sizable snacks in between. She was also given a daily amount of malt, concealed in large doses of pyrophosphate or iron.

At first Edith, who treasured her privacy, was disturbed at being under such close and unflagging observation—as though, she said, ghostly presences were peering in on her morning and night (Peter Quint and Miss Jessel, Berry suggested, fresh from a pleasurable reading of Henry James's new story, *The Turn of the Screw*). But gradually, in the untroubled atmosphere, free from household preoccupations and intimacies, and with the daily massage and electric treatment, Edith began to come back to life.

She gained an impressive number of pounds. Energy, both physical and mental, seeped back into her; the headaches diminished. She grew more cheerful and bought herself an expensive black fur ensemble. The doctors—rubbing their hands, so Teddy told Berry—encouraged her to take up her work. Edith sent to Scribners for the galleys of her stories and labored over them; she completed a new story, "The Portrait," a somewhat confused affair about an artist who for humane reasons paints an idealized portrait of a vulgar scoundrel—honesty in art was a minor theme for Edith Wharton—and implored Burlingame to substitute it for "The Lamp of Psyche" in the proposed collection.

As the time approached when Edith could be released from the Stenton Hotel, Dr. McClellan laid down the law against her returning to 884 Park Avenue and the housekeeping anxieties she had gone into seclusion to escape. He was willing to authorize another stay in Washington, and Berry found a house at 1329 K Street, available from early December to the end of May, at a total rental of $2,500. It fronted Franklin Square, had sunlight all day, and was splendidly furnished. When Edith learned that the "most gloriously post-restcure bed" in her room was imitation Florentine, she instantly let Berry know that she would wake in the night with spasms if she had to sleep on it; it was replaced by a specimen from the age of Louis XVI. But she was otherwise pleased, and in early December, Teddy wired Berry that they would take the house if the plumbing were tested and the stable put in order. "Ha! ha!" Berry exclaimed. *"Ca y est!"*

But it would still be some time before Edith could move in. At midnight on New Year's Eve, Berry, who had been imbibing and disporting with Teddy at 884 Park Avenue (the two got along famously at this time), wrote her: "The bells, whistles and horns are clanging, shrieking and tooting, and I'll risk the $1 I won from Teddy at pool tonight on a bet that I'm the first to give you luck for '99. No more rest-cures," he said, but "Pelicans galore." He jollied her further by reporting that a honeymoon couple had occupied the curtained berth opposite him on the night train from Washington and had kept him awake all night by the noisy vigor of their love-making.

Alone in the Stenton Hotel, Edith Wharton passed New Year's 1899 tidying up her volume of stories and inscribing ideas for new tales, with scraps of dialogue and character description, in what she called her *"donnée* book."

3

It was in the late autumn of 1898 that Walter Berry, without quite planning to, began to assume the role of Edith Wharton's literary counselor. With the good intention of shaking her out of her depression, he wrote a stream of letters full of vivacity and gossip; but he realized, to his credit, that what would most brighten Edith's morale was encouragement of her literary efforts.

Edith sent him proofs of "The Pelican"; Berry found it "first-rate . . . very clever and very amusing and heap original." He praised this choice of language and that, and admonished her only about a couple of well-worn similes. He worked with special care over the manuscript of "The Journey," an effectively macabre story about a young woman whose formerly radiant but now stricken husband dies on a train journey from Colorado to New York (an imaginative device, perhaps, for dispatching poor Teddy).

His remarks here and elsewhere had mainly to do with style, as to which he had a keen eye; but he said next to nothing about character, setting, or development of the plot. Nor was he particularly discriminating about Edith's work, tending to receive almost all of it as being of the same high order. And there lay his value for his unstable and insecure friend.

Walter Berry was the first individual in Edith Wharton's personal world not only to have recognized her talent, but more important, to have taken the measure of her belated literary ambition and fully sympathized with it. Others had been bemused or suspicious of her creative interests. Teddy wore a proud but unperceptive smile; hostesses at dinner parties in New York (Edith Wharton would recall) avoided any reference to Mrs. Wharton's unseemly métier. But Walter Berry—a Van Rensselaer, a remote cousin, a Harvard graduate, and an unimpeachable socialite—met Edith on her own terms. He took in the nature of her imaginative capacity, he praised her, he shared with her his other literary enthusiasms—Zola, Henry James, Stevenson—and by implication he drew her, as a writer, into the company of the living masters of fiction. In the long process by which Edith Wharton freed herself from the repressions of her background and from the internal disorders partly caused by them, Walter Berry played a major role.

Of the novelists just mentioned, Zola and Stevenson exerted no influence upon the early development of Edith Wharton, and Henry James less so than would be shortly alleged. The stories she wrote prior to the breakdown in 1894 can scarcely be said to have displayed any serious influence at all: traces perhaps of William Dean Howells' novels of Boston and New York; here and there the work of Henry Blake Fuller, the Chicago writer who was her sanction for combining realistic detail with a melodramatic plot; a passing hint of *Madame Bovary*.

But for the most part these early efforts were rather vague experimentations in different modes of fiction.

With *The Greater Inclination,* her first volume of stories, certain presences can definitely be felt. In 1898, the year before the collection appeared, Edith Wharton wrote down a list of "my favorite books." The first half-dozen names on the list have nothing to do with fiction: they include Goethe's *Faust,* the poetry of Walt Whitman, Pascal's *Pensées,* and the writings of Marcus Aurelius. Fiction, when it appears, is dominated by the French—in the order mentioned, Flaubert's *Madame Bovary* and *Bouvard et Pécuchet,* as well as his correspondence; Stendhal's *La Chartreuse de Parme* and *Le Rouge et le noir;* Abbé Prévost's *Manon Lescaut;* Benjamin Constant's *Adolphe.*

None of Balzac's novels was on this early list. Edith Wharton, already an apt student of the *comédie humaine,* was devoted to the work of the writer who first gave that phrase literary resonance, but at this stage she was evidently unable to choose among his many achievements. She would later specify as Balzac's great distinction his characterization of women: "as much compact of human contradictions and torn with human passions" as his male figures. The English novel, meanwhile, was represented in 1899 by Meredith's *Harry Richmond* and *The Egoist,* and George Eliot's *Middlemarch.* No American novelist was deemed worthy of inclusion, nor would one be until 1909, when James's *The Portrait of a Lady* appeared low on the list.

Needless to say, a writer's favorite books are not necessarily those which have most deeply nourished or challenged his own creative imagination; and it would be incongruous to match too closely the large accomplishments just named with the relatively modest offerings in *The Greater Inclination.* But it is possible to suggest, cautiously, the value for Edith Wharton's particular talent of George Meredith's adroit social satire and his sly feats of language; of the images in *Madame Bovary* and *Middlemarch* of a dream-ridden woman trapped in an unhappy marriage and a frustrating environment; even perhaps of Constant's artful working out of a deteriorating erotic relationship. The true value of these and other writings, however, would be more apparent at later moments in Edith Wharton's career.

The Greater Inclination was further delayed by Burlingame's desire and Edith Wharton's reluctance to include some of her earliest tales, at a minimum "The Fullness of Life" and "The Lamp of Psyche." In July 1898, Edith formulated her opposition:

> As to the old stories of which you speak so kindly, I regard them as the excesses of youth. They were all written at the top of my voice, and "The Fullness of Life" is one long shriek. I may not write any better, but at least I hope that I write in a lower key, and I fear that the voice of those early tales will drown all the others; it is for that reason that I prefer not to publish them.

Those stories, in other words, had been not only too direct an expression of her personal situation, but almost a lament about it; it was her aim now to render versions of her experience translated, so to speak, rather than copied. Burlingame continued to press for "The Lamp of Psyche," and Edith worked over it dutifully; but it refused to take on the quieter tone she sought for it, and so it was that she exchanged it for "The Portrait."

Edith Wharton urged Brownell to give the printing of the book to Berkeley Updike, who had designed the title page for *The Decoration of Houses.* Updike, a tall, large-eared, and somewhat provincial young bachelor and Newporter (Edith called him "Upsie," and wished he would travel more often in Europe), ran his own shop, the Merrymount Press in Boston, and was developing into the best commercial printer the country would ever know. Scribners was agreeable, and Updike in fact printed half a dozen of Edith Wharton's volumes.

The Greater Inclination (the title, which Edith Wharton hit upon after discarding four others, referred to a loftier as against a meaner moral propensity) appeared at last in the second week of March 1899. There were several flawed and amateurish items in the collection, but at least five of the eight stories range from competent to first-class, and it would be hard to name another fledgling volume of fiction in late nineteenth-century America with a comparable degree of verbal resourcefulness and ingenuity of composition, and, especially, so pronounced a strain of moral and psychological perplexity.

For Edith Wharton, the publication of the book was a major step in her many-stranded effort to escape, imaginatively and actually, from the world she had been born into. Paradoxically, one of the best stories in it, "Souls Belated," enacts the conviction that in social terms such an escape is not to be accomplished. Lydia Tillotson in that tale abandons her heavily conventional husband and the oppressive mansion on Fifth Avenue presided over by her imposing mother-in-law and flees to Italy with her lover Ralph Gannett. After the divorce she startles her lover by her expressed aversion to marrying him, thus bowing to the social decrees she had so recently run away from. "I didn't know we ran away to found a new system of ethics," Gannett says, smiling; "I supposed it was because we loved each other." Lydia makes a gesture toward departing on her own, but she turns wearily back, and at the end they are preparing to make their re-entrance, as man and wife, into the social order they had violated.

"Souls Belated" was the first of Edith Wharton's stories to employ conspicuously the image (it harks back to Egerton Winthrop's teachings) of the prison cell as life's characteristic setting. The narrative suggests that however deeply she might long to break free of the proprieties, a part of Edith Wharton was still bound to them, inexorably and discouragingly. It also suggests that she was finding the way to convert her sense of confinement into art, and to that extent, at least, to overcome it.

4

By the end of January 1899, Edith was settled with Teddy Wharton at 1329 K Street in Washington for a four months' stay. She was, however, far from yet being a well woman; her physical condition had much improved, but her wobbly mental state expressed itself in a series of resentful and complaining letters to her Scribners editors. Agreeing to a contract with a royalty of ten percent (on a list price of $1.50), she announced her displeasure at the skimpy advertising of *The Decoration of Houses* despite all the "many favourable press notices," and stressed the ominous fact that the new volume was not even mentioned as among the firm's forthcoming publications. The tardiness in sending her copies of her own book rankled, and in April she launched a long and bitter protest at the failure of Scribners to make use of some excellent comments on *The Greater Inclination* in an energetic advertising campaign. She had compared the methods of other prominent publishers—Macmillan, Dodd Mead, Harper's—with those of Scribners, and was convinced, she said, that she had been "unfairly treated"; indeed that Scribners had been so "essentially unjust" in her case that she was not inclined to offer them her wares a second time.

Edith Wharton's feeling of having been neglected by her publishers went beyond the familiar suspicions of apprentice authors to verge on paranoia. Yet there was a great deal at stake for her, including her identification and appraisal of herself; and there was in fact a real basis for her charges. Many of the reviews, as she pointed out, had been "not only approving but flattering"; Scribners may perhaps be taxed for recognizing too slowly the literary phenomenon they had introduced. The influential *Bookman,* for example, found the book "exhibiting in the highest degree that rare creative power called literary genius," and *The Dial* felt that "no conventional commendation would be adequate for such a book." The New York *Commercial Advertiser* declared it "quite unique" for its delicacy of tone and profundity of insight "among the books that have been sent us this year." The periodical *Literature,* after praising the near perfection of Edith Wharton's style, observed with no little acuteness:

Only a woman to the manner born in society, a woman, too, whose literary favorites or literary masters may have been Thackeray or James, since she partakes of the spirit of the one, and has followed the exquisite craftsmanship of the other, could have written "The Pelican" or "Souls Belated."

More than one reader remarked on Edith Wharton's talent for probing the female nature; her ability, as a woman reviewer put it, to bring to the surface "the underground movements of women's minds." The same note was struck by F. Marion Crawford (Margaret Chanler's novel-writing half brother), who wrote from his villa in Sorrento that "The Muse's Tragedy" was "as good as Henry

James's best, with the something more which we men grope after in vain when we try to describe women and which a woman does naturally." The citation of Henry James was not yet vexatious to Edith Wharton, particularly since it was being made in her favor. William Dean Howells, meanwhile, tactfully avoided any mention of his friend James when he spoke to Edith Wharton "of your old editor's—perhaps your first editor's?—very great pleasure" in the stories.

The Greater Inclination was selling unusually well for a first volume of short fiction. In June, Walter Berry, after a visit to the Scribners offices, calculated that 2,750 copies had been sold or requested; sales in America ultimately went just over three thousand. John Lane, the representative of the English publisher John Murray, came over to collect five hundred copies in sheets, and the book appeared in London to the accompaniment of a laudatory article in the *Times* by the ubiquitous shaper of opinion G. W. Smalley. Brownell was, a trifle belatedly, much impressed. The book "has been appreciated so much in so many directions that I have heard of," he wrote Mrs. Wharton, "that you can assuredly plume yourself on having joined the 'note' of universality to that of distinction."

5

While her initial feeling of having been insufficiently appreciated was thus being gradually assuaged, Edith passed an otherwise quiet winter and spring with Teddy in the elaborate comfort of the house on K Street. In mid-May the Whartons were in New York, spending a few days with Egerton Winthrop while Edith conferred with the publicity department at Scribners before sailing for England. In London they became aware that the English edition of *The Greater Inclination* had aroused a little flurry of interest, to the point where Lady Randolph Churchill, who was just starting a periodical called the *Anglo-Saxon Review*, wrote "Miss Wharton" to solicit a contribution, to go along with those already received from Henry James, Swinburne, and Oliver Lodge, and to ask about a possible meeting. (No record of any meeting has survived.) Crossing the channel, Edith and Teddy lingered several weeks in Paris, a city about which Edith had not yet made up her mind.

Then they made their way by easy stages across France and into Switzerland to Ragatz, a watering place sixty miles southeast of Zurich and standing some 1,700 feet above the left bank of the Rhine. Here by arrangement they joined Paul and Minnie Bourget, the latter having come to take the mineral baths at Pfäfers, three miles up the mountain road from Ragatz.

The friendship which had begun six years before, but had been interrupted during most of the intervening years by Edith's long illnesses, now began to ripen. While Minnie was obediently submitting to the baths and Teddy ambled off on his own excursions, Bourget and Edith wandered over the slopes, gazed down at the spectacular Alpine scenery, and breathed in the superb mountain air. Back at the inn by sunset, happily exhausted, they sat long over spaghetti and Chianti, making one another privy to their ideas and interests. Bourget, lured into autobiography, reminisced about his family origins, the early stages of his literary career, his lifelong reverence for Stendhal and Balzac.

It was at just this time that the former Captain Alfred Dreyfus was brought back from Devil's Island, where he had been sent in 1894 for life imprisonment after being convicted of treason, for a second court-martial at Rennes. The only cloud over the days at Ragatz was a disagreement between Bourget and Mme. Wharton over this internationally resonant case, which had been reopened by Zola's rousing manifesto "J'accuse" and by the unanswerable demonstration by the socialist leader Jean Jaurès that the "proofs" of Dreyfus' guilt had been forged by a Lieutenant Colonel Henry, who promptly committed suicide.

Unlike many other French writers and intellectuals—unlike Zola, Anatole France, and such younger men as Marcel Proust, Paul Valéry, and André Gide —Bourget was an implacable anti-Dreyfusard. His sympathies and beliefs ran with those of the *salons* in the Faubourg St. Germain (an area as savagely divided over the case as was every other part of French society) that remained royalist and nationalist, and that shared his absolute faith in the French military authorities. Bourget had written Henry James that general officers in the French army would not conceivably declare any person guilty of treason without "certitude founded on proofs," though no doubt reasons of national security might require withholding these proofs.

Bourget pronounced his fierce opinions to Mme. Wharton in private; because of the strong anti-Semitic element in the affair, no mention was made of it in the presence of the former Minnie David. Edith Wharton shared the belief of most interested persons outside France that Dreyfus was completely innocent, and the legal handling of the matter a disgrace. She could hardly have been satisfied by the weak-kneed verdict at Rennes, by which Dreyfus was again convicted, by a vote of five to two, but with an evasive reference to "extenuating circumstances." "Iniquitous, cynical, odious, barbarous," wrote a young American journalist named Morton Fullerton in the London *Times* about the judgment.

But it was clear to Edith that, however illiberal his stance, Bourget was genuinely grief-stricken at the rending effect "the accursed case" was having on France and on his social and intellectual circles. For the most part, she kept her views to herself, and when the two couples separated around the middle of August they were in warm accord about rejoining each other shortly.

The Bourgets returned to Paris, and the Whartons moved south to the little village of Splügen, just above the icy Splügen Pass from Switzerland into Italy. The landscape, which suited Edith Wharton's temporary mood, was simple, serene, uneventful—cool pine woods, cobbled streets which disappeared into mountain tracks, snow on the blunt distant peaks. But after dark each day the village suddenly came alive, as if summoned into being by a master theatrical director.

Edith and Teddy cut short their dinner at the inn to hurry out to the terrace, there to await the diligences from Thusis and Chiavenna. It was an engrossing scene. Edith, as what might be called her writer's personality emerged and took possession, had begun to observe the passing show of life with a fictive eye; and when the citizenry of the village gathered in the square for the daily excitement, she saw them as type characters in a comedy by Goldoni. There was the Inn-keeper, the Postmistress, the Syndic; there was the Man of Leisure with his long Italian cigar and his frisky Pomeranian dog; the Mill Owner with his air of importance; and the Young Man who never failed to issue forth from the post office at the key moment, conspicuously reading a letter.

Then the first coach arrived—a four-wheeled landau, drawing behind it a four-wheeled glass-enclosed "clarence"—and the passengers descended into a swirl of villagers busy about the horses and luggage. "Germans first," as Edith Wharton would describe it in an article for *Scribner's,* "—the little triple-chinned man with a dachshund, out of 'Fliegende Blaetter,' the slippered Hercules with a face like that at the end of a meerschaum pipe . . . shrill and vivid Italians, a pleasant pig-faced priest, Americans going 'right through,' with their city and state writ large upon their luggage; English girls like navvies, and Frenchmen like girls." When this richly mixed contingent had been taken care of, a second diligence swept up to the door, and the agitated ceremony was repeated. Finally the last of the guests vanished into the inn, the horses were led away, the lights went out. The comedy was finished.

Edith had further occasions to exercise her fictive eye during the summer of 1899. The Whartons made the spectacular and precipitous descent through the Splügen Pass into Italy and went on to Colico, at the head of Lake Como, where they had another rendezvous with the Bourgets. The party regathered with the intention of exploring the Bergamasque Alps, a domain they were drawn to by its very name (*"Quel nom!"* Bourget exclaimed in a letter to Henry James). "Bergamasque" refers first of all to the province of which the center is the town of Bergamo, the fortified hill town northeast of Milan; but it also denotes a rustic dance invented by the people of Bergamo, and for Edith Wharton the word conjured up scenes from the *commedia dell'arte.*

It was always the astounding variety of Italian scenery—its capacity to change strikingly from one mode of enchantment to another within a few miles—that enthralled Edith Wharton. Coming down the gentler slopes of the Aprica Pass into the Val Camonica, she found the open meadows and orchards of the Valtelline suddenly giving way to more enclosed settings, waterfalls tumbling below old mills, villages hidden by foliage, small mossy glades surrounded by trees. There was, she decided much later, "no more *riante* valley south of the Alps" than the Val Camonica, before the railroads invaded it.

In pursuit of one of those rumors that were a constant challenge to her, Edith led the others by carriage, covered cart, and foot to the nearly inaccessible high-perched village of Cerveno and an allegedly "interesting church" there. Here, in screened alcoves on the landings of a broad vaulted stairway, they came upon a series of colored life-size terra-cotta groups enacting the Passion. Edith, who may have underestimated it, thought the artistry not equal to the similar groups she had discovered at San Vivaldo. But if the main characters were conventional enough, she was struck by the variety of peasant figures—all recognizable types of the Val Camonica, and all with their scowling faces distorted by a stupid hatred of Christ.

The travelers' route took them next down to the tip of Lago d'Iseo and the town of Lovere, made famous in her old age by Lady Mary Wortley Montagu. They sailed down the lake next morning to Iseo itself, and each lakeside village appeared to Edith's vision to be the setting of a *settecento* comedy, peopled by Harlequin and Brighella, Dr. Graziano and his timorous ward, Rosaura and Leandro.

It was Teddy Wharton who, looking up from the guidebook in Brescia one morning, announced that they had never in fact been in the Bergamasque. The jagged semicircle they had described had just skirted the area at each turn. Not at all downcast, they determined to complete the circle by journeying west to Bergamo and thence, avoiding Milan, to Lanzo d'Intervi, a few hours' drive from Como, and 2,500 feet above Lugano: "an ideal location," in Bourget's opinion.

Writing a dozen years later to Bernhard Berenson, who had himself just completed a tour of the Valtelline and the Val Camonica, Edith Wharton said that she had nearly cried when she read Berenson's descriptions. The whole region, she said, "is the most beautiful scene in Italy to me—partly because I was so happy when I saw it."

She was indeed happier than she had ever been in her adult life. Her health for the moment was robust, her energy boundless. Her full thirty-seven-year-old figure, her glowing russet-gold hair, her vitality of expression, her infectious laughter: all this gave her a physical attractiveness beyond anything she had hitherto possessed, and she was conscious of it. If Teddy was not in any sense an active lover, he was at his companionable best: endlessly even-tempered and thoughtful, falling in with her every whim.

Her first book of fiction had been published to no little acclaim in the United States and England. She was well along on a more ambitious story, and in the towns and villages of northern Italy she had been collecting impressions for something more ambitious yet, a full-scale novel set in the Italian eighteenth century. Other fictional possibilities teemed in her imagination. And with the Bourgets, she felt in touch at last with the living and historical culture of Europe.

Their affectionate admiration gave her the sense that she was beginning to take some small place within the larger world of letters—though if she counted on Paul Bourget introducing her speedily to his literary friends (Henry James, for example), she was due to be somewhat disappointed. Bourget preferred to keep the most gifted of his associates to himself.

6

The moment of emotional poise did not long endure. By the middle of September the Whartons were back at Land's End, and Edith began immediately to feel the depressive effect of the Newport climate and the lack of intellectual stimulus. "The dampness here," she told Brownell, ". . . is making me unhappy as usual." Her unhappiness again took the form of querulousness toward her publishers. She demanded to know why she had received no royalties on *The Greater Inclination*, though a second edition had been in print for three months; Mr. Codman had received his check for *The Decoration of Houses*—where was her share? The inquiries were reasonable, but the tone was unduly aggrieved. Within days a check for $441 was in her hands. In reply to a complimentary note from Brownell, she remarked pointedly that she had known the volume of stories must be selling well "from the number of letters I have received from other publishers."

Before long, Newport became intolerable. It so happened that Pine Acre, the summer home of Teddy Wharton's mother and sister in Lenox, Massachusetts, was unoccupied, the Wharton ladies being abroad. On impulse Edith gathered up her husband, her servants, her dogs and her trunks and departed for Lenox. It was her first visit of any length to the place where, before very long, she would build herself a home.

Lenox, lying in the foothills of the Berkshires in western Massachusetts, was in 1899 at its peak as a fashionable summer resort. Like its rivals Newport and Bar Harbor, it had had its earlier moment of literary eminence. Hawthorne spent a brief but important period in Lenox, where he completed *The House of the Seven Gables* and found the name "Tanglewood" which he used for a collection of tales. Melville's Arrowhead Farm was not far from the village, and it was on an excursion up Monument Mountain, nearby, that Hawthorne and Melville had their first and memorable encounter. Dr. Oliver Wendell Holmes and Longfellow were sometimes in residence.

But again like its rivals, and beginning at about the same time, 1880, Lenox gradually became dominated by the new breed of millionaire cottagers. One of them, Anson Phelps Stokes, flung up a gigantic granite castle in 1893 called Shadowbrook; it covered a mountainside and contained no less than one hundred rooms. In 1899, at the moment Edith Wharton was paying her first visit, Giraud Foster was bringing the fashionable period of Lenox history to a climax by completing Bellefontaine at a cost of more than one million dollars. There was still a small residue of literary representation: George Dorr, the editor of the *Century* magazine, had a home on Laurel Lake; Owen Wister, author of *The Virginian*, showed up occasionally; the cultivated physician Francis P. Kinnicutt, who was just becoming the Whartons' family doctor, summered at Deepdene Cottage. But the style was set by the huge estates, the imitation Italian villas, the lavish horse shows, the exotic gardens. Edith Wharton would not be slow to contribute to this elegant display; but for the moment she was more concerned with the invigorating mountain air.

Walter Berry, who had been worried by Edith's despondent letters from Newport, congratulated her on getting away from "all that sogginess" and taking to the hills. The dry atmosphere, he felt sure, would soon put her "in tingling shape." So it did; and Berry, who was somewhat more than an amateur of scientific history, likened Edith to that subclass of fish having both gills and lungs "who, when removed to dry places, suddenly acquire lung-respiration and breathe atmospheric air." Edith was hard at work again; but she had unluckily committed herself to a visit with Teddy's brother William and his family, and Berry foresaw the worst. He urged her emphatically to put the visit off: it would mean only the ruin of her autumn, "littry biz null" and "general awfulness."

Edith nonetheless went with Teddy to the Whartons' home in Croton, Massachusetts, and the result was everything Berry had feared. Between Edith and her husband's brother and sister-in-law there was no possibility of communication. The Wharton ménage was a version of what Edith had been struggling to escape, and the fact that it was her husband's family was the opposite of helpful. It may equally be imagined that Edith was the most trying of houseguests: her habitual shyness and uncertainty would have taken the form of a more than usually imperious manner; and the Billy Whartons, too, were already suspecting that Edith was not the devoted wife to their beloved Teddy that she ought to be.

She returned to Newport in late November once again a prey to deep melancholy. She was "a helpless thing," she wrote Berry, and unable to write a line; she was even tempted to destroy the manuscript of her novella *The Touchstone*. Berry could not restrain his impatience: "I do wish you would take my advice just occasionally." But he sought to console her in her bleak creative doldrums, as he had before, by drawing a highly flattering analogy: George Eliot, in 1869, describing her "great depression of spirit," and her conviction that she could never "make anything satisfactory of *Middlemarch*."

The latter, as we have seen, was one of the two or three English novels Edith Wharton most respected, and Berry's reminder may have cheered her up. By Christmas, anyhow, reestablished at 884 Park Avenue, she was contentedly acknowledging a special white-and-gold holiday edition of *The Greater Inclination* and fairly vibrating with literary plans.

7. The Italian Novel

"Please don't forget," Berry wrote from Washington in the last days of December, "that I am coming c. January 8th next century." Turning up on schedule in New York to help Edith celebrate the arrival of 1900, he found his hostess brimming with vitality and what she called *bien-être*. Released, somehow, from the paralysis that had gripped her during the previous four months, Edith Wharton was now charged with a remarkable surplus of imaginative energy. She had begun to perform as that great American rarity, the genuine "man of letters"— that is, as a practitioner, and for the most part on a high level, of every one of the literary arts. Over the thirty months following, she would complete and publish a novella, a second volume of short stories, and a massive two-volume novel; she would write poems, travel sketches, and literary and dramatic criticism. She would compose two, perhaps three plays of her own, and for the American stage she would dramatize a novel from the French and translate another play from the German. In her *"donnée* book" she jotted notes for scores of other stories and novels. The opening of the new century was the occasion of a creative outburst unmatched, thus far, in her career.

Although she was working on several different enterprises at once, Edith Wharton's main preoccupation through the first months of 1900 was with *The Touchstone*. She had begun the novella in Washington, while awaiting the appearance of *The Greater Inclination;* temporarily forgetting *Bunner Sisters,* she had written her new friend Sara Norton (the younger daughter of Professor Charles Eliot Norton of Harvard) that it was her first venture into longer fiction and that she was not very confident about it. In late September 1899 she asked Brownell if Scribners would consider bringing out a book of no more than thirty or forty thousand words. Brownell replied that he would be eager to, and offered an advance of five hundred dollars and a royalty of fifteen percent. Burlingame also persuaded her to give it to *Scribner's* for serialization, and there *The Touchstone* duly ran, for a fee of $750, in the March and April 1900 numbers.

The Touchstone is another of Edith Wharton's stories in which a certain shabbiness of character is revealed in the chief male figure, and a subtle betrayal of that figure's relation to a woman who has loved him. In order to marry a charming but impecunious young woman, Stephen Glennard, a no less impoverished lawyer, secretly and through an intermediary sells for a large sum a bundle of love letters written to him over the years by Margaret Aubyn, a distinguished novelist who has recently died. (The latter—recalled by Glennard as "the poor woman of genius with her long pale face and short-sighted eyes"—is suggestively drawn from Vernon Lee; she was "incapable . . . of any hold upon the pulse," but when she spoke "she was wonderful.") Glennard's marital and legal careers flourish thereafter, until his miserable secret begins to haunt him. There comes the painful scene of confession, and in the evolving Edith Wharton manner the marriage, which had been dissolving under Glennard's moodiness, is restored on a lower and permanently scarred level.

Berry, whose enthusiasm for the story was unrestrained, said that it moved at a great pace, and added, "O, Edith, the great thing is that you never write *truck.*" *The Touchstone* is without doubt expertly written, and it contains a number of the beautifully articulated insights into the ambiguities of the moral life at which Edith Wharton was becoming a master. But the trouble is that the story does *not* have enough momentum; it strikes one as sluggish and long drawn out—as though the author wanted to prolong Glennard's agony of conscience beyond necessity. *The Touchstone* is at best a minor success.

It was well received, however. Berry rejoiced in a notice that it was on one of the best-seller lists, and sent on a review which in his phrase emitted "high cries of enthusiasm." He quoted North, the Scribners grave and conservative business manager, as saying to him that the novella was selling "largely, very largely indeed; a very satisfactory demand." By the end of 1900 sales had reached five thousand.

The Whartons were scheduled to sail for England on their annual trip around the middle of April, a month after the publication of *The Touchstone,* but Edith managed to delay things while she canceled reservations several times and made new ones. Her health was again worrisome, and she had put herself in the hands of a Dr. James. "It feels like a drink of Teddy's best Scotch," Berry wrote her, to know that so competent a physician was in charge. It was not until the second week of May that Edith and Teddy (and probably two servants) made their departure.

London was enlivening. The literary community was hospitable to the talented American newcomer, and Edith, who between stories had written a comedy of manners for the stage, also had occasion to confer with various theatrical people (including William Archer, the drama critic and the author, years later, of *The Green Goddess*) about a possible production. There was even talk about a London premiere in the fall, but the discussions lagged and the idea was abandoned.

Paris in early June, when the Whartons were visiting there with the Bourgets in their new apartment on Rue Barbet-de-Jouy (around the corner from the former one on Rue Vaneau), was the site of an enormous International Exposition, eventually attended by fifty million persons and emphasizing the new modes of energy and the technological advances which were heralding the start of the twentieth century. Edith Wharton no doubt visited the exposition with the Bourgets and studied, perhaps with mixed feelings, the brilliant display of electrical power, the track for the testing of automobiles, and the industrial exhibits. (It was in the exposition's hall of dynamos, at almost exactly the same time, that Henry Adams, as he would record it in his *Education*, was undergoing his greatest revelation about the nature and source of *power* in the modern world.)

But Edith had another engagement closer to her heart: she was collaborating with Minnie Bourget on a French translation of "The Muse's Tragedy," a story that may have attracted Mme. Bourget because of its northern Italian background—Lago d'Iseo figures in it—and the strange character of the world-famous writer Vincent Rendle. The translation, somewhat roughly done, appeared in the July issue of the *Revue hebdomadaire*, with a complimentary footnote by Paul Bourget.

The Bourgets once again accompanied the Whartons on a fortnight's tour of northwestern Italy, where Edith gathered further materials and visual glimpses for her *settecento* novel-in-the-making. It was another little period of happiness; and yet she had scarcely been back in Newport for twenty-four hours, at the end of June, before she was reduced to a state of melancholy exhaustion. She felt utterly helpless, she told Berry; drained of energy, unable to lift a finger. The prescription, as before, was a move to the Berkshires. By July 15 she could tell Brownell that she was "pretty well" and send him her article on the stay at Splügen the year before. Soon she was describing herself to Berry as "ridiculously well" and going ahead rapidly with a new volume of short stories.

2

The pattern of Edith Wharton's life in these years was now fairly clearly defined: increasingly extended fits of creativity, travel, stretches of glowing happiness abroad followed by nervous collapses of greater or lesser duration at home, and a gradual displacement from Newport to Lenox. Edith had arrived, one guesses, at a state where she *expected* not only to be bored but to be physically and psychically wretched in Newport. One notices too that in Lenox the improvement in her health and the stepping up of her productivity tended to coincide with Teddy's prolonged absence (in the summer of 1900 on a yachting trip) and with a visit by Walter Berry. It may be added that, since Edith's natural condition, as she was realizing, was one of immense and far-flinging energy, the ever less frequent moments of fatigue and despondency were the more harrowing for her.

Change of place, moreover, was always important to her. Edith Wharton, whose handling of the element of "place" in her fiction was one of her strongest features, tended in her life to dramatize a change of personal fortunes or of her sense of herself by entering into a new scene of residence. Her first experience of independence, a decade earlier, had led to the rental and then the purchase of a home in New York, and to another one at a remote point in Newport. Now, as she was becoming established as Edith Wharton, a gifted writer of fiction, she was taken by a desire to shift residence again. This time she would build a home of her own from the ground up. Lenox, with its bracing atmosphere and magnificent surroundings, was to be the place.

She stayed on in Lenox through the balance of the summer and through the fall and the first heavy snows of November. She was working alternately on short stories and the novel to be called *The Valley of Decision;* but in her free time she looked about for a possible site to build on, though without any immediate success. There were wordy exchanges with Scribners about serialization of the novel and the date of publication; then abruptly, in mid-November, she reported that she had temporarily abandoned *The Valley of Decision* and was giving herself entirely to the short stories. She hoped Mr. Brownell would not think her "a monster of inconsistency" or "vague and oscillating" (he kindly assured her that he did not), but she regularly needed the refreshment of change. She had completed one more story, and another was nearly ready. That made six in all; would seven be enough for the collection? If not, she said, "I could do an eighth"; in parenthesis she added "How queer that looks!" She was gratified, meanwhile, to receive checks in the amount of $514 for *The Touchstone*, which was also doing quite well in England—seven hundred copies sold in the first month, and some fine reviews, especially one in the gardening and farming periodical *Country Life* ("between ensilage and sheep-breeding").

The turn of the year 1901 found Edith Wharton, resettled at 884 Park Avenue, busy with the last item for the volume, "The Confessional," a tale of the Italian *risorgimento,* based on something she had read in a magazine article. It was taking longer than expected, she wrote Brownell in February; it required doing "on such a large scale, with so much broader strokes than most of my stories." There was a minor domestic upheaval when a housemaid drank a bottle of rubbing alcohol from Edith's dressing table and had to be discharged. But the story was finished by March 1, and the volume, finally called *Crucial Instances* (a title Berry declared presumptuous), came out on April 7.

The seven items in *Crucial Instances* are so clearly inferior to the best of *The Greater Inclination* that it has even been speculated that Edith Wharton had written them some years earlier and had dragged them out of her drawer in the winter of 1901 to meet contractual obligations. In fact, they were all written ("Copy," to be accurate, was rewritten) after *The Touchstone*—in 1900 and 1901. The relative imaginative softness one feels so often in the volume must be explained in other terms.

Berry, as always, applauded vigorously. "It's quite the best book of stories that is," he wrote; there was not a single entry "that isn't *fine.*" He took a personal pride in "The Angel at the Grave," to which he had made a valuable contribution. For this tale Edith had invented the figure of a long-forgotten New England philosopher of transcendental leanings, a friend of Emerson named Orestes Anson (Orestes Brownson is the obvious prototype), and she wanted to credit him with having made a major scientific discovery in his youth, before he took to the higher cerebrations. Berry suggested the discovery of the *amphioxus,* that species of tiny fish that is taken, Berry said, to be "the real missing link between vertebrate and invertebrate." He supplied a deal of scientific history and certain sonorous and polysyllabic phrases that went virtually intact into the story.

"The Angel at the Grave" is representative of the entire volume, insofar as it focuses on the fairly remote past and involves an effort to achieve or restore continuity (in this case via the philosopher's granddaughter) between the past and the present. This was also a developing theme in *The Touchstone,* and all the other stories in *Crucial Instances* without exception are variations upon it— the past in question being at one time as far removed as two hundred years, at another merely the earlier life of some individual. Such uniformity of imaginative concern at just this moment in Edith Wharton's life and literary career challenges interpretation. The following seems to be the case.

During most of the 1890s, Edith Wharton's most intense imaginative efforts and her actual physical gestures were toward liberating herself from the social and intellectual (that is, anti-intellectual) world she had grown up in and had continued to inhabit after her marriage: attempting this even though she seemed frequently to imply that total liberation was not only impossible, it was not altogether desirable. Nonetheless, by 1900 or thereabouts, she had achieved a very considerable degree of independence and was determined to create a new environment of her own design, in Lenox, to live and work in.

At this stage, what might be called the more traditional side of her nature began to reassert itself. What she now needed was to connect up her new state of being with her former self—to solidify her sense of herself by finding vital continuities between personal past and personal present; and more largely and perhaps more important, between herself and the older world of values she had been moving away from. But, to judge from the stories in *Crucial Instances,* the endeavor was not wholly successful. Edith Wharton had not yet found the terms of coherence in her ongoing life; the constant vacillations of travel and writing plans may reflect a similar uncertainty. "The Angel at the Grave" is also typical of the volume in having a happy ending which is at once unexpected and not quite persuasive. Since that ending consists precisely in a recovered continuity (as the dead philosopher's reputation is restored), the impression grows that Edith Wharton was insisting in her fiction upon a personal interior accomplishment that she did not altogether feel. The consequence, to repeat, is an odd softness of imaginative tissue that sets the book unmistakably below its predecessor.

3

In February 1901, Edith had gone up to Lenox to stay at the Curtis Hotel, a venerable inn in the center of the village, and enjoy a change of scene and a week of fresh air. Her larger purpose was to pursue her quest for a suitable site, and this time she was in luck. Before she came back to Park Avenue, she had begun negotiations for the purchase of a good-sized property, part of it overflowing the southwestern edge of town and part of it within the boundaries of the adjacent village of Lee. It consisted of 113 acres; Edith later added about fifteen acres more. The property sloped in slow majestic style from the highest point two miles down through woods and open fields, past its solitary farmhouse, to a small curving body of water known as Laurel Lake.

Laurel Lake Farm, as its name then was, belonged to the Sargent family. In the transaction the family was represented by Georgiana Sargent, a local water-colorist of no little freshness and grace (she seems to have been a relative of sorts of the portrait painter John Singer Sargent). On June 29, 1901, Georgiana Sargent signed the deed conveying the property to Edith Wharton for the sum of $40,600 (part of the cost was eventually to be paid by the sale of Land's End). In February of the following year, while the new home was being completed, Edith took a mortgage of fifty thousand dollars on the property, with the Berkshire Savings Bank in Lenox. Teddy Wharton, who had little income of his own, did not sign the original deed; the place was to be Edith's very own. But he did sign the document covering the mortgage, as "husband of said grantor," and thus assumed partial responsibility for that item.

The house, Edith decided, would be built at the crest of the slope, with a clear view of the lake, and her old associate Ogden Codman was the inevitable choice as architect. But Codman, who had been prospering visibly in recent years, demanded what Edith regarded as exorbitant advance payments even for his rough sketches (one of the items in *The Valley of Childish Things and Other Emblems*, indeed, had spoofed the size of Codman's bills for the work on Land's End). She broke with him, and turned to Francis V. L. Hoppin, who was earning himself an excellent reputation in New York. She spent hours during the spring with Hoppin, going over plans for the spacious building she had in mind; it was to be modeled on Christopher Wren's Belton House in Lincolnshire, which she had inspected and greatly admired during one of her visits to England. Edith had even more ambitious ideas about landscaping and gardening.

Only days before the purchase of the Lenox property in late June, Lucretia Jones died in Paris. She had been paralyzed and unconscious for the better part of a year. To Sara Norton, Edith spoke conventionally of the loss of "my poor mother"; to Brownell, she only mentioned the event after acknowledging the receipt of nine pounds and ten shillings from John Murray. It was not, obviously, as decisive a moment for Edith as it would have been a decade earlier.

For six or seven years Lucretia had been living in Paris, at 50 Avenue du Bois de Boulogne. Edith, who had stayed increasingly clear of her mother prior to the latter's remove from America, did look her up in Paris during the summer of 1899, and perhaps again in 1900. But on her annual European trips she seems not to have made anything like a regular detour for the purpose of spending time with Lucretia. Nor did she, apparently, write her very often.

Lucretia may well have resented this neglect, even as she was enjoying the solicitude of her two Europe-based sons. Her will, certainly, reflected a strong contrast between her feelings for her daughter and for Freddy and Harry Jones. Freddy was to receive outright the sum of $95,000 (which he later asked to be reduced to $50,000, the balance going to his daughter Beatrix). Harry was left $50,000. The rest of the estate was divided into three equal shares. One of these was bequeathed outright to Freddy and another to Harry. The third share was left to Harry Jones and a certain Henry B. Anderson as trustees for Edith. They were to collect any rents and profits accruing from the properties involved (mainly New York real estate), and after paying all incidental expenses should, in the will's curious language, "pay over the balance from time to time" to Edith.

The value of the trust eventually amounted to about $90,000. The annual yield of Edith Wharton's three inheritances—from each of her parents and from Joshua Jones—must at this time have been about $22,000.

By coincidence, Teddy Wharton, who had gone over to England alone in late May to see his own ailing mother, was able to attend Lucretia Jones's funeral— presumably having been notified of that event by the newly established transatlantic wireless telegraph. He accompanied the older Mrs. Wharton back to Lenox, arriving in time to encounter the worst heat wave of the summer. By this time, Edith found that she herself had to go to Europe. The entire trip was distasteful. The purpose was to persuade her brothers, as executors of Lucretia's will, to set up the trust fund more closely under Edith's control, with Teddy as one of the two trustees. Edith detested legal matters, and she felt almost the same way toward her brother Freddy, whom she had managed not to see for almost two decades. She sailed from Boston on the *Commonwealth* in late July, and though convinced that she had been poisoned by the food on board ship, she was able to make her way from Liverpool to London, where Freddy Jones was living, and conclude her business there successfully.

Edith Wharton was too preoccupied with her own affairs to be fully alert, for the moment, to the epochal change that had taken place in England since her last visit there the year before. On January 22, 1901, Queen Victoria died at the age of eighty-two and was succeeded by her portly, bearded, fifty-nine-year-old son Albert as King Edward VII, with his graceful and long-suffering Danish-born wife, Queen Alexandra. The champagne-and-sports-loving new monarch was already transforming the atmosphere, not only at Buckingham Palace and Windsor, but throughout the higher reaches of English society. The almost immeasurably long Victorian age was over (the nineteenth century was over), and the "Edwardian garden party" had begun—a time of extravagance, surging prosperity, peace, and new varieties of freedom of behavior; along with counter-stirrings further down in the social order that would make it (in retrospect) a period of glaring contradictions. Edith Wharton crossed the channel to France in August only indistinctly aware of any of this, but the Edwardian age in England—at least in its garden-party aspects—was the one that she would live most deeply into.

The three weeks in Paris were dismal, despite glimpses of the Bourgets and the easy settlement of her financial questions with Harry Jones. "I don't care for [Paris] at the best," she wrote Sara Norton, "and in August, and with law business on one's hands, it is decidedly arid." Six days in Belgium were an improvement; but on the return voyage from Cherbourg in September, her on-deck cabin leaked so much during the heavy seas that she was reduced to lying in bed with an umbrella over her head. She was the more gratified to be back at last in Lenox, to stroll over the newly acquired acres and to be restored—as she put it selectively —by "the dear dogs and horses and our own woods." She was anxious, too, to get down to the last stretches of *The Valley of Decision*.

4

"The Italian novel," as Edith Wharton first called it, had been conceived several years before, but she only began to work on it seriously while *The Touchstone* was going to press in 1900, and by the spring of that year she had a title and a substantial portion of manuscript. "Ave atque Valley," Berry had remarked as Edith was about to sail for England. He added strong words of praise for the parts he had seen. Edith was uncertain about the scope and direction of the narrative, but with Berry's steady encouragement she pushed ahead. The last section of the story, where the ironies of political and social life get peculiarly entangled, gave her trouble; but soon after New Year's 1902 she announced from 884 Park Avenue "the end at last." The novel appeared on February 21 (book-making was then an incomparably swifter process than it has since become).

The narrative portion of *The Valley of Decision* is a wide-ranging account of the career of Odo Vansecca, who, when we first meet him in 1761, is a nine-year-old cousin of the reigning Duke of Pianura, a realm modeled on Parma and Mantua in north-central Italy. By the untimely death of another cousin, Odo becomes heir-presumptive and finally duke. Before this, while at an academy in Turin, Odo had come under the influence of a group of freethinkers, among them a lovely young woman named Fulvia Vivaldi, the daughter of a learned professor of history. After his accession, with Fulvia at his side as mistress and chief privy counselor, Odo attempts to put through some of the reforms he and his teachers had long dreamed about.

The major change proposed is a new constitution which would radically curtail the power of the church. The ecclesiastics stir up popular resentment against Odo and Fulvia, and the night before the constitution is to be proclaimed there is an uprising in the main square, and Fulvia is shot and killed. But by now a lingering conservatism has led Odo to doubt the wisdom of moving so rapidly toward social and political change. He withholds the constitution, and his former liberal associates—who have joined forces with General Napoleon, descending from the north (the year is now 1795)—present him with an ultimatum. Odo abdicates and leaves Pianura, disillusioned and bleakly enlightened; what we would call an alienated man.

But as Edith Wharton told a friend, the book was intended as "a picture of a social phase, not of two people's individual history." It was an introduction to certain aspects of the European eighteenth century, a period which appealed enormously to the rationalistic side of her as a time when "new hypotheses, new theories of life [were] germinating as they never had since the Renaissance." Fulvia and Odo, accordingly, were conceived primarily as "little bits of looking-glass in which fragments of the great panorama are reflected."

For the sketching of that great panorama, Edith did a prodigious amount of authentic scholarly research. She made lists of books to consult—histories, reminiscences, dictionaries, travel writing; she made notes in the Lenox library; she borrowed an Italian phrase book and other items from Charles Eliot Norton; she had knowledgeable friends write off for information about the leading opponents of liberal thought in Italy and France during the period. Berry sent her Casanova's memoirs in brown wrapping; she went back over the pages of her beloved Stendhal, especially *The Charterhouse of Parma*, and his sketches of Rome, Naples, and Florence.

Her notebook is crowded with telling indications of *settecento* life: how the monks of Bologna bred lapdogs and broke their noses when puppies; what Venetian ladies wore (black silk cloak and draping over head); popular scents (jonquil water, jasmine, spirit of musk, rosemary); turns of speech; the fact that male "sopranos" wore stays like women; songs for the gondola ("La Biondin' in Gondoleta"); the way rich nuns met their lovers at night and dressed in white gowns with low bodices to receive them; the scene in San Marco Square in Venice; notes on muffs, gloves from Grenoble, diamond-hilted swords, curled wigs. As a result, and given Edith Wharton's remarkable ability to evoke place and time, the lingering survey of the Italian scene from the 1760s through the 1780s lifts the novel into a high category; and by sending Odo off on a series of extensive travels, she was able to introduce large stretches not only of the physical setting but also of the complex cultural and political milieu.

The Valley of Decision was the one of Edith Wharton's novels that owed most to *The Charterhouse of Parma*, but Odo Vansecca, it must be said, is invested with the least impelling qualities of Stendhal's Fabrizio: his indecisiveness, his unfocused sexuality, his fits of passivity. *The Valley of Decision*, moreover, ends where *The Charterhouse* begins, with the arrival in Italy of the troops of General Napoleon—for Stendhal, a moment of intoxicating liberation; for Edith Wharton (or anyhow for Duke Odo), a moment in the unfolding horror emanating from the bestialities of the French Revolution. Even so, Edith Wharton's novel was unmatched in its generation for its presentation of the conflict between the stiffening old and the radically new, in all areas of human experience.

And it is here that we come upon the book's profoundly personal element. Edith could, of course, bring to bear the notes and memories of her own Italian journeys, and the novel in fact is dedicated to Paul and Minnie Bourget "in remembrance of Italian days together." But there are also detectable similarities between both Odo and Fulvia and Edith's real or imagined self. We hear the author's voice, for example, in Fulvia's meditation on being "in spite of herself . . . a child of the new era," and her sense of the "sacramental nature of human ties." Closer yet is Odo's recurring desire, in a time of enormous change, to link up his personal past with his present—as he tells Fulvia, "to trace the thread of purpose" upon which the fragments of his past could be seen hanging.

It was that same thread of purpose that, to judge from all her fiction at this time, Edith Wharton was seeking as the old century gave way to the new. In *The Valley of Decision*, she was working out the question partly in political terms, by reference to the tension between Odo's liberal and conservative impulses. For Edith, the question was at once larger and more intimate: how to preserve, or recover, the best of the past—the values, styles, and associations of her past— while risking the new, the emancipated, even the unorthodox. In her notebook, under the heading "Odo's characteristics," Edith offered a kind of modest paradigm solution, carried typically by an allusion to house and garden: "A certain piety for the past, and catholicity of taste, makes Odo preserve the rooms and gardens of Pianura unchanged, while adding new galleries, mss., coins."

What Odo can accomplish architecturally, he is unable to do politically. But Edith Wharton made of his failure a fundamentally successful, though undoubtedly deeply flawed, work of literary art. And she did so by writing large her own piety to the past, both historical and personal; writing it so large indeed, and making it so present and palpable, that she achieved an interior equilibrium that had an air of permanence.

5

That air was, of course, deceptive, both in short-range and long-range terms. While the book was going through the press, Edith began to complain with some bitterness about a number of items: the make-up of the title page, in which she found four serious defects, adding that "lots more" criticism could be offered; the size of the pages, as to which, to her annoyance, she had not been consulted; the mishandling of galleys; and the price (two dollars).

These were danger signals. The previous May, when a reviewer claimed her books were never advertised, Edith had remarked in a fit of euphoria: "I wonder what paper he takes? Poor thing, he must be blind." But now the enormous effort of finishing her massive novel was taking a familiar toll. At the end of December she wrote Sara Norton that a "silly woman" who had read her palms told her she had "tired hands," and this, she said, the woman "might have applied to my whole body." She insisted then that her spirits were very good and that she was enjoying life more every minute. But in January she had a bad attack of grippe, and in February she collapsed.

It was a stretched-out nightmare of exhaustion, depression, and nausea, and after ten days of it, she said to Sara Norton in a rambling and incoherent letter, she felt "as lifeless, as inert, as unable to cope with life as I did in the beginning." It seemed to her worse than anything she had experienced since the breakdown in 1898. There were, evidently, several otherwise unrelated causes. In addition to her severe reaction to bringing the novel to completion—a task which required an incomparably greater commitment to her work than ever before—there was the unsettling fact of having turned forty on January 24. "I excessively hate to be forty," she told Sara Norton. She felt the years like a physical growth that might be removed by hospital surgery.

Worst of all, perhaps, given Edith's priorities of devotion, Mimi, her much-loved little dog of eight years, died at this time, and Edith was reduced to helpless tears for hours on end. Teddy Wharton for once was also suffering from ill health and had gone down to North Carolina to recuperate. On impulse Edith took the train to Washington, and there, separated from household cares amid the relative comforts of the Gordon Hotel, and with the lively and teasing companionship of Walter Berry—at social gatherings, the theater, the art galleries—she started to pull herself together.

As had been the case previously, the reception of her book helped speed the cure. *The Bookman,* which had praised *The Greater Inclination,* suggested churlishly that the undertaking Edith Wharton had assigned herself was beyond the capacities of a mere woman—her first experience of antifeminism in literary circles; several other reviewers apparently expected what Berry called the "When-Valley-was-in-flower" kind of romance, and were disappointed. But the New York *Sun* said the novel "will undoubtedly become a classic," and the Boston *Evening Transcript* declared that it "places Mrs. Wharton side by side with the greatest novelists." Commentators took to vying with each other in issuing thundering superlatives: a Chicago writer saw *The Valley of Decision* as "the most distinguished performance yet accomplished on this continent"; the spokesman for the Louisville *Courier Journal* pronounced it "the most splendid achievement of an American man or woman in fiction." Though Edith Wharton's grasp of previous American fiction was still an uncertain one (it would grow firmer), she regarded all this as rather embarrassing, and preferred the contention—it was only slightly more restrained but it was essentially accurate—of the New York *Mail and Express* that the book revealed her "as one of the great novelists of the day."

There were encouraging echoes from across the Atlantic. In London, the *Pall Mall Gazette* was full of praise; from Rome, the editor of the *Nuova Antologia*, having heard so well of the novel, wrote for a review copy; from Paris, Minnie Bourget passed on the word of a Tuscan visitor, the able and garrulous writer Carlo Placci, that *"l'on ne parle à Florence que de la V. of D."*

Edith was flattered, too, by the many letters she was receiving, especially from persons who could view *The Valley of Decision* with a professional eye. Among these were Dr. S. Weir Mitchell, "whom I know very slightly"; R. W. Gilder, the editor of the *Century;* and Edwin and Evangeline Blashfield, New York kinfolk of W. C. Brownell, who had collaborated on a respectable study of Italian cities in 1900, and who told Edith that they were reading their separate copies seated on either side of a table, keeping pace and exclaiming over individual passages. Morgan Dix, the rector of Trinity who had officiated at her wedding seventeen years before, compared the rhythm and beauty of her style to Hawthorne's, and associated himself emphatically with what he took to be her marked distrust of revolutionary idealism.

Even more inspiriting was a long passage Sally Norton quoted from a letter her professorial father had written to Sam Ward, the well-read playboy-lobbyist, beginning:

> A work of another woman of genius has been exciting my admiration during these last days and when you read Mrs. Wharton's "Valley of Decision" you will not, I believe, wonder it has done so.

After analyzing the novel with his usual cultivated shrewdness, Norton concluded; "It is a unique and astonishing performance. . . . It is too thoughtful and too fine to be popular, but it places Mrs. Wharton among the few foremost of the writers in English today."

No less heartwarming were the comments sent from a villa outside Florence by Eugene Lee-Hamilton, Vernon Lee's brother.

> It is easy enough to write novels about the Middle Ages or the Renaissance—probably all of them absolutely false:—I have just been doing so myself. But it requires a Stendhal or an Edith Wharton to write a Chartreuse de Parme or a Valley of Decision. All the good judges that I have talked over your book with—beginning with my sister—have been equally struck by it.

To be joined with Stendhal by the likes of Lee-Hamilton was, for Edith Wharton, heady stuff, as was the report that Vernon Lee proposed writing a learned article in Italian on the novel. Meanwhile, Henry Blake Fuller, the Chicago writer who alternated realistic fiction with such Europeanized and Italianate work as *The Chevalier of the Pensieri Vani*, chimed in with his own brand of enthusiasm.

Thanking Brownell for a two-thousand-dollar advance (Berry, always money-minded, berated her for not demanding more), Edith had expressed the hope that "it will return to you before many days." Before three months were out, and despite Charles Eliot Norton's prediction, it had done so, and the royalties began to accumulate—more than ten thousand dollars in a relatively short course of time.

The February breakdown notwithstanding, the tremendous call upon her resources made by the long novel seemed actually to have summoned up in Edith considerably more energy than the book demanded. It was, suddenly, as if nothing could appease her creative and critical appetite. In January alone, immediately after completing *The Valley of Decision*, Edith came out with three very different but almost equally impressive items. A charmingly accurate sketch of Parma appeared in *Scribner's*, and Burlingame wondered whether there might not be a volume of these things, including Mrs. Wharton's pieces on San Vivaldo, the coaching inn at Splügen, and the Bergamasque (eventually there would be). A poem about St. Margaret of Cortona in *Harper's* elicited an excited charge of blasphemy from a Jesuit priest and an inquiry from Brownell whether Mrs. Wharton might not put together a collection of her poems (not for many years to come). Edith at the same time sent Burlingame "The Lady's Maid's Bell," the first of a series of ghost stories which were to establish her as a major practitioner in this possibly minor genre, and a sign that her own ghost-haunted days were far behind her.

The mammoth engagement with the past represented by *The Valley of Decision* had fairly well used up Edith Wharton's prolonged obsession with that phenomenon. By mid-spring 1902 she was well into a novel set on the contemporary scene, in New York and Long Island, to be called "Disintegration." Burlingame was enthusiastic about the scenario, but for one reason or another Edith abandoned it the following fall, after writing seventy-four typescript pages and a dozen-odd by hand.

"Disintegration" was at the least an invaluable rehearsal for *The House of Mirth* three years later. It was her first large-scale look at social change and social pressure, and at the wounding effect both could have upon the young and sensitive. The social deterioration referred to in the title is the consequence of wealth without responsibility, and Edith Wharton begins to develop this theme amid a lively cast of characters. She distributes telling witticisms with an ever more lavish hand—the one respect in which Edith Wharton surpassed George Eliot was in the tough vivacity of her wit. There is one superbly entertaining scene of savory gossip and malicious one-upmanship, and the foreseeable plight of the heroine is not without poignance. But for Edith, the narrative perhaps lacked the necessary inner compulsion and decisive point of view, and she put it aside.

The story of Edith Wharton's life in this period is primarily the story of her abundant writing. Not content with all the other forms of expression, she turned in the spring of 1902 for the first time to varieties of criticism. At the request of William Dean Howells, she wrote a comparison of three versions of the Francesca da Rimini legend by F. Marion Crawford, Stephen Phillips, and Gabriele D'Annunzio—she utterly deplored D'Annunzio's flamboyance as a person, she remarked, but she could not but admire some of his work. For *The Bookman* she took on a verse drama, also by Phillips. She did not like it very much, but her tone was indulgent; she was not in a mood to be disdainful of the literary efforts of others. The performance of Mrs. Minnie Maddern Fiske in *Tess of the D'Urbervilles* so stirred her that she wrote a eulogistic piece about it. Mrs. Fiske's gratitude took the form of a free box for the rest of the season.

An article on George Eliot in the May *Bookman*—a review of Leslie Stephen's biography of the English novelist—contained several revealing paragraphs. Edith Wharton began by defending George Eliot against the charge of an inappropriate interest in nonliterary fields of knowledge. Milton and Goethe, though poets, were likewise students of the sciences, she pointed out: "Is it because these were men, while George Eliot was a woman, that she is thus reproved for venturing on ground they did not fear to tread?" She recalled Dr. Johnson's saying that portrait painting was "indelicate in a female" (perhaps she was hearing her elders say that it was "not nice" for a woman to write novels), and observed that "indications are not wanting that the woman who ventures on scientific study does so at the risk of such an epithet." Edith Wharton was herself passionately addicted to scientific study; her commonplace book lists the definitions of a large array of sciences and scientific philosophies; and she was, in addition, gathering her forces for a defense of women in an overwhelmingly masculine literary culture.

She was also prepared to sympathize with a woman of great ability who, like George Eliot, had in some manner violated the moral code. Contending paradoxically that the novels of George Eliot's maturity were at once her worst and her greatest, Edith Wharton suggested that the explanation for this "must be sought in her personal situation"—her long extramarital relation with George Henry Lewes. For George Eliot was

a conservative in ethics. She felt no call to found a new school of morals. A deep reverence for the family ties, for the sanctities of tradition, the claims of slowly acquired convictions and slowly formed precedents, is revealed in every page of her books. . . . All George Eliot's noblest characters shrink with a peculiar dread from any personal happiness acquired at the cost of the social organism; yet her own happiness was acquired at such a cost.

There was a daily contradiction between her personal course of conduct and her moral beliefs; and George Eliot consequently attempted to mitigate her sense of what she had done by the ethical stress of her fiction.

Unconsciously, perhaps, she began to use her books as a vehicle of rehabilitation, a means, not of defending her course, but of proclaiming with increasing urgency and emphasis, her allegiance to the law she appeared to have violated.

Those words are unmistakably drawn from the depths of Edith Wharton's self-definition and self-appraisal. Unlike Lydia Tillotson in her own "Souls Belated," Edith Wharton did not have the slightest desire "to found a new system of ethics." But if by the spring of 1902 she had not in any way violated the pieties and sanctities to which she gave allegiance, the heretical side of her nature seemed to be stirring again, and certain buried impulses and resentments of a private kind were implicit in her generous understanding of George Eliot's situation and its twisted reflection in her work.

For some time Edith Wharton had been attempting to write for the American and English stage (such an ambition being an old habit, almost an old failing, of American novelists). In 1900 she had completed a comedy of manners called "The Tightrope." The manuscript has not survived, but from some remarks about it by Walter Berry—who suggested it be subtitled "A Comedy of Distemperament," and spoke of a musicale and a ballroom scene as elements in the play—one gathers it may have been a dramatic version of what became *The House of Mirth*, which Edith was already sketching out in her *donnée* book under the title "A Moment's Ornament." Nothing was to come of it.

Edith next entertained the notion of basing a play upon a melodramatic episode in late eighteenth-century London. This was the story of young James Hackman, a former army officer who became an Anglican clergyman and who grew so maddened by unrequited love for a certain Martha Ray, the charming mistress of an English lord, that he shot her dead one evening as she was leaving the Covent Garden Theatre. James Boswell was among those who attended Hackman's execution in 1779, and Berry and Edith agreed that it would be great sport to present a play in which Boswell and Dr. Johnson figured (the *Life of Johnson* was long established as one of her favorite books). Edith did not in fact pursue the idea, but it was an early example ("The Duchess at Prayer" in *Crucial Instances* was another) of her lifelong fascination with plots that combined sexual passion with physical violence.

In 1901, taking time off from short stories and *The Valley of Decision*, Edith completed two acts of a play called "The Man of Genius" and an elaborate outline of the remainder of the action—the latter being chiefly a restrained and wrong-headed affair between an eminent English novelist and his secretary, and the separation and reconciliation between the novelist and his wife. The play may even (though the evidence here is fuzzy) have gotten into rehearsal, but it never reached production. This was hardly surprising, for "The Man of Genius" was alive with subtlety and wit, and deep insight into the creative life: elements that in 1901 the New York stage, which at its most adventurous had yet to get beyond *The Count of Monte Cristo,* was not prepared to accept.

If she could not make it on her own, Edith Wharton was willing to try to reach the stage as a collaborator. At the request of the English actress Marie Tempest, she set to work on a dramatic version of Prosper Mérimée's romantic nineteenth-century novel *Manon Lescaut.* It was quite a sizable task; but Edith completed the highly competent four-act work only to be told over supper in Marie Tempest's house in London that she had decided not to do any more costume plays.

Despite that experience, Edith Wharton in May 1902 let herself be persuaded by Mrs. Pat Campbell, that great and high-strung performer, to translate a tragic drama by Hermann Sudermann called *Es Lebe das Leben.* After seeing Mrs. Campbell perform early in the year, Edith had described her unkindly to Sara Norton as "a great ranting gawk" and "an elephant walking on the keyboard of a piano." But as to Sudermann, though she thought that as an artist he was uncertain whether to follow the example of Nietzsche (like every other German tragic dramatist of the time) or of Aeschylus, *Es Lebe das Leben* appealed to her —perhaps because of its well-developed analogies between political and sexual immoralities and its ironic and worldly view of the conservative-liberal debate in both those spheres. She labored over the translation through the summer and completed it in mid-September. The title was the hardest phrase she had to deal with. "Long Live Life" was as close as she could come; but Mrs. Campbell held out for "The Joy of Living"—hardly suitable for a play which ends with the exceedingly sympathetic heroine solving a number of grim problems by swallowing poison. The critics did not fail to chide Mrs. Wharton for the inaccuracy of the title, and used it to cast doubt on the translation as a whole. *The Joy of Living* had the briefest of careers on Broadway, but, much to Edith's surprise, in book form it sold quite well for a good many years.

6

During the period from the writing of the last story for *Crucial Instances* in February 1901 through the completion of *The Joy of Living* in September 1902, another major creation on which Edith was a collaborator was going steadily forward. Construction of the house on the outskirts of Lenox, which Edith had decided to call The Mount (after the Long Island home of Ebenezer Stevens), had begun in the summer of 1901. By June of the year following, Edith could inform Sara Norton: "Everything is pushing up new shoots—not only cabbages and strawberries, but electric lights and plumbing." In her insistence on installing the latter amenities, it should be remarked, Edith Wharton was well ahead of her time.

Edith and Teddy rented a house for the summer near Lenox, and every morning she drove out to The Mount to busy herself with the gardens and orchards, consult with the architect, and keep a sharp eye on the workmen. She took long carriage rides through the Berkshires in the afternoons, coming back "stupid with fresh air"; and she spoke of perhaps hiring an "auto"—she put quotation marks around this unaccustomed word—to drive up to the Charles Eliot Nortons' at Ashfield, some forty miles to the east at the other end of the Mohawk Trail. She spent some time helping to reorganize the Lenox library, in its extraordinarily handsome early nineteenth-century building on the village green. The remaining hours she whiled away working on the novel "Disintegration" and wrestling with Sudermann's German.

Teddy, who had again been feeling poorly, spent much of this period fishing for salmon in Canada. But he seemed so healthy on his return in August, and he had shown himself so discriminating about the interior design of The Mount, that Edith did not hesitate to let him take the house off her hands for a number of days while she paid a visit to Margaret Terry—who had been Mrs. Winthrop Chanler almost as long as Edith had been Mrs. Wharton—in Newport. Soon after Labor Day the Whartons moved in with Teddy's mother at Pine Acre. And on September 30, Edith exclaimed to Sally Norton: *"Finalmente!"* The long move was over, and they were settled in The Mount. Changing languages and misquoting very slightly from her prime favorite, *Faust*, she continued: *"Zwei Seelen wohnen, ach, in meine Brust"* ("Two souls there are that live within my breast"), "and the Compleat Housekeeper has had the upper hand for the last two weeks."

After forty years Edith Wharton was in a home not inherited or rented, not purchased and remodeled, but genuinely of her own making. She was in the physical location of her own choosing, where the views near and far were, as she said, exquisite, and where everything for the moment was peaceful and sylvan, and the lanes purple with Michaelmas daisies. The achievement coincided precisely with her recognition as the first woman of American letters. Her health and nerves were in splendid condition; and so, with some trifling exceptions, they would long remain. But in this regard the domestic balance was abruptly shifting: almost immediately after they moved into The Mount, Teddy Wharton suffered the first of a long series of nervous collapses.

8. Henry James and Others

During the week in August 1902 that Edith Wharton spent in Newport to escape from her labors at The Mount, she attended the christening of Theodore Chanler, the newly born son of Daisy and "Winty" Chanler. The child was named after his godfather, Theodore Roosevelt, an old friend of the Chanlers from their Washington days. Because of Roosevelt's presence at the occasion, the Chanler estate, overlooking the Atlantic on the northeastern side of the island, was alive with cordons of police on horseback and on foot, with secret service agents stationed at all strategic points. Roosevelt had been President of the United States since the day in September of the previous year when President William McKinley died as the result of bullet wounds received from a young anarchist of Polish descent committed to the assassination of the rulers of the earth.

Daisy Chanler moved through the well-protected festivities with ease and charm. She was a striking rather than a beautiful woman; her strong features glinted with intelligence and humor, and a readiness for affection. Edith found her old friend "dear and wonderful, serene and unhurried, among seven children and the turmoil of the Newport season." Later, Mrs. Chanler escorted the party to the Newport Casino to watch a championship tennis match, and Edith, "a devout spectator of that game" (as of no other), was enthralled.

It gave me the sense of being at a Greek game [she told Sara Norton]—the brilliance of the scene, the festal dresses, the grace and ease of the two players, and the strange intensity of silence to which the chattering was subdued. It seems to me such a beautiful game—without violence, noise, brutality—quick, graceful, rhythmic, with a setting of turf and sky.

But the chief stimulation for Edith Wharton was the two hours she spent in the company of President Roosevelt. Within the community of cousins to which she belonged, Edith was distantly related to the second Mrs. Roosevelt, the former Edith Carow. She herself had known Roosevelt, though only slightly, for a number of years. They were close to the same age, and had been born within a few blocks of one another in New York City. They had attended some of the same balls during the season, and had participated in the same cotillions. At Mary Cadwalader Jones's hospitable home on East Eleventh Street they had encountered one another from time to time, and Roosevelt called on the Whartons when he happened to be in Newport. But the deeper friendship dates from the Chanler christening party. "I do delight in him," Edith wrote Sara Norton a trifle defensively, aware of Charles Eliot Norton's contempt for the new President.

A week after that meeting Edith Wharton saw Roosevelt again, at a distance and under dramatic circumstances. The President's appearance in Newport coincided with a tour of New England and the Middle West, campaigning for the off-year elections and hammering away before huge crowds about the suit recently filed by the government against J. P. Morgan for alleged violations of the Anti-Trust Act. On September 5, as he was being driven in his barouche from Dalton to Pittsfield, his carriage collided with a trolley car. A secret service agent was killed, and Roosevelt, hurled from the barouche, lay by the side of the road till rescued by alarmed members of the presidential team. It was in fact a grave accident: Roosevelt's face was badly bruised, and one knee was so damaged that there were later rumors about a possible amputation; but he insisted on going ahead with the business of the day.

Edith Wharton was among the many who turned out to see and hear him in Lenox, and she reported on the event to Sara Norton:

I think if you could have seen the President here the other day, all bleeding and swollen from that hideous accident, and could have heard the few very quiet and fitting words he said to the crowd gathered to receive him, you would have agreed that he is not all—or nearly all—bronco-buster.

2

The October issue of the *North American Review* ran a somewhat occult poem by Edith Wharton called "Vesalius." Burlingame, the Scribners office expert on poetry, praised it warmly to his colleagues; at Charles Scribner's request, Brownell again asked Mrs. Wharton whether she had enough poems to make a volume: "We should be greatly pleased to publish it if you had." Edith demurred. She couldn't help writing poems, she said, but she had never thought them worth putting in a book. Brownell asked slyly if her prose works were so "Olympian as to lose by the proximity of their comrades from Parnassus?" A neat thrust, Mrs. Wharton admitted; she *did* think her prose was better than her verse.

And then there are degrees in prose and in poetry—below a certain point—well, it simply isn't poetry; and I am not sure I've ever reached the "poetry line." But if Mr. Burlingame likes Vesalius (which has made me want to hide under the furniture ever since I've seen it in print), there is no telling how I may rise in my own estimation.

Brownell persisted, contending that a book of her poems would be "an elevated, a dignified and a thoroughly personal, individual and characteristic volume." He gathered up all the poems by Edith Wharton published in several magazines and sent them on with the comment that "they seem to me to have an extraordinary number of fine lines," and that if there were not enough of them, no doubt within the year she would have added others "in the natural course of your mind's multifarious functioning." Her verse, he felt, was as superior to other current verse as her prose was to current prose.

There was something to this view. It was a slack and discouraging season for American poetry, with William Vaughan Moody being taken seriously as a major poet, one of the greatest since Shelley, and the tension-ridden poems of Edwin Arlington Robinson and the cultivated lyrics of Trumbull Stickney going almost completely unnoticed. But Edith Wharton's estimate of her own poetic achievement, though partaking of the usual self-deprecation, was a sound one. She was always a much better critic than a writer of poetry, and it would be another half dozen years before she would unmistakably cross the "poetry line." For the time being, the proposed volume was left in abeyance.

But Brownell's allusion to her "mind's multifarious functioning" touched another chord in her—the fear that she might be appearing in print too often. "I am annoyed to find myself figuring as a 'magazine bore' (a thing Mr. Burlingame once warned me not to become)." In recent months, indeed, her work had turned up almost simultaneously in *Scribner's, Harper's,* the *North American Review, The Bookman* (four times), and the New York *Commercial Advertiser.* "I hate to be bursting out simultaneously like an epidemic," she remarked. But an end was in sight. There would be a story in the December *Harper's,* then nothing for a number of months.

The demands of The Mount, still unfinished inside and out, were in fact getting in the way of new writing; and Teddy, in the wake of the summer attack of influenza, was suffering from some new illness, evidently serious but not easily diagnosable, which had darkened his sunny nature and made him impatient and gloomy. "I am bothered about him," Edith said to Sara Norton, "and tired with the house. There come weary stretches, don't there, now and then?" The doctors made the customary prescription of "southern climate," and just before Christmas the Whartons went down for a visit with their Newport acquaintances the George Vanderbilts at the latters' staggering creation, Biltmore, on an estate of 150,000 acres in North Carolina. But southern Italy seemed even more in order than Carolina, and Edith booked passages on the *Commonwealth* from Boston to Genoa for January 3, 1903.

As the year's end approached and the Whartons prepared to transfer themselves to the elder Mrs. Wharton's house on Beacon Street prior to their Boston embarkation, Edith remarked to Sara Norton: "I am hoping that Mrs. Jack will ask us to her *fête de Nouvel An,* and if she were any one but herself I should write and ask if we might come, for I should like to see it." The *fête* in question was the gala opening of Fenway Court, and Mrs. Jack was Isabella Stewart Gardner

—"Boston's most cherished institution," according to *Town Topics*, which also described her as the brightest and breeziest lady in the city, and expatiated on what it called her sparkling wit and charming coquetry.

Mrs. Gardner, twenty years older than Mrs. Wharton, was the daughter of a successful New York iron merchant. She became a Bostonian by marrying John Lowell Gardner of that city, a handsome and methodical businessman. Unable to bear children (after the loss of her little boy in 1865), and not herself creative, "Mrs. Jack" threw her immense energies into collecting: first, the most stylish, and in Boston the most scandalous, costumes from Paris; then precious stones; then, with the advice of Charles Eliot Norton, rare books; and finally the paintings of the Old Masters. Beginning about 1892, the Gardners acquired a remarkable number of now priceless works—some of them by the great Italian painters from Giotto to Titian, in the acquisition of which Mrs. Gardner had the inestimable aid of young Bernhard Berenson, already established as an expert in this area. After the death of Jack Gardner in 1898, his widow began to construct a tall and ample building on a reclaimed stretch of marsh on Boston's Fenway, modeled on a Venetian palazzo and with a quite breathtaking brightly colored interior courtyard surrounded by galleries; the building was intended to serve as both a home for the paintings and statuary and a town house for Mrs. Jack.

Edith Wharton and Isabella Gardner knew and were close to a good many of the same people over the years, but they were temperamentally unable to warm up to one another. Their comparable energies clashed; the assertiveness of each grated on the other; their assurance in matters of art and travel was in conflict. Edith, in addition, was never at ease with breezy and coquettish women—partly because, as she sometimes wistfully confessed, she would have liked herself to have more of those qualities.

She was, nonetheless, invited to the opening on New Year's evening, and the Whartons may have traveled from New York to Boston in the private car arranged for by Mrs. Gardner. Arriving at Fenway Court at nine o'clock, punctually, as the invitation requested, and no doubt after standing outside in the cold for some time while waiting her turn to climb the long curving staircase to greet her hostess, Edith Wharton inevitably found things to disapprove of, especially in the décor of the various rooms. During supper in the Dutch Room—where green brocades beautifully set off the Rembrandts—Mrs. Wharton is said to have murmured in French to her neighbor that the meal reminded her of the kind one was offered at a provincial French railroad station. Mrs. Gardner, on saying good-bye, is alleged to have remarked how happy she was that Mrs. Wharton had come, but that Mrs. Wharton need not worry about being invited again to eat at the station restaurant.

The story is probably apocryphal, in part or in whole. But it is characteristic of the anecdotes which were beginning to accumulate around the increasingly imposing public personality of Edith Wharton—elements in the mildly malicious comic image which American society, no less than French society, enjoyed weaving about its more distinguished members.

3

The Atlantic crossing seemed long to Edith, and the January sea gray and unusually rough. Things were pleasanter as the *Commonwealth* approached the Mediterranean, and an afternoon's sail along the Spanish coast struck her as "divine." But Genoa was chilly, and San Remo, to which the Whartons immediately repaired, left her bored and restive. There was no one to talk to and no books to be found; and for Edith the climate was so debilitating as to make work impossible. The tedious days spent seated aimlessly under a palm tree did Teddy much good, however, and by the time they moved on to Rome in early February, Edith's tone was more cheerful.

If the initial reason for this Italian visit was Teddy Wharton's poor health, another was a series of articles the *Century* magazine had commissioned Edith Wharton to write on Italian villas and their gardens. There was a symbolic ring to the invitation. William Dean Howells had been similarly commissioned by the *Century*, in the 1880s, to do a group of articles on Tuscan cities. Howells, all things considered, was probably Edith Wharton's closest predecessor in American literary history; and it was young Howells, just beginning his career, who had heard the venerable Dr. Holmes remark to James Russell Lowell, over lunch in Boston and nodding toward Howells: "Well, James, this is rather like the laying on of hands; this is an apostolic succession." If Edith Wharton knew of that much-quoted comment, she must, in 1903, have felt herself to stand in the same honorable line of succession.

In pursuit of her enjoyable assignment, Edith went out daily from the Hotel Bristol to examine the great villas of Rome, on her first visit to the city in more than eight years. She and Teddy caught one cold after another. But there was abundant sunshine; the February air was briskly stimulating; and if the floors of the Villa Borghese were glacial and required cork-soled boots, violets in the grass outside gave promise of things to come.

There was some literary business to discuss in Rome: the editor of the *Nuova Antologia*—whom Edith and Brownell referred to not without irony as "the *onorevole*"—spoke of wanting to run *The Valley of Decision* starting in the summer. He offered no advance and was vague about royalties, but Edith was eager for her novel to reach an Italian audience (which it would not do for many a year). And it would only be a few weeks before she received a check from Brownell for $7,963—the American edition had now sold well over thirty-five thousand copies.

In Rome as well there were old and new acquaintances. Edith was beginning a long friendship with Mary Crawshay, the sister of Sir John Leslie and hence the sister-in-law of Leonie Jerome Leslie and a more distant relative of Jennie Jerome Churchill. Mrs. Crawshay, then living in Rome with her husband, was a witty and warm-hearted soul who liked nothing better than putting attractive people in touch with one another. It was she who introduced the Whartons to William Hepburn Buckler and his wife.

Willie Buckler was the half brother of Julian White, on whose arm Edith Jones, trembling, had entered the Patriarchs' Ball that uneasy winter evening in 1883. He was married to Georgie Waldron, a niece of the historian James Anthony Froude, and himself displayed a sporadic interest in English history and archeology. The two couples took to each other at once, and Edith invited the Bucklers to accompany the Whartons in their landau from Rome to Siena.

With Buckler in charge of the maps, the foursome made their meandering way up through Viterbo, Orvieto, and Montefiascone, with frequent pauses while Edith inspected some famous if often out-of-the-way villa and garden. She took innumerable photographs, made extensive notes, and bought old books on each region in the hope of discovering the locations of forgotten villas and the original plans of their gardens. Buckler was taken aback by the crowded conditions of some of the villas—a great-aunt sleeping in a hallway, a grandmother dying on the library couch, the periodic cackling of the family lunatics in that part of the villa to which they were confined.

Buckler was more at home with sports than with art, but he found his hostess engagingly modest both about her literary attainments and her broad knowledge of Italian art and architecture. He later said about her in one of his favorite idioms that "she liked talking to be a game of ball, not a disguised lecture." For her, he remembered, "the appreciation of 'a sight' was co-operative," and her enjoyment was always the keener "because of your presence and fellow-feeling." Percy Lubbock, who in 1938, persuaded Willie Buckler to write down his memories of Edith Wharton, wrote "no, no!" opposite the last two remarks. But Lubbock's experience was of the later and more regal Edith Wharton. The companion Buckler was recalling was a woman who really did prefer to share, even if she sought to guide, the aesthetic pleasures of others.

As the Tuscan spring drew on, the Whartons left the Bucklers in Siena and drove slowly through the hills to Florence. From there Edith wrote R. W. Gilder at the *Century* to say that she had already seen twenty-six villas and anticipated seeing as many more, but that the expenses of the trip were a good deal greater than expected. "You know, of course," she remarked, "that I do not 'live by my pen,' and did not expect these articles to pay for the expenses of our Italian trip"; but she wondered if the fifteen-hundred-dollar advance might be increased to two thousand. Gilder was apparently agreeable.

Vernon Lee was awaiting the Whartons at her Villa Palmerino, a few miles above Florence, and she began at once to make herself indispensable. Her admiration for Edith had grown with the close scrutiny she gave *The Valley of Decision* while writing the promised article in Italian about it. She drew up a prodigious list of villas for Edith to see, organized expeditions, and gained access to villas normally closed to the public. Vernon Lee wanted to visit America the following autumn for what Edith regarded as the quaint purpose of seeing "the out of the way parts of New England," and to cover the costs of such a venture she hoped to arrange a lecture tour of some American women's colleges. Edith secretly deplored her topic, which was to be "aesthetics, 'Art and Life,' that kind of thing"; but in her gratitude, she was anxious to help. She asked Sara Norton whether Barrett Wendall of Harvard might give practical advice. The tour never took place, but Edith's gratitude was conveyed by the dedication of *Italian Villas and Their Gardens* to "Vernon Lee, who, better than any one else, has understood and interpreted the garden-magic of Italy."

To tea with Vernon Lee one April afternoon, Edith brought another New York friend, Bayard Cutting, and his wife of two years, Lady Sybil Desart, the daughter of an Irish peer. Bayard, some eighteen years younger than Edith, was the son of the forceful and cultivated railroad tycoon, whom she had come to know and admire in the time after her marriage. The younger Bayard was a man of enormous promise; he had inherited his father's resoluteness and energy, but had turned them toward political and intellectual affairs. George Santayana, a teacher of his at Harvard, said of him: "His intellectual life was, without question, the most intense, many-sided, and sane that I have ever known in any young man." Cutting gave up his senior year in college to become private secretary to the American ambassador in London, Joseph Choate, and it was while acting in this capacity that he met, fell in love with, and married Lady Sybil. The world seemed to lie all before him; but in the first winter after the marriage he had a hemorrhage and a spot was discovered on his lung. In the spring of 1903 the couple were snatching a fortnight in Florence after a dull convalescent winter on the Italian Riviera.

Lady Sybil had called on Edith at 884 Park Avenue on a snowy winter day soon after the Cuttings' post-honeymoon arrival in New York. The meeting was not a happy one. Edith cross-examined the young woman, in a cool and imperious manner, about a number of literary personages, like Henry James, whom Lady Sybil had never laid eyes on, and showed not the slightest interest in the high life at the Court of St. James', with which the newly married bride was more familiar. During an awkward moment Ogden Codman came in. Sybil hastened to take her departure, but as she was struggling with her snowshoes in the vestibule she heard Mrs. Wharton say in a very different voice, warm and humorous: "What do you think, Ogden—could one in a little house like this allow a Chippendale clock on the hall table, or should it be only a card-tray?"

The meeting in Florence was more fortunate. Edith swooped down on the couple in their rooms above the Piazza Goldoni, overlooking the Arno and the

Ponte di Carraia, and when told they were planning an afternoon of churches and galleries, said: "No, no—it's much too nice a day for that." They must come with her to Fiesole, where they could see a splendid villa, and meet Vernon Lee into the bargain. The Cuttings came along willingly. All the way up the Fiesole hill in Edith's carriage, Edith talked gaily and learnedly about Italian gardens. The afternoon came to its climax with the trenchant talk of Vernon Lee and the quick rejoinders and ringing laughter of Edith Wharton.

The next day Edith lured Lady Sybil away from a lecture on Dante to explore some antique shops on Via Maggio, on the other side of Ponte Trinità. It was a lesson in the ritual of shopping in Italy. Edith's eyes, bright and rapacious as a robin's (so Sybil Cutting would recall), darted from object to object until they lit upon something she coveted. They then became shuttered while she pointed out flaws in the articles—a pair of old chests, perhaps, for The Mount—and haggled in a desultory manner until the dealer agreed to the price Edith had decided on.

As it happened, both women were scheduled to go up to Salsomaggiore to take treatments for asthma. Salso, as they called it, was halfway between Parma and Mantua, and one of the few really ugly spots in Italy. Edith once said it reminded her of the backyards of Jersey City seen through a train window, but it had a good reputation as a health resort. The Cuttings joined the Whartons at their dining-room table and at times regretted doing so. Enticing dishes were whisked away by a wave of Edith's hand, the preparation being adjudged unsatisfactory; she badgered the manager, whom she nicknamed Twilight because of his melancholy manner and white tie, and kept the waiters running. After each crisis she was again all talk and laughter, and Teddy, leaning back, ran a hand through his hair in relief.

One evening as the Cuttings and Edith came out of the dining room, they noticed Teddy, who had preceded them, talking with a middle-aged woman whom Sybil recognized as an American-born duchess. Edith marched by with eyes averted. Teddy called out something about the duchess, but Edith continued regally to the elevator. Lingering, Sybil heard Teddy apologizing: "When she is taking the cure, Mrs. Wharton has to rest a good deal. She feels the cold, too." "Yes," the duchess said serenely; "I noticed a chill in the air."

Up in the Whartons' sitting room, Sybil found Edith muttering: "That dreadful woman," and when Teddy came in she said: "We never see her in New York—why should we see her here? You'll make Sybil think there is no difference between one sort of American and another." With this report of Sybil Cutting —no doubt passed around among her friends—another element was fitted into the comic image of Edith Wharton.

For the Whartons, there were further investigations in the Veneto and Lombardy, and ten days in Paris, before they sailed back on April 25. Lenox was something of a shock. A drought of more than two months had reduced the countryside and the estate at The Mount to desolation: dust everywhere, "the grass parched and burned, flowers and vegetation stunted." The gardener, whom Edith suspected of drink, was supposed to have spent a good deal of money on the place in the Whartons' absence, but to so little good that Edith dismissed him on the spot. It soon became apparent that much of the money had gone into the gardener's own pocket.

The malaise Edith began to feel after her return had another and stronger cause. This was the feeling, quickened by the wonders and beauties of the Italian trip, of being almost completely at odds with her native country and its inhabitants. She spoke about this at length to Sara Norton, and with an attempt at self-derision:

> My first weeks in America are always miserable, because the tastes I am cursed with are all of a kind that cannot be gratified here, and I am not enough in sympathy with our "gros public" to make up for the lack on the aesthetic side. One's friends are delightful; but *we* are none of us Americans, we don't think or feel as Americans do, we are the wretched exotics produced in a European glass-house, and the most deplacé and useless class on earth!

The outburst, she explained, was due to

> my first sight of American streets, my first hearing of American voices, and the wild, dishevelled backwards look of everything when one first comes home! You see, in my heart of hearts, a heart never unbosomed, I feel in America as you say you do in England—out of sympathy with everything. And in England, I like it *all*—institutions, traditions, mannerisms, conservatisms, everything but the women's clothes and the having to go to Church every Sunday.

It was a notable inventory of dislikes and likes; but Edith Wharton would discover before long that the entire matter of the European as against the American was more complicated, and her loyalties more divided, than she had realized.

Meanwhile, she added, "I try to console myself by writing about Italian gardens instead of looking at my own."

The focus in *Italian Villas and Their Gardens* is on the second of the two title phrases. Having drawn upon the interiors of the great European *palazzi*, town halls, and villas for *The Decoration of Houses*, Edith Wharton now studied a variety of Italian gardens, each one taken as "the prolongation of the house." The major principle of judgment was that the best kind of garden consisted in a cluster of carefully related enclosed spaces, rather than a single unbounded space disappearing into the surrounding terrain. The modern "landscapist," she argued, tended "to annihilate his boundaries," whereas the older garden architect proceeded on the analogy, warmly espoused by Edith, between the interior make-up of a house and that of a garden. Just as Edith's ideal house was "divided according to the varied requirements of its inmates," so a garden should not be merely one huge outdoor room but have its own logical divisions.

It must already be evident that Edith Wharton had a profound addiction, sometimes amounting to an obsession, with enclosed as against unbounded spaces: with houses themselves (her own and those of others), the arrangement of rooms within houses, the make-up of properly designed gardens, even with the sheltered settings of the Val Camonica and her Lenox landscape encircled by mountains. Elements like these were habitual sources of metaphor in her fiction. When it is added that those metaphors were almost invariably used to describe the inner nature of women—we have heard the woman in "The Fullness of Life" comparing her interior being to a series of receding rooms—we reach a point of speculation: Edith Wharton's intense, continuing interest in enclosures may quite likely be another register of her alertness to her own developing nature as a woman.

The matter, of course, is not as straightforward as that, and it would be tempting to pursue the inquiry further. In doing so we would remind ourselves, for example, that if Edith Wharton cherished certain kinds of enclosures, she also took the prison cell—the most fearful of shut-in spaces—as the image of a number of her characters' condition in life, and by implication of her personal state. Mention has been made of her aversion to being closed into a bedroom with her husband. Beyond that, one would be wandering into far psychological fields, possibly fascinating but increasingly remote from the human reality—from the emotions and impulses, the sometimes irrational gestures, all the rich texture of behavior and response that constitutes the flesh-and-blood woman with whom we have to deal.

Italian Villas and Their Gardens is a remarkable achievement. It draws on learning taken from books in four languages dating back to the seventeenth century, and includes brief biographical sketches of some sixty historically notable garden architects. About four-score villa gardens are examined, often with accompanying sketches. The section on the villas dotted among the hills around Siena —a perfect location for villa-building, as Edith observed—is particularly fine, and still regarded by experts as a major source of information on the subject. In the Florence chapter, it was the Villa Gamberaia above Settignano—with its superb organization of terraces, lawns, formal gardens with beautiful topiary and fountains, and small wooded areas (all this rising abruptly from the surrounding open countryside)—that Edith Wharton selected with all justification as her model.

Packed with a combination of first-hand experience and history, infused with a somber charm of style and a stateliness of movement, the book remains unique in this country. Nobody except Edith Wharton, one feels, would have had the tenacity, the knowledge, and the discrimination to write such a treatise. The composition of the individual articles kept her reasonably distracted during the summer of 1903, until further trouble befell.

4

Teddy, now fifty-four years old, was sick again, and more seriously than ever. He had had "a sort of nervous collapse," Edith wrote Sara Norton on August 9, "much like one he had last year after the influenza, but complicated with bad insomnia, which he does not bear as heroically as you do." The affair of the defaulting gardener had upset him beyond reason, and there had been other vexations connected with the completion of the house and grounds. "All these accumulated annoyances have taken a monstrous shape to his imagination, so that he cannot bear the slightest question about anything, and yet cannot bear to be excluded from things."

Edith was herself desperately tired from trying to keep Teddy calm, take care of his correspondence, and oversee the work on The Mount. But she was not without a genuinely sympathetic concern for her irascible, contradictory, sleepless husband—so changed, for the moment, from the easygoing, considerate person she had grown used to. "The insomnia makes him so nervous that it is pitiful to see him in the morning, and the sleeping mixtures which were given him had a very bad effect."

It was as though the rhythm of ebullience and collapse which had for a dozen years been a feature of Edith's life had now transferred itself to Teddy. Edith's only physical affliction had become the occasional bout of asthma, like the one which had driven her to Salsomaggiore in April; and although this had its psychological roots, as would become clear, her health for the most part held steady. But Teddy, who had been jauntiness itself on the Italian journey, had gone into a sharp decline within a month or so of returning to America, and an alarming pattern was beginning to establish itself. No one yet suspected that it might be the pressure of a life everywhere and altogether dominated by an affluent and brilliantly successful wife of strong personality that was at least one source of Teddy's instability.

Where Edith had found a clue to health in the shift from Newport to Lenox, the cure for Teddy seemed to require the opposite, a transfer from the Berkshires to the seashore. By mid-August, Teddy was persuaded to go to his brother William's summer home at Nahant, on the Massachusetts coast, and at the end of the month, somewhat refreshed, he joined Edith at Newport.

Land's End was no longer theirs and it seems probable that the loss of their island home of almost ten years was a contributing factor in Teddy's condition. On June 13, by deed of sale signed in Lenox, the property had been conveyed to Eleanor Beeckman, the wife of Robert Livingston Beeckman (good-old-family names indeed) of New York. The price was $122,500, Mrs. Beeckman also taking over what remained of the $50,000 mortgage.

Edith Wharton made it clear to Sara Norton, if not to Teddy, that her own presence in Newport was purely a matter of wifely duty. "Teddy is improving so much in this hateful place," she remarked in late August, "that I have decided to stay on till the 31st, though devoured by pangs of homesickness for my hills! How glad I am I insisted on going away from here. It seems to me the most miserable place to grow old in." A weekend with Mrs. Vanderbilt at her majestic home, The Breakers, and a few days with Egerton Winthrop on Bellevue Avenue did little to change her mind about "the inanities of Newport," and it was with heartfelt relief that she returned to The Mount at the start of September.

Teddy's condition, Edith told Brownell, put any "consecutive work" out of the question. The reference was to *The House of Mirth*, on which she was trying to make headway. But she was simultaneously involved with no less than four other volumes. She had just managed to send Gilder the last two "garden articles" before Teddy's collapse; the series was to begin in the November *Century*. There was further discussion back and forth, through September and October, about Scribners bringing out a collection of her other Italian sketches, but the book was postponed by agreement until 1905. More immediately on the horizon was Edith Wharton's next volume of short stories: she had ten items ready to choose from, and liked Brownell's proposal of the following April as a date for publication. More immediate still was a novella called *Sanctuary*, which ran serially in *Scribner's* beginning in July and appeared in book form on October 23.

Sanctuary is a relatively undistinguished piece of fiction. Edith Wharton may have thought so herself: it was referred to at The Mount as "Sank," and about none of her longer works did she have less to say during and after composition. The story breaks in two, each part turning on an intricate moral dilemma—the first being confronted by a young woman with an extraordinarily stiff conscience, the second, three decades later, by her ethically more pliable son. But it reveals Edith Wharton as engrossed as ever with the theme of a sensitive woman's disillusion (catastrophic disillusion in the first instance) with a man she has loved.

How much this was on her mind in her personal musings was implied by some quotations she wrote in her commonplace book at this time from Flaubert's *Madame Bovary*. She seems almost to have identified herself for the moment with the romantic yearnings and sense of suffocation of Flaubert's heroine. She copied out Emma Bovary's reflection that her husband Charles's conversation "was as flat as a sidewalk in the street." And she transcribed, underlined, and wrote marginal strokes next to another passage of particularly relevant imagery: "Her life was as cold as a garret whose windows face north, and boredom like a spider spun its web in the shadows, to all the corners of her heart."

It was an enchanting autumn in the Berkshires. For the first weeks after the Whartons came back from Newport Teddy was in good spirits, "and consequently," Edith wrote, "everything is easier." But the Lenox air that was bracing for Edith gradually told on Teddy's nerves, and before September was out he was once more in a state of collapse. Edith faithfully accompanied him to Newport again for a spell in October, but she was soon telling Brownell: "Alas, we are off again next month. I say alas because it is in no sense a pleasure trip. My husband is no better, and the doctor thinks he must get away as soon as possible."

Their departure was delayed by the sudden grave illness of Teddy's mother, who arrived from Boston to take to her bed in Pine Acre and further agitate her unhappy son. Cabins were booked at last on the *Cedric*, and Edith, addled with fatigue, sailed from New York with Teddy in the first days of December. Teddy would have preferred to go straight on to Italy, for he had come to dislike England rather irrationally. But Edith was determined to stop over for a while in London, where, she said to Sara Norton, "I hope to see a few people."

5

Much the most important of those few people was Henry James, who came up from his home in Rye in mid-December to have lunch and spend the afternoon with the Whartons at their hotel in Brooke Street. "He looks, without his beard, like a blend of Coquelin and Lord Roseberry," Edith remarked to Brownell. The references were to the great French comedian and the elegant, strong-featured, and society-loving Prime Minister under Queen Victoria, and it was a very fair description of the sixty-year-old novelist. "He seems in good spirits," she added, "and talks, thank heaven, more lucidly than he writes."

It was a meeting that had been delayed for more than fifteen years. In *A Backward Glance*, Edith Wharton tells of two earlier occasions when she and James had been guests at the same dinner party, on neither of which did James even notice her. The first, in 1887 or thereabouts, was in the Paris home of Edward Boit, a watercolorist from Boston whom Teddy had known years before. Edith wore her prettiest dress to the dinner, a Doucet gown, but James scarcely glanced her way, and Edith was too frozen with shyness to address a word to him.

The second non-meeting took place in Venice around 1891, at the Palazzo Barbaro on the Grand Canal. The Barbaro was owned by Daniel Curtis, a Boston gentleman who had been involved in a fracas several decades earlier, as a result of which he had removed himself and his family from America permanently and settled in Venice. Believing himself to have been gratuitously insulted by a perfect stranger, he punched the other man (who turned out to be a magistrate) in the face and broke his glasses. Suit was brought and Curtis was sent to jail for three months; released, and in a towering fury, Curtis put America behind him forever.

His son Ralph, a gifted if dilatory painter and a man of great personal zest, had known both Pussy Jones and Teddy Wharton in the old Newport and Boston days, and he was aware that Edith wanted nothing more than to meet Mr. James. This time she counted on a new hat to attract the great writer.

I was almost sure it was becoming, and I felt that if he would only tell me so I might at last pluck up courage to blurt out my admiration for *Daisy Miller* and *The Portrait of a Lady*. But he noticed neither the hat nor its wearer—and the second of our meetings fell as flat as the first.

Conversation of a sort began in the fall of 1900, when Edith sent James a copy of "The Line of Least Resistance," which had just appeared in *Lippincott's* magazine. The story had to do with a wealthy but put-upon Newporter who, after discovering that his wife had been unfaithful to him, weakly bows to the importunings of several social arbiters and takes her back. Edith believed it to be her finest story to date, and even planned to use its title for her forthcoming volume.

But "The Line of Least Resistance" was far from Edith Wharton's best. Henry James, replying at once from Lamb House in Rye, and after praising the tale's "admirable sharpness and neatness, and infinite wit and point," pointed to one central flaw and then suggested that the subject was really too big for short-story treatment. By implication, Mrs. Wharton should never have attempted it: such was James's way of moving slyly through approval to devastating criticism.

But he also offered serious literary advice: she should continue to explore in fiction the American world she lived in.

I applaud, I mean I value, I egg you on in your study of the human life that surrounds you. Let yourself go in it and *at* it. It's an untouched field, really: the folk who try, over there, don't come within miles of any civilised, however superficially, and "evolved" life. And use to the full your remarkable ironic and satiric gift; they form a most valuable (I hold) and beneficent engine.

This was entirely cogent and knowing; but James, typically, could not hold back from additional strictures. "Only, the *Lippincott* tale is a little *hard*, a little purely derisive. But that's because you're so young, and with it so clever." He concluded by urging her to send him more of her work, "and do, some day, better still, come to see yours, dear Mrs. Wharton, most truly, Henry James."

However gratified by the praise, Edith was stung by the rest of the letter; in 1900 she had not yet reached the stage where she could take such criticism in the fellow-artist spirit in which it was intended. She sent the letter on to Walter Berry, who suggested breezily that James must be losing his mind. To Brownell she wrote an elaborate explanation for suddenly wanting to remove the story not only from the title of the new volume, but from the volume itself. It had quite unintentionally, she said, caused pain to certain friends of hers in Newport. This may have been true, but Edith's smarting resentment was indicated a few months later in her comment to Sara Norton after reading James's *The Sacred Fount.* The novel was "ignoble," and she "could weep over the ruins of such a talent."

She also sought to ease her bruised feelings by composing a little parody of James's current style of writing (his "late style," as it has come to be called). This purported to be "advance sheets of Mr. Henry James's new novel," the latter bearing the title "An Open or Shut Question." It began with a gentleman named Mr. Valentine Grope reflecting with immense verbosity that, should he go out into the winter storm, his hat would be damaged.

It was, on the basis of any, even approximately, tenable conjecture becoming momentarily more patent to the incessantly exercised meteorological perceptions of Mr. Valentine Grope—excluding the at that season so obviously negligible hypothesis of a complete readjustment of the existing nebular contingencies—any head-gear exposed after five o'clock that afternoon to the unimpeded action of the climatic influences must, within less than the hour hand's gyration of the dial, be reduced to a condition warranting, if not necessitating, on the part of even the relatively unexacting, precipitate recourse to the (in expert judgment) so little better than provisionally restorative manipulations of the hatter.

It was not that, as Mrs. Byas said, one couldn't always buy a new umbrella.

And so on, for several more paragraphs.

A number of years later Edith forwarded the pastiche to her friend Gaillard Lapsley with the comment that it was a "wicked old opus." But it was not very wicked; indeed it rather missed its mark, and showed little of the insight into James's complexly rolling periods shown in Max Beerbohm's brilliant parody, "The Mote in the Middle Distance." Walter Berry, rejoicing loyally, said that people who thought Edith imitated Henry James in her fiction should see what she could do when she really tried. What is surprising, and suggestive, is that when she did really try, she quite failed to catch the flavor of James's style.

Twenty months later, in August 1902, it was James who took the initiative: first, by having Scribners send Mrs. Wharton "a rather long-winded (but I hope not hopelessly heavy) novel of mine . . . a thing called *The Wings of the Dove*"; and second, by writing her a long letter inspired by his reading of *The Valley of Decision*. About the latter James had already spoken warmly to Mary Cadwalader Jones, whom he had known for some time, when Edith's sister-in-law and her thirty-year-old daughter Beatrix had visited Lamb House. On her return to London, Mrs. Jones sent James the two volumes of Edith's short stories. James felt that the novel was a major advance over the shorter works, but he was taken by the stories as well—and by their author, with "her diabolical little cleverness, the quantity of intention and intelligence in her style, and her sharp eye for an interesting *kind* of subject." He went on from this perceptive praise to say that Mrs. Wharton's work made him "want to get hold of that little lady and pump the pure essence of my wisdom and experience into her. She *must* be tethered in native pastures, even if it reduces her to a backyard in New York."

To Edith Wharton, James delivered the same imperative, even more emphatically and at greater length, but only after extolling *The Valley of Decision* in the richest terms. His eulogy ended: "In the presence of a book so accomplished, pondered, saturated, so exquisitely studied, and so brilliant and interesting from a literary point of view, I feel that just now heartily to congratulate you covers plenty of ground." This was exhilarating, especially, as Brownell would say, since the letter's "strangulation is guarantee of its sincerity." But James had something more to say.

For a page or two he walked warily around it and toward it, worried lest it be "somehow mistimed while the air still flushes with the fierce fire of the Valley." His message emerged with a kind of stammering precision.

Let it suffer the wrong of being crudely hinted as my desire earnestly, tenderly, intelligently to admonish you, while you are young, free, expert, exposed (to illumination) —by which I mean while you're in full command of the situation—admonish you, I say, in favour of the American subject.

No more, in other words, of the eighteenth-century Italian subject. As to the native theme:

There it is round you. Don't pass it by—the immediate, the real, the only, the yours, the novelist's that it waits for. Take hold of it and keep hold, and let it pull you where it will . . .

What I would say in an word is: Profit, be warned, by my awful example of exile and ignorance. You will say that *j'en parle a mon aise*—but I shall have paid for my ease, and I don't want you to pay (as much) for yours. But these are impertinent importunities— from the moment they are not developed. All the same, *Do New York!* The 1st-hand account is precious.

It was the most important and the wisest literary advice Edith Wharton ever received, and it could not have come at a better moment. She sent copies of the letter on to Brownell (with an exclamation of astonishment: "I never send Mr. James my books, and should not have expected him to be in the least interested in 'The Valley' "), to Sara Norton, and no doubt to Walter Berry. Brownell, after remarking that it was a very nice letter to get, observed: "Well, you are going to do New York, anyhow, so your other admirers needn't speculate about the wisdom of his counsel." As he knew, Mrs. Wharton had already set about doing New York a few months earlier, with the novel "Disintegration." But perhaps one paradoxical result of James's letter was the abandonment of that work-in-progress—in addition to feeling some uncertainty about its development, she may have been aroused by James's remarks to the larger and more focused ambition that fulfilled itself eventually in *The House of Mirth*.

In declaring his wish for personal conversation with Edith Wharton, James had remarked: "I gather indeed from your admirable sister-in-law and niece, who have been so good as to come and pay me a little visit, that chance *may* favour your coming hitherward within the next few months. I shall pray for confirmation of this." Confirmation was duly received; Edith promised to come to Rye when she had completed her tour of the Italian villa gardens in the spring of 1903. But that enterprise proved more time-consuming than expected, and the Whartons returned to America without having set foot in England. James was disappointed. "Has Mrs. Wharton migrated to another planet or only returned to Lenox, Newport or whatever?" he asked Minnie Jones in June. "She promised herself to us here many, many weeks ago—I have her signed and sealed word for it. But darkness has since, to *my* vision, completely engulfed her, and silence to my ears." It was not until the following December that the two finally did meet up.

Apart from the little report to Brownell about the encounter—in which shyness, struggling with pride, produced a tone of seeming condescension— Edith's only reference was a laconic word to Sara Norton that Mr. James had come up from Rye and had been given Sara's message of greeting. James was more fulsome:

> I mustn't omit to tell you [he wrote Mrs. Jones] though you probably by this time know it that Mrs. Wharton has gone and come—gone, alas, more particularly, fleeing before the dark discipline of the London winter afternoon. I was in town for a day or two during her passage, and I lunched with her, with very great pleasure, and had the opportunity of some talk. This gave me much desire for more—finding her, as I did, really conversable (rare characteristic, *par le temps qui court!*) and sympathetic in every way. I count greatly on her return.

To other friends, however, James spoke of Mrs. Wharton as *"sèche"* and "slightly cold," though with a special grace of her own and a striking intelligence. A part of James's initial reaction, like that of Paul Bourget in Newport, appears to have been a certain alarm at the formidable intellectual gifts of so fashionable and wealthy a woman.

6

If Henry James always associated Edith Wharton with a shiny and resplendent new motorcar, it was because she and Teddy first appeared before the door of Lamb House in just such a vehicle. This was in May 1904, and by that time the car had already covered a great many miles. It was a Panhard-Levassor and had been purchased in Paris, whither the Whartons had repaired at the start of the year after ten days in England: "a 'motor-car' of moderate speed and capacious dimensions," Edith told Sara Norton, imploring the "shades of Ashfield"—where Professor Norton rejoiced in having no car, no telephone, and no electricity— not to shudder at such extravagant modernity. In acquiring a private automobile, the Whartons were again in the vanguard of things. Teddy, who had recovered swiftly once he arrived on the continent, took to the new machine like a duck to water, and broke it in by driving it down from Paris to Hyères, near Toulon on the southern coast, with Edith following at her leisure by train.

The Whartons spent a fortnight with Paul and Minnie Bourget at their villa, Les Plantiers, in Costebelle, a few kilometers from Hyères toward the sea. It was a charming place, with pine trees climbing the hillside behind it and from the terrace a dazzling view of the Mediterranean. But Edith felt that the Bourgets led an oddly restricted and self-absorbed life—the villa crouched almost invisibly behind high walls and locked gates—and that Paul kept Minnie in such a state of nerves about her health that the delicate Mme. Bourget sometimes seemed like an old woman.

As she herself grew ever stronger, Edith grew impatient with the ill health or alleged ill health of others. She insisted—and had her way—that Minnie was fit to accompany the Whartons on several little excursions through the local countryside, through olive groves and past fields aglow with roses and along the shores "of a radiant blue sea." These outings brought color to Minnie's cheeks, Edith noticed triumphantly; but Bourget stubbornly refused to let her go with the Whartons when they moved on eastward along the coast to Grasse.

From Grasse the Wharons proceeded (a word Edith liked to invoke, as the English did in speaking of the travels of royalty) to Cannes, driving over the stunningly beautiful old inland highway across the freshly snow-covered mountains. There they were stormbound for a week. In Monte Carlo, which they reached by mid-February, they again encountered intermittent bad weather. Edith and Teddy whiled away the hours playing Ping-Pong in the hotel game room. But on good days they explored the coastal region with mounting delight. Edith found that for the first time she could enjoy the Riviera, discovering a mountainous hinterland hitherto inaccessible, and "in a carriage of which the horses are never tired." She was already feeling, as she would say only a few years later, that "the motor-car has restored the romance of travel."

They had intended a "motor cruise to Italy," but got only as far as Genoa before the weather drove them back to Monte Carlo. Here, as the season abruptly turned damp and warm, Edith came down with a variety of miseries. Teddy, she informed Brownell, was now bursting with *bien-être*, but for her the seashore climate had brought on a series of severe headaches and nervous indigestion, culminating in influenza and laryngitis. She and Teddy, Edith wryly observed, "don't at all agree about climates."

Whatever its causes, the illness did not last very long and seems not to have been accompanied by the numbing depression that had marked the earlier crises. Before the end of March, Edith and Teddy had left Monte Carlo and were driving west across southern France. Though neither of them could know it, the decision to give up the Italian trip in favor of a French tour was a critical one. The Italian phase of Edith Wharton's life had in effect come to an end, and France would henceforth be her European home.

The Whartons motored over to Pau, along the border of Spain, and then up through Périgueux, Limoges, Bourges, and Blois to Paris. The car behaved splendidly, and as they passed through one new country scene after another, every step, Edith told Sara Norton, was a delight. "But the long day in the open air and the rush of new impressions had a stupefying effect, and I could not keep my eyes open at night when we reached our destination." One visualizes her sitting bolt upright in the high front seat of the Panhard, unprotected by windshield, side doors, or hood; Teddy beside her at the wheel, wearing goggles and a canvas coat; she herself veiled and swathed from head to foot in a long dust-covered cape, chiffon scarf flying about her hair, her hands clutching her head. By the time they drove into Paris, the enormous doses of fresh air had fully restored her.

They were back in London by late April, hoping to stay in England for several months. But word reached Edith that the servants in the lower echelons at The Mount were deserting her (for reasons unknown), so the visit had to be cut short. The Whartons had concluded, since they could not comfortably afford the heavy import duty on a French car, that they should sell "our dear motor, the most perfect of its kind," and they engaged in a last little frenzy of automobile jaunts.

A journey to Cambridge and a punting trip down the river past the enchanting "backs" of the colleges summoned up a lyrical outcry and a wave of melancholy at having to return to America:

. . . limes and beeches in fresh radiant leaf, the turf sown with daisies, the gardens glowing with spring flowers, the old mellow walls bathed in pale sunshine. How much we miss in not having such accumulated beauties to feed on now and then at home! I enjoy them so keenly that the contrast makes me miserable, and I think it almost a pity for an American who loves the country ever to come to England.

In early May they drove down to Rye, in Sussex, where, breasting the cobbled, curving little street, they arrived at last at Lamb House.

It was a snug little place, and included a wide enclosed lawn which contained a kitchen garden and some flowerbeds, and a "garden-room" which one entered by climbing a small flight of wooden steps, and where James, striding up and down in front of the big bay window, dictated fiction to his secretary every morning. The two spare rooms in the house were occupied by other guests, so the Whartons stayed at the nearby Grange.

There were "some good hours of talk with Mr. James," Edith told an English friend, "and a great deal of excellent food." James in turn pointedly remarked to Howells that "the Edith Whartons" had visited him "in force." They took a drive together in the afternoon, going as far as the Winchelsea home of the actress Ellen Terry. As they were churning through the mild Sussex countryside, Edith remarked, not without complacency, that she had purchased the Panhard with some of the proceeds from *The Valley of Decision*.

So legend avers, anyhow, and it adds that James digested the information in silence, brooding a little as he stared out at the slowly passing landscape. "With the proceeds of *my* last novel," he said finally, referring to *The Wings of the Dove*, "I purchased a small go-cart, or hand-barrow, on which my guests' luggage is wheeled from the station to my house. It needs a coat of paint. With the proceeds of my next novel I shall have it painted." Here we have an item not only in the developing image of Edith Wharton, but in the (much distorted) image of her relationship with Henry James—that of the wealthy *femme du monde* and the impoverished country squire.

Both James and Edith Wharton later agreed that their friendship had formed so rapidly, their social and intellectual rapprochement had begun with such immediacy, that neither of them could recall the exact times and places of these first meetings. Literature, the craft of fiction, fellow artists in several countries, mutual friends in two hemispheres, the varying fascinations of Europe and the finest niceties of the English language, a love of laughter: these and other things the two could enjoy together and discourse about endlessly. Yet there remained for the time one phase of the relationship that still disturbed Edith Wharton.

This was the imputation that she was a rigorous disciple, almost a slavish one, of the master. James himself had not been loath to propagate the idea: when he first saw some of Edith's work in 1899, he referred to her as "that almost too susceptible *élève*." But by 1899 it was already too late, and by 1904 much too late, for so resolute a writer as Edith Wharton to be anybody's *élève*. The cast of her mind and imagination, in addition, was (as her attempted parody of James demonstrated) more remote from James's than even she realized. It had both a tough and a tender femininity, a sense of the immediacies of social change, a taste for the scientific, and a distrust of the colloquial that were all quite missing from Henry James. And James, in the midst of his great period in the early 1900s— what would be known as his "major phase" *(The Ambassadors, The Wings of the Dove, The Golden Bowl)*—was producing work which, however extraordinary, was not likely to enlist disciples, though it might earn him worshipers at the shrine.

The claim persisted. Edith Wharton had not been idle during the long months of motor-cruising. She had completed several short pieces of fiction and, from a distance and with Brownell's unsparing help, had seen through the press her third volume of short stories, *The Descent of Man*. The book appeared in April, and in June, after the Whartons returned to Lenox, Edith asked Brownell to send her a sampling of reviews. She returned them on June 25 with a kind of despair, having come upon the same critical contention in a number of them:

I have never before been discouraged by criticism because when the critics have found fault with me I have normally abounded in their sense, and seen, as I thought, a way of doing better next time; but the continued cry that I am an echo of Mr. James (whose books of the last ten years I can't read, much as I delight in the man), and the assumption that the people I write about are not "real" because they are not navvies and char-women, makes me feel rather hopeless. I write about what I see, what I happen to be nearest to, which is surely better than doing cowboys *de chic*.

7

To this unusual outburst, Edith Wharton's first explicit effort to identify herself as a writer, Brownell wrote a long and thoughtful reply. "I sympathise with you about the James business," he said. "Of course it is unpleasant not to have one's uniquity recognised, but sometimes you seem to come out of the mix better than he does." As an example, Brownell quoted a newspaper which had referred to her as "a masculine H.J." He teased her a little for seeking to make an art out of fastidiousness on the one hand, and on the other seeming to wish her work were "gummed up and begrimed" by all those aspects of life she so carefully avoided. "I am trying, as you see, to be mischievous as a guarantee of my candor."

Continuing in this vein, he took note that a story called "The Letter" was in the English edition of *The Descent of Man*, published by Macmillan, but not in the Scribners American edition, and commented in mock amazement that he had never even heard of the tale. "*You* have never referred to it. Your brood is so numerous you don't keep track of stray chicks. . . . How reconcile such stony-hearted absence of vanity with 'discouragement' over the treatment of your progeny by—save the mark—the papers of our country which does not apparently contain a critic from Maine to California."

William Crary Brownell was fifty-three in 1904: an elegant and courtly man with a finely chiseled head and an immaculately trimmed beard; a combination of intellectual dreaminess (he looked, one of his associates said, like someone intimate with all the sorrows of the cosmos) and great practical energy. He had been born in New York, attended school in Newport, and graduated from Amherst in 1871. He worked on the New York *World* and spent almost four years in Europe before joining Charles Scribner's Sons in the mid-1880s as "literary consultant," a position he would hold for forty years.

His wife, the former Virginia Sherbourne of Newport, suffered a nervous collapse in 1897, and she passed the remaining dozen-odd years of her life between sanatoriums and a house at Narragansett Pier looked after by a nurse-companion. It was this circumstance that made Brownell, who was kindly by nature, peculiarly sympathetic toward the periodic breakdowns of Teddy Wharton, about whose health he never failed to ask. He had moved into the New York Athletic Club in 1900 and refused all social invitations, though he dined occasionally with his cousin Evangeline Blashfield and her husband (a couple he introduced to Edith Wharton). His favorite haunt was the Century, of which in the course of time he became a senior officer.

Brownell was an industrious literary critic, though possessed of no striking flair or special grace of style. He was one of the first to deal closely with nineteenth-century English writers as a group (*Victorian Prose Masters* in 1901) and their American counterparts (*American Prose Masters* in 1909), and he brought to these studies a capacity for detachment, a broad cultivation, and a learned affection for the subtleties of formal composition. His manner may be suggested by a comment on Poe: "It is the tragedy of American letters that the one absolute artist of our elder literature should, in any marked degree, require a chivalrous, rather than requite a critical, justification."

Such stately circumlocutions often characterized his editorial comments as well, and more than one of his authors was left in the dark as to whether Brownell was admiring or rejecting his manuscript. But it was against Brownell's policy to offer concrete advice about work he received at Scribners. "I don't believe much in tinkering," he once remarked to Edith Wharton, "and I am not *suffisant* enough to think the publisher can contribute much by counselling modifications." In this respect he differed significantly from Maxwell Perkins, his successor as fiction editor at Scribners. He did not conceal the fact that, like Henry James, he preferred that Edith Wharton explore the contemporary American scene rather than the Europe of former ages, but he never pressed the point. He was, meanwhile, a tireless and erudite copy editor, searching out the correct versions of archaic words and phrases, and checking lines from the French and German poetry Edith liked to draw upon.

With Mrs. Wharton (they never came remotely close to first names), Brownell was a friendly correspondent rather than an intimate. He had in fact very few intimates. "An only child, childless, and for many years a widower," his second wife said of him, with a formality she had perhaps learned from her husband, "he was not rich in the closest contacts." But he was able to strike just the right note of amicable joking in answering Edith Wharton's letters of complaint. Apologizing for having neglected to forward the advance on *Crucial Instances* in 1901, he wrote: "Pray excuse the delay . . . and do not take the same sinister view of it that you do of the advertising maw." When his own book on the Victorians came out in the fall of that year, he told Mrs. Wharton: "I am now writing my publishers that friends inform me they have seen no announcement, are unable to etc. etc."

Almost from the outset he appreciated Edith Wharton's most remarkable feature: her immense energy. When he suggested she produce four more stories to complete the volume later called *The Descent of Man*, he admitted it might seem odd to suppose she would have "the strength, the leisure and the inclination 'to furnish' in such short order," but "I know that both your imagination and energy are equal to tasks which it is difficult for me to conceive as readily executable at all—to say nothing of the time limit."

Edith Wharton had reason to be disappointed in some of the reviews of *The Descent of Man.* The volume is probably the best of her collections of short stories. With it she reached full maturity as a satirist of American manners—the latter term including not only minor social gestures and habits of dress and speech, but also attitudes to premarital and extramarital sexual experience, the precarious relations between parents and children, and the popular vulgarization of scientific thought. This is conspicuously a book written by no one other than Edith Wharton. The dominant tone is comic, and ranges from the exquisite satire (not unmixed with poignancy) of "The Mission of Jane" to downright fooling, even private joking—as in "Expiation," in which a bishop and his niece conspire to earn each other's fortunes, she by writing a mildly scandalous book, he by denouncing it from the pulpit; the book's title is that of Edith's adolescent melodrama, "Fast and Loose." In between, there is a story like "The Dilettante," in which a young girl is appalled (rightly so, one slowly realizes) to discover that her fiancé had *not* been the lover of the older woman he had been close to for many years.

Fresh aspects of Edith Wharton's character and opinions come surreptitiously into view in these tales. "The Mission of Jane," for example, says something about her feelings toward children in these years. A wealthy New York woman and her elegant, helplessly embarrassed husband adopt a baby girl; the latter develops into an unspeakable child, and then a very monster of a bossy young woman; her eventual marriage and departure, after hair-raising hesitation, are the making of her adoptive parents' middle-aged relationship. The story supports Margaret Chanler's remark that Edith "did not like children," and that if the devil ever appeared to Edith, he did so in the shape of a small child—"but he was never able to deceive her as to his true nature."

Edith Wharton's attitude toward the very young, however, was a complicated and changing one. She could speak scathingly about the children of her New York friends, and after contemplating one of them was even heard to remark to Teddy in a resonant voice, that perhaps it was just as well that they had never had a child of their own. But there are moments in her fiction—in the latter pages of *The House of Mirth* and more prominently in her work during the 1920s— that suggest a deep yearning for motherhood.

In "The Other Two," the most nearly perfect short story Edith Wharton ever wrote and a model in the genre of the comedy of manners, she reflected from a new viewpoint upon the question of identity. The story's climax is the belated discovery by Waythorn, his wife's third husband, that the woman he had thought so unique was (the figure is precise if disconcerting) like "a shoe that too many feet had worn. . . . Alice Haskett—Alice Varick—Alice Waythorn—she had been each in turn, and had left hanging to each name a little of her privacy, a little of her personality, a little of the inmost self where the unknown gods abide." If Edith Wharton could now so deftly describe the shredding identity of another kind of woman, it suggests that she was increasingly in harmony with her own inmost self and respectfully aware of "the unknown gods" that abode there.

9. The House of Mirth

As spring 1904 passed into summer, The Mount came alive. It was the first time Edith could truly enjoy her new home. During the periods she had previously spent in it, she had more often than not been too distracted by Teddy's ups and downs to be fully conscious of the place. It was a fairly massive construction, ascending from the kitchen, laundry room, and servants' dining room on the basement level up red-carpeted stairs from the elegantly arranged ground floor to the assorted bedrooms of the second floor. On the third floor, nine bedrooms for servants opened off the hallway (all told, The Mount could house over a dozen employees). Topping the edifice—and following the example of Christopher Wren's Belton House in Lincolnshire, which served as a general model for The Mount—was a cupola and a little balustraded walkway from which one had a handsome view down over the gardens and fields to Laurel Lake.

Edith at last had her own private suite, which occupied the eastern end of the long second-floor corridor: a large corner bedroom, decorated with prints of multicolored flowers, a dressing room, and a bathroom. Teddy's bedroom and bath came next along the corridor, and then four rooms for guests.

Social life at The Mount centered in the three spacious rooms which led one into the other on the ground floor. Each could also be entered from the fifty-four-foot gallery with a barrel-arched ceiling, and from each one could pass onto the terrace which ran along the front and one side of the house and which in warm weather was partly covered by a broad striped awning. The rooms possessed a high degree of individuality and distinctness, but they flowed together in quiet harmony: an arrangement which reflected not only Edith Wharton's taste in interior design, but her very sense of the variety and unity of life and the nature of human relationships. To one end was a nicely appointed library, with tapestries and a surprisingly small desk—at which, however, Edith Wharton wrote nothing but letters. Adjoining it was the high-ceilinged drawing room, about twenty feet by twenty-five, with gilt mirrors and a piano, and beyond that the dining room, whose stout-timbered table could seat ten persons. There was a marble fireplace with elaborate trimmings and moldings in each room, to fend off the chill of the autumn evenings.

From the terrace a wide stone staircase descended to the gardens, which, as might be expected, featured a pattern of intricately related enclosed spaces, with ponds and fountains and curving stone benches. Trees towered up from the sloping ground below The Mount, and there were literally hundreds of varieties of flowers and plants in the profusion of carefully laid out beds. On a stretch of lower lands was a stable with stalls for fourteen horses, a greenhouse, several small cottages (one of them inhabited by the butler, Arthur White), and a barn. A gatehouse stood guard at the eastern edge of the property, and to the south a lawn ran down to a rolling meadow, below which lay the wooded lake.

Gardeners, under Mrs. Wharton's direction, were planting a clump of white pines between the house and the stable in the summer of 1904, and with this addition The Mount was complete. The first of an unending stream of visitors began to arrive, and lights burned late on the terrace. Over the Fourth of July, the Whartons entertained Brooks Adams and his wife, down from Cambridge, and Bay Lodge and Walter Berry, who came up together from Washington: a lively occasion despite some domestic mishaps to which Edith alluded darkly in a letter to Sara Norton. Other guests followed, and Edith was a trifle put out when her brother Harry cabled from Paris that he wanted to come for a stay in September; she had visitors booked for six solid weeks, none of whom would easily be put off.

However full the household, Edith devoted her mornings single-mindedly to *The House of Mirth.* She also found energy to spare for village concerns: the Lenox Library Committee, the Village Improvement Committee, the Flower Show Committee. But the impulse to travel, to move, even if only on short jaunts through the New England countryside, was as strong as ever. She and Teddy, Edith told Sara Norton, had purchased "a little sputtering shrieking American motor," and perhaps they would drive up to Ashfield for a call. Her tone implied that nothing, not even an automobile, could match its European equivalent, but when Sara wondered whether the new car could make the eighty-mile round trip in a single day, Edith replied that Sally had insulted "our motor," and that Teddy had driven it over from Hartford, a matter of seventy miles, in no more than four hours. (If so, he had crowded the speed limit, which permitted the rapid pace of twenty miles an hour only in open country; in cities, no more than ten.)

In mid-August, on the circuitous way back from Groton, Massachusetts, the Wharton car broke down at Petersham, and Edith found herself forced to spend the night at a new hotel called the Nichewaug. Everything about it appalled her, and she took the occasion to declaim again on the crudity of most Americans.

I have been spending my first night [she wrote to Sara Norton] in an American "summer hotel," and I despair of the Republic! Such dreariness, such whining callow women, such utter absence of the amenities, such crass food, crass manners, crass landscape!! And, mind you, it is a new and fashionable hotel. What a horror it is for a whole nation to be developing without a sense of beauty, and eating bananas for breakfast.

Despite that wholesale denunciation, Edith's own sense of the beautiful was too true and generous not to respond to the peculiar appeal of New England, at least apart from its vile humanity. There was romance here too, she was discovering, in the somber and changing scene. Returning in mid-September from the long delayed trip to Ashfield, she gazed up at "a sky of flying gleams and leaden clouds," and it seemed to her "the most beautiful, perhaps, for our austere New England landscape." Passing Plainfield, they crossed a desolate region "of lakes and rolling fields and forest, enclosed in sombre hills, and so remote, uninhabited and tragic under the dark sky." The image clung in her memory until it went into the description of Starkfield in the remote little tragedy of Ethan Frome seven years later.

2

At The Mount and on excursions away from it, Edith Wharton was forging new friendships and strengthening old ones that added to the growing population of her literary, intellectual, and social world. It was on a little tour of New England with Berry in late August 1904 that she first met Gaillard Lapsley, an American who taught at Trinity College in Cambridge, England. He soon became one of the closest and most dependable of her friends.

Lapsley, who was careful to pronounce his first name "Gillyard," was nine years younger than Edith: a tall, lanky man with an owlish expression, an observant eye, and an assured manner. Within limits—and there were those who said the limits were unnecessarily narrow—he was knowing and intelligent. He was a New Englander by origin, and had attended Harvard College. His graduate study there was in the field of medieval English history. He eventually earned an appointment at Trinity, and by 1904, more English than the English, he had a solid reputation as a history scholar with a certain literary flair.

Lapsley's recollection of the encounter (it took place in the Massachusetts home of some Washington friends of Edith's), written down many years later, can stand as a portrait—not an altogether flattering one—of Edith Wharton in her forty-third year:

. . . slim, smartly dressed in pale blue with some kind of rose coloured trimming on the bodice, extremely décolletée, her hair parted in the middle, curling slightly at either side and fastened in a small chignon on the nape of her neck. She wore a few good jewels but no necklace and had a rather shabby thumbstall on her right hand which she had injured or lamed in writing. Her face was already worn and looked tired in repose, which it seldom was. There was [a] sort of metallic radiance about her matched by a like quality in her voice.

Lapsley was quick to accept an invitation to The Mount, and came to appreciate her genuine vivacity and enjoyment of sheer fun, not to mention an ability to be so convulsed with laughter that it positively hurt. In addition to his companionable intelligence, Lapsley's special value to Edith was as another bridge to European literary culture, above all nineteenth-century English fiction and the Victorian masters.

In September, Edith and Berry drove over to Ashfield for a day with the Nortons. They had made the trip three years before, but on that occasion the journey involved a change of trains and a ride up the mountain in a buggy drawn by a lively chestnut. Edith felt that much had been crowded into the little visit, which included a picnic amid the blueberries of what was known as "High Pasture," a slow walk down through the orchards, and a steady flow of the best conversation. "I can't plunge easily with most people," she wrote Sara Norton afterward, "though I may know that somewhere in the depths there is something worth diving for"; but her shyness was quite overcome in the presence of Sally and her father. The visit by automobile in 1904 was no less rewarding. Norton, though failing visibly, was able to talk with them for several hours, and Edith declared that she had been, as always, "kindle[d] through and through" by his wise and humane conversation.

Charles Eliot Norton, nearing eighty, had been retired from Harvard for seven years, and now presented to the world a sensitive oval face, deep watchful eyes, a head adorned only by wisps of white hair, a prominent, almost aggressive nose, and a thick white moustache. His father, Andrews Norton, had achieved prominence by denouncing Emerson's historic address to the Harvard Divinity School in 1838 as "the latest form of infidelity." Charles grew up in the family home, Shady Hill, an imposing colonial house on an estate of fifty acres within easy walking distance of Harvard.

From young manhood on, Norton drew to himself a host of European literary friends, in particular Henry James (also an old friend of his sister Grace) and John Ruskin, whom he met on a steamer crossing Lake Geneva (Edith Wharton put this encounter to good use in her novella *False Dawn*). It was from Ruskin that Norton imbibed his lifelong dedication to the moral—one might almost say the virtuous—aspect of great art; and it was this aesthetic approach that he promulgated in a series of articles in the newly founded *Atlantic Monthly* beginning in 1857 and as co-editor, with James Russell Lowell, of the *North American Review* from 1863 to 1868.

In 1862, the year of Edith Wharton's birth, Norton married Susan Sedgwick of Cambridge. It was as a summer home for his growing family that Norton bought and converted the spacious and charming farmhouse amid the trees just outside of the mountain village of Ashfield. In the wake of his wife's death, he accepted an invitation from President Charles W. Eliot of Harvard to become professor of fine arts, a position he held for twenty-three years.

It was Harvard's golden age of humanistic teaching: among Norton's colleagues were Barrett Wendell, Henry Adams, William James, George Santayana, Albert Bushnell Hart, and George Lyman Kittredge. The galaxy contained no livelier performer in the lecture hall than Charles Eliot Norton. Smiling and looking about him benignly, he condemned everything written or constructed since the late Middle Ages, everything American from the beginnings, all modern architecture and especially that of Harvard University. It was said that when

Norton died and went to heaven, he would recoil and exclaim: "Oh! Oh! So garish! So Renaissance!" In his later years, after struggling to awaken the minds of some 450 students, he would go home to inveigh against "this football generation . . . this generation without a poet."

He and Edith Wharton obviously had a good deal in common, including both spirited prejudices and an abiding love of Dante—of whose *Divina Commedia* Norton made what became a standard prose translation. But Edith did not share his views of the Spanish-American War, which he denounced as criminal and idiotic; for saying this he was vilified in the public press as being treasonably unpatriotic (he was not the last American academic to be so attacked for opposing an American military venture). And she differed with him decidedly regarding Theodore Roosevelt: "the good cowboy become President," Norton said.

Of Norton's six children, Edith had some acquaintance with Richard, was on terms of wary friendship with Lily (Elizabeth), and was growing fonder by the year of Sara. The latter, only a little younger than Edith, was a quick-minded, serious, and rather humorless person, a born spinster it seems, and selflessly devoted to her father. Edith began to correspond with her in early 1899; by February 1901 she was addressing her as "Sally" and signing herself "Edith or Pussy as you please."

Over the next seven or eight years, it was to Sally Norton that Edith wrote most regularly and personally—letters which Sally eventually said should, in case of her death, be returned to Edith: "She may burn the letters, I can't." They exchanged literary opinions and books, including Fitzgerald's translation of *The Rubáiyát* and the poems of "Mr. Santyana," as Edith first spelled the name. Edith alluded frequently, and with reverence, to the volume of John Donne's poetry which Professor Norton had given her. The two women differed about Turgenev, Edith finding the Russian writer "colourless," especially by contrast with Tolstoy. In January 1902, Edith spoke of reading Schopenhauer on "the ascetic life" in *The World as Will and Idea:* "How strange it is to rummage in all that old metaphysical lumber."

Comments were passed back and forth about world events. In the spring of 1901, Edith, describing herself as a "rabid imperialist," voiced her support of the British in the Boer War—a conflict which had ended the previous September, following the relief of Mafeking and the annexation of the Transvaal. Two years later she was expressing her and Teddy's excitement over the Russo-Japanese War and their sympathy for Japan, "though we don't quite know why, except that Russia seems to be at once false and brutal."

It was Sally Norton who, in 1899, had introduced Edith to Lucy Whitridge, the daughter of Professor Norton's friend Matthew Arnold and the granddaughter of the famous schoolmaster Thomas Arnold of Rugby. Lucy had married an American, Frederick Whitridge, and they divided their time between an English country home and a house in New York. It became a lifelong friendship.

3

Shortly after the middle of October, Henry James arrived at The Mount, bringing with him Howard Sturgis. It was James's first visit to the United States in more than twenty years—he was beginning the tour of the country that was the basis of *The American Scene*—and from his brother William's home in Chocorua, New Hampshire, he wrote Mrs. Wharton that her relative proximity in the Berkshires helped him feel that his "repatriation isn't a mere lurid dream." He also passed on from the Bourgets their admiring comments on her story "The Last Asset," which had appeared in the August *Scribner's* and was indeed one of her finest.

The combination of beauty and comfort at The Mount was a source of profound enjoyment for James. He was, he wrote, surrounded "by every loveliness of nature, and every luxury of art, and treated with a benevolence that brings tears to my eyes." Walter Berry was occupying another of the guest rooms, and James described him as charming; something in the nature of each of these two keen-witted and so differently cultivated bachelors responded at once to the other. James would lavish upon Berry some of his most rollicking and hyperbole-strewn letters, much of them devoted to extravaganzas about "the lady of Lenox."

The golden New England autumn amounted to a kind of "revelation" to James, and he even became reconciled to the automobile (about which he had previously spoken with stern disapproval), experiencing it now "from within," which was, he said, "the only way." There was a motor outing every afternoon, criss-crossing the slopes of their corner of Massachusetts with, as James put it, its extensive "mountain-and-valley, lake-and-river beauty," going once into New York State for a view of the Hudson, and another time to Lebanon, Connecticut, and the old Shaker settlement. As they drove slowly through the little New England villages, Edith regaled the fascinated James with reports that had reached her about the dark unsuspected life—the sexual violence, even the incest —that went on behind the bleak walls of the farmhouses.

After exclaiming volubly over these and other phenomena of the local land-scape during the afternoons, James further endeared himself to his hostess in the evenings by reading poetry aloud from the volumes on the library shelves: Browning and Baudelaire, Arnold and Leconte de Lisle, Emily Brontë (whose work Edith had not previously known). Edith had not heard James's perfectly modulated organ voice recite before, and the experience added to her sense of his greatness of soul. It was during this visit, apparently, that James read at length from Whitman's *Leaves of Grass*, an unforgettable occasion. James and Edith agreed in finding Whitman the greatest of American poets, and they talked about him long into the night, exchanging favorite passages. James finally brought the conversation to an end by crying, with a stammer and a twinkle: "Oh, yes, a great genius; undoubtedly a great genius! Only one cannot help deploring his too-extensive acquaintance with the foreign languages."

Howard Sturgis, the other visitor from England, was a person of remarkable qualities both of personality and mind—qualities which even such observers as Henry James, Edith Wharton, and Percy Lubbock, however much they rejoiced in them, found it almost impossible to convey. "Howard in his infinite Howard-ism," James once remarked helplessly; and Edith called him "the kindest and strangest of men." He was one of several children of Russell Sturgis (by a second marriage), an eminent Bostonian who had started on a banking career in the Far East and had wound up as a partner in the powerful firm of Baring Brothers in London. It was in London that Howard was born, in 1854, and he spent his entire life in that vicinity. Russell Sturgis died when Howard was still a child, but he left a sizable estate to his wife and his English brood—there was an American set back in Boston as well (George Santayana peripherally among them).

Howard grew up in Queen's Acre, a well-furbished household near Windsor, under the watchful domination of his mother, a woman as beautiful as she was severe. As a grown man and a gentleman of leisure, his favorite occupation was crocheting and needlework. Seated in his chintz chair at Queen's Acre, or "Qu'Acre" in the contracted form used by his friends, he would hook steadily and skillfully at his woolwork or stitch at his silken embroideries in a manner to arouse the liveliest speculation in anyone meeting him for the first time.

His nature was indeed at once feminine and childlike. He had the candid inquisitiveness of a child. Percy Lubbock, writing a memoir of Sturgis, had the distinct impression that Howard was looking over his shoulder "frankly and shamelessly interested in what I shall say." He also had the effect upon those around him of making them assume a childlike posture—a posture, that is, of spontaneous and dancing-eyed excitement. His friends expanded visibly in his presence, as though at a birthday party. "Our dear Howard is like a cake," James used to say, "—a richly sugared cake—always on the table. We sit round him in a circle and help ourselves." Howard's attractiveness was made up of a richly nourishing charm, sudden rushes of humor and playfulness which brought out all the wit and laughter in others, endlessly flashing conversation which could leave a friend out of training, as it were, exhausted after an evening of it, and withal, a capacity to cajole, flatter, advise, assuage.

In Edith Wharton's memory of Sturgis when she first came to know him, he appeared as a hefty, handsome individual, "with brilliantly white wavy hair, a girlishly clear complexion, a black moustache, and tender mocking eyes under the bold arch of his black brows." She had known him since a meeting in Newport not long after her marriage, but by the fall of 1904 she had not yet taken the measure of his delicately charged personality.

But even before Sturgis won her to him at The Mount, Edith had been trying hard to persuade Scribners to publish his novel *Belchamber*, which had been brought out in England the previous winter, and about which James had spoken to her during the London meeting with guarded enthusiasm. The narrative touched on adultery, illegitimacy, and various forms of ill-doing amid the loftier reaches of the English aristocracy, and Brownell, after inspecting the book, pronounced the subject unpleasant, esoteric, and non-American, and the whole thing in need of drastic cutting. Edith agreed about the cutting; but what completely took her aback was

the objection on the score of *moeurs* in a book of such serious purpose and tragic import, and secondly the view that it isn't American enough to interest American readers. It isn't American at all, of course—it is an English novel, to all intents and purposes by an English novelist—but is that a reason why it shouldn't "take" in America?

She compared it favorably with other books about allegedly "painful" subjects, among them *Red Pottage*, Mary Cholmondely's novel of 1899 about some scandalous goings-on in English society which had titillated and shocked readers in both London and New York.

But she was unable to break down Brownell's puritanical provincialism—of a kind that, from readers to reviewers, she too had suffered and was soon to suffer even more. *Belchamber* was eventually published in New York by G. P. Putnam's Sons in 1905, and though no sort of success, it gradually won a grudging critical admiration. It is a work of no little distinction, with moments of sheer farce as well as a steady tragic drift. In addition to the overt autobiographical elements, the central story of a marriage never consummated, an adulterous wife, and the early death of an illegitimate child constitutes a parable at several removes of Sturgis' own experiences and apprehensions.

4

The Whartons lingered on in Lenox through the later fall, with Edith, at least, reveling in the "glacial brilliant weather." The ground was snow-covered, the air was still and bright, the temperature hovered near zero each evening, the marble fireplaces blazed. When time came for the move back to New York, Edith was in despair at having to exchange "this delicious stillness" for "the noise and stuffiness of that execrable New York."

The return to 884 Park Avenue just before Christmas was the harder to bear since the Whartons had not inhabited the little house for two years. "This thrice loathed New York!" Edith exclaimed. Such bustle, such piled-up social obligations, so many cards and notes to acknowledge. To be sure, Edith Wharton enjoyed bustle betimes, and where there was none was apt to create it herself. But she was concentrating on the New York of the early 1900s all her growing disaffection for America as a whole. "I think the U.S. a bad dream," she had told Sara Norton a few months before; "but only man is vile, and oh, how enchanting the country is at this season." Even this was an oversimplification. At The Mount, "man" was represented by the highly agreeable society of friends and visitors carefully selected by Edith herself. But in New York she felt less able to choose the human beings she would run up against.

Her assorted complaints revealed a deep restiveness of both a personal and a traditionally American kind. The shortage in her native country of man-made beauty and cultural resonance periodically depressed her, as it depressed Charles Eliot Norton and a good many others; in one perspective, the most American aspect of Edith Wharton was exactly her impatient, Europe-oriented critique of the country. "I think I have found a way of summing up what ails 'our country' —that is, from the point of view of aesthetic interest," she once said to Sara Norton, ironically distancing herself from America by the use of quotation marks. "The American landscape has no foreground" (no villages, perhaps, quaintly perched on vine-clad hillsides), "and the American mind no background." But there was a private impulse as well. After a fortnight's stay in Paris she could burst forth abruptly: "I would give up all this fine civilization for a sight of my spring blossoms at Lenox." The fact was that she increasingly pined to be where she wasn't, where she had just come from, where she was next moving on to.

She was not at this time inclined to expatriate herself, though she considered the possibility. After one such meditation she announced with a sort of hard gaiety that she would stay on in America in order to criticize it from close at hand, and perhaps even to improve it. This would be a hidden motif of her literary work, and no doubt she heard Henry James's warning about "exile and ignorance" ringing in her ears.

In was, meanwhile, only in New York that she was hard put to find any residual charm or redeeming feature. She would eventually realize that the harshness of her attitude came from a buried loyalty to the earlier New York, that of the 1870s and 1880s, as to the earlier Newport. Those were worlds which combined elegance with simplicity, where there was physical and emotional space to move about in, and which, however narrow their mental outlook, possessed a clarity and firmness of moral vision. But the process of deterioration in those regards, which was already discernible in the 1870s as against the pre–Civil War condition, had, in Edith's view, accelerated rapidly and woefully. The simplicity was gone with the pushy displays of twentieth-century New York and Newport; the elegance had given way to vulgarity; the space had narrowed, and the vision had dimmed.

Henry James arrived at 884 Park Avenue on the day after New Year's 1905, to encounter at once the fourth snowstorm in as many weeks. It was an unusually severe winter in the city, culminating near the end of February with the heaviest blizzard since the famous one of 1888. Huddled inside the tiny house, James felt distinctly less at ease than he had amid the spacious surroundings of The Mount.

The amenities were superb as before, but James found that he and Edith and Teddy tended to bump into one another within the small compass and got a little on one another's nerves. Edith may have sensed her guest's mildly resentful discomfort. She took occasion, anyhow, to speak caustically to Sally Norton about James's most recent novel, *The Golden Bowl:* it might, she said, conceivably have possessed some greatness if only it had been written much more simply. Even so, when James departed in some relief for a stay with Mary Cadwalader Jones on East Eleventh Street, he left Edith with the very pleasant memory of an evening when, as they sat together before the fire, he read her the lecture on Balzac he was about to give at Bryn Mawr College and elsewhere.

Edith was busy with her own work. *The House of Mirth* was nearing its conclusion—as well it ought to, since it had already begun to appear in serial form beginning with the January issue of *Scribner's.* She was simultaneously completing several stories for her next book of shorter fiction, though one of them, "The Hermit and the Wild Woman," was giving her trouble, and had refused to resolve itself since she had first spoken about it to Burlingame the year before. As almost always, there was yet another book passing through the press—*Italian Backgrounds*, a collection of the sketches she had been writing off and on since 1894.

This volume, which appeared in March, is within its careful limits an expert and enduring series of images: of San Vivaldo and the coaching inn at Splügen, of Parma, of then unknown corners of Tuscany (Vallombrosa and environs), of less familiar sections of Milan. Its modest and well-illustrated thesis is that, confronted by scenes of a conventional and stylized nature, "it is only in the background that the artist finds himself free to express his personality." Such a thesis could also find application in Edith Wharton's fictional portraits of the stirrings of rebellious individuality within conventional society. Perhaps, more obscurely, it might have relevance to the outward and inward shaping of Edith Wharton's own life and personality.

5

On March 4, another snowy morning, Edith Wharton noted in her diary that it was the day of Theodore Roosevelt's second inauguration. Henry James, a week after leaving 884 Park Avenue, had written of his visit to Washington (a city, he told Edith, which seemed to cry out to one: "I am nothing, I am nothing!") and of his gratification over receiving diplomatic recognition "at Court." Roosevelt was on record as declaring James an "effete" and "miserable little snob," and James as declaring Roosevelt to be "a dangerous and ominous jingo." Nonetheless, the novelist was invited to the White House and placed at the President's table. Edith was soon able to match James's monarchical experience. On March 16, while staying with friends in Washington, she and Teddy also dined at the

White House, in the company of the President and Mrs. Roosevelt, the Bay Lodges, Mrs. Gifford Pinchot, the wife of the Pennsylvania politician, and Senator Cram of Massachusetts. She sat not only at the President's table, as she was quick to mention, but at his right hand.

The moment he spotted her, Roosevelt thundered: "Well, I *am* glad to welcome to the White House some one to whom I can quote 'The Hunting of the Snark' without being asked what I mean!" Apparently no one in his administration had read Lewis Carroll. Only a few days before, Roosevelt said, he had invoked Carroll's poem to remark to the Secretary of the Navy, *"Mr. Secretary, what I say three times is true!"* only to be met by the aggrieved reply: "Mr. President, it would never for a moment have occurred to me to impugn your veracity." Roosevelt and Mrs. Wharton then discussed *The Valley of Decision*, the President indicating that for all his great admiration he could not but wish that a higher moral code had operated in the story. Odo, he suggested, should have ceased his philandering early on and married Fulvia Vivaldi. Edith explained gently that such moral ideals did not happen to prevail in the decadent Italian states she had been describing. Roosevelt laughed, and agreed.

Three months later Edith Wharton, just back from France, drove over from Lenox to Williamstown to see Roosevelt receive the Doctor of Letters degree from Williams College ("a charming old institution"). The evening before the ceremonies, she attended a small reception in the house of Williams' President Hopkins. On this occasion, Roosevelt greeted her with an exclamation of surprised delight: "But you're the very person I wanted to see! Of course you've read the wonderful new book of de la Gorce's, the *History of the Second Empire?* What an amazing thing! Let's go off into a corner at once and have a good talk about it." Despite such exuberant flattery, Edith thought to herself next day that the President's speech, after the granting of degrees, was too long, too full of pauses and grimaces, and altogether quite inappropriate. It was a measure of Edith's concern over the Norton family's hostility to Roosevelt that she told Sally a downright lie, though a white and forgivable one. The rain, she said, had prevented her from going to Williamstown, so she had not after all seen the President receive his honorary degree.

Edith Wharton and the nonpolitical friends she shared with Theodore Roosevelt entertained no conviction that their relation with the President made them participants in political power. Not that Edith was immune to pleasure in the company not only of Theodore Roosevelt but of the country's chief executive, though it was probably less the man's power than his energy and many-sidedness that appealed to her. But the relationship between Edith Wharton's circle and the President rested rather upon belonging to the same social class, on reading the same books and enjoying the same jokes, and in the case of some of the male members, on having graduated from the same college. Walter Berry, who had met Roosevelt at a wrestling match during their undergraduate days at Harvard, could invite him cheerily to the annual jollification of the Columbia Bar Association and ask his help in organizing an American lecture tour for the French playwright Edmond Rostand. Mary Cadwalader Jones could send him a learned volume of early English history and speak of having seen their friend Henry Adams in Paris. Edith Wharton could write and consult him about works of history and literature, and Teddy could commiserate with him on the illness of his wife.

The presence of Roosevelt could be vaguely felt in the story Edith Wharton wrote in the wake of her visit to the White House, "The Best Man," which Senator Lodge liked especially, but which in fact only showed the author's lack of sureness in dealing with political figures. The man himself would appear more plausibly in *The Age of Innocence* as governor of New York, banging on the table and chewing on the earpiece of his glasses while he tells Newland Archer that Archer is just the kind of person the country needs and wants.

6

The annual trip to Europe in the spring of 1905 took the form of a health cure. Edith's health had been generally excellent, though she drove herself so hard both creatively and socially that her face sometimes wore the strained expression noticed by Gaillard Lapsley. But in April she was again suffering from asthma —from a severe difficulty in breathing caused perhaps by a reaction to finishing *The House of Mirth* against a deadline and by being cooped up at 884 Park Avenue with her husband. When Edith sailed for Europe she was accompanied only by Gross, her faithful housekeeper-companion.

There followed twelve rather lonely days in Paris, driving about the city in hired carriages. No doubt she called upon the Bourgets, but the French Academician was not yet prepared to introduce her to his friends among the aristocratic and intellectual gatherings in the Faubourg St. Germain. (It was at this time that, temporarily surfeited with the churches and galleries of Paris, she expressed her sudden longing for the spring flowers of Lenox.) At the start of May, Edith and Gross went via Milan to Salsomaggiore for the cure and then sailed home after another uneventful week in Paris.

The Berkshires were in the midst of another long drought; the countryside was parched, Edith observed, and the vegetation stunted. It was not a very auspicious moment for Henry James to pay a visit, especially since he was in a state of exhausted demoralization (he told Mary Cadwalader Jones) at the end of his long and grueling tour of the United States and "reduced to impotence by . . . the snapping of the cord of my long tension." But the atmosphere of The Mount was relaxing, and James willingly went with Edith on a drive to Ashfield for a visit with the Nortons. The trip back, through Northampton and Westfield and over Beckett Mountain, provided them, James remarked, with "a bath of beauty."

During the rest of the summer and on into the fall, Edith indulged in a frenzy of social entertainment. In addition to a succession of Lenox neighbors coming to tea or dinner, there were dozens of houseguests—some coming more than once, all of them for a number of days, and several for longer stretches. It was a rare period of creative inactivity: almost the only creative gesture was Edith's contribution to the flower show in mid-August—July thunderstorms had cleared the air, and the garden at The Mount was now "in perfection"— at which she won seven first prizes. Her energy was otherwise given over to her guests.

Among the latter were familiar old friends: Walter Berry, Sara Norton, Bay Lodge, Egerton Winthrop. Most of the others belonged, though in most cases to no very lasting effect, to the world of art and letters. There was the printer Berkeley Updike and Moncure Robinson, an amiable person with a face like a cherub, who had illustrated some of Edith Wharton's work. Ralph Curtis (who once, in Venice, had tried in vain to introduce Edith to Henry James) came by in September; after exhibiting some of his paintings years before, he had virtually given up trying to make his way as an artist and devoted himself to collecting Far Eastern art and living the good life, mostly in Europe. A more impressive and equally diverting companion was Edward Robinson, the head of the Metropolitan Museum in New York, a tall, spare man with a Teutonic manner which belied his talent for comical anecdotes.

A frequent visitor was Walter Maynard, nine years younger than Edith and the director, by inheritance, of a New York company which published books, mostly for elementary schools. Edith had already known Maynard's bride of two years, the former Eunice Ives, since the latter had been spending her summers in her parents' home in Lenox. While courting Eunice, Maynard had been observed in the Lenox church by a lady who declared him the "wickedest looking man" she had ever seen, and this was the epithet that Edith delightedly applied to him thereafter.

There were others still who began to make a stay at The Mount a regular affair, and to whom Edith would also extend her hospitality later in Paris. Of these, Eliot Gregory, just over fifty in 1905, was one of the most charming and least effectual. He wrote articles discussing and passing judgment on the social manners of the New York elite under the title of "The Idler"; these were collected in book form, and one of them, The Ways of Men in 1900, had been dedicated to Edith Wharton (who had probably supplied him with the title, after discarding it herself in favor of The Greater Inclination). Johnson Morton, more or less Edith's age, had been the editor of the Youth's Companion but gave it up for a modest career as a writer. He was an exceedingly kind man who worked hard amid the poor and wretched of Boston, but he could also write and tell a sprightly story.

And there was William King ("Billy") Richardson, a Boston lawyer specializing in patents and trademarks; something of a dandy, with a handlebar moustache and deep mournful eyes. Though he was well traveled, his literary qualifications were nonexistent; but his appeal to Edith is suggested by one of the apocryphal stories he mischievously spread about her. An opulent woman in the Berkshires neighborhood, while showing Edith through her house, remarked at one point (so Richardson claimed): "And this I call my Louis Quinze room." To this Edith, staring about through her lorgnette, replied, "*Why*, my dear?"

The visitor most accomplished in literary terms (needless to say, apart from Henry James) was Robert Grant, a boyhood friend and college classmate of Teddy Wharton's, and a tall, stooped gentleman of great formality of style. He had been a trustee of Harvard since 1895, was a judge of the Probate Court in Boston, and a prolific novelist of uncertain merit. Edith particularly admired *Unleavened Bread* of 1900, with its naturalistic vision (it quite fitted her own deepest view of life) which perceived no escape from the entanglements of experience except for the brutally insensitive and the ruthlessly grasping. She was to say that the novel anticipated the best work of Theodore Dreiser and Sinclair Lewis, and it undoubtedly had an influence upon her own most pitiless work, *The Custom of the Country.*

But it is misleading to list these individuals seriatim, as though each came and went quite independently of the others. They were not only visitors but friends of Edith Wharton's. She was only just now exercising to the fullest her remarkable capacity for warm and enduring friendship—the quality which, almost without exception, her guests best remembered and valued about her. But at the same time, Edith put them in touch with one another. At The Mount they motored together, they exchanged opinions and swapped jokes, they inquired eagerly about the absent ones and passed on the latest news. Within the larger world, with its array of dissatisfactions, Edith was creating a small human community, a society of friends, and the first of a series of its kind. This too was in response to a deeply felt personal need; for Edith, it was not a matter of keeping busy as a much-admired hostess, but of surrounding herself with genuine and like-minded companions.

Not that every visitor saw it that way. Lily Norton, Sara's rather inflexible older sister, thought that the house and garden were as perfect as money, taste, and instinct could make them, but that they were cold. "There was never the sound of young and ardent feet," she remarked a bit unfairly, nor of large romping dogs. If there was a piano (and Lily seems somehow not to have noticed it), there was no music lying about on it; and in general "the sense of *home* was not there." (Percy Lubbock, editing this memoir, noted sagely opposite the latter remark:

"Nobody thinks a *home* can be very different from his own.") But Eunice Maynard looked back fondly on the picture of Edith greeting her at the front door of The Mount, holding in her arms a Pekinese—perhaps too small a beast to be reckoned a real dog by Lily Norton—and recalled both the house and its mistress as not only beautifully ordered but gay.

Berkeley Updike, who had thought that Land's End lacked intimacy, regarded The Mount as a complete success: "I do not remember any house where the hospitality was greater or more full of charm." Everything was arranged in the most civilized manner, yet the atmosphere was informal, even unsophisticated. Updike was astonished to what absurdities and childish games the cultivated visitors, under Edith's prompting, allowed themselves to descend. Updike was interested, too, in Edith's relations with her Lenox neighbors. He could be bored by her interminable conversations with others about gardening and the relative merits of various English seedsmen, but he enjoyed her acid comments on some of the local inhabitants—as when, driving back after dinner with a stodgy couple, Edith remarked: "The So-ons tell me they have decided to have books in their library." He understood why Mrs. Wharton was not popular in all quarters.

Edith Wharton was herself, of course, the one who supervised the manifold concerns of life at The Mount, and she reveled in every detail of it. When one visitor, Marion (Mrs. Gordon) Bell, gave a cry of pleasure at discovering an exquisitely carved desk in her bedroom and "everything conceivable needed for writing," Edith replied with a deprecating smile: "Oh, I am rather a housekeeper-ish person." But she had a great deal of well-organized help. Teddy Wharton, too, had an eye for detail, and perhaps an even greater zeal for perfection than his wife. He seemed his old self again in the summer of 1905, and he amiably drove into town for groceries or escorted a guest in his Mineola cart on a tour of the region while Edith guided another through the woodlands on horseback. It was Teddy who was in charge of the wines. Edith attributed her dislike of wines to her brothers' premature attempt to develop her interest in them; but though she took the occasional glass of Cointreau or Dubonnet and liked champagne (of which she always had a bottle ready for guests arriving after a long railroad journey), she had in fact little discernment in this matter. Teddy's taste was superb, and the finest wines were served at the table.

Gross, more like a bulging rubber ball than ever, and Arthur White divided the general running of the household. Beneath them, and apart from Edith's personal maid, were housemaids, footmen, a cook, and one or two kitchen boys. A man named Reynolds commanded the little squad of gardeners. The basic staff at The Mount had been completed the previous summer when the Whartons took on a resident chauffeur, Charles Cook. Cook, from the adjoining town of Lee, was a lean, laconic young man in his twenties, quintessentially New England in speech and manner, and a most competent driver and mechanic.

Cook was at the wheel, occasionally spelled by Teddy, when a motor trip interrupted the ongoing rush of life at The Mount. In July, Bay Lodge accompanied Edith and Teddy on a drive as far as South Berwick, Maine, the home of Sarah Orne Jewett. A month later the Whartons and Maynards set out in two cars for a run along the Connecticut River and lunch in Cornish, New Hampshire, with Maxfield Parrish, who had supplied the romantic, richly tinted illustrations for *Italian Villas*. Afterward Parrish took Edith to meet Winston Churchill, the American writer whose very popular novel *The Crossing* had appeared the previous year. The Whartons' car thereupon broke down, as it regularly did, and Edith drove back unprotected from the pouring rain in the Maynards' automobile, Teddy having gone on to Boston.

One other indispensable member of Edith's household was Anna Bahlmann, the quiet German-born spinster who had tutored the Rutherford children, and for a period in her adolescence Edith herself, in German literature. She had been employed for a time by Minnie Jones, and seems to have been taken on by Edith in 1904. Anna now served as Edith's secretary and literary assistant, and as a liaison between Mrs. Wharton and her publishers; to the latter end, she spent much of the year at 882 Park Avenue. She was anything but a beauty, and Edith felt that she lived a rather starved life; but she was extremely valuable, the more so as *The House of Mirth* moved toward publication.

7

The House of Mirth was published on October 14, 1905, in a first edition of forty thousand copies. When, late in the previous March, Edith noted in her diary that the novel was done, she commented that she had begun work on it "about Sept. 1903." This was accurate in the sense that only then did she finally determine the theme of her story: a theme, in her telling of it, that emerged as much from literary and dramatic meditation as from private reminiscing. As early as 1900, in fact, she had been mulling over the subject—fashionable society in New York and perhaps in Newport—and had hit upon several of her characters' names. But though New York society was something she knew intimately, she also knew it to be a futile and insubstantial affair. The problem, as she recalled telling herself, "was how to extract from such a subject the typical human significance which is the story-teller's reason for telling one story rather than another. . . . The answer was that a frivolous society can acquire dramatic significance only through what its frivolity destroys."

The answer, she declared in summary, was to be the sensitive and vital heroine Lily Bart: and the story would be Lily's slow destruction by a grossly indifferent society. Lily Bart, though distantly perceived and named in 1900, was not truly born until the end of the summer of 1903.

Work on the novel was delayed nearly a year by Teddy's collapses and the enforced departure for Europe and by other literary obligations. It was Edward Burlingame, apparently, who drew Edith back to it in August 1904, by begging her to have the novel ready to begin serialization in *Scribner's* the following January, since another story due to start then had fallen through. Edith worked harder and more steadily than she ever had in her life. It was this experience, she would contend, that finally taught her "the discipline of the daily task" and transformed her once and for all "from a drifting amateur into a professional" —though an outsider might suppose that the author of nine books in eight years had long since acquired that discipline and become a professional. After a period of "black despair," the novel began to go with a rush; by early October, Edith could tell Brownell that she was "fatuously pleased" with it. She managed to have enough of the narrative in shape by the time requested, and *The House of Mirth* ran through eleven issues from January to November 1905.

As the time for book publication approached, Mrs. Wharton flooded Brownell with her customary queries and suggestions, but they were all made with a kind of lordly good humor. Only when she saw the wrapper on the first copies did she rebel. It declared that "for the first time the veil has been lifted from New York society" and further words to that garish effect. "I thought that, in the House of Scribner, the House of Mirth was safe from all such Harperesque methods of *réclame,*" she wrote spiritedly. "[Please] do all you can to stop the spread of that pestilent paragraph, and to efface it from the paper cover of future printings. I am sick at the recollection of it!" The paragraph was removed at once.

Ten days after publication Brownell notified Edith Wharton gravely that "so far we have not sold many over 30,000, but perhaps that will satisfy your expectations for the first fortnight." He warned her, more seriously, that the sales would probably slacken off, especially since the story had little love interest, though others at Scribners were talking about "high figures." The figures did indeed continue to climb. Edith observed in her diary that 20,000 more copies were being printed by October 30, and 20,000 more on November 11; by this time Brownell had assured her that the novel was having "the most rapid sale of any book ever published by Scribner." One hundred thousand copies were in print as of November 20, and 140,000 by the end of the year. Over the first two months of 1906, Edith could several times record that *The House of Mirth* was still the best-selling novel across the country, as it continued to rival or surpass such other current successes as *The Garden of Allah*, *The Clansman* and Upton Sinclair's *The Jungle.*

For the serial rights, she had been paid an outright fee of $5,000. The contract for the book itself (studied and witnessed by Walter Berry) granted her a royalty of fifteen percent of the list price of $1.50, and by the end of 1905 she had been paid $7,500 against accrued royalties of more than $30,000. Altogether, in the course of that year, Edith Wharton's literary earnings amounted to more than $20,000 (including $2,200 for several short stories, a $1,500 advance on a novella, $1,800 from *Italian Villas*, and another advance of £250 from Macmillan, the English publisher of *The House of Mirth*). It is next to impossible to translate the meaning of income from one period to another with any accuracy; but given the absence of income tax in the United States of 1905 and the rate of inflation in our own time, one should probably multiply the figure of $20,000 by eight or nine to get some sense of its dollar value today. Edith Wharton's annual expenses, it may be added, were almost always identical with her income.

Edith received a deluge of letters, many from total strangers. One woman said that when she read the final installment, she was so overcome that she telegraphed a friend "Lily Bart is dead." Another reader enclosed a two-cent stamp and begged Mrs. Wharton to write and say whether it might not have been possible to allow Lily Bart to live and marry Lawrence Selden. Still another woman, Edith Wharton told Burlingame, wrote: " 'I love, not every word in the book, but every period and comma.' I hope she meant to insert an 'only' after the 'not' . . . Well, it's all great fun, and you did it all by accepting 'The Last Giustiniani.' Do you remember?"

She was especially gratified, as before, by letters from fellow practitioners of fiction. Charles Eliot Norton huffed a little and laid it down that no woman not spotlessly virtuous (which ruled out Lily Bart) could be the heroine of a truly serious novel. But from Queen's Acre, Howard Sturgis wrote pages of exclamatory and discriminating praise:

How good! How good! It is to *my* mind the best thing you have done, so sustained, so closely woven, so inevitable, so living! I am lost in admiration. . . . Except, perhaps, for our beloved Henry, I think you are head and shoulders above any other writer of fiction of the present day in English (poor dear George Meredith no longer counts as "of the present day"). You will be overwhelmed with congratulations, of course, but I am not going to make any pretty minauderies [coquettish airs] about your not caring for my humble opinion. On this one subject (and possibly embroidery) I know what I'm talking about.

Hamlin Garland, the author of *Main-Travelled Roads*, wrote appreciatively, as did R. W. Gilder of the *Century*. From his retreat in New Jersey, Owen Wister sent congratulations and called the book *"un ouvrage parfaitement distingué,"* adding: "You have set the world discussing. Whenever I emerge from my isolation they're hard at it agreeing and disagreeing."

The eighty-two-year-old Thomas Wentworth Higginson, whose literary acquaintanceship went back to his baffled espousal of Emily Dickinson decades before, said that *The House of Mirth* seemed to him "to stand at the head of all American fiction, save Hawthorne alone." S. Weir Mitchell ceremoniously took his hat off "to the writer of *The House of Mirth*, cruelly descriptive name." From Knightsbridge in London, the novelist Mary Cholmondely found herself "quite unable to put into words" her delight and admiration: "I would give anything to see as deep into life as you do, to know what you know about it, to write as you write about it."

Literate New Yorkers recognized at once that *The House of Mirth* was the first American novel to give an accurate, if also devastating, portrait of their society (Howells and Stephen Crane having attacked society at lower levels). Winthrop Chanler sat up late on an October evening in his upstate New York home, sipping coffee and brandy and reading the novel. He paused to write his wife: "It is a very remarkable book. New York Society as it really is, as one really knows it, has never been written about before. The satire is so right, so deep, and so true to life. One knows all the people without being able to name one of them. Save I think Walter Berry is the hero." Chanler, who had thought that the women in Edith Wharton's earlier stories had sinned rather with their minds than their bodies, was enchanted with Lily Bart. Daisy Chanler surely passed on at least the gist of this, omitting "Winty's" later verdict that the second part of the novel drooped at times.

A long letter from Henry James was more ambiguous. He had spoken to Edith's sister-in-law, in a curiously low-keyed way, about "Mrs. Wharton's pleasantly palpable hit. I much admire the book myself," he said, "though I find it two books and too confused." To Edith herself he described *The House of Mirth* as "altogether a superior thing," instantly modifying that remark by saying that "it is better written than composed," and that Lawrence Selden, the chief male figure, "is too *absent.*" But the old master put his finger unerringly on the novel's major achievement. He was, he said, thinking of writing a lecture about "the deadly difficulties" of the novel of manners in America: "When I do that I shall work in a tribute to the great success and the large portrayal of your Lily B. She is very big and true—and very difficult to have *kept* big and true."

There is no evidence that Edith Wharton was put out by James's strictures. She respected him too much; and she had, besides, reached the point where praise as such held relatively little interest for her. Sara Norton was not alone in feeling that what most impressed her about Edith Wharton was "her fine indifference to praise, her conscious sense that her performance, judged by the standards *she* held, was but a slight affair." It might indeed be said that the only illusion she had about her work was the illusion that it was not as good as it actually was.

Her high standards, professional dedication, and general lack of vanity were reflected in a letter to Brownell, after Brownell had read the novel for the first time, in proof. "There can't be two opinions," Brownell insisted. "The way in which the study of *moeurs* melts into a novel of character—ah, well, it's the whole shooting-match. It must seem nice and easy to have done an incontestably big thing." How could she possibly develop any further as an artist? "Would it not have been cannier to postpone perfection till you could use it as the cap-sheaf of your oeuvre?" And he had special praise for the way in which the beautiful texture of the novel's substance could be seen "interpenetrating the sapient grand construction."

It was the latter phrase that did most for Edith's morale.

I was pleased with bits myself; but as I go over the proofs the whole thing strikes me as so loosely built, with so many dangling threads, and cul-de-sacs, and long dusty stretches, that I had reached the point of wondering how I had ever dared to try my hand at a long thing. So your seeing a certain amount of architecture in it rejoices me above everything. —My theory of what the novel ought to be is so exorbitant that I am always reminded of Daudet's *"Je rêve d'un aigle, j'accouche d'un colobri"* ["I dream of an eagle, I give birth to a hummingbird"].

For all its huge commercial success, *The House of Mirth* did not earn uniform approval in the press. Edith was attacked for having provided a warning about modern American society rather than a hope; for not having shown a means of escape for society's victims; for having chosen a subject which was "utterly unsuitable for conversion into literature, which demands ideals and humor"; for not having introduced finer specimens of humanity, and for not exposing enough good in the characters she did present. Such was a large portion of the atmosphere in the American literary marketplace circa 1905.

Even so, the unfavorable commentary had the air of being made knowingly in a lost cause. What permeates the reviews of *The House of Mirth* is the sense, as of a settled fact, that Edith Wharton was one of the two or three most serious and accomplished writers of fiction on the American scene and that the new novel was undeniably her most important work to date. The hostile sought to pick flaws in what was taken for granted to be a novel of distinction. Amid the favorable, the issue was whether *The House of Mirth* could be adjudged a masterpiece or whether it fell just short of that final accolade. It may be added that enlightened critical opinion remains today at that same stage of uncertainty.

The House of Mirth, as its very title suggests, was Edith Wharton's first full-scale survey of the *comédie humaine*, American style. It is set in a time contemporary with its composition, and it covers the last seventeen months in the life of Lily Bart, a beautiful and fashionable but also penniless and imprudent young woman in her late twenties. The action moves between various segments of New York society and an American gathering on the French Riviera, and it is spurred by Lily's extraordinary capacity to get herself, at least half innocently, into situations of a doubtful, even of a scandalous, nature. In Edith Wharton's brilliant characterization of her heroine, Lily Bart possesses a stronger moral *consciousness* than most of her associates, but a wholly insufficient moral *constancy*. With her several special and immensely attractive qualities, she is all too much a product of the environment indicated by the title—a phrase taken from

Ecclesiastes: "The heart of fools is in the house of mirth."

The nature and status of women in that society are suggested by the other two titles Edith Wharton originally contemplated. The first was "A Moment's Ornament": women were regarded as ornamental, beautiful objects to be collected and displayed; they were expected to strike elegant attitudes and poses; and their career was a fleeting one. But women were also required to appear flower-like, gentle, fragile, innocent, lovely; the second title was "The Year of the Rose." Lily Bart was an exceptional flower, but only to a degree. At the end, refusing a gambit which would have restored her social and financial fortunes, she takes an overdose of a sleeping potion and dies.

"Lily" was the name given Edith Jones by the Rutherford children in the Newport days, and Lily Bart undoubtedly incorporates some of Edith Wharton's features. She is endearing, proud, sensitive, and exasperating by turns. Through Lily Bart, moreover, Edith Wharton conveyed her sense of herself as essentially unfitted for the only American society she knew, and as gravely misunderstood by that society. By the same token, if she pointed to no means of escape for Lily, it was because she was aware of none—or any viable alternative life to the one she depicted.

Lawrence Selden, the attractive and seemingly astute lawyer who is drawn to Lily in the opening phases of the narrative, is the one human being who might have supplied such an alternative. He has a vision, about which he is given to holding forth, of what he calls "the republic of the spirit," where the keynote is freedom and where only two or three are encouraged to gather together. But although this betimes was also one of Edith Wharton's ideal images, Selden himself, as she told Sara Norton, was "a negative hero," a sterile and subtly fraudulent figure whose ideas were not much to be trusted.

Selden was also an emblem of masculinity in Edith's world. Fond as she was of her Walter Berrys, her Egerton Winthrops, her Eliot Gregorys—and Selden has a little of each—she knew they had insufficient blood in their veins and could provide little of what an intelligent and ardent woman might crave.

There were, of course, enormous differences in the outward and material circumstances of Edith Wharton and Lily Bart; a reviewer might well be skeptical about the mistress of The Mount coming truly to grips with the downward spiral of Lily's life. Yet behind the trappings of Lenox and Park Avenue was a soul that was familiar with pain, with the feeling of entrapment, with psychological and physical deprivation. The crucial difference between the author and her heroine was Edith Wharton's unshakable belief in the possibilities of life. In the spring after the publication of *The House of Mirth*, Edith wrote Sally Norton about a mutual friend who was gravely, perhaps critically, ill, but whose zest was undiminished.

And how I understand that love of living, of being in this wonderful, astounding world even if one can look at it only through the prison bars of illness and suffering! *Plus je vois,* the more I am thrilled by the spectacle.

Nothing that Edith Wharton said in these years more aptly formulated her consciousness of her relation to the world she lived in.

Paris and M.F.: 1906-1909

PART THREE

10. The Faubourg

On Thanksgiving Day 1905, amid icy weather at Lenox, the Whartons (in Edith's diary note) gave thanks for the best period of their lives. *The House of Mirth* was selling at a tremendous rate. Edith had started work on a new novel tentatively called "Justine Brent," bearing in mind no doubt Charles Scribner's jocular request that "in your next book you must give us a strong man, for I am getting tired of the comments on Selden." Bay Lodge and Walter Berry had come and gone; Lodge stayed long enough to enjoy a visit to The Mount by his closest friend, Langdon Mitchell—the son of Dr. S. Weir Mitchell, and one of the few American playwrights with an authentic sense of the theater (his best and still amusing play, *The New York Idea*, would be staged a few months later). At the same time a clue to Edith Wharton's more hidden urgings was provided by an intent reading, on a December afternoon, of Plato's two great dialogues about erotic and transcendent love, the *Phaedrus* and the *Symposium*. She found them overpowering, and transcribed a long passage from each in her commonplace book, that from the *Symposium* declaring that "love will make men desire to die for their beloved . . . a woman as well as men."

There was a blizzard in early December, and on the eighteenth Edith recorded that she and Teddy had "left our dear Mount with deepest reluctance for the winter." They were briefly in Washington, then down to Biltmore for Christmas with George and Edith Vanderbilt. Henry James, who had preceded them there earlier in the year, had told Edith that the gargantuan construction was a huge and deplorable waste, but Edith herself was entertained by the seasonal ceremonies—which included the distribution of presents to 350 guests in the vast banquet hall—and found much to interest her in the expansive shrubberies and nurseries which she explored on the days after Christmas. She came back to Washington alone—Teddy stayed behind for some shooting—and passed the year's end with Bay Lodge and his wife of several years, the former Elizabeth Frelinghuysen Davis; a beautiful and, in Edith's view, thoroughly engaging young woman, who counted a United States Senator and other valued public servants among her forebears. "Goodbye to the good year 1905," Edith wrote in her diary on New Year's Eve, and greeted 1906 with the satisfied observation that her novel was still the best-selling book in New York.

A concern for small animals preoccupied Edith during much of the winter of 1906. January was not a week old before it became necessary to chloroform her little Pekinese, Miza. Miza had been with the Whartons for thirteen years, since the first days at Land's End, and her extinction was no minor event. When Edith drew up a list of her "ruling passions" in life, many years later, dogs were high on it:

Justice and Order
Dogs
Books
Flowers
Architecture
Travel
A good joke—and perhaps that should have come first!

Pride of place was given to the suggestive combination of justice and order (not, it should be stressed, "law and order"), and Edith's irrepressible love of laughter received its due. But it was a fact that dogs—small dogs and preferably Pekinese —were among the main joys of her being, and had been since she was a child. She also nourished an affection for horses. But her general attitude to animals, as it developed over the years, was both imaginative and equivocal. She once defined a cat as "a snake in furs." And in a remarkable and poetic diary entry in 1924, she confessed:

> I am secretly afraid of animals—of all animals except dogs, and even of some dogs. I think it is because of the *us*ness in their eyes, with the underlying *not-us*ness which belies it, and is so tragic a reminder of the lost age when we human beings branched off and left them: left them to eternal inarticulateness and slavery. Why? their eyes seem to ask us.

As to Teddy, he loved all the cows, sheep, ducks, and hens at The Mount so much that he could not stand to slaughter any of them. Edith was left, meanwhile, with Miza's male companion, Mitou—a gallicization, one fancies, of "Me, too!" the cry that Edith, straining to hear dogs articulate to her, could detect in the Pekinese's frantic barking whenever Miza was served her meal first.

The status of animals even entered her intellectual musings. Her attention was drawn to a passage in Paul Sabatier's *Life of St. Francis of Assisi* in which the author argued that the saint's "sympathy for animals had none of the senti- mentality so loudly displayed by certain contemporaries." Here, she felt sure, was the familiar Roman Catholic fear of the heresy that attributed souls to animals; on the basis of it, the Pope was refusing his support of the Society for the Prevention of Cruelty to Animals in Italy. That Mitou had a soul, Edith obviously did not doubt for a moment.

2

A late-winter bout of influenza and bronchitis delayed the sailing for France, and her miseries did not increase Edith's fondness for New York. She found herself longing equally, and characteristically, for the Berkshires and for Europe. "I am wretched at being in town," she told Sara Norton. "Oh, to live in the country all the year around." But there was the even stronger appeal of France and England, and the "mental refreshment that I can get only *là-bas*"; she lamented "the curse of having been brought up there, and having it ineradicably in one's blood." Still, from her sickbed, she reaffirmed her disinclination to expatriate. "One would feel, I am sure, if one lived in another country, the alien's inability to take part, help on, assert one's self for good. . . . But," she concluded, "I speak through wool, darkly," fevered and congested by flu.

She and Teddy sailed on the *Philadelphia* on March 17. There had been a heavy snow two days before, and Edith grumbled a little when it took an entire hour to drive through the snow-laden streets from East Seventy-eighth Street to the dock in Walter Maynard's car.

It was snowing lightly in Paris, too, when the Whartons arrived there on the afternoon of the twenty-fifth after debarking in Cherbourg before dawn that morning. They took a suite of rooms on the second floor of the Hotel Domenici, on Rue Castiglione near the Place Vendôme. Edith discovered at once that, as the author of *The House of Mirth*, she had suddenly become the object of considerable interest in certain quarters of French society, particularly in the Faubourg St. Germain. Paul Bourget judged it now propitious to introduce his accomplished American friend into the intellectual and social circles where he wielded such influence. He had read Mme. Wharton's novel with the closest attention, and held it to be admirable. More, he put his Academician's stamp of approval upon Edith Wharton herself as that excellent combination, a *femme du monde* who took her creative work with the utmost seriousness.

Bourget began to bring his highborn and gifted friends to tea at the Hotel Domenici, and Edith Wharton had her first glimpses of the milieu she had long heard about, where the artistic and intellectual mingled easily with the socially distinguished. Among the earliest of her new French acquaintances was Comtesse Charlotte de Cossé-Brissac, a beguilingly ugly woman from one of the oldest families in France; cultivated and cosmopolitan, multilingual, and with a penchant for gossip and earthy jokes. To know the comtesse was to know her intimate friend the renowned Byzantine historian Gustave Schlumberger ("Schlum"), a vastly read and entertaining man with a violent temper. One invariably encountered them together, seated on opposite sides of the fireplace in Comtesse de Cossé-Brissac's apartment in Rue Vernet, she teasing him as though he were a large and clumsy dog; he perhaps growling with fury when the comtesse outraged his Protestant nature by speaking disrespectfully of the Bible.

For Edith Wharton, the most arresting person she met at this time was Comtesse Anna de Noailles, whom Bourget brought to tea on a Sunday in early April. She was the daughter of a Rumanian prince and a Greek woman, and the not very attentive wife of Comte Mathieu de Noailles, a silent blond gentleman of ancient lineage. Just thirty in 1906, she was beautiful, diminutive and intense, with dark hair cut low on her forehead, deep melancholy eyes, and sensuous lips. She was a rapid and indefatigable talker. When Edith Wharton first met her, Comtesse de Noailles had published two volumes of poetry, one honored by the Académie Française, and three short novels, each exploring the psychology of women in love. Marcel Proust was among those she received regularly at 40 Rue Scheffer, just off the Place du Trocadéro, greeting them from a chaise longue or stirring about restlessly on her blue-and-white bed.

In Edith Wharton's view, she was "quite exceptionally interesting," picturesque and fanciful, brilliant in conversation, and "like a little exotic bird." Something in Edith responded at once to the young woman's passion for life and for letters, to the rush and gaiety of her talk, and to what Edith intuited as an undercurrent of sadness and dissatisfaction. She was, as well, "indescribably" attracted to Anna de Noailles' poetry, fusing, as it did, romantic evocations of natural landscapes with expressions of erotic desire and the subtle disclosure of the wounded heart.

A very different new acquaintance was Charles du Bos, an able young man, a friend of André Gide's and a follower of Paul Bourget's, but a person hampered by indecisiveness and periods of sometimes imaginary ill health. The Bourgets introduced du Bos to Mrs. Wharton at the theater one night. It was a calculated moment. Minnie Bourget had spoken to du Bos about Edith Wharton, their travels together, and her book *The House of Mirth*—her "first great modern novel," in Mme. Bourget's phrase; she urged du Bos to read it, and he devoured it at once. There had, meanwhile, been several applicants for the French translation (there were also nearly twenty requests for the German rights, and the novel was about to appear serially in Sweden, a country curiously hospitable to Edith Wharton's work). Edith had decided to leave the choice of translation up to Bourget, and he chose du Bos for the job. Du Bos was English on his mother's side and was bilingual, though he spoke and read English aloud with a marked accent.

It was to be a test case. But Bourget, a firm believer in the gospel of work for literary people, was concerned about his young friend's tendency to procrastinate. But Edith Wharton, who was fascinated by questions of translation, threw herself into the task of advising du Bos, and the novel, under the title of *La Demeure de liesse*, eventually began to run in the *Revue de Paris*. The experience convinced du Bos that criticism rather than translation was his métier, but he would feel that it was Bourget and Edith Wharton, between them, who started him on his career.

The rhythm of their relationship was typical of what regularly befell Edith Wharton. At their first meeting Edith found du Bos "a clever and agreeable young man," but du Bos himself was made decidedly uneasy by what seemed to him Mrs. Wharton's excessive self-assurance and by the bewildering range of her talk. Only in the course of time did he realize that it was by no means self-assurance but rather an intense and concealed shyness that was her chief characteristic. Shyness, he wrote, was and remained her "inveterate trait, and . . . constituted the key to all her social demeanor outside the circle of close friendship." Nor could he at the start comprehend the special phenomenon represented by Edith Wharton: that "personal shyness may co-exist with the swift and unfailing sureness of step that I so admired in *The House of Mirth.*" As these things came home to him, Charles du Bos grew not only to admire but to love Edith Wharton.

As to the quality of her conversation, du Bos discovered that "Edith always considered the interlocutor her equal: it was the finest characteristic of her wholly civilized politeness, but on that very account she postulated in me a range of culture which I did not possess, and I often missed the point of her rich play of allusions." Here we observe another facet of Edith Wharton's "American-ness": for in talking with a European, the truly cultivated American (partly because of the relative sparseness of his native culture) tends to wander over the literature and thought of many countries, while the other is likely to be more confined within the boundaries of his own rich national traditions.

Nevertheless [du Bos continued], for the literary apprentice, to drop in at tea time at the Hotel Domenici, to listen to a talk even but half apprehended, to think of Lily Bart with whom I was a little in love, all that had the flavor of a *romanesque* adventure.

3

In the same memoir, du Bos recalled that "Bourget always called Edith *Le Velasquez*, and the name suited her high restraint, that quality of the subdued everywhere present and around her." Such was the image Edith Wharton presented to French society as she began to move into it. The air of restraint was far more notable in Paris than amid the sometimes exuberant playfulness at The Mount; but even so, Edith at this time appeared to all but her intimates as a woman of unusual self-control.

Physically, she held her sturdy body straight, whether standing or sitting, as though in willed repose. There was a strong set to her jaw and mouth, which made her sudden smile the more winning; her eyes were wide and alert—the apprehensiveness and strain that had characterized her expression from early childhood onward were no longer visible. She dressed with extreme and becoming elegance, in the attractive flowing style of the day. Dining out of an evening, she would wear a gown cut daringly low above a pinched-in waist, with tufts of lace covering the lower expanse of white bosom. A choker of pearls encircled her throat, and a bracelet her left wrist. The general impression was one of fashionable and handsome stiffness.

Personally, too, she seemed to hold herself firmly in check. The discipline she had achieved as a professional novelist had, over the years, been extended to her personality in anything approaching its public appearance. She could speak of her astonished delight in the human scene, but she believed her own inner nature to be now immune to emotional disturbance of any sort, either in the way of suffering or excitement. She struck the less intuitive among her French friends as simply repressed.

Something of Edith Wharton's sense of herself in 1906 went into her portrait of the American-born Marquise de Malrive in *Madame de Treymes*, a novella which ran in the August *Scribner's* and was brought out in book form the following February. It was the first fruit of her dip into Parisian society, and that contradictory world is appraised with a discerning eye: an eye sharpened, it seems, by a re-reading of Henry James's novel of 1877, *The American*. Edith Wharton's personal feelings are evident in the contrast registered by the chief male character between the "unenlightened ugliness [of] his own lamentable New York" and the graceful contours of the Faubourg, "shining in the splintered radiance of the sunset beyond the long sweep of the quays." But it is the figure of the youthful marquise who captures one's attention.

As Fanny Frisbie in her New York days, she had been lively, dashing, and free-spirited. Now, married to a dissolute French nobleman and hemmed in by the invincible forces of the Faubourg aristocracy, she has become a very different person. She has in some ways been enriched by the association, but she has also been subdued by influences which had "lowered her voice, regulated her gestures, toned her down to harmony with the warm dim background of a long social past." If there is a gain in refinement, there is a loss of resilience and spontaneity.

Fanny de Malrive enacts another, Paris-based version of Edith Wharton's dominant theme. She has escaped New York only to be imprisoned within a disastrous marriage—an entrapment more complete than anything Edith had contrived for the women in her American tales. The twists and turns of the plot (in which Fanny's desperate and passionate sister-in-law, Mme. de Treymes, plays a key role) conclude with a demonstration that freedom is to be achieved only at fatal cost. With this, the latest in a long series of stories upon the same or a closely related theme, Edith Wharton seems to have been suggesting that the psychic imprisonment of women could occur anywhere and even under the most gracious of conditions.

4

In mid-April, Edith accepted an invitation from her brother Harry to move over to his *hôtel* (town house), fronting a tiny square which he had recently acquired at 3 Place des Etats-Unis. She was beginning to feel that Paris, and specifically the Faubourg St. Germain, might be where she belonged: all her early aversion to the city melted away as she came to appreciate the coherence of life there, the almost effortless intermixture of the artistic and the fashionable, the steady nourishment of "the warm dim background of a long social past." Nowhere in England, the only other possible European choice, was there so unmistakably a *center* for the exercise of her various faculties. The presence of her brother was another attraction, and she started to look about in the ancient quarter for a home of her own in which to pass half the year.

Teddy, meanwhile, was off to London with the mission of buying a second-hand automobile, and at the end of April, after a final gathering with Mme. de Cossé-Brissac and others, she left to join him. An immediate breakdown of the twenty-four horsepower Panhard prevented Teddy from coming down to meet the channel steamer, but Henry James showed up as arranged. *"Bien sur que* I'll meet you at Dover on the 25th, or anywhere in the world—this world," he had promised, addressing her tentatively as "Dear Edith Wharton." They dined together and had a look at Canterbury before Edith went on to London. The next morning Edith and Teddy set forth on their first motor tour of England.

They drove south to Portsmouth, crossed to the Isle of Wight for an evening, then headed north through Salisbury to Bath, pausing periodically to inspect cathedrals and closes, colleges and bishops' palaces—Edith's enthusiasm for the like being shared in only the faintest degree by her husband. James joined them at Bath, and they moved on through pouring rain with the intention (Words-worth's lines echoing in their heads) of getting as far as Tintern Abbey. They were held up, however, at Malvern by the rain and by James's insistent attempts to give directions. He knew Malvern very well, he assured them, and since its geography was difficult he proposed changing places with "Edward" and sitting next to Cook, the chauffeur. The party circled the city in rain-swept darkness while James strove to remember which street led to their hotel. In Edith Wharton's later account:

At each corner (literally) he stopped the motor, and we heard a muttering, first confident, then anguished. "This—this, my dear Cook, yes . . . this certainly is the right corner. But no; stay! A moment longer, please—in this light it's so difficult . . . appearances are so misleading . . . It may be . . . yes! I think it *is* the next turn . . . a little further lend thy guiding hand . . . that is, drive on; but drive slowly, please, my dear Cook; *very* slowly."

Cook finally turned down a street at random, and soon brought the hungry and exhausted group to their lodging.

It was still raining hard when they awoke, and James departed in discouragement for London. The weather promptly cleared, and the Whartons made the long swing eastward through Stratford-on-Avon to Cambridge, where Gaillard Lapsley was ready to greet them and escort them by moonlight through the vast beautiful courtyards of King's College and his own Trinity. Cambridge rather than Oxford was Edith's favorite English university town, and had been since Harry Jones had made a show of studying law there forty years before; similarly, the Englishmen she was coming to know and who introduced her one to another tended to be Cantabrigians (like the anglicized Lapsley and Howard Sturgis) rather than Oxonians.

"I left the rich, rushing, ravishing Whartons under stress of most ill weather (at Malvern)," James wrote Lapsley, "whereupon, their luck quite changing, they went and threw themselves into your arms." But to Mary Cadwalader Jones a few weeks later, and in a manner that was becoming habitual with him, James offered a far more questioning view of the Whartons:

> They had, the W's, I thought, a rather frustrating, fragmentary merely-motory trip to have crossed the dreadful sea for—though it was what seemed to suit them best. . . . Poor Célimare [the name James fancifully used for himself in writing Mrs. Jones], always moralising on everything, only rather thanked goodness, as he observed, that such fantastic wealth and freedom were not *his* portion—such incoherence, such a nightmare of perpetually renewable choice and decision, such a luxury of bloated alternatives, do they seem to burden life withal. However, I had some very charming and enjoyable, even if half wealth-blighted hours with our friends.

It was a brilliantly worded analysis, shrewd enough up to a point, but ultimately off target. For James, also a passionate observer of the human comedy, the Whartons' way of life, as they sped from hotel to hotel, could only have seemed a chaos of meaningless alternatives—a "fantastic freedom" based on great wealth and entirely bereft of such significant pressure as might force them to make one choice rather than another. What he failed to understand at this time—he would never understand it fully—was that for Edith Wharton the "perpetually renewable choices" were *not* the ingredients of a genuine freedom. Where her French friends missed the deeper pulsations of her nature behind her outward self-control, James saw nothing but a frantic and uncharted dash at experience.

The options between which Edith Wharton was oscillating—Lenox, Paris, England; the next city on the itinerary; the newest social milieu—were in fact beckoning symbols of self-completion, each upon inspection seeming to be lacking in some crucial element. They were the hypothetical settings of the liberated life. The constant movement, the dizzying changes of direction, were signs of a sometimes desperate search for the great good place, something she had in fact already found in the old Faubourg, without yet fully knowing it.

To be sure, Edith Wharton, on a simpler level, was relishing the opportunity her money and the Panhard gave her to see fresh scenes and revisit familiar ones, make new acquaintances and catch up with old friends. It was a way of casting her net at once more broadly and more tightly about the human and physical world she inhabited. At lunch in Cambridge, Lapsley introduced her to the adroit political philosopher G. Lowes Dickinson. After a night in London, the Whartons drove out to Windsor for a meal with Howard Sturgis at Queen's Acre, returning there three days later, with Henry James, for the night.

It was on the latter occasion, apparently, that James put on one of his most memorable performances as a direction finder. Cook was on vacation, and in Windsor the temporary chauffeur, Dobson, was unable to find the King's Road, on which "Qu'Acre" was situated. James beckoned to "an ancient doddering man" who was staring at them in the rain and darkness, and in the most ornate Jamesian style, full of interpolations and asides, sought to ask his advice. The old man merely looked dazed, and James continued his labyrinthine interrogation until Edith, unable to stand it, said, "Oh, please, do ask him where the King's Road is."

"Ah—? The King's Road? Just so! Quite right! Can you, as a matter of fact, my good man, tell us where, in relation to our present position, the King's Road exactly *is?*"

"Ye're in it," said the aged face at the window.

Queen's Acre was not a particularly handsome house, outside or in. Wooden balconies and deep eaves marked its exterior, and the rooms within were crowded with chintz and cushions, tables covered with books, and walls smothered by watercolors—striking one young visitor as "a period piece from an age not yet quite old enough to charm." But the atmosphere was immensely charming, and the mode of life a delight: "a place," said the same source, "where breakfast in bed was the rule and not the indulgent exception, a house where there were books in the lavatories." All this was the creation of the host. James had complained to Edith Wharton earlier of Sturgis' "neurosis" and his "strange drop into dullness." But neither on this occasion nor any other did Edith find Sturgis guilty of dullness.

On her arrival at Queen's Acre with James, Edith encountered a long-limbed, quiet, observant young man named Percy Lubbock. In his late twenties, with a malleable personality and a self-effacing interest in others, Lubbock was a product of Cambridge University, where he had become friendly with Gaillard Lapsley and via Lapsley with Howard Sturgis. He was also one of the most fervent among those literary apprentices who regarded Henry James as the Master. His own first book, only recently published, was a fictionalized biography of Elizabeth Barrett

Browning. Biography, memoirs, and tasteful editing were to be his special province, along with a singularly felicitous prose style.

With James and Sturgis beside her to join in extravagances of gossip and literary give-and-take, Edith Wharton scarcely noticed Percy Lubbock at this initial meeting; he was, to adopt the phrase of Robert Burns, a child among them taking notes. But he was soon to become a cherished member of her slowly assembling "inner circle"—of which Queen's Acre in May 1906 provided the earliest partial gathering.

Back in London, there were continual visitors to the Whartons' hotel rooms at 34 Brooke Street. The sixty-eight-year-old Sir George Otto Trevelyan, the author of *The Early History of Charles James Fox*, sometime member of Parliament, and good friend of Henry James's, dropped by with Lady Trevelyan to issue an invitation to their home near Stratford-on-Avon at Whitsuntide. Owen Wister came to lunch with Henry James. The aging poet laureate of England, Alfred Austin, appeared on the scene; Edith had spent an evening with him a few years before in Fiesole. Although he had published almost twenty volumes of verse, Austin was the least distinguished laureate in English history; he had been an odd choice by Lord Salisbury, Queen Victoria's Prime Minister, to succeed Tennyson. Edith Wharton was under no illusion about the quality of his work: "I can't take Alfred to my heart (I mean as a poet)," she told Sara Norton. But for all his strutting and the comical smallness of his stature (he was no more than five feet tall), there was something appealing in his innocence and love of country, his conversation was not without charm, and he had a keen eye for current events. Edith was easily persuaded to go down to Ashford, not far from James's Lamb House, for a two-day visit in the Austins' home.

5

But France was calling, and Edith was ready to cross the channel again for a more extensive look at what was becoming her adopted country. Dobson was waiting at Boulogne, and Harry Jones arrived, bringing with him Nicette, the replacement for Miza. In mid-May the party started on a two-week exploration of France, the first of several Edith was to make this spring and the one following, and which she described in a series of articles for the *Atlantic Monthly*. They were collected in a volume called *A Motor-Flight Through France*, published in October 1908, perhaps the best of Edith Wharton's always superior and original travel books.

This first swift-moving excursion took the Whartons and Harry Jones south through Amiens and Beauvais, over to Rouen, down the Seine to Fontainebleau. Without pause, the Panhard turned farther south—to Orléans, Tours, Châteauroux, and southeast to Clermont-Ferrand, along a succession of white roads that flung themselves "in great coils and arrow-flight" across the changing landscape;

finally north through Bourges and Orléans back to Paris. It was indeed a "flight," but even James, when the trip was reported to him by Edith, was prepared to believe that the days in France were "more successful"—more meaningful—than those in England.

For Edith Wharton, the high moment of the tour was not the cathedral at Amiens (its façade "surely one of the most splendid spectacles that Gothic art can show") or Beauvais ("the great mad broken dream of Beauvais choir—the cathedral without a nave") or the journey down the Seine (past "bright gardens terraced above its banks . . . moist poplar-fringed islands . . . low green promontories deflecting its silver flow"). These had been scenes overwhelming or exquisite, which Edith conjured up in print with a greater accuracy and a richer appreciation than anyone in her American generation or later. They spoke to her variously and compellingly about one of the things she herself most sought after in both her personal and artistic life—the deep desire "to keep intact as many links as possible between yesterday and tomorrow, to lose, in the ardour of new experiment, the least that may be of the long rich heritage of human experience."

But for all her reverence for that long heritage, Edith Wharton, as a woman and as a writer, was herself by no means without ardor for new experiments. What stirred her most during the fortnight was a visit to Nohant, a little to the east of the town of Châteauroux, and the former home of the adventurous French novelist who took the name George Sand. (James, when he learned of this intended visit, gave vent to a marvelously exaggerated expression of envy, pain, and rage, culminating in: "They're on their way to Nohant, d—n them!") George Sand had been dead for thirty years, but to Edith Wharton—strolling the grounds, examining the stable, chapel, and family graveyard, peering up at the large placid house set back undramatically behind the trees from the country road —the former Baronne Aurore Dudevant came into distorted but powerful existence.

Here again was a woman of immense talent and an irregular private life (like George Eliot and Anna de Noailles) with whom Edith could feel an affinity that was almost a self-revelation. George Sand had made a conventional marriage with a local squire named Casimir Dudevant, and had separated from him only after putting up for a number of years with his bouts of brutish drunkenness and unconcealed affairs with the housemaids. She had already written several vividly erotic novels which conveyed the unhappiness of her condition and her growing hostility to the institution of marriage. Then, in pursuit of her own dream of freedom, she had gone on to several passionate love affairs, most notably with Alfred de Musset and Chopin. For a long period George Sand led what Edith Wharton, unconsciously echoing Henry James's words about herself, called an "incoherent and inconceivable existence." But later in life, in an imaginative return to her old countryside, she wrote a series of what many readers have thought to be the best pastoral novels in French; and Edith was tempted to wonder whether in her old age George Sand might not have "gradually conformed the passionate experiment of her life."

Perhaps, she fancied, it was the very house which, in its sobriety and conformity, had exerted "an unperceived but persistent influence" over the writer's restless nature and brought her at last to acknowledge the strength of the household pieties. It was surprisingly dignified and decent, and showed no outer mark—as Edith, always sensitive to the analogy between houses and persons, had rather expected it to do—"of that dark disordered period . . . when the timid Mme. Dudevant was turning into the great George Sand." But there was a lingering sadness in Edith's meditation, as though somehow she regretted the toning down of George Sand's personality and the gradual conforming of her way of life.

6

The Whartons came back to Lenox in the second week of June and settled into the now familiar summer routine. Edith returned to work at once on the novel which she was still calling "Justine Brent." It was due to begin in *Scribner's* the following January, but she had barely written forty thousand words and had not touched it for three months. "I am really hungering to get at it," she wrote Sally Norton. Over the next month she added fourteen thousand words, while at the same time completing a five-thousand-word article, for Bliss Perry at the *Atlantic*, covering the first phase of her recent French "motor-flight."

There was, again, a stream of houseguests with whom Edith could mingle after the morning's work: Berry, Eliot Gregory, Updike, Billy Richardson—Edith had browbeaten the latter into buying all the available writings of Henry James. Willie Buckler, last seen in the Whartons' carriage on the Italian trip in 1903, paid his first visit to The Mount, as did Edith's cousin Herman Edgar, a New York lawyer.

Florence La Farge was especially welcome. The wife of the architect Grant La Farge, who was the eldest son of the painter John La Farge, Florence was a dynamic bluestocking whom Edith had known for several years. She was said, by those who knew them both, to be the only woman who could outtalk Edith Wharton on both social and literary matters—a fact that did not diminish Edith's enjoyment of her company.

Bay Lodge appeared with his wife, Bessie, two persons particularly appreciative of Edith Wharton's home. "A really beautiful house," Bay told his mother; ". . . the sort of house one longs to live in because of its exquisite harmony throughout and its real luxury and distinction." He took particular delight in the swift verbal exchanges between Edith and Walter Berry, "whose keen little minds crackle and sparkle together unremittingly as of old, reminding one, for sheer continuity of sharp explosive wit, of some endless string of small prompt firecrackers."

It was to hear Bay Lodge read the annual Phi Beta Kappa poem at Harvard that Edith drove over to Cambridge in late June. The poem was an austerely intellectual long blank-verse work called "The Soul's Inheritance," dealing in ponderous vocables with the pursuit of "imperishable Truth." Lodge's recitation, from memory, received an ovation, but both Edith and Sara Norton were disappointed. Sally thought that what Bay lacked as a poet was a more intimate experience of Europe; Edith, however, observed more accurately that it was not "opportunity of any kind that he lacks," but rather any real sense of "visible beauty." "He doesn't see things in images."

Not long after, Edith took Sally to task for some poems of her own. In forwarding them Sally had defended their formlessness on the grounds that what she sought for was simplicity and a natural tone. Drawing upon her own not very satisfactory efforts, Edith gave a short discourse on the subject:

I think you are trying to skip a necessary *"étape"* on the road to Parnassus. Such bareness as "she neither hears nor sees" [from one of Wordsworth's "Lucy poems"] is a result of a great deal of writing, of a long and expert process of elimination, selection, concentration of ideas and expression.

"Personally," she said summarily, "I think a long apprenticeship should be given to form before it is thrown overboard."

As autumn approached, Edith prepared to leave for Buffalo, where, supposedly, the play version of *The House of Mirth* was due to have its trial run. The previous December, Clyde Fitch had called at 884 Park Avenue to propose that he and Edith collaborate on the dramatization. Fitch was at the time the most popular living American playwright, counting among his most recent hits the entertaining farce *Captain Jinks of the Horse Marines* in 1901 and *Her Great Match*, written for Maxine Elliott in 1905. Edith had not been very much impressed with such of Fitch's work as she had seen, but she thought him probably more gifted than any of his rivals, and she admired both his practical grasp of the theater and his "sense of the irony of life." She could not but be flattered by the suggestion from this famous figure, and she was taken by Fitch himself: a "plump showily dressed little man, with his olive complexion, and his beautiful Oriental eyes full of wit and understanding." From the outset, their discussions were sprinkled with personal anecdotes on both sides.

A contract was signed with the producer Charles Frohman in January 1906. Edith was to write the dialogue, and Fitch to have charge of the construction and movement of the play. For Edith, it was uncommonly hard work, sandwiched in, as it had to be, between the novel, the "motor-flight" articles, *Madame de Treymes*, and some short stories, but it aroused in her a fresh interest in the theater. She began to read more widely in dramatic literature: Greek tragedy, the plays of Shakespeare, French comedy, neoclassic tragedy, and more modern examples. In Paris, where Fitch showed up for a couple of days of intensive talk, she went to the theater almost every night, watching the performances now with a would-be professional eye.

Fitch arrived at The Mount in August for a four-day session. On the last day Edith, who had grown increasingly dissatisfied, tired, and confused, burst out: "I can't see how you could ever have thought there was a play in this book." Fitch replied in astonishment that he never *had* thought so, and it gradually became clear that each had been led to believe that the other desired the collaboration, and each had been unable to resist the flattery implied. The conversation ended in shouts of laughter, but from that moment Edith held out little hope for the play. She claimed not to be particularly concerned. "I don't regard a dramatisation as a real play," she remarked to Sara Norton, "and therefore don't feel strongly about it, but I naturally hope it will succeed."

Fitch wired in late August that the cast was enthusiastic and the rehearsals going well. At the last minute the opening was shifted from Buffalo to Detroit, and Edith went out by train on September 14 with Teddy and Walter Berry. It was her first and last journey any real distance west of the Hudson River, and she was not converted to the American midlands. Nor were her spirits lifted by the "vile hole" opposite the railroad station which had the only rooms available in the city. But the Detroit Opera House was full, and the performance was greeted by a great deal of applause.

The opening at the Savoy Theater in New York on the night of October 22, however, was anything but a success. Edith, who attended the event with Teddy, Berry, Gregory, and another couple, was inclined to blame its ineffectiveness on the actors, though Lumsden Hare and Grant Mitchell were in the cast, along with the accomplished Fay Davis as Lily Bart. They were, she said, so tired and so poorly rehearsed that they left out some of the most important lines. After the final curtain, enough applause was engendered to encourage Clyde Fitch to lead Mrs. Wharton onto the stage; both withdrew without saying the customary few words. The press reviews were wretched. "A doleful play," *The New York Times* proclaimed in its headline. "Not a success," said the *Herald* loudly. The theatrical career of *The House of Mirth* was brief.

Looking back a few days later, Edith suspected there had been no chance for it from the start: "I now doubt if that kind of a play, with a 'sad ending,' and a negative hero, could *ever* get a hearing from an American audience." This may have been her own reformulation of the "lapidary phrase" she would attribute to William Dean Howells as they left the theater together: "What the American public always wants is a tragedy with a happy ending."

Edith took the whole experience in her stride; she called it "instructive," and was enduringly grateful for the friendship with Clyde Fitch that came out of it. The day after the opening found her with the Tom Newbolds at Hyde Park, rejoicing in the "wonderful colours of foliage." The following afternoon she was back among her own glowing autumnal foliage at The Mount and playing hostess to Minnie and Beatrix Jones.

Minnie, a city woman to her fingertips, could scarcely tell one shrub from another. Her daughter "Trix," however, already far outstripped Aunt Edith in matters horticultural and was on her way to becoming one of the great landscape gardeners of her generation. Tall and reserved and with somewhat masculine good looks, Trix at thirty-four had behind her a decade of productive work. She was a fellow of the recently formed American Society of Landscape Architects and was accepting commissions from Maine to California, and in England.

Snow fell early and heavily that fall in Lenox, and there was "beautiful sleighing" on the November afternoons. Sara Norton came, and Moncure Robinson. Teddy absented himself for a fortnight's hunting. Since their return in June, he had been away more than usual: some six weeks in all, fishing or shooting, or enjoying himself in New York as a bachelor clubman. He was beginning to feel a little out of things at The Mount, amid the company that typically gathered there. Edith had looked forward to spending Christmas in Lenox, but Teddy announced he had to be in the city. They passed the holiday with Egerton Winthrop, whereafter Teddy left for his brother's home in Groton and Edith went down alone for a few days in Washington.

7

In early January 1907, Edith and Teddy sailed to France on the German ship *Amerika*. "Splendid voyage on splendid ship," she wrote with unusual warmth. Edith rarely commented on an Atlantic crossing, unless the seas were rough or her accommodations inadequate; incessant traveler though she was, it made her nervous to be aboard a steamer in midocean. But she rejoiced audibly on this occasion over the Louis XVI boudoir of their suite (it served as Teddy's bedroom at night), the writing desk, the azaleas on the center table, and the telephone. She was also feeling a rising excitement at the thought of returning to Paris and was inclined to take pleasure in everything connected with that event. She was, moreover, going to France well ahead of her normal schedule, and she planned to stay longer than ever before.

She had arranged with the George Vanderbilts to rent their apartment at 58 Rue de Varenne, and she and Teddy were settled there in time for her forty-fifth birthday. "There was a curious strangeness," she wrote Sally Norton, "in keeping a birthday in my own home, as it were, yet in a 'foreign' place." It was, of course, not altogether her own home, it had been furnished by other hands. But she was thrilled by its beauty and surroundings:

We are peacefully established in this very beautiful apartment, with charming old furniture, old Chinese porcelains and fine bronzes, against an harmonious background of *real* old boiseries (the hotel was built in 1750), in the heart of the most delightful part of Paris, and just two steps from my dear "Minnie-Pauls" who are well and cheerful, unusually, and with whom we "voisiner" very much.

We also know, partly from Henry James's constant teasing references, that the drawing room at 58 Rue de Varenne was graced by a crimson Aubusson carpet.

"The most delightful part of Paris" was the Seventh Arrondissement, a lozenge-shaped section on the Left Bank that descended in narrowing fashion from the long stretch of quais (Branly, d'Orsay, and others) along the Seine to the point where the Avenue de Suffren and the Rue de Sèvres intersect. The heart of it was the age-old Faubourg St. Germain.

Faubourg is a variously translatable word—"quarter" is perhaps the nearest English equivalent for this use of it; and as to the Faubourg St. Germain, it yields less to a geographical than to a social, historical, and intellectual definition. It was the town seat of the most imposing of the French nobility; an aristocratic society slowly being penetrated by bourgeois artists and intellectuals; the standard of social behavior for the other faubourgs in Paris; an atmosphere, a cluster of traditions, a wholly assured but to the outsider a strangely inconsistent human world. It was the setting of those great *salons* which the thirty-five-year-old Marcel Proust was at that very moment beginning to contemplate exploring in a long novel, having already written half a dozen articles for *Figaro* about the most worldly of them.

Whatever its contours, the Rue de Varenne undoubtedly ran across its center. A narrow, quiet, tree-lined street, it made its brief way, between the high indifferent walls of the *hôtels*, west from the Boulevard Raspail past the Rue du Bac and Rue Vaneau down to the Boulevard des Invalides. It was on the last corner, in the Hotel Biron, that Rainer Maria Rilke would install himself in a year or so and persuade Rodin to join him and set up a studio; soon afterward young Jean Cocteau, scarcely out of school, would come to live there as a sort of houseboy.

France in 1907, and especially Paris, was in the midst of what the French, looking back nostalgically, came to call *la belle époque:* the period from the turn of the century to the outbreak of the Great War in 1914. The phrase conjures up a richly assorted spectacle: the waltzes of Franz Lehar's *The Merry Widow* and *The Count of Luxembourg;* elegantly attired aristocrats and expensively gowned if suspect ladies gathering after midnight at Maxim's in the Rue Royale; bearded gentlemen wearing dark clothes and bowler hats in the winter, white linen and Panama hats in the summer; women wearing long, flowing, brightly colored dresses and hats with plumes and artificial fruits and flowers, bosoms accentuated by hidden supporters, waists held in tight by belts; the worldly *salons* of the idle nobility along the Champs Elysées and near the Place d'Etoile, the more traditional and intellectual ones peopled by Proustian figures in the Faubourg St. Germain; apéritifs at Fouquet's, boating on the Seine, the Tuesday evening galas at the Comédie Française, and everywhere a riot of the peculiarly intense Paris colors.

The period had indeed an air of unshakable stability, even of permanence. The incessant changes of government reflected little change of political position or program, and in fact the ministry of the fiery Clemenceau, which had come to power in the fall of 1906, would endure for the relatively long stretch of almost three years. Housekeeping costs had scarcely varied in thirty years. The Whartons probably paid the equivalent of about eighty dollars a month for one of the more luxurious apartments in the city—six or seven rooms, a kitchen and pantry, and two baths; no more than they would have paid in 1875. Long-established and seemingly unchallenged class distinctions were evident in the very cut of the beard and shape of the moustache.

The arts were flourishing as never before, and with them the theaters, galleries, bookstalls, cafés, and music halls. In fiction, it was a time of work as varied as the psychologizings of Paul Bourget, the delicate eroticism of Colette in her "Claudine" novels, and the adventures of Maurice Leblanc's attractive gentleman-rogue Arsène Lupin. Poetry had fallen below the peak of the previous generation, but poets swarmed across the literary foothills. In drama, Rostand and a host of others; in music, Debussy and Saint-Saëns; in painting, Impressionism was giving way before the achievements of Cézanne, Matisse, Picasso, and Gauguin. It was a time, too, of great performers, from the aging but still formidable Sarah Bernhardt and Coquelin to Mistinguette and the young Maurice Chevalier with his cane and bowler.

The most visible changes seemed all for the better, in the way of convenience and adventure. The Métropolitain underground railway had opened just after the Exposition of 1900, with three wooden carriages proceeding at twenty miles an hour; by 1907 the Métro had been vastly extended and transported scores of millions of passengers a year to all parts of Paris. Automobiles named for their builders—Peugeot, Renault, Panhard-Levassor, Mercedes—were increasing in numbers; by the time Edith Wharton bought her first Panhard, about one out of every eight thousand Parisians owned an open two-seater or a four-seater. Daring men, meanwhile, were testing the possibilities of aircraft: the November before the Whartons came to the Rue de Varenne, one man flew a distance of some 225 yards at a height of thirty feet above the ground.

For the watchful, at the same time, there were very different signs—of distress and foreboding. In 1907 two-fifths of all the private apartments in Paris were declared unsanitary. Strikes were proliferating, most markedly after the miners' rebellion in 1906 that followed a catastrophe costing more than a thousand lives; in 1907 some 1,300 strikes of varied size and duration were counted. The intermittent bomb threats and the news of assassinations from other parts of Europe and America were reminders of the spread of anarchism.

Edith Wharton, for the moment, saw only the best, the most stimulating and nourishing, of all this. The Faubourg in 1907 still bore the ineradicable psychological scars of the Dreyfus affair (which had come to an end in the summer of 1906 with the full exoneration and reinstatement of the French army officer), but it was at its apogee of fashion and influence. Edith's situation in it seemed to her a perfect combination of privacy and easy access to the social and intellectual life. From her bedroom, as she sat writing the final pages of the novel called *The Fruit of the Tree*, earlier called "Justine Brent," she could look down not onto the street but onto a wide courtyard protected by a heavy iron gate: a somberly handsome enclave in which she could feel luxuriously shut off from the world about her. At the same time, the Bourgets were only two blocks away; the *salon* of the Comtesse de Fitz-James, which she was beginning to frequent, was around the corner in the Rue Constantine; next door was the ducal family of the Lévis-Mirepoix.

The Faubourg also represented another combination upon which Edith Wharton's health of spirit depended: the sense of continuity and the sense of personal freedom. The stately houses, with their air of concealing some secret, had survived, virtually unchanged, since the days of the later Bourbon kings—the *hôtel* at 58 Rue de Varenne, as Edith had said, since 1750. More important for an observant American novelist of manners, the noble families retained their age-old pattern of domestic and social behavior: the Faubourg in the twentieth century, one commentator remarked, was "a piece of the *ancien régime* set in contemporary Paris." This was why, when a bourgeois intellectual was admitted to an aristocratic *salon*, it was likely to be a historian, an expert in the past, rather than an artist, literary or otherwise—unless of course the latter happened to be a member of the Académie Française, like Bourget, in which case all doors were open. The hospitality, it may be added, did not extend to the wives of historians. "Why do you want me to receive the person who cooks his food?" one nobleman asked indignantly; it was widely believed in the Faubourg that university professors customarily married their cooks or maids.

The author of *Madame de Treymes* had shown that she understood the terrible iron authority of the Faubourg matrons, those dowdy old ladies in uniform black with their sloping aristocratic noses. But Edith Wharton believed nonetheless that the Faubourg manner of living also encouraged a certain experimenting with life which she simultaneously felt the need of: the assertion of one's individuality, an expression of the self (or *quant à soi*, as she called it) to a degree beyond that of New York society, where for all its greater looseness of social gesture, social existence was more public and more stereotyped.

8

The Whartons had brought with them on the *Amerika* no less than six servants, as well as two dogs. Gross and Edith's personal maid certainly "lived in," but the others—including White, who was married now and the father of a son— probably had rooms elsewhere. Cook, when he drove in from Le Havre with the car, proved himself, in Teddy's words, to be "a perfect wonder," finding his way about Paris as if he had lived there for years. Teddy busied himself doing over the automobile for his wife's pleasure, closing in the body, installing an electric light inside, and adding "every known accessorie and comfort." He might be, as he told Sara Norton in his schoolboy hand, "no good on Puss's high plain of thought," but he looked upon Edith as "a wonderful person," with "a nice, to me, worldly side" that he enjoyed catering to.

It was in the remodeled Panhard that Teddy and Edith, in March and after the entire household had undergone a siege of influenza, set forth on a second "motor-flight" through France. Henry James joined them on this occasion. He had congratulated Edith some months earlier upon hearing that she was moving into the Rue de Varenne apartment, and had agreed to come over and accompany her on an automobile trip. He also besought her to steer clear of the Franco-American subject in future writings: there was too much disparity between French ways and American. (Since Edith had already written *Madame de Treymes,* the advice was a little late.) But as before, James turned the next day to Mary Cadwalader Jones to speak with dark ambivalence.

I brace myself—all appreciatively—for the prospect of the pilgrimage to the (to me) formidable Paris that this very interesting event opens up. It would still be interesting even if as only illustrating further, to my slightly troubled and bewildered eyes, the wild, the almost incoherent freedom and restlessness of Wealth and its wonderful art, when it combines with ability of harmonising the same with literary concentration of so positive and productive an order.

Edith, unconscious of these half-fearful, half-admiring reflections, pressed James for a specific date. This was translated by James for Mrs. Jones's benefit. Mrs. Wharton, he said, had been " 'ordered off in the motor,' alas into which she drags poor H.J. *à tour.* He likes an occasional day, immensely, but abhors long continuance." But he abandoned that posture soon enough, especially since Edith made a point of speeding due south the first day (March 20) through Châteauroux to Nohant and the home of George Sand.

James had known personally a number of the great figures—Flaubert and de Maupassant among them—who used to come to Nohant in what Edith described as "the serene old age of its tumultuous chatelaine," and he was absorbed by every aspect of the place. His presence led to their being admitted to the ground floor, where they could see the old marionette theater and the two hundred figures carved by Maurice Dudevant and costumed by his mother, George Sand. Later they wandered out into the garden and looked up at the windows, speculating as to which visitor might have peered out from each of them. James, pondering, suddenly murmured: "And in which of those rooms, I wonder, did George herself sleep?" Then, with a twinkle, he turned to Edith and added: "Though in which, indeed, in which indeed, my dear, did she *not?*"

After leaving Nohant they went west along the Creuse to Poitiers, then darted south through Angoulême and Bordeaux to Pau. Here they paused for a week, while Teddy was hotel-bound with flu, making day-long excursions into the Pyrenees, over to St. Jean-de-Luz on the Spanish border, and down to Lourdes and Cauterets. For Edith, as no doubt for the others, Lourdes was "a loathsome place," "a congeries of pietistic hotels, *pensions,* peddlars' booths and panoramas . . . [a] vast sea of vulgarism"—and expressing a cynical, grasping side of the French character which other foreigners had taken note of but which Edith had not before encountered. Now the route was eastward, and the Panhard devoured the miles to Toulouse, Albi, Carcassone, Nîmes, Aix, Hyères at a pace which even today might seen breathtaking.

One wonders how there was time to absorb anything—for example, the cathedral at Albi, shaped like some upright prehistoric animal: "So strange, so monstrous, so 'hallucinated,' " as Edith put it to Sara Norton, "that I already began to think I dreamed it, we all three dreamed it, in the hot sun and the mistral—a huge evil pink vision of a church in which black mass might have been said." But as that passage and the subsequent *Atlantic* articles demonstrate, Edith's cultivated eye registered a very great deal—no doubt more than usual, with James there to point to particularly fascinating and subtle details.

For all his histrionic apprehensions, James bore up bravely during a trip of fairly "long continuance"—three weeks from door to door. And whatever may have been his private feelings as the party rushed on, for Edith he proved himself perfect company.

> This part of France was unknown to Mr. James, and it is delightful to show him all its beauties, and to see his appreciation of them. Never was there a more admirable travelling companion, more ready to enjoy and unready to find fault—never bored, never disappointed and never (*need* I say) missing any of the little fine touches of sensation that enrich the movements of the really good traveller.

From Hyères the Panhard plunged north, back through Aix to Avignon, and up through Montélimar, Valence, and Lyons to Dijon. One of the curiosities in Edith's re-creations of these trips is that she scarcely said a word about the inns they stayed in; and to judge from her accounts, one might think they never took time out for a meal (though James spoke of "inveterately good grub"). But the *haute cuisine* of Burgundy was a phenomenon not to be passed over without comment, and Edith lavished some of her most Dickensian prose on a "luncheon . . . in the grimy dining-room of the *auberge* at Précy-sous-Thil," where "a flushed hand-maid, in repeated dashes from the kitchen, laid before us a succession of the most sophisticated dishes—the tenderest filet, the airiest *pommes soufflées*, the plumpest artichokes that ever bloomed in the buffet of a Parisian restaurant."

So back they came through Auxerre and Sens to Paris, feeling at first, as they entered the city after their weeks in the open country, a "terrific pressure . . . of converging masonry," but quickly succumbing to "the curves of the lifted domes, the grey strength of the bridges, and all the amazing symmetry of what in other cities is mean and huddled and confused." They had not been back at the Rue de Varenne a week before Gaillard Lapsley showed up to propose "a little trip near Paris." James was by now no less disposed than Edith to setting forth again. By common consent, they retraced their route southeastward through Avallon and Auxerre, experiencing once more what Edith called "the strongly marked *personality* of Burgundy" and "the mellowest of French civilizations."

Lapsley departed, but James stayed on for more than a month, dining out and visiting countesses, as he put it, having his own first introduction to Paris's *haut monde*. Mrs. Wharton, a friend of James's complained mildly, "kept a pretty tight clutch on him," but James frankly enjoyed it. "I have had a very interesting agreeable time," he wrote, "one of the most agreeable I have ever had in Paris, through living in singularly well-appointed privacy in this fine old Rive Gauche quarter." When at last he went back to England, he took with him social impressions "of more or less intimate French kind that I had *never* had." And he spoke without irony or reservation about "a great deal of wondrous and beautiful motoring."

Edith's appetite for motoring had not been assuaged, and to escape the Whitsun crowds in Paris she and Teddy made a rapid circuit through Rheims, Laon, and St. Quentin. It was a last outing before the return to Lenox. *"Non regionam',"* she said mournfully to Sara Norton as the sailing date approached. But a strike of the French maritime workers canceled their voyage on the *Provence* and gave them several days' reprieve, during which they drove in a leisurely manner down to Cherbourg, stopping overnight at an old gray inn at Bayeux and going to see "the really epic, Homeric, 'Tapestry.' "

They embarked on the *Adriatic*. It was the pride of the English passenger fleet, but Edith, in her resentment at leaving France, referred to it disrespectfully as "this last new White Star tub, which has taken nine mortal days to drag itself across the brine."

9

She was in no mood to look kindly on her native land and snatched at reasons to cavil. A newspaper announcement that President Eliot was instituting a course in business at Harvard sent her into a rage. "It is bad enough to break with all that charms life, as one does on leaving Europe," but to come back to business courses and skyscrapers! "Alas, alas!" Fresh from the great cathedrals of France, Edith took skyscrapers as a particularly evil symbol of the state of things cultural in America, and reported with a kind of shudder that the heirs of a recently deceased millionaire were constructing a tall office building as a memorial to him. Even her gardens did not, for the moment, provide solace. "The place looks well, in its dry, spare, *reluctant* New England way," she remarked, ". . . but, oh, how the landscape and the life *lack juice.*"

Slowly the summer life at The Mount had its curative way with her, and by July 4 she was prepared to admit that the garden was "unfolding beautifully." It was a season considerably less active than the two preceding years. Apart from the annual flower-show and village committee work, Edith was occupied chiefly with the publication of *The Fruit of the Tree.* The novel appeared on October 19, in a first edition of 50,000 copies—"exhausted," so Charles Scribner told her, in advance. Edith had a sudden pleasing image of a heavily fatigued edition being restored to life by the tender care of the publisher.

In fact, the novel had a short life span. A second edition of thirty thousand was printed at once, but as late as the following February less than ten thousand of these had been sold in the United States and Canada. The news from Macmillan in England was, relatively speaking, a bit better; but the American sales of *The Fruit of the Tree* never did get much beyond sixty thousand copies. This was certainly a respectable figure, but it was a disappointment after the record-breaking career of *The House of Mirth,* which was still selling fitfully in a cheap edition. Charles Scribner and his associates, observing that "the book has been well received everywhere," were inclined to blame its limited commercial success on the financial panic which, accompanied by a brief depression, occurred in the fall of 1907—a panic due to financial irregularities and overproduction, and one from which the country was quickly rescued by the valiant efforts of J. P. Morgan, abetted by his sometime enemy President Roosevelt.

Edith Wharton's literary earnings in 1907, in any case, were less than half those of the preceding year. In 1906, when *The House of Mirth* alone brought in $23,700—to which were added $900 for the "motor-flight" articles and an advance of $5,000 for *The Fruit of the Tree*—her income from writing amounted to almost $32,000. In 1907 the total dwindled to about $13,500, though another installment of $5,000 on the novel was due immediately after New Year's. In summary: over the three-year period between 1905 and 1908, Edith Wharton accumulated some $65,000 in advances, serial rights, royalties, and other fees.

The reviews were indeed good, several of them declaring *The Fruit of the Tree* to be superior to its predecessor. With this judgment, Henry James concurred—he was never able to regard *The House of Mirth* as more than a lucky hit. But the new novel simply failed to capture the reading public as had the story of Lily Bart; a lady from Winona, Minnesota, in fact, wrote furiously that she would have nothing to do with the book's heroine, Justine Brent, because of her allegedly dishonorable conduct, the facts of which the lady got slightly wrong.

Edith Wharton seems not to have been quite sure what she was up to in this 630-page novel, and one sign of uncertainty was the succession of unrelated alternative titles she proposed before settling for the least communicative of them all. There are too many "subjects" in the book. One of these was euthanasia. Edith had read newspaper accounts of an actual case of mercy killing in New England, and she had privately endorsed such an act with regard to a fatally injured friend. In the summer of 1905, Ethel Cram, a Lenox neighbor for whose intellectual capacities and moral perceptions Edith had a high esteem, was thrown from her pony cart and had her skull fractured by a kick from the horse. She lingered on for a month without regaining consciousness, and during this period Edith spoke to Sara Norton about the desirability of putting an end to her sufferings with a dose of morphine.

In *The Fruit of the Tree* it is Justine Brent, a former nurse, who performs the act of mercy killing by dispatching (with the use of morphine) the painracked Bessie Amherst, who has also had an accident while out riding. Justine subsequently marries Bessie's widowed, mill-owning husband, but as the result of certain melodramatic developments her deed comes to light. There is a painful confrontation, after which—as persistently in Edith Wharton's fiction—the marriage is resumed on a more confined and guarded level. "Nothing," Justine tells herself, "was left of that secret inner union which had so enriched and beautified their outward lives." The enactment in *The Fruit of the Tree* of marital disillusion is perhaps subtler than before. Justine's action may be roundly debatable, but John Amherst reveals a stubborn moral obtuseness in not understanding her soul-twisting dilemma, and there is little left of the passionate idealist Justine had first seen in him.

Another subject is industrial reform in a New England town very like North Adams, Massachusetts. About this, Edith Wharton was scantily informed. She had made a tour of a cotton mill in North Adams, but her guide did not know who she was or what she wanted, and in any case the din was so terrible that she missed half of what he said. After the first portion of the book ran in *Scribner's*, she received several letters from literate mill workers kindly pointing out various inaccuracies.

But in Justine Brent, Edith Wharton created one of her most comely and intriguing heroines, and she lent to her a number of her own features: her ironic temper, her cultivated and amused sense of human incongruity, her quickness and warmth of spirit, her intense if uncertain moral seriousness. It is suggestive that Justine is the first of Edith's women to have an undeflected awareness of her body and her physical needs; but she is also made to carry Edith's feeling that "fate had held her imprisoned in a circle of well-to-do mediocrity"—from which, like Edith, she had fled into the darker prison of a disappointing marriage. If Edith Wharton had clung to her first intention of calling the book "Justine Brent," and if, doing so, she had written a tightly packed novella devoted to that young woman's moral and psychological crisis, she might have composed one of her strongest shorter works of fiction.

10

Over the late summer and early fall of 1907, Edith fussed sporadically with book-making details. When she saw the first illustrations by Alonso Kimball, she uttered a cry of dismay. Kimball, she thought, had done surprisingly well by *Madame de Treymes*, but now he had depicted a "lumpy dumpy Justine, with a face like a town clock" just opposite a description of her that was all the opposite. There was also a long and intricate to-do about the spacing of dots at the end of sentences left unfinished in the text—to the point where Edith wondered dourly why the English handled their galleys so much better.

Otherwise, when she was not busy with the last of the "motor-flight" articles, she occupied herself of an evening with a new diversion which she called "star-charting." She had come upon a little volume called *A Fieldbook of the Stars*, and with its aid, standing on the terrace after dinner, she mapped the heavens, locating among others Capella, "a handsome new luminary" that appeared in the east about nine thirty in the evening. She drew her guests into the game, and, focusing a flashlight on the star chart, she lectured them on her findings. Johnny Morton, she reported, was haunted by the news that "we are moving toward Vega at the rate of sixty miles a second—or some such rate."

It was a scientific exercise of sorts: "There is nothing," she told Sara Norton at this time, "like the joy of a good scientific book." But there was also something uncharacteristically romantic about this new nightly ritual.

Writing from Paris the previous April, Edith had spoken to Sally Norton about "your friend Fullerton, whom we see frequently." Morton Fullerton, an American journalist who for some years had been the Paris correspondent of the London *Times*, had been a student of Sally's father at Harvard, and was a friend of the Norton family. He was, Edith went on, "writing a series of charming articles" on the Rhone valley for the *Revue de Paris* and had been most helpful in arranging for the serialization of *La Demeure de liesse* in the same periodical. "He is very intelligent, but slightly mysterious, I think," Edith concluded in a tone quite unusual for her.

Fullerton was also one of the most promising of Henry James's younger friends and admirers, and when he came to America in October 1907 to visit his family in Brockton, Massachusetts, he carried with him a letter from James urging him "to let Mrs. Wharton know of your American presence and whereabouts, that she may ask you to come to her at Lenox—as she earnestly desires to do." Stressing the "tenderness" he felt for Fullerton, James said "that sentiment is singularly served by this lively hope of your not missing a very valuable and charming American impression, quite a particular and (of its kind) highly characteristic."

When in due course Fullerton reached The Mount for a visit of several days, among the innumerable things he and Edith discussed was an essay he was completing on Henry James's fiction. Edith, listening to the piece, found it "very original, but too emphatic," and she sat up late on the chill New England evening trying to persuade Fullerton to moderate its style. But Fullerton announced his determination that for once an American audience should have driven home to it the full achievement of the great writer, and both impressed and amused his hostess by refusing to "abate a jot."

Lenox had its first snowfall of the year shortly before Fullerton arrived. Driving through the Berkshires on the second day of his visit, Edith and Fullerton paused to sit on a wet bank and smoke a cigarette while Cook put chains on the Panhard's wheels. Near them, as they talked, they noticed a shrub known as witch hazel, its delicate yellow flowers just coming into bloom. Each took a sprig, and Edith felt, suddenly, a personal symbolism in the juxtaposition of autumnal snow and the blossoming witch hazel: in botanical lore the shrub, which only begins to flower when other plant life is dying, is sometimes called "the old woman's bloom." In Fullerton's presence something seemed unexpectedly to quicken in Edith's forty-five-year-old life, and Fullerton shared the feeling.

Or so he seemed to say when, taking his departure, he enclosed his sprig of witch hazel in a note of gratitude more intimate than weekend guests at The Mount customarily offered. Three days later, on October 29, Edith began a private journal addressed directly to Fullerton, though not at this time destined for his eyes. It was an act of secret but wistfully hopeful communion:

> Finding myself—after so long!—with some one to talk to, I take up this empty volume in which, long ago, I made one or two spasmodic attempts to keep a diary. For I had no one but myself to talk to, and it is absurd to write down what one says to one's self; but now I shall have the illusion that I am talking to you, and that—as when I picked the witch-hazel—something of what I say will somehow reach you . . .

And then, on November 27, after Fullerton had returned to Paris, a brief inscription, like a sigh: "Your letter from Paris . . ."

2

William Morton Fullerton had just turned forty-two when he came to Lenox. The eldest of the three children of Bradford and Julia Bell Fullerton, he had been born in Norwich, Connecticut, and had passed his childhood in the small New England town of Waltham, Massachusetts, a few miles from Boston, where his father was the Congregational minister. Until he went to Phillips Academy at Andover around 1880, he had, as he put it, experienced nothing beyond "the prehistoric simple life" of Waltham, "with its town-meetings, its Moodey and Sankey revivals, its spelling-bees, its sleigh-rides." Growing up in a clerical household, he was almost naturally of a studious and religious disposition—as an adolescent, he remarked, he was more at home on the shores of Lake Galilee than on those of Lake George (where he spent a summer camping) and could more readily draw a map of the Acropolis in Athens than of the Atlantic coastline.

Andover and then Harvard, which he entered in 1882, helped confirm this part of his nature by providing him with "seven years of the sheerest idealistic education." He was a brilliant undergraduate, winning the esteemed Bowdoin Prize for literature in his junior year and graduating *magna cum laude* in 1886. Charles Eliot Norton admired and liked him, and Barrett Wendell was so taken with his English themes that he kept them as models for later generations of students. Fullerton gravitated inevitably to the literary community at college, helping to found the short-lived *Harvard Monthly* and serving on its board with the twenty-one-year-old George Santayana and a young Lithuanian immigrant of awkward speech and remarkable abilities named Bernhard Berenson.

After two years as literary editor of the Boston *Daily Advertiser,* Fullerton went to England with Richard King Longfellow, a classmate and a nephew of the poet, put in a number of months as a freelance writer, and in 1890 was appointed to the staff of the London *Times.* It was in this period that he came to know Henry James, and through James other figures in the English literary and artistic world.

In James's view, Morton Fullerton was all wonderfully incomplete, a cluster of promises and bound to develop in many admirable directions. (To his mistress at this time, Fullerton confided: "I have in me 100 men instead of one.") James and Fullerton frequently dined together at the Reform Club and talked over theories of literature; after Fullerton transferred to Paris, James showered him with letters, often beginning with the phrase "Dear Boy," a sign that he had taken the younger man into his inner circle. At the same time, in London, Fullerton was privy to another circle from which James absented himself: that of Oscar Wilde and his entourage, in particular the talented sculptor Ronald Sutherland, Lord Gower.

In 1892 or early 1893, Fullerton was assigned to the Paris office of the *Times,* working there under the colorful, majestically proportioned, and authoritarian editor Henri Stefan Opper de Blowitz, who scooped the world more than once on epoch-making international news. Friends from England continued to seek the young man out. In a small pocket diary in which he jotted occasional notes, Fullerton recorded in April 1893 taking James to lunch at Le Doyen with the Marquess of Lorne, Princess Louise (the daughter of Queen Victoria), and Ronald Gower. Later, after calling regularly on James at the Hotel Westminster in the Rue de la Paix, he observed with satisfaction: "All this month James."

But he was also becoming an increasingly accomplished journalist, with a special skill in reporting to the English on French political developments. He covered the Dreyfus case—that affair that wound its way through French social and political history, and in its reverberations through Edith Wharton's life— from the inquisition of Emile Zola through the second trial of Dreyfus at Rennes and the final chapter. It might be added that, though Fullerton only observed from across the channel the trial instigated by Oscar Wilde's libel action against the Marquis of Queensbury—the second of the two cases which most shook European society in these years—he was brushed lightly by its epilogue. When Wilde came to Paris in 1899, broken and ill after his release from Reading Gaol, he sent Fullerton a copy of his play *The Importance of Being Earnest* and asked him for a loan of a hundred francs. Fullerton wrote so ornate an apology for not being able to come to the aid of so great an artist that Wilde was moved to remonstrate mildly: honest feeling, he said, was never in need of stilts.

Fullerton found time as well for writings of his own: on Cairo, on George Meredith, on new departures in scientific thought. In 1905 he published *Terres françaises,* a series of sensitive and well-informed sketches written in graceful French and drawing upon a tour of Burgundy, the Franche Compté, and the Narvonnaise. It was *couronné* by the Académie Française, a testimony not only to the book's qualities but to the author's excellent standing with the French establishment.

Upon de Blowitz's retirement in 1902, Fullerton was in effect made his successor, an unusual appointment for however talented an American. He remained the chief Paris spokesman for the London *Times* until 1907: a familiar and yet oddly elusive and solitary personality in Parisian circles and on the boulevards, delighting and puzzling his journalistic associates with a manner of speaking as intricate and hesitant as that of Henry James, and even more fully sprinkled with idiomatic French phrases. He was a slight, trimly built man, five feet six inches in height, with gentle blue eyes, a thick, well-manicured moustache, and dark brown hair which ran straight back from his forehead. He was always extremely precise in dress, even something of a dandy, appearing more often than not in morning coat and glossy hat. To the world Fullerton presented a simple and unaffected manner and a quiet glow of idealism that elicited a sort of smiling fondness from nearly everyone with whom he came into close contact.

Considering the part he was to play in the life of Edith Wharton, almost everything about this man interests us. There was indeed a strong if somewhat dreamy vein of idealism in him, and an inherited interest in religious matters: meditations on proofs of the existence of God alternated in his pocket diary with references to politics, literature, and art. But religious idealism mingled in Morton Fullerton's make-up with a no less positively marked erotic impulse and a strong sexual appeal.

The clergyman's son made note in his diary of the arresting disclosure by a friend of Guy de Maupassant's that the writer had " 'had' 14 women in one day." When a sprightly young cousin came to Paris in 1905 on a last little fling before her forthcoming marriage, Fullerton escorted her about the city and paid court to her till she quite fell in love with him, telling him so in long letters from home and begging him not to be shocked. "With all your frankness and cordiality, you are a bit dignified, and I haven't a spec—not a spec. And my heart is bigger than my head—a great deal bigger. After I am married I hope you will come to see Mr. T—— and me." Almost simultaneously, the free-moving American woman who wrote under the name Blanche Roosevelt was telling Fullerton firmly that she would not again visit him in his rooms alone "unless expressly invited—*parole de bonne fille,*" only to add yieldingly: "When am I to see you again, Adonis— do you wish me to cry for the moon . . . ? I believe you do."

But as regards Fullerton's later relationship with Edith Wharton, a more important liaison was with Margaret Brooke, the Ranee of Sarawak. The former Margaret de Windt, descendant of an aristocratic French family with which Dutch and English blood had mingled, was married in 1869, at the age of twenty, to Sir Charles Brooke, a first cousin and close contemporary of her mother's. The year before, Sir Charles had succeeded his uncle, the prodigious Sir James Brooke —who had become the first white rajah of the country by putting down a rebellion of Dyak headhunters in 1841—as Rajah of Sarawak, a small, independent, and multiracial state in northwest Borneo. It was a loveless marriage on both sides, but Margaret had a certain admiring affection for her dedicated, grim-spirited husband, faithfully performed her ceremonial role as ranee, and bore Sir Charles seven children in as many years. (The first four all died within a matter of days during a cholera epidemic in 1874.) But the climate, the isolation, and the unending public and marital demands finally told on her; she had recurring illnesses, all diagnosed as hysteria, and in the late 1880s she returned to England with her three sons and settled in a small attractive house in London.

Her title gave her entrée everywhere, but her eager, untutored interest in art and letters led her to cultivate, in particular, persons such as Henry James, Oscar Wilde, Burne-Jones, Paul Bourget, and Swinburne. It was probably James who introduced her to Morton Fullerton, soon after the young American's arrival in England. She was immediately captivated by him—to a degree, she was soon confessing, beyond anything she had ever experienced. The rapid progress of their relationship was reflected in the changing mode of her address to him in letters, from "Dear Friend," to "Dearest," and then "My Darling"; by 1890 they were lovers.

The ranee was of middle height, with a generous, full-bosomed figure and a broad, uncompromising face. Her commanding presence gave her such an air of propriety, she told Fullerton, that people would be incredulous at the *"passionate, true"* letters she wrote him almost daily. It was indeed about the reaction of the world at large, should it learn of their affair, that she worried most. "I don't want the low vulgarly minded people to jeer at me for loving you—a man young enough to be my son," she wrote in September 1890, seeking to arrange a rendezvous in Paris. "In the eyes of the world I am a fool to love any one so much younger —15 years . . . only think." To this Fullerton (who had made similar protestations to a somewhat older American woman some time before) replied: "I understand your bothering about age and things like that. Believe me, it has never come to trouble me. . . . You forget, dearest, you forget I love you and you love me. That is the only fact to be considered."

Margaret's letters were vivacious and meandering, full of gossip about Henry James (whom she quoted as saying that "love was not the most necessary thing"), Oscar Wilde (she expressed surprise that Fullerton was surprised at her liking Wilde so much), Burne-Jones, and the others. But she constantly returned to her feelings for Fullerton, with the attractive Victorian blend of sexual honesty and euphemism, sometimes conveying them in French: *"Je t'aime de tout mon coeur —et je t'embrasse."*

Fullerton's letters were at once more ethereal and more literarily erotic. They alternated allusions to their eternal souls with professed longings to feel their lips together, accompanied, as it might be, by a quotation from the Greek pastoral poet Bion: "That thee I may feel in my arms, and kisses with kisses may mingle." His most effective tactic—and one takes note of it for future reference—was to appeal dramatically to the grand moral independence which he and Margaret shared in common:

> The beauty, the safety of our love is . . . our deliberate calm reckoning of the circumstances that have to do with it, that make it what it is, unique. We are both supremely self-reliant and intolerant of any laws that others make for us. We must create our own worlds. This may be sublimely, Satanically immoral, audaciously Promethean; but it is the way we are bound to love and be.

Even before Fullerton moved to Paris, the affair was beginning to run its course. Reporting mournfully, on a Sunday midnight in 1892, that she had spotted three more gray hairs that morning and would assuredly be snow white within the year, Margaret also passed on the rumor she had heard that "you supped and breakfasted and dined and—I think slept—at a certain woman's house perpetually." But she held back from reproaching him. "I don't allow myself to be too absurd—and like Mme. S. and others tell you that I should expire from grief if you left off loving me." Fullerton did gradually leave off loving her, though they were together a few times during his first Paris years. Margaret Brooke, far from expiring from grief, had many decades to come of an amply rewarding and stimulatingly complicated life.

3

Another glimpse into Fullerton's special brand of sensuality is provided by an early morning dream which he recounted in his diary in February 1894 (between a quotation from Keats and notes on an exhibition of paintings). "I dreamed," he wrote, "that I was in a splendid palace in the midst of a luminous green country, a palace of long corridors and high ceilings and airy rooms." Returning to his chamber from a walk, he heard behind him the step of a woman who occupied a room near his and who had already enchanted him by her "magnificent beauty."

> She was of perfect classic beauty, divinely tall, and divinely fair, magnificently serene in her movements, big-browed, gentle-eyed, with round arms and fully modulated curves of breast, and belly, I was sure, like the goblet-belly of Canticles, and light hair waved as naturally as the whorls of a shell, and with far more beautiful freedom of curve. She was very grand, and as big, I swear it, as the ladies of the Erectheion. I wished to worship at her shrine; I prayed God to give her eyes to feel the worshipful heart within me, to know that I adored her and would pour out libations of my very blood if she would raise her eyelids slowly with a smile and let me lie between her breasts.

She was, his dream-self told him, as lovely as Aphrodite, and one "of those great women . . . who can share their persons as others dispense kind deeds without loss of their integral beauty, or other sense than that of having been generous, as their mother the earth." At her chamber door, this resplendent female turned and, "with a joyous intoxicating look of love," whispered: "I will come to you."

She came, draped only like a figurine of Hellas. She flung aside the mantle. I seemed lost in her effulgence like an asteroid near the sun. She was more grand and beautiful than I had dreamed. Lying on the cushions of a silk divan she seemed a goddess come on an errand of mercy.

But as Fullerton approached her, he woke up—or his imagination ran out. For whatever else it may be, this Aubrey Beardsley vision is scarcely recognizable as a dream: it has been too much meditated and smoothed out. Something of Margaret Brooke may linger in the statuesque earth-mother, enlarged and beautified into Fullerton's image of the ideal female. But one hesitates to interpret so literary a performance. What is unmistakable, in this description by a relatively small and relatively young man, is the stress upon the size and grandeur of the mythic creature. Fullerton seems to have been periodically obsessed by a dream of older and bigger women; but amidst all the elaborate lyricism of the account, with its Biblical and classical allusions, one does not fail to notice the lavish anatomical, not to say orgasmic, detail.

Fullerton's waking life, meanwhile, continued to be busy enough. In 1902, when de Blowitz retired, he was living at 2 Rue de Chausée d'Antin, near the Opéra and just off the Boulevard Haussmann. At the same address, and possibly the owner of the building, was a certain Mme. Henrietta Mirecourt, and with this lady, who also seems to have been considerably older than Fullerton, he had been carrying on an affair for several years. From references to her, she appears to have been an intelligent, even a cultivated person, and perhaps part English. She was undoubtedly a passionate, mercurial, and demanding woman.

Then, in 1903, with virtually no one in Fullerton's circle, then or later, being aware of it, he married. His wife was Victoria Camille Chabert, sometimes called "Ixo": a striking young woman of twenty-four from the Dordogne in central France, who was already making a name for herself as a *chanteuse* in the Opéra Comique in Paris. A daughter, Mireille, was born of the match; it may well be that the child's imminent arrival explains the double phenomenon of marriage and with so young a woman. The marriage, in any event, lasted scarcely a year.

Fullerton evidently had no intention of giving up his other relationships, particularly that with the possessive and curiously irresistible Henrietta Mirecourt. In May 1904, Camille wrote her husband a letter which—according to the paraphrase of it in a court document—charged him with maintaining several mistresses and "of having, as a result, refused to grant her his caresses." The letter added "in wounding terms that her confidence in him had disappeared." These statements became the basis of Fullerton's suit for divorce against his wife. He was adjudged to have been "injured" by the accusations, and the decree was granted him in November, by virtue of a court order which referred to Camille as "the Fullerton woman," required her to pay all the expenses of the case, and then tailed off indecisively with a semicolon. It was one of the more perplexing additions to French judicial history; but the legal and political rights of women during *la belle époque,* though sporadically agitated for, remained negligible.

One of the features of Fullerton's erotic career is that his women almost never entertained the slightest rancor toward him following the separation. Three years after the divorce, Camille—obviously a warm-hearted as well as a gifted woman —was addressing him as *"Mon bien cher Will."* Writing from Fiume, where she was to sing the lead in *Thaïs* for the first time (she had by then become a *tragédienne lyrique*), she said: "Our correspondence seems to me so bizarre and at the same time so delicate that I really do not know what tone to give it. May I write you? Dare I write you? Do my artistic affairs interest you? In a word, I am still dazed and stupefied by everything that happened, and the more I think about it, the more I understand the folly of it." A decade later she was still signing herself *"Camille, qui t'adore."*

But if Camille Chabert kept her balance, Fullerton's parents in America (the family had long since moved to Brockton) were increasingly bewildered by the turn of events in Paris. They had always been selflessly devoted to their elder son and had rejoiced proudly in his journalistic successes, reading aloud to one another the clippings he occasionally sent them. Julia Fullerton—and here, plainly enough, is another key to Fullerton's nature and conduct—concentrated a passion of maternal love upon him. "I long for you with such an intensity of feeling," she wrote him, "that it almost makes me sink with exhaustion some-times." She described him lovingly, in an impulsive and even girlish manner: "Your methods of thought, your way of looking at things, your ideas of friendship —your great sociability and enjoyment of people and yet your fondness for not being disturbed—your enjoyment in doing things your own way all appeal to me." She thought they were very much alike, and was the more shocked and disturbed to learn belatedly of his marriage. She wrote in such agitation that she misdated the letter by a decade, telling him of her deep unhappiness at his not informing them "when you were in love, and surprising us by news of marriage, and *then* not writing."

Julia and her husband were able to accept the fact of the marriage, especially since Camille had been writing faithfully. But the clerical couple found the continuing involvement with Mme. Mirecourt incomprehensible. As far as they could make out, Fullerton in the spring of 1904 was married to Camille but was sharing an apartment with Henrietta—and was being pressed by his mistress not only to help with the rent but to pay her two hundred francs a month in addition. How could Morton be so dominated by "this scheming woman"? Fullerton, writing back for funds from his insurance policy, spoke rather formally of his "profound sympathy and affection" for Mme. Mirecourt, but was bound to report that in her financial demands—which he felt obliged in all honor to meet —she grew by turns excited, tearful, beseeching, rampaging, and threatening. Bradford begged him to settle the affair once and for all with a lump sum, since the suffering his mother had undergone had brought her to the verge of her grave.

Fullerton, as has been seen, extricated himself from the marriage with almost disconcerting ease. But the *affaire Mirecourt* would endure for a number of years longer and would have its unsettling effect upon Fullerton's relations with Edith Wharton.

4

Within a few days of Fullerton's departure from The Mount in October 1907, Edith advanced her sailing date to France from early January to December 5, giving it out that with the autumn's unusually heavy snow and long cold spell, the servants' quarters were too chilly to be occupied. After a rough crossing and few days in Normandy with Harry Jones, the Whartons came to Paris, Teddy to leave at once for a visit with the Walter Gays at their villa, Le Bréau, Edith to spend a week in Harry's *hôtel* on the Place des Etats-Unis. She thought nostalgically of Christmas in the Berkshires, but she also admitted to being "sunk in the demoralising happiness which this atmosphere produces in me." Returning to 58 Rue de Varenne on Christmas Eve (they had rented it for another season), she found the apartment and its surroundings more endearing than ever. Fullerton was in attendance at once, escorting her to a lecture on the Elizabethan playwrights by the American professor Frank Baker, and later bringing Baker to call.

The city was blanketed in snow on New Year's 1908 and extremely cold. Edith, descending daily, well muffled, for a stroll through the Faubourg or a drive to some social or artistic engagement, became more than ever aware of what she called "the subtle beauty of Paris in winter." And yet another phase of her state of mind at the start of 1908, and one that perhaps gave special poignance to her sense of happiness and beauty, was suggested by two quotations she entered at the front of a page-a-day diary that she began to keep.

The first was from a love poem by Pierre Ronsard, the leader of the group of sixteenth-century French poets known as the Pléiade:

> *Une tristesse dans l'âme close*
> *Me nourrit, et non autre chose.*

(A sadness in my shut-in soul
Nourishes me, and no other thing.)

The second was taken out of context (Edith had come upon it in a life of John
Addington Symonds) from *Canti popolari Toscani* by the obscure mid-
nineteenth-century Tuscan poet Giuseppe Tigri:

> *Sono stato all' inferno e son tornato;*
> *Misericordia! La gente che c'era.*
> *V'era una stanza tutt' illuminata,*
> *E dentro v'era la speranza mia. . . .*

(I have been to hell, and I have come back.
Great God! How many people were there.
There was a chamber, all illuminated,
And within was my loved one.)

Edith had taken to employing a private literary code—quotations from poetry
and fiction—as a way of hinting to herself about her most private feelings. One
should be cautious in deciphering it, especially since the quotations by no means
always the carry the meaning they had in the original work. But the juxtaposed
lines from Ronsard and Tigri are, obviously enough, variations on her recurring
theme of imprisonment—of being shut away from the sources of emotional
fulfillment. The quotation from Ronsard, which was accumulating immense
significance for her, indicates that, while conscious of a desolation at her core,
Edith could nevertheless find a certain sad sustenance in the imprisoned condition. As to the passage from Tigri, she had literally been to America and had come
back to Paris; but "hell" is not at all to be equated with America, much less with
Lenox. It was, rather, a situation, a manner of existence which she periodically
faced up to. The two taken together are a version of her image of herself (to Sally
Norton) as gazing out through the bars of a prison at the procession of life.

The pattern had crystallized after the sudden deterioration of Teddy's health.
He had maintained a fairly steady keel for four years, but soon after their arrival
in Europe in December he had fallen into a "nervous depression" and was looking
and feeling "very dolorous." It was a collapse, Edith thought, very like the one
that had lasted six months in 1903, and she was at a loss to explain it. Only dimly,
and for the most part in retrospect, did she understand what some of her friends
were quicker to perceive: that the environment she was building about her in
Paris was suffocating to the easygoing lover of fishing and the looser amenities
of American social gatherings. Teddy was as stifled by the *salons* of Paris and the
French literary acclaim of his wife (as the successive installments of *La Demeure
de liesse* appeared in the *Revue de Paris*), not to mention his total financial
dependence upon her, as Edith was by what she regarded as the inescapable
bondage of her marriage. But the diagnosis of Teddy's condition had a great deal
farther to go than that, and had to wait upon other varieties of symptoms.

Teddy's numbness of spirit combined with Edith's uncertainty about Morton Fullerton to provide a serious distraction from writing. Over the early months of 1908, however, she made extensive notes for two related essays: one, a sober appraisal of Walt Whitman's poetry, its major themes, techniques, and imagery; the other on Anna de Noailles and her poetic and emotional affinities with Whitman. Neither reached print, but the second of them occasioned a statement from Edith that, though partly playful, was a sign of the direction her mind and temperament were taking.

Brownell made an amicably skeptical comment about the Whitmanian element in the Anna de Noailles essay, and replying, Mrs. Wharton declared she had "reeled under the shock" of discovering that her editor was *"not* a Walt-ite." Despite Brownell's praise for so much of the piece as he had seen, she was sure there must be a "sardonic laugh between the lines."

If one isn't *for* Walt, one is so indignantly and contemptuously against him! But being a Whitmanite, like being an agnostic, cultivates forbearance and humility, since the anti-Whitmanite and the Christian are licensed to say what they please about one's belief, while it's understood that one may not talk back.

She also managed two short stories during the winter—not among her best, but each in its way having a certain special interest. The first of them, "The Verdict," has to do with a popular American painter who abruptly and cheerfully accepts the fact that he is no more than second-rate, marries a rich widow, and settles down to a well-cushioned life on the French Riviera. This was almost a point-by-point replica of the situation of Edith's old acquaintance Ralph Curtis, who had tried his hand at painting, not without success, but had given it up— very likely (for he was a man of genuine artistic discernment) for the reason alleged in the story. He had married the former Lise Colt of Providence, Rhode Island, the decidedly wealthy widow (after a short marriage) of Arthur Rotch, and now lived in mild splendor at the Villa Sylvia in Beaulieu, near Monte Carlo. Lise, who could hardly have been pleased by the portrait of her as a woman of beaming stupidity, took enduring offense.

The other story arose from a suggestion by Henry James. In a letter written in early January, James elaborated upon an anecdote he and Edith had discussed the previous spring—about an Englishwoman who pried, James-like, into the emotional problems of various persons and came upon some startling discoveries. The incident seems to have involved James's neighbor at Rye, a brilliant member of the Foreign Office and friend of the Bloomsbury group, Sidney Waterlow; and in real life, James told Edith, the "pretext" for the actions discovered remained unknown. Edith could make free with this happily inconclusive material.

She absorbed it quite artfully into a story called "The Pretext," which was essentially an oblique statement about her relationship with Morton Fullerton—

or her worst apprehensions thereof, as Fullerton seemed not inclined with the passing days to carry forward from the moments at The Mount. It tells of the middle-aged wife of a sedate American professor at a small New England college reminiscent of Williams. A much younger visiting Englishman presses his charming attentions upon her, and she has a fleeting vision of escape from the stolid mediocrity which surrounds her. She is the more saddened and embittered to learn that the visitor had pursued her only as a pretext for lingering in the neighborhood while wooing and winning the hand of another woman. The tale was not only shrewd in its appraisal of the characters involved (and its evocation of remembered scenes), but up to a point, as we shall see, remarkably intuitive.

5

Henry James, after his long stay at the Rue de Varenne apartment the year before, had spoken appreciatively of the "singularly well-appointed privacy in this fine old Rive Gauche quarter," and indeed Edith Wharton in the Faubourg was as carefully protected from the more strenuous and showy aspects of the Paris of 1908 as she had been, when a debutante, from the similar aspects of old New York. But she was not unobservant of developments in the larger world, and showed some discernment as to which were of special import. On February 1, for example, she made mention of the assassination of the King and Crown Prince of Portugal, one in a series of such events that reflected the murderous restiveness among certain elements of the European population. A week or so later she went to the Chamber of Deputies and occupied a box seat supplied by the American ambassador Henry White to listen to the debate on the Morocco question.

That always vexatious issue had come up again because of Germany's fury over the arrest of three of its nationals in Casablanca. Edith Wharton listened while Jean Jaurès, the great and far-seeing socialist leader, urged a pacific course between France and Germany. Her reaction is not recorded, but she later came to regard Jaurès with great hostility. His words, in any event, were only partly attended to in the Chamber, and in retrospect the parliamentary debate could be seen as a moment in the zig-zag course which eventually brought *la belle époque* to an end.

Edith Wharton had, meanwhile, much to occupy her in her daily life. She worked hard on her French and Italian lessons, one session of each per week. She attended lectures: on Venice in French poetry ("idiotic"); on Shakespeare; on Racine by Jules Lemaître (one "very good," one "very dull"). She went frequently to the theater with friends—to the Français to see Mlle. Barlet perform splendidly in *Andromaque*, to the Théâtre Marigny to see a company of Sicilian actors in *Cavalleria rusticana* and D'Annunzio's *La figlia di Iorio*. Toward the end of January, Bourget took her to the Vaudeville for the dress rehearsal of his play *Un Divorce*, shortly to be the hit of the Paris season. *Sherlock Holmes* at

Antoine's, three nights later, she dismissed as "perfect rubbish."

But the chief feature of the winter was the extraordinary bustle of her social life. During the first six weeks of 1908, Edith Wharton lunched or dined out, or took tea with friends, or had guests to lunch, tea, or dinner no less than thirty-nine times. On a number of these occasions she was in the company of the Proustian aristocracy—those members of the French nobility whom Marcel Proust would draw upon for his depiction of the Faubourg St. Germain ("the Guermantes way") in *Remembrance of Things Past.*

Among these—their names follow one another in Edith's diary—was the Duchesse de Rohan, the charitable and energetic hostess whose *salon* was as likely to be crowded with poets as with aristocrats, and her daughter Princesse Marie Murat. Edith re-encountered Comtesse Mélanie de Pourtalès, whom she remembered from her days in Cannes almost three decades earlier; once a lady-in-waiting to the Empress Eugénie, the countess was still a beautiful and forceful woman. She saw something of Comte Aimery de Rochefoucauld, whose family had once owned the *hôtel* at 58 Rue de Varenne, one of the foremost noblemen of France and a man passionately concerned about social precedence and his proper place at the table. She caught glimpses of Boni de Castellane, once regarded as the most brilliant man in Paris society but now beginning a long period of financial and social decline, following his divorce from the person and the money of the dowdy American millionairess Anna Gould.

These and others were apt to be Edith's fellow guests in the *salon* of Comtesse Rosa de Fitz-James in the Rue Constantine. Rosa, with whom Edith struck up a lasting friendship, was a Vienna-born woman of Jewish descent, the daughter of a wealthy banking family; like several others of her co-religionists in Paris, she had been volubly anti-Dreyfus. She was somewhat older than Edith, slight and slender, with white hair and bright, questioning eyes; she walked with a slight limp, leaning on a cane. Her husband, Robert de Fitz-James, was an acid and notoriously faithless fellow (and a descendant, via a mistress, of King James II of England). Rosa's life centered in her *salon;* at her Wednesday dinner parties a dozen or more guests assembled in the several, and as Edith thought, characterless, drawing rooms of her eighteenth-century *hôtel.*

The invaluable Bourget had placed Edith under Rosa's wing the previous winter, and Edith found the company at the Rue Constantine *salon* stimulating in a variety of ways. Writers and intellectuals were drawn to Rosa's table, though their hostess was relatively unlettered. She sprinkled her eccentric English with the phrase "Isn't it?" and Edith would recall her asking, after struggling with a new book by some Academician: *"Tell me, my dear, is it any good?"* Aristocrats and diplomats appeared at her gatherings, as well as men and women of letters. At dinner on January 29, for example, there were Paul Bourget; Paul Hervieu, a highly successful playwright; Comte Alexandre de Laborde, an authority on illuminated manuscripts; Princesse Henri de Ligne; Francis Charmes, an editor of the *Revue des deux mondes;* and the recently installed and exceedingly able American ambassador, Henry White, with his wife, the former Margaret Rutherford, the friend of Edith's adolescence in Newport. At other times Edith found Charley du Bos and the charming young woman he had recently married, Zezette; Anna de Noailles; and the man she was now indicating in her diary by his initials, M.F.

Talk in the *salon* wandered in a sometimes leisurely, sometimes flashing manner among the vocations and the personal interests of the cunningly selected guests. Edith discovered to her pleasure that it was an ensemble affair in which everyone participated as the occasion arose. Younger writers were on their mettle to show themselves worthy, by the brilliance of their literary comment, of future election to the Académie. Women on the whole were expected to listen attentively to the interchanges between the gentlemen, mentally preparing their contribution to fill in the pauses. To this, Anna de Noailles was a striking exception: she was an inveterate monologuist who even waved her hand wildly for silence while she interrupted her discourse to take a swallow of wine.

Edith Wharton, it has already been remarked, was a woman who felt a need not only for friendship, but for something larger: for a community of friends. During the four or five years preceding, she had created a community of sorts at The Mount; now during her second winter in the Rue de Varenne, partly out of the individuals she was meeting in the *salon* world, she began to put together a Paris version.

In addition to several of the names just mentioned, Charlotte de Cossé-Brissac belonged to it—Edith saw her or had her to tea perhaps once a fortnight; and Gustave Schlumberger, still fuming over the total vindication of Alfred Dreyfus. There were Louis Ganderax, the influential taskmaster of the *Revue de Paris,* and Victor Bérard, a large, good-looking man, given to little explosions of intellectual excitement, a Greek scholar of note and the director of the Ecole des Hautes Etudes. Edith was also coming to know and admire André Tardieu, Fullerton's keen-minded friend, whose long political career was just getting under way with a number of brilliant articles in *Le Temps,* of which he was an editor.

Turning up frequently at the Rue de Varenne was Vicomte Robert d'Humières, to whom Edith had taken an immediate liking. He was an accomplished linguist and a translator of English fiction, as powerful of mind as he was engagingly gentle in manner; he was in fact a circumspect homosexual, a fact known only to a few, including his friend Proust and his own somewhat nervous-looking wife.

The most regular and for Edith the most entertaining new member of her French circle was Alfred de St. André, a man with no visible achievements, no vocation, and for that matter no very large income. But he had astonishing staying power as a friend and was inveterately good company, especially with

Americans and English in Paris. Even his intermittent periods of gloom and declared loss of self-confidence had their odd and restful charm. St. André was a great gourmet and a connoisseur of out-of-the-way restaurants; for Edith and others, he was an unfailingly dependable guide to delightful but little known haunts in Paris.

A little American constituency was forming around her as well, alongside the French group and sometimes mingling with it. Throwing herself wholeheartedly into the social whirl, Edith arranged several lunch and dinner parties each week, and included at some of them were the Harry Whites (Edith had attended their first ambassadorial party and sat next to the Austrian ambassador); Edith's gregarious and much younger second cousin Le Roy King, who was much in Paris these days; and M.F.

Coming in periodically from their country home, Le Bréau, on the road to Fontainebleau, were Walter and Matilda Gay. The latter, whom Edith had known since childhood, was the daughter of the popular and outspoken William Travers, a leading light of old New York society. She was a frail and most attractively stylized woman, with a long thin face and a thin, authoritative nose. If she did not inherit her father's wit, she exerted a presence in its way no less compelling; and she could, as well, be an unconscious source of amusement. Once when she had bought a powerful new automobile, she remarked to Edith: "Yes, I believe that it has the power of 40 horses, but of course I don't allow our chauffeur to make use of them all." People were tremendously fond of her.

Walter Gay, a well-known figure in Paris and notably hospitable to visitors from home, was gaining a good reputation as a painter with a subtle eye for color and light. He did quite exquisite interior scenes, but his best works were vigorous architectural watercolors: some of these would shortly be on exhibit at the Georges Petit Gallery. Walter took life perhaps with less severity than Matilda; certainly he was a less devout Catholic. When he would make gestures toward skipping Sunday morning Mass, Matilda—after a silence in which icicles could be felt forming—would begin to ask in a sepulchral voice: "Walter, can it be . . ." Walter hastily prepared to accompany her.

Other old friends reintroduced themselves: James Van Alen, the Whartons' escort on the Aegean cruise in the late 1880s; Giraud Foster, in whose colossal mansion in Lenox Edith had been an occasional visitor; Comtesse Jane d'Oillamson. Edith had known the comtesse years before as the Princesse de Polignac in Cannes, the daughter of yet another American woman married into the French nobility. Jane was now the wife of an immensely rich French *aristo*, but she had a good deal of money of her own, beginning with a pension of six thousand francs established by Louis XVI in requital for the accidental killing, on a hunt, of one of Jane's ancestors by the dauphin. Jane proposed occupying her time by translating a few of Edith Wharton's stories into French. They settled down together on "The Reckoning," the sad tale of the emancipated Julia Westfall, who, after jettisoning one husband on the proclaimed principle of being faithful to one's sexual urgings, is herself set aside by her second husband on the same grounds.

6

Over this entire period, from Christmas to the middle of February, Morton Fullerton, in an idiom of the day, had made her no sign. They had been together frequently enough. Fullerton was constantly at lunch or dinner, with other guests or by himself; he came to tea, bringing André Tardieu; he dropped in of an afternoon, or in the evening after staying late at the Chamber of Deputies. He dined with Edith and Le Roy King and accompanied them to *La figlia di Iorio:* "unforgettable hours," Edith wrote in her diary. They talked together at length about his still unfinished essay on Henry James. But he said nothing to renew the intimate communion Edith had been so sure they had created at Lenox.

"I thought after all I had been mistaken," she told him forlornly in her journal. Picking up the theme from the Ronsard quotation, and employing her favorite image of herself, she said: "My poor *'âme close'* barred its shutters and bolted its doors again, and the dust gathered and the cobwebs thickened in the empty rooms, where for a moment I had heard an echo." She thought of leaving Paris for a trip to the south.

Fullerton, if the truth be told, had a good deal on his mind. He had scarcely returned to Paris the previous November before Henrietta Mirecourt began making another series of tempestuous demands: that he come back to live with her; better, that he marry her at once; and in any case that he again provide financial support. To these there were now added what for Fullerton were somewhat unnerving threats. During his absence in America (so one reconstructs the case), Henrietta, rifling through Fullerton's desk, had come upon a batch of potentially damaging letters. She understood their import with surprising facility, and she now proposed that, if Fullerton did not comply, she would publish abroad to his friends and to his family in Brockton the evidence that he had had an adulterous affair with the Ranee of Sarawak. More and worse, she also threatened to charge Fullerton with having had homosexual relations with Ronald Gower, a person known at one time, as it has been put, to be an uninhibited homosexual (though unlike his friend Oscar Wilde, he had stayed clear of public scandal).

The moment the danger became apparent, Fullerton wrote his old friend Henry James, giving him a guarded account of the situation and asking for a loan of money. James replied at once in a burst of sincerity, conveyed by a stammering complexity of syntax, to say there was a "portent of better days" in the mere fact of Fullerton's having at last and after so long spoken out about "what there was always a muffled unenlightened ache for my affection in not knowing." He advised Fullerton to sit tight and *do* nothing, except look for the money to buy Mme. Mirecourt off—as to which James himself was unable to help, sending instead his "ever so much wasted and wandering wealth of affection."

By return mail Fullerton sent an even more agitated letter. James, offering the wisdom of his own experience, urged Fullerton to "throw yourself on your work, on your genius, on your art, on your knowledge"; these would rescue him from his anxieties. But when Fullerton replied with another long cry of alarm, James, losing patience a little, took up the details of the case. Fullerton, he said, by living ill-advisedly under the same roof with Mme. Mirecourt, had been hypnotized into thinking she could have a really damaging effect upon him. She was, in James's view, no more than "a mad, vindictive and obscure old woman" with whom Fullerton had lived for a few years and who was now only "wreaking her fury" at Fullerton for not marrying her, as it was incredible that he should do.

Letters to Fullerton's family, James was sure, would be burned on the spot. And nobody else would even listen to the particular accusations:

> No one will *touch*, or listen to, e.g., anything with the name of the Ranee in it. . . . As for R.G., he is very ancient history, and, I think, has all the appearance today of a regular member of society, with his books and writings everywhere, his big monument (not so bad) to Shakespeare one of the principle features of Stratford on Avon.

Fullerton was quite aware that the report of his affairs with Margaret Brooke and Ronald Gower would be no news whatever to his parents. In one of the most forthright letters a clergyman father can ever have written to a wayward son, Bradford Fullerton in May 1904 had outlined Morton's erotic career. After alluding to "the two or three early love episodes in this country which seem to be excusable because of your youth," he went on to list the European adventures: "the lamentable Kellogg affair. Afterwards Percy Anderson, Lord Gower etc. associations, the dangerous complications with Lady Brooke . . . and the cruel Gould matter in which you had proceeded even to house-hunting. Within the last few years, Mme. Mirecourt has reigned supreme with you," even though Morton was legally married to Camille Chabert.

It is not clear why Fullerton was so disturbed by Henrietta's threats, especially since he seems to have invariably confided to each new mistress or lover the names of their predecessors. Perhaps he shrank from the thought of his parents actually perusing the letters from Margaret Brooke (and presumably from Gower, though these are not extant) and of having his habitual methods of courtship made public. In fairness, it may be added that he might also have been recalling his promise to Margaret to guard her reputation.

After a brief passage of time, Fullerton could tell James that matters looked more hopeful. He was not actually living in the same apartment with Mme.

Mirecourt, he explained, but only in the same building, so as (he insisted defensively) to keep an eye on her. With regard to this particular affair, he was slowly recovering his equilibrium, though, he feared, trouble might erupt again at any time. But as winter arrived and 1907 gave way to 1908, there was someone else on Fullerton's conscience, and perhaps more worryingly than Henrietta Mirecourt.

This was Katharine Fullerton, the young woman who had been brought up in the Fullerton household believing herself to be Morton's sister, but who had belatedly learned that she was in fact his first cousin. Katharine, born in 1879, was fourteen years younger than Morton (there was another brother, Rob, a businessman, married and the father of two). From the time she was a child she had worshiped the man she thought to be her older brother: at the age of six, when Morton was at Harvard, she sent him a carefully printed note vowing that "I will learn very much and be clever and wise write stories for the papers." It was Morton who directed her education at school and later at Radcliffe, which she entered in 1896: passing judgment on her program of courses with Mr. Copeland, Mr. Wendell, Mr. Santayana, insisting that despite her initial aversion she read widely in Henry James, seeing to it that the taboo writings of the French novelists came into her hands, and in every way encouraging her literary ambitions.

By the time she graduated in 1900, the six-year-old's promise was beginning to be fulfilled. She was a cultivated and articulate—as well as an intense, romantic, and inward—young woman, and she launched her career by winning the *Century* prize for the best short story by a recent college graduate.

During her senior year at Radcliffe, Katharine's feelings for Morton, poured out in letter after letter, grew markedly more serious. "My brother, whom I love absolutely," she addressed him, and writing to him at Rennes, where he was covering the Dreyfus trial, she told him: "My latest paradise is a place where we shall be together." Two months later, in October 1899, she was expressing her belief that "of all the relations of friendship in the world . . . that of brother and sister seems to me to contain the most elements of perfection."

But six weeks after that, in a long open-hearted letter, she was viewing their relationship in a different light. She had changed in recent months, Katharine said; she was becoming a woman; she could say things she would not have dared to utter only a little time earlier.

> It is not the ordinary relation of brother and sister, still less is it the friendship conventionally known as "Platonic." It would never have been, if we were not brother and sister, but it is as far as possible from the usual feeling of brother and sister for each other. . . . You will always be, as you have been, my beloved and reverenced older brother (no one knows what, in that role, you have been to me), but now I am a woman, and I claim you for my friend, my comrade. . . . You know that nothing can ever prevent me from being, heart and soul and mind—your loving Katharine.

Katharine spent another year at Radcliffe earning a Master's degree, and following this she accepted a position as reader in English at Bryn Mawr College. It was in her second or third year at Bryn Mawr—probably in 1903—that she learned that she was an adopted child. She was the daughter of Bradford Fullerton's younger brother, and hence not Morton's sister but his first cousin.

The discovery removed the last barrier to an entirely honest statement—to herself as well as to her adoptive brother—of her feeling for Morton. She was inclined at first, in the fullness of her joy, to be gay-spirited and sportive: "I love you so much that nothing matters or could matter. I should always love you. Does that do you any good, I wonder? It may some day, when you have broken all the Ten Commandments" and been cast out by society. But then there came the shattering revelation that Morton had married Camille Chabert. Four years later Katharine could still confess that the whole period had been a ghastly one and that she would never get over it. Even after the divorce, and with a stretch of somber wit, she said that she felt as if she were Morton's widow—"in the sense Meredith meant when he said of the hero of *Vittoria* that merely to have known him was, for all women, a kind of widowhood."

In October 1907, when Fullerton came to America, carrying with him James's letter enjoining him to visit Mrs. Wharton at The Mount, he made Bryn Mawr his first stop. They talked long in Katharine's rooms in Low Building, and hitherto unacknowledged emotions came slowly into the open. Morton told Katharine that he was in love with her and had been for years, that he could have made the confession "ten years ago, five years ago, one year ago." He insisted, with the gentle sadness that had proved so irresistible to so many women, that "without marriage, there is no life for you nor for me." They engaged themselves to each other, and agreed to meet in a few days in Brockton to discuss it all with the older Fullertons. Morton thereupon left for Lenox.

Edith Wharton, consequently, was intuitive in drawing a portrait, in "The Pretext," of a young man coming from abroad to pay court to an older married woman as a device for affiancing himself to another young lady. Katharine and Morton were, it seems, formally engaged at Brockton: the understandably skeptical elder Fullertons were persuaded to give their approval and consent. But undefined difficulties remained—something, Katharine imperfectly understood, to do with affairs in Paris. She was willing to wait.

But she found herself in a storm of feeling. Though long since informed of their true blood relationship, she continued to invoke her old name for him, as with a kind of *frisson* of pleasure: "My darling brother, you have only to bid me live and I will live; only to bid me die, and I will die. . . . If I could choose, my brother, I would choose, held close in your arms, to die—our breaths falling at the same instant." On the evening of November 1, while Morton was saying his good-byes to the others, Katharine sat in the living room writing a letter to him: "There is nothing to say except that I love and love and love you; that I trust you to the end of time. . . . Remember, darling. *Souviens toi de mes baisers quand tu es loin de moi.*" During a weekend by herself, while Morton was at sea, she tried to take stock, feeling at one moment that her very identity was dissolving in passion, and at another that she had been granted the treasures of the earth. "You did me the honour, I believe, to fall in love with me? Then to me 'the kingdom and the power and'—ah, I won't take to myself words meant for God, *par exemple!* We need God, you and I, more than most people." She ended, as regularly, by beseeching him to destroy her letter, but it is hard to blame Fullerton for not destroying these heart-filled documents.

Morton, writing twice a week from Paris in the waning year, oscillated in his customary manner between expressions of idealized love and declarations of strong physical desire. He kept coming back to "our strange and romantic story" ("and it's all you love me for, that so romantic story," Katharine told him fondly), and became lyrical over how "wonderful in its wretchedness as is our fate." He had proposed earlier that Katharine should be to him as Beatrice to Dante, and Katharine had rebelled: "I will not be your Beatrice, to triumph in some fantastic heaven. You shall have me—flesh and blood on this earth." Now he sent her a letter of such undisguised passion that it shook her to the core. "The mere saying of your written words made my heart beat suffocatingly fast. It means more than all the figurative sense of it has ever meant—that *you can make this heart of flesh beat loud and fast,* by telling me your passion for me. It frightened me: that flush of emotion." And she came back, time and again, to the urgent question: "I do not know what, with perfect feminine grace, a woman may ask a man—tell a man; but I beg you, so soon as it is right and possible, to marry me. I would not beg it of you if you had not begged it of me."

Morton let her know about the distracting harassment from Mme. Mirecourt —"the sordid and painful maneuvers," as Katharine called them, assuring him of her confidence that he would triumph over them nobly. He sent her Henry James's letters on the subject. "They are right and wonderful, those letters," Katharine agreed. *"He* is right and wonderful." Even worse than those difficulties as obstacles to her happiness was the atmosphere in the Fullerton household, where during a Christmas visit Katharine felt "flayed alive." Bradford and Julia were again looking askance at the entire situation. Could they not see that it was inevitable? Quoting her childhood note to Morton, Katharine said: "Why didn't they see . . . that I was as done for at six as I am at eight-and-twenty?" Julia alternated chatter about the details of the wedding breakfast with a survey of Morton's amorous escapades over the previous decade, and explained to Katharine that it was purely a matter of chance that Morton had "taken pity" on her.

Katharine felt a lurking suspicion of the accuracy of such insinuations, and she was seized with racking doubts about her own worthiness and as to whether they ever would in fact be married. Morton seemed clearly to be cooling.

7

In Paris, as the winter weeks wore on, Fullerton began to emerge from his various entanglements sufficiently to concentrate more of himself on Edith Wharton. As to Henrietta Mirecourt, he had once more escaped, for the time being, by following James's advice and doing nothing. To his fiancée, waiting miserably back at Bryn Mawr, his letters grew infrequent, brief, and evasive. He was, to say the least, a man who lived almost entirely in the moment, and by mid-February 1908 the moment was represented by Edith Wharton and 58 Rue de Varenne.

On February 12, Teddy Wharton went down for a stay at Beaulieu with Rafe and Lise Curtis. The next afternoon Fullerton lunched alone with Edith and remained for several hours of talk about plans for a variety of outings. On the cloudy afternoon of the fifteenth they drove up to Herblay, and their relationship took a definite turn.

It should be explained at this point that during the first half of 1908 Edith kept two separate and overlapping "diaries." The first, begun the previous October in Lenox, is a private *journal*, written in a plain hardbound notebook. The first thirty-odd pages have been ripped out: no doubt they contained the "spasmodic attempts" of an earlier time she mentioned in the first entry. The journal is addressed to Morton Fullerton in the second person, and it deals exclusively with the growth of their relationship. Edith conceived of this journal as a narrative, with a definite theme. She gave it a title, "The Life Apart," which was her rendering of the phrase from Ronsard which was currently haunting her and which she added here in parentheses: *"L'Ame Close."*

The other is a standard page-a-day *diary*. It is headed "Paris. 58 Rue de Varenne," and it begins with the passages from Ronsard and Tigri already quoted. In the diary Edith recorded the daily weather and Fahrenheit temperature; listed the various individuals she entertained day by day and those she encountered in the Faubourg and elsewhere; and described briefly the lectures and plays she attended. The entries contain little of a private nature—with one major exception.

Filtered through the pages are allusions to M.F., and sometimes her afterthoughts about particular moments with him. Many of these are in German, as though, by speaking of Fullerton in a language not only other than English but other than that of the city and country in which they both resided, she could set their relationship at a distance, distinguish it from all the rest of her ongoing life, almost, in a sense, enshrine it. After the evening together at the D'Annunzio play, she had written: *"Unvergessliche stunden"* ("unforgettable hours"). And she recorded in German Fullerton's reading aloud to her his essay on James: *"Er kam um 5 Uhr and wir lasen sein Aufsatz uber H.J. Er blieb bis 7."* ("He came at 5 o'clock, and we read his essay on H.J. He stayed until 7.")

Saturday, February 15, Edith reminded Fullerton in her journal, was "a cold, sad winter day, with the wind beating the bare trees, and a leaden Seine between brown banks." They left Paris after an early lunch, driving west up the steep curving road that led through the regal village of St. Germain-en-Laye and beyond it through the well-stocked forest of St. Germain. They paused at Conflans (the confluence of the Seine and Oise rivers) to inspect the beguiling and unpretentious church, with its commanding view of the Seine and the slowly moving river traffic. They drove on to Herblay, a few miles to the east, and here they left the car with Cook in the village square at the foot of a hill and walked up to the church. It stood on a high promontory next to a small grassy cemetery, and through the bare branches of the trees they could see the Seine dividing around wooded islands, and far off, the dark mass of the forest.

The vaulted church, with its twelfth-century steeple and sixteenth-century choir and nave, was not without interest, but their quest that afternoon was literary rather than architectural. They had come to find the home of Hortense Allart, a little-remembered early nineteenth-century French novelist. Edith admired her to some degree, despite her lack of "long vibrations"; but she appealed to Edith even more because of her energetic adulteries—she was the mistress of Chateaubriand and Bulwer-Lytton among others—and the candor with which she discussed her experiences in her letters. Hortense Allart was added to Edith's growing list of talented and unconventional women, headed by George Sand; and although Henry James expressed impatience with Mlle. Allart's unending talk about her "copulations," he confessed, on being informed of the visit, that "I ache to have been—or not to have been at Herblay with you and Fullerton—fancy there being a second and *intenser* Nohant."

Fullerton, conversing with the *curé* inside the church, discovered that the priest had never heard of the village's one literary celebrity. Edith was periodically discovering, and forced thereby to modify her views of the French, that country-people in France often knew nothing of the great ones who had lived near them. The visitors later decided that Hortense must have lived in a little house opposite the church and had enjoyed from her garden the same fine vista of the river and the islands.

Seated in a quiet corner of the dim nave, watching Fullerton make his inquiries, Edith felt a special richness in the moment, and was suddenly conscious of a surge of unaccustomed or forgotten emotion. She indulged herself in the fancy that a veiled figure stole up to look at her, and wondered whether its name might possibly be "happiness." That evening when she wrote her account of the visit to Herblay, Edith invoked for the first time the simple German phrase she would always use to indicate an experience of deepening intimacy with Fullerton:

"Wir waren zusammen" ("We were together"). She concluded by citing line 48 from Canto XXX of Dante's *Purgatorio*, which (carrying as it does the additional echo of Dido's admission of sexual desire in the *Aeneid*) formulated her sense of the stir of feeling within her: " *'Conosco i segni dell'antica fiamma'* " ("I recognize the tokens of the ancient flame").

Very different, and yet another stage in their evolving relationship, was an exchange two evenings later. Edith, after going with Matilda Gay to a Dante reading and taking tea at the Duchesse de Trevisée's with an assortment of comtesses and baronnes, entertained Fullerton at supper. *"Er kam zum aben-dessen,"* she wrote, and then, shifting back to Dante, " *'Quel giorno più . . .'* "

The phrase comes from the Paolo and Francesca episode in the *Inferno*, but Edith quoted it—with a mixture, one imagines, of irony and frustration—to an effect opposite to that of Dante. In the *Commedia*, Francesca, a young married woman, is explaining to Dante how it came about that she and her lover Paolo had yielded to sexual impulse. One afternoon they were reading together the story of Lancelot and Guinevere, and it so aroused their own erotic feelings that before long they let the book drop and fell to the sin of adultery:

> *La bocca mi baciò tutto tremante:*
> *Galeotto fu il libro, e chi lo scrisse;*
> *Quel giorno più non vi leggemmo avante.*

> (He kissed my mouth all trembling:
> A Galeotto was the book, and he who wrote it;
> That day we read no further.)

What happened in Edith's living room was something quite otherwise.

"At first it was exquisite," Edith wrote. Fullerton, seated near the lamp, began to read aloud from an article on George Meredith by André Chevrillon, a nephew of the great philosophical historian Hippolite Taine and the author of several books on English literature; Edith had just come to know him personally. She sat nearby with her sewing, exhilarated by the movement of Fullerton's mind as it singled out the "finer values" in the article that she herself had missed, as it "discriminated, classified, with that flashing, illuminating sense of differences and relations that so exquisitely distinguishes your thought."

> Ah, the illusion I had, of a life in which such evenings might be a dear accepted habit! At that moment, indeed, "the hour became her husband."

And then Fullerton broke the spell by saying something, saying several things apparently, that distressed and confused her. He seems to have made, and a little too rapidly, one of his characteristic swings from the intellectual to the erotic. The special quality of mental communion was shattered; and yet, after Fullerton had taken his departure, Edith felt to her bewilderment more emotionally bound to him than ever.

Why did you spoil it? Because men and women are different, because—in that respect—in the way of mental companionship—what I can give you is so much less interesting, less arresting, than what I receive from you? It was as if there stood between us at that moment the frailest of glass cups, filled with a rare colourless wine—and with a gesture you broke the glass and spilled the drops.

You hurt me—you disillusioned me—and when you left me I was more deeply yours . . . Ah, the confused processes within us!

Fullerton, she thought, unsatisfied in his masculine way with a mere union of minds, was demanding of her something that she had no capacity to engage in, no real experience of. She felt, simultaneously, eager to invite him into a closer kind of intimacy and frightened that, if he responded, she would fail him. Such ambivalence was the import of the "Herblay sonnet," which she wrote seated alone later the same evening, and in which she tried to organize her contradictory emotions about the state of things between them.

It, too, is called "Ame Close," and draws upon the familiar house image. She likened her soul to an abandoned house wherein no light can be seen by those dwelling nearby. Its owners, the neighbors say, must long since have died or departed. The door latch is rusted and covered with ivy; the chimney rises coldly against the sky; the flowers have turned to weeds, the paths have decayed.

> Yet one stray passer, at the shut of day,
> Sees a light trembling in a casement high.
>
> Even so, my soul would set a light for you,
> A light invisible to all beside,
> As though a lover's ghost should yearn, and glide
> From pane to pane, to let the flame shine through.
> Yet enter not, lest as it flits ahead,
> You see the hand that carries it is dead.

12. The Journal

Teddy Wharton came back from Beaulieu on February 21, and opportunities for Edith and Fullerton to be alone together were scarce. There was need, in any event, for the greatest discretion, and life was constantly intruding to dash Edith's hopes. On the twenty-second the two had planned to drive down for the day to Montfort l'Amaury, thirty kilometers south of the city, on the road to Chartres. But Jane d'Oillamson called to suggest a long afternoon and evening of work on the translation of "The Reckoning," and Edith could think of no excuse to put her off. She sent "a vague note" to Fullerton postponing the trip; Fullerton was hurt, and Edith was disappointed to the verge of desperation. "How can I ever dream that life has in store for me a single moment of happiness?" she asked him in her journal.

> This is the day on which we were to go to M . . . l'A . . . a whole day together in the country!—I said to myself all the week: "I have never in my life known what it was to be happy (as a woman knows happiness) even for a single hour—now at last I shall be happy for a whole day, talking *à coeur ouvert*, saying for once what I feel and *all that I feel*, as other women do." *Ah, pauvre âme close! Y ai-je vraiment cru un seul instant? Non, je savais trop bien que quand il s'agit de moi les Erynnies ne dorment, jamais, hélas* . . . ["Ah, poor shut-in soul! Did I really believe in it for an instant? No, I knew only too well that when it comes to me, the Furies never sleep, alas!"]

The soft springlike day, she went on, was "some other woman's day, not mine." In her diary she quoted the refrain of one of the favorite poems of her childhood, Joseph Schliffel's "Der Trompette Peter von Säckingen": "God keep you! It would have been too beautiful. God keep you, it was not to be!"

There was only the occasional moment, sometimes the accidental moment, to be seized and treasured. A few evenings later, after dining at the Café Anglais, Edith went on with the Bourgets to the Renaissance to see Lucien Guitry perform in a play called *La Femme nue*, and Fullerton joined them for an act. "*Ach Gott—Gott,*" Edith murmured in a kind of anguished ecstasy in the diary; and to Fullerton in the journal she confided:

> The other night at the theater, when you came into the box—that little, dim beignoire (No. 13, I shall always remember!)—I felt for the first time that indescribable current of communication flowing between myself and some one else—felt it, I mean,

uninterruptedly, securely, so that it penetrated every sense and every thought . . . and said to myself: "This must be what happy women feel."

Her whole being was beginning to vibrate to the longed-for but entirely novel sensation of human intimacy. There was another half hour of happy and unexpected closeness the following Sunday, after Edith and Teddy had driven across the river to St. Cloud to lunch with André Chevrillon and his wife. Fullerton was there, along with Robert d'Humières and the Frank Bakers; Harry Jones came by to drive Teddy back to Paris, and Edith and Fullerton returned together. Snow was falling in the afternoon dusk, and the flakes froze on the car windows. Edith had the sense of being beautifully shut away with Fullerton from the rest of the world, and that, in their privacy, her true nature was revealing itself at last to the man beside her.

I felt your *dearest* side then, the side that is simple and sensitive and true . . . and I felt that all that must have been, at first, so unintelligible to you in me and in my life, was clear at last, and that our hearts and our minds met.

Such evanescent moments of womanly happiness were, Edith suspected, the most that life would ever accord her, and she was half willing to accept the fact. "I should like to be to you, friend of my heart," she told Fullerton with romantic wistfulness, "like a touch of wings brushing by you in the darkness, or like the scent of an invisible garden, that one passes on an unknown road at night." But the resolve belies itself in part by the literary quotation Edith smuggled into it, perhaps unthinkingly. "Friend of my heart" is the mode of address by which Clelia Conti, in *The Charterhouse of Parma*, invites Fabrizio del Dongo after years of hesitation into her boudoir and into her bed, in the pitch darkness that permits her to keep her vow never to see him again.

For the time being, Fullerton could only be one of the many individuals whom Edith ran into during the frenetic round of social affairs or whom she invited with others to lunch or dinner. The phrase *Er kam* shows up repeatedly in the diary, but usually he came with company: on March 8, for example, with Jane d'Oillamson, Charles du Bos, and Le Roy King. However openly she might speak to him within the pages of her journal, their outward relations, in the drawing rooms and the theaters and at the tables, were determinedly casual and decorous. Fullerton indeed served to make Edith more aware of the banality of some of the larger social events, which, nonetheless, she continued to attend almost daily. On another March morning he turned up on their doorstep as the Whartons were going out and drove with them to the office of the *Revue de Paris*. "How happy, how blissful I always am when I am near him," she reflected in her diary German; by comparison, the big crowd at the American Embassy that afternoon seemed "horrid" to her.

It was an uncertain and unsettled period, and Edith was experiencing an ebb and flow of hope and happiness. In early March, when she was recovering from a bad cold which kept her in bed for several days, Fullerton came by to cheer her up; the visit left her feeling that she was being reborn emotionally as well as physically, and she inscribed in her diary: *"Qui comincia la vita nuova."* But "the new life" did not last very long; after another visit, during which Fullerton no doubt again exhibited his worldly and insistent as against his gentle and sensitive side, Edith summed up the afternoon as consisting of *"zwei traurige Stunden"* ("two sad hours"). The situation, however, was about to change.

On March 21 Teddy Wharton sailed for New York on the *Philadelphia*. His melancholy condition, despite some effort on his part, had remained virtually unchanged since their arrival in France three months before, and now he was also having "terrible sensations in his head," Edith told Sally Norton. It may be surmised, in the light of later developments, that his general physical and psychic unhappiness (whatever its other sources) was aggravated by the constant presence of Morton Fullerton and by Edith's responsiveness to her new friend. With Walter Berry, Teddy had had his own partly independent and cheery relationship; but it must have been evident that Fullerton came round almost entirely to see his wife. As to Edith, she was genuinely worried about Teddy; but he appears, in her references to him, more as a distracting burden than anything else, and as a person with whom she had otherwise very little to do. It was her husband's illness, she told Brownell, that prevented her from making much progress on her new novel. *Scribner's* wanted to begin serialization of *The Custom of the Country* in January 1909, but she now doubted she could meet that deadline.

To Edith's relief, Teddy's sufferings were diagnosed as being due completely to gout, and it was arranged that he should go to the fashionable Hot Springs, Arkansas, for the cure. Charles Scribner thought it odd that Mr. Wharton should be coming home for the cure: "that is something for which every one went abroad a few years ago"; but the plan had its attraction for Edith. The day after Teddy's departure, and following a lunch party that included M.F., her rising spirits were conveyed in a second evocation of the phrase *la vita nuova*. And such was her delight at the prospect of many hours alone with Fullerton—she was not expected back in Lenox until the end of May—that she also added another portion of Francesca's confession about her lapse into sin: " '*Galeotto fu il libro*' " If not itself a confession, literally, on Edith's part, it was at least a spirited declaration of intent.

She and Fullerton took to strolling amid the leafy shrubs and blooming crocuses of the Bois de Boulogne and in the woods of St. Cloud; they lunched together quietly; they attended the opening of Walter Gay's exhibition. Edith felt that the large throng in the gallery was rather too public a setting for them. But of a visit to Montmartre that same afternoon, when, bending over the high parapet side by side, they had studied the city of Paris spread out and closely packed below them as in an old map, she could say contentedly, *"Wir waren zusammen."* Fullerton was Edith's supper guest on April 7. In her diary for the day she filled out the line from Dante she had half-quoted in February, but in a voice from which irony had been banished by joy: " '*Non vi leggemmo avante.* ' "

A few days later, after her brother Harry Jones had left for America, Edith gave up the apartment in the Rue de Varenne and moved with her staff into Harry's comfortable *hôtel* in the Place des Etats-Unis. It was not far from the Arc de Triomphe, and was sufficiently distant from the attentive eyes (what in another context she called "the grave offending eyes") of the Faubourg. It was a portentous moment. For anyone whose imagination was as sensitive as Edith Wharton's to the dramatic significance of place, and especially change of place, this move carried a weight of symbolism and promise.

The postponed day in Montfort l'Amaury had finally taken place: a leisurely morning's drive through Pont Chartrain, a climb to the old château abreast the hill, lunch in a local hotel, a walk through the ancient burying ground. "We were together. Blissfully happy hours." Even more stirring, and somehow completing a circuit of emotion for her, was the long day of April 18, when, on a cold gray morning, they made the run of eighty kilometers southeast through Joinville and Brie to Provins—to the almost preternaturally quiet "old town" perched high above the modern village, and a wandering inspection of its aged tower and church, its fragmenting Roman wall, its peaceful lanes and gracefully compact town square. "We were together," she said again; and, underlining heavily, *"The sweetest hours of my life."*

Edith was now deeply, helplessly in love, and a prey to thoughts, emotions, desires she had never dreamed herself capable of and with which she scarcely knew how to deal. In her own view (and in that of most others), she had rigidly guarded herself against such emotional buffeting; she had created a personality severely immune to the enticing dangers of life. That personality was, suddenly, being swept away by Fullerton, but even as she clutched after it in bewilderment she was ravaged by the thought of their impending separation. "I didn't know what it would be like," she had written Fullerton in a letter, when she first felt the onset of the ancient flame; openly acknowledging at last the intensity of her love, she discovered it to be at once unbearably exalting and unbearably shattering.

"I have known 'what happy women feel,' " she wrote on April 20, "—with the pang, all through, every moment, of what heart-broken women feel!" The heartbreak was suffered in anticipation of the moment when she must leave Paris.

For a month now I have been here alone—in another month I shall be gone. *It will be over.* Those four words are always before me, day and night; and yet I don't understand them, they mean nothing to me . . . What! I shall be gone, I shan't see you, I shan't hear your voice, I shan't wake up to think: "In so many hours we shall meet, my hand will be in his, my eyes will be in his" . . . ? But what shall I *be* then? Nothing else lives in me but *you*—I have no conscious existence outside the thought of you, the feeling of you.

And she came back—in a manner very reminiscent of Katharine Fullerton only a few months before—to the way in which her slowly acquired strength of spirit had been devastated. "I, who dominated life, stood aside from it so, how I am humbled, absorbed, without a shred of will or identity left! All I want is to be near you, to feel my hands in yours. Ah, if you ever read these lines, you will know you have been loved!"

They were not yet lovers in the full physical meaning of the word, but Edith had moved well beyond the state of mind expressed in the "Herblay sonnet" where she feared, metaphorically, that the hand carrying the light through the abandoned house, as a signal to the lover without, was "dead." She had meant by this not so much that she might be too old for sexual adventure, but that her erotic nature had long since been fatally sealed away. But now the tremendous impact of Morton Fullerton and the resulting shock to her psychic being had sprung loose impulses buried deep from the time of her young womanhood.

What was shaken to the surface in particular were the two major impulses of her much younger life: the religious and the erotic impulse; and for a time, as both intensified within her, she oscillated between them. Fullerton, it seems, was pressing his court in his characteristic way, and felt that the hour had arrived for intellectual and aesthetic companionship to yield to a different kind of union. At one moment Edith resisted the plea on the grounds that the marriage of minds was closer and mystically truer than that of bodies; at another moment she longed almost uncontrollably for physical union.

Sometimes I am calm, exalted almost, so enclosed and satisfied in the thought of you, that I could say to you as I did yesterday: "I never wonder what you are doing when you are not with me." At such moments I feel as though all the mysticism in me—the transcendentalism that in other women turns to religion—were poured into my feeling for you, giving me a sense of *immanence*, of inseparableness from you.—In one of those moods, the other day, when you were reproaching me for never giving you any sign of my love for you, I felt like answering: "But there is a contact of thought that seems so much closer than a kiss" . . .

Then there are other days, tormented days—this is one of them—when that sense of mystic nearness fails me, when in your absence I long, I ache for you, I feel that what I want is to be in your arms, to be held fast there—"like other women!" And then comes the terrible realization of the fugitiveness of it all, the weariness of the struggle, the *à quoi bon?*, the failing courage, the mortal weakness—the blind cry: "I want you! I want you!" that bears down everything else . . .

And sometimes you say to me: "*Ah, si vous m'aimiez d'amour*"—*Si je vous aimais, mon amour!*"

It may be added that Fullerton had picked up the phrase *aimer d'amour*— as it were, to love with total self-giving love—from his cousin Katharine, who had employed it rather to his amusement in the first stages of their engagement and had explained that she herself had learned it from her old French teacher.

2

Despite such emotional upheaval, Edith joined with Fullerton in maintaining outward propriety and continued to display to the world an air of cool self-possession. One or two of her American friends in Paris came to have a dim awareness that something had developed between Fullerton and herself, but the members of her widening French circle never had the slightest inkling.

Had they done so, they might well have asked each other how on earth Mme. Wharton had the time to carry on any sort of liaison, considering the teeming nature of her social life. Her calendar of engagements was never more crowded, and not infrequently she took part in three or four different matters in the course of a single day. On April 13, as an example, after a morning walk she went to lunch at Durand's with an American couple; went to call on her cousin Herman Edgar and his wife; dropped in for tea at the home of Marie Lee Childe; worked with Jane d'Oillamson over more tea on the translation of "The Confessional" (Jane had also completed "Souls Belated"); entertained Egerton Winthrop, passing through Paris on his way to Rome; and dined with Rosa de Fitz-James, among the thirteen guests being Prince Gortchakoff, Abbé Mugnier, Charles du Bos, Jacques Emile Blanche, and Fullerton. During the day she also found time to move herself and her household from the Rue de Varenne to the Place des Etats-Unis.

The nobility continued to come trooping, and Edith to accept invitations to their elegant houses. In her autobiography she would speak deprecatingly of the more purely fashionable aspect of the old Faubourg, but her diary overflows with aristocratic names—she never referred to a *monsieur* when it was possible to identify him as a *duc*, a *marquis*, a *comte*. This was snobbery, to be sure, but of no simple sort.

Edith Wharton was not snobbish in the familiar American way—as perfectly described by a Boston visitor to New York in 1882 who had said of the New York girl: "She is afraid of her position. She 'does not know if she can know certain people.' . . . The Duchess of Sutherland can know anybody." Edith was, rather, *très snob* in the then contemporary Parisian manner, as was once said of Walter Berry by the Vicomte Charles de Noailles (a younger and remote relative-in-law of Anna de Noailles). When Berry saw a duchess, de Noailles has remarked, he saw two hundred years of duchesses. Edith did the same. It was her fondness for lineage and continuity that expressed itself; her snobbery was an integral part of her historical imagination. In Paris the former and (in American terms) well-born Edith Jones could do what was possible only in a limited and prosaic manner in her own American society. She could mingle with the living representatives of the oldest regimes.

Her French milieu was further solidifying itself as one social encounter followed another. Among her new friends were Comte Othenin d'Haussonville and his tall, imperiously beautiful wife, Comtesse Pauline. D'Haussonville, a courtly man with an ironic expression and a dangling monocle, was a member of the Académie Française; intellectually gifted noblemen forgathered in the *salon* on the Rue St. Dominique (which ran roughly parallel to the Rue de Varenne, three streets away). He could trace his ancestry back to the court of Louis XIV and beyond, but he was something of a liberal, politically speaking; he had given a certain ambiguous support to the cause of the Dreyfusards.

A very different friend, and before long a closer one, was Jacques Emile Blanche, a man of Edith's age and a gifted if unadventurous portrait painter. He was a hefty individual with a strong square jaw, and a fluent and malicious conversationalist, much of his talk being given to allusions to his aristocratic friends in France and even more (he was an Anglomaniac) in England. Edith quite enjoyed his genial pomposity.

After being introduced to Blanche in Rosa de Fitz-James's *salon,* Edith went with Morton Fullerton, on a cold and overcast Easter Sunday, to lunch at the Blanches' home in Passy. There she found a characteristic international assembly, with society and the arts equally represented. Violet Granby, the Duchess of Rutland, was among the guests: a quite delightful lady, conspicuous in London social circles and herself a portrait sketcher of considerable skill. There were also her daughter, the lovely Lady Marjorie Manners; Prince Brancovan, the Rumanian father of Anna de Noailles; Prince Antoine Bibesco, of a most cultivated noble family; and Henri Bernstein, a popular and pugnacious French playwright. Most interesting, perhaps, for Edith Wharton was the former Consuelo Vanderbilt, now the beautiful and unhappy wife of the Duke of Marlborough and the mistress of Blenheim Palace. Edith had known her a little, years before, at The Breakers, her parents' stupendous "cottage" in Newport.

Blanche was an acute observer and collector of modern painting, as well as an artist, a writer, and something of a musician. In the high-ceilinged living room where the guests were served tea, Edith Wharton had her first guided introduction to paintings by Degas, Manet, Corot, Renoir, and Whistler. In the upper gallery she was shown Blanche's portraits of celebrated literary contemporaries, the work on which his fame chiefly rests—among them, that Easter day, Thomas Hardy, George Moore, Aubrey Beardsley, and the lesser known Marcel Proust.

But of all her new French acquaintances the dearest to Edith's heart was the Abbé Arthur Mugnier, a little plump person of about fifty-five with bespectacled smiling eyes and a tuft of gray hair that leapt up from his forehead. Mugnier was probably the best-loved man in Paris, then and for several decades to come. He lived in deliberate poverty, but since 1896 he had been vicar of the ultrafashionable church of Ste. Clothilde, in the heart of the Seventh Arrondissement; and he was, as it has been said, the apostle to the Faubourg St. Germain. Clad in a rather disreputable soutane (he only had two), he appeared constantly in the great *salons,* where he was the gentle but resolute arbiter of opinions and where his soft sayings were handed around like gems. Edith thought she had never known anyone in whom the keenest intelligence so combined with inexhaustible kindness. When asked once if he believed in hell, the abbé replied: "Yes, because it is a dogma of the Church—but I don't believe there is anyone in it."

This witty saint was an immensely well-read lover of literature, and he concerned himself in particular with the state of grace of his many literary friends, beginning with Huysmann, whom he converted in 1892; it was said that the most convinced atheist was in danger in Abbé Mugnier's presence. But he also had a profound compassion for the poor ("he throws communion-bread to the sparrows," Bourget grumbled), and a year after Edith met him he was given every chance to exercise it. He fell from favor after trying to reconvert an unfrocked married priest, and was sent into the Paris wilderness as an almoner to a mission in the Fourteenth Arondissement. But he made his way back to the Faubourg tables with regularity, and much later a fund (in which Edith joined) was raised to supply him with a daily taxicab for the journey.

While visits to the *salons* and dinner engagements *chez les heureux du monde* were providing a satisfaction to Edith's social appetite and a distraction for her troubled spirit, she continued to be much in the company of other Americans. It would not be long before Henry Adams (himself due in Paris in a fortnight) could say: "Our little American family-group here is more closely intimate and more agreeably intelligent, than any now left me in America . . . [and] Edith Wharton is almost the center of it."

The *hôtel* in the Place des Etats-Unis was becoming a home away from home for old friends. Willie Buckler came in from Madrid for a few days and was promptly invited to lunch. Clyde Fitch was in town and came around for an hour or two. Egerton Winthrop returned for a week's stay; Edith toured the galleries with him and had him to tea and dinner. Moncure Robinson showed up, followed by the affable Eliot Gregory. On the Tuesday after Easter, Edith was hostess at lunch to Charles Scribner, Gregory, and Fullerton.

The next day Edith drove out with the Courtlandt Bishops, friends from Lenox, to Issy-les-Moulineaux to watch the testing of a new Voisin biplane, piloted by an enthusiastic sportsman named Léon Delagrange. The strong winds (April was still stubbornly wintry) made the test less than satisfactory, but Edith was fascinated with this latest twentieth-century invention and was gratified when Delagrange showed her about the airplane. (Two months later he set a new French record by flying more than fifteen miles in half an hour.) On Friday evening, April 24, Edith and Gregory went to the Gare du Nord to meet Henry James.

3

For several months James had been adamant about the impossibility of his coming to Paris. He had been full of happy hyperbole about Edith's settling there —"a most majestic manoeuvre," he called it, which displayed "an almost insolent *maîtrise* of life." But he was resolutely determined not to stir from Lamb House.

> Your silver-sounding toot that invites me to the car—the wondrous-cushioned *general* car of your so wondrously india-rubber-tyred and deep-cushioned fortune—echoes for me but too mockingly in the dim, if snug, cave, of my permanent *retraite.*

He was definitely on the shelf, he assured her; but from the shelf he would watch the proceedings on the Rue de Varenne, enthralled and envious:

> I shall watch you on the Aubusson carpet! Dear old Aubusson carpet—what a more and more complex minuet will it see danced with the rich Oriental note of Rosa flushing through (doubtless more closely still) and binding and linking the figures! What sequences you will see to what beginnings, and into what deeper depths of what abysses you will find yourself interested to gaze.

James concluded this elaborate hilarity by urging Edith to persuade Walter Berry to come over from Washington and join the fun, if only so that he, James, might receive a regular account of the doings. As to Fullerton, James was uncertain what part he might play: "he's so incalculable."

James's interest in Edith's literary career, meanwhile, had taken the form for a brief period of his proposing to write an article about her in connection with *The Fruit of the Tree*—of addressing a few thousand words "to the mystery of your genius." (This sounded, Edith remarked to Brownell, asking him to send the novel to James, "as if he meant to make mincemeat of me.") A literary agent in New York had told James that Mrs. Wharton had indicated a desire that he write about her work. Edith, when informed, denied with some indignation that she had ever said any such thing, and James soon agreed that the claim was "really, evidently, a barefaced lie, and, as I judge, a common trick of the trade." But he still wanted to write something if invited to by the *Atlantic Monthly* or the *North American Review:* "I *want* to enthuse over you, I yearn to, quite." Having now read *The Fruit of the Tree*, he could not enthuse over it without reservation. It was infirm in its composition, he told Edith candidly and accurately; nonetheless, "you have to my mind produced a remarkably rich and accomplished and distinguished work of more kinds of interest than anyone now going can pretend to achieve." The article was never written.

In the same letter (of the previous November), James reiterated his determination not to come to France, then or ever: "The truth is I shall never, never, never cross the channel again." Warding off Edith's continued solicitations, he combined a word of welcome as she was about to reach Paris in December with another refusal: he sent her greetings as she "set foot on the dear old Crimson Carpet even at the cost of seeming wantonly to remind you that *my* feet are no more to know that softness." But by the turn of the year he was beginning to change his mind.

He had completed one major portion of the enormously demanding work on what would be known as the New York edition of his fiction; and, more immediately important, he had written a light comedy that "may have on my scant fortunes, a far-reaching effect." The play, under the guidance of Forbes Robertson, was to be presented in Edinburgh in March and, if successful, to be brought to London in May. In between, he might be able to come to her for fifteen days.

The great observer's appetite had been whetted by Edith's accounts of the Paris scene. "It's horrible," James said, "not to know the Minnie-Paul, the 'Charley,' the d'Humières, the *Fullerton-Hervieu.*" If he underlined the latter names, it was to convey his sense, slyly, that something was now afoot with Morton Fullerton; Edith had let on more than she realized. "What you tell me of your seeing dear Fullerton, whom I am really very fond of, gives me the greatest pleasure," he wrote her; and (in early March, after hearing of the trip to Herblay and the search for Hortense Allart) "I rejoice afresh—*tell* him please—that you have dear Fullerton a little 'on toast.' "

He agreed finally to come over in the third week of April. Edith suggested that they join up in Amiens and asked if he would mind Fullerton's being with them. "It will be adorable to have W.M.F.," James replied. "Kindly tell him so with my love." And Amiens was a splendid meeting place. It was decided, however, that James should come directly to Paris. There was only one thing about which James professed anxiety—Edith's bright allusions to the many people in Paris who kept asking about him. "Let me say, alas, that it is just those admirable and amiable enquiries for 'cher James' that profoundly terrify me in advance." He begged for a minimum of social activity. "Let me come please incognito—masked wholly in motor goggles—removable for Rosa—once."

Edith responded to this plea by limiting James to a mere dozen social events during the first week of his stay. Some of these were small affairs. There was only Gregory at lunch the first day, and only Fullerton at dinner; in between, Edith and James went to a theatrical exposition and took tea with a Mme. de Gheest. The next day, after Fullerton had come to lunch, the three of them went to the Blanches' Sunday open house in Passy, where *cher James* consorted with Rosa de Fitz-James and a good many others. They were back at the Place des Etats-Unis in time to receive Harry White and six or seven additional guests; in the evening they joined a large and resplendent assembly at Rosa's which included the d'Haussonvilles and Prince Gortchakoff, as well as Abbé Mugnier and Alfred de St. André. They were again at Rosa's three nights later in a goodly company, among it Countess Hohenfelsen, the wife of Grand Duke Paul of Russia. There were also more modest dinner parties at the Embassy and at the home of the du Bos', and small lunches in the apartment.

At Passy, Edith had helped persuade James to sit for a portrait by Jacques Emile Blanche, and James spent part of each of the next few afternoons in Blanche's studio. The immediate result, James thought, made him look " 'brainy' and awful"; but Blanche later redid it with the help of photographs, and when James saw it exhibited in London he conceded that it had "a certain dignity of intention." Edith, proud of her part in the enterprise (she may have paid for it, if anyone did), always regarded it as the best portrait of Henry James ever done.

4

A letter from Fullerton, written the night before on lined notebook paper in a restaurant near his office, was delivered every morning with Edith's breakfast tray. It provided an exquisite daily ritual: the letter left unopened while she poured the tea, savoring as long as she could "the joy that is coming"; the little silver knife slipped cautiously under the flap of the envelope (nothing must be torn); and then—

the first glance to see how many pages there are, the second to see how it ends, the breathless first reading, the slow lingering over each phrase and each word, the taking possession, the absorbing of them one by one, and finally the choosing of the one that will be carried in one's thoughts all day, making an exquisite accompaniment of the dull prose of life.

These letters have not survived, but from others of Fullerton's that have, one may readily guess that they were devoted to close readings of their relationship, now lyrical and allusive, now fiery, now dilating on the grandeur of their love: and all this adapted to the special personality—as Fullerton imperfectly understood it— of Edith Wharton.

On Edith's part, she felt that their shared love was the fulfillment of every experience of beauty in her past life and every thwarted desire to communicate that experience, to participate in it with another person. Having fallen passionately in love for the first time, in her mid-forties, she knew a desperate need to seize wholly on every passing phase of it, as though in requital for the lost years. "How I see in all this the instinctive longing to pack every moment of my present with all the wasted driven-in feeling of the past! One should be happy in one's youth to be happy freely, carelessly, *extravagantly!*"

Even the occasional poems she had written out of her imagination and long before she had met Fullerton—"when a wave of Beauty rushed over me, and I felt that *I must tell some one!*"—now seemed to her anticipations of her feelings about him. One such was "Artemis to Actaeon," a poetic monologue published in *Scribner's* six years before. Edith wrote Burlingame asking him to send her a copy; rereading it, she found in it a precise statement of the impulse that was gripping her, to crowd a lifetime into a single moment of passion. To the mortal Actaeon in the poem, the goddess Artemis says that his rash attempt to spy upon her while she is bathing naked shows his desire

> to reach the heart of life, and lie
> Bosom to bosom in occasion's arms.

She will grant him his wish and join herself to him in love, though it will mean his death (in the classical legend, Actaeon is changed into a stag and destroyed by his own hounds). But he will experience the only immortality available to humans, which is

> to drink fate's utmost at a draught,
> Nor feel the wine grow stale upon the lips,
> To scale the summit of some soaring moment,
> Nor know the dulness of the long descent.

Edith's thoughts about Fullerton and those she exchanged with him were ever more strongly colored by emotion. She had spoken to him knowingly enough about "the thoughts that are closer than a kiss"; and when one afternoon she had said something that led him to exclaim: "Oh, the joy of *seeing round things together!*" she was sure he understood what she had meant by the phrase. But she was also, as she acknowledged, beginning to perceive "how thought may be dissolved in feeling," and simultaneously how feeling may be magnified and clarified by thought, as in the line she quoted from Dante: " *'Donne che avete l'inteletto d'amore'* " ("You women who have the intellectual intuition of love").

These were the meditations of calmer moments. More often, as the days passed, she felt simply consumed, in her own metaphor, by the blaze of her passion. She looked again, with growing incredulity, even with a certain *pudeur,* at what had become of her former self.

Malgré moi, I am a little humbled, a little ashamed to find how poor a thing I am, how the personality I had moulded into such firm lines has crumbled to a pinch of ashes in this flame!

Not only was she unable to write a line of fiction, she was no longer even able to read: "I hold the book in my hand, and see your name all over the page." Her self-assurance, previously, had been integrally related to her proud sense of herself as a woman; but now she was wondering, a little appalled, whether it might not be the destiny of women to find their individuality blotted out by love.

I am stupefied, *anéantie* . . . There lies the profound difference between man and woman. What enlarges and enriches life for the one eliminates everything but itself for the other. Now and then I say to myself: *"Je vais me ressaisir"*—*mais saisir quoi?* ["I must take hold of myself." But take hold of what?] This pinch of ashes that slips through my fingers? Oh, my free, proud, secure soul, where are you? *What were you*, to escape me like this?

On the first of May, Edith drove with James and Fullerton to Beauvais for the day. Fullerton had not wanted to go, maintaining a little sulkily that with James along it would not be like their excursions *à deux*. Edith, humbling herself, begged him to change his mind, and he grudgingly did. But in his letter next morning, he said he wanted her to know "how delicious" it had all been.

I really think you found it so [Edith replied in her journal] . . . Alone with you I am often shy and awkward, tormented by the fear that I may not please you—but with our dear H.J. I felt at my ease, and full of the "motor-nonsense" that always seizes me after one of these long flights through the air.

And what a flight it had been!

History and romance and natural loveliness every mile of the way—across the windings of Seine and Oise, through the gray old towns piled up above their rivers, through the melting spring landscape, all tender green and snowy fruit-blossoms, against black slopes of fir.

In Beauvais they took a leisurely lunch in the courtyard of the Hotel d'Angleterre, accompanied by the sound of canaries singing, dogs barking, and the thin shouts of children. After coffee and a cigarette they wandered along the little streets to the church of St. Etienne, through the displays of a town fair which was filling the Grande Place, until, coming up behind the cathedral, they saw "far up against the blue, the soaring, wheeling choir."

Inside this fantastically beautiful but never completed edifice, they felt "the sense of glad upward rush of all those converging lines—'gladness,' as H.J. said, is the dominant note within the church." While James explored the ambulatory, Edith and Fullerton sat outside in the sunshine on the shallow stone steps. Turning to her, Fullerton asked quietly: "Dear, are you happy?" The question, Edith felt, made the whole so immeasurably rich moment "all yours and mine, [and] drew the great miracle down into the compass of our two hearts—our one heart."

From Beauvais, Edith and James sent a postcard to Walter Berry, toiling in his Washington office (Fullerton, who was not yet acquainted with Berry, did not sign it). James liked what he had seen of Berry at The Mount and in New York, and contrived a Jamesian message: "We try not to miss you so, but only succeed in so wanting you." Back in Paris by nightfall, the three dined together in the Place des Etats-Unis. After dinner James read aloud his recently written one-act play, *The Saloon*, a dramatic version of his story "Owen Wingrave" (about a young pacifist who is killed by the ghost of a militaristic ancestor). It was probably this same evening that Edith, by way of reply, read her poem "Artemis to Actaeon."

Edith kept James going at an only slightly reduced pace during his second and final week in Paris. The day after the Beauvais venture she took him to the Walter Gays at Le Bréau, where Lady Sassoon, St. André, and Eliot Gregory were also in attendance. The following evening, after the threesome had reunited for lunch, Edith assembled an agreeable group: the Harry Whites, the Charles du Bos', Jane d'Oillamson, and Blanche. At lunch next day she submitted James to a bevy of princesses and marquis, but she let him off on his own that evening, and she herself enjoyed the time alone with Fullerton: "We were so happy together."

At tea the same day James encountered not only André Tardieu, but his old friend of many years Henry Adams. Adams, who had been in town only a few days, sent around to James at the Place des Etats-Unis his annotated edition of *The Education*, privately printed in Washington the year before. Acknowledging the book, James remarked upon the tenor of his life at Mrs. Wharton's: "I am kept here in golden chains, in gorgeous bondage, in breathless attendance and beautiful *asservissement.*" James came upon Adams again at the American Embassy when he went there for lunch with Edith, and also an older and dearer friend, William Dean Howells, whom Edith was no less pleased to see. There was time for a visit to the Théâtre des Arts with the d'Humières to watch the dress rehearsal of Shaw's *Candida* in French. But finally, on the warm cloudy morning of May 9, James escaped his gilded bondage, and Edith saw him off for England at the Gare du Nord. He would never set foot in France again.

5

Seated alone at her desk in the Place des Etats-Unis on the night of May 13, Edith wrote Fullerton: "Something gave me the impression the other day that we are watched in this house . . . commented on. Ah, how a great love needs to be a happy and open love! How degraded I feel by other people's degrading thoughts . . ." They were actively lovers by this time, and had been for several days—though not in the manner Edith would have ardently preferred.

She had been arguing out the matter with herself and with Fullerton in the journal. In a long postscript to her account of the visit to Beauvais, she had reflected on the intolerable pain, after such an experience, of an entire day without seeing him, and marveled at her inconsistency in constantly reaching out "for more and more. I used to think: 'If I could be happy for a week—an hour!' And now I am asking to be happy all my life . . ." Pondering thus, she arrived at a vision of what might give her a life-illuminating satisfaction:

> Sometimes I think that if I could go off with you for twenty-four hours to a little inn in the country in the depths of a green wood, I should ask no more. Just to have one long day and quiet evening with you, and the next morning to be still together—oh, how I ache for it sometimes!

But even as she wrote the words, she knew that she would ache for it even more when it was over, and foresaw what "sweet, vain impossible pictures it would evoke." Even so, she made her decision: *"I will go with him once before we separate."*

As her thoughts flowed on in that same entry of May 2, she expressed surprise at her readiness for such an action. Mingling echoes of Nietzsche, her poem about Artemis, and medieval theology—her cultivated side, as it were, coming to the support of her erotic desire—she concluded:

How strange to feel one's self all at once *"Jehnseits von Gut und Böse"* ["Beyond Good and Evil"] . . . It would hurt no one—and it would give me my first last draught of life . . . Why not? I have always laughed at the *"mala prohibita"*—"bugbears to frighten children." The anti-social act is the only one that is harmful "per se." And, as you told me the other day—*and as I needed no telling!*—what I have given you is far, far more . . .

It was of course the lingering puritanical strain in her that gave the issue its transcendent importance; a woman of a different temperament—say, Anna de Noailles with her impetuous affairs—would have undergone no such painful intellectual and moral conflict. For Edith Wharton the act of adultery had, potentially, a sort of absolute significance, and had to be contemplated within the most challenging context. The latter did not include traditional Christian teaching; Edith was now a declared agnostic and put no stock in the notion that certain acts were evil and prohibited "per se." Her religious sense at this stage was a combination of a private mystical streak and a belief in the sanctity of other persons. Religion, too, had become inseparable from a concept of civilization: the "reverence" which the cathedral at Amiens suggested to her was, precisely, a "reverence for the accumulated experience of the past."

So it was not some abstract morality, but rather the civilized order of life that —as she puzzled it out and an antipuritanical feeling arose in her—must never be violated. Like the fictional characters of George Eliot, in Edith Wharton's description of them six years before, she shrank "with a peculiar dread from any personal happiness acquired at the cost of the social organism." It is not too much to say that, for her, the fate of society—as the embodiment of civilization—hung upon every important moral decision. This was the shape of her own moral imperative. And she was telling herself insistently that in the present instance no damage would follow a yielding to her sexual inclinations. This was the full import of her contention that "it would hurt no one" and that "the anti-social act is the only one that is harmful 'per se.' "

By a subtle, instinctive gesture of her mind, she sought not to set the act of love against the civilized order, but rather to set it *within* that order—by journeying with Fullerton toward consummation through the "history and romance and natural loveliness" she had described on the trip to Beauvais, to "a little inn in the country, in the depth of a green wood." It would be somewhere, she would soon be saying in another poem, where she and Fullerton, intimately united, could feel "the tides of time / Coil round our hidden leafy place."

But Morton Fullerton was incapable of comprehending his mistress's complex, romantic, and morally refined desires. The little inn was never visited, and the physical unions began to take place (with some regularity, one gathers, and protected by such massive displays of tact by Gross as can only be guessed at) in the Place des Etats-Unis. Edith's fear that the two of them were being watched and commented upon may have reflected a certain distaste for the situation. Continuing the entry of May 13, she spoke of their having walked to the Luxembourg Gardens and sat for a long time in a quiet corner under a tree. It was pleasant, but could he not understand that what she really longed for "these last days, is to be with you alone, far off, in quietness—held fast, peacefully, 'while close as lips lean, lean the thoughts between.'" (The line is from a blank-verse poem she wrote at the time, beginning "Such music as the hearts of lovers hear . . ." and ending, six lines later, with "Such music once I heard.") She dreamed of a simultaneous wedding of mind and body, of thoughts and lips, accomplished in the green silence of their own private world. Fullerton could not grasp this: "There is no use in trying to look at things together," she concluded sadly; "we don't see them any longer."

That mood, however, was transitory, though it would recur. Before it and after, in this new phase of their relationship, Edith was seized with a feeling of sheer radiant happiness and at times was almost beside herself with excitement. Fullerton had given her courage—just as he had with Margaret Brooke many years earlier—by appealing to her staunch moral independence, declaring in his practiced way that she and he stood together beyond the world in a shared posture of proud unconventionality. "We are behind the scenes together," he wrote her one morning, "—*on the hither side.*" Coming almost immediately upon Edith's citation of Nietzsche's *Beyond Good and Evil*, the remark seemed to clarify and confirm her own state of mind. Thus fortified, she was able to feel herself a transformed being, at the dawn of a new existence: "I appear to myself like a new creature opening dazzled eyes on a new world. *C'est l'aube.*"

A main element in that "new world" was an intensity and variety of sexual experience such as Edith Wharton had scarcely dreamed of. Having decided at last to enter into an active relationship, Edith now knew virtually no restraint. A good many years later, Fullerton would remark to Elisina Tyler, who was proposing to write a biography of Edith Wharton, "Please seize the event, however delicate the problem, to dispel the myth of your heroine's frigidity." He went on to compare his former mistress to George Sand, in the quality of her passion, and to speak in the most extravagant—and unfortunately not altogether legible—terms of her adventurousness as an erotic companion. Fullerton's comments would sound like old-age preening, on Fullerton's part were it not for other evidence. But the latter (for example, the fictional fragment "Beatrice Palmato," included as an appendix at the back of this book) suggests that Edith Wharton was indeed, of a sudden, an uninhibited woman, eager to experiment—with a kind of generous and imaginative energy—in all the modes of sensual enjoyment. The suppressed ardor of more than thirty years was released, in Fullerton's description of it, with something approaching violence in the spring of 1908.

There were, of course, quieter and more purely tender moments. A day at Senlis, northeast of the city, seemed to her perfect beyond anything that her "exacting, scrutinising, analytical" character might ever have expected to enjoy. They went by train to Chantilly, then drove to Senlis, where they wandered through gardens, sat long on a terrace above the Roman wall looking out over the north front of the cathedral, and dined under a lilac arbor at the hotel. The excursion did not conclude at an inn in the depth of a green wood, but on the train coming back, as they sat alone in their compartment, gently exchanging caresses and watching a full moon rise in the warm spring evening, they heard a thrush singing on the verge of the woods, "filling the night with what was in our hearts." Edith felt that her moment of fulfillment had come:

I knew then, dearest dear, all that I had never known before—the interfusion of spirit and sense, the double nearness, the mingled communion of touch and thought . . . One such hour ought to irradiate a whole life.

To celebrate the day, Edith composed an eight-stanza poem called "Senlis. May 16." It spoke of her consciousness, on the terrace before dinner, of experiencing the ideal combination of private intimacy and enveloping history:

> We watched, and felt the tides of time
> Coil round our hidden leafy place,
> Sweep on through changing race and clime
> And leave us at the heart of space.

And it ended with an evocation of the thrush at moonrise, when, as the train paused, "Some thrush from immemorial throat / Poured all the sweetness, all the pain."

Two days later they went together to the Théâtre Français to see the dress rehearsal of Albert Samain's play *Polyphème*. Watching Fullerton as he sat beside her in a balcony armchair, absorbed by the performance, Edith experienced an overwhelming sensation not only of physical and emotional closeness but, more deeply, of achieved physical possession.

I don't suppose you know—since it is more of my sex than yours—the quiet ecstasy I feel in sitting next to you in a public place, looking now and then at the way the hair grows on your forehead, at the line of your profile turned to the stage, your attitude, your expression—while every drop of blood in my body whispers: "Mine—mine—mine!"

. . .

Later in the afternoon they went to the Tuileries, where they found a quiet spot under the trees from which they could look down onto the Seine. They sat for a while in silence, until Fullerton exclaimed softly: "My love! My darling!"— "while people walked up and down before us, not knowing—not knowing *that it was not worth their while to be alive!*"

6

Edith conceived of her journal as a literary work—personal experience was never entirely real for her until it had been converted into literature. It was also a long love letter; and, speaking to Sara Norton a little later about the quality of love letters as one read them in reports of divorce proceedings, she said that they might have been written by a child of ten. "Yet the emotional inspiration," she argued, "ought to help expression in love as in architecture!" In her own case, it led to a mode of expression that was at times uncharacteristically adolescent (not surprisingly, perhaps, since urges stifled since adolescence were among those being brought into play), and it did not always escape the clichés upon which strong emotion tends to fall back. To speak in chillingly aesthetic terms, the journal cannot be ranked among Edith Wharton's best efforts. But there is a wealth of honesty at its core, and behind the exclamations and the underlinings there lie that toughness and fortitude of spirit that were of her essence.

Apart from the journal, her only writing in the spring of 1908, until after her departure in late May, was the occasional letter to Sara Norton; the story she had promised *Scribner's,* to follow "The Verdict" and "The Pretext," failed to materialize. She had been giving Sally Norton a selective account of her Paris days, and her friend may have been astute enough to detect a rather different tone in the letters, as though Edith were answering questions no one had asked. "I shall stay on quietly in Paris," she wrote when Teddy was about to sail, "till I join him in Lenox at the end of May." "I am well and happy and busy," she said a week later, adding again that she would remain "quietly" in the city for another two months.

Sally may also have noticed that Fullerton, who had figured so regularly in Edith's letters the previous fall and immediately after her return to Paris, had disappeared from them entirely. And she may have wondered a little at Edith's enthusiasm for the letters of the morally questionable Hortense Allart, "an extraordinary woman . . . a George Sand without hypocrisy."

During her last fortnight in Paris, Edith saw a good deal of Henry Adams, and it is from this moment that their friendship can best be dated. They had known each other slightly for many years and had long had a number of friends in common—Bay Lodge, Walter Berry, Margaret Chanler, and the Walter Gays among them. Their earliest encounters appear to have been in Paris rather than in Henry Adams' Washington. In December 1891, for example, Adams' darkening spirit had been briefly cheered by a glimpse of Edith Wharton in Paris, looking as "fragile as a dandelion in seed" and talking with brisk confidence about things artistic and literary on the Paris scene. There were other brief meetings over the years, but only beginning in May 1908 were they at all regularly in each other's company.

Adams, just turning seventy, was by this time more or less commuting between Washington and Paris. His wife, the former Marion Hooper, had died tragically, by her own hand, in 1885; the long subsequent period of wandering, in the South Seas and elsewhere, was behind him. He had completed *Mont-Saint-Michel and Chartres* in 1904 and *The Education of Henry Adams* three years later, though it would still be five and ten years respectively before either saw public print.

In Paris, Adams could invariably be found at 50 Avenue du Bois de Boulogne, a little street near the Etoile and an easy walk from the Place des Etats-Unis. It was the Paris home of Elizabeth Cameron, and Adams stayed there when Mrs. Cameron was off on one of her frequent travels, withdrawing himself and his books and belongings, upon her return, to another apartment farther along the avenue. Adams had for long stood in ambiguously ardent relation to "Liz" Cameron, the beautiful estranged wife of Senator James Donald Cameron of Pennsylvania, and at forty-nine (in 1908) some twenty years younger than her scholarly lover. It was at Mrs. Cameron's brilliant *salon* in Lafayette Square in Washington that Adams had centered his American life. Now that her daughter Martha was to marry Ronald Lindsay, a most promising younger member of the British Foreign Office, she was about to give up the Washington home and divide her time chiefly between England and Paris. Edith Wharton had also known Mrs. Cameron for a number of years, though they remained thus far on fairly formal terms.

With his trim gray beard and his small erect figure invariably clad (like Mark Twain's) in a white suit, Adams had become a striking figure on the boulevards and in the art shops and libraries. He was well looked after by Mrs. Cameron and others among his favorite ladies—his "wives," Edith Wharton called them—and by an assortment of nieces, mostly young Hooper girls. Nieces by the score, he said, flattered and petted him; Edith, who now found herself immensely drawn to him, began to refer to Adams, like almost everyone else, as "dear Uncle Henry."

Adams spoke mockingly of Mrs. Wharton's "saloon," but he enjoyed himself there and derived pleasure from the teasing exchanges with his hostess. He was even persuaded to go with Edith to dinner at Rosa de Fitz-James's, though he otherwise showed far more resistance than did Henry James to Edith's efforts to lure him into the social depths of the Faubourg. For her part, though she felt that Adams' profoundly skeptical mind and his inveterately sardonic and tired manner tended to drain life of its "vital juice," Edith rejoiced in his piercing destructive wit and the sheer range of his knowledge, which alone in her Paris community greatly outmatched her own.

It had been a high point for Edith when, at tea one May afternoon, she found herself flanked by Henry James and Henry Adams. Later Adams drew her a comical portrait of the two elderly gentlemen "drivelling" at her in front of the fire and besought her to accept *that* situation as her best fate rather than to abandon them all and sail back to the United States.

The days sped on. As often as possible, Fullerton came along to lunch or supper. On May 22, the day before her departure, he spent two late-evening hours in the apartment. "God keep you," Edith wrote, revising the old German poem, "it *was* too beautiful." When he left, Fullerton took the journal with him. "My two months, my incredible two months, are almost over," the most recent entry began. "I have drunk of the wine of life at last, I have known the thing best worth knowing, I have been warmed through and through, never to grow quite cold again till the end . . ."

Her parting message to Fullerton was one of overflowing gratitude to life. Her trust had been rewarded, her aching conviction justified that an experience of vital beauty was yet awaiting her, somewhere; she had been right not to accept along the way "any lesser gift, any small happiness than this that you had in store for me."

How often I used to say to myself: "No one can love life as I do, love the beauty and the splendour and the ardour, and find words for them as I can, without having a share in them some day"—I mean the dear intimate share that one guessed at, always, beyond and behind their universal thrill.

Her "day" had finally come,

and I have poured into it all my stored-up joy of living, all my sense of the beauty and mystery of the world, every impression of joy and loveliness, in sight or sound or touch.

On the last day she stood in the apartment in the midst of open trunks counting over the dresses, cloaks, hats, and tea gowns she had worn in Paris over the months, as they lay strewn on the bed, the sofa, the chairs. Perhaps only half-consciously, she was reliving a crucial moment in *The House of Mirth*, on the last evening of Lily Bart's life. Lily, rehearsing her adult life, had surveyed her various dresses while the scenes in which she had worn them arose in her mind. "An association lurked in every fold," Edith Wharton had written about her doomed heroine; and so it was for Edith herself. "There is the black dress I had on the first time we went to the Sorbonne to hear B[aker] lecture last December. I remember thinking: 'Will he like me in it?' . . . There is the tea-gown I wore the first night you dined with me alone . . . You liked it, you said. . . . And here is the dress I wore the day we went to Herblay, when, in the church, for a moment, the Veiled Happiness stole up to me."

The next morning, May 23, Edith left on the boat train for LeHavre. Fullerton joined her in the Gare du Nord, and they sat together for some minutes in her compartment. He returned the journal, having written several lines in it (the page has been ripped out); but there was no possibility of intimate talk. Other people were milling in and out, suitcases were being piled on the racks, and then Le Roy King—"good gay L.R.K."—showed up, "all unconscious, and lingering between us to the last." But at least they were together: "Our eyes could meet, I saw your forehead, and the way the hair lies on it—when shall I see that again?"

As the train pulled out, she saw Fullerton still standing on the platform, waving at her. She waved back and smiled: "to smile at that moment!" By two in the afternoon she was at LeHavre and boarding the *Provence*. An hour later the big liner pulled up anchor. "It is over, my Heart, all over! . . . *Et on n'en meurt, hélas!*"

7

The third day at sea, Edith wrote Fullerton a poem:

> When I am gone, recall my hair,
> Not for the light it used to hold,
> But that your touch, enmeshèd there,
> Has turned it to a younger gold.
>
> Recall my hands, that were not soft
> Or white or fine beyond expressing,
> Till they had slept so long and oft,
> So warm and close, in your possessing.
>
> Recall my eyes, that used to lie
> Blind pools with summer's wreckage strewn.
> You cleared the drift, but in their sky
> You hung no image but your own.
>
> Recall my mouth, that knew not how
> A kiss is cradled and takes wing,
> Yet fluttered like a nest-hung bough
> When you had touched it like the Spring.

Always the connoisseur of names and of their special poetry, Edith walked the decks reciting to herself the names that conjured back the whole experience:

Herblay . . . Montfort l'Amaury . . . Provins . . . Beauvais . . . Montmorency . . . Senlis . . . Meudon . . .

What dear, sweet crowding memories! What wealth for a heart that was empty this time last year. How the witch-hazel has kept its promise, since it flowered in our hands last October!—Bring me, magic flower, one more day such as those—but dearer, nearer, by all these death-pangs of separation with which my heart is torn.

On the fifth day out, in a burst of savagery and despair, she wrote at one sitting a five-thousand-word story called "The Choice," about a married woman who wishes above all other things that her husband would die. Cobham Stilling, like Teddy Wharton, is a trustee of his wife's estate, and as the story opens (this, as will be seen, represented something of an intuition on Edith's part), has speculated or gambled away a good portion of it. But it is not impending financial ruin, it is the man himself who has driven Isabel Stilling to the verge of frenzy and into the arms of a lover. Strutting and vainglorious, Stilling is addicted only to good cigars and water sports, at the moment to careening around the lake at Highfield in a ten-thousand-dollar motor launch.

Huddled in the darkness of the boathouse with her lover on a summer evening, Isabel voices her dearest hope: "That he may die!"

> "You wish that too?" he said.
>
> "I wish it always—every day, every hour, every moment!" She paused, and then let the words break from her. "You'd better know it; you'd better know the worst of me. I'm not the saint you suppose; the duty I do is poisoned by the thoughts I think. Day by day, hour by hour, I wish him dead. When he goes out, I pray for something to happen; when he comes back I say to myself: 'Are you here again?' When I hear of people being killed in accidents, I think: 'Why wasn't he there?' When I read the death notices in the paper I say: 'So-and-so was just his age.' . . . Night after night I keep myself from going to sleep for fear I may dream he's dead."

Cobham Stilling comes staggering drunkenly down from the big house to see that the launch is properly moored. The lovers break apart; there is a confused scuffle, and both men are plunged into the water. Only one of them survives: needless to say, it is the husband.

The writing of this story had a good therapeutic effect upon Edith's creative energy: immediately after it, she returned to her novel *The Custom of the Country* for the first time in half a year, making a start on the seventh chapter. For the rest, she divided her time on the voyage, typically, between R. H. Lock's scientific *Heredity and Variation* and a spirited account of George Sand's love affair with Alfred de Musset, which the author, Paul Marieton, had presented to her just before she sailed. The latter book, she told Sara Norton in an echo of James's remark at Nohant, was "well done and interesting—as when are they *not*, the darlings?"

Things were even worse than anticipated when the boat docked in New York and, with Teddy, she took the afternoon train to Lenox. Back at The Mount, she rehearsed the homecoming to Fullerton in her journal. On the train she had been struck by a particularly interesting passage in *Heredity and Variation* and held the book out to her husband, saying, "Read that."

> The answer was: "Does that sort of thing really amuse you?" I heard the key turn in my prison-lock. That is the answer to everything worth while!

Oh, Gods of derision! And you've given me over twenty years of it!
Je n'en peux plus.

"At sea I could bear it," she wrote. *"Ici j'étouffe."* In the turmoil of remem-bered ecstasy and present despair, it did not occur to her that a technical treatise on heredity was not the aptest greeting for a nonintellectual husband whom she had not seen for two months and who had only precariously recovered from a serious illness. Her consciousness was too full of her return to a prison now palpably bleaker (and, via the key-turning image from Dante, more infernal).

I have stood it all these years, and hardly felt it, because I had created a world of my own, in which I lived without heeding what went on outside. But since I have known what it was to have some one enter into that world and live there with me, the mortal solitude I come back to has become terrible . . .

A letter from Fullerton came with every steamer, and Edith noted the event in her diary with the word *geschreiben.* But the letter which reached her on June 11 spoke ominously about the uncertainty of his plans. He definitely could not come to America until the autumn, and he was not at all sure where he would be the following year. He had resigned as the regular Paris correspondent of the London *Times,* and everything was in doubt. Edith wrote back frantically:

Don't write to me again! Let me face at once the fact *that it is over.* Without a date to look to, I can't bear to go on, and it will be easier to make the break now, voluntarily, than to see it slowly, agonizingly, made by time and circumstance. But oh, my adored, my own love, you who have given me the only moments of real life I have ever known, how am I to face the long hours and days before I learn again the old hard lesson of "how existence may be cherished, / Strengthened and fed, without the aid of joy"? I knew that lesson once, but I have unlearned it—you have kissed away the memory of it.

She knew she should be grateful for having had her hour, "but the human heart is insatiable, and I didn't know, my own, I didn't know!" She recalled what she had written after the day at Senlis: "One such hour ought to irradiate a whole life," and confessed wretchedly, *"Eh bien, non—ce n'est pas assez!"*

Edith's first reaction was to rush instantly back to France. The new emotional crisis had helped bring on an attack of hay fever: the sense of psychic stifling *("Ici, j'étouffe")* had expanded into one of physical suffocation. She felt unable to breathe, and wrote Sally Norton of her desperate need for ocean air and her thought of going to take inhalations at Aix or Salsomaggiore.

Typically, she sought to appraise her situation—and its components of pas-sion, infidelity, suffering, and intellectual challenge—by juxtaposed quotations in her commonplace book from the writings that had seized her attention. She covered more than thirty pages with such borrowings in 1908, much the most of any year in which entries were made. From William Morris' "Defence of Guenevere" she took eleven lines of the queen's reflective account of the adulterous affair with Lancelot: "So day by day it grew, as if one should / Slip slowly down some path." She borrowed Baudelaire's admonition to his own grief *(Receuillement)*, that it be sensible and hold itself more quietly. A formula of her own devising was jotted down: "There is the rain-grief and the lava-grief . . . and when the cloud gathers, who knows which it will be?"

A burgeoning quarrel with religion in general and Christianity in particular became evident as the quotations followed one another. From Matthew Arnold's dramatic poem *Empedocles on Etna* she drew the contention that man's inability to understand all things "Affords no ground to affirm / That there are gods who do." Stendhal supplied the witty proposition that "the one thing that excuses God is that he does not exist." The English biologist Thomas Huxley—one of several scientists made use of—was quoted as to his absolute refusal "to put faith in that which does not rest on sufficient evidence."

But it was Nietzsche who for the moment most absorbed her. Goethe's *Faust* still led the list of her favorite works, and she felt that Goethe contained most of Nietzsche, including his image of Superman ("and most of everything else! He was the Super-est of them all," she wrote a Paris correspondent). But she was intently reading Nietzsche's writings—*Beyond Good and Evil*, *The Will to Power*, and *The Genealogy of Morals* were all in her inventory of favorites this year—and she found them full of originality and poetry. She was alert to the role of Stendhal (still her leading novelist) "in the formation of Nietzsche" and detected the voice of Walt Whitman in such of the German writer's sayings as "Man is a *sick animal.*"

What she especially admired was Nietzsche's exhilarating "power of breaking through the conventions," and she thought that it was "salutary now and then to be made to realise '*Die Unwerthung aller Werthe*' ["the reevaluation of all values"] and really get back to a wholesome basis of naked instinct." Thus enthralled, Edith Wharton shared for the time Nietzsche's driving hostility to Christianity as an emasculating force and a repressive "instrument of culture." She applauded Nietzsche's concept of "the blond beast," a mythic embodiment, as it were, of naked instinct: an unfettered animal impulse that Nietzsche believed needed to erupt from time to time in an assault upon traditional culture and upon Christianity's influential distrust of the human body. "There are times," Edith wrote Sally Norton, "when I hate what Christianity has left in our blood—or rather, one might say, what it has taken out of it—by its cursed assumption of the split between body and soul."

It was of course the affair with Fullerton that had aroused Edith to these considerations of naked instinct and the status of the body. She had always had a healthy regard for the human body itself, which she once described as "that glorious and ignoble, that magical and mysterious Ark"; and she had come to be on equitable terms with her own body. Her mother's disapproving evasions had confused her, and her personal sexual life had been inactive for more than twenty years, but she had long ceased to be prudishly ashamed of her body (if indeed she ever had been) or embarrassed by it. She referred to it with un-Victorian candor, she liked to adorn it, and was not without pride in the curves of her figure. Yet before she knew Fullerton she had no intimation of the excitement and fulfillment that could be found in physical love, most especially when there occurred a simultaneous communion of body and spirit. Meditating on these matters, she now felt—and would soon be saying so in a poem—that the experience had moved her into a strange and alien land; one remote, in its sexual energy and its belief in the instinctual, from the Christian world she had for long ostensibly inhabited.

In fact, her allusion to Christianity's "cursed assumption of the split between body and soul" was not altogether fair or accurate, though the churchmen she had listened to and the Protestant sermons she had read in her youth probably seemed to be pressing such an assumption. But Abbé Mugnier could have told her otherwise; and as to Christian teaching, her literary understanding was sounder than her theological ruminations.

Alongside the passages from Nietzsche in her commonplace book she wrote three stanzas of John Donne's "The Extasie," a poem that addresses itself to the very question she was confronting. She also transcribed the resounding inquiry in Donne's "The Good Morrow": "I wonder by my troth what thou and I / Did, till we loved"; and even more pointedly from "The Blossom": "A naked thinking heart that makes no show / Is to a woman but a kind of ghost." She cited as well a recent article in praise of Donne by young Desmond MacCarthy. Edith Wharton, first guided in this direction by Charles Eliot Norton, was astutely enamored of Donne many years before he became enshrined in Anglo-American criticism.

"The Extasie" speaks about the "interanimation" of two souls, but argues precisely that if one soul is to flow into another, it must "to the body first repair," and that communion begins with the senses:

> So must pure lovers' souls descend
> To affections and to faculties,
> Which sense may reach and apprehend,
> Else a great Prince in prison lies.

Edith strongly underlined that last particularly appealing image, and went on to copy the key lines:

> To our bodies turn we then, that so
> Weak men on love revealed may look;
> Love's mysteries in souls do grow,
> And yet the body is his book.

Walter Berry came up from Washington for a few days in the middle of June. The visit helped Edith's morale, as did a new friendship with a cultivated and entertaining young oceanologist named Carl Snyder, and she threw herself into her work. Her worst fears about Fullerton gradually quieted, and with them the hay fever: "After six weeks of torment," she observed in mid-July, "the fiendish thing has subsided." By early August she felt she had earned a respite, and planned a trip to Boston and points north with Berry.

But the example of Hortense Allart was still alive in her thoughts, and she continued to press Sally Norton to appreciate her. The circumspect New Englander evidently found the unconventional Frenchwoman rather rich for her blood, and Edith was moved to explain just what it was in Mlle. Allart that she responded to. It was "her frankness, her absence of 'the man tempted me' element, her fearless way of looking life in the eyes."

13. Interlude in England

A literary observer in the late summer and fall of 1908 would have found Edith Wharton as energetically productive as ever. *The Hermit and the Wild Woman,* her fourth volume of short stories, was published in September; *A Motor-Flight Through France,* its luminous text nicely illustrated by photographs and etchings, followed in October; new work was appearing in both New York and Paris periodicals. The display, however, was slightly deceptive. Most of the items in the new collection had been written in previous years (one as early as 1904), and after a hard month's work in July, *The Custom of the Country* again came to a standstill. The hay fever had been overcome, but now Edith was suffering badly from insomnia. She began to talk about returning to Europe ahead of schedule and in advance of Teddy.

"The Choice," the story written on shipboard, was not included in *The Hermit and the Wild Woman;* Edith had perhaps recoiled a little from its naked virulence, though after revising it somewhat (and after another period of life with Teddy), she liked it well enough to give it to the *Century* for an autumn issue. It would have fitted with several other tales in the volume about unhappy or disastrous marriages—"The Pretext," "In Trust," and especially "The Last Asset," an expertly contrived account of an affable old codger, estranged from his social-climbing wife, who is persuaded to feign marital harmony and parental approval by attending his daughter's wedding in Paris, since the groom's aristocratic French family would otherwise forbid the match.

The familiar themes—domination, entrapment, the longing and the failure to escape, along with considerations about the nature of artistic commitment—palpitate unevenly in the book, and the irony is pervasive. Some reviewers complained that the cumulative effect was depressing and lamented the absence of any "relieving touch of cheerfulness." On the whole, though, the volume was well received. *The New York Times* called the stories uniformly delightful, and it was generally acknowledged that the book was up to the high standards of subtlety and artistry that Mrs. Wharton had led readers to expect. The sales were relatively modest: only a little more than four thousand copies; Edith did not earn back the advance of one thousand dollars. Her total literary income for 1908 was about fifteen thousand dollars; most of it royalties on *The Fruit of the Tree.*

In September, when Francis Charmes of the *Revue des deux mondes* asked for another story, Edith—feeling suddenly sick, as she told Brownell, "of the arid work of translating"—said to herself: "Hang it, I'll write him one in *French.*" It was called "Les Metteurs en scène" ("The Stage Managers"), a bitterly ironic tale about a young American woman who makes her living arranging marriages between rich American ladies and the nobility of the Faubourg. She admitted to Brownell that she would never dare look him or Henry James in the face after this rash venture.

When she met up with James in London, soon after the story's appearance, she found to her dismay that he had given it a close look. Some third person asked James if he did not think it remarkable for Mrs. Wharton to have done such a thing. "Remarkable—most remarkable," James replied; "an altogether astonishing feat." Then, swinging around to Edith, he went on: "I do congratulate you, my dear, on the way in which you've picked up every old worn-out literary phrase that's been lying about the streets of Paris for the last twenty years, and managed to pack them all into those few pages." To another friend he said in all seriousness: "A very creditable episode in her career. *But she must never do it again.*"

In fact, her chief literary attention was in this period being given to poetry rather than fiction. "I have perversely and inexcusably taken to warbling again, instead of sticking to prose," she informed Brownell in October. For her novels and stories Edith Wharton drew systematically upon incidents, persons, and places she had herself known; but for the expression of her own most private and vital emotions, she turned to poetry. The relationship with Morton Fullerton was not yet wholly accessible to her novelistic imagination (though it would become so); however, it was the source of at least ten poems in 1908 and 1909, several of them ambitious ones, and most of them addressed directly to Fullerton, as the journal had been.

We have already seen the Herblay sonnet, the little work celebrating the day at Senlis, the shipboard poem of farewell and remembrance, and the one containing the phrase "When close as lips lean, lean the thoughts between." Soon after the return to Lenox, when despite her sense of suffocation she retained a stirring memory of days and evenings with Fullerton, she wrote a poem called "Life." It is a high-spirited allegory of sexual and psychic arousal, in which Life rescues her from a condition of slumber, pours "wild music" through her, and escorts her on a Whitmanian flight across the universe to a pinnacle of experience where she and Love become the piper and Life dances to their joyous tune.

A far more elaborate, searching, and problematic survey of the relationship was given in "The Mortal Lease," a sequence of eight sonnets composed over the autumn months. Here at last Edith Wharton crossed what, in the letter to Brownell some years before, she had called "the poetry line." The sequence has a certain opacity, beginning with the title—which might be translated as "the limits of mortality"; though, noticing how often and in how many contexts Edith was using the word "mortal," one suspects that a poignant pun on her lover's first name was echoing half audibly in her mind. But "The Mortal Lease" has an arresting complexity of feeling and a sometimes startling originality, even a waywardness, of phrasing.

It is a reenactment, at a sufficient distance of time and space, of the journal she had addressed to Fullerton: a rehearsal, made more orderly in retrospect, of the stages she had passed through in the evolving relationship. The opening sonnets pick up the Nietzschean theme in an effort to reconcile the primitive nature of their passion with the civilized concerns acquired in the long course of history:

> Because the currents of our love are poured
> Through the slow welter of the primal flood. . . .
>
> Shall we deny the journey's gathered lore—
> The great refusals and the long disdains. . . .
> And all mortality's immortal gains?

As the sequence moves forward, Edith Wharton repeats in fresh language the incredulity expressed in the journal that she, who had stood aside so from life and intellectualized it, should now be visited and almost overwhelmed by sexual passion.

Again the religious and the erotic impulse play against each other. In her own image of herself, she had been like

> the nun entranced
> Who nightlong held her Bridegroom in her soul.

But now she is ready to abandon herself to pagan recklessness and plunge wildly into the waters of experience:

> And I would meet your passion as the first
> Wild woodland woman met her captor's craft,
> Or as the Greek whose fearless beauty laughed,
> And doffed her raiment by the Attic flood.

The lover in the sequence is heard voicing his insistence, in the Fullerton manner, that one must put aside otherworldly thoughts and simply "live today":

> And every sense in me leapt to obey,
> Seeing the routed phantoms backward roll.

At this stage, Edith found a new metaphor for the decision she had reached the previous May, in which had figured the little inn in the green woods:

> Yet for one rounded moment I will be
> No more to you than what my lips may give,
> And in the circle of your kisses live,
> As in some island of a storm-blown sea.

The speaker is alone now (as Edith felt herself to be), but she is sure that she has won something to prize in her solitude:

> And some mute angel in the breast even now
> Measures my loss by all that I have kept.

Hers is a different way of life: a way, one gathers amid the flow of metaphors, of stoical acceptance and solitary artistic endeavor. The stoical writings of Seneca remained high among Edith Wharton's literary preferences; but we shall shortly see how little Edith was actually willing to accept things as they were.

Edith felt that some, at least, of her new verse was "creditable," and talk was soon renewed with Brownell about the possibility of a volume of her poetry. Her first thought was of a limited private printing, but she cautiously changed her mind when word was passed on that Charles Scribner favored a trade edition. The important thing, she wrote Brownell, was not to claim too much for her work:

> If Mr. Scribner thinks a small edition of the volume would be worth while, perhaps it would be less "precious" to do it in that way than "for private circulation." I can't make up my mind what is the simplest, least pretentious thing to do. As I reread them: a few seem to me worth the very relative longevity of a "volume," and yet I should like it known how little I mean when I say that!—Poetry is to me so august a thing that I always feel that I should be struck by lightning when I sidle up to the shrine.

Her first collection of poems, *Artemis to Actaeon*, was published by Scribners in April 1909. It contained "Life" and "The Mortal Lease" as well as the title poem and a good many others composed over the years; no other of the poems to Fullerton was included. The volume further confirmed Edith Wharton's position as a woman of letters: she was alone among living American novelists in being capable of such genuine if modest poetic accomplishment.

The return to poetry, meanwhile, led her to reflect, almost for the first time, upon the American achievement in poetry, and by extension on the American literary achievement in general. As to the former, she summed it up in the course of asking Brownell when his projected essay on Poe would appear: "I should like to get in that Nicaean bark with you—and in time gently steer it toward the 'far-sprinkled systems' that Walt sails among. Those two, with Emerson, are the best we have—in fact, the all we have." On another occasion, getting back to Emerson "after several years of neglect," she declared herself "amazed at his facilities, and his clear cold amenity, flushing now and then like some beautiful bit of pink crystal." It was primarily Emerson's poems that drew her, but she admired his essays in particular as providing a major influence, even greater than that of Stendhal, upon Nietzsche: Nietzsche, she said, was Emerson's *chef-d'oeuvre*.

Poe resonated less in her imagination, and when it did it was likely to be his fictional dramas of the trapped consciousness (which had their effect, for example, upon her story "The Bolted Door"); but she brought the actual Poe, marginally but sympathetically, into her novella *False Dawn* in the early 1920s. Walt Whitman was, of course, the lyric poet she esteemed above all others, ranking him even more highly than Keats and Shelley. Edith Wharton was a close student of poetic technique—to Brownell she held forth on Milton's artful violation of metrical rules—and no poet did she scrutinize more carefully in this regard than Whitman. Commenting to Bliss Perry about his essay on Whitman (1906), she found herself wishing Perry had "gone into more detail about his rhythms. It seems to me on *that* side that he was the great and conscious artist, and the great Originator, and most likely, therefore, to live on and be fruitful."

Her own emotional agitation in the fall of 1908 was such that what especially interested her in major American writers was their treatment of the emotional life, their investment in their work of their deepest personal feelings. Whitman seemed to her preeminently effective in this regard—and Hawthorne decidedly lacking. Anticipating a forthcoming essay by Brownell on Hawthorne, she remarked that she was "counting the minutes till I see the egregious Nathaniel expire without shedding of blood." After reading the essay a month later, she hurried to tell Brownell that she

especially enjoyed your bringing out his lack of poetry and his lukewarmness. . . . My only two quarrels with you are for calling the Scarlet L. "our one prose masterpiece"—I'd so much rather we had more than that one; and for saying that his prose has a classic quality. It seems to me about as classic as a bare hotel parlour furnished only with bentwood chairs.

But, oh, the good things you say by the way! How the *marble* was what he saw in sculpture (that is the key to so much of him); how he dwelt apart, and was therefore taken for a star; how there can hardly be a more barren state than revery for the production of anything beyond "conceits."

It was a curiously grudging reading of Hawthorne, whose impact upon *Ethan Frome* a few years later would be unmistakable. But Edith Wharton had reached that stage in her career as a writer when it becomes necessary to denigrate one's most important predecessors as a way of affirming, of gathering together, one's own literary identity. At the same time, in her eagerness to deny or escape Hawthorne's influence upon her, she was tacitly admitting his importance, and her emerging place in the still publicly unrecognized American literary tradition.

2

Edith Wharton had ended "The Mortal Lease" upon a note of resignation, but this was far from her fundamental mood—as she indicated in a sudden outcry to Sara Norton in a letter of October 17. Charles Eliot Norton was dying, and

Sara had written in a distraught manner to ask whether over the years she might have done better or differently by her father. "Alas," Edith replied, "I should like to get up on the house-tops and cry to all who come after us: 'Take your own life, every one of you.' " The exclamation was not a summons to suicide. On the contrary, it was an urgent appeal to others—and most particularly to self-sacrificing women—to lead *their* individual and personal lives, the only lives that would ever be accorded them. It was Edith Wharton's heartfelt rendering of Lambert Strether's outburst in Henry James's *The Ambassadors:* "Live all you can; it's a mistake not to. It doesn't make so much matter what you do in particular so long as you have your life. If you haven't that what *have* you had?"

It may have been with those words in mind that Edith, in early October, wrote James two evidently despairing letters describing her situation: a marriage that had become intolerable and a sense of hopelessness about Morton Fullerton. James cabled at once, expressing his "earnest hope" that she would come to Europe very soon so that they might talk at leisure. He followed with a letter that has been much quoted and, for lack of evidence, misinterpreted as referring to her relations with Walter Berry:

> I am deeply distressed at the situation you describe and as to which my power to suggest or enlighten now quite miserably fails me. I move in darkness; I rack my brains; I gnash my teeth; I don't pretend to understand or to imagine.

All he could suggest was that Edith must hold back from any final decision, any irreversible action:

> I am moved to say "Don't *conclude!*" Some light will *still* absolutely come to you—I believe—though I can't pretend to say what it conceivably may be. Anything is more credible—conceivable—than a mere inhuman *plan . . .* Only sit tight yourself *and go through the movements of life.* That keeps up our connection with life—I mean the immediate and apparent life, behind which, all the while, the deeper and darker and unapparent, in which things *really* happen to us, learns, under that hygiene, to stay in its place.

As to Fullerton, he had heard almost nothing directly: "I have had but that one letter of weeks ago—and there are *kinds* of news I can't ask for." After repeating his hope that she would come speedily to Rye for long talks "*à perte de vue,*" he ended:

> Believe meanwhile and always in the aboundingly tender friendship—the understanding, the participation, the *princely* (though I say it who shouldn't) hospitality of spirit and soul of yours more than ever, Henry James.

To this letter, one of James's most generous and compassionate, as well as wisest, verbal gestures, he added a postscript in a quite different tone of voice: "I can't tell you what hearty joy I take in Walter B.'s beautiful appointment. I delight, I revel in it—I infinitely desire to see him."

3

Berry's "beautiful appointment" was to a judgeship on the International Tribunal in Cairo, Egypt, a well-deserved testimony to his accomplishments in the field of international law. He joined the Whartons at Egerton Winthrop's house in New York, and on October 30 he sailed for Europe on the same liner with Edith, Teddy for the time being moved around to the Knickerbocker Club on Fifth Avenue. To Sara Norton on the day of her father's funeral (and offering to send a "plain black tailored coat and skirt" and a black veil, to save Sally the distraction of being measured for such an outfit), Edith remarked that she and Teddy would not be in Paris until January, "and I am not sure the decision was wise, because I am not sure of anything. But I *had* to choose without further delay."

According to an enigmatic note Edith sent to Bay Lodge, Berry's conduct during the voyage was offensive to her: probably he flirted more flagrantly than usual with other women. It seems likely that Berry intuited, and resented, the fact that he was not for the moment the first man in Edith's life—not that, either then or later, Edith Wharton was unequivocally the first woman in *his* life. James alluded gaily to a certain Lady G. into whose arms Berry was alleged to be flying; and there were always other ladies, American and English, with whom he could be seen consorting—at this time, more often than not, Rita (Mrs. Philip) Lydig, an authentic beauty of Spanish descent. But there was a strong vein of selfishness in Berry's character, and a felt slackening in Edith's response to him could easily have led to a stagy display of independence.

The performance was repeated once or twice in England. Before that, however, there were a few days in Paris, at the Hotel Domenici, a visit which may have vexed Berry still further. "I'm in Paris, unexpectedly, instead of Rye," Edith wrote Gaillard Lapsley disingenuously; but Berry could observe that she had made a diversion to the city to snatch a few hours with an American journalist he now met for the first time.

By November 8 they were in England, and Edith launched upon a social whirl that fully matched the most strenuous season in the Faubourg: her first deep immersion in English social and literary life. Before it was over, it had evolved into something of a triumphal tour for Edith Wharton and her English circle had expanded to take in several important new members.

Her old friends were on the alert for her. James, announcing Edith's impending arrival, urged Howard Sturgis to "be kind to her," though for all his knowledge of her troubled state he could not resist adding: "*What* an incoherent life! It makes me crouch more dodderingly than ever over my hearthstone." "She arrives Sunday p.m. with Walter Berry," he reported a few days later, "and I take rooms for her (not *them*) at the Berkeley." James, who knew better than anyone that the parenthetical assurance was beside the point, may have been deliberately hiding the trail.

In London the inner circle quickly formed about Edith and Berry: James staying on, Lapsley coming down from Cambridge, and Sturgis in from Windsor. With four of the men Edith liked best in the world, she lunched, dined, laughed, and toured the galleries. She began to sleep better. "The change and movement carry me along," she told Sally Norton, and helped create a better "surface" to her being; she was perhaps recalling James's advice about her "immediate and transparent life." "But the mortal desolation is there, will always be there," she added, without explanation.

With James and Berry, Edith drove down through Dulwich to Canterbury, where they paused to watch the sunset, then across the marshes in the dark to Lamb House. The next day Berry was driven to Dover, whence he departed for Cairo.

On their way to Howard Sturgis at Queen's Acre on November 16, James, overcoming Edith's extreme reluctance, persuaded her to make a stop at Box Hill and be introduced to George Meredith. Edith, as she told Sally Norton, felt that such unannounced visits were "rather an intrusion," but she yielded out of her immense admiration for Meredith's novels: *The Egoist* and *Harry Richmond* had yet to be dislodged from their place among her eight favorite novels in any language. As they were shown into a tiny, low-ceilinged room, she found a huge gentleman who turned out to be a Mr. Morley Roberts; Howard Sturgis' handsome sister-in-law; and a trained nurse stolidly eating her supper at a table next to Meredith's chair. To her surprise and delight, the eighty-year-old Meredith got to his feet and approached her with outstretched hands, exclaiming: "My dear child, I've read every word you've written, and I've always wanted to see you! I'm flying through France in your motor at this moment"—and held up the book.

Meredith was almost completely deaf, but his organ voice flowed over Edith as he continued praising her work and asking questions about it. He seemed to her to be "radiating light and life from every feature, and every tone of voice— so different from the ruined man I had had described to me!" Edith then discreetly retreated to talk with Roberts and Mrs. Sturgis, and to watch, fascinated, as Meredith engaged in a long, rich monologue for Henry James's benefit: "James, benignly listening, Meredith eloquently conversing, and their old deep regard for each other burning steadily through the surface eloquence and the surface attentiveness." As they went out into the dusk, James said, "Wasn't I right?" and Edith could only agree.

The Edwardian age was in full flower, and though it would technically end with the death of King Edward VII in the spring of 1910, it survived in essence —like *la belle époque* across the channel—until the terrible summer of 1914. In retrospect, it seems to have an even clearer historical outline than its French counterpart. The coincidence of the death of the old queen and the start of the new century gave even the men and women of the time the strongest sense of having entered into a new epoch of English life.

We see now that it was a time of strain, unrest, and fateful change as well as of confidence, optimism, elegant sophistication, and well-bred adultery in high places. Connecting the Edwardian world with the periods that followed it, one's eye is inevitably drawn to signs of dislocation and perhaps of progress: to the stunning victory of the Liberal Party in 1906 that sent Tory England to its grave; to the failure of the Liberals to solve the enormous political and social problems of the day, and hence to the rising influence of the loosely knit socialist movement and the eventual rival efforts of Beatrice Webb's Fabians and H. G. Wells; to the intolerable gap—the worst in British history—between the ever poorer poor and the ever richer rich, and the half million men who went on strike at one time or another in the single year 1910; to Baden-Powell's Boy Scout and Girl Scout organizations, created as one way to reverse the decline of imperial prestige; to Havelock Ellis' *Studies in the Psychology of Sex,* clamor over change in the divorce laws, and heated words about contraception; to the sometimes violent agitation—incomparably greater than in France—over women's rights, especially voting rights.

These were, certainly, prominent features of the age. But if, as it has been remarked, the *époque* in France did not always seem very beautiful to those who lived through it, to the Edwardians the period did not always appear one of unmanageable restiveness and uncontrollable change. It was not only that a certain amount of Victorianism persisted in institutional life and social manners. It was also that in parts of London and the English countryside there was a graciousness, a subdued alertness to the possibilities of life, a newly candid grappling with reality, and an imaginative energy in the air.

It was with these more pleasing aspects of Edwardian England, in any case —the England of James Barrie and Henry James, of George Bernard Shaw and H. G. Wells, of Rudyard Kipling and John Galsworthy, of country estates like Cliveden and Stanway—that Edith Wharton came in closest contact.

After the stay at Queen's Acre and a day at Eton to see King Edward and Queen Alexandra open a new hall, Edith went on to London and Lady St. Helier's house in Portland Place. The former Mary Mackenzie of Scotland, a singularly charming and hospitable woman, had been married briefly to Colonel Stanley of the Coldstream Guards; after his death she married Francis Jeune, who became the first Baron St. Helier around the turn of the century. Perhaps the most notable event of an otherwise rather slack season had been the marriage in September of Mary St. Helier's grandniece Clementine Hozier to young Winston Churchill, the member from Manchester and president of the Board of Trade in Herbert Asquith's recently formed Liberal cabinet.

The fine weather, Edith reported, permitted "pleasant sight-seeing prowls" in the morning, and at tea and in the evenings at Portland Place she had her first close-up glimpse of the British aristocracy—including, at one gathering, the Duchess of Manchester, whom she had known in the old days at Newport as

Consuelo Yznaga; their friendship would reestablish itself periodically over several decades. Some of the same guests were on hand when, the weather changing, Edith drove through a white late-November mist to Cliveden, the three-hundred-acre estate above the Thames of the expatriate William Waldorf Astor and his brilliant and authoritarian second wife, the former Nancy Langhorn.

James was back in London and was prevailed upon to stay at Portland Place instead of the Reform Club. In early December, with James and Sturgis, Edith was the guest of James Barrie for dinner in the Savoy Grillroom; they all went on to see Gerald du Maurier in Barrie's *What Every Woman Knows*—a work which gently spoofed the male ego (or Barrie's somewhat distorted view of it), to Edith's womanly amusement. She lunched at the House of Lords with its librarian, Edmund Gosse, a gossip-loving old friend of Henry James's, a writer of uncertain talent, and a trusted liaison officer in the London literary wars: "the official British Man of Letters," H. G. Wells would call him. Gosse, whom Edith Wharton thought "quick and flashing," introduced her in turn to Max Beerbohm, the dapper and distinguished drama critic, caricaturist, and fable spinner who had already earned for himself the adjective "incomparable," which would cling like a first name or a title.

Dinner parties at Portland Place were not as spectacular nor the guests as varied as they had been before Lord St. Helier's death—in earlier times one could encounter people as diverse as Carlisle, Gladstone, and Mark Twain—but the widow's hospitality was still boundless, as Edith Wharton remarked. Thomas Hardy, an intimate of the St. Helier household, was present on several occasions. Edith managed what she called "a mild chat on literary matters" with Hardy, but the nearly seventy-year-old novelist seemed to her exceedingly shy and not much interested in current literary developments or critical talk about their common craft.

To entertain her American guest one evening, Mary St. Helier invited a group which included Sir Philip Burne-Jones, Princess Marie Louise of Schleswig-Holstein, and John Galsworthy. The first and best of Galsworthy's novels in the Forsyte series, *The Man of Property,* had been published two years before; Edith was not unimpressed by it, though, as so often, she thought the man more interesting and enjoyable than the work. But she warmly agreed with the observation of a new young English friend—after seeing Galsworthy's play *Justice,* which spurred Winston Churchill to modify English prison regulations—that Galsworthy was "the kind of man who thinks that a few bye-laws would solve the dark human problem."

A few days later Edith went to Stanway, at the foot of the Cotswold hills in Gloucestershire, for a weekend party arranged in her honor by Lord Hugo and Lady Mary Elcho. Elcho, a member of Parliament and an ardent card player, was the elder son of Francis Charteris, the tenth Earl of Wemyss (pronounced to rhyme with "dreams"), a Scottish family with a Jacobite background. The most memorable Wemyss in recent history had been Hugo's grandfather, known for his exploits as "the Hunting Earl"; Hugo remembered him as a frail old man shooting at game with a valet standing behind him to catch him when he reeled backward from the kick of the gun.

Stanway was one of the most beautiful, though not the largest, of English aristocratic homes, and the Edwardian world glimmered there as perhaps nowhere else. Talk at other house parties tended to be the vapid accompaniment of incessant eating and drinking, the display of new coiffures and parasols, and the *sotto voce* making of assignations. But at Stanway the conversation ranged brilliantly over literature, science, politics, and art—it was the Stanway constituency which made these interests fashionable in a society led by a king who rarely opened a book.

The most frequent and celebrated visitor over many years was Arthur James Balfour, the Tory leader and, from 1902 to 1905, Prime Minister: an erudite, philosophically minded man with penetrating eyes and an elastic step. Around him gathered persons like H. G. Wells, James Barrie, Harry Cust, the Duchess of Rutland, and Balfour's devoted friend and hostess, Mary Elcho herself. Many years before Edith Wharton's first visit, one noble gentleman, after listening to the group discoursing, dubbed them "the Souls," since that phenomenon seemed to be their chief topic.

The name stuck, and the Souls were a major element in the Edwardian age; but the epithet inevitably drew such counter-comments as that the group was more pagan than soulful, and that " 'the Souls' so often discovered they had bodies too." Stanway was no more immune to the Edwardian habit of discreet adultery than any other estate. Balfour and Mary Elcho had a liaison going back to the first days of her marriage. Hugo Elcho, meanwhile, found satisfaction for years with a tough-minded noblewoman separated from her husband. And Harry Cust, whose remarkable beauty of body and mind made him the helpless prey of one adoring woman after another, was said to be responsible for the unusual number of sapphire-eyed children in the nurseries of the peerage.

It was most probably in December 1908 that Edith Wharton first met Harry Cust, editor of the evening paper the *Pall Mall Gazette:* "Noblest and Best of Editors," in the words of H. G. Wells, who, with Kipling, Balfour, and others, wrote for him; a man of extraordinary promise never quite fulfilled; a person who, as it was said, always lived "at concert pitch," reading the *Georgics* on his way to a hunt, comparing quotations from Horace coming home from a dance in the early hours. With Edith Wharton, as she recalled pleasurably, he swapped examples of great kisses in literature: in *Antony and Cleopatra, Troilus and Cressida, The Red and the Black.* Edith, after meditating, confessed surprise that Henry James had contributed only two great kisses: in *The Spoils of Poynton* and *The Golden Bowl.*

Despite the affairs that flourished at Stanway, the Elchos were an affectionate and closely knit family, and theirs was a most comfortable and inviting home. Lady Elcho was a lovely and captivating creature: tall, queenly, impulsive, self-deceptive, scatterbrained, and given to mystical visions of hopeful or fearful variety. Edith was smitten by her, and in later years Mary, Countess of Wemyss (as she had become) would be the Englishwoman to whom Edith Wharton was most devoted.

4

In the eighteenth-century drawing room at Stanway, with its Tudor ceilings and Queen Anne mirrors and log fires that warmed only so much of the body as was turned toward it, Edith Wharton that December weekend was introduced to two young Englishmen of particular interest to her. These were an agreeable man named Robert Norton, and John Hugh Smith, "the most brilliant young man I have met in England." Both became part of her inner circle—Hugh Smith at once, Norton more slowly—and remained within it for almost thirty years.

Norton, then forty years old, was a man of such striking dark good looks (a picture of him reminds us, today, of Anthony Eden) that he was known to his intimates as "Beau Norts." He had been educated at Eton and, for a year, at Cambridge, the university which had been as hospitable to Edith Wharton's English male friends as Harvard was to her American. In 1890 he had been appointed clerk in the Foreign Office, later served in Stockholm and Paris, and became the private secretary of Lord Robert Salisbury, the Conservative Prime Minister at the turn of the century. But his real interest was in landscape painting. In 1903 he left the Foreign Office and went into business in "the City," where he was so adroit that at the time he met Mrs. Wharton he was about to retire and devote himself to watercolors.

He had a decided talent, although not much ambition; he also dabbled at writing nature poems and love poems, and did some verse translations. But as his lifelong friend Gaillard Lapsley would say of him, it was life that he chiefly cultivated as a fine art: painting, reading, conversation, European travel, and such gentlemanly exercises as swimming and walking. For Edith he would provide a calm, steady, and disinterested friendship, and perhaps the most relaxing company she would ever know.

John Hugh Smith, at twenty-seven, was considerably younger. He was a small, strongly built man, with a powerfully etched face, a bullet head, and a little moustache. He had a keen, deeply cultivated, and inquiring mind—habitually, pinching his lips, he would pursue his interlocutor's most casual remark—and an educated taste in women beyond that of most of the bachelors in Edith's personal community. He was also very much of a gourmet, with an admirable knowledge of burgundies; but he was oddly unfastidious in dress and was likely to appear in a rumpled, even a shabby, suit.

This was not due to economic need. Hugh Smith came from a well-to-do and influential family of landed gentry which had produced bankers, admirals, and tea merchants, and he was himself beginning to carve a career of his own in banking, with a special interest in Anglo-Russian financial affairs. (It was his father, incidentally, who added the name "Hugh" to the family surname.) He had been a friend of Percy Lubbock's since their Cambridge days together, and of late had been listening with interest while Lubbock praised Edith Wharton's writings and expressed his bewilderment that she expected him to be as well informed on whole ranges of subjects as she was. "I was right," Hugh Smith wrote Edith soon after their first meeting; "you alarm poor Percy, but his admiration for you is that of all sane men."

Having encountered each other at Stanway, they met up again at Cirencester, Abingdon, and Queen's Acre. "I am pleased to think," Hugh Smith told Edith on December 19, "that during the last week I did not miss one hour of your society that I could possibly have taken." Looking back years later, he recalled a woman in her mid-forties with a youthful figure, very good clothes, and a lined face, and a gift for the most entertaining and stimulating conversation he had ever heard.

He thought her fascinating and possessed of an exuberant vitality, rather than charming in any literal sense. This was a judgment in which Howard Sturgis concurred. Sturgis had just come to know a Lady Bective (an acquaintance of Edith's as well), and was so charmed by her that he suggested the word "bective" as a synonym for charming. There were, Sturgis said, beaming around at his guests and elaborating on the idea in his customary manner, people who were "bective" and those who were "abective"—"like you, dear Edith," he remarked benignly—and finally people who were *"absoulment imbectes."*

Charming or no, Edith Wharton struck John Hugh Smith as complete "mistress of the civilised life" in an unmistakably American fashion. He fell, in fact, more than a little in love with her. One of his brothers told Sturgis, who hastened to pass it along to Edith, that John was "incomprehensively interested in a 'married American female novelist.' " (That description, Edith observed to Hugh Smith, "is specific enough for a manual of zoology.") He sent her Yeats's poem, derived from Ronsard, to Maud Gonne: "When you are old and gray and full of sleep / And nodding by the fire"; and begged her to send him some casual verses she had written when they sat together in her car. He told her he wished his "business in life was to motor every day with you and not to urge *'l'âme Russe'* along paths which should lead me and it to affluence." He described his depression over the many weeks that must pass before he could "have nine or even three hours' conversation with you."

Speaking of their forthcoming reunion in Paris, after Edith had left England, Hugh Smith braced himself to make a small confession:

And now I want to say something that I find rather difficult to express. When I see you again our friendship will have one quality which has not been altogether present here in London. The fact of such an obviously brilliant person such as you being so exceptionally kind to me has at times made me a little self-conscious—even when I was alone with you. And the simplicity I sought was not helped by Howard Sturgis's and Mr. James's amused though perfectly kind remarks. . . . In Paris we shall be able to go ahead and eliminate this Jacobean element in our relation.

Though acknowledging her pleasure in their friendship, Edith was not inclined to encourage quite that degree of the personal in their intercourse. From Avignon, on the day after Christmas, she replied:

Was I—or were you—all the complicated things you say? It seemed to me so much simpler! I'm afraid I always go with outstretched hands toward any opportunity for a free and frank exchange of ideas, and am too much given to omitting the preliminary forms where I find a fundamental likeness of mind!

It was a great pleasure to wander over the cosmos with you in that easy fashion, and if you liked it too, for whom are you concerned, and why do you plan better things for our next meeting? Beware of gilding the lily!

Yet, as the months passed, it was often to John Hugh Smith that Edith was drawn to confide her strongest feelings about her own condition of life.

"Ah, my dear young man," Henry James wrote him, "you have made friends with Edith Wharton. I congratulate you: you may find her difficult, but you will never find her stupid, and you will never find her mean." Difficult, Hugh Smith would learn, Edith could certainly be, especially when the restless fit was on her. Never once did Edith appear to him stupid; he stood in awe of the "noble curiosity" that James so rightly attributed to her, and was impressed by the way her fund of knowledge and high intelligence were tempered by humility. Like many others, he felt that Edith Wharton held too low an opinion of her work. "She knew that it was all right and competent and never amateurish," he said later; "she did not think it was in any way of the same kind as the really first-class stuff." As to meanness, Hugh Smith discovered that Edith was remarkably devoid of malice, except in one or two cases (and this too was much later) when some woman or other had offended her. "I do not like the women friends of my men friends," she used to admit, but it rarely showed.

To Edith herself, James wrote to say that he was "intensely wondering" if Hugh Smith had found her *"de choix,"* as James was sure he must have. James had been following her progress through England with the liveliest interest and with ornate speeches of encouragement. "I gather from Howard," he had said in November, "that you are making as many *gestes* as possible, for which I heartily applaud and commend you. . . . Keep at them, keep at them, and when you've made a *great* many *gestes*—well, you'll see! So I rejoice that circumstances make for the multiplication of them." He spoke to Sturgis of "the most brilliant of women and of all the light she sheds—in the form of far-scattered *paillettes* [sequins]—as well as in others." Her procession across the country in what he was beginning to call her "chariot of fire" seemed to him "glorious and godlike— almost too insolently Olympian."

At the same time, he was disturbed by the rush and movement of Edith's existence, the plunge from one great house party to another, even though he knew the value of all this to her for the moment. "The arrangement of [Edith's] life," he wrote Lapsley, "is to me one of the prodigies of time." A few months later he summarized the entire English visit as "a social 'time' worthy of her. General eagle-pounces and eagle-flights of her deranging and desolating, ravaging, burning and destroying energy. . . . The Angel of Devastation," he said, inventing an epithet that would endure, "was the mildest name we knew her by."

He wrote much the same, and at greater length, to Walter Berry in Egypt, with an air at once marveling and consternated:

> I should like to tell you *par le menu* the entire sequel to that poignant hour of our loss of you, mine and the Lady of Lenox's. . . . But the theme is too large, and the whole thing defies, by volume and quantity, my lame epistolary muse. She has been having, indeed, after a wild, extravagant, desperate, detached fashion, the Time of her Life. London, and even the Suburbs, have opened their arms to her; she has seen everyone and is even now the occasion of some great house party away off in the midlands (Stanway —the Elchos!) whence she comes back to more triumph and will, I imagine, be kept here in one way or another, till the New Year and the arrival of Teddy. She has really been much amused and pleased, and with her frame of steel, it has been remarkably good for her. But what a frame of steel, and what a way of arranging one's life.

It may be doubted that Hugh Smith, for example, would have recognized the woman described in those tempestuous adjectives. And though James did perceive, as none other, that the interlude in England was "remarkably good for her," one wonders if beneath the frame of steel he also sensed the continuing mortal desolation. The more James knew and observed Edith Wharton, the more some part of him grew positively alarmed by her energy, her curious insatiable zest for life, and what seemed to him her "fantastic freedom." He felt inexplicably threatened by her, to the point where he missed the capacity for suffering which gentler-minded and less probing friends perceived rather quickly.

14. "Terminus"

During Edith Wharton's absence from Paris, in the later summer and autumn of 1908, Morton Fullerton's emotional interests were again taken up by his cousin Katharine, who came to Europe on a year's sabbatical leave from Bryn Mawr. She arrived in a state of trepidation. Morton's messages, mostly on postcards, had been few, and she felt tormentedly uncertain about the engagement. She approached her fiancé cautiously, and only after some weeks in England, which included a visit to Oxford and several days in London, where she met and quite lost her heart to the beautiful Mrs. Bertrand Russell, the former Alys Pearsall Smith. From London, Katharine wrote a wary letter to "Dearest Will," entreating him to write his parents and saying that he had a terrible ability to inflict pain. There was some talk of their going to Lamb House together; nothing came of it, but Katharine's spirits brightened a little.

In Paris she took rooms in the St. James and Albany on the Rue de Rivoli, insisting on having a sitting room, expensive as that would be, so that they could have a place to talk. "What a damnable world it is that puts every kind of convention between us!" Her position seemed to her extraordinarily ambiguous, and there were times when she "would give everything to be your own sister." As the autumn deepened, the relationship seemed, to her troubled, hopeful mind, to have been reestablished.

Morton and Katharine were daily in each other's company—as was observed by a sprightly young woman named Doll, who appears to have been one of Fullerton's lesser *amours*. "So you are always with your sister," Doll wrote him in slovenly French. "*You play with fire too much.* You tell me that your little sister loves you. Don't break her heart if you are not capable of attaching yourself to her. I should talk to you about morality," Doll went on. "Wednesday or Thursday my lover arrives. He will stay here 8 or 10 days. As soon as possible after that, I hope to see you again. I embrace you tenderly." Fullerton seems to have enjoyed referring to Katharine as his sister, even after, presumably, explaining the true relationship: Camille Chabert also wrote a worried, affectionate letter urging him not to trifle with his sister if he were not serious.

But then there came what Katharine called "that bitter midnight hour." One can only guess, but it seems likely that Morton (this was his custom) told her in some detail about the affair with Edith Wharton, with the implication that their engagement was at best in a highly doubtful state. Katharine fled to the Convent of the Sacred Heart near Tours and settled there for the winter to get on with her work, a first novel. When Morton asked her to return to Paris, she refused: if she were to do any work, it must be apart from him. But her work did not progress.

We may glance ahead to follow this story to its conclusion. When Katharine returned to America in the summer of 1909, the situation was bewilderingly unchanged. They were still engaged, as far as she could make out. They had seen each other several times during the winter and spring, but Morton continued to be an infrequent and incommunicative correspondent. From Bryn Mawr on November 1 she wrote asking if Morton's silence meant that "you have grown to hate me: to suspect me of wanting to clog your feet. Please do not think such ugly things of me." At the same time, she could not resist passing on word from an American friend, the wife of a Frenchman, whom she had seen much of in Tours: "She doesn't like Mrs. Wharton, who looks worn out and nervous and wants too much 'homage.' I ought not to tell you this."

By the end of the year Katharine was in a "tumult of perplexity." Gordon Gerould (the name was pronounced "Gerald"), a highly gifted young instructor of English at Princeton, had proposed marriage, and Katharine was more than half inclined to accept him—if marriage with Morton was truly and finally out of the question. But was it? She had heard nothing for months except, in answer to a distracted inquiry, a cable saying "Wait letter."

Katharine's letters, and especially her last long one to Morton in January 1910, were embellished by the literary flourishes of an able writer and teacher of literature, but they have an air of passionate honesty, and it is hard not to be moved by them. "I would rather live alone with my dream of you—if I can't have you—than forego that dream for whatever recompense"; but she was shaken by the fear that Morton's "unintended unkindness" and the long silence would so weaken her that one day she would discover the dream of him had evaporated: Morton's obdurate refusal to write, to answer her pleas, was an unending agony for her. "I do not believe you have ever treated another woman so ill." She had asked before, and now asked again, "for nothing explicitly save that you should explicitly throw me over. That oughtn't to be hard, if you don't care for me. . . . Oh, my own, trust me and send me some word."

This time, it would appear (again, one guesses), Morton wrote to say in effect that he did love and want her, but that his own situation was too confused for him to contemplate marriage. Perhaps he said that he would accept the fact of her becoming the wife of another man, however much it might wound him. In February, when Katharine became engaged to Gordon Gerould, she sent Morton a cable saying: "Courage dear." In June she and Gerould were wed.

Katharine Fullerton Gerould's first work of fiction, *Vain Oblations*, appeared four years later. She had sent the manuscript to Edith Wharton in Paris, and it was Mrs. Wharton who successfully pressed it upon Scribner's—as the work, so she put it, of the cousin of an old friend (Fullerton had obviously explained the actual degree of his kinship with Katharine). Mrs. Gerould went on to produce a sizable number of volumes—novels and collections of stories—over the next three decades, a portion of it, at least, a decided cut above the "magazine writing" usually attributed to her. The debt to Henry James was obvious at the outset, so much so that James was embarrassed by a story of Katharine's that Fullerton sent him in 1902. "Am I so much that *as* that?" he asked. But Mrs. Gerould's more mature work, at its rare best, is a curious and attractive blend of Edith Wharton and Joseph Conrad: with something of Edith Wharton's poignant irony and sense of the relentless power of piety, mixed with an interest in the exotic, the violent, and the primitive.

The former Katharine Fullerton waited a dozen years after her marriage before drawing upon her relationship with Morton in a story called "East of Eden" (in *Valiant Dust*, 1922). The tale is, in fact, almost a reversal of the story of Katharine and Morton Fullerton. On a South Sea island a young missionary named Roger Twining meets and falls deeply in love with Letitia Quayle, the daughter of a visiting anthropologist. The two grow so much in love that, to the narrator's view, they begin to resemble each other in speech and gesture. On the eve of the wedding, it is discovered that they are in fact brother and sister, each having been taken by foster parents. With a kind of desperate defiance, Letitia offers to stay with her brother despite the relationship:

> If you choose, I'll stay forever. I don't understand anything; I don't believe anything; and nothing they say makes a difference. I love you better than the whole world, or what you call God, or anything. No one is real but you.

But Roger sends her away.

2

The week before Christmas 1908, Edith crossed from England to France with Howard Sturgis. They celebrated Christmas in the Rue de Varenne and then drove rapidly south and east to Dijon—a motor tour which Edith described as an "elopement," taking note of a letter from an unnamed gentleman "who wanted to elope with me to see Stromboli in action" (that volcanic Sicilian mountain having undergone one of its irregular eruptions). They swept down to Avignon, where, of all southerly places, there was a blizzard, and the two fled to the snug comfort of 58 Rue de Varenne for New Year's Eve, and the start of Edith's third season in the Vanderbilt apartment.

That same night, in search of true Paris "life" and celebration, as Edith put it, they dined at the Café de Paris, where, inevitably, they saw only other

Americans and English "in quest of the same elusive element." But this first introduction of Sturgis to the old Faubourg was enjoyable for all concerned, and Henry James felt that the combination was a very happy one. It was delightful for Sturgis to be there, he wrote Edith, and "delightful for you to have had him —so genuine and special and charming a social value—to produce in a society so deeply sentient of such value."

Edith's household was beset by small afflictions in the wake of Sturgis' departure. "I, for whom the domestic ship usually runs with miraculous smoothness," she wrote Hugh Smith, "have been having what Mr. James calls 'a hell of a time' (he really does!)." James wrote commiseratingly: "What fell things can happen in the *grande vie*"; but he still had the impression of dash and glitter in and around the Rue de Varenne.

Matters were not improved by the arrival of Teddy Wharton from New York on January 18. He was in a most wretched condition. The insomnia which Edith had overcome during the English weeks now seemed to have transferred itself to Teddy; his body ached in various places; he was morose and pain-ridden. Edith was forced to realize that his basic trouble was nothing so obvious as gout, and that the "cure" he had taken the spring before in Arkansas had been temporary at best. Upon arrival in Paris, Teddy also came down promptly with a case of the grippe which refused to respond to medication.

He had to be excused from Edith's dinner parties, though the latter were in fact abruptly curtailed since, as Edith said with attempted lightheartedness, her husband needed constantly to be "cheered at the family fire-side." She escaped at least once from the depressing atmosphere for an evening at Jacques Emile Blanche's, one moment of which did her soul good.

Among the guests was George Moore, the fifty-seven-year-old Irish writer and man of many escapades, whose autobiographical *Confessions of a Young Man* in 1888 had perhaps done the most to secure his literary reputation. Moore, according to Edith, "revealed himself so monstrous, incredible and repulsive a bounder that I had to annihilate him." Moore had remarked with some complacency that the women he had written about had, oddly enough, been flattered by his doing so. "I should think *you* would have been flattered at their ever having heard of your book," Edith replied acidly; and, as she reported, "having tasted blood I proceeded to wade in it."

Despite such occasional satisfaction, she was beginning to feel like a "shabby, close-to-the-ground and frequently eclipsed planet," and not at all an "unclouded luminary," as John Hugh Smith was depicting her. It was with young Hugh Smith during this difficult time that Edith was growing most confidential. Though she had, at first, artfully eluded his verbal advances, she was beginning to be playful, even flirtatious, in her letters to him. "Dear Mr. Smith," she wrote, "(or Hugh-Smith?? Well, at any rate, Dear Mr. John!)"; and when she learned that his first initial was A., she wrote: "Dear A. John Hugh (though why 'a' when you're so obviously *the?* and how often has this been said to you?)." She signed herself "your affectionate friend Edith," and took to praising his artistic discernment: "you who have a scent for the rare and fine" and an "admirable instrument of apprehension."

In early February, Hugh Smith remarked that he and Percy Lubbock had seen Mrs. Pat Campbell in a play by Rudolf Besier, *Olive Latimer,* and had disapproved of it because it was weighted too heavily on the side of its main female character, a discontented wife. "Dear me!" Edith answered. "What *jeunes féroces* you and Percy are. . . . If what you said had been addressed to Mrs. Campbell's acting, I should have understood; but no, it's the subject you scorn." She then let herself go in one of the most outspoken statements she ever made about both her own situation and her habitual choice of subject matter for fiction.

My first impulse, of course, was to truckle—but, as I cast my eye backward over literature, I seemed to remember a few other neurotic women who were discontented with their husbands and relations—one Clytemnestra, e.g., and Phaedra, and Iseult, and Anna Karénine, and Francesca da Rimini—who still live in the imagination, and will I fancy, outlast Shaw—not to speak of Barrie!

And I wonder, among all the tangles of this mortal coil, which one contains tighter knots to undo, and consequently suggests more tugging, and pain, and diversified elements of misery, than the marriage tie—and which, consequently, is more "made to the hand" of the psychologist and the dramatist?

How close this was to an appraisal of her personal dilemma was made evident in the next letter, in which Edith admitted that "things have not been going better" with her and Teddy and that her outburst had been a "way of relieving the tension." In response to repeated invitations, Hugh Smith came over for a brief visit and helped lighten a little the gloom spread by the despondent Teddy. Upon his return to London he sent Edith, as he had promised to, a handsome cigarette case (along with a bottle of "Rose Tooth Wash," at Edith's request, from Floris' in Jermyn Street); thanking him, Edith said that the "admirable" case had arrived at just the moment "when it needed all the robustness of the self-conceit which Howard deprecates in me to convince me that you wouldn't after all, think better of your intention."

For his part, Hugh Smith was also feeling restive, and spoke of the fact that his banking activities did not challenge his deeper energies; but, he added, "I won't bother you with my troubles." Taking him sharply to task, Edith in effect repealed the veto implicit in the earlier letter. After their London days together, she wrote,

I thought we had reached a point where one doesn't have to make speeches of that sort, and that the joy of reaching such a point is precisely that of being able to speak one's mind to the "party of the second part" without the paralysing fear of being a bore or a bother.

You see I am going very far back in our correspondence. . . . I go back because what you said struck such a chord of sympathy. I've known, in the past, so many such blank bits of time, out of which one felt one might have made something delightful—"lovers and lamps," as Walt says, if only—!

She struck a Jamesian note: "I wish I could talk it all over with you here and now, instead of groping about in the darkness of my ignorance! But write me, and tell me more." And she ended with the acknowledgment that she too was going through "weary weeks."

In an effort to provide Teddy with some distraction, Edith at the end of February took him on a ten-day motor trip through southern France. They had "splendid sunshine" and fresh air, but the trip did Teddy no visible good, and he was soon pleading to go back to Paris. There, under the direction of a specialist, he began the kind of massage and electric treatment from which Edith had benefited to a considerable degree a decade before in Philadelphia.

Under the circumstances, large-scale literary work was next to impossible. *The Custom of the Country* was abandoned once more (this novel, arguably the most powerful Edith Wharton ever wrote, was also the one that suffered most from interruptions of several kinds). But Edith did not allow the season to pass without a new volume: her first book of poetry, *Artemis to Actaeon*, was published in the third week of April. She was, meanwhile, producing short stories at almost one a month, and had already decided upon the title and nature of her next collection: *Tales of Men and Ghosts*. But the half dozen stories written in 1909 are dismayingly below her best achievement; one has the sense that her imagination was simply not focusing, that in her daily stint she was only going through the motions, her thoughts elsewhere.

Too often, a good fictional idea gets smothered in tricky turns of plot. In "The Bolted Door" (published in March), for example, the real theme is that of the "prisoner of consciousness"—the feeling on the part of the main character that he has been "visited by a sense of his fixed identity, of his irreducible, inexpugnable *selfness*, keener, more insidious, more unescapable than any sensation he had ever known." This could have been a fascinating variation on Edith Wharton's central theme of entrapment: in this instance, within one's own mental skin—a sensation Edith herself no doubt was experiencing as her mind throbbed with clashing and irresolvable concerns. But the idea is fleshed out in a Poe-esque tale of a man who has murdered his cousin and is unable to persuade anyone—his lawyer, his best friend, the district attorney, an alienist—that he is guilty of the crime. Percy Lubbock, reading the story in *Scribner's*, dismissed it as a "rotten little melodramatic anecdote" of the sort Mrs. Wharton had no business writing, and remarked again that Edith herself was "cleverer and more alive and finer than her books."

"His Father's Son," which came out in June, has on the biographical side a certain potential interest. It was the first of several stories Edith would write on the theme of illegitimacy, and although there is not much evidence to support it, it may be that it was only at this time that Edith first heard the rumor about her own irregular paternity. If so, the story implies that she rejected it derisively.

There are, nonetheless, one or two interesting parallels. Edith Jones, born in January 1862, was, according to allegation, not the daughter of the soberly upper-middle-class George Frederic Jones, but of the cultivated foreign-born tutor of her brothers. In "His Father's Son," young Ronald Grew persuades himself that he is not the son of the solidly bourgeois buckle manufacturer Mason Grew, but of the distinguished European pianist Fortuné Dubrowski, whose relationship with Mrs. Grew appeared to have begun in January 1872. But it is all an innocent hoax and a misunderstanding; Mrs. Grew had never even met Dubrowski, and the tender letters she was supposed to have written him were in fact composed, for a variety of reasons, by her husband.

It might be argued fancifully that Edith Wharton's best contribution to fiction in the spring of 1909 was the part she innocently played in Henry James's story "The Velvet Glove." After reading it Edith wrote James to say that it was "really good," and to this James answered that two American periodicals had turned it down, which was like "declining *you*, since *bien assurément* the whole thing *reeks* with you—and with Cook and *our* Paris (Cook's and yours and mine) so no wonder it's 'really good.'"

The story harks back to James's visit to Paris in the spring of 1908, and behind that moment to the proposition put forward in the name of Edith Wharton that James devote an article to Mrs. Wharton's writings. James was fully persuaded that Edith had made no such suggestion, but he was characteristically intrigued by the thought that she might have done so. In "The Velvet Glove," the novelist-playwright John Berridge is approached by an intermediary at a reception in Paris and told that a highborn lady is eager for him to write a preface to her next book: in the lady's own words a little later, a "lovely, friendly, irresistible log-rolling preface." Berridge gracefully declines and urges the lady in effect to remain a *grande dame* and forgo literary activity.

The tale, as Leon Edel has demonstrated, is packed with echoes of Edith Wharton and allusions to her work and her manner of life. The lady's most recent novel is called "The Top of the Tree." She is an American-born princess, like several of Edith's Paris friends; *la princesse lointaine* (the phrase taken from a verse play by Edmond Rostand) was one of the innumerable epithets James applied to Edith. The princess is introduced amid a swirl of references to Artemis, Astarte, and other classical deities whose names throng Edith's poem "Artemis to Actaeon." Her motorcar is described as a "chariot of fire," and there is a gleaming evocation of the Paris through which Cook had driven Edith and James the year before.

Edel finds a note of hostility in the story, as though James were warning Edith

Wharton to confine herself to her lavish social existence and not to poach on his literary grounds. In this Edel may be right; there would be further evidence of muffled envy and apprehension on Henry James's part toward Edith Wharton. But Edith, rejoicing in the story and praising it, sensed no such element.

3

Edith was once again conserving her truest creative energies for poetry, and in the spring of 1909 her most cogent writing was another series of poems to Morton Fullerton. Things had evidently cleared up a good deal between them the moment that Edith's return to Paris had made possible private conversations. In James's brisk paraphrase, Edith spoke guardedly about "Morton's hell of a summer"; one speculates (with reason, as will be seen) that Henrietta Mirecourt had been raising a fresh storm, and there was the question of the ambiguous engagement to Katharine. But Edith was soon able to provide James with an encouraging report, and James applauded. "I couldn't accept the possibility of a non-clearance," he wrote, "from the moment a *meeting* remained possible. . . . Glad am I that we 'care' for him, you and I; for verily I think I do as much as you, and that you do as much as I. We can help him—we can't *not*. And it will immensely pay."

For several months, however, Edith was too busy looking after the nearly helpless Teddy to have much time for Fullerton. It was only—the pattern of 1908 in part repeating itself—after Teddy left for America in mid-April that the relationship could bestir itself anew. New poems were among its first fruits.

One of these, dated April 23, repeats what Edith had said in the 1908 journal: that poems written out of some solitary aesthetic or emotional impulse before she knew Fullerton were all unwittingly directed forward to her lover and their love. More arresting is a three-part, forty-two-line work bearing the title "Colophon to The Mortal Lease." A colophon is a concluding stroke or inscription placed by the printer at the end of a book; but these straining stanzas would have sounded odd indeed at the close of that sonnet sequence. They have to do in all candor with the immediate experience of sexual love and its aftermath, and in a manner somewhat to belie the import of the last original lines.

The experience is shrouded in elaborate similes of far-off empires, garlanded city streets, "star-sown melodies," and "the long winding of the mystic way"; but its successive stages emerge clearly enough. "Beat by beat," the speaker says, "my body hears the coming . . . of surging ecstasies." There occurs the act itself and the climax:

> I tremble into flower and flame to meet
> The fury of the cymbal and the song—
> Till suddenly the flood of rapture falls
> And silence darkens down the temple walls.

With her lover she had ascended to a mysterious height where sense and spirit had seemed perfected to commingle; she marvels at the complex power of sexual love, which, with its beauty and its terror, gathers to itself the whole of life in a single instant—a single murmur of the senses.

Yet, the poem says sadly in closing, it had been in part a delusion. Looking into the eyes of her lover, lying still beside her, the woman seeks to recapture "What sights beyond all seeing we have seen," only to realize that the event, the physical and spiritual communion, had not been as fully shared as she had supposed. "Ah, close your eyes," she says. "They see not what I saw." Exactly so had Edith felt during a transient moment the previous spring: "There is no use in trying to look at things together; we don't see them any longer." Fullerton, in the handwritten copy of "Colophon" that Edith sent him, with a dedication to "M.F.," added a postscript: "I saw not what she saw, and that's the tragedy of it."

But very much as before, the sad sense of failed communion was swept away in renewed sexual fulfillment, and a long remarkable narrative poem called "Ogrin the Hermit," written in May, testifies to the event. The handwritten copy Edith presented to Fullerton was inscribed *"Per Te, Sempre Per Te."* The poem contained Edith Wharton's passionate and triumphant defense to herself of her adulterous conduct.

"Ogrin the Hermit" takes as its epigraph a line from a recent prose version of the story of Tristan and Iseult: *"Vous qui nous jugez, savez-vous quel boivre nous avons bu sur la mer?"* ("You who judge us, do you know what drink we drank upon the sea?") The source is Joseph Bédier's imaginative retelling of the old legend. Tristan and Iseult, having drunk of the love potion together, flee Iseult's husband, King Mark, and arrive, faint and exhausted, at the forest hut of the hermit Ogrin. At first Ogrin deplores the lovers' sinful conduct, even while pitying them; but he is slowly persuaded by Iseult that their love has its own powerful pre-Christian sanction and springs from realities of nature older than the church.

The poem constitutes Edith Wharton's most searching examination of the clash she was so conscious of in herself at this time, between piety and sensuality —more abstractly, between Christian teachings, as she understood them, and such anti-Christian postures as she was drawn to in the writings of Nietzsche. She had dramatized this conflict (as its very title suggests) in a tale of medieval setting, "The Hermit and the Wild Woman" of 1906: a story strangely prophetic, in its contrast between austerity and the ecstatic pleasure of bodily refreshment, of actual experience to come. In "The Mortal Lease," she had virtually duplicated the theme in the opposing impulses to be "the nun entranced" and "the first wild woodland woman."

In "Ogrin the Hermit," all the phases Edith Wharton had passed through are evoked and drawn together: the adolescent eroticism and the adolescent religiosity; the fatal sexless marriage; the subsequent years of invulnerable self-control, during which any concern with either sex or religion lay buried; the explosion of desire in the spring of 1908 and its transforming effect upon Edith's sense of herself; the intent religious questioning it had stimulated.

As the narrative goes forward, the erotic element is unmistakably the victor. With Tristan away hunting, Iseult comes daily to the hermit's hut to hear his "words of holiness," but she listens, gently, like some visitor from a foreign land (as Edith, in her journal, had felt herself to be)—like one "in whose ears an alien language dwells, / Of some far country. . . ." In her replies to Ogrin, Iseult's utterance has a kind of "heathen innocence" that has nothing to do with lust or pride, but partakes of the essence of the natural life.

Iseult's vision communicates itself subtly to the holy man, and when he kneels in predawn prayer he begins to be aware of strange presences about him—"the old gods" hidden in the woods. The moment comes when Iseult must return to her husband. Ogrin sends her on the way in an attitude not only of forgiveness but reverence:

> For meet it was that a great queen should pass
> Crowned and forgiven from the face of Love.

What might be called the hermit (or nunlike) side of Edith Wharton's nature was thus for the moment—so the poem suggests—made subservient to the Iseult side, the side that was willing to risk the conventionally tabooed experience. But the adjustment was a precarious one, and depended for its continuance not only on Edith's special strength and cast of mind, but on outside factors she could scarcely foresee.

4

The lease on 58 Rue de Varenne ran out soon after Teddy left for New York in April; Alice Gwynne (Mrs. Cornelius) Vanderbilt was due to take over. Edith shifted to a commodious suite in the Hotel Crillon, high enough above the Place de la Concorde to have a panoramic view of the city. She had no plan, this time, to follow Teddy back to Lenox. The year 1909 was, in fact, the first in three decades that she spent entirely in Europe.

One reason for staying put, she told Henry James, was that she was simply too tired to travel. James sympathized. He too had had a "bad and worried and deprived and inconvenient winter," with heart trouble and a threat of jaundice; and he apologized for his silence "during a period of anxiety and discomfort on your part which I all the while feared not to be small—but which I now see with all affectionate participation, to have been extreme."

"Poor dear Teddy," James felt, was not made for such miseries as he had suffered. But he was aware that Edith's fatigue was as much due to other affairs, social and personal, as to concern over Teddy. " 'Tired,' you must be, even you, indeed," he wrote; but to his "wincing vision" (he was altogether committed to his "dusky village" and to "peace at any price"), Paris figured as a great blur of intense white lights and revolving wheels. And he ached for further news—"the real, the *intime*"—of herself and Fullerton.

Another reason for remaining in Paris was Edith's determination to find a place in the Faubourg where, with or without Teddy, she could settle more or less permanently. Before the spring was out, her brother Harry Jones found another apartment on the Rue de Varenne, this one at No. 53, on the other side of the street from No. 58 and a few steps nearer the Rue du Bac. It was available for an indefinite lease at something like seventy-five dollars a month.

The apartment had a series of balconies giving onto the street, but the interior was designed to face away from the traffic and to look down onto the privacy of a large courtyard; next to it were the attractive little Cité de Varenne (a small enclosed residential area which the English would call a close) and the gardens of the Doudeauville *hôtel*. It was considerably larger than the apartment at No. 58. Teddy, Edith reported, would no longer need to leave his boots in the library and could leave his room without having to pass through the *salon*. But this was a typical understatement.

In addition to the library, the spacious, high-ceilinged drawing room, the elegant dining room (all in a row above the court), and a good-sized kitchen and pantry, there were half a dozen bedrooms of various sizes, another sitting room —probably for Gross and Edith's personal maid—and several inadequately equipped bathrooms. The apartment contained what amounted to a guest suite: a bedroom and bath, and for private access a back stairs leading down to the courtyard. Unlike the apartment at No. 58, that at No. 53 was entirely unfurnished, and it was no small task, or expense, to put the place in order. Happily, and in a leisurely manner, Edith began to rummage through the Paris bazaars and the Faubourg antique shops in pursuit of one of her favorite occupations— keeping an eye out, too, for that most urgent necessity, a porcelain bathtub.

And then, of course, Paris also meant M.F.

James, who was holding firm to his vow never to leave England again, kept urging Edith to come over to him, promising to meet her in London if necessary. On June 3, Edith and Fullerton drove to Boulogne and crossed to Folkstone, where they spent the night. The following day they went up to London and took Suite 92 at the Charing Cross Hotel—two bedrooms and a sitting room. James joined them there for dinner.

It was a vivacious evening with a certain *fin de siècle* atmosphere: champagne, dim red lamps, laughter and lively talk, and in the late hours after James had gone back to his club, very considerable passion. Fullerton was due to sail next morning for a visit with his parents in Brockton; James arrived at ten to accompany him to Waterloo Station and the boat train for Southampton. As he was leaving the suite, Fullerton looked back to see Edith, propped up in bed with a writing board across her knees, scribbling the first words of a poem—typically (and it was a sign of her authenticity as an artist) she began to make a literary transcription of the adventure almost before it was over. There was just time for Fullerton to send a bunch of roses to the room from Waterloo. At sea that evening he received a loving message by telegram.

The fifty-two-line poem Edith wrote over the next days about their night together was called "Terminus"—a name chosen to indicate both that the experience occurred in a station hotel and that it marked a temporary end to their relationship. All things considered, it is an extraordinary document. It begins with startling directness:

Wonderful was the long secret night you gave me, my Lover,
Palm to palm, breast to breast in the gloom. The faint red lamp
Flushing with magical shadows the common-place room of the inn,
With its dull impersonal furniture, kindled a mystic flame
In the heart of the swinging mirror, the glass that has seen
Faces innumerous and vague of the endless travelling automata
Whirled down the ways of the world like dust-eddies swept through a street,
Faces indifferent or weary, frowns of impatience or pain,
Smiles (if such there were ever) like your smile and mine when they met
Here, in this self-same glass, while you helped me to loosen my dress,
And the shadow-mouths melted to one, like sea-birds that meet in a wave—
Such smiles, yes, such smiles the mirror perhaps has reflected;
And the low wide bed, as rutted and worn as a high-road,
The bed with its soot-sodden chintz, the grime of its brasses,
That has born the weight of fagged bodies, dust-stained, averted in sleep,
The hurried, the restless, the aimless—perchance it has also thrilled
With the pressure of bodies ecstatic, bodies like ours,
Seeking each other's souls in the depths of unfathomed caresses,
And through the long windings of passion emerging again to the stars . . .
Yes, all this through the room, the passive and featureless room,
Must have flowed with the rise and fall of the human unceasing current,
And lying there hushed in your arms, as the waves of rapture receded,
And far down the margin of being we heard the low beat of the soul,
I was glad as I thought of those others, the nameless, the many,
Who perhaps thus had lain and loved for an hour on the brink of the world,
Secret and fast in the heart of the whirlwind of travel,
The shaking and shrieking of trains, the night-long shudder of traffic;
Thus, like us they have lain and felt, breast to breast in the dark,
The fiery rain of possession descend on their limbs while outside
The black rain of midnight pelted the roof of the station;
And thus some woman like me waking alone before dawn,
While her lover slept, as I woke and heard the calm stir of your breathing,
Some woman has heard as I heard the farewell shriek of the trains
Crying good-bye to the city and staggering out into darkness,

And shaken at heart has thought: "So must we forth in the darkness,
Sped down the fixed rail of habit by the hand of implacable fate—"
So shall we issue to life, and the rain, and the dull dark dawning;
You to the wide flair of cities, with windy garlands and shouting,
Carrying to populous places the freight of holiday throngs;
I, by waste land and stretches of low-skied marsh,
To a harbourless wind-bitten shore, where a dull town moulders and shrinks,
And its roofs fall in, and the sluggish feet of the hours
Are printed in grass in its streets; and between the featureless houses
Languid the town-folk glide to stare at the entering train,
The train from which no one descends; till one pale evening of winter,
When it halts on the edge of the town, see, the houses have turned into
    grave-stones,
The streets are the grassy paths between the low roofs of the dead;
And as the train glides in ghosts stand by the doors of the carriages;
And scarcely the difference is felt—yes, such is the life I return to . . . !
Thus may another have thought; thus, as I turned, may have turned
To the sleeping lips at her side, to drink, as I drank there, oblivion.

After the final line, Edith wrote: "VI, 1909."

Edith placed the poem in Fullerton's hands when he returned in July, with a note saying: "I beg you dear, send back the poem soon. *Je suis si heureuse*—it breaks over me like a great sweet tide." Fullerton complied, but not before copying the poem out and adding a word about its actual and literary origins. Fullerton's note gives the number of the suite at the Charing Cross Hotel. It also claims that the rhythmic pattern of "Terminus" derived from Goethe's *Römische Elegien*. Edith Wharton was undoubtedly fond of that handsome poetic sequence. But the American reader of "Terminus" is more likely to be reminded of the expanding rhythms and long lines of Walt Whitman—which Edith Wharton more than once singled out as the most striking and original aspect of Whitman's verse. "Terminus" can remind one as well of Whitman's expression of union with all of suffering humanity.

Edith Wharton once read about herself in a review, and wryly recorded the comment, that she was a woman who had never known passion. "Terminus" dispels that still obstinately lingering legend. Nothing she ever wrote out of her own actual experience speaks for itself more forthrightly than this poem, with its moving combination of candor about the act of love and compassion for the forlorn and weary.

5

Edith stayed on in England during the rest of June and until the middle of July. On the afternoon of the day Fullerton left for America, she and James drove down to Guildford and thence, in James's phrase, "by a beautiful circuit to

Windsor and Queen's Acre." James could remain only for the weekend, but Edith enjoyed what she called "this green refuge" for another ten days—green was now established as the color she deployed in describing anything particularly dear to her heart.

She then betook herself to London, to Lady St. Helier, for a dip into the London season and another exploration of the social world presided over by King Edward. She told Sally Norton that everyone was busy, but she managed to lunch and dine several times with the Duchess of Manchester; to see Lord Burghclere, the Liberal politician, and his wife, Winifred, a writer of history and a woman of charm; to lunch at Cliveden with the Astors (and bow out of a large house party there). At Cassiobury, not far from London, she visited with the former Adela Grant of Boston, now the wife of the seventh Earl of Essex, a friend of Jennie Churchill's and of the king's. "All the mightiest of the land" were there, Edith reported.

In the town house of the immensely successful novelist and antisuffragette leader Mrs. Humphry Ward, Edith met at lunch George Protheroe, the editor of the *Quarterly Review,* and his pert and animated wife, Fanny, a confidante and neighbor of Henry James's. Also on hand was General Sir Ian Hamilton, a brilliant soldier and a classically good-looking man who was equally at home with poets, politicians, and persons of fashion. At Stocks, the Wards' country estate, Edith found various members of the Trevelyan family, Lady Stanley of Alderley (Mary St. Helier's sister-in-law), and the original and talented American monologuist Ruth Draper, who performed to the company's, and especially James's, delight.

It was all highly diverting, but Edith was discovering that she cared "less and less for 'general society,' and more and more for just a few friends." She abandoned London and contented herself by commuting between Queen's Acre and Lamb House, with stops in Oxford and in Gaillard Lapsley's Cambridge.

The friends in question had the impression of incessant motion, of a regal figure sweeping down upon them and then soaring away to other conquests. Edith, Percy Lubbock observed, "came & went & came & went—and Henry was snatched down to Windsor more than once"; but Lubbock found her "very kindly," and they hit it off better than ever. Observing Edith's galvanic flights, Sturgis composed a comic fable about "the *oiseau de feu*" and "the majestic Paddingtonia," borrowing the title of Stravinsky's ballet for Edith and basing the other mythic creature upon Mrs. Paddington, James's matronly and autocratic housekeeper of some years.

Edith was undoubtedly experiencing a tremendous surge of vitality in the wake of the night described in "Terminus," though the nervousness and impatience she felt while waiting for Fullerton to return gave her "a furious case of hay-fever." But then Fullerton was back after the briefest of visits with his parents, and the hay fever disappeared. When Sturgis learned that Edith and

Fullerton, after another night in London, were moving on from the Alfred Austins in Ashford to Lamb House and a motor tour with Henry James, he wrote her with a sort of fanciful shrewdness: "Keep it up—run your race—fly your flight —live your romances—drain the cup of pleasure to the dregs."

As for James, he said about "our aquiline Edith"—Edith as eagle was another of the figures now being invoked—that *"elle plane,* for the hour, just over this province," and that he hoped for "her *séjour* with me" at any moment. On July 12 he noted in his diary: "E.W. and Morton Fullerton arrived to dinner and the night." Next day the three of them drove along the coast to Eastbourne and lunch with James's crippled old friend Jonathan Sturgis (no relation of Howard), then on to Chichester and a night at the Dolphin. After another run to Canterbury and Folkstone, they parted company; Edith and Fullerton spent another day in Folkstone and one in Boulogne before making their way back to Paris.

The sixty-six-year-old James at once put on an air of total exhaustion. To Sturgis he declared that he had come back to Lamb House "more dead than alive" after being carried along "at the tip of our *so* high-flying kite" through most of Essex. He referred to Edith's "ineluctable descent" and her "unappeasable summons," and said that though Edith had been "convulsed . . . and infinitely charmed" by Sturgis' fable about her and had recited it for his benefit, it was not,

I make bold to say, to her faintest amendment or amelioration. Her amusement at any cost and in any quantity that suits her she *will* have, let who will pay (vitally, conveniently, and temporally speaking) the piper. So she set the pipers piping hard—and I danced till my aged legs would no more—and (the worst of it) it was all beautiful and interesting.

The final phrase was characteristic of the about-face Edith's most critical friends were always finding themselves forced to make, in all honesty; but for the rest, the language seems unduly strong to describe a visit of less than three days and a drive to Chichester and back.

In fact, it was not Edith who issued the "unappeasable summons," but James himself, by telegram to the Austins urging her to come down to Rye with Fullerton and take them all on a tour. So Edith told John Hugh Smith, adding that upon receipt of the telegram, and realizing that James was "inflamed by jealousy" over the report of her excursions, she had postponed the channel crossing and "turned Hortense's prow westward" (the car had been baptized in honor of Mlle. Allart).

A month later, nonetheless, James was still expostulating to Lapsley over Edith's visit, though here he seems to have been referring to the entire six-week stay rather than the last brief appearance at Rye:

The Angel of Devastation has become a mere agitating memory, but nothing could have exceeded the commotion and exhaustion produced by her prolonged stay. Devoted as I am to her I feel even as one of those infants of literary allusion whom their mothers hush to terror by pronouncing the name of the great historical ravager of *their* country, Bonaparte, Attila, or Tamerlaine.

During the trip to Chichester, Edith consulted with James and Fullerton about a plot she had been hatching, the aim of which was to rescue Fullerton once and for all from the menace of Henrietta Mirecourt. The latter was again making direct threats and more pressing demands. The previous uproars had ended in a kind of compromise, Mme. Mirecourt calming down after Fullerton returned—part time, so to speak—to her company, but continuing to hang on to the precious papers. She may now have added to her store the many letters from Edith Wharton; but by the same token, Fullerton, this time, had not only the moral support of Henry James but, in Mrs. Wharton, a wealthy mistress who was ready to take more practical action.

Edith's plan was in two stages. Frederick Macmillan had invited her to write a book about Paris for a series in which James was to do one on London (a task he never got around to). Edith replied that she, regretfully, was too busy to take on the assignment, but warmly recommended Morton Fullerton, who had lived in Paris for many years and knew the city in all its aspects: "I know no one half as well qualified to do the work charmingly as well as thoroughly." Fullerton was duly commissioned, and received an advance of one hundred pounds.

The literary enterprise would itself benefit Fullerton importantly, as James and Edith realized. "It will help him to write it," James remarked, "and he will help it to write *him*, which he hasn't for a long time been able to help anything efficiently to do"; Fullerton's only recent products had been a few excellent but brief articles on political conditions in France. But Edith had a further proposal, according to which an additional one hundred pounds should make its way stealthily into her lover's pocket.

The method of payment worked out was remarkably roundabout. Edith was to write James a check for that amount. James in turn was to suggest to Frederick Macmillan that he, James, should supply funds for a second advance which would come as though from the publisher. Into this charade James entered with enthusiasm, even though, as he pointed out, "it puts *me*, poor impecunious and helpless me, in the ridiculous nominal position of a lender of *de fortes sommes!* That, however, is *la moindre des choses;* so please consider that I will play my mechanical part in your magnificent combination with absolute piety, fidelity, and punctuality." On July 26 he wrote Macmillan to say that Fullerton had many sudden expenses because of his father's illness, and was badly in need of money: "I should like to send you a cheque for 100 pounds, say, that he may profit to that end, *without his knowing it comes from me.*"

There is no doubt whatever that Fullerton knew all about it, and had been privy to the plot from the outset. He may have demurred a little, but he allowed himself to be persuaded to go along. James wrote him urgently: "You will give me as much pleasure by accepting as you can have done by any act in your life." One can only marvel at the exquisite scruples of all three persons as they participated in this circuitous undertaking; Edith might have quietly put the money directly into Fullerton's hand. But one surmises that such an act would, for Edith, have verged on the sordid, with the words of "Terminus" still echoing in her head; and this way, besides, the one hundred pounds could be associated with a literary venture.

James sized it all up in terms of high moral drama, and found Fullerton's acquiescence precisely the element that completed the splendid pattern.

That he should *let* you do it will seem to me in that case almost as beautiful as that you should do it, in converting a stricken and comparatively sterilized life into a life worthy of his admirable intelligence and capacity, I can't speak in terms adequate—or without emotion. Therefore I regard it as *all* worthy of three children of light and honour.

Macmillan countered with the suggestion that he himself would forward the one hundred pounds (for which read today the respectable sum of more than three thousand dollars). James would stand surety if Fullerton failed to write the book; he never did write it, but Macmillan did not call in the note. Before the month of August was out, Edith could report that Fullerton had "recovered his possessions," and could give an affirmative reply to James's inquiry as to whether "the accursed woman" had, finally, "surrendered the papers, letters, scraps of writing containing references to people, etc. which he mentioned to me originally."

When the plot had first gotten under way, James wrote Edith: "What a *détente*, what a blest and beneficent one, poor tortured and tattered W.M.F. must feel!" Now he wound up the episode by saying that, though Fullerton had been tormented, "he will also, D.V., have been redeemed." Using such language, James must have thought that by some incalculable conversion of art into life he had been helping to act out a drama similar to that in his own novel of 1902, *The Wings of the Dove*. In that story, an attractive but indecisive young journalist named Merton Densher—an obvious play on the name of James's young friend Morton Fullerton—is at a critical moment offered a large sum of money by an exceedingly wealthy American woman who is in love with him, and by whose love, the novel says, he has been "blest" and "redeemed."

The Neurasthenic: 1909-1913

PART FOUR

The news from Teddy in America was mixed during the spring and summer of 1909. He had still been suffering from a variety of aches and pains when he left Paris in April, but in June, Dr. Francis P. Kinnicutt, who had been Teddy's personal physician for a number of years, wrote from his New York office that the serum treatment Teddy had been given in Boston had been partly successful. The "facial neuralgia" had been cured, and the pain in his feet relieved. But Dr. Kinnicutt was now convinced—and this seems to have been the first time the matter was broached—that Teddy's trouble was basically a mental one, and he could be no more than moderately optimistic. "Local irritations and suffering directly affect the deeper evil," he wrote. "Remove them and by just so much you retard the progress and manifestation of the other." Edith wrote gloomily about her husband to Henry James, who declared in turn to Lapsley that he gravely feared Teddy might be "cerebrally compromised."

Around the middle of July, Teddy's widowed mother, Mrs. Nancy Spring Wharton, fell seriously ill, and on August 17 she died in her Lenox home; Teddy erected an oddly shaped marble slab and drinking fountain in her memory in the Lenox cemetery. Edith had long felt that Teddy was perhaps excessively attached to his mother, and now thought that her death might be a release for him. A letter from the younger Nancy Wharton ("Nannie") a month later seemed to fulfill that prophecy.

Edith had received one thousand dollars as a legacy from Teddy's mother and proposed using it to buy books for the Lenox library. Nannie wrote twitteringly that this was not the idea at all; her mother had wanted Pussy to buy something for *herself*, perhaps an article of furniture for the new apartment. She then offered a glowing and repetitious account of Teddy's state of being:

> He, Ted, seems *perfectly* well and *perfectly* normal now. He sleeps well, eats well, and looks very well. . . . You need have no anxiety about him physically or mentally now, for he seems perfectly well in all ways. No pain in feet, hands or face and his whole aspect is that of a perfectly healthy person.

He had bought himself a new car and was enjoying a series of drives around the countryside. More than that, he had shown himself to be something of a genius in his handling of Edith's estate, displaying "immense energy and great astuteness" in venturesome transactions in steel.

It was not entirely clear, as the autumn weeks passed, why Teddy was staying on in America. Dr. Kinnicutt grew troubled over reports that reached him of Teddy's zestful conduct. Mr. Wharton, he thought, sounded "in a distinctly exalted state"; the physician had already observed a certain large oscillation of spirit in Teddy's case. During a short stay in his own summer home in Lenox, he made a point of calling at The Mount. They had only an hour together, and in the company of others, but the doctor was forced to admit that Teddy struck him as "very natural; keenly interested in all he showed us, interested and interesting in his plans for the further development of The Mount."

With this in mind, Dr. Kinnicutt wrote Mrs. Wharton a cautious letter of warning.

> From the reports which I have mentioned, from my knowledge of his past, and from my experience in similar cases, I am not free from anxiety about him. My fear is that on his return to Paris, in an environment which does not appeal to him apart from the helpfulness of your presence, there may be another swing back of the pendulum.

The tactful implication was that Teddy flourished to some extent in places—like The Mount and the salmon rivers—that were suited to his nature, but that the highly charged social and intellectual life of the Faubourg bored, wearied, and depressed him. The doctor urged Mrs. Wharton not to allow her husband's interest and involvement in The Mount to flag: "At present it is the one place in the world which he is most fond of."

2

On the evening of Thursday, September 30, 1909, Bernhard Berenson went to Voisin's in Paris to dine with Henry Adams, his friend of several years; Voisin's, on the corner of Rue Cambon and Rue St. Honoré, was probably the greatest of the Paris restaurants at this time, though closely rivaled by Larue's, Paillard, Laperouse, and one or two others. Somewhat to his surprise, Berenson was not shown to Adams' usual ground-floor table but was led upstairs; here Adams greeted him and took him to a table by the window where a lady was seated. No introductions were made; dusk had fallen, and the strange lady was wearing a black lace veil so that Berenson could not make out her features. But he soon found himself engaged in liveliest conversation with her; they touched on art, literature, and mutual friends, and their minds seemed to meet at many points. When, eventually, the lights were turned on, Berenson discovered to his astonishment that the lady was Edith Wharton. The astonishment was due to the fact that on his only other meeting with Mrs. Wharton, some years before, he had found her thoroughly disagreeable.

Such was Berenson's reconstruction of the event forty years later in *Sketch for a Self-Portrait*. The reality was less dramatic. Edith was not alone, having come on the arm of Morton Fullerton, and Elizabeth Cameron was there as well, with her daughter Martha. The conversation was more light-hearted than Berenson recalled; there was no problem of visibility; and in any case Berenson had seen Mrs. Wharton in Adams' apartment only a few days earlier. They had even been in correspondence about the dinner engagement. Nonetheless, the September 1909 meeting was a momentous one for both persons, and Berenson's subsequent dramatization was unconscious testimony to his awareness of the fact.

In March 1903, when Edith was in Florence during her tour of Italian villa gardens, a meeting had been arranged between her and the Berensons by Henry Cannon, a Philadelphian and a long-time friend of Mary Berenson's; he was sure they would all like one another. The encounter took place at Cannon's home, the Villa La Doccia, an imposing edifice (now the Hotel San Michele) whose long, balustraded covered terrace loomed up above the road coming down from Fiesole.

Mary Berenson arrived late, with her brother Logan Pearsall Smith. Alfred Austin, the little poet laureate who also maintained a home in Florence, was there, and Robert Underwood Johnson, the editor of the *Century* magazine (for which Edith was writing the garden articles), and his wife. "The great Edith Wharton," Mary informed her diary that night, had been purely hateful. "We found B.B. there, already, it was clear, loathing her. We also disliked her intensely." Mary had an impression of "intolerable miffiness, rudeness, self-absorption," and Berenson said later about Edith that "she sniffed, she sneered, she jeered, she lost no occasion for putting in the wounding word, the venomous phrase." When, long afterward, Edith and Berenson, now firmest friends, talked about the disastrous evening, Edith said she had had no idea of appearing so repellent; it was only that, as so often, she had been petrified at being in the presence of a man whose work and the quality of whose mind she so greatly revered.

Berenson, meanwhile, had been careful to stay out of Edith Wharton's way in the years following, but he and his wife took occasion to comment spitefully on Edith's work. Mary reported with some glee that a highly intellectual Spanish woman friend had thought *The House of Mirth* "a rotten novel," and was incredulous that, if the novel were accurate, fashionable American society avoided the one justification for its very existence—which was, of course, illicit love-making. Coming upon Edith's article about the terra cottas at San Vivaldo, the Berensons went to look at them and returned scoffing at Mrs. Wharton's preposterous suggestion that any of them could have been by one of the della Robbias.

On his arrival in Paris in September 1909, however, Berenson ran into a kind of conspiracy to bring him and Mrs. Wharton together. Adams spoke with unusual warmth about Edith and declared he wanted to arrange a dinner for the two of them; Berenson, straining for politeness, said he would be charmed. Driving back from a visit to the Henry Whites' country place, he listened as the former Margaret Rutherford held forth on Edith, claiming that "no higher bred woman existed in America, and that she was above all littleness." As he was about to take his leave from Adams' apartment in the Avenue du Bois de Boulogne one afternoon, Elizabeth Cameron showed up, no doubt by preconcerted plan, bringing Edith Wharton with her. "She did not look the least like the woman we met 6 or 7 years ago," Berenson wrote Mary, back in Settignano.

There followed swiftly the dinner at Voisin's. "It was very nice and we all were 'merely human,' " Berenson told his wife; "chatting, gossiping, exchanging limericks, etc. Mrs. W. was affable to the last degree, and so I buried the hatchet, and called on her yesterday."

Bernhard Berenson (he would not drop the "h" from his first name until after the outbreak of the war) was forty-four in 1909. He was of Lithuanian Jewish background and had come as a child to Boston with his parents. At Harvard he did brilliantly, and served on the literary *Monthly* with Morton Fullerton, among others ("Fullerton," he told Mary after the evening at Voisin's, "looked pretty much as he did 23 years ago, altho' graver, and maturer. He seemed perfectly simple and likeable and I shall try to see him again"). After graduation he continued his studies of art history, concentrating gradually on the Italian Renaissance, with the help of stipends provided largely by Mr. and Mrs. Jack Gardner. In 1894 he became Mrs. Jack's European agent, and in her name, for large sums, he purchased painting after painting for the planned gallery at Fenway Court: a Botticelli, a Rembrandt, a Titian, a Masaccio. By 1909 he had also become the chief agent for the Duveen brothers—Joseph, Louis, and Earnest—and was beginning to earn a small fortune, and more, for his services of "expertising." He lived well and enjoyed it: the Ritz Hotel in Paris, he told Mary comfortably, was very expensive but was worth the money.

Berenson had become widely recognized as the most distinguished and original living student of Italian Renaissance paintings. His four volumes on Florentine, Venetian, Northern Italian, and Central Italian painters of the period had already appeared by 1909, along with two series of essays on Italian art. It was Berenson who determined most of the different "schools" of the artistic epoch, and he had introduced phrases like "life-enhancement" and "tactile values" into the vocabulary of art criticism. He was without rival in the work of identifying the authors of disputed paintings and correcting wrong attributions, and seems to have regarded Edith Wharton's venture into this field, at San Vivaldo, as an effort to preempt his function.

In 1900, after a liaison of some years, Berenson married Mary Costelloe, who had just become the widow of an Irish Catholic barrister. She was the former Mary Pearsall Smith of a Philadelphia Quaker family—Mary regularly addressed her husband as "thee." A large handsome woman of Berenson's age, she had great vitality, a quick intelligence, a strong sense of humor, and a freedom, even a rashness, of spirit that led to erotic entanglements before and after marriage.

The Berensons made their home in the Villa I Tatti—no one has ever discovered the origin or meaning of the name—which they first rented from a Lord Westbury in 1900. They had just completed purchase of it at the time of the 1909 meeting, had enlarged it considerably, and laid out a beautiful design of terraces, gardens, and lawns. The villa lay on the Vincigliata slope below the village of Settignano, some five or six miles northeast of Florence. The interior was richly hung with the late medieval and Renaissance paintings Berenson had acquired for himself in the course of time, those by Simone Martini and other Sienese artists being perhaps the most striking among them.

Bernhard Berenson was a slight, slender man, with a sensitive, fine-boned face adorned with a carefully trimmed beard and moustache. He had bright watchful eyes, often crinkled in concentration, and a delicately charming and rather flattering manner. An ardent conversationalist, he was at home in half a dozen languages; a sometimes oddly displaced kind of English was his own preference. Edith, unconscious at the 1909 encounter of the *brutta figura* she had made six years before, found him even more remarkable than his great work. For his part, Berenson was a little intimidated by Mrs. Wharton: a matter for surprise, since he was on easy terms with the wealthy, the aristocratic, and the artists and writers of several countries. But he had perhaps never before met an American woman who combined the creative and intellectual gifts, the social background and the money, of Edith Wharton.

3

Getting out of her car in front of the Crillon late one October afternoon, Edith noticed several people standing transfixed and staring up at something. Glancing up herself, she saw a tiny airplane sailing lazily through the skies high above the Place de la Concorde, heading toward the river. It was a Wright biplane, piloted by the Russian-born Comte Charles de Lambert, who had been a pupil of Wilbur Wright's and in fact had the American aviator in the seat behind him. In what was said to be the first time a plane had flown over a major city, Lambert had come in from the gates of Paris at a height of more than a thousand feet—about three hundred feet had been the average altitude attained to date—and had cruised past the tip of the Eiffel Tower, a few yards to the right of it, before circling over the obelisk in the Place de la Concorde and wandering away.

Edith invested the technological achievement with romance and poetry:

It sailed obliquely across the Place, incredibly high above the obelisk, against a golden sunset, with a new moon between flitting clouds, and crossing the Seine in the direction of the Pantheon, lost itself in a flock of birds that was just crossing the sky, reappeared far off, a speck against the clouds, and disappeared at last into the twilight.

Edith took pride in the recent ascendancy of the French in the field of aviation. She had rejoiced no less than her Paris neighbors the previous July when the heroic Louis Blériot won the London *Daily Mail'*s prize of twenty-five thousand francs by being the first man to fly the channel. Taking off from a point near Calais, he made the thirty-mile trip in thirty-eight minutes and landed on the Dover cliffs, where his approach was guided by a journalist wildly waving the tricolor.

With the vision of Lambert's plane still in her imagination, Edith went off for a few days with Jacques Emile Blanche at Offranville, in Normandy near Dieppe. It was a good change, but once back in the city she began, in her own phrase, to feel "Paris-stale." She hoped that when Teddy arrived they might go away on a more prolonged motor trip. But when her husband did appear, soon after the first of November, he was in very questionable shape.

It is as well at this stage to rehearse the history of Teddy's various troubles and changes of personality and conduct. Until his fifty-third year (in 1902), he had been invariably robust physically and alert mentally. Fishing, shooting, and riding were among his favorite occupations; he loved dogs as much as Edith did and had himself photographed with a Pekinese on either knee; he also loved all other animals. According to virtually unanimous testimony, Teddy was warm-hearted, gracious, and utterly accommodating—whether of his wife's interests or those of their guests. He had an intuitive good breeding which at least one friend of the Whartons thought went deeper than Edith's. He was much more knowledgeable than she about fine wines; after a discourse with Berenson concerning some rare vintages, Edith wrote with wan pride that *that* was something Teddy really did know.

Teddy was given to reading mystery stories and sports magazines—though he bravely made his way through Henry James's *The Golden Bowl,* recording his conservative opinion that it was one-quarter too long; he was devoid of Edith's interest in philosophical and scientific writing. But he had an enormous admiration—sometimes reverential, sometimes amused—for his wife's attainments, even if it remains unclear how attentively he read her books. Once at Lenox, walking with Walter Maynard a few paces behind Edith, he pointed ahead and said: "Look at that waist! No one would ever guess that she had written a line of poetry in her life." He told Maynard proudly and with a sense of wit that in order to build a new piggery which they had felt they could not afford, she had dashed off a poem and sold it to a magazine.

He had no vocation and no great sense of civic duty, but as Gaillard Lapsley once said about him, his "idleness was busy and innocent." He was busy particularly, as co-trustee with Harry Jones, with the management of his wife's estate: the property at Lenox and the complicated list of stocks and securities. This was his chief labor in life, and he gave himself to it with a skilled devotion. Even finding and settling in a new apartment in Paris without Teddy, Edith had learned, was an unfamiliar burden to her.

For the rest, he was spruce but not foppish, debonair without in any way being a snob. Above all, perhaps, he had a bubbling good humor, an addiction to the good story, and a gift for repartee.

The first period of Teddy's sporadic illnesses lasted something over a year and a half, from the summer of 1902 to the moment in the winter of 1904 when Edith reported, almost resentfully, that he was "bursting with *bien-être.*" Melancholy, insomnia, and intermittent nervous irascibility were the chief symptoms at this time. Whatever the other possible causes, it is hard not to suspect that one underlying source of these afflictions was the extensive change in Edith's position in life. During the year 1902 Edith Wharton published to considerable acclaim her first full-scale novel, *The Valley of Decision;* began to earn a great deal of money from her literary work, which was itself astonishingly varied and prolific; closely oversaw the completion of The Mount, her own creation from the ground up and the first home of her own design; and fully recovered her health for the first time in a dozen years. Teddy had always had something not unattractively childlike in his nature. His collapses were in part, one surmises, ways of drawing attention to himself in the midst of his wife's widespread recognition and her achieved independence and well-being.

Teddy was now in the hands of Dr. Francis Parker Kinnicutt, one of the leading physicians of New York. Dr. Kinnicutt had married the daughter of a highly successful New York banker, and the Kinnicutts lived in something of a grand style. He was a general practitioner rather than a specialist, but he was as shrewd medically as he was kind personally; his early diagnosis, quoted above, was as sound as that of any of the specialists Teddy was later forced to consult. He became the most trusted of the Whartons' medical advisers, and he was a valued friend, in his courteous way, of both husband and wife.

After Teddy's return to good health and fine spirits in 1904, his condition was generally excellent for four years. This was the time of the first motorcars and the excursions in New England and across France; Teddy much enjoyed sharing the wheel with the chauffeur. It is true that Teddy began to absent himself from The Mount more often than hitherto, for fishing or shooting or for family visits. The flood of vaguely intellectual and artistic houseguests was more than Teddy could comfortably stand without periodic refreshment in the woods or on the river. Nor did Edith always make the effort to turn the conversation into areas where Teddy could participate. One of the visitors to The Mount has remembered the awkward and slightly tight-lipped silence that would fall upon the company when Teddy smilingly joined them on the terrace.

Teddy's second series of nervous and physical disorders coincided with Edith's remove to Europe for part of each year, and in particular with the taking of the Faubourg apartment in 1907. Friends of the couple have said that Edith might have preferred a place in England and that Paris was Teddy's choice. If so, it was a most unhappy one: for with little opportunity for his favorite forms of recreation, Teddy, in Berkeley Updike's words, "found himself stranded in a society for which he was neither adapted nor inclined." His command of French was limited; and in any event, what had he to communicate with Anna de Noailles, Paul Bourget, Jacques Emile Blanche, Gustave Schlumberger? Small wonder that his previously sunny nature should occasionally be clouded.

But it was, of course, far worse than occasional fits of ill temper. Teddy survived the first Paris year with only minor ailments, but the reentry into 58 Rue de Varenne in the winter of 1908 coincided with the severest attack of "nervous depression" in five years. Never thereafter could the seemingly hearty condition he sometimes attained be counted on to last. He continued morose and racked by headaches through the winter, until he betook himself to Hot Springs. By the winter of 1909 it was evident that Teddy, now nearing sixty, was in the grip of some profoundly serious illness.

It took two forms. The physical manifestation was an assortment of acute pains in his head, face, teeth, arms, thighs, legs, and toes. The mental symptom had become a long alternation between high, sometimes wild exuberance and frozen melancholy, each state enduring for several months or more but the one passing into the other with lightning speed.

4

Teddy arrived in Paris in November accompanied by his sister Nannie; the latter, following the death of her mother and the break-up of the homes in Boston and Lenox, had decided to address her discordant energies to her brother. To Edith, Teddy appeared "much *too* well": very excitable and given to rattling on incoherently about his business triumphs. Within a matter of weeks there occurred what Dr. Kinnicutt called the "swing back of the pendulum." "The breakdown," Edith wrote Sara Norton, "has come exactly *as* and *when* Dr. Kinnicutt told me it would," and she was exasperated that Nannie Wharton, with the evidence before her eyes, had persisted in an "incredible blindness and stupidity and determination not to recognise *any* nervous disorder."

Edith proposed a motor trip to get them both out of Paris, but Teddy seemed too depressed for such an effort. Nannie thereupon announced that she wanted to go to Pau in the Basse Pyrenées, and Edith was given a taste of the capacity of brother and sister to wrangle over plans and change their minds from one moment to the next. She summarized the discussions to Sally: "After numerous plans, and variations of plans, and modifications of the variations, and deviations

1. Edith Jones about age five

2. Edith in 1870, age eight

3. Edith in 1876, age fourteen

4. Edith in 1880, age eighteen

5. Interior of the house on West Twenty-fifth Street, New York, about 1884

6. The New York home of Edith and Teddy Wharton at 882-884 Park Avenue, in the 1890s

7. George Frederic Jones in 1880

8. Harry Jones about 1890, age forty

9. On the lawn at Newport around 1884. Sitting, left to right, Hoyt Gould, Lucretia Jones, and Teddy Wharton; standing, Miss Edgar, Edith's cousin, and Edith Jones

10. Edith Wharton, age
twenty-eight, in 1890

11. Edith Wharton in 1897

12. Teddy Wharton with his dogs, 1886

13. The Mount in Lenox, Massachusetts, about 1905

14. Edith Wharton, Christmas 1905

15. Walter Berry, about 1905

16. Teddy Wharton and Paul Bourget, with Minnie Bourget standing, at Les Plantier in the early 1900s

17. Outside The Mount, 1904; Teddy Wharton and Cook in front, Edith Wharton and Henry James behind

18. Henry James at Northampton, Massachusetts, 1905

19. The exterior of 58 Rue de Varenne about 1908

20. Edith Wharton in Paris, 1908

21. Morton Fullerton, around 1908

22. Elisina Tyler and her son Bill, about 1913

23 Philomène de Lévis-Mirepoix at Hyères, about 1922

24. Edith Wharton, 1925

25. Walter Berry in 1925

26. Pavillon Colombe in the 1920s

27. Ste. Claire in the 1920s

28. Bernard Berenson and Edith at Ste. Claire about 1931

29. Edith Wharton in 1934

30. A Christmas party at Ste. Claire, 1936. Sitting, left to right, John Hugh Smith, Mme Homburg, Edith Wharton; standing, Robert Norton and Gaillard Lapsley

from the modifications, it was settled that Teddy should 'run' her down to Pau"
and Edith should go off to Germany for a week with Anna Bahlmann, she also
having recently come over from America.

The two women had several amiable days in Munich, where they stayed at
the Vier Jahreszeiten. Edith caught cold in the "sepulchral damp" of one of the
galleries, but she enjoyed a performance of Schiller's *Kabale und Liebe* in the
Schauspielhaus and liked roaming the National Museum. They went on to see
the Tiepolo paintings in Würzburg, and to Bruchsal and Karlsruhe, before returning to Paris. A "very 'rococo' trip," Edith admitted; she was always drawn to the
German eighteenth century and to the spirit of her idol, Goethe, enshrined there.

From Pau, Nannie wrote to say that the drive down had been splendid and
Teddy as wonderful as always. "Spite of rain, we did have a very pleasant time
together, Ted and I, and the parting with him yesterday was awfully hard." On
December 8, Edith and Teddy rejoined each other at the Crillon.

That same evening Teddy came out suddenly with a most unexpected confession. He told Edith that the previous summer he had converted a number of her
holdings, including those in steel, into cash, had speculated on his own behalf,
and then had purchased an apartment in Boston. He had established a young
woman there as his mistress and lived with her for several months. He also
claimed to have let out the spare rooms to several chorus girls as tenants; and he
added other picturesque details.

After a stunned silence of a few days, Edith wrote Nannie to ask what she
knew of this affair. Nannie wrote back in a splutter of remorse. She acknowledged
that Teddy had been in a very excitable state during the summer and fall, and
that she and her brother Billy Wharton had been very worried about him. On
the trip to Pau he had been "in a terrible state of mind," and it was only then
that he revealed "what he had done with your money. . . . You can imagine what
an awful blow it was! Of course I knew last summer that he was speculating, but
had no idea that it was with your Trust Funds." She was only thankful her mother
was no longer alive.

It would have killed her and for us all it is a hard blow. You have much to forgive,
dear Pussy, and I feel so sorry you should be called upon to go through such a terrible
ordeal.

There was but one thing for Teddy to do: return to America at once and "settle
everything"—as now, with the legacy from his mother, he was fortunately able
to do. The poor dear fellow had already suffered a good deal after realizing what
he had done.

As to the other matter, Nannie said, she had felt that *something* was wrong,
but could not, of course, speak to Teddy about it. He had written her about this
too, however, in a note that had just arrived from Paris.

My dear Pussy there is nothing to say, except that you have my *deepest sympathy* and I try to dwell upon the fact that he was not responsible for what he did last year. Which is my only comfort. Fortunately everything can be all arranged at once and no one except ourselves will know about the sad story and he will thus be sheltered and spared any extra mortification. He has to bear that at any rate alone.

Edith wrote a guarded account of the developments to Henry James, apparently stressing the financial aspect of the matter, and James, who had always spoken most affectionately, and of late most commiseratingly, about Teddy, now turned against him with a kind of majestic ferocity. Writing on Christmas Eve from Lamb House about Teddy's "depredations," he told Edith he had long feared something of the sort, but that Teddy "can do—can intervene and bedevil —no more; as co-trustee he *has* to liquidate," and so make amends. He did not hold back from implying that Edith was quite affluent enough to survive this particular financial calamity. To Sturgis he was more vehement:

Bear you lightly on [Edith] in thought; she has had and is having great anxieties, inconveniences and complications about Teddy (who has had no "melancholia" but on the contrary excess—quasi-demented excess—of levity and gaiety which has translated itself into incongruous and extravagant forms and consequences). I can't say more—and *don't know this from me please.* I can't speak of it, mustn't yet. What a nightmare the Paris history is . . .

"I wish I had better impressions of this particular phase of the situation of the Angel of Paris," James confided to Lapsley on New Year's Day, 1910; "but those I have are pretty bad. . . . The unspeakable Teddy," he said, had been "sinister, even very sinister, in a financial way." Teddy had misbehaved "with a great deal of fatuous and misapplied energy and ambition," and poor Edith had been through some dreadful weeks. "I greatly pity her. I can't help regretting, however, that an *intellectuelle*—and an Angel—should require such a big pecuniary base."

Abjectly remorseful and humbled—though full of protestations (so Nannie said) about Edith's nobility, understanding, and forgiveness—Teddy sailed back to Boston just before Christmas, presumably to set about making restitution. In the first week of January, Edith braced herself to write at length to Dr. Kinnicutt. The latter, on receipt of her "amazing account of the past six months," immediately communicated with William Wharton in Groton, Massachusetts, and began inquiries into the entire episode.

Dr. Kinnicutt gave it as his judgment that Billy "in justice to his brother . . . should persuade him temporarily to take up residence in a sanatorium. By doing so his irresponsibility for his actions during the summer would be acknowledged and the moral slate of the previous six months would be wiped clean." Billy answered that he and his wife were ready to accept Dr. Kinnicutt's analysis but that Teddy could not be persuaded to enter a sanatorium. Dr. Kinnicutt countered with the proposal that Teddy be sent south in the care of a physician, and after a week's discussion this was arranged; Edith received a cable to that effect.

Teddy, who was being given very little say in these conferences, then begged not to be sent away, but allowed instead to go back to his wife; he sent a letter to the doctor pleading his case. This was conveyed to Edith, who cabled that she was quite willing for Teddy to return to her and would send White by the next steamer to accompany him, or if necessary would come herself. Dr. Kinnicutt, with whatever reservations, consented to this solution, saying that White would do very well; and Teddy, his brother informed the others, at once became "much more content and quieter with the settlement of the matter."

The truth of what had happened emerged only in installments, as it is likely to with investigations into even the most modest iniquities. Dr. Kinnicutt's findings, sent on to Edith in early February, indicated that Teddy's confession had been unnecessarily lurid. He was at pains to make the adventure sound as mild as the evidence allowed.

The fact remains that for a short time he did live quietly with a woman in a small flat which he purchased for $16000 or $17000 I am told. I am also informed that she was not a woman of the town, a woman of perhaps 33 or 4.

The story of chorus girls etc filling his flat as tenants and many other stories told by himself I find had no foundation. As you know, all this has been finally settled and your husband's unhappiness and shame about the whole miserable business is very great.

Dr. Kinnicutt added one piece of gentle advice: although "the opinion of the world may be disregarded at times," he hoped that in this critical case Mrs. Wharton would return to The Mount in the conspicuous company of her husband the following summer.

But it slowly came out that Teddy had embezzled—and spent—not less than fifty thousand dollars from Edith's several trusts. The "small flat" turned out, according to the deed of sale, to be "a parcel of land with buildings" on Mountfort Street, near Beacon Street in one of the most desirable sections of Boston and near his mother's former home. Teddy appears to have rented the property during the summer but not to have purchased it until sometime in the autumn. There must have been a good deal of extra space, and there is no reason why Teddy should not have rented some of it out to other persons, though not necessarily to ladies of the chorus.

As to restitution, Teddy had to draw upon his recent inheritance. By the terms of his mother's will, he received one-third of two hundred thousand dollars, along with some valuable land. His brother arranged for fifty thousand dollars of Teddy's share to be transferred to one of Edith's trusts. Teddy thus saw the major portion of his fortune snatched away almost before it came into his hands, even as the sky fell in on him immediately after the first transaction of any size he had ever made on his own account.

Edith must have reflected, with what bitterness one can only guess at from later evidence, upon the ironic possibility that the start of Teddy's affair in Boston had coincided with her nights together with Fullerton in London. She would learn belatedly that Teddy's provable adulteries had begun the year before, in 1908, apparently at just the moment when the relationship with Fullerton was first being consummated. This may well have made her wonder about the exact nature of Teddy's behavior during those periods when he absented himself from The Mount to enjoy the clubman's life in New York.

Running through fifty thousand dollars in half a year's time, Teddy, in a fevered way, had no doubt been enjoying himself hugely; but apart from that, his actions have the air of childlike revenge, at once financial and sexual. For a good many years Edith Wharton had been an extremely wealthy woman. Teddy, on the other hand, had only a rather small allowance until his mother's death; he had inherited nothing from his father, whose estate went intact to his widow, and had been making do with about two thousand dollars a year—and with the shared use of his wife's money. For a man approaching sixty, however normally easygoing, this could not but have been galling, especially since his chief association with Edith's fortune was in the handling of it.

How heavily the sexlessness of his marriage over more than two decades weighed upon him cannot be known; but there is no doubt that Teddy had a perfectly normal, even a vigorous, sexual nature, though like Edith's it did not erupt until fairly late in life. For a number of years, meanwhile, he had witnessed his wife's heightened enjoyment in the company, first, of Walter Berry, and then of Fullerton. He seems to have been aware that Berry was no real threat, and Berry was besides a pleasant male companion with whom Teddy could exchange jokes and stock-market tips. But Teddy could not have failed to detect, in the Paris winters of 1908 and 1909, that something more was in the air than Edith's customary enjoyment of the conversation of other males, and that Morton Fullerton was playing a role in her life very different from that of the others. It is not unlikely that, by way of recompense, the fact induced him to step up, if not to initiate, his own program of misbehavior.

But such an interpretation should not leave out of account Teddy's fits of nervous excitability and melancholy, his severe physical sufferings, and his lapses from rationality. What all this amounted to was to be made clearer in the sequel.

5

Edith moved into the apartment at 53 Rue de Varenne around the first of the year 1910 and busied herself with the final arrangement of the furnishings she had acquired so lovingly over the months. The little twin houses at 882 and 884 Park Avenue, which the Whartons had not occupied for several years, were about to be sold for an undisclosed sum; and Edith's secretary, Anna Bahlmann, who had been living at 882 as Edith's New York representative, had come over to join the Paris household. On January 24, Edith passed her forty-eighth birthday "sadly and soberly."

But for the moment she hardly had time for her personal troubles, in the excitement and danger of an event that was engulfing half of Paris. It had been raining heavily and steadily for days. On the day before Edith's birthday, and by a very rare coincidence, the rivers Yonne and Marne, which feed the Seine, flooded over at the exact instant when the Seine itself flooded. There followed the worst inundation the city had experienced in 170 years.

Miraculously, Edith's stretch of the Rue de Varenne was largely spared. But a few yards to the left of her apartment, the river waters poured down Rue Vaneau into Rue Bellechasse; to the right, the Rue du Bac was transformed into a lake, with wooden bridges hastily erected for pedestrians to cross it. Moving about cautiously, Edith observed the footman going up by rowboat to the front door of Rosa de Fitz-James's *hôtel* in the Rue Constantine, where she had dined two nights before. Other boats transported passengers down the Rue St. Dominique, where the d'Haussonvilles lived; the Walter Gays, who had just moved into a new apartment nearby, were without light and heat, and the family below them had to evacuate.

The ladies and gentlemen of the Faubourg and the Jockey Club offered their services to the Red Cross and other centers of assistance for the many thousands of refugees. There were very few casualties, and no serious epidemics. But as Edith told Elizabeth Cameron, it would be months before the ravages could be repaired. "If it could only have happened to Omaha!"

Edith had grown closer to Mrs. Cameron. She now addressed her as "dear Lizzie," and spoke warmly about their "good moments of cameraderie" in Paris before Mrs. Cameron left for England. She even confided some of the more intimate details of Teddy's financial misdemeanors. Perhaps something in the delicate ambiguity of Elizabeth Cameron's relations with Henry Adams touched her sympathy; certainly, Mrs. Cameron evinced a deeply sympathetic understanding of Edith's present situation.

It was thanks in part to Mrs. Cameron that the household at 53 Rue de Varenne was able to begin functioning when it did; she lent Edith, from her Paris apartment, a set of flat silver for twelve, with four dozen knives, blue-glass salt cellars, and two pepper pots. Her new home, Edith wrote, was a "paradise," and so clean and smiling that it was "almost as nice as a baby." The sun poured into the drawing room with such force that Edith had to put up awnings.

She was seeing very few people, Edith remarked to Liz Cameron; "and no one talks of anything but flood and *Chanticler.*" The latter reference was to the most recent verse play of Edmond Rostand, which had just opened (February 7) at the Porte St. Martin. Rostand, the most gifted and inventive of the verse playwrights of his generation, had—after *La Princesse lointaine* and one or two others—achieved a towering success with *Cyrano de Bergerac* in 1897; the great French comedian Coquelin played the durable, large-nosed poet-hero with unforgettable verve and poignancy. Rostand also wrote *Chanticler*, a beast-fable about the self-deluding fantasies of the cock Chanticleer, for Coquelin; upon the latter's premature death, the part was taken over by Lucien Guitry. The play ran for 322 performances, but Edith had heard that it was "the saddest of failures." When she went to see it a little later, with Fullerton, she rendered a firmly negative verdict; even so, it provided a diverting topic of conversation for a number of weeks.

Edith could claim a remote acquaintance with Rostand. Walter Berry had represented him successfully years before in Washington, in a suit for plagiarism brought by an American writer over *Cyrano de Bergerac,* and Berry had brought him together with Mrs. Wharton. But she saw much more of Rostand's sister, Jeanne de Margeries, a cultivated and warm-hearted woman who, in the course of time, became one of the best of Edith's Parisian friends.

"Flood and *Chanticler"* provided helpful distractions as the winter weeks passed and letters were exchanged between Paris, Groton, and New York. Edith was also writing a little; not surprisingly perhaps, considering the nightmare she was going through, she was writing ghost stories: "The Triumph of Night," about financial corruption and a mysterious death; and "The Eyes," which came from far lower depths of her psyche.

In February, *Scribner's* published her graceful little tribute to Bay Lodge. Bay, who had suffered from heart trouble from time to time, had died the previous August 21 of a heart attack brought on by food poisoning; he was thirty-six, and left behind his wife, Bessie, and three young children. Senator Lodge expressed to Edith the strong hope that she would write something about his son: "I need not tell you how much he loved you—how grateful he was to you for all your sympathy and kindness. . . . You I know loved him. You are the one person of all others that I would have write about him."

In her article Edith recalled first meeting Bay in Washington in the late 1890s, and stressed his boyishness and freshness of spirit, his endearing capacity to give of himself. About his poetry, which Edith was unable to rank at all highly, she spoke with careful restraint. But her sense of personal loss was great. She had never realized, she told Bessie, how "luminous a presence" Bay had been in her life; and she lingered in memory over their times together, especially on the thyme-scented slopes above Lenox, with a grieving fondness.

In *A Backward Glance,* Edith Wharton would speak of Bay Lodge with immense affection, but she also took him, in a very shrewd passage, as an example of one kind of intellectual failure in her American generation. The passage points, as well, to the particular limiting environment she had herself been spared, and suggests retrospectively that the aridness of her own youthful surroundings had had a certain negative value. Bay's fate, she wrote,

was the reverse of mine, for he grew up in a hot-house of intensive culture, and was one of the most complete examples I have ever known of the young genius before whom an adoring family unites in smoothing the way. This kept him out of the struggle of life, and consequently out of its experiences, and to the end his intellectual precocity was combined with a boyishness of spirit at once delightful and pathetic.

What Bay Lodge suffered from most, she went on, was "the slightly rarefied atmosphere of mutual admiration, and disdain of the rest of the world, that prevailed in his immediate surroundings." There were those, it should be added, who felt that Edith Wharton in her maturity herself inhabited a disdainful sphere of mutual admiration. Insofar as she did, she must be credited with refusing to let the atmosphere shape and confine her.

Edith shared her grief with Henry Adams, who was about to embark on *The Life of George Cabot Lodge,* and William Sturgis Bigelow, a longtime friend of the Lodge family and a Harvard classmate and intimate of Bay's father. Bigelow, then nearing sixty, had violated the family tradition by abandoning medicine after a promising start, and betook himself to Japan for eight years, building a fine collection of art treasures and converting to northern Buddhism. In 1908 he had been made lecturer at Harvard on Buddhist doctrine.

Bigelow was a hefty individual, bald but with a white moustache and tufted beard and an air of slightly disheveled distinction. He was a curious mixture: one of his friends said that he "emanated a peaceful radiance mingled with a faint fragrance of toilet water," and that he combined the mystical with the epicurean; at his home on Tuckernuck Island, off Nantucket (where Bay Lodge spent his last days), women were forbidden and the gentlemen sat around all day in pajamas, discussing the universe between dips in the ocean.

For the moment, however, Edith Wharton and Sturgis Bigelow (who was himself in Paris for reasons of health) came together on the ground of their common loss. After Teddy reappeared, around the first of March, Bigelow proved himself an invaluable ally. Teddy was pathetically glad to be back and pleased with the new apartment, but he was too depressed to be left alone for a minute. He seems to have worn a continuous hang-dog expression; and for Edith, who must be imagined silently harboring guilt feelings of her own, it began to turn into the darkest period of her life. "My days are terrible," she wrote. Bigelow came by regularly to take Teddy motoring and attempt to instill some cheer into him.

Bigelow also knew a little about mental trouble. He was related to Marion Hooper, Henry Adams' former wife, who had committed suicide, and he used to confide to his friends that the reason he had not himself married was his fear that—Mrs. Adams being an example—there might be mental instability in his family. He was now willing to offer a diagnosis of Teddy's condition.

Following a long phone conversation, in which he accepted an invitation to dine with Mrs. Wharton and Adams, Bigelow dispatched a hand-delivered letter to 53 Rue de Varenne. It touched on Teddy's and Nannie Wharton's extraordinary changeability and forgetfulness: "He changes oftener but seldom more quickly or completely." Worse than that, Bigelow said, was the inability of Teddy's family to face the reality of his situation.

> It is astonishing that neither she nor Billy seem to grasp the fact that Ted's melancholy and exhilaration are not the only trouble with him, but that his mind itself—his consciousness and reasoning powers—are not connected nor consecutive. They still consider him, or seem to, as if he were a reasonable being like the rest of the world, capable of consecutive thought; and do not recognize that what he says is only true, even to him, while he is saying it, and is certain to be changed soon to the opposite. The increasing *rapidity* of these changes, which now occur in the time it takes to get from one room to the next, is I take it one of the things which make Dr. Isch Wall [a leading Paris nerve specialist] think him worse. Of course their *number* increase proportionately. The extreme condition is when they come as fast as a man can talk. This, with the concomitant of an imagination running riot, is a condition familiar in the hospitals.

Thus the analysis of Dr. Sturgis Bigelow: increasing mental derangement displaying itself in what would later be called manic-depressive behavior.

6

Edith was not entirely confined to the gloomy household, or without sources of support. Her family rallied. Minnie Jones came for a stay. Fond as she was of her sister-in-law, Edith was sometimes so exasperated by her unquenchable patriotism and her ignorance of botany that she declared her intention of killing Minnie and then instantly erecting a monument in her memory; but in moments of stress, Minnie was splendid. Harry Jones, Edith told James, was being a great strength and comfort to her, and her cousin Herman Edgar was in town and standing by. She moved about among the reduced circle of her friends and saw what she could of Morton Fullerton. With Fullerton she worked over the proofs of his long-delayed article on Henry James, which appeared at last in the April issue of the English *Quarterly Review*. Edith took some modest credit for this excellent study, which disclosed as nothing hitherto had done the great scope of James's major theme: "the clash between two societies," American and European, as dramatized by the invasion of Europe by American women. James was "embarrassed . . . fairly to anguish" when he read the highly eulogistic manuscript.

But matters were not growing better in the Rue de Varenne in the spring of 1910, and they were made measurably worse when Nannie Wharton came back to Paris after several months in the Pyrenees and began to interfere with every sensible proposal for Teddy's welfare. Teddy had himself decided he wanted to try a rest cure, and one was elaborately arranged for him in a nursing home in Neuilly, just outside the city. "But when it was proposed to Nannie, she became violently excited, said she was absolutely opposed to it, and—what is really unpardonable—told Teddy so, and excited him so much that it is now useless to refer to that subject."

I can only watch passively [she continued to Robert Grant], shelter Teddy as much as I can from the curiosity and comments which are inevitable when a man in his condition attempts to live in the world, and be prepared for the fact that any day he may yield to some impulse like those which wrought such havoc last summer.

Their Paris physician gave Teddy clearance to travel, and in late March Edith took him on a flying trip to England to call on Henry James, who had been extremely poorly on and off for several months. To the series of "beautiful and interesting and thrilling letters" Edith had addressed to him, James had responded faithfully, uttering kindly little cries of sympathy and support, while reporting without self-pity his own intermittent lapses of health. "Your immersion," he said, "must be grand and horrible." Some of his otherwise surprising adjectives reflected James's watchful interest in Edith's relations with Fullerton and in her literary activity, as well as his concern over the dilemma posed by Teddy and his sister. "I make out what I can," he wrote, "by Morton's playing flashlight," and what he made out only enhanced his admiration. "What dire complications—and you knocking off 'sellers' in the midst of them. You are prodigious and magnificent."

Edith thought James looked better than expected, during an afternoon at Lamb House, and James was able to say that he had had a thorough and cheering examination in London by Sir William Osler, who had assured him that he was "splendid for his age." The English visit was momentarily refreshing for Edith, but it left Teddy unchanged; Paris and April, to which they quickly returned, provided nothing but further darkness. Consultation with an eminent neurologist in Lausanne proved valueless; from Aix on the journey back Edith wrote Berenson despondently that nerve doctors seemed simply unable to treat Teddy's kind of trouble.

The daily conversations at 53 Rue de Varenne thereafter turned wearily and incessantly on alternative possibilities, Edith trying her best to find out what, if anything, Teddy really thought would help him to improve. She suggested a long leisurely drive across the continent; she expressed herself willing to go back with Teddy to The Mount; when he mentioned a desire to speak with Dr. Kinnicutt and the Boston physician, she at once agreed that White should make the journey with him. Each of these was ultimately rejected by Teddy, who now began to talk vaguely about traveling in the United States as far west as California. Suddenly, he seized upon the initial proposal of a sanatorium and chose on his own the well-known Kuranstalt Bellevue at Kreuzlingen, near Konstanz, in Switzerland. White accompanied him there in early June, and Teddy had not been in residence a week before he was clamoring to be released.

The first report from Dr. Binswanger, the obviously able and humane director of the sanatorium, was cautiously optimistic. He knew that Mr. Wharton had been writing his wife that the place was making him worse, not better, that there was no one to talk to, that no golf was available, and so on. Those were the same complaints that Mr. Wharton made to him every morning. What the patient was probably not saying was that there were good hours each afternoon, when he worked in the garden and engaged in animated talk with the friend of a friend who had also just arrived. For all his grumbling, Mr. Wharton was following "with admirable precision" the planned treatment (which was step for step the one invented by S. Weir Mitchell, including isolation from family): massage, hydrotherapy and electrotherapy, rest, lots of food, puttering in the garden. He was eating and sleeping well and had already gained a few pounds. The pains in his legs were troubling him less, though he was now speaking of toothaches.

Dr. Binswanger was convinced—and had so written Dr. Isch Wall—that Mr. Wharton's condition was entirely curable and that they had only to fear another fit of exaltation. He made a special point of saying that Mrs. Wharton's husband was an exceedingly sympathetic person to the whole staff, and that "even in his illness we recognise very well his excellent character."

7

Alone at 53 Rue de Varenne, Edith felt with enormous relief that the very worst part—the "dreadful months" when she had been "stretched to the snapping point, from fatigue and worry"—was at last behind her. Looking about in a slightly dazed manner, she also found, as she wrote Berenson, that she was "humiliatingly free from evening engagements," since she had not known from one week to the next where she would be. But, though she could not have known it, the days of the social extravaganzas in the Faubourg were drawing to an end. She would entertain apace and she would dine out, but the personal excitement and turmoil of the previous two and a half years had left Edith less eager for the whirlwind life. Assuring Berenson that there would be only one or two others at dinner on June 22, she declared: "I can imagine no happiness in human intercourse except when a *very* few are gathered together."

The friendship with Berenson was solidifying. Berenson was in and out of Paris a great deal in the summer and fall of 1910, mostly on business for the Duveens, and he quickly became one of Edith's regulars. They lunched and dined together; they talked at length; they went to the Opéra with Fullerton and Berry on July 3 to watch the prodigious leaps of Vaslav Nijinsky in *L'Oiseau de feu,* the new ballet by the unknown thirty-year-old composer Igor Stravinsky, with costumes designed by the painter Léon Bakst. It was only the second Paris season for the Ballet Russe, under the direction of Sergei Diaghilev, but the city had been conquered almost at once by the impeccably rehearsed performances.

Berenson had initially expressed surprise that Edith had seemed so genuinely delighted to see him when he came to call. Now he was saying to his wife that "I like Mrs. Wharton better and better." To Edith herself he confided with a show of awkward sincerity: "How much I had got attached to what is you in particular.—But no more. At 45 I am still shy." ("Thee has a misleading pen for ladies," Mary Berenson once told him, after receiving a letter full of gallantry at just the moment she had come upon some love letters from her husband to the widowed Sybil Cutting.) Edith remarked to Hugh Smith that she found Berenson "extremely interesting, with *lots more of him* than there is in his books."

Walter Berry, who had begun to join the gatherings with Berenson, had resigned from the International Tribune in Cairo, effective June 20. There had been moments in Egypt which he enjoyed, but two years away from the main centers of his interest were enough. It was his idea to settle in Paris, if he could find a suitable position there. By July 1 he was installed in the guest suite of the Whartons' apartment and was searching for a place of his own. He remained there almost six months.

In the rhythm of Edith Wharton's personal life, Berry's temporary establishment in her household marked the start of his gradual replacement of Fullerton in her deepest affections. This, to be sure, may have been just what Berry had in mind. But the fact was that the Fullerton affair was drifting to a close, for reasons that can only be guessed at—though given all the circumstances and the personalities involved, one can guess with a certain confidence.

On Morton Fullerton's side, the time elapsed was about normal for a love affair. Margaret Brooke, Camille Chabert, Katharine Fullerton: Morton's intimacy with each of these women had lasted about three years. The one striking and inexplicable exception was Henrietta Mirecourt, who managed to hang on to Fullerton, or recall him to her with threats and appeals, for the better part of a decade. With the others there had been a recurring pattern of gentle idealism, slowly rising passion, an intense physical affair (with Katharine, of course, only stirring talk about the possibility thereof), and another process of absenteeism, silence, and gradual withdrawal.

It is never easy to date affairs of this kind with any precision, but it can give an approximation to say that the essential affair between Edith Wharton and Fullerton had its subdued start in the fall of 1907 and came to an end in the summer of 1910. This is to say that it coincided very closely with Fullerton's involvement with Katharine (who, it will be recalled, became Mrs. Gerould in June 1910), to the extent that one must suppose some cause-and-effect relation between the two simultaneous episodes—as though Fullerton somehow needed each as a buffer of sorts against the other. For Edith Wharton, Fullerton would be much on the scene for the next half dozen years, and occasionally after that; but not to put too fine a point upon it, she had ceased being his mistress by the time Berry showed up as her houseguest.

The "terminus" was without doubt due as much to Edith's inclinations as to Fullerton's. The situation had become, on the face of it, an impossible one. It is not difficult to imagine that, in the light of Teddy's revealed conduct, the physical relationship had lost a good deal of its exhilarating and poetic appeal. Perhaps in her somber meditations Edith was even led to equate the two adventures in moral and aesthetic terms, which would be drastically to reassess her own experience. There would be evidence to support this.

It is likely, too, that she had undergone a delayed reaction to the business of offering her money to buy back Fullerton's compromising letters. Such anyhow was partly the gist of a story, "The Letters," which she was writing in the early summer of 1910. That story, with another written a few months earlier, "The Eyes," suggests that she was definitely making a reappraisal of Fullerton's character and of his fitness to be her intimate companion.

"The Letters," a touching if rambling tale set in Paris and its environs, is a mélange of incidents culled from Edith Wharton's and Fullerton's lives, separately and together. It concerns Lizzie West, a young American woman adrift in Paris, and Vincent Deering, an expatriate American painter who employs Lizzie to tutor his little daughter. While Mrs. Deering (the "Teddy-figure" in the story) remains invisible upstairs, stricken with headaches and reading cheap novels, Lizzie falls in love with Deering, and he professes his love for her. Mrs. Deering dies, and, the daughter stowed away with relatives, Deering hurries to America to settle his wife's estate. For some time Lizzie showers passionate letters upon him, but after tenderly answering the first two or three, Deering lapses into absolute silence.

A year or so later Lizzie receives an unexpected legacy, and soon thereafter Deering turns up in Paris. He reestablishes himself, they marry, and Lizzie bears him a son. She also provides the money with which Deering can rescue the trunk he had left with his landlady in New York when he fled with the rent unpaid. Glancing through its contents one day, Lizzie finds her letters to Deering, with the seals of the envelopes unbroken; not one of them opened or read. He had lied to her, she realizes, and had only sought her out when he learned that she was rich. Yet she decides not to leave him, but to adjust to a new image of him: "not the hero of her dreams, but . . . the man she loved, and who had loved her."

In addition to allusions harking back as far as Joshua Jones's unexpected bequest in 1888, the story draws directly upon more recent episodes. The New York landlady—"that awful woman," says one of Lizzie's friends in a mild echo of Henry James—is an American version of Mme. Mirecourt, and Deering's good-natured approval of his wife's supplying "the liberating draft" of money suggests the manner in which Fullerton had been coaxed into accepting the conspiracy involving James and Macmillan. Deering, indeed, is almost to a detail an ironic though tempered portrait of Morton Fullerton: a seemingly gifted but irresolute artist, "a gentleman of melancholy elegance" with a gentle soulfulness and an insinuating eloquence of speech. In the description of Lizzie's growing response to him, Edith Wharton borrowed richly from the 1908 journal and the poems to her lover.

At the same time, Deering's comportment with Lizzie is, up to a point, so exactly like Fullerton's with Katharine as hardly to need comment: the pact seemingly made between them, the first overwhelmingly beautiful letters from across the Atlantic, the falling utterly silent, the rumor of other affairs. The wording of Lizzie's anguished effort to reestablish communication ("in the first weeks of silence she wrote again and again to Deering, entreating him for a word, for a mere sign of life") is so close to Katharine's that it seems certain Fullerton had not only recounted the whole story to Edith but had even lent her some of his cousin's letters. If so, this may well have been another reason for Edith's taking a fresh and clear-eyed look at her lover.

Yet the portrait is not, finally, without affection. Edith's days together with Fullerton are poignantly remembered: their excursions to nearby places "where now and then, in the solitude of grove or garden, the kiss renewed itself, fleeting, isolated"; dinners in the private upper rooms of a restaurant on the Seine, "with the lights of the river trembling through their one low window, and the rumor of Paris enclosing them in a heart of silence." By the summer of 1910, Morton Fullerton was no longer for Edith the man she had once dreamed of, but he was still—undependable, weak, and irresistibly attractive—the man she had loved and who had loved her. But there was to be no further intimate commerce between them.

"The Letters" was written, as it were, from the top of Edith Wharton's imagination, possibly with the relevant documents spread out on her writing board. The ghost story called "The Eyes" is a very different affair, and appears to be a powerful collaboration between her unconscious and her creative genius.

The tale is told by Andrew Culwin, a middle-aged dilettante, before the fire one evening, to the narrator and Culwin's newest protégé, young Phil Frenham. It turns on two ghostly visitations. The first occurred after Culwin, in what he took to be a spontaneous act of compassion and generosity, had engaged to marry his artless cousin Alice Nowell. That same night Culwin wakes to find a pair of hideous red eyes glaring at him in the darkness. The experience so unnerves him that he packs and flees to Europe without a word to his fiancée, with whom indeed he never communicates again.

A parallel incident takes place a couple of years later in Rome. Culwin has taken up with Gilbert Noyes, an enchanting and beautiful youth with a burning ambition to write, and no talent of any kind. When the boy shows Culwin his would-be masterpiece, Culwin, instead of proclaiming it the disaster that it is, praises it to the skies. That very evening the eyes return: more beastly than before, sneering at him venomously, seeming to contain the essence of accumulated evil. They appear nightly until Culwin, exhausted, tells Noyes the truth about his literary capacity and departs for Frascati.

The story, certainly one of the finest Edith Wharton ever wrote, is a subtle study in human egotism at its most extreme and most self-deceiving. When it has been interpreted biographically, it has always been assumed that Andrew Culwin—unshakably self-centered, cultivated but cold-spirited, witty but spiteful, and latently homosexual—was based on Walter Berry. Yet Edith, at the time of writing the tale, had seen next to nothing of Berry for two years, while he was serving his term on the court in Cairo. During that period it was not Berry but Morton Fullerton who had aroused and engaged Edith's passions. And in fairness to Berry, it must be acknowledged that it was not he but Fullerton who had been erotically involved with members of both sexes; there is some question that Berry was ever thus involved with a member of either.

The traces of Fullerton are there to recognize in the portrait of Culwin: what might be called a sort of sexual indecisiveness, the sense of unrealized literary gifts, the cunning use of language in conversation; even more, the engagement to a first cousin, followed by flight to Europe and absolute silence. One of the phrases used about Culwin—"the humorous detached observer of the immensely muddled variety show of life"—is taken almost verbatim from Fullerton's report to his Harvard class secretary in 1910. There is in Culwin something as well of Howard Sturgis, sitting amid the comfortable debris of his library, with his circle of friends to which a neophyte is now and then added. But the great and ultimate distance between Culwin and either of his prototypes is provided by the element of evil in his spirit, and this was contributed by Edith Wharton's imagination, working out of depths rarely plumbed by it and with an intensity of concentration rarely achieved.

8

With the passing weeks at Kreuzlingen, it was clear that Teddy was not improving to any appreciable degree. At the end of June, Dr. Binswanger arranged for White to return to Paris so that Teddy would no longer have someone ready at hand to complain to. Teddy was put in the charge of a Swiss-German steward with whom, largely due to an inability to communicate, he got on rather well. He was playing tennis and gardening, except when a bruised finger interfered with those activities; the pattern of his day was despair, interrupted by grumbling, in the morning and a certain animation and bridge playing until late in the evening. The unhappiest sign was a frequent rush of self-accusation and self-reproach.

His letters to Edith were dejected. In reply to one of them in which Teddy wrote glumly that she would probably not even want to answer him, Edith, addressing him as "Dear Old Man," urged him to give the sanatorium a fair trial of at least three months, as he had promised to do.

I know—we all know—that you are not well, and that anything in the nature of a nervous breakdown is hard to struggle against; but you are a perfectly reasonable being, and capable of the struggle, and also of seeing how impossible it is for anyone to help you if you won't make the effort yourself.

Teddy was particularly downcast at the prospect of being merely a "passenger" in Edith's life for the rest of his days—in Edith's paraphrase, of "not being able to manage my money affairs and decide about household matters." On this important point Edith was unyielding: "I can do nothing to alter these conditions."

[They] are the result of your nervous breakdown, nor can I help the fact that your having lost part of your fortune weighs with you more than the fact that, when you came back last year, I was ready to overlook everything you had done, and to receive you as if nothing had happened.

She asked him to reconsider the notion he had mentioned of a long trip to the American West after leaving Kreuzlingen. Johnson Morton could go with him, and they could leave in time to savor the autumn weather in the Rockies, and then go on to southern California and tarpon fishing. She was sure he would enjoy the trip more by car than by rail: "And I am so flush now, thanks to my 'sage economies,' that I should like to offer you a small car of the kind you have always said you would prefer for such a trip. . . . Yours aff.," she signed herself, "E.W."

"Dear Heart," Teddy wrote back: she must not worry about him and should think only of herself; he would stay at Kreuzlingen as long as she wished him to —he would be no more exhausted there than anywhere else. He felt wretchedly about her, and above all he so longed for another chance; how much he would give for the opportunity to take over her vexations for her, as he formerly had. On this, Edith refused further comment.

By mid-July he had grown far less irritable, and he struck Dr. Binswanger, who had become fond of him, as merely tired and sad. The doctors agreed that he could leave the sanatorium at the end of the month, but that he should not go directly back to Paris. Dr. Isch Wall, deposing that Mme. Wharton was still weak, fatigued, and in need of *"grand repos physique et moral,"* urged her husband to travel in Europe for several months. This communication led Teddy to say that he was not fit to live with Edith, and that he would make no attempt to do so until he could carry on a normal life.

Nothing, he said, would give him greater pleasure than the trip with Johnnie Morton; he accepted everybody's advice about this. But just before departure day he cabled that the trip was "impossible," and that he was going to Thun to join his sister and to Bern to consult with a famous Swiss surgeon; at the same moment, he was informing Dr. Binswanger that he was not ready to leave Kreuzlingen, that his big toe was hurting badly and he needed further treatment. Edith returned doggedly to the debate. Why impossible? she asked. The motor tour was surely his best chance to get well. If it was the large expense that worried him, "that is too foolish to discuss with you. There is plenty of money to do what you like, and if you really want to get well, and help me, you will carry out this plan, now that the chance presents itself."

From the Thunerhof in Thun, Nannie Wharton commented with much satisfaction that now Teddy "can be looked after *properly* for a few days." But she thought they should all go slow—he was likely to be excited after the confinement and discomfort of Kreuzlingen (to which she had been volubly opposed). Teddy was given a thorough physical examination by the surgeon in Bern, who then wrote Dr. Dupré in Paris that Mr. Wharton was suffering from "sclerosis of the peripheral arteries of the lower parts of the thighs, very pronounced, much more than in any other part of the body."

Edith managed a few days in England in early August, and a visit to Lamb House—the latter also a depressed household, since Henry James's brother William, who was staying there, had a grave heart ailment. William had been most appreciative, the previous April, of Mrs. Wharton's "exquisitely generous and tactful offer of the car and chauffeur" at a moment when it was Henry who was feeling badly and needed to be taken out of himself. He had shared with Edith his enthusiasm over a speech Theodore Roosevelt had delivered at the Sorbonne: "I myself regard Roosevelt, with all his faults, as a tremendously precious natural asset." In May he had come to call at the Rue de Varenne, and the philosopher and the novelist had their first view of each other. But now William, after an attempted cure in Germany, had entered his final illness.

Lamb House was a little island of anxiety within a country in official mourning: King Edward VII had died on May 6. His son and successor, George V, was an unknown quantity except for his exploits as a sailor; the new king's ignorance of national politics and foreign affairs was cause for apprehension. Leaving a Lamb House burdened with worry, Edith Wharton carried her own inner troubles to a London filled with unease, to meet Minnie Jones and Beatrix and to dine with Berenson.

In Paris a letter was waiting for her from Sturgis Bigelow. He had been thinking hard about her problems, and found they divided into two almost equal parts: "1.—Nannie. 2.—Ted." Nannie Wharton's entire attitude since she came to Paris, Bigelow observed, had been one of "persistent, dogged and indiscriminate opposition to all suggestions about Ted," even if they came from some of the best physicians in Europe. Her unchanging stance was: "I will take no responsibility whatever, but I am absolutely opposed to"—whatever the proposition happened to be. Edith should tell Nannie flatly that one or the other of them must have full charge of the case; Nannie could decide.

Teddy's extreme volatility, meanwhile, did not augur well for the expedition with Johnson Morton. Bigelow could easily imagine him starting out for California in the morning and then wanting to hurry back in the afternoon. Bigelow himself had no doubt what should be done:

> *He ought to be put under restraint, and the sooner the better.* It ought to have been done a year ago. I cannot imagine what Billy was thinking of that he did not do it. It was very like criminal neglect.

He ended this severe commentary with a plea to Edith not to allow herself to be alone with Teddy unless someone were within call. One could not tell "what mental tension may have accumulated since you have seen him, nor how explosive it may be."

Teddy was more forlorn than explosive on his return. Berenson, after lunching at the Rue de Varenne, wrote his wife that Mr. Wharton looked terribly aged. Berenson was himself in a melancholy frame of mind. He was in the throes of a helpless and debilitating love affair with Belle da Costa Greene, a New York art librarian, and not even the presence at lunch of Morton Fullerton and a new French acquaintance, a cultivated and ironic mining engineer named Léon Bélogou, could stir him from his misery.

For a fortnight Edith, while keeping a wary eye on her husband, worked over the proofs of *Tales of Men and Ghosts* and tried to overcome a predictable attack of her recurring affliction, hay fever. "I have been really *ill,*" she told Brownell, "—there's no other word for it!" Toward the end of the month she and Teddy wandered south to the Cote-d'Or, and then to a *"petit trou"* not far from Mont Blanc. Here, in the quiet and the cool crisp air far above the foliage line, she began suddenly to flourish.

The place enchanted her: a former Carthusian monastery—"a *real* Chartreuse," she said, thinking of Stendhal's novel—which had been turned into an inn the year before. She was sure it was destined to failure, since it was too remote and ineptly run, but for Edith it was a rare experience. Bancel La Farge, a younger son of the painter John La Farge, was also there with his family (Edith had been seeing something of them in Paris). His seven-year-old son Henry stored up the memory of Mrs. Wharton as an elegantly attired woman who held them all in sway with a series of not-to-be-interrupted monologues. "We are pic-nicking in large bare vaulted 'cells,' " Edith informed Sally Norton, ". . . and walking along echoing stone cloisters to our *very* bad meals.—It's really 'the Great Good Place' of H. James's tale."

It was in this monastic retreat that Edith learned of the death of William James on August 26. The brothers had gone back to William's home in Chocorua, New Hampshire, arriving there on August 18; eight days later William was dead.

"My beloved brother's death has cut into me, deep down, as an absolute mutilation," Henry wrote Edith. He spoke of his brother's "beautiful genius and noble intellect," and said that he felt "stricken and old and ended." But the familiar strength and resiliency were already beginning to stir; even in the first days of terrible grief he could respond to "the thin, empty, lonely, melancholy American 'beauty,' which I yet find a prudish charm in." He was able to remember sympathetically Edith's own portion of sorrow and had a sudden biting word for "that brutal slut" who was again, apparently, harassing Fullerton, and for "those vulgar and odious people"—possibly the new directors of the London *Times*, from which Fullerton had now totally dissociated himself. "Oh, how I want to see you both."

That latter wish was soon granted. By the third week of September, Edith and Teddy were at the Belmont Hotel in New York, and Johnnie Morton—the kindly Bostonian who was a regular visitor at The Mount, and who wrote light fiction and verse for magazines—was hovering nearby waiting to take Teddy off on what had now been enlarged into a trip around the world. There was a last nerve-racking delay when Dr. Kinnicutt became ill, and Edith spent ten dreary days staring out balefully from the windows of their lofty suite onto the New York scene

> looking over the brick and iron landscape of this appalling city . . . [which] looks exactly like a Mercator's projection of hell—with the river of pitch, and the iron bridges, and the "elevated" marking of the bogie, and Blackwell's Island opposite for the city of Dis.

Berry and Fullerton, both in America on family affairs, had rallied round for a little, but were now gone.

Berenson, to whom this dismal report had been dispatched, cabled words of encouragement. The doctor recovered, made his examination, and gave his medical blessing for the expedition, now set to begin on October 16. Edith thereupon fell ill for several days, but even so, was "passionately, immoderately anxious to get away" on the first possible boat. "I have seen no one to *speak* to for ten days!" she complained to Berenson, but then instantly added:

> This sounds *odious*, and I am ashamed of having written it; but you know what I mean by "speak to." Lots of the kindest friends can't be communicated with; and the few who can—oh, how seldom one is with them, and how the time flies when one is!

The connoisseur of friendship was about to have a feast. Henry James came down from Cambridge and Morton Fullerton from Brockton; Walter Berry made his way back from Washington. All forgathered at the Belmont. Teddy departed on schedule—in James's diary note, "with brave charming Johnson Morton." On Monday evening, the seventeenth, Edith found herself at table in the Belmont dining room with three of the men who were the dearest and most important to her in all her life. The next day she sailed for Europe on the *Prinzessin Cécilie*. James, Fullerton, and Berry enjoyed a gentlemen's lunch together. Berry took the train for Washington; at dinner that night there remained only James and M.F.

16. Ethan Frome *and Other Dramas*

As Henry James sympathetically and admiringly surveyed her, Edith at the Belmont had been in "nervous and intimately personal . . . *rags*," but had also been "as sublime and unsurpassable and as *pailletée* as ever." In Paris she allowed herself to go quietly to pieces for a short while and to succumb to exhaustion and nervous indigestion—"the one always follows the other with me," she wrote Sara Norton. She rested a good deal and underwent daily massages; by mid-November she was feeling a trifle more human.

Berenson thought she looked a wreck when she first arrived. He had postponed his departure from Paris primarily to be with Mrs. Wharton. "She *may* mean something to me," he wrote Mary, "for she really seems just now to care for me." In his continuing wretchedness over his insufficiently requited love for Belle Greene, he felt a special tenderness for anyone else's private affliction. "My present state," he said, "makes me into a sort of water finder or dowser for everybody's loneliness, love-hunger and unhappiness."

Edith, Walter Berry, and Berenson were together frequently, Berenson observing that "we make a good trio, and have got to terms of real affection." But he had it fixed in his head that Edith's emotional commitment was exclusively to Berry, and had been for many years.

> Loafed in the afternoon with Mrs. Wharton and Berry. Mrs. W. is one of my realest friends now, but her heart is Berry's, and she could not have it better placed. I envy them both such a friendship. . . . I can see perfectly that she still would rather be with him than with me for instance, and that everything is planned for him.

Berenson's jealousy of Berry, here only faintly masked, was one reason why he would eventually turn against the other man, and out of the same emotion Berenson helped create the exaggerated image of Edith's long-standing infatuation with Berry.

Letters and postcards were flowing in from Teddy. He and Johnnie Morton had reached southern California and were due to sail on November 22 for the Far East. Nannie Wharton, staying at the Crillon, declared her faith that the worst was over and that the long trip would complete the cure. She was eager for Edith's account of the departure from New York, and in a hand-delivered note she asked her sister-in-law to send back word with the bearer whether Edith could see her that same afternoon. Edith made it emphatically clear that she could not, neither then nor in the foreseeable future. There had been a set-to the previous August when Edith had gone to Vevey to accompany Teddy back to Paris, and for Edith it had been the last straw.

I have come back feeling very tired and unwell, and after your treatment of me at Vevey—which I overlooked at the time on Ted's account—I can see no use in exposing myself once more to having my conduct criticised and my word doubted as they have been by you for the past year whenever, out of consideration for Ted's family, I have reported to you the Drs.' advice, and the plans which I had made for him in consequence.

Billy Wharton could tell her everything she wanted to know,

and I shall be spared what would probably be as trying and unprofitable as all our former talks on the subject.

I will therefore ask you to excuse me if I am not able to see you at present.

As the winter wore on, Edith's life became even more carefully restricted. She dined at home almost every evening and issued no formal invitations of her own for weeks on end. Her "group" gradually dwindled to Berry, Fullerton, and Paul Bourget; the latter had, disconcertingly, developed the habit of telling exceedingly bawdy stories in a nearly inaudible voice. Berry was still occupying the guest suite in Edith's apartment, but he had found himself a permanent residence in the Rue St. Guillaume, just off the Rue de Grenelle and a stone's throw from the Rue de Varenne: an attractive set of rooms, full of light and air and surrounded by gardens. He was busy arranging his huge collection of books and preparing to move in.

Fullerton, as has been said, had left the *Times* once and for all, after a long wrangle with his London superiors, and was devoting himself to freelance writing. He professed himself delighted to be free from bondage, and to his class secretary, on the twenty-fifth anniversary of his graduation from Harvard, he wrote with the faint pomposity he was beginning to display:

After twenty years of strenuous service as a foreign correspondent I have severed my connection with the Times. I am now an unattached critic of the great spectacle of things. . . . I am rejoicing in the discovery that my spirit has not been entirely broken by my long discipline as an anonymous portion of a great machine. Out of the fragments of my shattered *âme de fonctionnaire* I am piecing together my real self. This occupation is amusing and edifying.

Edith too felt the change was working wonders, and reported proudly on the stream of articles that began to appear under Fullerton's name in newspapers and periodicals. Most of these had to do with current political affairs ("When England Awakens" was the characteristic title of one of them), and out of them, a few years later, he would produce his one solid achievement, *Problems of Power*.

2

Sending Berenson greetings at Christmas, Edith remarked that the new year of 1911 "owes us all something, don't you think?" In fact, by this time she was in surprisingly good spirits. Her health had much improved; she had recovered her "lost balance"; and she was working again after many "wasted months"—working steadily, and working better than she had for a long time. She had begun a "new opus," and it was proving enormously stimulating.

Tales of Men and Ghosts had come out in October to a mixed and even a confused reception. It contained one small masterpiece, "The Eyes," and another ghost story, "Afterward," which begins promisingly but wilts into melodrama; and several other tales not without interest, such as "The Letters," "His Father's Son," and "The Debt." Some reviewers dismissed them all as no better than run-of-the-mill magazine fiction; others, on the contrary, accused Mrs. Wharton of an excess of subtlety beyond anything the average magazine reader could enjoy. The latter charge, it might be said, could be justifiably leveled against "The Blonde Beast," whose Nietzschean title is only skimpily fulfilled in the story, which has to do (apparently) with an unprincipled young man acquiring a moral sense. Edith agreed with Hugh Smith that she had failed to pull it off—that "it *was* a good subject," but she had written it at a bad moment. The volume sold about four thousand copies, the figure around which her collections tended to hover.

The new opus was called *Ethan Frome*, and it had its origins in an exercise she had written—probably in 1907—for her French teacher in Paris. In *A Backward Glance*, Edith Wharton recalled that when she first settled in Paris, she became aware that her spoken French derived largely from her reading in seventeenth-century literature, so much so that Bourget teased her for speaking "the purest Louis Quatorze." She asked Charles du Bos to find some young professor who could help her bring her idiom up to date. The amiable youth who took on the job suggested she prepare an "exercise" before each visit. For Edith, this meant writing a story, and for a few weeks she plodded ahead with what would be the French seed of *Ethan Frome*. The lessons were given up and the copybook mislaid; but the basic motif returned to her mind in December 1910.

The exercise, untitled, dealt with an impoverished New England farmer named Hart, married to an ailing and complaining wife, and in love with his wife's niece Mattie. Anna, the wife, of a sudden, declares that Mattie must be sent away. Hart offers to go with her, but Mattie, insisting in tears that Anna had been kinder to her than any other relation, refuses to let him do so. Out of this fragile piece of fiction Edith Wharton kept the basic situation and a part of its development, one proper name, and a few telling images and details.

When Edith began writing *Ethan Frome*, she conceived of it as a longish short story to be finished in no more than a fortnight; she was amused and surprised at the way it grew under her hands. Soon after the first of the year, she told Berenson:

> I am driving harder and harder at that ridiculous nouvelle, which has grown into a large long-legged hobbledehoy of a young novel. 20,000 long it is already, and growing. I have to let its frocks down every day, and soon it will be in trousers! However, I see the end.

She had gotten past "the hard explanatory part" (the sketching in of the backgrounds of the three central characters), "and the *vitesse acquise* is beginning to rush me along." The scene, she said, "is laid at Starkfield, Mass., and the nearest cosmopolis is called Shadd's Falls. It amuses me to do that décor in the rue de Varenne."

When Berenson inquired about further progress on her "novel," Edith replied in late March: "My 'novel' doesn't deserve the name. It is a hybrid, or rather a dwarf form, of the species: scarcely 40,000 words." But when she received the proofs of her "winter's work" in April—the story was due to begin in the August *Scribner's*—she confessed to being in a "state of fatuous satisfaction."

The latter remark suggests what *A Backward Glance* confirms: that Edith Wharton was *happy* while she was writing *Ethan Frome*—happy as the artist is always happy when creative energy is responding successfully to the most severe demands that can be put upon it. She told Hugh Smith in January that "my writing tires and preoccupies me more than it used to"; but the fatigue and the preoccupation were themselves components in her happiness, and an earnest of her artistic involvement. And yet even to Berenson she felt impelled to conceal her sense of creative well-being, to label the work ridiculous and to speak of the fatuity of the pleasure she took in it. The fact is, there remained a growing tension in Edith Wharton's attitude toward her writing and herself as a literary artist; it became the more pronounced when she was engaged in work she felt to be of her best.

Percy Lubbock, in his subtly denigrating *Portrait of Edith Wharton*, implied that Edith's concern with art was at best superficial, adducing her enjoyment of company "in which art is an amusement, not a life to be lived." But this was woefully missing the point. Edith Wharton certainly did not have the visionary dedication to art, and the life of art, of a James Joyce or a Henry James. Her attitude was more modest, but in its way it was also more contradictory.

From middle age onward, she talked restrainedly about her work-in-progress with a few of her men friends, but for the most part she seems to have limited the talk to matters of technique and organization. She found it hard to believe herself worthy to discourse, from a personal standpoint, upon larger questions of the art of fiction and the creative experience (her collection of essays in this area, in 1925, addressed itself typically to the *writing* of fiction). When she was completing *The Reef* in 1912 and her domestic life was again collapsing around her, she told Hugh Smith that her writing was simply not good enough to act as a solace. "If only my work were better, it would be all I need. But my kind of half-talent isn't much use as an escape—at least more than temporarily."

Still, it was not only skepticism about her creative capacities, as measured against those of the undoubted masters, that led to such poignant disavowals. The old conflict had assumed a new form. A part of her had, after all, become the qualifiedly devoted artist in letters, and she had begun to locate herself—with a certain assurance, though without vanity—in the developing course of American literature. But in another part of her, there remained something of the conviction drilled into her in old New York that it was improper for a lady to write fiction. One could do so only if one joked about it—if one treated it, to borrow Lubbock's word, as "an amusement." She sometimes sounded as if her writing were her entertainingly guilty secret, and in her memoirs she referred to it (borrowing the title of popular children's book of her own New York youth) as her "secret garden."

But in the winter of 1911, as on perhaps half a dozen other occasions, it was the believing artist that was in the ascendancy during the hard-driving morning hours.

3

Barrett Wendell had come to dinner around New Year's, with Berry and Fullerton. The restless, forceful, tawny-bearded professor of English at Harvard was on his way to India and the Orient, carrying with him introductions to high personages from his friend President William Howard Taft. Berry and he had known each other distantly in college, and Fullerton had been one of his favorite students during Wendell's first years as an instructor in composition. With Edith Wharton he had had only a nodding acquaintance, but they shared a strong mutual admiration, and they had a host of friends in common, a number of whom were also known to Edith's other two dinner guests.

Among the friends who might have been inquired after were Dr. Washburn of Calvary Church, the father of Edith's girlhood friend Emelyn—Wendell had gone to Europe with him as a youth, and had persuaded him to increase the daily tipple from a pint to a quart; Ralph Curtis, a fellow undergraduate with whom Wendell had helped found the Harvard *Lampoon;* Robert Grant, another college mate and *Lampoon* editor—it was Grant who, as an overseer of the university, had confided to Wendell his appointment as professor in 1898; Bernhard Berenson, whom Wendell had enlisted as the fourth editor-in-chief of the Harvard *Monthly.* A letter from Berenson arrived while the foursome were still at the table, and the chorus of welcome, Edith remarked, must have been audible on the Settignano hillside.

Wendell was also well acquainted with the Jameses, the Adamses, the Lodges, the Nortons. It was partly through the good offices of Edith Wharton that Wendell had come to meet Paul Bourget in Paris when the distinguished American scholar had, in 1904–05, given a series of lectures at the Sorbonne, the first of a long line of visiting Harvard professors.

With his wife and daughter, and a courier, Wendell moved on to Genoa and from there by steamer to Ceylon. They crossed to the Indian mainland and journeyed north to Calcutta, and here they encountered those other world travelers, Teddy Wharton and Johnson Morton (still another student of Wendell's), who had reached the subcontinent from the opposite direction. Fullerton had urged his old teacher to send him any news he might acquire about Teddy's condition, and Wendell dutifully did so.

His communication from Calcutta was disturbing. Both Teddy and his companion were in a state of "unusual nervous tension"; even the staunch Johnnie Morton had, evidently, found the going a severe strain. Teddy's facial muscles were rigid, and worse yet, in Wendell's opinion, he seemed uncharacteristically inward and withdrawn, and showed a disposition to be left entirely to himself. The two parties met up again at the hotel in Agra, and by this time Wendell was inclined to modify his first impression.

Calcutta, he now felt, had itself been a main source of difficulty: a most uncomfortable hotel, and nothing in the city to distract from the "manifold inconveniences." Agra, however, was "really comfortable, and has architectural beauties of a kind I have never seen elsewhere." Teddy's face was relaxed, he was much more sociable than before, and he had begun again to talk in the old amusing and observant manner. When they visited the Taj Mahal, Teddy's response, Wendell thought, had been more acute than his own, and he fell in cheerfully with the plan of an all-day motor excursion the following day. Morton too seemed a good deal easier, and Wendell was glad that a reassuring telegram had been sent to Teddy's sister in Pau.

Temporarily comforted, Edith turned her attention to a scheme she had had in mind for some time. This was an organized effort to secure the Nobel Prize in literature for Henry James. It was a suitable moment, with the immense New York edition of James's novels and tales so recently completed (though selling depressingly little); and Fullerton's discerning article had been timely. Edith prodded into action several members of the English nominating committee, including Edmund Gosse, who joined the enterprise with alacrity, even while warning Edith that a parallel attempt was being made for the American Winston Churchill, the author of *The Crisis* and other popular novels. Rudyard Kipling, the winner of the prize in 1907, was said to have given his vote to James.

Edith reported these findings to William Dean Howells, who thought the notion "wonderfully good and fit" and only wished it had occurred to him first.

Minnie Jones, just beginning to act as Edith's American lieutenant for various purposes, served to relay information back and forth. What was being stressed, as Edith told Robert Grant, was not only the sheer quality of James's literary achievement, but a "self-denying and life-long service to letters," with material returns of only the slightest. "All and singular the authors of America will favour getting the prize for James," Howells promised.

Perhaps they did, but not to any persuasive effect upon the academicians in Stockholm. The jury passed James by without visible interest, and the prize in 1911 went to Maurice Maeterlinck, the Belgian playwright and author of the fairy-tale work *The Bluebird.*

In the ups and downs of Teddy's condition, according to the reports thereon, the symptoms again grew discouraging as spring approached. "I am rather doleful myself," Edith told Berenson in early March (she was now addressing him as *"Cher ami"* and "My dear friend," when she was not invoking Dante's phrase for Aristotle and calling him *Maestro di color che sanno*); "tired and worried and weary." Teddy was due in Marseilles on April 6, and the very prospect seems to have helped bring on an attack of "my tiresome hay (or rather dust) fever," though she attributed it to a long stretch of rainless weather. Her husband, she said, "is no better, and I am much bothered about the future. Enfin."

She was also feeling somewhat at loose ends and lonely. Fullerton was busy writing the numerous articles on which he depended for a living, and Berry had moved out into his new apartment. Edith had only Anna Bahlmann and the dogs for company. Earlier in the winter there had been a dance concert by the thirty-four-year-old Isadora Duncan, just beginning to achieve world fame under the direction of Michel Fokine, and Edith was looking forward to the next visit of the Ballet Russe in May. But meanwhile she had not "dined anywhere or done anything worldly for a month, and I don't feel as if I should ever want to again."

Teddy arrived on schedule, and there instantly began a wrangling over money matters—Teddy alternately begging and demanding that he be allowed to handle Edith's affairs and then agreeing miserably that he was not well enough to do so, Edith adamantly refusing to go back to their former arrangement. She would (in the rather stiff language she used a little later) "never consent to your having anything to do with the control of my money, whether income or capital." An offer had come unexpectedly to buy The Mount, where Edith had not made an appearance for nearly three years. Edith was willing to leave the decision up to Teddy, but Teddy maintained that he would not live with her at The Mount unless he were allowed to run the place. For the first time, it seems, it occurred seriously to Edith that perhaps they would have to separate.

After six days of this, Teddy dashed off with White to London to have himself fitted for a new wardrobe; whatever his other failings, Teddy knew where in Europe the finest clothing for gentlemen could be acquired. There was the familiar indecisiveness about travel plans, until Teddy, whose hands and feet had started hurting again, possibly as a result of the quarreling, chose to hurry back to Boston for treatment. He left before the end of April, and a fortnight later Edith, her hay fever having grown intolerable, was at Salsomaggiore.

Edith had hoped that Berenson might join her there; he had asked, in his engagingly formal way, if it would be "proper" for him to do so, and Edith had replied spiritedly, "I hope you'll come *even if it is.*" Berenson was not, finally, able to get away. Relaxing at Salsomaggiore—and pausing only to refer disrespectfully to the local English doctor, who was "about on the veterinary level, like most English doctors at continental water places"—Edith got to work on what she called "a *vast* novel" *(The Reef),* and was content with solitude and quiet for the time being.

Her peace was abruptly shattered by a letter from Herman Edgar, her first cousin and the son of her mother's younger sister Eliza who had drowned when the *Ville de Havre* went down many decades before. Since Teddy's collapse in 1909, Edgar had been Edith's chief financial as well as her legal adviser. Immediately upon reaching Boston, Teddy had written Edgar, in a manner at once jaunty and touching, seeking in effect to resume control over his wife's finances. He asked for a total accounting of what had happened to all properties "from the time of my collapse to date" and a complete list "of the three trusts and of Puss's individual things," with an indication of any changes made. He gently criticized some of Edgar's transactions, and went on to say:

> You know just the spirit I write you in. For 25 years I looked after Puss's affairs and I did well until I went to pieces 2 years ago. I still take a great interest in them and I don't want to give it all up. I want to feel still that I know about them and can be of some use to her.

In some bewilderment, Edgar passed this along to Edith with a covering note, and Edith girded herself for action. "I am surprised and discouraged," she wrote Teddy, "at your manner of keeping the agreement which I thought had been made between us when you left." She rehearsed their many discussions in Paris and her settled decision that he was to have no part in the handling of her estate. In view of his recent effort to intervene, she now proposed another major step: namely, his removal as trustee.

> In order that no further questions of this kind should come up, the only thing left for me to do is to suggest that you should resign your Trusteeship, as you have so often proposed to do during the last two years. Your health unfortunately makes it impossible for you to take any active part in the management of my affairs, and this being so, you yourself will probably be more content, and less disposed to worry over the subject, once your resignation has been decided on.

Whether Edith herself believed the prophecy of Teddy's greater contentment, it is hard to say. But she was determined to spare herself any more *talk* about money, the chief and exhausting topic of conversation between them of late. To drive it home that he was to consider himself altogether out of things, she added: "I want to remind you again, before we meet, that this applies not only to talk about the management of my property, but to the question of managing household affairs for me"; in other words, of running The Mount.

She would be sailing for New York on June 24, and promised her husband to have their Lenox home ready for him when he came back from his fishing trip with his brother William. On her way to Paris she lingered a few days in Parma, reading and thinking and trying to take stock. From Parma she sent a wistful postcard to Morton Fullerton with the soft-spoken plea, "Take care of me": "*Géris moi,*" she wrote, in a minuscule hand.

4

What James would describe to Edith as "the storm and sorrow of the last act of your personal drama" began at The Mount on Saturday, July 8. The first days were far from sorrowful: they were indeed, for Edith, an unalloyed joy. She had reached New York on the *Philadelphia* the week before and had gone directly to Lenox to open the house, no small undertaking after so long an absence. On the eighth, the clan gathered: another coming together of those few with whom Edith could commune and renew herself. Henry James was met at the Springfield station just after noon; there was a pleasant run through the hills and lunch in a shady place; by two thirty they were at The Mount. John Hugh Smith, on his first visit to the United States, made an appearance an hour later, and that evening Gaillard Lapsley came over from Narragansett, where he was paying his annual visit with his family. There was champagne at dinner, and with Teddy away for yet a few more days, Edith could savor the atmosphere of her own special, exclusive, and lofty-minded republic of the spirit.

The Mount and its surroundings had never seemed more beautiful. The mere possibility of selling her American home lent the place a singularly idyllic quality, with its deep stillness, its greenness, its riot of flowers, the scent of hemlock from the woods, and in the warm July evenings, moonlight on the long terrace looking down toward the lake.

Everyone seemed at once to relax and expand. James in particular was at his resplendent best. Edith, as she would put it, had never known him more completely and lavishly himself, and felt again that *"greatness"* in him that was the encompassing fact of his being. The months he had spent in America following William's death had done much to restore him, and he was now meditating his next, and last, major literary enterprise, his autobiography (the first volume, *A Small Boy and Others,* would appear two years later). As a consequence, he was in a mellowly reminiscent mood.

One evening, as the party sat late on the terrace and the moon reflected dimly in the lake through the dark trees, James happened to mention his Albany relations, the Emmet and Temple families. He had just been visiting the former, and someone said, "Oh, tell us about the Emmets!" Recalling his response in *A Backward Glance*, Edith Wharton contrived a fine impressionistic account of James's style of speaking:

> For a moment he stood there brooding in the darkness, murmuring over and over to himself, "Ah, my dears, the Emmets—ah, the Emmets." Then he began, forgetting us, forgetting the place, forgetting everything but the vision of his lost youth that the question had evoked, the long train of ghosts flung with his enchanter's hand across the wide stage of the summer night. Ghostlike indeed at first, wavering and indistinct, they glimmered at us through a series of disconnected ejaculations, epithets, allusions, parenthetical rectifications and restatements, till not only our brains but the clear night itself seemed filled with a palpable fog; and then, suddenly, by some miracle of shifted lights and accumulated strokes, there they stood before us as they lived, drawn with a million filament-like lines, yet sharp as an Ingres, dense as a Rembrandt; or, to call upon his own art for an analogy, minute and massive as the people of Balzac.

"Were ever such splendours poured out on mortal heads," Edith asked Lapsley a few days later, "as descended on ours that fiery week?"

Hugh Smith's initial impressions of America had not been very favorable, and the critique he put forward was warmly seconded by James. Somewhat to her surprise, Edith found herself defending her native land: the thought of cutting her last ties with it had caused her to reconsider her ambivalent feelings about the country, both as an American and as a writer. "America," she wrote Hugh Smith soon after the party had broken up, "can't be quite so summarily treated as our great Henry thinks." She admitted that "at the present stage of its strange unfolding it isn't exactly a propitious 'ambiance' for the arts, and I can understand his feeling as he does." Nonetheless, she argued, Balzac would have seen its possibilities. America, or a part of it, was still, she was forced to realize, her own central and abiding subject for fiction.

Hugh Smith left on July 12, and Lapsley the following morning. That afternoon Edith and James paced the grounds, escaping from the severe heat into the cooler woods, and talked long about her domestic anxieties. With regard to the two most pressing questions facing her, James on the whole took the position that Edith should sell The Mount and that she should not continue to live with Teddy. Edith was not fully convinced.

There followed a little comic interlude, before the more somber drama got under way. James was finally overcome by the roasting temperature, and observing its calamitous affect upon him, Edith proposed that she telephone to Boston to arrange an earlier sea passage than the one on which James was booked. The suggestion threw James into a kind of fit. How could she have possibly imagined he could make so impetuous a move? What of the heavy luggage at the James home in New Hampshire, and the laundry he had sent out to Lenox the day before?

Between the electric fan clutched in his hand, and the pile of sucked oranges at his elbow, he cowered there, a mountain of misery, repeating in a sort of low despairing chant: "Good God, what a woman—what a woman! Her imagination boggles at nothing! She does not even scruple to project me in naked flight across the Atlantic."

James recovered in time to stand by when Teddy arrived, and to be startled by his performance. Physically, Teddy was remarkably well: springy, athletic, eager for the golf course and the tennis court. Psychologically, he was in a distressing state. He plunged at once into the discussions about money that Edith had made him promise to forgo. He accused Edith of having been cruel and vindictive, and of inflicting upon him a terrible humiliation in demanding that he resign his trusteeship. He grew more heated and incoherent by the moment, and abusive almost to the point of violence—only to collapse into fits of weeping, self-reproach, and pleas for forgiveness.

"The violent and scenic Teddy," James reported to Lapsley, "is negotiable in a measure—but the pleading, suffering, clinging, helpless Teddy is a very awful and irreducible quantity indeed." James was due to go to an old friend in Nahant on July 14; he was reluctant to leave Edith, but she assured him she could manage, and Cook drove him through the cold rain (the weather having broken at last) to Pittsfield. From Nahant he again summarized his views to Lapsley:

She has only to take her course—quietly, patiently and firmly; he can hold or follow no counter-proposal, no plan of opposition, of his own, for as much as a minute or two; he is immediately *off*—irrelevant and childish. But I didn't mean to go into this—one's pity for her is at the best scarce bearable.

5

But to take a course and hold to it was exactly what Edith found it difficult to do. If things went from bad to worse over the next ten days, it was in part due to Edith's own state of uncertainty regarding both The Mount and her life with Teddy. When the abusive mood was on him, Teddy extended his list of accusations to include Edith's having been personally and financially mean to him, of having sent him to Kreuzlingen so that he would be "locked up there and kept out of the way," of seeking to sell The Mount behind his back and then lying to the gardener by saying it was not to be sold. Teddy, as had been his option, had turned down the offer received in Paris and, given his seemingly excellent health, Edith rather approved the action. But as the days went by and Teddy became, intermittently, the more uncontrolled and insulting, she began to reconsider; her impulse, indeed, was to leave Teddy then and there.

Matters came to a climax on the twenty-second. Early that evening Teddy came to Edith's room in an extremely apologetic frame of mind, asking her forgiveness for his conduct over the past days. They had a long and—for this stage in their relationship—unusually amicable talk, and out of it came the following agreement. They would hold on to The Mount. Assuming that Teddy could "keep on pleasant terms" with her, Edith would remain another few weeks. She would then return to Europe, and Teddy would join her at the Rue de Varenne in March. Meanwhile, he would have sole and total charge of the Lenox home, and to this end Edith would deposit five hundred dollars each month which Teddy could expend in any way he saw fit. He *must,* however, resign as co-trustee. And the agreement would be off the moment Teddy began to argue about money matters, or "should he, by his tone or attitude toward me, make it impossible for me to lead a peaceful life with him."

That was at eight o'clock, and the last phrases quoted were contained in a letter Edith immediately wrote to Teddy's brother Billy. The missive, which recapitulates the developments of the previous few months and sets forth the agreement, sounds a little like the terms of peace dictated to the losing side by the fairly generous-minded victor. Teddy, she said, had spoken "in a tone of voice which was completely unjustified by any act or word of mine, and which I could not and would not tolerate."

I told him this frankly, and I added that, in the circumstances, I felt it would perhaps be better to sell The Mount after all, since it seemed as difficult to live here as elsewhere without raising questions that make reasonable and peaceful relations impossible between us.

At ten o'clock, Teddy again presented himself in his wife's room. Edith showed him the letter to Billy Wharton and asked him, in effect, to countersign it as an indication that he "agreed to the conditions as I have stated them." Teddy glanced through the document and at once flew into a towering rage. He declared the whole substance to be untrue, since it implied strongly that Edith had been "behaving well" throughout, whereas in fact she had treated him very badly in the matter of resigning the trusteeship. This, he insisted, he had never agreed to, and moreover—so Edith put it in a second letter to her brother-in-law, enclosing the earlier one:

If I still made it a condition, it was useless for us to try to live together either here or elsewhere, and that for his part he thought there had better be a final break between us at once, as he should take no interest in managing The Mount and running the household if I turned him out of the fund.

From Edith's point of view, there seemed nothing more to be done. The last ten days had shown her that "the fact of my meeting all his wishes, even to giving him the control of a large part of my income is not enough to satisfy him. I have therefore reluctantly concluded that . . . it is best that I should take him at his word and put an end to this last unsuccessful experiment." She would still place five hundred dollars monthly at his disposal, and she was sure that he would find a happy mode of life once he was "removed from the associations which my presence seems to suggest."

Two days later Edith dispatched a letter from her bedroom to that of her husband saying much the same thing. She recounted her version of the successive phases, to the point where she had consented not only to stay with him but to give him full charge of The Mount. Despite this, she told him, he had "reopened the question of the trust, accusing me of seeking to humiliate and wound you by the request, abusing me for my treatment of you during the last few years, and saying that, rather than live with me here or elsewhere after you had resigned the trust, you preferred an immediate break." She had hoped against hope that Teddy would "regain a normal view of life."

But your behavior since your return has done nothing to encourage this hope, and as nothing I have done seems to satisfy you for more than a few hours, I now think it is best to accede to your often repeated suggestion that we should live apart.

I am sorry indeed, but I have done all I can to help your recovery and make you contented, and I am tired out, and unwilling to go through any more scenes like those of the last fortnight.

In a postscript she added the notation that H. Edgar would deposit the monthly check in Teddy's Boston bank. (These various letters exist in Anna Bahlmann's transcription of them. Edith Wharton left them behind as a sort of posthumous brief for her defense against the charge of having mistreated her husband.)

Here we may shift perspective a little. Behind Teddy's irascibility and tears, his contradictory demands and contentions, his shouting and his no doubt sometimes maddening behavior, it is possible to discern a pattern of motivation that is logical, familiar, and human. In his conduct during the summer and fall of 1909 —the business of the Mountfort Street property and the mistress installed there —a portion of vengefulness had mingled with a desire for self-assertion. But by the summer of 1911, Teddy might be said to have been fighting for his life: that is, he was fighting in no very coherent manner for his identity.

One cannot be sure about the exact terms in which Teddy abused Edith "for my treatment of you during the last few years"; it may well be that he flung Fullerton's name in her face as a counter to the facts of his own infidelity. No more miserable exchange can be imagined; but even so, what most agitated Teddy was the issue of his financial function. Teddy Wharton had for many years been a vocationless individual in an American society which retained the old Puritan habit of identifying a man by the kind of work he did. His job in life had gradually become that of managing his wife's large estate and overseeing the many needs of The Mount. The greater part of that function was now about to be taken from him, and he was invited to accept the limitation as being for his own best good. Little wonder that a few months before, Dr. Dupré, an expert on nervous diseases, had predicted grimly that M. Wharton would end by killing himself.

Teddy was also hopelessly outnumbered. He had already, two years earlier, experienced the amount of sheer power that Edith and her associates could bring to bear upon a temporarily wayward spouse. Now, seeking to regain his lost financial authority, he had run up against a swift and decisive exertion of counter-force which demanded his resignation as trustee. He could expect little moral support from the likes of James, Hugh Smith, and Lapsley, or from the others who customarily filled the Lenox and Paris homes. The only recourse left to him was futile rage and recrimination.

Something of this was intuited by William Wharton and his wife, Susan, who were understandably disposed to see things from Teddy's point of view. Edith, having communicated to her husband and to his brother her determination that she and Teddy should separate, made the gesture of going over to Newport for a few days, there to visit with Egerton Winthrop and see Walter Berry (the latter had been briefly at The Mount and had been privy to some of the scenes before escaping to the shore). On her return to Lenox she found a letter from Billy in response to hers of the twenty-second. He and Susan, Billy wrote, felt sure that Teddy's illness and misery were—in Edith's paraphrasing—"caused in great degree by the realisation that he and I were not so happy together as we used to be, and that we were getting estranged from each other more and more each year."

Edith was altogether indignant. Apart from everything else, she said, it might have occurred to the Whartons that "a wife 'estranged' from her husband, in however slight a degree, would hardly have behaved as I did, when I learned, two years ago, of Ted's conduct in Boston," or have proposed that he be given charge of The Mount. Writing and revising with the care she would have given to a work of fiction, Edith went on, after a final review of events:

I absolutely deny that there has been any change of behaviour on my part, or any cause of "estrangement," save that produced within the last three or four months by his own disregard of all courtesy and self-control in his behaviour to me.

If Teddy had been able to admit this freely, she would have been willing to give him another chance. "As it is, your letter only convinces me of the uselessness of all I have done in the past, or might be disposed to do in the future."

Despite such disingenuous statements, Edith was an enormously troubled woman. Once again, her impulses, her inherited beliefs, her allegiances and convictions, her accumulated sense of herself, jostled and warred with each other. She foresaw in the sale of The Mount the abandonment of her last American home and the loss of a central element in her own identity; not to mention the seat from which her imagination might gather in the materials for its special workings. Separation from her husband was more momentous yet. She was aware of marriages dissolving on all sides, yet every traditional piety she clung to argued against such an action. And buried under her most forthright assertions of blamelessness, there must have remained a strong residue of guilt. There was, too, her deep natural fastidiousness, her detestation of emotional clamor, and her hitherto carefully protected psychological privacy. No one shrank more from having to discuss or defend, or listen to dissections of, her inmost personality and domestic conduct. Given all this, her sheer survival as a reasoning and, more, a productive human being is almost a matter for wonder.

6

Ethan Frome, which ran in *Scribner's* from August through October and was published in book form at the end of September, was in good part the product of Edith Wharton's personal life during the previous few agitated years. Into no earlier work of fiction, not even *The House of Mirth*, had she poured such deep and intense private emotions. *Ethan Frome* in this regard was a major turning point, whether or not it was also the very finest of her literary achievements. Edith had hitherto reserved her strongest feelings for poetry; henceforth, they would go into her novels and stories. The experience of writing the fictively conceived 1908 journal had served her well. From this moment forward, and with obvious exceptions, Edith Wharton's fictional writings began to comprise the truest account of her inward life.

One event external to her life also contributed to the climax of *Ethan Frome*. In March 1904 there had been a disastrous sledding accident at the foot of Courthouse Hill in Lenox (Schoolhouse Hill in the novella). Four girls and a boy, all about eighteen and all but one juniors in Lenox High School, had gone coasting after school on a Friday afternoon. They made several exuberant runs down the mile-long slope, a descent on which a tremendous momentum can be achieved. On their last flight the young people's "double-ripper" sled crashed into the lamppost at the bottom of the hill. One of the girls, Hazel Crosby, suffered multiple fractures and internal injuries; she died that evening. Lucy Brown had her thigh fractured and her head gashed, and was permanently lamed. Kate Spencer's face was badly scarred.

Ethan Frome, when the narrator meets him at the opening of the tale, walks painfully with a lameness that checked "each step like the jerk of a chain"; there is an angry red gash across his forehead. The story that Ethan eventually unfolds for his visitor, and that the latter pieces together from other sources, goes back nearly thirty years to events leading up to a sledding catastrophe.

As a young farmer in the New England village of Starkfield, Ethan had married an older woman, Zenobia, a morose figure victimized by real and imaginary ailments. Her cousin Mattie Silver had come to help with the household chores and the work on the hard-pressed farm. Ethan and Mattie, much of an age, fall in love, even while realizing that there is no future for the two of them together. When "Zeena" announces that Mattie is to be sent away and replaced by a more efficient housemaid, the lovers determine to kill themselves by crashing their sled into the big elm at the foot of the hill near the main road. The attempt is hideously unsuccessful. Ethan is merely lamed and Mattie crippled for life. They live on now in the joyless ménage dominated by the abruptly recovered Zenobia.

In her description of the bleak village of Starkfield and the allusions to nearby places like Bettsbridge, Corbury Flats, and Corbury Junction, Edith Wharton was drawing upon her memory of Plainfield and Lenox, of the Berkshire scenes she had so frequently passed through on the drives to Ashfield and back. She was re-creating the spell that the New England landscape had laid upon her, its dark somber beauty, its atmosphere (for her) of the haunted and tragic.

The treatment both of setting and character shows Edith Wharton in perfect command of the methods of literary realism; in its grim and unrelenting way, *Ethan Frome* is a classic of the realistic genre. At the same time, it is Edith Wharton's most effectively American work; her felt affinities with the American literary tradition were never more evident. A certain Melvillian grandeur went into the configuration of her tragically conceived hero. Despite her early disclaimers, the spirit of Nathaniel Hawthorne pervades the New England landscape of the novella and lies behind the moral desolation of Ethan Frome—a desolation as complete in its special manner as that of his namesake, Hawthorne's Ethan Brand. The sense of deepening physical chill (the French translation was called *Hiver*) that corresponds to the inner wintriness is similarly Hawthornian in nature. The role of the inquisitive city-born narrator is deployed with a good deal of the cunning and artistry of Henry James.

But the great and durable vitality of the tale comes at last from the personal feelings Edith Wharton invested in it, the feelings by which she lived her narrative. *Ethan Frome* portrays her personal situation, as she had come to appraise it, carried to a far extreme, transplanted to a remote rural scene, and rendered utterly hopeless by circumstance. As she often did, Edith shifted the sexes in devising her three central characters. Like Edith Wharton, Ethan Frome is married to an ailing spouse a number of years older than he, and has been married for about the same length of time as Edith had been tied to Teddy. Ethan sometimes wonders about Zeena's sanity, and he daydreams about her death, possibly by violence (one recalls "The Choice"). He looks about frantically for some avenue to freedom, but his fate is conveyed to him in Edith's regular image for her own condition: "The inexorable facts closed in on him like prison-warders handcuffing a convict. . . . He was a prisoner for life."

The relationship between Ethan and Mattie Silver contains memories of Morton Fullerton (even the names echo faintly) and passages transposed from the 1908 journal. Ethan and Mattie go star charting together; he feels that for the first time in his life he has met someone who can share his sensitiveness to natural beauty. During their one evening together, he with his pipe and Mattie with her sewing, Ethan lets himself imagine—as Edith had done on a winter evening in the Rue de Varenne—that their evenings would always be so. But in the savage quarreling between Ethan and Zeena, in the latter pages of the story, we hear something of the bitter recriminations Edith and Teddy had begun to visit upon each other. And in the denouement—where the bountifully healthy and vindictive Zeena commands a household that includes Mattie as a whining invalid and Ethan as the giant wreck of a man—we have Edith Wharton's appalling vision of what her situation might finally have come to.

It was quickly recognized by reviewers that *Ethan Frome* was one of Edith Wharton's finest achievements, though some of them found the concluding image too terrible to be borne. The entire tale, said a writer in *The New York Times*, was an exercise in subtle torture. A library guide declared the book too pessimistic to be recommended to the general reader, and the critic in *The Bookman*—confusing Edith Wharton's judgment on life with her personal attitudes—could not forgive her her cruelty toward both her characters and her readers. But there was a great deal of praise, and almost every reviewer had admiring words for the story's construction and style.

Gratifying letters poured in on Edith. Dr. Kinnicutt told her prophetically that *Ethan Frome* was "a classic that will be read and re-read with pleasure and instruction," and was astonished at what she had been able to do in the midst of her "pressing anxieties." James expressed total admiration. He had been jovially skeptical about the narrator's opening remark: "I had been sent by my employers . . ." the notion of dear Edith being sent anywhere by anyone, he commented, boggled belief. But when he finished the story he found, with his usual critical exactness, that it contained "a beautiful art and tone and truth— a beautiful artful kept-downness." Others, if less eloquent, were equally warm in their enthusiasm.

Ethan Frome was Edith Wharton's sixteenth book in thirteen years. Between *The Greater Inclination* in 1899 and *Ethan Frome* in 1911, there had been only one year, 1906, when she failed to produce at least one volume; and she made up for it by bringing out a novella, a full-length novel, a book of short stories, and a collection of travel sketches in the next twenty-four months. Nor would her phenomenal energy flag in the years to come. The war was an inevitable interruption, but beginning with *The Age of Innocence* in 1920, she continued to appear at the rate of a volume a year until her death. Of all these manifold and varied writings, *Ethan Frome* has been much the most widely read and admired.

It was not, however, an immediate commercial success. In some small circles, especially in England, the novella was recognized almost at once as a work that approached greatness; but it did not otherwise exert a very broad appeal. It was not until the 1930s—surprisingly, given the public's aversion to literary realism during the Depression years—that the sales suddenly picked up, and a long-running dramatic version was produced on Broadway. It has since become a standard classroom text, Edith Wharton's one sure contribution—though *The House of Mirth* and *The Age of Innocence* are being given increasing attention —to surveys of American literature. *Ethan Frome* has also been translated twice into French, half a dozen times into Italian, and into Swedish, Russian, and Japanese.

Edith was dismayed and resentful at the slowness of the sales in 1911. She fell to bickering with Scribners in a manner reminiscent of earlier days, but this time with more fateful consequences. Soon after publication she told Charles Scribner that the book seemed to be having an immediate success and asked for a second advance of one thousand dollars, taking the occasion to remark that the volume had been "*very* badly printed. . . . I have never seen so many defective letters and various typographical untidiness in any book you have published for me, and I think a protest ought to be made." Scribner, who had pointed out that shorter books never did as well as full-length novels, reported that as of mid-November, *Ethan Frome* had sold a little over four thousand copies, as much as her two most recent collections of short stories had sold since publication.

Edith expressed puzzlement over the figures: friends in Boston and New York had told her the first edition had sold out and the book was unobtainable; a bookseller at Brentano's observed that "they had more demand for it than any novel published this season." "Nothing," Scribner replied patiently, "is more difficult to meet than the statement of an author's friends who report that a book is selling tremendously or cannot be had at the best bookstores. Retail clerks are very apt to say whatever they think a customer wishes to hear." He enclosed a week-by-week breakdown of sales in four Boston stores (300 in all) and in Brentano's (283). By late February 1912 sales of *Ethan Frome* had reached nearly seven thousand, and it was "still in active demand."

When it became evident that *Ethan Frome* was not to be a major commercial success, Mrs. Wharton reverted to the charge that it had been sparsely advertised, and trusted that her next novel, *The Custom of the Country*, would be given much better publicity. Scribners contended that they had in fact spent more than they could afford for a book of its small price, and promised the new work would be pressed hard. Edith Wharton's subsequent communication, dated May 3, announced that her next novel turned out to be *The Reef* and that she had given it to Messrs. Appleton, who had made a "very high offer for it." She had no doubt that this would work to Scribners' best interest: *The Reef* would probably reach a rather different public and hence would "in some sort be a preparation for *The Custom of the Country.*"

It would take a month for Charles Scribner to bring himself to reply to this news. It was the first stage in Edith Wharton's slow disaffiliation with her long-time publishers.

7

The upheaval at The Mount in July 1911 was not, after all, "the last act" of Edith's personal drama. Henry James, who had thought that it could not help but be, gave Howard Sturgis a reading after returning to Lamb House. Edith was in very deep waters, he said, and before coming over she would probably sell The Mount and separate "finally and 'legally' " from Teddy. As to the latter, he was

perfectly sane and in the stoutest, toughest physical health, but utterly quarrelsome, abusive, perpetual scene-making and impossible. He simply and absolutely, otherwise, will do her to death, and then where shall we be?

Yet by early August some kind of reconciliation had been effected, and things quieted down once more.

Edith was now determined *not* to sell the Lenox home, on the chance (as she wrote Hugh Smith) that Teddy might improve and benefit from the life there. During the interval of tranquility, and following a visit from Morton Fullerton, she indicated to Lapsley the two matters of closest concern to her by sending on, without comment, two newspaper clippings: one about the divorce of a rising young novelist (Upton Sinclair), the other about Harold Bell Wright's novel, *The Winning of Barbara Worth,* selling over one million copies.

There was no further talk, for the time being, of separation, legal or otherwise; but before August was out, the decision regarding The Mount had again been reversed, for the fifth or sixth time. It was simply too expensive, she wrote Lapsley, "unless I continue to drive a successful quill"; the offer to buy it was a very good one, and the place was indeed almost sold. Teddy was "unspeakably worried" by the prospect. She sailed for Europe on September 7, leaving it to Teddy to take final action.

The sale of The Mount finally did go through, in a long-drawn-out business that began with a petition filed in Lenox in early November. Two weeks later Edith wrote Robert Grant: "The sale of 'The Mount' is a great regret to me, and was done against my wish and without my knowledge. As you know, surprises of that kind have not been infrequent lately." The statement is as mystifying as it is bitter. There is no doubt that Edith enormously regretted the loss of the home she had built; to this extent, it could be said to be against her wishes. But the sale can hardly be said to have been negotiated behind her back. On September 2, before sailing for Europe, Edith signed a document making her husband her "true, sufficient, and lawful Attorney" for any action involving The Mount; giving him "full power to rent said real estate and personal estate on such terms and for such times as he may see fit"; and "especially" granting "full power to negotiate a sale of said real and personal estate, at his sole discretion." Teddy was legally entrusted with absolute authority.

Perhaps she was merely trying to dissociate herself from an act of which Robert Grant was likely to disapprove; or perhaps, in the pain of her loss, she was moved to present Teddy in the worst possible light. She seems at times to have welcomed the commiseration she received because of Teddy, and to have discovered that up to a point martyrdom has certain advantages. The sale, at any rate, was completed the following June, Edith co-signing (in Paris) with Teddy. The purchaser was one Albert Richardson of Greenwich, Connecticut; the sum was unannounced (save for the legal evasion of "One Dollar and other valuable consideration"). Edith Wharton's American life was at an end.

17. Divorces

In the fall of 1911, Edith Wharton made her first visit to the Villa I Tatti, the Berensons' home in the hills above Florence. She had had only a week in Paris (at the Crillon) after returning from Lenox, days spent mostly with Berenson and Adams; there had followed an interval at sticky, fly-blown Salsomaggiore. Liberated from the spa, with Berry at her side and Cook at the wheel, she set off on a slow circling tour of central Italy. It was a rainy season and the roads were bad, but Edith took delight in her new fifty-horsepower Mercedes—a great improvement, she felt, over "our old plodding Hortense." They made their way through Parma and Mantua to Verona, and from there via Vicenza to Arquà, pausing every other day to fire off a postcard to Henry James.

James, in the course of turning down an invitation to join them, had expressed his wormlike hope that they would "peck" at him with their "beaks" now and then, and on the back of a card bearing a photograph of Petrarch's home in Arquà, Berry scribbled a bit of light verse:

> Without the worm, the Beaks are growing starker,
> The more so in This Room; and if Petrarca
> Could live again he'd sing: "We want the aura
> Of Henry more than all the lures of Laura."

In Ravenna, with thoughts in her mind of Lord Byron and the last of his mistresses, Edith advanced the versified question:

> In such a place, with ties unholy,
> How could he live with La Guiccioli?

The weather turned magical as they continued on through Urbino and up to Rimini, on the Adriatic; and the latter setting inspired Berry to send James

> A flashing word to mark the giro's gesta
> Merceding through the land of Malatesta.

On October 15 they drove out of Florence on the long, climbing road to the little *frazione* of Ponte a Mensola, and up the Vincigliata slope to I Tatti.

Mary Berenson, after doing much to prepare for the visit, had slipped away. Hearing this, James remarked to Mary Cadwalader Jones that there appeared to be "a bad split there, too"; but not even James, the most passionate observer of his time, could fully grasp the special marital arrangements of Bernhard and Mary Berenson. Berenson's temporary solitude was perhaps not displeasing to Edith Wharton, who described the tenor of the days at I Tatti in gleeful rhymes:

> Climbing cliffs and fording torrents
> Here we are at last in Florence,
> Or rather perching on the piano
> Nobile, at Settignano.
> Doing picture galleries? No, sir!
> Motoring to Vallombrosa,
> Piacenza, Siena, tutte quante,
> High above the dome of Dante.

Berenson took his guests to call on Florence Baldwin, an American woman living nearby, and her daughter by a former marriage, Gladys Deacon. The latter was an attractive, eccentric woman of about thirty, with a rollicking sense of humor; Berenson had not failed to have an affair with her, though now, it was said, she was the mistress of the Duke of Marlborough. Later—after an extravagant negotiation with the Vatican which led to the annulment of the duke's marriage to Consuelo Vanderbilt—she became his wife. Edith Wharton thought her flamboyant and likable.

In early December, Edith exchanged the quiet rush of Paris for the bustle of London. She went primarily to see Henry James, with whom she dined several times, and whom she accompanied to a performance of *Kismet*. The ten-day visit turned out, unexpectedly, to be another triumphal procession; if *Ethan Frome* had not sold very widely, it had obviously sold in the right places. The ever cordial Mary Crawshay, in Upper Berkeley Street, took Edith in tow, remarking later that "Mrs. Wharton . . . had a wild success in London over the little masterpiece *Ethan.* It is quite great." Everyone, said Mrs. Crawshay, "insisted on worshipping her and making her do things she didn't want to do."

Relaxing at Queen's Acre with Howard Sturgis, Edith was happy to meet and to come on friendly terms with Logan Pearsall Smith, whom she had not encountered since the debacle at the Villa La Doccia eight years before. The brother of Mary Berenson was forty-six at the time and had been living in England for more than twenty years. After a period at Harvard he had transferred to Balliol College, Oxford, and later withdrew to an eighteenth-century farmhouse in Sussex, with a small but adequate income.

Tall, heavily built, and good-looking, like his sister Mary, Pearsall Smith was one of the witty and amusingly malicious bachelors to whom Edith was periodically drawn. It was in Sussex, in 1902, that he put together *Trivia*, the first of four mandarin volumes of aphorisms and reflections on the curiosities of life and a variety of well-bred discomfitures. The book rather irritated some, who felt it was not the time for such verbal niceties when there were so many social and ethical issues to be met. But Pearsall Smith was gradually revealed as one of the most graceful prose writers alive, and his several anthologies displayed both his erudition and wit, and his dedication to literature.

2

The situation with Teddy was heavy with ambiguity. The decision to separate had been abandoned, but it was unclear how they might set about living together again. In October, Teddy visited a spa in French Lick, Arkansas (while Edith, in James's phrase, was at "Italian Lick, Lombardy—what a dividing abyss"). Teddy's big toe was hurting so badly that he asked to have it operated upon; this request was denied by the doctor in charge, who was convinced that all Teddy's troubles were pyschosomatic.

Forwarding this opinion, Dr. Kinnicutt remarked: "It is all very sad and it is difficult to advise. . . . I think we must accept the fact that Mr. Wharton is suffering from a psychosis, and the prognosis is an unfavourable one." Both he and his colleague urged that Teddy be placed in a sanatorium: "It would be really helpful to him, not perhaps as regards the ultimate outcome but in relieving some of his unhappiness." Just before Christmas, Teddy cabled that he wanted to come over to Paris at once. Edith dispatched White to escort him, but upon his arrival White learned that Teddy had suddenly changed his mind and was determined to go down to Bermuda for several weeks.

These changes of direction may have contributed to the attacks of vertigo that Edith began to experience shortly after New Year's 1912. There was also the fact that on January 24 she reached her fiftieth birthday, though this seems not to have distressed her greatly. The chief symptom was the feeling, when she saw anything drop, that she herself was about to fall down; on the street one day a man let a book slip out of his hands, and Edith almost tumbled at his feet. She understood her doctor to say that the condition was due to "tension in the *'labyrinthe de l'oreille'* " (inner ear) related to anemia; she was told to avoid all hurry and rush, and to keep out of doors as much as possible. She was also taking "all kinds of blood-makers, and not doing much with my head, or such poor pulp as it contains."

It was not until February that White finally brought Teddy back to France. Berry immediately returned to the guest suite in the Rue de Varenne, to act as a "shock-absorber." He stayed several weeks and, digesting Berry's report to him, James observed that Teddy seemed amazingly "well and strong and normal—but only the more hopelessly futile and arid and *énervant,*" and though "it be true that with his restlessness he can't 'endure,' so on the other hand, and from the same cause he can't be endured, or scarcely." James was appalled at the prospect that the situation might go on forever. He told Sturgis, however, that he himself was feeling so poorly, and so unable to help, that he could not bear to think about "Teddy's victim"; he asked himself "why cultivate, in the commotion, a mere

Platonic horror—which permits me neither to hold her hand nor to kick his tail."

But the intent student of the troubled life could not long withhold his attention from the state of things in Paris, and to Sturgis he summarized his terrible sense of them:

> What comes to me most is the thought of how it must come to poor Edith, in these dark vigils, that she did years ago an almost—or rather an utterly—inconceivable thing in marrying him. As how superfluous, irrelevant, incoherent an act (with all its futility in its face—as in *his!*) it must now press upon her; and there *is* the intolerable pressure!— her bed is made, and such a great big uncompromising 4-poster.

Here again, as in the summer of 1909, James was exploiting his own fiction for an appraisal of actual life. The image of Edith Wharton in her dark Parisian vigil pondering her deadly marital imprisonment springs from what is perhaps the most brilliant narrative passage James ever wrote: the long vigil of Isabel Archer in *The Portrait of a Lady,* sitting late in the darkened room of her Roman palazzo meditating her disastrous choice of a husband and the course of her psychic incarceration by him.

Unlike Isabel Archer, however, Edith Wharton had a number of close and warmly supportive friends. Fullerton was in particularly fine fettle. It was, James said, "as if he were engaged for the moment almost in a gay Nijinsky *pas,*" with a proliferation of essays and articles, some of which Edith seems to have had commissioned for him. Berry, now established in an important and lucrative position as head of the American Chamber of Commerce in Paris, was faithfully at hand, as were du Bos, Bourget, and Saint André, with James, Berenson, Hugh Smith, Lapsley, Sturgis, and others at a quickly reducible distance.

Edith's community of friends was never more needful to her; yet she was wistfully aware of the limits of any conceivable relationship under her present circumstances. The deepest and completest kind was, she felt, denied to her, and this she made manifest one afternoon to Charles du Bos. She had driven over to St. Cloud, where du Bos and his wife were staying with Zezette's parents. After lunch Edith took Charles to see the church at Montfort l'Amaury, which she had first visited with Morton Fullerton. The memory of that earlier visit may have stirred thoughts in Edith's mind; in any event, the two of them began talking about their favorite works of modern literature that dealt with love between man and woman.

As to fiction, both agreed on the supremacy of *Anna Karenina* and *Middlemarch;* in poetry, Edith chose Browning's "Any Wife to Any Husband," and du Bos "By the Fire-side" by the same poet. Du Bos then quoted a remark by Dorothea Brooke in *Middlemarch:* "Marriage is so unlike anything else. There is something even awful in the nearness it brings." It was at this point that Edith burst out: "Ah, the poverty, the miserable poverty, of any love that lies outside of marriage, of any love that is not a living together, a sharing of all." It was the bitter fruit of almost five years' experience.

A comparably bleak perception was conveyed in the story "The Long Run," which appeared in the *Atlantic Monthly* and helped to sell out the issue in two days. Although the tale is set in the upper echelons of New York society around the turn of the century and deals with the unexceptional "people of the old vanished New York," it has an aftermath almost as harrowing as that of the rural-based *Ethan Frome*.

It tells of Pauline Trent, married to a rigidly correct gentleman, and Halston Merrick, an artistically ambitious young man with whom she falls in love. Pauline arrives at Merrick's home in Riverdale one rainy evening, offering to go off with him for good. Merrick, though no less in love, is dismayed, and gives a flurry of confused arguments to the effect that he cannot take advantage of her rash impulse. Listening to him with sad gravity, Pauline suggests that "one way of finding out whether a risk is worth taking is *not* to take it, and then to see what one becomes in the long run, and draw one's inference." What the two of them become in the long run are the corpses of their former selves.

Merrick and Pauline linger on like Ethan and Mattie, psychically if not physically mutilated; both were broken at the instant of their parting, Merrick turning into a platitudinous bore, Pauline married a second time to an oafish "good fellow" and appearing at the correct social occasions with a strained artificial smile and unswervingly proper sentiments. It is a brilliant and cruel story, and seems to say again what Edith Wharton had learned: that although marriage may be intolerable, "any love that lies outside of marriage" is likely to be miserable and impoverished.

3

It was a period of confusion and drift, of hectic traveling and aimless loitering; with little interruption of work, yet with a sense of desolating uncertainty about her situation. She was, Edith told Berenson, feeling the "dead weight" of her life with Teddy. But Teddy spoke of returning to America in early May 1912, and she whiled away part of the interval by taking him to Madrid for Easter, indulging herself on the long drive back by detouring to the magnetically attractive Nohant. In Paris, though she declared herself exhausted—"morale fair" but physical condition "the downest"—she kept herself so busy socially that she earned from James the epithet *grande viveuse*. Teddy took his leave, and Edith moved on to Salsomaggiore, her third enforced visit to that unbeguiling resort in twelve months. Some of the treatments gave her chills and fever and made her bones ache, but they also did her good, and the routine was a steadying one: "Fiction in the morning," as she put it to Berenson, "and friction in the pomeriggio."

There then began a stretch of what James called her "whirligig" life, some five months of travel and adventure in Italy, England, and France, with only the briefest appearances in Paris in between. What is to be remarked is that Edith completed the last sizable portion of *The Reef*, her most tightly drawn novel, while thus almost constantly on the move.

Berry had joined her upon her release from Salsomaggiore, as he had the previous autumn. They thought of going into the Abruzzi, a relatively primitive and gauntly beautiful section of east-central Italy with which Edith was unfamiliar. But Berenson, when they stopped by at Settignano to chart an itinerary with him, was doubtful: Berry had had a siege of enteritis, and Berenson warned that changes of temperature and food might make it flare up again. He was entirely right. Berry was so obviously in pain by the time they reached Rome that Edith declined to proceed further. They started back by what were supposed to be easy stages to Venice and a few days' rest.

The journey in fact developed into a series of misadventures and borderline catastrophes which Edith described in a letter to Berenson. The first day they went as far as Spoleto, Berry insisting that en route they go over to San Oreste; he grew sulky when Edith refused to climb Soracte in the blazing afternoon sun. Next morning, after studying the map, he proposed that they drive into the hills north of Arezzo and look in on the monastery of La Verna—where, in 1224, St. Francis of Assisi received the stigmata—before going on to that of Camaldoli. Here is Edith's account:

> We started about 10 o'c, and were to "do" La Verna and dine at Camaldoli. Ye Gods! At 11 P.M. we were hanging over dizzy precipices in the Appenines, unable to turn back and almost unable (but for Cook's coolness and skill) to go on. Our luggage was all taken off and hauled behind us on a cart by a wild peasant, others escorted us with big stones to put behind the wheels at the worst ascent, and thus, at 11.30, *fourbus*, we reached the gates of La Verna, where it took us a good half hour to rouse the Frati, and Walter, under their relentless eyes, had to sup on oil soup and anchovies and cheese before they'd let us go to bed.

La Verna squats imposingly at the edge of uncommonly steep chalk cliffs; even today it is no small undertaking to reach it by daylight on the narrow, winding country highway, and for Cook to grope his way up to it at nighttime along what was then no better than a mule track was a decided feat.

> Further dangers and troubles ensued; "the Furies had only taken their apéritif!"

> The next day the car had to be *let down by ropes* to a point about 3/4 of a mile below the monastery, Cook steering down the vertical descent, and twenty men hanging on to a *funa* [rope] that, thank the Lord, *didn't break*.

This too was an achievement that would have had to be seen to be believed. But as if the oil soup and salty anchovies had not given Berry sufficient agony in his intestines, he now suffered a hideous inflammation in a tooth. They had "to speed *ventre à terre* from Bibbiena to Florence," where the dentist told him it would take ten days to heal.

Berry chose to hurry on to Paris, and an almost fatal disaster awaited them on the way.

As he preferred motoring on account of the heat, we started for Milan where he was to take the night train. We went over the Abetone, and just after we left Modena a crazy coachman drove full tilt out of a side road (Cook "horning" hard at the time), lost his head when he saw the car, and smashed straight into us. A pile of stones saved us from pitching into the deep stream by the roadside, but my poor maid was thrown out and nearly drowned. All the glass was smashed in front, and when we finally got patched up again I had to sit till 11.30 P.M. holding my umbrella open (inside the car) to keep the night wind off my maid's dripping head and Walter's tortured tooth! We reached the station 3 *minutes* before his train left, and I crawled back to the Cavour for two days' rest. *Et voila.*

Edith put in a few days in the Rue de Varenne while making plans for a three-week visit to England, as a substitute for the aborted Italian venture. Her announced plans threw Henry James into a paroxysm of alarm. The sixty-nine-year-old writer knew that a visit from Edith meant a flurry of motor trips of shorter or longer duration and a severe interruption to his work on *A Small Boy and Others.* He gave vent to a number of excited forebodings, and it was largely out of James's reactions to this 1912 visit that there grew the fanciful image of Edith Wharton descending upon Lamb House with remorseless frequency to destroy James's peace of mind and wreak havoc with his work.

Edith proposed that upon her arrival they should go instantly to Queen's Acre, pausing there—so James understood—only to gulp a hasty cup of tea before racing on to Lady Ripon's for dinner. To Mrs. William James he admitted that he would probably "enjoy it as much as I *can* enjoy it with an irritated and distressed sense of interruption and deviation." But to Howard Sturgis he sent a letter dated "Reign of Terror, *ce vingt Juillet* 1912," containing a "signal of distress thrown out . . . at the approach of the Bird o' freedom—the whir and wind of whose great wings is already cold on my foredoomed forehead! She is close at hand, she arrives tomorrow, and the poor old Ryebird . . . feels his barnyard hurry and huddle, emitting desperate and incoherent sounds." The Angel, he declaimed, planned to carry him off "struggling in her talons" whither she would and at her own pace. At the same time, he begged his friend and neighbor Fanny Prothero to pray for him "while I am hurried to my doom."

Edith drove into Rye on July 21, and James, who had been elaborately imploring her to come and had expressed vast delight when the dates were agreed to, now set himself in his accommodating way both to participate and to observe, performing the latter function with professedly mounting consternation. Edith took him on a hour-long drive to Crowborough; from the Reform Club in

London, James permitted himself to be carried down to Windsor for dinner and the night; he went with Edith to the Waldorf Astors at Cliveden for tea, both promising to return within the week.

In the intervals Edith went about London, visited the art galleries with Berenson, lunched with Walter Berry (when the latter was not squiring about the glamorous Elsie Goelet, with whom he was about to sail for America), and went on her own to Coombe Court in Surrey—the scene of some of the most lavish of all Edwardian house parties. Her host, the Marquess of Ripon, was reputed to be the finest shot in England; he was once said (implausibly) to have brought down twenty-eight pheasants in sixty seconds. His wife, Gladys, was a statuesque, beautiful, and imperious woman whose love affairs increased the Edwardian average.

But the Marchioness of Ripon was also a leading patroness of the arts, and at Coombe Court that weekend Edith Wharton found a gathering that included Nijinsky and Diaghilev, Rhoda Broughton (a competent minor novelist and friend of Henry James's), Bernhard Berenson, and Percy Grainger, the Australian pianist and composer of "In a Country Garden." There was also present the Princesse Edmonde de Polignac, another product of old New York: the former Winaretta Singer, the daughter of the inventor of the sewing machine, she was a sternly ugly woman and the chief backer of Diaghilev's Ballet Russe. Edith was especially pleased to see Mary (Mrs. Charles) Hunter, the delightful and muddle-headed mistress of Hill Hall, near Epping. She and Edith had spent some time together at Salsomaggiore the year before, and Edith thought her mad but charming. In Berenson's view, Mrs. Hunter was "full of unconscious venom against poor Edith"; in fact, the two women struck it off handsomely.

A few days later Edith accompanied James and Sturgis to Ascot to have tea with the aging, by now extremely bizarre, and still fascinating Margaret Brooke, the Ranee of Sarawak, who at this time was given to reclining regally in large armchairs with a huge and terrifying scarlet-winged macaw on her wrist. Edith undoubtedly knew, as of course James did, that she had been Morton Fullerton's mistress twenty years before. The intellectually ardent Vernon Lee was also on hand to Edith's pleasure—though not necessarily to that of Henry James, who had steered clear of her after a bad falling-out at an equally early date. The conversation, one can only suppose, must have been guarded.

A tinge of tragic drama clung to the assembly at Cliveden when Edith and James went back to that huge estate. Among those staying in the mansion was young Mrs. John Jacob Astor, who had suddenly and devastatingly become a widow the previous April 14 when the *Titanic* bumped into an iceberg and plunged to the bottom.

The loss of the greatest ship afloat, on its maiden voyage and seeking to break the record for the passage from Cherbourg to New York, was a disaster unparalleled in seagoing history. The doomed passengers, it was said, were as calm as the moonlit sea; but some fifteen hundred lives were lost—the ship, incredibly, had a thousand fewer places in its lifeboats than there were persons on board—and among them a number of the world's richest men. The most famous was John Jacob Astor, whose wealth was reckoned at 150 million dollars. The catastrophe was traumatic for the imagination of the Western world. In retrospect one sees it as symbolizing the beginning of the end of "the beautiful epoch"—of the age of expansion, of psychological and economic confidence, of total faith in science and technology, and of veneration of the very rich: the end, almost, of a way of life that saw nothing amiss in a few persons spending four thousand dollars on a five-day trip when the average American family income was less than a thousand.

Henry Adams took the event particularly hard. "The *Titanic* blow shatters one's nerves," he wrote. "We can't grapple it." A week later he suffered a stroke largely as a result of it. A worried Edith Wharton summarized for Berenson distressed cables about Adams ("alas and alas"), and said the worst danger was that he might live on with his mind affected.

Accompanying the nineteen-year-old Mrs. John Astor (who was pregnant) at Cliveden was her twenty-one-year-old stepson, Vincent. Edith's impressions of the pair are not recorded. Nor are those of her hostess, Lady Astor-to-be, the future leader of the sociopolitical "Cliveden set," and the gadfly of Parliaments. James regarded her as "a reclaimed barbarian." It is improbable that Edith was much taken by her aggressive vitality, her domination of social talk, and her odd antics at the dining-room table.

Edith and James of an evening walked down through the beautiful gardens to the Thames and along its banks; they strolled the grounds and wandered into the Taplow woods. After one of these little excursions James suffered a "pectoral attack," he noted in his diary, "through too much hurry and tension on slopes and staircase." Edith took alarm, and on August 2 drove James to Windsor for a quiet lunch and then lent him her "admirable car and dear Cook . . . for a most beautiful and merciful return, by myself, across country back to Rye."

After a visit with the Alfred Austins at Ashford, Edith came down to Lamb House on the eighth. Her twenty-four-hour visit elicited further reaches of eloquence from James. Even as he wrote, he told Sturgis, "the fire-bird perches on my shoulder. . . . She had held us . . . this pair of hours, by her admirable talk. She never was more wound up and going, or more ready, it would appear, for new worlds to conquer." But at the rate at which she consumed worlds—"eating up one for her luncheon and one for her dinner"—there would soon be none left. That headlong pace, James felt, was the terrible thing about (and *for*) a nature and a life in which a certain saving accommodation or gently economic bias seem able to play so small a part. She uses up everything and every one by the extremity of strain or the extremity of neglect.

Before she left, she had the entire small gathering at Lamb House in rags and tatters—"ground to powder, reduced to pulp, consumed utterly."

He outdid himself in a letter to Mary Cadwalader Jones which contained a similar mixture of awe, dazed horror, and glowing admiration.

She rode the whirlwind, she played with the storm, she laid waste whatever of the land the other raging elements had spared, she consumed in 15 days what would serve to support an ordinary Christian community (I mean to regulate and occupy and excite them) for about 10 years. Her powers of devastation are ineffable, her repudiation of repose absolutely tragic and she was never more brilliant and able and interesting.

The note of the mock-heroic—whereby a 140-pound fifty-year-old woman is transformed into the embodiment of a hurricane of mythic proportions—is splendidly done. Yet again it is possible to wonder just why Edith Wharton's manner of life should stir James to such a violence of metaphor.

One understands James's justifiable impatience at having his work broken into (how many more years of work could he be sure of?), his settled conviction that extreme wealth threatened its owner with psychological disarray, and even the actual exhaustion that a couple of hours of Edith Wharton's intense and prehensile conversation—not to mention her constant impulse to be up and going —could produce. But there seems to be something still unaccounted for. These tempestuous periods obviously gave James's rhetorical soul a great deal of pleasure; yet even allowing for James's love of hyperbole, his image of being seized and carried off in the talons of some monstrous female bird of prey might well carry for the post-Freudian (or even post-Jamesian) reader a suggestion of something bordering on sexual panic. Margaret Chanler, the recipient of the letter just quoted, was not alone in thinking—though she could adduce no clear reason— that James was sometimes positively frightened by Edith Wharton. Like several of his fictional characters, in any event, James seems occasionally to have been tempted to flee, with many histrionic gestures, before the approach of a certain kind of forceful woman.

4

It was rather different in the "leafy quiet" of Offranville and the seventeenth-century manor house of the Jacques Emile Blanches to which Edith now repaired. She customarily stayed about a fortnight; while she was there, Blanche would say, ". . . our home assumed suddenly another air; there was something brighter in the atmosphere." Edith had given the Blanches sound advice about the planting of trees and the laying out of gardens. In return they accompanied her on motor runs to old châteaux in the Normandy neighborhood and took her to call on the eccentric aristocrats who occupied them, supplying her with useful anecdotes about the lives of these gentry.

It was at Offranville that Edith first met Jean Cocteau—"little Cocteau whom I delight in," as she said to Berenson; "I don't know of any other spectacle in his class." Cocteau, twenty-seven years younger than Edith Wharton, had just published his third volume of somewhat derivative poetry; his more dazzling achievements lay in the future. But already brilliant and mercurial in his early twenties, he was cutting a dash in French literary circles and was frequently to be seen with Anna de Noailles, Proust, Blanche (who had recently added him to his portrait gallery), Maurice Rostand, and others of the upsurging younger generation. He had done some work for Diaghilev, and his fruitful association with Igor Stravinsky was about to begin.

Cocteau was a slender and theatrically good-looking young man, with a manner that tended toward the clownish; Berenson, when he met him in Edith's apartment, thought him beautiful but insolent. Edith would have rather the memory of

a passionately imaginative youth to whom every great line of poetry was a sunrise, every sunset the foundation of the Heavenly City. Excepting Bay Lodge, I have found no other young man who so recalled Wordsworth's "Bliss was it in that dawn to be alive." Every subject touched on—and in his company they were countless—was lit up by his young enthusiasm.

At Offranville, Blanche and Cocteau wrote a light comedy for Sacha Guitry's theater at St. Wandrille, and Cocteau read it aloud for the company; Edith, all attentive, offered some helpful hints about technique. At 53 Rue de Varenne, Berenson looked on, amused but puzzled, while Edith, Cocteau, and the Abbé Mugnier engaged zestfully in long verbal sparring matches.

Mme. Jacques Emile Blanche was among those French acquaintances who believed Edith Wharton to be seriously devoid of a sense of humor. She delivered herself of the opinion that Edith never had "a real, good ringing laugh," and that her infrequent smiles looked "forced or condescending." One can only meet this contention—as Percy Lubbock did, citing it—with an astonished stare, and wonder how annoyed Mme. Blanche may have been by Mme. Wharton's preference for the company of her husband. As to Edith Wharton's capacity for laughter, a much more typical testimony is that of Gaillard Lapsley:

She never failed to rise to a fly that was fantastic or absurd. She would laugh with the sincerity of complete surrender to every paroxysm that followed a fresh vision of the ludicrous, with shoulders shaking and the tears running down her cheeks, lift a deprecating hand that bade you spare her another turn of the screw, or at least to "give her ribs of steel." ... What she loved above all was *fun*—the farce of life in its wildest and subtlest surprises; and how wild they could be, and how subtle, how blandly disguised, there was none like her to discover.

It was at Pougues-les-Eaux, which she described as a squalid hole, that, near the end of August 1912, Edith Wharton finished *The Reef.* For the moment she was elated, and prepared to take a celebrational drive into southern France. But by the time the book came into print, two and a half months later, she had suffered a revulsion of feeling. "I'm sending you my book," she wrote Berenson, "though I don't want to, because I'm sick about it. . . . *Please* don't read it! Put it in the visitors' rooms, or lend it to somebody to read in the train and let it get lost."

Part of her hostility seems to have been aesthetic: the novel, she had come to believe, was no more than a "poor miserable lifeless lump." Ralph Curtis' mother declared accurately enough (according to Ralph) that the end was not up to the beginning and the whole not up to *The House of Mirth.* Yet for about half its length, *The Reef* promised to be Edith Wharton's surest accomplishment in long fiction to date, and Berenson was probably not alone in thinking that the novel had fulfilled its promise: "I think it better than any previous work excepting *Ethan Frome,"* he told Henry Adams. It is in the latter portions of the story that the work loses a certain coherence.

George Darrow, a youngish American diplomat with an interest in political and economic affairs, is en route from London to join his fiancée, the widowed Anna Leath, at her château in France, when he is put off by a curt and cryptic telegram. During the channel crossing, he makes the acquaintance of a vivacious and impecunious young woman, Sophie Viner, who is herself fleeing an appallingly vulgar London household; a strange little creature, quite knowing about the more sordid ways of the world but otherwise, to Darrow, appealingly ignorant and inexperienced. In Paris, embittered by the lack of further word from Anna, Darrow assuages himself in Sophie's company, and the relationship ripens into intimacy over the better part of a week in a station hotel. When he at last reaches the château at Givré—where Anna lives with her stepson Owen, her young daughter, and her mother-in-law—Darrow finds Sophie Viner not only installed as the little girl's much cherished new governess, but also engaged to marry Owen Leath.

Attitudes and relations thereafter shift almost from page to page—until Anna, hitherto eager to help the young lovers, learns of the Paris adventure, turns against Sophie, and sends Darrow away. Sophie also disappears, and Owen, stricken and mute, goes off for a trip around the world. Anna Leath, in an effort to fortify herself against marrying her besmirched fiancé, seeks out Sophie in Paris, with the intention of declaring she has renounced Darrow. Sophie, however, has left for India, reattached to her former crude household.

When the word "cruel" is used about a story by Edith Wharton, it usually means (as it has meant earlier in this book) that she has displayed a compassionate awareness of the cruelty that inheres in human experience. Not that Edith would always admit as much. Once, when a friend said that she had wept through the whole of one of her books, Edith responded icily: "I am never interested in the misfortunes of my personages, only in their psychological evolution." The friend refused to believe it: "You may like to *think* that, but no one could possibly have written that story without a deep feeling for the tortures of the human heart." At this, Edith gave a half apologetic, half rueful smile, and busied herself in being "very sweet and human in many little ways" to the friend. The latter's claim was largely true; yet about the final disposition of Sophie Viner and George Darrow there is a cruelty that, seemingly, was uncharacteristically supplied by the author.

It was almost as though Edith Wharton were engaging in a mode of *self-punishment*. Half a dozen years later, replying to a letter of praise for *The Reef* from Brownell, she was able to say candidly that his words went to her "innermost heart, because I put most of myself into that opus." But to Berenson, at the time of publication, she said in a troubled way: "It's not me, though I thought it was when I was writing it." Both remarks may have had to do primarily with the book's composition and its moral posture; but in other regards *The Reef* was all too much her, and possibly the most autobiographical work of fiction she ever wrote. The personal element extends even to the portrait of Anna Leath's American-born mother-in-law, Lucretia, who comes to France to grow expensively old, a person with "a sort of insistent self-effacement before which everyone about her gave way"; originally unpredictable, now staid and narrow and aroused only by questions of fashion and propriety—Lucretia Jones as ever was.

In the presentation of Anna Leath, Edith Wharton almost literally began to write her autobiography. The story of Anna's life to the moment when the novel's action begins is such that Ralph Curtis could say quite rightly that it was "a masterly self-diagnosis, as I knew [Edith] at Newport." I have not myself scrupled to draw upon it for a description of Edith Jones as an uncertain, secretly gifted young woman in New York society, less pretty and clever than her feminine peers, but with a talent for the enjoyment of life. It likewise provides the best available source for understanding Edith's state of mind after Walter Berry vanished from Newport without proposing, and when Teddy Wharton arrived fortuitously on the scene.

But one must look elsewhere in the book to find the reason for Edith's rejection of it. The London experience in 1909 out of which Edith wrote her poem "Terminus" is reenacted in *The Reef* at the Terminus Hotel next to the Gare du Nord in Paris, where Darrow and Sophie Viner are sharing adjacent rooms. It is raining steadily in the fictive Paris of 1912, as it had been in the actual London of June 1909, and the room in which the act of love takes place, as Darrow surveys it, is a replica of the bedroom in the suite at the Charing Cross Hotel as Edith described it in "Terminus." The "common-place room" and the "dull impersonal furniture," the "bed with its soot-sodden chintz" and "the grime of the brasses" in the poem are matched in the novel by "the featureless dullness of the room," "the grimy carpet and wall-paper," and "the high-bolstered counterpaned bed."

But where Edith in her rapture had poetically transformed the original love scene into a place of beauty and compassion, Darrow, before the week is out, has come to loathe every aspect of it. Darrow, that is, represents the Edith Wharton of 1912 rather than of 1909: the person whom other events—chiefly Teddy's simultaneous and sordid-seeming liaisons—had caused to look back on the London adventure with a good deal of distaste. It was a revulsion against her own behavior: a feeling still not entirely devoid of remembered pleasure, but strong enough to make her bear down harshly on the two partial images of herself, and to leave her with a feeling of general disaffection with the novel.

Henry James, though he had a few reservations about *The Reef*, mentioned none of them to Edith Wharton, to whom he declared that the book had a "psychological Racinian unity, intensity and gracility," that the narrative was a triumph of method, and that the two main figures were "admirable for truth and *justesse.*" With the latter verdict, it can be noted, Ralph Curtis heartily disagreed, as many readers since have done: never, he wrote Berenson, had there been a person as boring as Edith's heroine, and Darrow was "Walter Berry distorted into a somewhat shifty prig." Curtis only hoped that Sophie Viner would marry a peer's son in Simla and end up the intimate friend of the Mayfair aristocracy. Yet he had nothing but admiration for Edith's style: "Since Stevenson I know nobody who can festoon English words together with such Gallic grace."

The character of Sophie and the style of writing were about all that came in for praise by the reviewers, who otherwise thought the story was sordid and the novel a failure. It sold little more than seven thousand copies. Appleton had given Mrs. Wharton an advance of fifteen thousand dollars, incomparably the largest she had yet received. The publishers came nowhere near getting their money back, but they had never made a wiser investment.

5

With the last chapters of *The Reef* dispatched to Appleton, Edith was restive as always without a manuscript in the making, and wrote Hugh Smith—after alluding to several books of high distinction—that she was eager to tackle "the last book of another masterpiece, *The Custom of the Country.*" She was nonetheless quick to rendezvous with the Berensons at Avignon in early October, to tour the area and travel on with them to Portofino, on the Italian coast south of Genoa. It was her first real opportunity to come to know Mary Berenson. The latter had begun to speak more kindly of Edith as her husband warmed to her. But Mrs. Berenson was inclined to be wary toward Mrs. Wharton; it was not until the war years that cautious admiration grew into genuine affection. Edith, against her habit with the women of her male friends, appears to have taken to Mary from the outset.

At Portofino, Edith begged a few days' solitude: she had hit upon a new notion for the next chapters of *The Custom of the Country* and wanted to get down to it at once. Watching intently from afar, James, after the last bulletin, gave out that "the greatest known to us, or to the annals of man, is revolving at a maximum pace to Avignon and the territories beyond. . . . *Il n'y a qu'elle—* long life to her," even at the cost of a shorter one to her friends and companions. Edith caught up with the Berensons at I Tatti, spent a week there, paused for a time at La Spezia, and in the first week of November resettled in Paris. Her whirligig life was over for the moment, and sobering days lay ahead.

Bernhard Berenson had now joined that circle whose members passed much of their time telling one another the most recent news about the movements, the accomplishments, and the "situation" of Edith Wharton, with reactions, delighted or uneasy, to her personality. Edith and Berenson had had a three-hour talk over lunch the previous July 4, and for the first time Edith rehearsed in considerable detail the events in her private life over the past few years. "Her adventures," Berenson wrote his wife, "were even more gruesome than I had supposed, including an awful case of blackmail." The allusion was to Edith's efforts to rescue Morton Fullerton from the blackmailing claws of Mme. Mirecourt, though Edith clearly said nothing about her intimacy with Fullerton. But her personal narrative served to bring them much closer together, and gave Berenson a sympathetic understanding of her conduct of life which, however it might falter betimes, he was never entirely to lose.

Not long after that conversation, Berenson lunched with Henry James at Claridge's in London and listened with some impatience to James's description of "Mrs. Wharton's restlessness and insatiability." The fact was, Berenson contended, that James's language exactly fitted him, Berenson; he had himself the same avidity for motion and travel, "and I don't find myself such a distressing case." What it amounted to, he said with great acuteness, was that "H.J. is 'complete,' and wants no more stimulus, having had enough from without and possessing within more than enough to keep him going for the rest of his day."

The growing relationship was not without strain. There would always be times when, in Berenson's view, Edith treated him as a potentially unruly schoolboy; and he vowed periodically never again to visit an art gallery with her. ("She was simply impossible," he had fumed recently after his cultivated analyses of the pictures had failed to hold her interest, "—unless indeed she was in one of her famous possessed moments.") But his expanded knowledge of her life led him to see her as more rational and coherent, more attuned to common reality, than James could quite credit her with being. Her fiction, Berenson thought, had the same qualities. Meditating the fact that one responds to a fictional character insofar as the latter "calls to life dormant parts of one's self," he observed to Mary that "the more everyday side of me is responded to in that way by no one better than Mrs. Wharton," while what he thought of as his "aloof and lofty" aspect was evoked rather by Dostoyevsky. The latter claim was greeted at I Tatti, by Mary and her brother Logan, with shrieks of laughter.

No one, except possibly his own wife, was more convinced than Berenson that Edith was deeply in love with Walter Berry and almost certainly having an affair with him. Here we have to reckon with the Berensons' theory of human behavior, which was that virtually every normal close relation between a man and a woman must have an active sexual element in it. "Every woman who lives for society," Mary wrote her husband in the summer of 1912, ". . . craves the excitement of sex in any man she is attracted to." By the same token, she went on, "how few men care for *us* unless we are sexually interested in them." The letter was in response to Berenson's account of the long lunch conversation with Edith, in the course of which he recorded, in the curiously knotted English he was sometimes prone to, that "she spoke of [Berry] with a detachment feigned but no longer conscious, and oozing devotion." As to this, Mary thought that Edith had developed a "habit of deceit where W.B. is concerned" which had become simply second nature to her, and part of "the necessary decorum of life." She disagreed with her husband, on general principles, only in rejecting his idea that many women could be sexually aroused by intellectual conversation and "chatting on *literary subjects,*" but suspected that "Mrs. Wharton and Mme. de Cossé and the Countess Serristori and (possibly) Mme. de Ludres are exceptions."

Berenson, in any event, was under no illusion that Berry fully reciprocated Edith's devotion; he had too often observed Berry enjoying other female companionship. Deprecating his own considerable assays in this direction, he remarked that "I am not in it as a lady's man with W.B." and quoted a woman friend as saying that "Walter Berry is the most noted lady's man in America" and was far more attached to Elsie Goelet, for example, than to Edith Wharton. Some time later he passed on to Ralph Curtis the *mot* of Frank Crowninshield, the editor of *Vanity Fair.* How was it, someone had asked at a New York club gathering, that Walter Berry was able "to seduce the minds of our women," especially the most intelligent of them. "If only he left them in an interesting condition," Crowninshield had sighed.

6

Around the turn of the year, events on both sides of the Atlantic helped to quicken Edith's interest in political matters. Her old friend and political idol, Theodore Roosevelt, having been denied the 1912 Republican presidential nomination, had bolted to form his own Bull Moose party, carrying with him a number of key Republican figures and a sizable constituency. As the November election approached, it became ever more probable that his defection would ensure the victory of the Democratic candidate, Woodrow Wilson. Edith was prepared to dislike Wilson, or any other person of his political stamp, but she was perhaps more impressed by the dramatic than the political aspect: by a drama, as she saw it, of rebellion and dark revenge. "Our Theodore," she wrote Mary Berenson, "is a good deal more saga-like than anything in *Wuthering Heights.*"

On January 17, 1913, Edith was smuggled into the Salle de Congres in Versailles by Paul Bourget to hear the new President of France proclaimed. Raymond Poincaré, who had been Premier for twelve months, won fairly easily with 483 votes to his opponent's 296. It was, Edith said, "really an *emotionnant* moment, for feeling ran high and everybody had the sense that history was being made." It was indeed. His opponent had warned that the election of Poincaré would make war inevitable between France and Germany, and one of the first acts of Poincaré's seven-year term was an extension of military conscription from two to three years. The German army was estimated at about 870,000 men; the new French law (which actually reestablished an old law) gave France a force, at any moment, of 700,000—which was enough, the experts said, since part of Germany's strength had to face eastward toward Russia. It is hard to imagine any French government failing to take steps to bring the country to some sort of military equity with her old enemy. Nonetheless, war was undoubtedly drawing closer.

For a number of months Teddy Wharton had been living in Boston, conspicuously doing without a servant, in Berry's gossipy newsletter to Berenson, in order to give the impression of "poverty and neglect." In fact, so the word went around, he had ten thousand dollars a year of his own, and Edith contributed again as much (she probably supplied more like six thousand); by implication, he was enjoying himself. During the summer, after much troubled thought, Edith wrote him offering to sublet the Rue de Varenne apartment, set up house for the two of them somewhere in New York City, and then look for another country house for the permanent future. Teddy cabled back excitedly that he entirely disapproved, that she was not to come to America, and, in effect, to leave him alone.

He was squired over to London by White in the late fall. On her return from the month-long jaunt from Avignon to I Tatti, Edith found "a shattering account of Teddy's state in a letter from White, and painful corroboration in several letters from Teddy." He notified her firmly, among other things, that she was under no circumstances to join him in London. For Edith, who had been saying with dogged hopefulness that Teddy was sounding much better and that they were shortly to reunite in England, this was a decided, even a mortifying rebuff. She wrote that her husband was "again in full crisis of megalomania" and referred, borrowing from Nietzsche, to "the eternal return." But the truth was that Teddy, passing beyond both abusiveness and self-pity, was beginning to assert a total independence of action and spirit.

Harry Jones, who happened to be in England, investigated the situation at his sister's request and wrote that Teddy seemed in fine condition and there was really nothing to worry about. This exasperated Edith almost beyond speech, especially since she had just learned from some other source that Teddy was again living with a woman and was running about London calling on all her friends. James spoke of receiving "rockets from poor mad T.," all written "with the last and crudest extravagance"; it was "a peculiarly damnable case." Edith felt buried beneath "big black bales of worry and weariness."

There were compensations, however. *The Custom of the Country*, though far from finished, had begun to appear serially in the January issue of *Scribner's*, and James cheered Edith by saying that he was reading it with a beating heart. At the same time, she had discovered the fiction of Joseph Conrad, in particular *The Secret Sharer*. "What a man!" she exclaimed to Lapsley about that masterful little drama of identity, and she was moved to express her enthusiasm to Conrad himself, with an inquiry about a possible translation of it into French. "The appreciation of a fellow worker of such great and distinguished gifts," Conrad replied, "can't but be precious to me." He doubted the wisdom of translating it: the story was all too English in its moral atmosphere. But he took Mrs. Wharton's letter as a Christmas present to him, and asked if he might *"venir vous saluer"* some time in London: *"Votre très devoué confrère et serviteur fidèle."* Edith Wharton went on to acquire all of Conrad's writings.

There were always cherished friends to visit with or worry about. Elizabeth Cameron came for a stay, and in response to Edith's "piteous appeal," Percy Lubbock and Gaillard Lapsley crossed over for a New Year's visit of ten days; she was touchingly grateful for their coming "when and *as* you did." The widowed Bessie (Mrs. Bay) Lodge arrived in Paris with her three children, and Edith busied herself finding them a place to live and a school for the boys, John and Cabot.

There then occurred another racking upheaval in Edith's life, this one wholly unexpected. Her brother Harry, without warning, exploded in a long and bitter denunciation of her unkindness to him. Harry, who had grown rather stout but was ever more courtly (he was often observed, in the idiom of a former day, "making a leg" in the Edwardian drawing rooms), had been living for two years with a countess of Russian extraction named Tecla, and was about to marry her. He now accused his sister of pointedly refusing to make friends with her and of having turned against him as well.

As of January 1913, Edith was only vaguely aware of the woman's existence; Harry, according to Edith's distraught and bewildered letter to Lapsley, had never even mentioned her, and Edith had no notion that the relationship was a serious one. It now turned out that on the part of both Harry and Tecla, resentment at what they took to be Edith's stiff moral disapproval had deepened into downright hatred.

It was an enormously unsettling discovery, the more so at that moment of trial, and coming as it did on top of her loss of The Mount and any home base in America, and her partial break with Scribners. Harry had been the warming presence during her lonely childhood, and since her father's death thirty years before he had been the one member of her family to whom she could turn for comfort and support. (Her older brother Freddy—Minnie's divorced husband, whom she had not seen for twenty-five years—had long been a resident of Paris, but Edith was careful never to lay eyes on him; she had been unresponsive to the report, a year before, that he had suffered a stroke.) Harry's residence in Paris had been a main reason for Edith's choosing to settle in the Faubourg. There had been motor trips together and exchanges of hospitality; it was Harry who had found the apartment at 53 Rue de Varenne. Henry James had characterized him to Edith as "your best of brothers."

She felt that her personal world was giving way on all sides. It was imperative that she get on with *The Custom of the Country*, but for the moment she was immobilized. "I try to say to myself that poor rags like those two can't really touch me," she wrote Lapsley, during a few days in Versailles; "but they *can* stop my work, and they have, and I've been sitting here paralysed looking at my last two chapters and unable to feel anything about them." In her own phrase, she kept gnawing at herself over the breach with Harry, and returned to Paris with the manuscript untouched.

Yet the breach, as a final straw of sorts, seems to have brought to an end her year-long period of indecisiveness in the more important matter. She at last allowed herself to recognize that her marriage to Teddy was finished and that nothing remained except legal action.

7

Teddy appears to have been of a similar mind. Even while Edith had been making the final and not ungallant gestures toward patching things up by creating a new home for them in America, Teddy had been announcing his marital freedom in an undisguised manner. Word of his sexual exploits in Boston drifted down to New York, over to Settignano, and back (in letters from Mrs. Berenson) to Paris. When Teddy stopped over in the city for a brief spell in December, he did not bother to call at the Rue de Varenne but put up in an apartment on the Rue Volney, off the Place Vendôme.

He had come abroad with a high-powered car and a chauffeur, and Edith heard at second hand that he was driving about the continent. He was then reported at Monte Carlo, cutting a broad swath. Ralph Curtis, who always found Teddy highly entertaining, said that "he was in tremendous form—and was capital company." Curtis noted admiringly that Teddy had encountered a certain M—— S——, an attractive American woman, in the street one morning and had carried her off to lunch at the Ritz and on to the theater; the lady, captivated, had kept things alive by taking Teddy to dinner and to another theater, before the two of them disappeared from view. "That's going some," Curtis remarked, in a current idiom.

Herman Edgar, when Teddy's whereabouts were established, hurried down to Monte Carlo to talk with him and found him leading a life that, on Edgar's return to Paris, "he couldn't describe to me except in gestures of disgust," Edith told Mary Berenson, "and I couldn't have listened to if he *had.*" Her friends and relations in America, she continued, "have been writing me on all sides that I must 'act'; so I hope something may soon be decently, silently and soberly arranged."

The decision to divorce was the most painful one Edith Wharton was ever required to make. The case was clear enough. As Edgar, acting on her behalf, began to piece together the evidence, it was learned for the first time that Teddy's infidelities had begun at least as early as 1908, a year before the Mountfort Street adventure; and there was little difficulty in collecting proof of flagrant adultery on later occasions. Teddy, Edith discovered, insouciantly "registered his various temporary brides as 'Mrs. Wharton' in the hotels they frequented" across Europe. Even so, divorce was profoundly abhorrent to her.

She recoiled, of course, from the sheer messiness of the situation. Her pride and her dignity were offended nearly beyond repair by the discussions and exposures the action inevitably led to. But divorce itself was something it pained her even to contemplate. She knew perfectly well that divorce had become common, even casual, among the younger American generation of the best society; for example, in *The New York Idea,* the witty and popular play of 1906 by Langdon Mitchell, the very "idea" alluded to was that of divorce as the fashionable solution to domestic and erotic problems. But her own fifty-one-year-old character had been shaped by the conventions and pieties of a much older and narrower New York, one which never fully recovered from the shock and titillations of the divorce proceedings against her mother's errant cousin, Mary Stevens Strong.

Edith was also exceedingly apprehensive about the figure she would cut as a divorced woman in the social circles back home. She had expressed something of this fear in one of her most poignant tales, "Autres Temps . . . ," first published in the *Century* in 1911, at a time when she was tentatively deciding to separate from Teddy. Mrs. Lidcote in the story had scandalized New York many years before by divorcing her husband and has been quietly living ever since in exile in Florence. When she learns that her daughter Leila has just shed one husband and is about to marry another, she returns in haste to America with the thought that Leila will need maternal aid to get through the bad days. But social mores have changed radically over the years: in Leila's bright young set, no one gives a second thought to these substitutions of spouses. Things have changed—but only for the young. For a person of Mrs. Lidcote's generation (which was also Mrs. Wharton's), the stigma is still attached. The ambassador's wife snubs her, her daughter keeps her hidden away from the company on the second floor, and the man she had begun to think might comprise a future for her reveals himself as no less chained to the moral attitudes of the past.

It was the possible reaction in Boston that most worried Edith, and at her request Berenson sounded out his old teacher Barrett Wendell and President Lowell of Harvard. The responses, which Berenson passed on to Edith, were encouraging, though even in her appreciation she found Wendell's letter "funnily solemn and ceremonious," like everything else in Boston: "even I'm sure to the performance of the *derniers outrages."* Wendell's message, which has not survived, was probably much the same in tone as his letter to Lapsley some months later:

[Mrs. Wharton's] own troubles are now known here—so far as I have heard them mentioned with full sympathy for her. The pity of it is that Teddy could not have been committed, some time ago, to formal guardianship of some kind.

In Wendell's view Teddy was entirely irrational and irresponsible, and "as for her, I cannot imagine more admirable and simple devotion than she has shown as long as it was in any way possible."

Edith was much moved, as well as relieved. "Considering the extraordinary attitude of Teddy's family from the outset, I hardly hoped that any one in Boston would see the situation as it really is, and that Mr. Wendell . . . should take the view he does is a great comfort to me—for I do sometimes feel a great soreness and indignation at the way in which the Whartons have treated me."

Once the fateful decision had been made, Edith's spirits began to rise. She still felt wrung out, but she was able to convey her state of being with a little of the old-style vivacity. When, in mid-February, a scheduled brief visit to England was canceled because of the simultaneous illnesses of Henry James and Howard Sturgis, she remarked to Lapsley how lucky it was that she *hadn't* gone: "Henry and Howard would both have ascribed their attacks to my devastating presence!" Lapsley should only know "how devastated is the Devastatress at present," and she congratulated him on receiving word of her proposed visit "without a complete breakdown." She felt muddied by the whole situation; but when, to Berenson, she again invoked her obsessive image of imprisonment, she contrived a grimly witty formula to describe herself as locked up in a *"prison de suie"* (soot). And she went on at once to say: "You mustn't think there haven't been bits of blue sky all the same; there always are with *me;* I can hardly ever wholly stop having a good time!"

Good times were made more frequent by the reappearance from America of Walter Berry, rejoicing that his mother's estate had been equally settled (she had died more than a year before), and walking around, Edith said, "with his hands in his bulging pockets, wondering what to buy! It's too delightful to see him." Her "beloved Bélogou" was also back from Ceylon, bringing her a star sapphire. Edith was cultivating Berenson's highly intellectual friend Mme. de Ludres, though she thought that a dinner given by the latter was rather too "Ritzian." This, for Edith Wharton, was a term of severe reproof; she cherished a singular animosity to that famous hotel. When Adams had counseled against holding the meeting of September 1909 at the Ritz and had suggested Voisin's instead, he had remarked to Berenson that the Paris ladies of his acquaintance were divided into two classes: "Ritz vs. Anti-Ritz. The Anti-Ritz class contains only Mrs. Edith Wharton."

Edith had been suffering from some sort of intestinal disorder, but Dr. Isch Wall had solved that mystery, "and calm reigns below the belt." In fact, she thought, if only she had sufficient help—"someone to run the house, pay the bills, oil the machinery, and *See Bores For Me*"—she would be well in an instant. Gross and White could run the house, and Anna Bahlmann pay the bills; but given the unavoidability of bores, Edith declared herself resigned to being incurable.

The case seemed to drag on interminably. "I'm at the mercy just now," Edith told Berenson wearily in late February 1913, "of circumstances created by a person over whom no one—least of all himself!—has any control." Teddy had vanished after leaving Monte Carlo and was gallivanting about somewhere out of touch with his friends; until he showed up again in Paris, "nothing can be done; and even if and when he does, it's still all a big'?'." But three days before Easter, Teddy suddenly appeared on the scene. He was immediately served with a summons, and all preliminaries were completed within twenty-four hours. Edith had only to wait for the court's post-holiday sitting.

Letters of support continued to flow in from Boston and New York. Both sides had closed ranks in the familiar manner, each putting out its own version of the marital crisis—though the Wharton side, it should be observed, comes down to us only in accounts by what must be called hostile witnesses. According to W. K. Richardson, the Whartons were saying that Teddy was "a sort of suffering martyr," and by implication that Edith was heartless, cruel, and a bad wife. Whenever he heard such echoes, Richardson tried "tactfully and without detail, to convey an adumbration of the truth." Robert Grant, too, had sought "to counteract the effect of such misrepresentations as reach me," and assured Edith of his "hearty and loyal sympathy."

None of Edith's Boston friends had the slightest doubt that divorce was the only solution. Meanwhile, her New York cousin Tom Newbold was proving an unexpected source of strength. He conferred almost daily with Herman Edgar and Egerton Winthrop and went as envoy to Boston to survey the battlefield.

"I want you to know," he wrote, "that I approve most *warmly* of everything you have done," and he felt that the whole ghastly business was being "most satisfactorily arranged," with very little talk and no newspaper publicity. He urged Edith to think only of the future: "Your life and work are far too important to be interfered with by these horrid annoyances."

Egerton Winthrop, Edith's treasured friend of thirty years, wrote in a series of agitated and scarcely decipherable letters that Teddy had been behaving and talking wildly and that Billy Wharton was being severely criticized. The Bostonians, he remarked, "are persuaded that [Teddy's] mind has gone, that he is going as his father did, and that nothing he says is worth listening to." He concluded in words that must have gone to Edith's heart:

> No one knows better than I what the last four years have been to you in nerve waste and health waste, [and] that there is relief in sight for you from the anguish of mind and body is a source of inexpressible joy to me. There was no way out of the misery but the one you took.

Edith Wharton's divorce decree was granted on April 16, 1913, in the Tribunal de Grande Instance de Paris. Edith was represented by André Boccon-Gibbod, a young Parisian lawyer she had met through Léon Bélogou only a few months before, and who would become one of her most admiring friends. On the basis of documents submitted, the court ruled that

> *le sieur WHARTON a entretenu à Boston en mil neuf cent huit et mil neuf cent neuf des relations adultères,*

and also that

> *récamment malgré le pardon accordé par la dame WHARTON qui avait consenti à reprendre à Paris la vie commune le sieur WHARTON s'est affiché tant à Londres qu'à Monte Carlo avec differentes femmes et a eu avec elles des relations d'un caractère gravement injurieux pour la demanderess.*

> (Mr. Wharton maintained adulterous relations in Boston in 1908 and 1909 . . . Recently, despite the pardon granted by Mrs. Wharton, who had consented to take up their life together in Paris, Mr. Wharton attached himself to various women both in London and in Monte Carlo, and had relations with them of a character gravely injurious to the petitioner.)

These facts, the court pronounced, constituted sufficient grounds to justify Mme. Wharton's petition. Divorce was thereupon decreed as between *"Les Epoux WHARTON,"* and M. Wharton was instructed to pay all the expenses of the case.

The War Years: 1913-1918

PART FIVE

18. Customs and Countries

During the fifteen months that followed the divorce Edith Wharton traveled farther and more constantly than ever before in her life: traveled, almost compulsively, in seven countries and on three continents, and even to scenes that lay quite outside the range of her previous experience and cultural traditions. With the termination of her marriage after twenty-eight years, she felt propelled out of her metaphorical prison and really had begun to exercise what Henry James had called a fantastic freedom. Her new sense of herself as both a liberated and a divorced woman gave her a more than customary restlessness. She was determined, she told Berenson, to eat the world "leaf by leaf"—almost as if she foresaw the fact that the historical world she had known had not long to endure, and she was launched upon a prewar tour of it. Much of her great energy, in short, went at this time into the exigencies of travel; but during the first part, and despite fits of abject weariness, she also managed to complete *The Custom of the Country*, her most substantial and far-reaching novel, and one that introduced the most restless and devastating of her heroines.

Still pinching herself, as she said, and feeling "as if Pelions and Ossas had been lifted off of me," Edith drove out of Paris with Walter Berry toward the end of March 1913, heading for a leisurely drive down the Italian peninsula and a tour of Sicily. But she had not yet passed the French border before a cable from Sturgis Bigelow, in Boston, threw her into one of the worst turmoils of her life.

The cable had to do with a gift of money Edith had been helping to arrange for Henry James's seventieth birthday, on April 15. It was to parallel the effort of a number of James's English friends—Percy Lubbock and Edmund Gosse among them—to raise money enough to buy James a silver-gilt porringer and bowl and to commission a portrait of him by John Singer Sargent. Edith had hoped that she and a few other Paris-based Americans might be allowed to join the English enterprise; when this proved impossible, she took thought to organizing an independent American effort.

Berry agreed that "we *must* do something of the kind," and, Edith told Lapsley, "as I'm too tired and generally collapsed, he is going to take it in hand." Since Berry did so, there was a certain thin accuracy to Edith's later claim to James that she "had nothing to do with originating the birthday plan." But the circular that went out from Paris in mid-March was signed by Edith Wharton and William Dean Howells, and it read in part:

April 15th next is Henry James's 70th birthday.

His English friends and admirers have raised a fund to present him with a portrait. We believe that his American friends will be at least as eager to ask him to accept a gift commemorating this date.

In view of the shortness of time, such commemoration, we think, might most appropriately take the form of a sum of money (not less than $5000) for the purchase of a gift, the choice of which would be left to him.

The circular urged that "this proposal should be kept *strictly confidential,*" and added that checks should be drawn to the order of Edith Wharton and mailed to 53 Rue de Varenne.

The appeal was sent to some thirty-nine individuals, among them Mrs. Jack Gardner, Henry Adams, Sturgis Bigelow, George Abbot James, Mrs. Cadwalader Jones, Senator Lodge, Barrett Wendell, Robert Grant, the Norton sisters, Dr. S. Weir Mitchell, John Jay Chapman, George Vanderbilt, Robert Minturn, and Charles Scribner. Money began to come in immediately: what Edith regarded as no more than a "gift-mite" from Mrs. Jack Gardner, $250 from George Vanderbilt, and intermediate sums that gave Edith confidence that the amount aimed at would be raised in time. Then, on March 30, the whole affair was called to an abrupt halt.

George Abbot James—no kin but a long-standing friend of Henry's—had broken the news to the widow and sons of William James. Word got to Henry, who cabled back at once: "Immense thanks for warning. Taking instant prohibitive action. Please express to individuals approached my horror. Money absolutely returned." In a following letter James declared: "A more reckless and indiscreet undertaking, with no ghost of a preliminary leave asked, no hint of a sounding taken, I cannot possibly conceive—and am still rubbing my eyes for incredulity." Sturgis Bigelow was called in, and after a melancholy afternoon's conversation with Barrett Wendell, Bigelow cabled Edith Wharton that the undertaking must be abandoned.

Howells pulled out at the first sign of trouble, sending Edith what she described as "an ineffable letter . . . senile and querulous—*how* it explains his novels!" Far more disturbing was what seems to have been a deeply offended message from James himself. "My trip has been completely poisoned by Henry's letter," Edith wrote Lapsley from La Spezia. "There was nothing on earth I valued as much as his affection. I can never get over this." In a distressed reply to James, she deprecated her part in the effort; but she implored Lapsley, who had been one of the prime movers, to talk with James

and tell him the idea was that he should choose a fine piece of old furniture, or something of the kind. *Above all, please* make him understand that in answering his letter I could not have been more explicit than I was without breaking my promise not to reveal the English plan.

James in fact knew all about the English plan, and had allowed his scruples to be overcome regarding it. But he had the distinct impression that the American intention, prodded by Edith Wharton, was simply and even crudely to put into his hands a fat sum of money.

Edith once told Berenson that over the course of time she had suffered "a series of resounding whacks" from fate, and that life had "slain" her "at least once a year since five." It was a piece of high rhetoric, part of a little lecture on the need for moral stamina; yet during this period and for several years to come, the frequency with which the blows descended on Edith Wharton scarcely permits of exaggeration. But she invariably rallied, and in the present instance her anguish, while real and intense, was not long-lived. A month or so after the debacle Henry James was once again writing her in the old grandiloquent, teasing manner, marveling at the "epic story" of her Italian flight and expressing gratification at the divorce. The friendship had been only briefly impaired.

There were a few reverberations elsewhere. Ralph Curtis elaborated the whimsy that James, after the event, was now himself engaged in a fund-raising effort, the aim of which was to create "La Societé Internationale des Amis de Edith Wharton." "The chief object of the movement," Curtis explained, "is to prevent her making any banal finale." A number of others found the affair more unfortunate than amusing, and wrote Edith to say so. Wendell was particularly upset. He felt, after their talks in Paris, that he and Mrs. Wharton had become genuine friends: "wherefore, I suppose, what touches you has come to seem more nearly to concern my own life than by any right or reason it should." Deplorable as the "birthday matter" was in its outcome, he said, "I cannot a bit regret it. There could never be impulse or sentiment more gentle than that which possessed us all. That is what lingers in memory, rather than the tactless or malicious breach of confidence which brought it to nothing."

Edith Wharton undoubtedly made the original proposal on the assumption that James would deploy the money to select an appropriate object for his household. But she had failed to reckon with James's enormous unease at any seeming allusion to his personal financial needs, and never quite understood James's complex attitude—in which a portion of envy at her literary earnings may have mingled with a more detached moral judgment—toward her own wealth. She denied that she was "a meddlesome philanthropist." Yet, however generous the idea, the strategy behind it was ill-considered; in this instance Edith Wharton lacked the kind of fine psychological vibration that she so admired in other characters, real and fictional.

At the same time, James was largely right to intuit a wish on Edith's part to come to his financial rescue. Nor would he ever have in hand the evidence that would have dismayingly confirmed his guess.

A few days after Sturgis Bigelow's shattering cable, Edith took great solace from the news, via Charles Scribner, that an altogether different secret enterprise involving Henry James had been successfully carried through. During her "reign of terror" visits with James the previous summer, Edith had interpreted his expostulations about the hazards to his work as simply a sign that his novel was not progressing as it should, and this she laid to money worries. She thereupon wrote Scribner proposing that he offer James a sizable advance on the novel— it was *The Ivory Tower*—with funds provided by her. Scribner, who still hoped that Mrs. Wharton's defection to Appleton (for *The Reef*) was temporary, accepted the idea.

The negotiation went forward during the fall. James learned to his astonishment and pleasure that Scribners were so eager to have from him, as soon as possible, "another great novel to balance *The Golden Bowl*" that they were prepared to offer him an advance of eight thousand dollars, half on signing the contract, half upon receipt of the manuscript. In January 1913 an agreement was drawn up between Charles Scribner's Sons and Edith Wharton which spoke of the contract with James as having been "entered upon at the suggestion of Mrs. Wharton and upon her promise to supply the money for the said payments." On April 2, Scribner wrote Mrs. Wharton enclosing a letter from James acknowledging with "lively appreciation" receipt of the first half of the promised eight thousand dollars, minus the agent's commission (the goodly sum, in short, of thirty-six hundred dollars), and adding that the advance was so handsome that he would be worried if his work had not been going so well. On his side Charles Scribner remarked glumly that "our fell purpose was successfully accomplished. I feel rather mean and caddish and must continue so to the end of my days. Please never give me away."

Edith, who read the two letters during a pause with the Berensons at Settignano, felt anything but mean or caddish, nor was she at all dubious about the manner in which James's sensibilities had been outmaneuvered; the outcome of this scheme went far to assuage the extreme soreness caused by the birthday calamity. In a note "for my biographer," scribbled some fourteen years later, she declared: "I gave Mr. Scribner this $8000 from the earnings of *The House of Mirth* to encourage H.J. to go on writing, as he was so despondent about his work. The result was successful and no one ever knew." (Edith Wharton's memory was at fault in this notation. *The House of Mirth* had brought in next to nothing in the way of royalties for a number of years. The money probably came from the fifteen-thousand-dollar advance given her by Appleton for *The Reef*—in which case irony was being added to irony: Mrs. Wharton was using Scribners as a secret conveyor of money supplied her by the house for which she was gradually abandoning Scribners. Since James did not live to finish *The Ivory Tower*, Edith was not called upon to furnish the remaining four thousand dollars.)

James, at least, remained happily in the dark. He had been privy to the comparable—but quite overt—plan, in 1909, to pass money over to Morton Fullerton in the guise of a publisher's advance, and had indeed relished the little drama in which he had served as Edith Wharton's agent. But he had no faintest inkling, as he contemplated the largest advance he had ever received, that he was now the beneficiary of a parallel strategy.

2

After consulting with Berenson, Edith and Berry drove down into the austerely craggy mountains southeast of Siena to visit the fourteenth-century abbey of Monte Oliveto Maggiore: a stupendous affair, a majestic and remote entity unto itself with proliferating smaller churches and cloisters. From this quiet and bracing atmosphere they descended to the little Renaissance hillside town of Montepulciano, the home of the *quattrocento* humanist and writer of graceful Latin verses, Politian.

They crossed to Sicily in mid-April. As they crisscrossed the mountains from shore to shore over a fortnight, Edith felt that her first experience of the island was "one long radiance." Another sort of experience was provided by the hotel authorities in Trapani, on the coast southwest of Palermo. After Berry had visited Edith in her rooms once or twice, a message was slipped under her door stating: *"Le signore sono pregate di ricevere le visite dei signori nel salone pubblico, per riguardo agli usi severi del paese."* ("Ladies are requested to receive visits from gentlemen in the public salon, out of consideration for the severe customs of the region.") The author of the ongoing serial *The Custom of the Country* fairly snorted as she passed this on to Berenson. "What desperate days," she commented; "though I may add that in the restaurant, which thronged with commercial guests, *le signore* seemed to be exercising the traditional privileges of the priestesses; nor do I think that the rites were concluded in the *salone pubblico.*"

Were Edith Wharton and Walter Berry lovers on this journey—or at any other time or place? Henry James seemed to think so: observing them depart on still another trip, he remarked that they were traveling together "even like another George Sand and another Chopin." This may have been only a piece of James's magisterial fooling, for he rarely joked about an actual illicit affair, but the analogy was a telling one given Edith's sense of imaginative kinship with the free-spirited French novelist. (Morton Fullerton, many years later, stressed that affinity by declaring roundly that Edith Wharton in love had displayed the uninhibited passion of "a George Sand.") Edith herself appeared obliquely to be confirming the general suspicion when, late in life, she observed to Fullerton that only with him and one other man—the reference was obviously to Walter Berry

—had she wanted the relationship to be "total." Many of her French friends took it for granted, as did the Berensons, that an affair had been in progress for a good many years. Yet a doubt persists.

The doubt springs in part from one's appraisal of Walter Berry's character. He seems to have been a "ladies' man" only in the sense of a man who enjoyed the company, in public, of a series of glittering females—among them Rita Lydig, Elsa Goelet, and Ava Willing, the former Mrs. John Jacob Astor and now the wife of the aging and withdrawn Lord Ribbesdale (once lord-in-waiting to Queen Victoria). He had a reputation for dry gallantry but, Berenson's joshings aside, none at all for sexual promiscuity. No few women, indeed, were put off by Berry's muted but unremitting sarcasm and his habit of lightly tapping his mouth with his fingers in a scarcely disguised effort to conceal a yawn. "My dear," Mary Berenson wrote consolingly to her husband, when Berenson was chafing under Edith Wharton's supposedly strong preference for Berry's company, "how *les dames* dislike Walter Berry!"—and how much they deplored Edith's devotion to him. Berry, constantly reporting to Berenson on what he called *"ces girls,"* sometimes appeared as the prototype of the old-time American dandy who ogled the ladies, tugging at his moustache, and archly drew his male companion's attention to some particularly attractive woman passing by: the perennial bachelor.

There seems, in fact, never to have been any serious question of marriage between Edith and Berry. Those same French friends who misjudged Mme. Wharton in other regards told one another knowingly that Berry had inflicted the gravest of humiliations upon Edith by failing to marry her after the divorce; but other testimony is more convincing. Jacques Emile Blanche cornered White one day to ask, as many others were doing at this time, if it were true that Berry and Mrs. Wharton planned to marry. White only laughed at the question. "That'll never come off, sir," he said with assurance. Had "Mr. Walter" ever intended to marry, he would have done so long since; and in any case, White said, "out of the many beautiful ladies always making up to him, Mrs. Wharton is the last one he would have sacrificed his liberty to." Mr. Walter and Mrs. Wharton, White deposed, were equally lacking in patience. As to remarriage, almost all the evidence agrees that Edith Wharton was twice shy. And there is no reason to believe that she had abandoned the conviction she voiced to Charles du Bos about "the miserable poverty of any love that lies outside of marriage."

The word "lovers" is, of course, an indefinite and flexible one, hardly less so than the word "love." To say that Edith Wharton and Walter Berry were not lovers is to adopt the meaning implicit in the remark to du Bos: at no time did they actually share the same bed. But it is safe to assume that there was a hovering and gratifying sexual element in the relationship, and that Edith embraced Walter Berry with special tenderness. She loved him very much.

The travelers were ravenous by the time they reached Palermo; after a hearty dinner Edith sent Berenson a postcard on which, adopting the Italian suffix which means "large" and even "outsize," she wrote: "For our first menu we venture to suggest: minestrone—ravioloni—polloni di Bressoni—sparagoni—articiocchoni —ed altri generoni." They spent a relaxing week in Palermo, including a "shivering afternoon" at Monreale, where they studied the overarching sweep of the incomparable mosaics. By early May they were back in Naples. The place was crowded with German tourists, to whom Edith, preening herself over the pun, referred as a horde of *"Ja-*hoos." Cook then escorted them up to Settignano.

On the long drive back to Paris, Geoffrey Scott made a third passenger. Tall and thin, in his early thirties, and with a mass of untidy black hair, Scott was an interesting combination of the temperamental and the scholarly. The former was attested to by swift changes of mood, fits of moroseness followed by charming bursts of gaiety and wit; the latter hinted at by the pince-nez which clung to his weak eyes. He was an English protégé of sorts of Bernhard Berenson, but though he was a man of considerable intellectual and literary gifts, he was only beginning to find his proper calling. In the spring of 1913 he was completing his first book, *The Architecture of Humanism,* which, when published a year later, quickly established itself as a classic of cultural history. For Edith Wharton, Scott was "a traveler after my own heart"; by the time they reached Paris they were already fast friends.

At 53 Rue de Varenne, Edith was immediately submerged by piled-up mail, telephone messages, compatriots eager to call—and the first proofs of *The Custom of the Country.*

3

Although the novel had been running in *Scribner's* since January, it was far from ready for book publication. The final seven or eight chapters were yet to be written, and there were large changes to be made in the magazine version; more than two months of severely demanding work lay ahead. No novel of Edith Wharton's was longer in the making than *The Custom of the Country.* She had begun it in the lively spring of 1908, with an unusually clear idea of what it would consist of—the marital adventures, in Europe and the United States, of a certain type of predatory young American woman. But she had been periodically distracted from it, setting it aside to devote herself to short stories, to *Ethan Frome,* and to *The Reef.* As she got back to it upon the return from Italy, however, Edith was spurred on by the warm responses to the serial and by the buzz of discussion it was arousing in literary journals.

Charles Scribner was hardly less pleased. He had gradually rallied from the shock of Edith Wharton's having given *The Reef* to Appleton; and when Edith informed him from Palermo that a New York magazine had offered $12,500 for the serial rights to her next novel, Scribner was able to tell her, barely wincing, that *Scribner's* was prepared to match it. He was also happy, he said, at the reception shown to Morton Fullerton's expert analysis of international affairs, *Problems of Power* (dedicated to Theodore Roosevelt), in which the acute reader might discern portents of evil things to come.

While driving hard toward the finish of *The Custom of the Country*, Edith still had time to pursue a variety of other interests. Berenson came to Paris, and Edith invited a succession of people to lunch and tea with him: Henry Adams, the Bourgets, Bessy Lodge, Rosa de Fitz-James, Abbé Mugnier. In Berenson's view Edith seemed to have gained a good deal of weight—the dinners at Palermo had had their effect; but she spoke of suffering from mild heart palpitations and of still feeling rather battered. The two consulted on a household question: on an earlier visit of the Berensons, Edith's young footman Henri had fallen in love with Mary's personal maid. Edith submitted gracefully to Henri's being transferred to the staff at I Tatti, but warned that he needed a strong hand.

At the end of May, Edith went to the newly built Théâtre des Champs Elysées to see the Ballet Russe perform Igor Stravinsky's *The Rite of Spring*. It was the artistic event of the spring of 1913 in Paris, and Edith did not hesitate to call it "extraordinary." Her opinion was not shared by the majority of those attending the premiere. Stravinsky himself described the music and dance as representing "the violent Russian spring that seemed to begin in an hour and was like the whole earth cracking," and after the opening soft sounds, the first crashing chords had scarcely been struck before the entire theater was in an uproar. Most of the audience erupted in a storm of booing, shouting, and whistling; but there were also immediate adherents to what became recognized as a landmark of modern music, and opponents and enthusiasts literally spat at one another.

In mid-July, Edith gave herself a ten-day break in London, staying at the somewhat racy Cavendish Hotel in Jermyn Street. The Cavendish was owned and presided over by Rosa Lewis, one of the most remarkable representatives of Edwardian womanhood. The daughter of a London clockmaker, she began her career as maid-of-all-work in a middle-class home, then moved on to become chief kitchen maid in statelier town houses. At a weekend shooting party in the 1890s, the tall, swanlike Rosa caught the eye of the Prince of Wales, and thereafter was in steady demand as the caterer at garden parties where Prince Albert was expected. During the coronation year of 1902 she made so much money from the lavish dinners she prepared that she was able to buy the Cavendish Hotel. It became a favorite meeting place for the well-born and influential, both English and American—and the site of utterly discreet assignations and amours. "Secrecy, unique cooking and Rosa's Cockney wit," Anita Leslie, the granddaughter of Edith's friend Leonie, has remarked, "kept the Cavendish Hotel famous for forty years."

It is suggestive that Edith Wharton found the atmosphere at the Cavendish so much to her taste. In Mrs. Lewis' high-spirited memoirs of 1925 she spoke of Mrs. Wharton, taking her as an example of "the very best Americans." Rosa's comment was uncommonly perceptive:

> She struck me as having a very fine mind, but a very shy and retiring disposition, very difficult to get at. . . . I think she's never been really unlocked, and that most of her emotions have gone into her books.

Edith had Berenson, James, and Lapsley to lunch at the hotel. Berenson thought James oddly shy of him at first, but things eased and everyone was "very *drôle.*" Edith spent time, as usual, with Leonie Leslie and her circle, and with Berenson and Lady Sybil Cutting had a second view of *The Rite of Spring.* "Curious" was the strongest word Berenson could summon for the controversial and, in Stravinsky's word, "prehistoric" ballet.

Edith passed a weekend at Mary Hunter's genuinely stately home near Epping, Hill Hall: a rust-colored mansion part Elizabethan and part William and Mary, and surrounded by breathtakingly lovely country that fell away from the superbly tended grounds toward Epping Forest. The gathering was "a mixture of Society and Bohemians," as one of the guests put it; the gentlemen engaged in endless sets of tennis, and in the evening Percy Grainger entertained the company by playing the piano "like an angel."

The most interesting person there, from Edith's point of view, was Edward Marsh, an elegant and cultivated bachelor of forty-one who had been Winston Churchill's private secretary since 1905. Able in his official duties, Marsh was also widely known as a bemonocled and top-hatted man about town and inveterate guest of Edith's friend Lady Elcho of Stanway and the Duchess of Rutland. He was, in addition, largely responsible for defining the English poetic spirit of the age, in a series of anthologies called *Georgian Poetry;* the first edition, just published, had included work by John Masefield, Walter de la Mare, and Marsh's close friend Rupert Brooke.

At Hill Hall, Edith quarreled with him enjoyably about D. H. Lawrence's recent novel *Sons and Lovers,* professing amazement that he could approve "such bungled stuff." Marsh, who delighted in the exchange, admitted to liking Edith Wharton very much. They sat across from each other at another dinner, in Lady Hamilton's London home. William Butler Yeats was there, looking "fluffy and lovable," but, probably out of her habitual shyness (for she admired Yeats's poetry more than that of any other English-language poet alive), Edith did not attempt to engage him in conversation, and spent the evening instead leaning forward to hear Marsh's flow of anecdotes and exploding with laughter at them.

During a second visit to Hill Hall—the guests on this occasion including

Victoria Sackville-West and Feodor Chaliapin, as well as Berenson and Walter Berry—Edith made a little foray to inspect a nearby property called Coopersale, she was thinking of buying. The eventful change in her life and even in her identity brought about by the divorce had led inevitably to thoughts of a major change of place, and she was feeling more drawn to England all the time. She longed to hear English spoken on all sides for at least part of the year; she longed as well for quieter surroundings. She was becoming almost as distracted as Marcel Proust by the increasing noise and roar of Paris; once when she was writing a letter to Sara Norton at her desk in the Rue de Varenne, the commotion caused by workmen remodeling the building next door made her so nervous that she forgot what she was saying. And there was the lure of the country; for all her urbanity, Edith in a part of her was always very much a countrywoman, and the loss of her Berkshire home still rankled and saddened her.

Coopersale seemed ideal, as Berenson and Berry agreed when they went with her after lunch one day to look at it. The privacy and quiet were almost absolute. The main building, which Edith described as a "dilapidated sort of wood-cut house," was set far back from the high enclosing walls on the peaceful village road; there were over a hundred acres, gardens exquisitely landscaped in the English manner, a running brook and a cluster of orchards. In the word Howard Sturgis instantly coined, Edith determined to "Cooperbuy" and made an offer of six thousand pounds. The agent regarded this as inadequate, and discussions continued in a desultory way through the winter and into the spring of 1914. Eventually and reluctantly, Edith decided against buying. The British government, she learned, levied a heavy income tax on foreign residents, and she felt that Coopersale was after all too close to London—it was about eighteen miles north. By this time, too, the shadows were visibly thickening over Europe, and Edith may have thought it not the moment for a transfer across the channel.

4

It was on August 4, 1913, that Edith told Berenson—who was waiting impatiently for her to join him on a much-delayed tour of Germany—that she had completed the last chapter of the novel.

The Custom of the Country, her most powerful if not her most beguiling novel, gave Edith Wharton her best opportunity thus far to draw upon her bountiful accumulated knowledge of the recent history of American and European society. It is essentially the saga of the beautiful and ruthlessly grasping Undine Spragg and her successive marriages over about a dozen years (roughly from 1900 to 1912): to Ralph Marvell, the gentle and vulnerable representative of the older New York; to the Marquis Raymond de Chelles of the old French aristocracy, with homes in Burgundy and the Faubourg St. Germain; and to Elmer Moffatt, formerly of Apex City, Kansas, a robust member of the new

American social breed who had been Undine's first husband in a brief-lived secret marriage before becoming her fourth and last.

Only about Apex City could Edith not speak from first-hand experience, but she was sure that her conscientious reading of newspaper articles supplied her with all the information she needed. When Berenson chided her for employing such implausible names as Undine Spragg and Indiana Frusk (Undine's childhood friend), Edith replied: *"Naïf enfant.* And how about Lurline Spreckels . . . and Florida Yurlee, two 'actualities' who occur to me instantly? As for similar instances, the 'Herald' register will give you a dozen any morning."

Edith Wharton exploited these materials to draw a remarkably subtle and convincing pattern of suggestive contrasts and arresting similarities between a variety of customs and countries, of social structures and social types. The old New York of Ralph Marvell is pitted against the new invaders and conquerors as represented by Peter van Degen, the gross millionaire playboy who takes Undine as his mistress for a two-month period. After Marvell's suicide and Undine's marriage to de Chelles, she finds confusedly that "the usages of her adopted country" are oddly similar to the rituals and expectations of the Marvell set. But the great strength of the novel derives from Edith Wharton's imaginative understanding of what was *happening,* historically, to the American and French aristocracies in the first decade of the twentieth century. Both were giving way before the two major forces of the historic moment—sexual power and financial aggressiveness. Those forces combine, in the second marriage between Undine and Elmer Moffatt (now a billionaire), to form a huge metaphor of the enthralling and terrible ongoing process of the age.

No less than its predecessors, *The Custom of the Country* teems with the personally remembered and experienced—settings, encounters, journeys, persons. Not surprisingly, given the time of the novel's completion, the subject of divorce and the attitudes toward it come in for a thorough airing. In Marvell's circle it is a scandal and a disgrace, something not fit to be mentioned in polite company; but within the new breed, as Undine learns, "couples were unpairing and pairing" with astonishing ease and rapidity. In the unrestrainedly satiric final portion of the story, Undine de Chelles is divorced from the marquis at breakneck speed in Reno, the judge, immediately after scribbling the decree, leaping into an automobile with Undine and Moffatt to accompany them to the justice of the peace, where he acts as best man.

On deeper levels, each of the four main characters bespeaks a portion of Edith Wharton herself and tells us a little more about that complex nature. Ralph Marvell in his musings suggests Edith's growing tenderness toward the vanishing New York she had known, and which now seemed to her to display virtues she was inclined to honor. Marvell also, as it were, embodies Edith's feminine side; Moffatt her masculine side, her immense energy, her decisiveness in action, the vigor of her ironic humor. This aspect had long been recognized by Morton

Fullerton, who addressed her at times as *"Cher ami";* and Henry James in a commentary would point to a certain masculinity, a toughness of mind, in the very texture of the novel. Edith Wharton's commitment to the traditional French way of life, meanwhile, and her gathering disgust at some of her rootless compatriots as they blundered about in the Old World are voiced in an outburst of articulate rage by Raymond de Chelles.

But the most of Edith Wharton is revealed, quite startlingly, in the characterization of Undine Spragg. No one (except possibly Ethan Frome) would at first glance seem more remote from Edith Wharton than Undine: a crude, unlettered, humorless, artificial, but exceedingly beautiful creature, with the most minimal moral intuitions and virtually no talent whatever for normal human affection. Undine did, undoubtedly, stand for everything in the new American female that Edith despised and recoiled from. But the matter, as it turns out, is much more interesting than that.

There are smaller and larger telltale similarities. As a child Undine, like Edith, enjoyed dressing up in her mother's best finery and "playing lady" before a mirror. Moffatt addresses her by Edith's youthful nickname, "Puss." Edith's long yearning for psychological freedom is queerly reflected in Undine's discovery that each of her marriages is no more than another mode of imprisonment; and Undine's creator allows more than a hint that the young woman is as much a victim as an aggressor amid the assorted snobberies, tedium, and fossilized rules of conduct of American and, even more, French high society. Above all, Undine suggests what Edith Wharton might have been like if, by some dreadful miracle, all her best and most lovable and redeeming features had been suddenly cut away.

So imagined, we see in Undine Spragg how Edith sometimes appeared to the view of the harried and aging Henry James: demanding, imperious, devastating, resolutely indifferent to the needs of others; something like an irresistible force of nature. James's image of Edith as a cyclone is borrowed (Minnie Cadwalader Jones probably showed her the letter) to describe the uproar Undine caused on one occasion, when "everything had gone down before her, as towns and villages went down before one of the tornadoes of her native state." Marvell thinks of his young bride as an eagle, and one has the decided impression of a number of men carried off seriatim, "struggling in her talons." No character Edith Wharton ever invented more closely resembles that bird of prey by which James, Sturgis, and others so often, and only half-jokingly, portrayed Edith herself. Undine Spragg is, so to say, a dark Angel of Devastation: Edith Wharton's anti-self; and like all anti-selves, a figure that explains much about its opposite.

When it appeared in October, *The Custom of the Country* received a generally excellent press. The *Saturday Review* observed with considerable prescience that the entire novel should be read as a fable for the times, and there was nothing but praise for the brilliance of the narrative technique and the lack of sentimentality. One commentator grumbled, with reason, that Undine Spragg was the most disagreeable girl in American fiction, and another solemnly declared that the book constituted a slander on most American men and women. But most reviewers shared the private opinion of Ralph Curtis' ever astute mother, who declared to her son that *The Custom of the Country* was "the cleverest women's book she had ever read." Edith Wharton's position as a woman of letters was never more secure. One can go further: in 1913 and for some years thereafter Edith Wharton may be reckoned as the most accomplished practicing American novelist.

The Scribners sales figures for the novel have unfortunately not survived. But to judge from Edith Wharton's royalties, it appears to have sold more than any of her books since *The Fruit of the Tree*, of which sixty thousand copies were disposed of in 1907. *The Custom of the Country* also had more staying power than most of Edith Wharton's other volumes.

5

During the July break in England, Edith and Berenson had talked about making a tour of Germany together, but she had teasingly refused to be pinned down about dates. She insisted that she still had an indeterminate number of days' work on her novel; but Berenson, who was curiously insensitive about the demands of the creative imagination, refused to credit this, and after their return to Paris he jealously attributed her reluctance to leave the city largely to her concern over the slightly ailing Walter Berry. "Between him as sun and her writing as moon," he complained to Mary, "her life oscillates. All else is meteoric drift." He took off impatiently for Brussels. Edith wrote him there saying she was dead tired and asking if he might give her three or four days in "some green, woody, *walky* place where I can recover my nerves before we attack the big towns. Don't be hard on me or think me uncertain or capricious," she added, noting a little wistfully that Mary Berenson did for him everything that she, Edith, had to do for herself: "household, cheque book, publishers, servant questions, business letters, proofs —and my work!"

"She protests too much," Berenson said, and described himself as "amusedly curious to see what particular specimen of womanliness she is going to treat me to." Even after the novel was finished, there was a further delay caused by an infected foot, by which, Edith wrote, she was embarrassed and annoyed. "There is truth in it," Berenson mused, ". . . but still more Walter." On August 7 they met at last at the Grand Hotel in Luxembourg, Edith arriving worn out in general, and tired in particular by the ten-hour run.

Over the following four weeks, as the two of them made their way from Luxembourg to Berlin, Berenson enacted the classic pattern of emotional response to Edith Wharton's conduct and personality—the pattern one observes time and again with others of her closest friends—in long swings of feeling between indignation and resentment (in this case, at her indecisiveness and changes of mood) and the keenest and most affectionate delight in her company. Berenson's daily letters to his wife comprise one of the closest, if not always the most dependable, glimpses of Edith Wharton on record.

The addict of the Ritz Hotel in Paris looked askance, to begin with, at the grandeur of Edith's style of traveling: she reached Luxembourg accompanied by Cook, White, and a new traveling maid acquired at the last moment when Gross had fallen ill; her small dog Nicette was in her lap. After an evening's conversation which touched on Freud, Berry's horror of fat women, and Edith's hatred of beards, however, Berenson admitted that she was "excellent company." He also acknowledged that "she is tuckered out, and no mistake." But he failed to understand how enormously exhausted she really was, or the sources of her condition: the huge expenditure of energy required to complete a massive work of literary art, and a deep delayed reaction to the internally disruptive act of divorce.

On August 11, in the Hotel du Nord in Cologne, Edith abruptly collapsed, and announced that she was unable to go on. She urged Berenson to continue without her and offered him the use of her car, with Cook, to travel as far as Copenhagen, if he wanted, or anywhere else. Berenson at first agreed, but was then stricken by compunction: "She seemed so genuine and so generous . . . that I really could not bear to leave her by herself. So we are going to a quiet place in Thuringia for some days where she can rest. As a matter of friendship, I can do no less."

A few days later, in a leafy little resort called Oberhof, Berenson began to wonder whether Edith were not "half shamming illness so as to have her way," and in mounting irritation offered a summary indictment: "What is clear is that *surmanager* takes the form in her of flaccid indecision mixed with obstinate opposition to her companion's plan." He might have been quoting from Edith's assessment in 1910 of her sister-in-law Nancy Wharton. But in a following letter to Mary, after saying that the only motive he could now conceive of for ever taking another trip with Edith Wharton was the pure desire for her company, honesty compelled him to add:

Her company *is* delightful. She is ready to talk and to listen on so many topics and nothing is too small for her if it is characteristic or significant on a point of contrast.

He continued in a full tide of appreciation to say that her sense of human motivation was as acute as the best of the French, and more so than "any other English-speaking person I know." He only felt "how much better she might have been had she fallen on better hands! With her beginnings and her Ted and even her W.B., she has turned out so much better than one could have expected.

... I am here chiefly to study her," he decided, and agreed with Mary that the trip was "a *discipline* as well as a pleasure" for him.

Mary Berenson had been eager to join the travelers and had written her husband several times to suggest places of meeting. Berenson fended her off with agility, enjoining her to stay at home and go on with her medication. The tactic evidently stirred in Mary a growing resentment against Edith. Earlier in the summer, after a talk with Edith, Mary had written: "Edith is *very* fond of thee, Bernhard, lucky man"; but now she began to inveigh against Edith's "unseemly and misplaced archness and coquetry," and even her deceitfulness (so Mary said) in anything that involved Walter Berry. Her love affair with Berry was a matter well known in America for many years, and there had been considerable support for "poor Ted" in the divorce case. "But of course that makes no difference to her. She must be well used to criticism and quite indifferent." The truth was, Mary said, that Edith was completely spoiled, self-satisfied, unreasonable, and immature. Berenson's women friends tended to repeat themselves about one another: the time would come when Edith would level almost identical charges against Mary.

On the drive through Goethe's Weimar to Dresden, Edith seemed to Berenson to be on the verge of hysteria. She kept whining about the squalor of the villages and the ugliness of the countryside (he wrote) as if it were all his fault; and each time Cook made a wrong turn she fell back in her seat in all but a faint. In the Dresden museums she was at her most annoying: Berenson's eloquent discourses had little effect upon her, and he declared with cold finality that "art is a sealed book to her."

Writing to Mary Berenson herself, Edith confessed apologetically that she had thought Claude and Poussin to be the same painter, but that B.B. had borne with her ignorance graciously. She also passed along a fragment of conversation between an American couple who were contemplating a painting by Rembrandt:

She—That's Rembrandt's portrait of himself with his wife.
He (not a man to be fooled)—Ugh! How on earth could he paint himself?
She—Well, he *did*—
(They walk away)

On August 25 they reached the Hotel Esplanade in Berlin and here remained for ten days. It was Edith's first view of the city, and she greeted it, Berenson reported, with a minor fit of hysterics because the bed in her hotel room was not properly situated; not until it had been moved to face the window did she settle down and begin to find Berlin "incomparable." Berenson thought this an absurd performance; but because Edith never harped upon the physical requirements of her literary life, he did not quite realize that she worked in bed every morning and therefore needed a bed which faced the light. It had been her practice for more than twenty years; and for a woman in as uncertain a state of nerves as was Edith Wharton in August 1913, and who clung so tenaciously to her daily stint, the need was a serious one.

Edith was too harried to pay much attention to conditions in Germany: to the intellectual and literary ferment in Munich and Heidelberg or the upswelling of belligerent patriotism in Berlin. In the latter city, had she listened, she could have heard talk of a typical piece of bombast by the crown prince a few months before, about "the holy duty of Germany above all other peoples to maintain an army and a fleet ever at the highest point of readiness." The German army, now increased to a million and a half well-trained men, was indeed at a high point of readiness, and Germany, exemplified by the vainglorious and impulsive Kaiser Wilhelm II, had reached a mood of extreme militancy. The "gigantic conflagration" to which the crown prince looked forward was being soberly prepared by military men along the lines laid down by Count Alfred von Schlieffen.

For Edith and Berenson these matters were, so to speak, drowned out by the sound of music—the other dominant feature of Germany in the prewar years. In Dresden they had seen Richard Strauss's *Der Rosenkavalier* (first produced in 1911), the hauntingly beautiful masterpiece of the most acclaimed composer of his time. In Berlin, Edith was enraptured by *Faust:* "When she is appreciative," Berenson wrote, "she is splendid." They attended the whole of Wagner's *Der Ring des Nibelungen,* and at the performance of *Siegfried* on August 29 they were joined by Rainer Maria Rilke (whom Berenson had known before) and the poet's massive and brilliantly lively patroness, Princess Marie von Thurn und Taxis. Edith's reverence for Rilke's poetry froze her, as usual, into total silence.

While Edith was gathering herself to start back for Paris, Berenson, suddenly discovering how much he was going to miss her, summed up his feelings for Mary's benefit:

> Spoiled, luxurious, *difficile* as she is, she is infinitely preferable to most women, for she can talk and think and feel and listen to a million things most people have no sense for. So I shall part with her feeling forlorn and more devoted to her than ever, but knowing in the future what to avoid.

"I enjoy her more and more," Berenson said just before bidding her good-bye. It would be something of a relief to be free of her for a while; but in Edith's absence, the next evening, Berenson felt decidedly let down.

6

Despite Mary Berenson's accusations, Edith was entirely aware of having been a difficult and changeable companion in Germany. From Baden-Baden, where she went for a week of complete rest, she wrote Berenson a wistful note: "I wish

I had been in better trim for your delectable company and our good trip. You must give me another chance. This time, everything I looked at hurt." The only good thing about her incapacity was that it had brought out "such treasures of indulgence and dearness" on Berenson's part.

The hurting did not quickly let up. Her memories of the year past—the venomous attack by her brother Harry, the agony of the divorce proceedings, the dislocating breach with Henry James—throbbed in her mind, and during a night in October they were translated into a dream which she wrote down in a notebook:

A pale demon with black hair came in, followed by four gnome-like creatures carrying a great black trunk. They set it down and opened it, and the Demon, crying out: "Here's your year—here are all the horrors that have happened to you and that are still going to happen" dragged out a succession of limp black squirming things and threw them on the floor before me. They were not rags or creatures, not living or dead—they were Black Horrors, shapeless, and that seemed to writhe about as they fell at my feet, and yet were as inanimate as bits of stuff. But none of these comparisons occurred to me, for I *knew* what they were: the hideous, the incredible things that had happened to me in this dreadful year, or were to happen to me before its close; and I stared, horror-struck, as the Demon dragged them out, one by one, more and more, till finally, flinging down a blacker, hatefuller one, he said laughing: "There—that's the last of them!"

The gnomes laughed too; but I, as I stared at the great black pile and the empty trunk, said to the Demon: *"Are you sure it hasn't a false bottom?"*

"Yes—one gets over things," Edith told herself some time later. "But there are certain memories one can't bite on."

By the time Edith was back in Paris, she felt well enough to observe with interest new fashions on the local scene. The chief of these was the tango, a dance form that had been imported from Argentina and for the moment was more popular than the fox trot or the one-step, and in some quarters the waltz. It was a dance, remarked a friend of Edith's, that permitted "an unbecoming and unsuitable license of movement," and at dance halls like the Sans Souci the display was startling. Edith looked on with amused skepticism. When she heard of an acquaintance taking tango lessons, she commented: "It always seems so funny to me that people need to be *taught* to tango. Nature used to do that for us when I was young. Ask Freud." The Archbishop of Paris shared that opinion so warmly that he put out an edict forbidding young Catholic girls to perform the dance. But it was reported that when the Pope had a couple demonstrate the tango for him, his only reaction was: "My poor children! It can't be much fun."

An important event was about to take place in the American branch of the Jones family. Edith's niece Beatrix was to marry Max Farrand, a professor of history at Yale, the date fixed for just after Christmas. Beatrix Jones, at forty-two, had earned an international reputation as a landscape gardener and had most recently designed a new garden at the White House for Mrs. Woodrow Wilson. Max Farrand was an able scholar and a charming individual, as Edith—whose first conventional reaction was that he sounded rather dim—immediately discovered when they met. She had not been inclined at first to go over for the ceremony; but then, as she said to Lapsley, she decided she ought to be present "to represent our dwindling family." She sailed on the *France,* put up at the Ritz-Carlton, and played her matronly role at the wedding.

"New York," she said of the city she had not seen, except for the most fleeting glimpse, in nearly eight years, "is overwhelming and I am overwhelmed." But she was touched by the affectionate welcome she was given on all sides, particularly by Mary Cadwalader Jones, the mother of the bride, and by Walter and Eunice Maynard, and she spent hours on the long-distance telephone communing with absent friends. She was enormously in demand, lunching and dining out daily; Berry, who had followed her across the Atlantic, described her as "eating her way through the new New York, and pleasantly *ahurie* [bewildered]." Gradually, however, the bewilderment became more than she could accommodate. She had the impression, she told Berenson (who was in Boston), that her individuality was slipping away amid the frenzy of New York's "queer, rootless life," and that she was no more than a *"jeton* in a game, that hurried and purposeless hands were feverishly moving from one little square to another—a kind of nightmare chess without rules or issue."

According to another, not unprejudiced, report, this sensation of being constantly and heedlessly pushed about had certain unfortunate consequences. "Edith was in a very desolating mood when she was here," Mary Berenson wrote Geoffrey Scott from New York in January. "She spoiled several evenings especially arranged for her by evidently hating everything and has left some bitter enemies behind her." She must have been as *"indiablée,"* Mary thought, as on the occasion of their first meeting in 1903. Mary did not hesitate to ascribe the source of Edith's conduct: she was "so nervous with jealousy" over the equally pressing social engagements that kept drawing Walter Berry from her side "that she could not control herself." Berry was alleged to have told "everyone" how much he hated Edith dragging him away from the city before he was ready to go.

Edith's analysis of the experience, needless to say, operated on a rather different level. There was, she said, little of the sort of conversation she relished and needed, and what most put her off was a new self-consciousness on the part of New Yorkers about their native city. "New York" was tediously woven in and out of every topic of conversation.

Boston always *has* been self-conscious about Boston, but the one distinction of ugly, patchy, scrappy New York was that it didn't get off from itself and measure and generalise; it had that in common with Paris and London. But now it hasn't any longer.

It was a telling insight by one of the most knowing observers in her generation of the great cities of the Western world. But she concluded that the visit had, after all, been a great show, though it left her "absolutely inert and inarticulate" by the time she and Berry embarked on the *France,* a week after New Year's. She would come to America only one more time in her life—and that not for nearly a decade, and for an even shorter stay.

Sending Berenson greetings on New Year's Day, Edith had expressed "the modest wish . . . that 1914 may not be like its predecessor." It was the kind of wish that fate, or history, tends to grant in a manner quite alien to the spirit in which it was voiced.

7

Fresh from Italy, England, Germany, and the United States, Edith, in her Paris apartment early in the year, began to make plans for a tour of North Africa. Having surveyed so much of the Western world in recent months, she now felt impelled to explore a different and more ancient culture. As we have seen, Edith Wharton had long shared the currently fashionable appeal of the primitive, of Nietzsche's attacks upon civilization and Stravinsky's *The Rite of Spring,* and the Parisian vogue for Africa. The same strain, working strongly against her conservatism and rationalism, would be evident in her next important work of fiction, *Summer.* The divorce had in some way intensified her attraction to the exotic; she talked of later trips to Baghdad and Beirut, after North Africa, and Walter Berry had meanwhile set the example by taking, as he put it, "passage to India."

As traveling companions she sought to enlist Gaillard Lapsley and Percy Lubbock. Lapsley demurred: he was due to spend some time at the Riviera home of a lady under whose spell he had fallen. To this Edith responded, after she met the woman, by suggesting that she must have put on a good deal of flesh—or had she always been "on the Statue-of-Strasbourg order"? When Lapsley finally gave in, Edith exclaimed: "Oh *law!* Can't we—won't we—have fun?" In fact, Lapsley joined the party late, instantly succumbed to dysentery, and crawled back alone to Europe.

Lubbock posed a more delicate problem. Edith had grown fonder by the year of this lean, intelligent, unfocused young man, and she knew he was in bad financial straits. He had had a job of sorts in Vienna, but it was coming to an end, and he had written Edith, in the habit of young Englishmen, to ask if she could take him in for a while. Edith's hope was that he would be as agreeable to her paying his expenses as he was to sharing her hospitality. Lubbock arrived in late February, and after beating around the bush for a few days, Edith—who was learning to move more cautiously where philanthropy was concerned—put the question to him as one *confrère* of the pen to another. Lubbock accepted the proposal with all simplicity, grace, and satisfaction.

Edith was immensely excited. There were, she said, only five or six people she could really stand traveling with, and her two escorts-to-be were among them (the others, at this stage, included Berry, Berenson, and Geoffrey Scott). She armed herself with letters of introduction to an assortment of officials in Algeria and Tunisia, studied the maps, and began to lay out the itinerary.

It should not be supposed that the notion of purchasing a home in England or the contemplated foray into North Africa in any way meant that Edith was cutting her ties with Paris or the French. On the contrary, the city in the winter of 1914 seemed to her more alluring than ever. The season was unusually mild and mellow. Her group was somewhat diminished, but the Bourgets were "fond and faithful," and with them and others Edith dined out at her regular pace. After her days in New York, she particularly relished the fine French conversation, and in general what she called the "amenity and *civility* of this pre-eminently conversable race. . . . If one cares very little for society," she thought, "it's really the only society one *can* care for." During an evening of talk with Paul Bourget, Edith proudly made her first joke in French. It was an elaborate one. Bourget had been telling a series of off-color anecdotes, in his slyly lascivious way, about nightwalkers and *demi-mondaine* actresses and restaurants which provided private rooms for illicit assignations, and finally Edith broke in with: *"Oh, taisez-vous, Bourget. C'est le cloaque de Chez Maxim."* Only the cultured and discerning, she averred, would appreciate the *mot*.

"I like Paris in winter more and more," Edith told Sara Norton, faintly anticipating a much later popular song by the composer that Berry and others would refer to as the Coleporter. Edith was taking in a number of concerts: the *Well-Tempered Clavier* series, which she attended religiously each week; and several performances of Beethoven. It was at this time that the Paris musical world (possibly recoiling from Stravinsky) abruptly rediscovered Ludwig von Beethoven; his work could be heard almost nightly in one hall or another. Edith declared that Beethoven was the "deepest musical experience" of her life, and about the Ninth Symphony she wrote in her notebook that "when it ceases one feels that its harmonies must have passed into some other form of beauty: sunsets or statues or poems." The woman who had once spoken so contemptuously of an interest in music was now fairly well at home in both its classical and modern modes.

She was working hard every morning, probably on an ambitious novel called "Literature," which was never to be completed. But upon all these activities and diversions, developments on the European political scene were impinging ever more alarmingly. On March 14 there occurred one of the most sensational and fateful incidents—or better, *scandales*—in the history of the period, and Edith was given virtually an eyewitness account of it.

Joseph Caillaux, the cabinet minister who spoke most vigorously for a policy of reconciliation and rapprochement with Germany, had drawn to himself a number of increasingly virulent and powerful enemies, among them President Poincaré. It happened that there fell into the hands of Gaston Calmette, the editor of *Figaro* and a strong supporter of Poincaré's anti-German stance, a batch of extremely compromising letters from Caillaux to his former mistress. They were written while Caillaux was still married to his first wife, and were a queerly reckless mélange of the political and the erotic. Calmette announced his intention of publishing them.

Hearing of this, the former mistress, who was now the second Mme. Caillaux, procured herself a pistol, stormed into the offices of *Figaro* and, shouting incoherently, shot Calmette several times, mortally wounding him. Paul Bourget appeared on the scene, making a routine visit to *Figaro*, tried in vain to provide first aid to the dying man, and helped calm down the agitated murderess. While his wife was being taken off to the St. Lazare prison, Caillaux handed in his resignation—and with him went one of the last influential voices for peace in France.

Edith listened eagerly to Bourget as he bounded back and forth between the Chamber of Deputies and the Faubourg, full of patriotic exuberance and the latest bulletin. "What a seething political cauldron you're coming back to in this hemisphere," she wrote Berenson as the latter was about to sail from New York. "I wish you'd been in Paris during the week after the Calmette murder. It was extraordinary!" The combination of violence and sex always held a special fascination for Edith Wharton; but she was also struck, as others were and would be, by the tendency of political scandals in Europe—as against those of her native land—to contain a potent element of the erotic.

The party which sailed on the S.S. *Timgad* from Marseilles to Algiers on March 29 was almost a royal procession: with Edith Wharton as the queen-empress, Lubbock her equerry, Anna Bahlmann her royal secretary, Cook (after carefully stowing away the big car on board) her private chauffeur, and a young woman named Elise Duvlenck her personal maid in attendance. The pink-cheeked and rather breathless Elise had only recently joined Edith's household. Edith at first regarded her as "full of merit, but lacking her predecessor's commanding genius"; but after the group began its jaunts, Elise proved her ability by taking charge of most of the luggage and conveying it from place to place by train, while the others traveled in the Mercedes. As time passed, indeed, Elise came closer in Edith's affections than anyone in her household except Gross. On her side Elise, who was soon declaring that she alone knew how to look after Mme. Wharton and her wardrobe, developed an almost mystical reverence for her mistress.

The travelers covered only the extreme northwestern slice of the continent —driving down from Algiers through Orléansville to Oran, then over to Biskra, and through Constantine into Tunisia—but every step of the way was a fascination for Edith Wharton. Here and there they came upon vestiges of the Europe they had left behind: at Timgad, the Roman ruins (which had a suitable effect on what Edith called the Timgadabouts), and in Carthage, which she thought "august and shadowy," the remains of a Roman theater and memories of Virgil's Dido and of St. Augustine. But it was not for such that Edith had come to Africa.

What she looked for, and found, was a world, as she said to Sara Norton, "far from everything I know," and one that steeped her in "immemorial things." At Biskra, in the Sahara, she stood with Lubbock and watched the moon rise over the vast sand dunes. "I had no idea what desert magic could be," she wrote; having experienced it, she felt she had it in her bones forever and scarcely knew how she could return to her normal life. With the noise of Paris still in her ears, it was above all the uncanny quiet of her surroundings that pleased her. Even the human element seemed noiseless, and she later compared her "beautiful silent swift Arabs" to the "strident apes" she unkindly described as reencountering in Naples.

As she felt the "western fever" further receding, it seemed to her that the entire Eastern world was slowly revealing itself. But at Timgad another and perhaps not less characteristic aspect of that world was disclosed. After visiting the ruins there the party took rooms in a lonely inn nearby, from which they could have another look by moonlight. As they stared out, hypnotized, Edith remarked to Lubbock: "This is the way my grandparents saw the Forum, in the days when it was dangerous to sleep at Radicofani on account of the brigands." She then went to her room, aware that Cook and Elise were installed down another passage. In the middle of the night she was awakened by a slight noise in the room. As she groped for matches beside the bed, she touched the hand of a man bending down over her.

Edith sprang up in a panic. There was a brief, furious scuffle in the darkness; she found herself in the grip of a small man—not, she thought later, an Arab, but a strong, wiry creature. She escaped from his embrace, struggled with the door latch—which stuck for a hideous moment—and plunged screaming into the deeper blackness of the corridor. After a moment Cook and Elise shot out of their rooms, followed by others carrying candles. The intruder apparently slipped out behind Edith and disappeared before anyone else showed up. When the bleary-eyed waiter arrived, he displayed almost complete skepticism at Edith's frantic story, made a desultory search of her room, and went back to bed.

It was, as Lubbock said in his account of it to Lapsley, the old familiar tale of a man hiding under the bed of a solitary woman—banal enough in all truth, "but so deadly real when it happens." "Don't let *anybody* talk to me about being frightened," Edith wrote Berenson, "who hasn't known that sensation" of awaking to feel the hand of a strange figure in the dark of one's room. "I would rather have given him my cheque book than gone through that minute when I touched him. Brrr!" But she recovered quickly, refusing to let the hateful episode cast any pall over their adventure. "Her gallantry has been amazing," Lubbock reported. She was able to joke that she had, after all, lost nothing but her voice, which her succession of piercing screams reduced to a squeak for a day or two.

During a week in Tunis and southern Tunisia, she absorbed still another image of the Arab world. In Algiers the natives had seemed possessed of a noble beauty; now she was confronted by a vision of "effeminacy or obesity or obscenity or black savageness." In the sun-sprinkled depths of the vaulted bazaars in the native quarter, she felt she had stumbled into an "unexpurgated page of the Arabian nights" and reveled in the fantastic variety of types. The crowded scene, constantly astir, seemed to her charged with sexuality. She responded by purchasing several erotic gifts: a phial of essence of sandalwood and sycamore, "which, diluted with the purest alcohol, is said to—*mais ne précisons pas!*"; some perfumes; and from a black prostitute in Sfax, a love charm in the form of an ambergris necklace. Edith attempted to explain circumspectly to Anna Bahlmann the alleged power of the necklace to attract and arouse young Arab men, but, while Lubbock choked with suppressed laughter in the background, Anna prudishly failed to understand.

The trip ended with a drive to Kairouan, Susa, and Gabès, over steep gorges above roaring torrents, with enormous vistas which would become familiar to American troops in the Second World War. They went by car and train and car again to Tezeur and Nefta, said to be the best "oasis-towns" in Tunisia. "But it's *all* best to us," Edith exulted; "—it's attar-of-roses all the way." As the party sailed to Naples and went on through Rome to Florence, she felt that she had been pulled out of her familiar orbit, and was infected with a passion for Africa which could never be cured. To what extent she might have pursued this passion and entered more deeply into the so invitingly alien and exotic world—as a source of personal enlargement and perhaps of literary stimulus—is not to be known. She would revisit North Africa, but events not three months distant would draw all her strongest allegiances back to the traditions and the civilization which were her own.

8

The return journey was dimmed momentarily, at I Tatti, by news from Egerton Winthrop in Paris that Teddy was in the city with his sister and very ill. It was "an attack like the others, but much more acute," Edith told her hostess in a handwritten note asking to be allowed to withdraw immediately after dinner. She felt "rather sad," and cabled Winthrop for further information. Teddy recovered sufficiently to start back to America before Edith reached the Rue de Varenne.

For the most part Teddy was in fact well enough, and would be for some time to come, to career about Boston and elsewhere in a high-powered automobile, delighting and alarming his female passengers. At sixty-four he still retained considerable charm and bonhomie; one of his much younger female acquaintances has recalled him as being on occasion a "disturbed" individual, but very far from insane. Edith, however, felt that since the divorce, Teddy had been behaving in a way that in former days would have filled him with "disgust and contempt." There was a wrangle over dower rights—the rights to Teddy's property that Edith might legally claim. Teddy's lawyer, Edith told Judge Grant, was demanding that she surrender all such rights in return for being permitted to use the name of Mrs. Wharton in France. Edith was anxious to do this so as to avoid publicity, but she regarded the transaction as an act of blackmail.

Life in the Faubourg, in Edith's phrase, jogged along as usual. Berry was on hand, thinner than ever and full of accounts of his trip to India, very knowledgeable now about Indian art. Berenson came for a long stay; there was a dinner under the trees in the Bois de Boulogne and a drive to St. Cloud to call upon Charley and Zezette du Bos.

Edith had succeeded in renting for the summer the English house known as Stocks, near the village of Tring in Buckinghamshire. It belonged to Mrs. Humphry Ward, whom Edith had come to know in earlier Edwardian days— having known her cousin Lucy Whitridge and her daughter Dorothy for almost fifteen years. Mrs. Ward's earnest, rather preachy novels (someone in the Queen's Acre set had coined the phrase: "Virtue is its Humphry Ward") were not selling very well, perhaps on account of her unpopular opposition to the suffragette movement. Her card-playing son was also a financial strain, and the rent money would be useful. Edith began to spread her net for summer gatherings, with a special eye on Henry James, an old habitué of Stocks. To Lapsley she remarked in an allusion to her Undine Spragg side: "I feel less and less like the lurid exotic flamboyant *volatile* [Henry] persists in calling me—but I'll do my best to fly up to the hauteur when we celebrate his promised visit to Stocks."

But still another motor tour was in order before the departure for England. Edith had been having throat and eye trouble, and her doctor advised her to "get a little high air before I plunge into English greenery." On July 10 she left with Walter Berry and her staff, circling down through Albi and over the Pyrenees into Spain. For three weeks they wandered across Spain, a country that Edith found it hard to make her way into, imaginatively. The high point of the trip was an exploration of the caves at Altamira, where the walls were covered with ancient drawings of bisons "roaring and butting and galloping over the low rock roof." Berry bumped his white linen hat against one of the figures, and thus, Edith said, carried off "prehistoric stigmata" in the form of red chalk marks. It was indeed not Christian Spain but the Spain of prehistory that finally touched a chord in Edith Wharton.

"The international news in this morning's paper here is pretty black," Edith wrote Berenson from Pamplona on July 26. "I wonder." They drove back into France twenty-four hours later. On the next to last day of July they were in Poitiers, ready to start on the final day's run north to Paris.

19. The Refugees

Edith Wharton would remember July 30, 1914, as a day when she felt singularly attuned, in a sort of ultimate peacefulness, to everything that was enduring, strong, and beautiful in France. Motoring north from Poitiers, the party had lunch by the roadside, under apple trees at the edge of a field. In the noonday quiet Edith surveyed the "sober disciplined landscape" which spoke to her of the steady attachment to the soil of generations of workers in the field. The serenity of the scene, she thought, simply smiled away the war rumors which had hung around them for several days. It was just over a month since the Austrian Archduke Franz Ferdinand, the heir to the Hapsburg throne, had been assassinated at Sarajevo. Austria-Hungary had declared war on Serbia, and on the day Edith and Berry reached Poitiers, Russia mobilized for the defense of her little neighbor. Germany seized the occasion to issue Russia an ultimatum; two days later Germany and Russia were at war.

To the travelers all this seemed unreal, remote stage posturings. The town of Chartres, which they entered at four in the afternoon, was saturated with sunlight, and the cathedral was an extraordinary contrast of dark shadows below, pricked only by a few altar lights, and above "great sheets and showers of colour" from the amazing stained-glass windows. "All that a great cathedral can be, all the meanings it can express, all the tranquillising power it can breathe upon the soul," Edith wrote, ". . . the cathedral of Chartres gave us in that perfect hour." It was sunset when they drove into Paris. There was a pink-blue luster on the Seine; the Bois held the stillness of a summer evening; the currents of life flowed evenly and quietly along the avenues. At that moment in history, in Edith Wharton's sad imaginative words, "the great city, so made for peace and art and all humanest graces, seemed to lie by her river-side like a princess guarded by the watchful giant of the Eiffel Tower."

But next day and the day after, there was talk of nothing but war. As Edith made her way about the Faubourg she heard on all sides expressions of disbelief, amid a tenseness of waiting for the next edition of the newspapers and the latest announcement from Poincaré's government. "We don't want war," everyone told her, *"mais il faut que cela finisse!"* German arrogance must be put a stop to, but better by any means other than war. At Edith's dressmaker's the fitters looked pale and anxious. Elsewhere, however, there were signs of a developing mania. On July 31, Jean Jaurès—France's last spokesman for peace, however ineffective he had been of late—was shot and killed in a Paris café by a white-faced lunatic. The next afternoon, passing by the Ministry of the Navy, Edith saw a sign pinned to the wall: "General Mobilization."

Two more days passed before Germany formally declared war on France, giving as its reasons a series of nonexistent acts of hostility; by this time German forces had occupied the Grand Duchy of Luxembourg and were ready to sweep through Belgium en route to the long-planned conquest of France and the mastery of Europe. England, for reasons of its own, dawdled another twenty-four hours until German troops had actually crossed into Belgium before casting its lot against the Central Powers. Its official reason for acting was its long-standing guarantee of Belgian neutrality—a claim which caused the German chancellor to sputter indignantly that England was turning a limited conflict into a general war "for just a word—'neutrality'—just for a scrap of paper." By August 4 the Great War had begun.

In Paris there was no panic and no tumult, not even very much excitement; in Edith's view, only a staunch subdued readiness for whatever must come. On the evening of August 1 she dined with friends at a restaurant in the Rue Royale. Through the open window next to their table, she could see the first hordes of conscripts trudging stolidly down the street toward the railroad station, carrying their luggage and accompanied by families and friends. All were on foot: every taxi and bus and almost every private car had abruptly vanished from the streets, commandeered by the War Office. The crowd was orderly and restrained. Edith was impressed by the calm faces of the women, and observed with pleasure that many of them were holding small dogs. Inside the restaurant the red-coated Hungarian band played patriotic music, requiring the clientele to stand up between courses for the "Marseillaise," "God Save the King," and the Russian national anthem. From other restaurants toward the Madeleine, similar stirring music drifted down to them.

There was a sudden total change in the look and atmosphere of the city. Edith took rooms for a few days at the Hotel Crillon, and from its long balustraded terrace high above the Place de la Concorde she looked down upon an eerie spectacle. There was virtually no motor traffic, except for the occasional taxi darting across the Place taking military personnel to their appointed destinations. The Seine was emptied of its little steamers, and the canal boats were gone or lay motionless. Not a gardener stirred in the Tuileries. The movement of summer tourists had ceased entirely, after frantic and useless efforts and hours of waiting at Cook's travel agency. In the hotel itself the halls were porterless, the lifts immobile, the dining room without waiters. There was only the endless procession along the streets of *poilus*-to-be, joined, as the days went forward, by legions of volunteers from Italy and Rumania, and North and South America.

Then they were gone too, and the long stately avenues stretched away silently to "desert distances." Two-thirds of the shops in Paris were closed, their managers and salespeople caught up in the military machine. The street lights were dimmed at night. With the other remaining residents, Edith Wharton, now reinstalled in the Rue de Varenne, settled down to life controlled by martial law.

2

Looking back, half a year later, on the first days of the war, Edith found that they now struck her as curiously idealized and abstract. The tremendous sense of political and social unity; the abeyance, as she put it, of every small and mean preoccupation in the effort to serve *la patrie;* the "clearing of the moral air"— all this gave her the impression, in retrospect, of having been "reading a great poem on War rather than facing its realities." She had spoken of the "horrors" she had come back to from Spain, but she also confessed to finding the general scene thrillingly interesting. It seemed, for the moment, not the end of *la belle époque,* but its grandest hour.

Like all her friends, she was convinced that the war would be a short one. In this they were at one with the German and French high commands, each of which had a carefully worked-out plan which envisaged a swift and crushing victory over the enemy. Only a very few persons foresaw the length of the agony to come—Lord Grey, the British foreign secretary, staring down from his Whitehall window as the street lamps were being lit and murmuring: "The lamps are going out all over Europe; we shall not see them lit again in our lifetime"; Lord Kitchener, recalled as war minister, speaking candidly of his belief that the war would last a minimum of three years; the glum-spirited Helmuth von Moltke, German chief of staff, joining in the same opinion. In Paris there was the belief, put forward by Walter Berry in Edith's circle, that the German people would soon revolt and a provisional government would come to power and sue at once for peace. News from the battle areas in August 1914 was sparse, contradictory, and often inaccurate; but what was touted as French successes in Alsace seemed to bolster these expectancies.

Even so, Edith wasted no time in finding herself a useful wartime occupation. The fashionable ladies in the Faubourg had taken to sewing garments for the troops: an admirable activity which had the immediate effect of throwing the local seamstresses out of work. Government policy allotted military allowances only to persons with near relatives at the front, something that did not hold true for many of the newly unemployed. Within a fortnight of the outbreak of hostilities Edith had established an *ouvroir* (workroom) in the Rue de l'Université, a few blocks from her apartment, and had admitted several dozen seamstresses.

Eventually the *ouvroir* employed up to a hundred women at a time, drawn from all over the city. Each woman was given a franc and a half a day, free lunch and medical attention, and a supply of coal in the winter. Seamstresses could stay for two or three months, and after an interval could apply for readmission. A main part of Edith's task was to procure sizable work orders—of lingerie, dresses, handkerchiefs, stockings, children's clothes—through her far-ranging connections in France and America. For this and all other later enterprises, Mary Cadwalader Jones was Edith's irreplaceable representative in the United States. There was also the problem of fund raising: Edith soon acquired two thousand dollars, enough to get on with, and appointed an able-seeming woman as manager of the workroom.

She had her own money troubles, and perhaps thought of her parents' stories about their financial anxieties in Paris during the revolution of 1848. She sent cables to bankers in America, but even cables had to be censored by the police; there was no guarantee of their arriving, and if they did the reply was likely to be: "Impossible at present. Making every effort." But Walter Berry, exploiting his position as president of the American Chamber of Commerce in Paris, was able to get his hands on sums large enough to tide her over, and he acted as banker for a good many other Americans in the city.

Edith was luckier and more comfortable than most, and she knew it. She was well looked after by three devoted women, and the household staff was otherwise in good repair. Frederic, the footman who had replaced Henri, was lent to Henry James, whose man-of-all-work, Burgess, had been called up, but Henri himself was due back from I Tatti for a stint with Mme. Wharton while waiting for conscription. There were also unexpected attractions to Paris. Amid all the restrictions of life, there was the freedom of walking the beautiful trafficless summer streets. And the silence, particularly in the evening, was incredible; the Faubourg was as hushed and still as the African desert. Edith could hear a hoofbeat half a mile off, and the tread of the policeman guarding an embassy across the way sounded like pistol shots. She was awakened one morning by what seemed a rattle of noise in her very room: it turned out to be a low-voiced exchange of *Bon jour* in the street below.

She saw no reason, however, for abandoning the stay in the English countryside, and White was already at Stocks organizing matters. Even so short and familiar a trip had become a laborious affair. After an interval, there were now occasional seats for civilians on trains going out of Paris, but one had to walk the long way to the Gare du Nord and undergo endless delays before tickets were issued. The tickets then had to be visaed by the police, and this meant climbing dark stairways and (something peculiarly repellent to Edith Wharton) being jostled by swarms of perspiring fellow aliens. For once, Edith had to do these chores herself, as she had had to secure her own identification papers, a new requirement for foreign residents, by interminable visits to the consulate, the chancery, and the police station.

Edith and her attendants managed to cross to England toward the end of August, and Berry, using all his considerable influence, succeeded in having the car shipped over; in a few days he came himself. Stocks was the loveliest kind of English country home, and Edith perhaps enjoyed occupying and paying for the residence of a woman who was in some sense her literary and social rival. But the place felt cut off and lonely at this historic moment, and Edith was annoyed to find that, inconceivably, it had no telephone. For a day or two she meditated turning part of the house into a convalescent home for wounded soldiers; but giving that up, she moved instead, bag and baggage, to Mrs. Ward's London house at 25 Grosvenor Place, which had also been turned over to her.

Looking in at Windsor, she found Howard Sturgis in an intensely nervous state and unwilling to have the war so much as mentioned in his presence. At Lamb House, on the contrary, she and Berry were delighted to discover a new and "martial-truculent" Henry James. James had been much quicker than she to make out the scope of the disaster and what it appallingly revealed about the hidden processes of recent history (this, he wrote Sturgis as early as August 4, was what all "the treacherous years" of apparent progress toward decency and enlightenment had in actuality been leading to). He sought to bring home to her that the war threatened nothing less, in his phrase, than "the crash of civilization." But the daily bulletins in the latter days of August and early September were almost enough to persuade Edith of that.

Liège in Belgium had fallen by mid-August, despite the extraordinary valor of the Belgian troops and the exemplary courage of King Albert; on August 25 the Germans put to the torch the medieval city of Louvain and its world-famous library as a warning to the world of what resisters might expect. During the third week in August the French experienced one disaster after another and suffered 140,000 casualties; before the month was over a million German soldiers had entered France. A sizable portion of the country was in German hands by September 5, and the armies of General von Kluck were scarcely an hour's drive from Paris. For the first time there was alarm, even panic, in the city; on September 2 the French government had crept away from Paris in the dark and made for Bordeaux. The old Schlieffen plan was, apparently, being executed to perfection; Germany was within a day or two of winning the war.

Edith was at Stocks while the Battle of the Marne, probably the most crucial of the great turning points in the war, was waged between September 6 and 12. It was General J. J. C. Joffre, the French commander in chief, who made the decision to make a stand along the river and who forcibly persuaded the vacillating Sir John French, the British commander, to risk his relatively small expeditionary force in the action. Joffre commanded the battle with a sort of stolid brilliance; the British advanced cautiously into a suddenly perceived gap between the German First and Second Armies. General Joseph Simon Gallieni, the distinguished and resolute military governor of Paris, sent six hundred taxicabs racing to the front carrying six thousand troops. The German armies faltered, retreated, and fell back to a static position on the Aisne River. The possibility of a *Blitzkrieg* defeat of the Allies in France was over once and for all; yet the Allies had not won a victory sufficient to push forward decisively against the foe. There lay ahead years of indescribably costly trench warfare.

Watching these epochal events from the other side of the channel, Edith Wharton sought desperately to get back to France. The French Embassy in London, in the person of her friend Paul Cambon, the ambassador, provided the necessary papers but could guarantee no transport for her party. The news from the little *ouvroir* was aggravating as well: the manager Edith had left in charge had vanished, taking with her the two thousand dollars; things were pretty much at a standstill. After what seemed an eternity, places were found on trains and boat, and just before the end of September, Edith sank down again, exhausted, in the Rue de Varenne.

3

Edith's life in wartime Paris now really began, and there was to be a great deal less soaring and swooping. She speedily tracked down the defaulting manager of the *ouvroir* and recovered the money; a Mlle. Renée Landormy, the niece of a well-known music critic, took over the supervision of the workroom, and Zezette du Bos came in to help. Edith, attending to administrative details and to the search for funds and work orders, kept at the job from early morning until dinner time. To Berenson she passed on her new axiom: "It takes a great deal more time to do good than to have fun."

But Paris had recovered its poise and its vitality after the panic of early September; most of the "fluffy fuzzy people," in Edith's phrase, had disappeared, and only the hard-working remained. There were even occasions for fun: on the last day of September, Fullerton, Berry, and Victor Bérard dined at Edith's apartment, "and we laughed till 11:30." Fullerton, it might be said, was probably the least surprised American in Paris when war broke out. As long before as 1906, in a report to his Harvard class secretary, he had spoken ominously of the threat to European peace posed by the policy and character of the German emperor, and said that "some big and terrible things are shortly to be feared."

Edith ventured to the Ritz one January evening to dine with Mrs. Waldorf Astor and Lady Adela Essex and found the experience "spectral." Only four other tables were occupied, and a single ghostly waiter in a long apron shuffled up and down the "empty vistas" of the chill dining room. All her old dislike of the Ritz returned, and it only deepened when, some time later, the hotel came back to life as the popular and crowded meeting place for Allied officers. "I can't stand that scene of khaki and champagne," she told Henry James. One of her complaints about Walter Berry was that he spent too much time there, and when James asked guardedly whether there was some sort of little rift between them, she replied: "It is not a little rift but a little ritz that's between us just now."

She was in fact undergoing a temporary disenchantment with Berry. In December he made a short tour of Germany (as American civilians were of course still able to do), going as far as Berlin; his account of the trip struck Edith as flat and imperceptive. "I can't *see* anything he has seen," she wrote Berenson. "Somehow his imagination seems much less sensitive than it used to be, and what I call (in novel-writing) 'the illuminating incident' doesn't seem to have caught his attention."

The truth was that, under the strain of wartime living, Edith was feeling a certain dissatisfaction with most members of her group, and she admitted to loneliness. Bourget, she said to Berenson in a roundup of her friends, was dear and sensible and solid, but he was also whimsical, fanatical, and foolish. Abbé Mugnier was pleasant but somehow inadequate—she was evidently unaware that he spent much of his time at the railroad stations hearing the last-minute confessions of French soldiers heading for the front lines. Blanche was lucid but depressing, and Léon Bélogou was caught up in a love affair that did not in the least become him. As to Fullerton, she remarked to James a little later that "Morton . . . has completely abandoned me." Even when Anna Bahlmann underwent an operation for cancer, Fullerton failed to telephone for news of her or of Edith herself. "He will turn up again when I can be of use to him," she said with acid shrewdness. *"Enfin!"*

Nonetheless, she clung more than ever to her circle, and to those members of it who were not on the immediate scene. Never in her life had she been more profoundly conscious of the importance of her community of friends—those persons who shared one another's values, habits of perception, and, now, memories of better days. Her little community, she believed, was a human embodiment of what was at stake in the great war. She shared, it seems, the sentiment of Justice Holmes, who once declared that civilization amounted to no more than two thousand persons. Edith Wharton may have reckoned it at even fewer; in any case, the fate of civilized society was, for her, genuinely implicated in the survival of her own group.

"*My* sense," she wrote Lapsley in November 1914, "is completely of living again in the year 1000, with the last trump imminent." The Battle of the Marne had taught her how woefully wrong she had been in her estimate of the nature and duration of the conflict, and she dissociated herself from all those who did not share her apocalyptic vision and who continued to "serve up the old optimistic sugar plums of last August." She compared them to "left-over dead flies shaken out of a summer hotel window curtain. We shall never lodge in *that* summer hotel again." So there was a special poignance and urgency in her invitation to Lapsley to come to Paris for a visit:

It's a time when people who are fond of each other ought to try to be together when they can. . . . Do come, my dear, and let us warm both hands a little at the good fire of our old affection for each other.

Edith's conviction that it was to be a long and bitter struggle was reinforced by some of Berry's findings (he too had changed his mind): that most Germans thought the war had been forced upon them by the British, and that, far from there being an incipient revolt in the ranks, there were fresh and eagerly pugnacious troops everywhere. Reappraising the situation, Edith looked about for an occupation of greater range and more widespread usefulness than her little *ouvroir*.

She found one almost immediately in what developed into an enormous effort to provide succor for the civilian refugees who straggled into the city, driven from their homes during the Battle of the Marne, and even more in the savage fighting in October around Ypres—the town in Flanders, which the British Tommies, who fought so valiantly there until four-fifths of the first British Expeditionary Force had been killed, called "Wipers." They began to arrive in great waves, utterly destitute, deafened by the bombardments and dazed with the horrors they had seen and undergone. They slept on benches in the street and on straw in the railroad stations; by day they wandered helplessly about—some of them, the Flemish, unable to speak French—looking with little success for food and shelter. They brought with them stories that froze the blood and wrenched the heart, stories they mumbled out between appeals for help while their children stared ahead with vacant eyes.

Edith discussed this ghastly business with French friends who were forming a rescue committee called the Foyer Franco-Belge. She then set about creating her own group, and for this, after a short time, the Foyer served as a reception headquarters, classifying the refugees according to their needs and recommending the most desperate among them to the American center. Between them, as of the end of October, the two groups had no more than five hundred dollars and a few bits of broken furniture. But several houses were put at Edith's disposal by wealthy and generous associates, and the immense work got under way.

In her entirely unaccustomed role as administrator—of what became known as the American Hostels for Refugees—Edith Wharton displayed something amounting to organizational genius. Anna Bahlmann said about her, wonderingly, that her energies went in twenty directions at once, and so they did; but in supervising the expanding hostels, and despite lapses, confusions, and disappointments, she showed a remarkable flair at coordination.

The first requirement, obviously, was lodging and food. The building in the Rue Brochant supplied free furnished rooms for families with seven or more children and for husbandless women with children; the place on the Avenue Félix-Faure rented housing to some two hundred refugees at the equivalent of

$1.50 a month per room, with light, heat, and washing included; the large apartment house in the Rue de la Quintinie took in as many more. In the Rue Taitbout, meals were distributed at nominal prices to nearly six hundred persons a day.

But these were only a portion of the proliferating enterprise. Almost all the refugees were sick, some of them perilously so, from hunger, fatigue, and horror, and in the Rue Taitbout, Edith also set up a free clinic and dispensary, where two skilled Parisian doctors gave their services free of charge and two trained nurses were in daily attendance. The refugees arrived with nothing but the rags on their backs: Edith opened a clothing depot in the Rue Boissy d' Anglas, and in response to her appeal clothes and boots of all sizes and description began to flow in from France and America. At the same time, she had a workroom fitted up, and here some sixty women worked to turn out clothes for the depot, also taking modestly profitable orders from the hospitals. A grocery-distribution point came into existence in the Rue Pierre Charron, thanks largely to Edith's accommodating new friend the Comtesse René de Béarn; refugees showing food tickets could purchase groceries here at a forty percent discount. And in the cold season Edith saw to the delivery of more than two thousand fifty-kilo bags of coal.

There were other matters to be considered. The children of the seamstresses and other workers had to be looked after, so Edith brought into being a day nursery in the Rue Boissy d'Anglas house, a big pleasant room opening onto a court where the young people could play. Singing classes were held there, and lessons in sewing and English. Having thus, with a tremendous outburst of energy, organized a vast apparatus for the refugees' immediate needs, Edith began to think about their future. The refugees, shattered by having their homes destroyed or overrun, were further demoralized by weeks of dreary idleness and a sense of hopelessness about what lay ahead. Amid the most trying of circumstances, Edith started an employment agency, and while waiting to find work, large numbers of men and women were given small sums of money to keep them going.

When, near the end of 1915, the American Hostels celebrated their first birthday, Edith could announce the following results: 9,330 refugees had been assisted during the year, 3,000 of them on a permanent basis; 235,000 meals had been served, and 48,000 garments handed out; 7,700 persons had received medical care; jobs had been found for 3,400. The whole undertaking had cost $82,000 in the first year, and monthly expenses ran to $6,000. To Sara Norton, Edith reported with exhausted pride that she had collected more than $100,000 in the preceding twelve months.

To carry out the complex work of the hostels, with their units dotted all across the city, Edith created a network of interlocking committees, no less than nine in Paris, and eventually three more in New York (Minnie Jones, chairman), Philadelphia, and Boston. The seventeen-member Franco-American General

Committee, of which Edith herself was chairman, included Walter Berry, Edith's lawyer friend Boccon-Gibbod, Charles du Bos, and Matilda Gay. An unexpected addition to this assembly was André Gide, whom Edith now met for the first time. She described the most esteemed writer and editor of the younger generation as "a man of quivering sensibilities" who "invents grievances when he can't find them ready made. Luckily he is so charming that one ends up by not minding."

Elizabeth Cameron, back in Paris for a long stay, served on the Investigating Committee and worked long hours at the important task of determining the status and needs of individual refugee families. Another member of the General Committee whom Edith had come to know recently was the beautiful and fashionable Mildred Bliss, formerly of New York—"Perfect Bliss," as Berenson and others of her admirers sometimes called her. She was younger than Edith and of a younger disposition, with an elegantly modernist side to her; their work forced them to see much of each other, and they would never lose touch, but their friendship was not without strain. Mildred's husband, Robert Woods Bliss, was a capable and cultivated member of the American diplomatic service, who had been secretary of the Embassy in Paris since 1912.

The *sine qua non* for the running of the American Hostels was Elisina Royall Tyler, another young woman of authentic beauty—she must have been one of the best-looking women in Paris—who became Edith's acknowledged aide-de-camp (especially by those who saw Edith Wharton less as a chairman than as a commanding general) during the war and for the rest of Edith's life.

Elisina Palamadessi di Castelvecchio had been born in Florence, the daughter of Conte and Contessa di Castelvecchio. The title had been created by Emperor Napoleon III for the illegitimate son of Louis Napoleon, the ruler of Holland; in one portrait of her, Elisina markedly resembled Laetizia Ramolini, the Tuscan mother of Napoleon Bonaparte. Elisina had been married for some years to Grant Richards, an English publisher and sometime novelist. Elisina had three children by Grant Richards, but in 1910 she separated from him and married Royall Tyler, already, in his late twenties, an accomplished scholar and art historian, specializing in Spanish studies. He was a descendant of the Royall Tyler who, with *The Contrast* in 1787, became the first significant American playwright.

"Peter" Tyler, as his intimates called him, was an invariably well-dressed, stocky man of middle height, with a thrust of jaw that suggested both strength and sensitivity; his presence was a vital one—the atmosphere grew subtly changed the moment he entered the room. Berenson, who doted on him from the instant Edith introduced them to each other, spoke of Tyler as "the most attractive and finished and cultivated person of his age I've met for a long time . . . perfectly genuine and very lovable, a real scholar and a man of taste." Edith would have agreed with every word.

The Tylers, with their infant son, Bill, had not been long in Paris before Elisina—in the spring of 1912, and perhaps at the suggestion of their mutual friend John Hugh Smith—began to call on Mrs. Wharton. In Edith's word of twenty-five years later, the two women "clicked," mysteriously and almost completely, from the outset. This quickly aroused the jealousy and suspicion of Edith's other friends, few of whom looked upon Mrs. Tyler with the same admiring regard as did Edith. Tall, slender, and handsomely dressed, with a classically lovely Florentine face, Elisina was a strong-minded and aggressive woman. But for the work of the hostels, her talents were exactly what Edith stood in need of: great stamina; a positive enjoyment and mastery of committee work; a total command of English and French, as well as Italian; an ability to subordinate her own potent personality to Edith's sufficiently for the large tasks at hand. Edith, addressing her as a "good angel," called her in early in the game, and Elisina became vice-chairman and frequently acting chairman of the General Committee. She was also in charge of housing and worked for the day nursery and the workroom. As time went on, indeed, it was Elisina who oversaw the actual workings of the apparatus, while Edith spent more and more time on fund raising.

Edith Wharton's dedicated work for the American Hostels revealed again that Whitman side of her which had expressed itself in the poem "Terminus": the periodically overflowing compassion for the wretched of the earth—in the present case, for the victimized, the uprooted, the sick and the shattered. She probably thought of Walt Whitman walking the Washington hospitals during the Civil War, bringing solace to the wounded, writing their letters, holding up the dying ones in his arms. A decade later, in her novella *The Spark*, she would offer a quirky image of Whitman the wartime healer.

Not that she displayed any great show of emotion, much less any earnest pride. On the contrary, what won her new affection from her friends was that she took herself lightly in her new role: however forceful she might be as an organizer and supervisor, she struck no one as officious or as a busy do-gooder. Percy Lubbock, who came for a visit in December and watched her dashing from one *maison* to another, holding conferences, and making endless phone calls, told her he could forgive her zealous activities because she so obviously hated what she was doing.

Such, anyhow, was Edith's exaggerated and self-derisive report to Berenson; and in her only work of fiction to come out of the experience, "The Refugees," she made a gentle mockery of it all. In the short story, Charlie Durand, an American professor of languages, is swept from France to England with a horde of refugees in September 1914, and at Charing Cross in London is mistaken for one of the unfortunate fugitives by a timid spinster who carries him off to her baronial home in the country. The collecting and care of refugees has become the fashionable sport with the English gentry, and seeing his hostess's air of shy triumph in having gathered one for herself, Durand plays up and lets her show him about as a prize possession.

4

By February 1915 the face of Paris had again changed. It was still deathly quiet at night, and the streets were so dimly and sparsely lit that groping her way back through the winter fog to 53 Rue de Varenne from dinner or a visit to a hostel was for Edith an adventure not lacking in romance. But by day there were boats once more on the river, taxis could occasionally be found, and there were even a few private cars in the streets, while the additional and incessantly rushing military traffic made life even more perilous than usual for the Paris *piéton.* Many shops had reopened, including the big department stores, and Edith began to indulge herself, after many months, in the joy of shopping—shopping, as she carefully explained, rather than mere buying; "the voluptuousness of acquiring things one might do without."

Though the war had receded geographically from Paris, a new element in the population, the wounded, was a steady reminder of it. Edith watched the limping figures and pale bandaged heads on the pavements, in passing carriages, at concerts. Most of them were very young, and Edith was stirred by the expression on their faces: grave, calm, meditative, and to her vision "strangely purified and matured," as though what they had undergone had burned them "down to the bare bones of character."

Surveying them, Edith felt as her one consoling thought that "the beastly horror *had* to be gone through, for some mysterious cosmic reason of ripening and rotting." The crash had perhaps come at a time that found the Allied nations "*morally* ready." She only wished she could include the United States, she said to Lapsley,

but it sticks in my innards that the great peace-treaty-Hague-convention protagonist shouldn't rise in its millions to protest the violation of the treaties she has always been clamouring for. We *are* smug just now, aren't we?

She deplored the posture of neutrality taken by the President of the United States (who had urged "neutrality in fact as well as in name") and by Pope Benedict. She understood that each sought to play a critical peace-making role in world affairs as a result of the stance, but she spoke venomously to Berenson about "two such Panteloons as Wilson and Benedict the Last (I hope)" holding the threads of destiny.

She remarked to Berenson that the sword Italy had been threatening to draw must have gotten stuck in the scabbard, though perhaps the *"valore Italiano"* might be about to boil over again. She wrote scathingly about the pro-German position of his neighbor, the brilliant Spanish-born Countess Serristori, whom Edith had long and vigorously disliked.

Toward the end of February, Edith and Walter Berry made a visit to the front lines in the Argonne, east of Paris, to deliver supplies to the hospital units and to examine conditions and needs. Driving out of the city with its atmosphere of workaday security, she was startled to find signs of the ongoing war within twenty miles: the desolate countryside, the abandoned farms, the empty open doorways. Beyond Meaux she came upon more positive signs—the sentry posts where permits had to be looked at; the constant movement of military trucks, staff cars, motorcycles carrying dispatch riders; columns of "French 75's" being hauled up the hillside.

At Châlons, on the road to Verdun, Edith and Berry took lunch in the crowded restaurant of the Hotel Mère-Dieu, the army headquarters, squeezed in between great numbers of officers and men. Puzzling out the variety of uniforms and studying the different types of people, Edith thought that they all seemed quietly tough and determined, and began to understand why the French said of themselves (as Churchill and de Gaulle would again proclaim in the Second World War): *"La France est une nation guerrière."* Outside the hotel she watched the long lines of *éclopés:* the unwounded, but battered and half-paralyzed with fatigue, on their way by the thousands to rest and rehabilitation centers.

Northeast of Châlons they passed a series of villages almost totally destroyed during the fighting in September, and in Clermont-en-Argonne they gazed across the valley at an actual battle. The war in Europe had by this time settled into a virtual deadlock, each side, refusing to accept the fact, launching a series of militarily wrongheaded and hopeless frontal assaults on nearly unassailable positions. The network of trenches rendered the preliminary artillery barrages almost useless, and the troops advancing behind them were simply mowed down by the enemy guns. The British lost 60,000 men at Ypres in March; six months later in a combined attack that gained the British nothing and the French eight miles, the British (at Loos) and the French (in Champagne) lost a quarter of a million men between them, while managing to slaughter about 150,000 Germans.

But the tactic of nibbling away, at whatever cost, at the enemy forces had become the accepted procedure: and it was just such an effort, on a minute scale, that Edith and Berry witnessed from a terrace full of soldiers and nuns, looking through binoculars provided by the gallant Sister Gabrielle Rosnet. There was the rush of French infantry up the slope and into the "fire-tongued wood," the drift of French gunsmoke from below, and from the crest along the skyline where the little village of Vauqois was perched, the red streaks and white puffs of German artillery. Vauqois, which had been taken in late September, was nearly impregnable, but that afternoon the French gained the ridge and reoccupied part of the village. And several hundred new casualties were delivered to Sœur Rosnet's care.

Edith thought the spectacle awe-inspiring, and that she had never been closer to history in the making. But her mission was a medical one, and she drove on with Berry to Verdun, where there were fourteen hospital units within the old walls of the half-destroyed town. All were badly overcrowded, and the arrangements were primitive. The great need everywhere, she was told, was blankets and underclothes; the wounded came in encrusted with frozen mud, not having been able to wash or change for weeks.

Next day, while the boom of cannonading filled the air, they made their way through a snowstorm to sectors north and south of Verdun, and by nightfall they were back in Châlons. A new contingent of troops had arrived, and there was not a bed or even a sofa in the lounge of the Hotel Mère-Dieu. Headquarters, which could offer no alternative, suggested giving them a pass to return to Paris, but Edith had no stomach for a drive of 125 miles through the icy dark, with every chance of being turned back en route too late for reentry into Châlons.

Walking uncertainly along the street, Edith ran into Jean-Louis Vaudroyer, a gifted and sophisticated young writer, a friend of Proust's and a frequent visitor to the Rue de Varenne, who was now a member of the headquarters staff. Vaudroyer knew of lodgings to be had nearby, and gave directions for finding them through the maze of dark streets around the cathedral. As they separated, he whispered the password for the night: "Jena." Edith felt a sort of slippage in time at thus being rescued in the heart of the war zone by a man who used to come to dinner and talk about new books and plays.

Edith Wharton made several other visits to the battle areas in the course of the next six months, and in the dispatches she wrote about them (for New York newspapers and for *Scribner's*) she appeared in still another role—that of journalist, a practitioner of what, fifty years later, would be called the "new journalism." Her articles—they were later collected in *Fighting France*, one of the best of her volumes of nonfiction—were colorful and personal in the now contemporary manner, with character portraits and little dramatized scenes, but with less intrusion of the ego than we have recently become used to, and no rhetorical capering.

At the start of summer Edith spent a number of days driving in Belgium, and at St. Omer and Cassel she had her first view of the British forces: cavalry, artillery, infantry, lancers, sappers and miners, trench diggers—a river of war, Edith thought, winding its way north. The hotel in the little medieval hilltop town of Cassel swarmed with khaki-clad tea drinkers, and at improvised camps along the road there was the surprisingly cheery spectacle of shirts drying on elder bushes, men polishing their boots and rubbing down their horses, others communicating mysteriously with young girls and children. There was a positive "gayety of war," and the scene led Edith to reflect: "It is one of the most detestable things about war that everything connected with it, except the death and ruin that result, is such a heightening of life, so visually stimulating and absorbing." She remembered the phrase that recurs in *War and Peace:* "It was gay and terrible."

5

The Belgian tour, which included a conference with Queen Elizabeth of the Belgians at La Panne, was partly in connection with still another enterprise—in addition to the *ouvroir* and the hostels—which Edith had started upon the previous April. When the heavy shelling of Belgium began, among the worst victims were untold numbers of children, who were belatedly picked up in the cellars of wrecked houses and from the rubble in the streets, on abandoned farms and in burned-out villages. Trainloads of them arrived in Paris, accompanied by Sisters of Charity and little huddles of aged and infirm people left behind by the fleeing civilians. The Belgian Ministry of the Interior, knowing of Mme. Wharton's other work with refugees, cabled one morning to ask if she could receive sixty children within the next forty-eight hours.

Mme. Wharton could; she was on the phone at once and quickly located an empty and serviceable schoolhouse in Sèvres, just outside the city. The children were delivered—the first group were all girls—and installed. Like the older refugees, they arrived sick with privation and filth, and stupid with terror: one child had been rescued from a farm where she had been left alone without food for five days; two other girls were lifted from the arms of their dead father. They were bathed, clothed and fed, and turned out into the garden to play. The Sèvres experiment was so successful that the Belgian government asked if Mme. Wharton could take in another six hundred.

The Children of Flanders Rescue Committee, which was eventually running an organization almost as large as that of the American Hostels, was primarily a Wharton-Tyler affair. Boccon-Gibbod faithfully helped out, and so did the Walter Gays and eight or nine others; but Edith was president, Elisina Tyler vice-president, and Royall Tyler secretary and treasurer. Before the year was out there were six homes in operation, in and around Paris and as far away as Arromanches, on the Normandy coast across the bay from Le Havre. It was to the latter place that the most sickly of the children, some of them with tuberculosis of the bone, were sent, eighty at a time, for a period of three months.

Once again, Edith and Elisina took thought for the whole of their wards' lives. Schools in lacemaking were established for the older girls at Sèvres and St. Ouen, and classes in French were started for those children who spoke only Flemish. Edith sought funds to open a school in industrial training for the boys and, looking ahead, further money to supply the children with clothing and small sums when they returned to their ravaged country. By the end of 1915 the Rescue Committee had taken care of 900 persons, 750 of them children.

Her work with the children of Flanders was, Edith declared in a brochure, "my prettiest and showiest and altogether most appealing charity"; any view of her attitude to the young, which has often been adjudged severe and uncomprehending, must be modified in the light of it. To be sure, it was easier to raise money for these bewildered waifs than for the adult refugees (some of whom, Edith had to admit, were hard to help and morosely unappreciative of anything done for them). But her heart was undoubtedly engaged by the undertaking. She never forgot the day when, with some friends, she was standing amid the fine old trees of the park at the Villa Bethanie in Montsoult: the gates opened and in came a procession of crippled old men, a dozen Sisters of Charity with their white caps, and about ninety small boys, each with a little bundle on his back. The old folk were too weary and confused to know where they were, and the nuns were weeping from fatigue and homesickness. But the grave-faced boys took in the rose borders, the haycocks, and the hospitable-looking mansion and broke spontaneously into the Belgian national anthem.

The range of Edith Wharton's activity in 1915 staggers the mind. She continued to oversee the *ouvroir*, the complex system of American Hostels, and the extensive new apparatus for the Flemish children, and was growing concerned, and thinking what practical steps might be taken, about the widespread tuberculosis among both the military and civilians. By midsummer she had made five tours of the front lines from Dunkirk to Belfort (in Alsace) and had written a series of journalistic articles which, when collected, amounted to a 250-page book. She arranged two benefit concerts at 53 Rue de Varenne by Vincent d'Indy, the distinguished sixty-four-year-old composer and disciple of César Franck, promoted other concerts in the United States, and put together rummage sales and fund-raising art exhibitions. She had to keep busy every minute, Edith declared; otherwise, her awareness of the horror would be too much for her.

When Mary Berenson arrived for a few days in mid-July, she found Edith exceedingly tired, gloomy about the war—which she was beginning to believe would never end—and impatient with the sputtering British campaign in the Dardanelles, where her peacetime friend Sir Ian Hamilton was directing the proceedings on land. It was during this visit that Mary Berenson yielded to Edith at last, in almost total admiration and in growing affection. Only a few days before, Mary had spoken with customary disdain about Edith's eloquent article in *Scribner's* on "The Look of Paris": "singularly trivial," though with some good *little* points. Now she saw Edith in an entirely new way.

"I can't tell thee how many Committees she is chairman of," she wrote her husband, "and where she is chairman she does all." Echoing Percy Lubbock's reaction, she added that Edith "speaks less of her good works than anyone I know," and when she did refer to them she "turns them off laughingly." Mary also found herself companionably and amusedly eye to eye with Edith on various

human phenomena. There arrived for dinner one evening Nettie Johnstone, the
wife of Sir Alan Johnstone, a British diplomat, and the sister of Gifford Pinchot,
chief forester of the United States under President Roosevelt. "Lady Johnstone,"
Mary told Berenson, "was full of a Field Hospital she has got some man in a soft
moment (probably in bed, Edith said) to give her for the front," and as she
postured on about it, she made what the two women thought between themselves
was a nearly indecent spectacle.

Edith struck Mary as nearly at the end of her tether and desperately in need
of intelligent secretarial help. Anna Bahlmann was lying sick in America, and
Edith had been trying to make do with a Miss Dolly Herbert, lent her, apparently,
by Lady Sybil Cutting; but Dolly was a frail, pathetic, and only minimally
competent young woman, much occupied with an invalid mother. Mary Berenson suggested that Geoffrey Scott would make an ideal administrative secretary,
if her husband could do without him. But it would be a number of months before
Scott became available.

"All the Belgians in Paris are feeding out of Edith's hands," Walter Berry
remarked to Berenson; "she's half a wreck but keeps on *quand même.*" And
quand même, she threw herself into still further undertakings. The most demanding of these found her shifting roles, in the summer of 1915, from journalism to
editing.

The work in question was a volume called *The Book of the Homeless,* which
was given simultaneous October publication by Scribners in New York and
Macmillan in London. It contained prose, poetry, musical scores, and illustrations
of several kinds, all contributed to the volume at Edith's solicitation. The proceeds went to the American Hostels and the Children of Flanders Rescue Committee.

The book opened with a tribute from Marshal Joffre, written on August 18
from the headquarters of the Commander in Chief of the Armies of the French
Republic:

The United States of America have never forgotten that the first page of the history
of their independence was partly written in French blood. Inexhaustibly generous and
profoundly sympathetic, these same United States now bring aid and solace to France in
the hour of her struggle for liberty.

Theodore Roosevelt followed with a ringing declaration that it was "not only a
pleasure but a duty to write the introduction that Mrs. Wharton requests," and
that "we owe to Mrs. Wharton all the assistance we can give. We owe this
assistance to the good name of America, and above all for the cause of humanity
we owe it to the children, the women and the old men who have suffered such
dreadful wrong for absolutely no fault of theirs."

There were an array of poems, most of them new, among others by Rupert

Brooke (who had by now fulfilled his poetic prediction of death), Paul Claudel, Cocteau, Robert Grant, Howells, Anna de Noailles, Edmond Rostand, George Santayana (a serene lament for "The Undergraduate Killed in Battle"), Barrett Wendell, and Edith Wharton herself. Thomas Hardy sent in what Edith called a "jolly malediction," a three-stanza work addressed to Germany as "Instigator of the Ruin." William Butler Yeats composed a crisp statement of the poet's credo in wartime, "A Reason for Keeping Silent":

> I think it better that at times like these
> We poets keep our mouths shut, for in truth
> We have no gift to set a statesman right;
> He's had enough of meddling who can please
> A young girl in the indolence of her youth
> Or an old man upon a winter's night.

Sarah Bernhardt and Eleanora Duse issued passionate outcries of distress for the occasion. Edith's policy was to ask the artists to provide pictures of other contributors: Blanche gave photographs of his portraits of Hardy, George Moore, and Stravinsky, Leon Bakst an unpublished crayon sketch of Cocteau, Sargent a replica of his painting of Henry James, and Theo van Rysselberghe portraits of Gide and d'Indy. Max Beerbohm lent a caricature, and Walter Gay a watercolor; Charles Dana Gibson sketched the Gibson Girl as "the Girl he left behind him"; Claude Monet sent in a lovely early pastel landscape and a crayon drawing. D'Indy contributed part of the score of his hybrid work *La Legende de saint Christophe* (oratorio, opera, symphony), and Stravinsky the entire score of *Souvenir d'une marche boche,* composed in September.

Prose was represented by writers from several countries: Joseph Conrad in a long piece called "Poland Revisited"; James in an intricate tribute to the British soldier touched off by a personal memory of the Civil War; Bourget, Maurice Barrès, Edmund Gosse, Maeterlinck, Paul Elmer More. Rudyard Kipling declined to contribute on the grounds that he felt unable to write during the war. Reporting this to Max Beerbohm, Edith Wharton remarked: "As Mr. James says, 'I kinder see' a portrait of Mr. Kipling explaining the fact to a French refugee who happened to have read his *France!!?*" She began to ask whether Beerbohm might persuade "dear Mr. Wells" to appear in Kipling's stead, but then added, "No, I'd rather not make any other suggestion, because no other could be as good."

Altogether it was a stupendous compilation, and an editorial triumph of sorts, Edith's work including translations of all the French poems except that by Rostand. Financially, however, it was rather a disappointment. Delays and unexpected expenses kept the amount going to the causes to about eight thousand dollars; a later auction of the manuscripts, and some of the art brought in seven thousand dollars more.

6

Edith's mid-August visit to the front lines took her to reconquered Alsace, far to the east of Paris. The climax of the tour was a long ascent of a mountain on muleback, to the point where the party came upon the marker of the former boundary between France and Germany: an insignificant stone with *D.* on one side and *F.* on the other. Colmar, in Germany, was clearly visible from the ridge, and beyond it the Rhine; Edith and the others sought a sheltered place to unpack their lunch baskets and listen in safety to the heaviest and closest firing Edith had heard yet. Many years later a chance encounter with an officer of the troop holding the sector brought back to Edith an image of herself on that summer morning: "an eager grotesque figure, bestriding a mule in the long tight skirts of 1915, and suddenly appearing, a prosaic Walkyrie laden with cigarettes, in the heart of the mountain fastness held by the famous *Chasseurs Alpins.*"

But it was time to get away from the overwhelming demands of the refugee work, and away too from the heart-sickening scenes of destruction. Early in October, Edith secured the necessary papers to cross to England and passed a somewhat aimless week in London, trying without much success to see something of Henry James. She found him "very preoccupied and not very well," and decided that it was "useless to 'sit around' here without being much use" to him.

The tone reflected the last vestige of Edith's grievance over an action James had taken that summer. On July 28, James had become a British citizen and had taken the oath of allegiance to King George V. The process was speeded by the Prime Minister, Herbert Asquith, abetted by the home secretary; the London *Times*, speaking for "all lovers of literature in this country," gravely applauded "the decision of this writer of genius." Much of the American reaction, however, was sharply critical, and Edith Wharton was among those who looked askance at the news. She shared to the full James's feelings about the war—she had been instructed by them; but she saw herself and her compatriots in France and England performing their tasks amid the horrors precisely *as* Americans, in some small way mitigating their country's failure to enter the conflict.

To Alfred Austin, at the end of July, she wrote: "You don't really expect me, as an American, to think Mr. James has done well to leave us? It has made me very sad. . . . We don't care much for defections." Taking note of the newspaper encomia, she observed to Geoffrey Scott, pointedly rewording the opening line of Browning's "The Lost Leader": "All for a mouthful of drivel he left us." But before September was out, her attitude was relaxing. She regretted James's "change of nationality," she told Austin, but it did not touch their friendship: "Such a man never *could* do anything that would affect one's devotion to him."

With Lapsley she went from London to Windsor, where Sturgis and Lubbock were waiting for them. Edith sat up most of the night talking with the other two, but Sturgis was in a sorry condition. His dear friend Wilfred Sheridan, Clare Frewen's husband, was believed (rightly) to have been killed in action, and Sturgis was numbed by the news.

"But which of us isn't shattered in some such way?" Edith asked. "And the only thing to do is to hug one's friends tight and do one's job."

Death was all around her. Among the first of Edith's Parisian friends to die in battle—Edith, with emotional exaggeration, spoke of him as "my best friend in France"—was Robert d'Humières, who had graced so many gatherings at the Rue de Varenne, at Rosa de Fitz-James's, and elsewhere. During his free moments the expert translator of Kipling and Conrad had been at work on a translation of *The Custom of the Country.* He had dined with Edith only a few weeks before to discuss this undertaking, had returned to the front, and was killed almost at once. And Henri had died. The little footman who used to burst into tears when his ears were boxed by White for some household lapse had arrived from Settignano ablaze with patriotic bellicosity. He insisted on being sent to the Dardanelles and fell there in late summer.

But other losses were due to the ravages not of war but of life. In July, Anna Bahlmann was operated on for cancer and her condition was discovered to be worse than expected. She lingered on for a few months, but then Edith was bereft of the woman who had served her with such single-minded fidelity—first as governess and language teacher, later as secretary and liaison with publishers— for more than forty years. "The only object I have had in life," Anna had told Mary Berenson during Mary's recent visit, "has been to help Edith and spare her trouble and fatigue."

The worst news of all, as the year 1915 drew to its close, was of the decline of Henry James. He had suffered a fairly bad heart attack not long after Edith's return from England in October, and from Minnie Jones, who had talked with James's doctor, Edith learned that the physician was not very reassuring. In early November, Theodora Bosanquet, James's invaluable and fine-spirited secretary, wrote Mrs. Wharton at James's request to say he was somewhat better. But on the morning of December 2, in Cheyne Walk, Chelsea, he had what his maid —who discovered him lying on the floor—described accurately as "a sort of stroke."

Edith was taking a rest at Costebelle, near Hyères, with Bourget and Robert Norton (on leave from his wartime duties with the Admiralty) when she heard the news by a cable from Mary Hunter. She at once said good-bye to James mentally and began to talk about him in the past tense. "His friendship was the pride and honour of my life," she wrote Lapsley. *"Plus ne m'est rien* after such a gift—except the memory of it." All her "blue distances," she felt, were forever shut out; but she echoed Lapsley's cry: "Thank God, *we never wasted him!* No, not a fraction of a second of him."

Sturgis wrote in a storm of distress. "Oh, it is going to be terrible to lose him. . . . I'm all dissolved in grief, Edith, and I know what you are feeling too. We both adored him." During January 1916, James had intervals of coherence and even wit, but there were intermittent bouts of delirium and hallucinations, and Edith could not bear the image which reached her of the "shadowy being" carried daily over to the window to watch the boats passing along the Thames. He died on the afternoon of February 28.

In her immediate sense of irreparable loss, Edith groped for a new mode of communion, in a shared memory of Henry James. "Dearest Gaillard," she wrote, "let us keep together all the closer now, we few who had him at his best." "Yes," she said a few days later, "we had a Henry that *no one* else knew; and it was *the* Henry we had!" The thought was consoling, but Edith was aware that some huge reality—in her own figure, some mountainous reality—had been abruptly removed from her world, leaving a space nothing could ever fill.

She was still struggling to adjust, six weeks later, when she learned from New York that Egerton Winthrop was dead: "My dear and good and wise friend whom everyone misunderstood but the few people near him." Their friendship, extending over three decades, had begun with counseling on scientific theory and French fiction and with many hours of companionable traveling; it had gone on to include personal advice as sympathetic and understanding as any Edith ever received.

For Edith Wharton, James and Winthrop were associated in their lives as in their deaths. "Between them," she told Berenson in a kind of settled grief, "they made up the sum of the best I have known in human nature." And to Sara Norton: "Though they seemed the poles apart, and one was a genius and the other simply an *'honnête homme'* in the fullest sense of the word, they were akin in all their deepest feelings and instincts, and their beauty of character was of the same kind." There was not an ounce of humbug in either, "and both their hearts were as tender as their judgment was wise."

Even as these recurring losses made her feel more than ever the need for the survivors to cling together in a saving remnant, so they heightened her Whitmanian compassion for the afflictions of others. "My heart is heavy with the sorrow of all my friends who are in mourning," she said, "or trembling for the lives of sons and husbands." She felt "the weight of the war as a horrible inescapable oppression."

20. Within the Tide

In the unfolding history of the Great War, 1916 was the year of two successive catastrophes, each agonizingly long drawn out. From early February until late June the German forces attacked east of Verdun, inching their way through heavy bombardment and vicious fighting to the last height guarding the city, before tidings from another sector of the front brought things to a halt. Insofar as the German aim was to "bleed the French white," the campaign was successful: nearly 300,000 Frenchmen were slaughtered. The Germans, however, lost nearly as many. At the beginning of July the British and French launched a counteroffensive along the Somme. During the first day's battle the British lost 60,000 men almost at a stroke; by mid-October the Germans had been pushed back about five miles and the British casualties had risen to 420,000. The French suffered another 200,000 losses, and the Germans more than 275,000. Nothing in the grander horrors of the Second World War equaled these devastations, in psychological effect and historical consequence. A European generation was being all but wiped out.

Against this most somber of backgrounds, Edith Wharton and her associates carried on their day-by-day rescue work. Edith had the sense, as she put it to Minnie Jones, of waking "in the middle of the night with a black abyss where one's heart ought to be." "The sadness of all things is beyond words," she wrote Sara Norton, "and hard work is the only escape from it." Keeping at it from breakfast to dinner virtually without break, Edith moved from office to workroom to dispensary; met with committees; wrote daily letters and cables to her representatives in America; drove into the country to inspect the various units— fourteen of them by the fall of 1916.

In the spring of that year Edith helped inaugurate a cure program for *les tuberculeux de guerre:* French soldiers who had contracted tuberculosis in the filth and cold of the forward trenches. It was, she thought, "the most vital thing that can be done in France now." To this, the fourth of Edith Wharton's rescue organizations, she could only allot enough of herself to act as vice-president. The president was Mrs. Edward Tuck, wife of a wealthy philanthropist and art collector whose Paris home was near Edith's. Walter Berry took time off from his duties with *les mutilés de guerre* (he had one thousand such under his care at the time) to become treasurer, and the secretary was a new young American friend of Edith's named Ronald Simmons.

After a year and a half the entire outfit—funds, property, and equipment amounting to about 1.7 million francs—was taken over by the International Red Cross. By that time Edith had turned her attention to civilians suffering from tuberculosis, which they either brought with them or, sleeping nine to an unheated attic room, contracted in Paris. With the quickly responsive help of generous American friends, Edith opened two "American Convalescent Homes" at Groslay, just north of Paris, and two more for children at Arromanches. The indefatigable Elisina Tyler took charge of these well-supplied centers.

There were, somehow, moments during the day for still further undertakings. In connivance with Elizabeth Cameron, Edith raised one hundred thousand dollars from a New York war relief committee to furnish a number of "Mobile Hospital Convoys"—ambulance groups—for the Red Cross. And, again working with Mrs. Cameron, she successfully solicited funds to be passed along through local agencies to the Russians and Serbians.

Edith had taken a great fancy to the Tylers' only child, Bill, now in his sixth year. Emotions in wartime, though intense, tend to be elemental, and in the spectacle of new life embodied in a lively little boy Edith seems to have found something to counter her unending experience of death.

William Royall Tyler had no little of his mother's headstrong character and was given to fierce, short-lived tantrums; he also had a breezy and sometimes impudent humor. He greeted a French surrealist painter just back from the front —so commonplace had death become—with the cheery question: *"Comment, tu n'es pas encore mort, toi?"* And once when he had sought to visit violence upon his nurse and had been warned by Elisina never again to raise his hand to a woman, he replied that he had not raised his hand, but his foot. These were not among the first qualities that endeared him to Mrs. Wharton, who was not patient with the unseemly precocities of the very young. But to Edith, young Bill was for the most part bright and affectionate and amusing, and he drew from her communications that displayed a warm appreciation of what children respond to.

Exchanging presents at Christmas (probably 1916), Edith wrote Bill in large capital letters: "I thank you for your beautiful white tree: and send you a kiss as big as my writing and a brave French soldier to guard your toys when you are out walking. Your friend Edith." For his next birthday Edith—eventually to be known by both Bill and his father as "Edoo"—sent him a stuffed parrot, apologizing for not being able to attend his party but providing a "little pet" as her replacement: "and as he is very handsome and beautifully dressed I am almost sure he will remind you of me."

As you know, parrots talk, and I have asked this one to give you my love and wish you a great many happy returns of the day.

If he does this prettily and politely you may give him a bit of cheese I am sending with him; but if he is noisy and vulgar, as I am told parrots sometimes are, you had better have him cooked and give him to Béguin [the Tylers' dog] to eat.

I want very much to see you again, and hope you will come to lunch with me. If your mother is very good perhaps you might bring her too.

There were other consolations and distractions. Geoffrey Scott came over from Settignano soon after the first of the year, and occupied the guest suite in the Rue de Varenne for almost four months. His professional assistance was invaluable; but he also provided the kind of intellectual companionship of which Edith stood in even greater need, and the evenings were lightened by what others would remember as the "flashing play" of their conversation. In February, Mary Berenson paid a visit. Quite reversing her tone of three years before, Mary, observing Edith's activities, remarked to her husband: "What a blessing she got rid of Teddy—he would have spoiled all this splendid work." She repeated her more recent judgment: "And she is so gay and un-pompous about it all, so ready not to speak of it, so keen about other things. I am amazed at her. Surely a very rare character."

"And this is what is so charming," ran another report about Mme. Wharton's enterprises. "This enormous and varied work is a silent work; this energy, this apostle's faith, are hidden beneath an air, hard to describe, of deceptive nonchalance, of smiling grace—an air of having really nothing to do in life and no other concern except to observe approvingly the good things being done by other people." Such was the conclusion of an article in *Figaro* on April 8, 1916, announcing that Edith Wharton, *femme de lettres*, had been made a Chevalier of the Legion of Honor.

The order was the highest that the President of France could dispose of, and it was the more exceptional, as the papers stressed, since the French government had just decreed that it would grant no more awards to civilians or foreigners until the end of the war. Edith Wharton was being recognized for "having given all possible assistance to refugees from those areas of France and Belgium invaded by the enemy." But the press, rehearsing her literary career, including the book *Fighting France* (which had been translated as *Voyages au front*), made much of the fact that it was "America's most celebrated writer" who had performed these great services. It was an occasion for an outburst of emotional journalistic enthusiasm for the United States, and for "our noble American friend."

Edith was overwhelmed by messages of congratulations—eighty-seven letters in a single day. Egerton Winthrop's cable from New York, "Congratulations with all my heart," were his last words to her; two days later he was dead. Abbé Mugnier cabled with characteristic finesse: "All the world will applaud this act of justice but nothing will equal the joy of those who have the honor and the good fortune to know you." Anna de Noailles sent around a letter of praise to the *"grand écrivain et à l'admirable, à l'efficace amie de France que vous êtes,"* and

Edith's old friend J. J. Jusserand wrote from the French Embassy in Washington to *"Madame la Chevalière"*: *"Brave, vous l'avez été, et habile, et de bon conseil et de bon cœur."* Maurice Barrès and the Abbé Bremond chimed in, along with several French generals; but Edith was perhaps most touched by a scroll designed for the event by the seamstresses in her *ouvroir*. It displayed two pillars and winding around them a ribbon listing her various *oeuvres*. "For a long time," the message ran, "we have been dreaming of your receiving a recompense worthy of your great devotion to our country." It offered her "warmest felicitations" and sent "deepest thanks"—"above all for your attachment to this *Ouvroir* which you love so much and which has kept us alive now for twenty months." It was signed by fifty-seven workwomen.

Two years later King Albert of Belgium presented Edith Wharton with the Medal of Queen Elizabeth. Edith's reaction to this was said to be one of impatience, even anger—probably because the decoration was a minor one after the Legion of Honor; though Elisina interpreted her friend's feelings as arising from the generous belief that Elisina herself should have been the one to be decorated. A year after the war King Albert satisfied Mme. Wharton by naming her Chevalier of the Order of Leopold.

2

Edith was not in Paris when the Legion of Honor award was made public: "Mme. Edith Wharton was not even there," observed *Le Temps;* "she does good works without seeming to notice it." She was again, in fact, at Costebelle, near Hyères on the French Riviera, seeking to regather her energies and making a determined start on a new work of fiction. Truth to tell, she was worn out, not only by the day-by-day demands of her several *oeuvres*, but also by the personal stresses and strains involved.

Charitable work often brings out the worst in human nature, and Edith Wharton's organizations were as prone as others to bickering, jealousy, and inane struggles for authority among the underlings. There were tensions on higher levels. Mildred Bliss and Edith Wharton simply could not get along, though the need to cooperate over the Mobile Convoys and other Red Cross affairs (Mrs. Bliss's main concern) forced them to try to. After a long planning session in July 1916, Edith confessed helplessly to Elisina: "I seem to poison her after I've been with her half an hour and she gets perfectly horrid." More rancorously and indeed more injuriously, Mildred Bliss spoke to Elisina and the Red Cross authorities about Mrs. Wharton's "incredible ruthlessness and lack of consideration" (the words are Elisina's), contending that she let other people slave away for her and then assigned the credit capriciously to some new person who struck her fancy, and in general ended up by alienating everybody. As an image of Edith Wharton in action, this one does not easily square with most others; but the distemper caused by overextension under wartime conditions is quickly recognizable.

Elisina Tyler was herself too much of an individual not to have moments of impatience and even rebelliousness; her developing relation with Edith corresponds closely to the pattern we have observed in other instances. Elisina found Edith by turns fidgety, nervous, and too tired to operate well; she complained of Edith's interminable letters about the workings of the *maisons* and her habit of canceling meetings and rescheduling them at impossible moments. Edith's fussing over minuscule details sometimes drove Elisina to distraction. But, like Berenson, Elisina invariably came around to an expression of unstinted and loving admiration. "Edith does lean on me, I know, and I must play true," she wrote her husband in the midst of a variety of recriminations. "She is such a valiant soul herself, and I don't like at all the idea of falling below what she expects of me."

Edith was capable of astonishing Elisina, the Florentine, in other ways. Edith arrived at a committee meeting in July in a black dress and hat, and (as Elisina put it) "with her charms showing outrageously." She flung herself into a chair; then, noticing that Charlie du Bos's tie was askew, she sprang up and straightened it—only to sink back in the chair, blushing furiously. Looking on, Elisina reflected on the strange varieties of *pudeur.*

By the summer of 1916, Edith had become sufficiently convinced that she had no real taste for what she later called "organised beneficence." She was well aware of other women who were finding their own vocation in such activities, but for her it was much rather individual cases of distress that truly appealed. Gaillard Lapsley, speaking with precision not about her "charitable works" but her "charity," would declare without reservation that Edith "possessed, indeed was possessed by, a sense of compassion deeper and more authentic than I have seen in any other human being." It was the more authentic, Lapsley felt, because it was not dependent upon any abstract theory of justice (though "justice and order," it may be recalled, was Edith's chief passion, according to her own notation), and sometimes not even personal liking. Lapsley too observed that it was the individual instances that most stirred her:

> The knowledge that there was mitigable suffering in a particular man or beast was enough to unseal the spring of her pity and she was not content to give money alone, she was ready to submit to boredom and something close to disgust if she was assured (as she was in two cases I have in mind) that she herself and not merely material relief was what was needed.

In later years Edith would have her fill of individual charities. Indeed, she was already giving her hard-pressed sister-in-law, Minnie Jones, a gift of four hundred dollars each Christmas, and the pitiful and muddled Dolly Herbert and her mother would soon be receiving regular deliveries of groceries and clothes. But for the time being, Edith stuck doggedly to her intricately organized hostels and *maisons*, reduced though she might be, in her own phrase, to the status of a "dowdy drudge."

3

The work took its periodic toll. In early November, Gross came into the drawing room at 53 Rue de Varenne to find her mistress stretched out on the floor in a dead faint. "I have never before done anything so romantic," Edith wrote Berenson during a few days in bed. She had attempted a period of rest at Fontainebleau and its environs during the summer, but, as Walter Berry remarked unsympathetically (he was growing bored with refugee work, though he did not slacken his efforts), she was constantly dashing back to Paris "for meetings and a hundred other God-knows-whats."

She rallied in time to enjoy the company of Berenson, who spent the whole of November in Paris. He had now dropped the "h" from his first name, presumably as a mild anti-German gesture. Blanche and Cocteau were summoned to the Rue de Varenne several times, and Abbé Mugnier: a group that, as Berenson enviously put it, made particularly diverting company as they fired intellectual challenges at one another. Bourget, on the other hand, was "wallowing in woe" over the progress of the war and had a dire respect for German military might. There was a dinner amid the elaborate tapestries of the Edward Tucks's *hôtel:* possibly a somewhat strained affair for Edith, since she found herself flanked by Mildred Bliss and by Lise (Mrs. Ralph) Curtis, who had shown no sign of forgiving Edith for her story "The Verdict." Edith said next day that the meal had given her food poisoning.

All Paris, Berenson said, was talking about Edith's inexplicable *engouement* for the Comtesse de Béarn, whom Berenson thought to be a most inferior lady with a mouth that opened like a fish when she began to speak. This was a surprising judgment: the former Martine de Béhague was an extremely handsome Jewish woman with a strong and engaging personality. Her marriage was an unhappy one, and her energies were directed toward art and music and putting together what became one of the great private collections of paintings in France. At the time she was a powerful and generous ally of Edith's in the *oeuvres;* Edith periodically fled to Mme. de Béarn's country home at Fleury, near Fontainebleau, for restful weekends.

For Americans in Paris the most important event in the fall of 1916 was not military but political: the national election in the United States. Edith Wharton shared Walter Berry's view, much promulgated, that Woodrow Wilson stood no chance of reelection. Berry, it should be said, was making a rousing public speech almost daily, with the aim of inflaming his countrymen and, through them, of exerting pressure to bring America into the war. One saw him in the newsreels and read about him in the papers; he was becoming one of the best-known and most popular Americans in France. And it was just the stubborn refusal of Wilson to lead the United States into the great defense of Western civilization that so aroused Edith's hostility. Even the sinking of the British ship *Lusitania* in May of the previous year, with a hundred American citizens among the casualties, failed to shake the President's neutrality. But Wilson's professorial rhetoric also grated on Edith's nerves, and as late as the end of September both she and Berry were looking forward to a victory by Charles Evans Hughes.

Both of them, however, also wished ardently that Theodore Roosevelt were the Republican candidate. In a letter of March 1915 which gave an account of one of her visits to the front, Edith Wharton had written Roosevelt to thank him for all that he was "doing and *being*," and to say that, even if he were not himself "in the chair of Lincoln," he was making the present incumbent squirm. Roosevelt's reply, marked "private" and dispatched from Oyster Bay, arrived two months later.

If I had been President, I would have acted within twelve hours, indeed as a matter of fact within six hours, of the sinking of the *Lusitania;* and if Wilson had done his duty I and my four boys would now be training for positions in the trenches.

The old Rough Rider warmed to his theme:

I think Wilson the very worst President we have had since Buchanan. The dreadful part of it is that the educated people have backed him up. The college presidents, the philanthropists, the clergymen, the editors of the papers that call themselves cultivated . . . praise him to the skies.

In another letter Roosevelt labeled Wilson "if possible an even worse President than Taft," adding that "the shifty, adroit and selfish logothete in the White House cannot be kicked into war." Support for Wilson's neutrality, Roosevelt was convinced, was due to a serious slackening of both moral and physical muscle:

They do this from sheer physical cowardice—at any rate from softness and flabbiness. Until this nation realises that no man is fit to be called a man unless he is ready to fight for what is right, and, therefore, until he has trained himself to do so in body and mind, and until we understand that war and death are preferable to certain kinds of peace and life, we shall cut but a poor figure in the world.

Edith Wharton and Roosevelt had kept in touch intermittently since the meeting at Williams in 1905 when the President received an honorary degree. During Roosevelt's world tour in 1910, Edith, with the French ambassador J. J. Jusserand, had arranged a large (and not very successful) reception at 53 Rue de Varenne. She sent John Hugh Smith on to Roosevelt in the late summer of 1911 with a letter of introduction, and a week or so later she and Teddy spent the night at Sagamore Hill. From the *Provence,* Edith wrote: "You and Mrs. Roosevelt, on the too rare occasions when I am with you, always make me feel as if each of our fleeting encounters were the renewal and the reaffirmation of a real friendship."

They exchanged literary views and information. About Roosevelt's article on arbitration, Edith selected for praise its "good sound ringing English"—as important a contribution to the American scene, she thought, as his political wisdom. She thanked him for telling her of Gilbert Murray's book on Greek literature and drew his attention to H. O. Taylor's masterful study *The Medieval Mind*, about which Roosevelt promptly wrote two articles. He in turn told Mrs. Wharton that when Mrs. Roosevelt was recovering from a bad accident (she had been unconscious for a fortnight), almost the first thing she did was to read *Ethan Frome:* "one of the most powerful things you have done." When Edith sent him *The Reef*, he remarked guardedly that despite his natural inclinations, she was perhaps "educating my taste to the point where I really can like the 'unpleasant side of philistine home life'!" His whole family, he said later, had loved Edith Wharton's satiric short story "Xingu."

Edith also remained in touch with Roosevelt through several of her closest friends. Minnie Jones, who had a vast respect and liking for the former President ("You have led us all and re-taught us a virtue we were by way of forgetting—courage"), passed on firsthand news from time to time. Morton Fullerton was nearly overwhelmed by Roosevelt's review of the book Fullerton dedicated to him in 1913, and said in acknowledgment: "There must have been much with which you could not agree, but you have generously looked to the broad lines of my argument, and in a beautiful spirit of fair play given me the most magnificent chance." Walter Berry turned to his old college mate to seek sponsorship for an American lecture tour by Edmond Rostand to raise money for Edith Wharton's refugees. Roosevelt answered that he would greatly value such a tour, but feared that his endorsement might in some quarters do more harm than good.

When it became evident after a tense period of waiting in November 1916 that Wilson had won reelection by the narrowest of margins, it was Berry who most forcibly voiced the sentiment of Edith Wharton's circle. "G—d d—n it all to H—l," he wrote Berenson with self-censored explosiveness. "Four more caterpillar years—as they might have said in Egypt in plague time. *C'est écœurant* [sickening]."

A more positive tribute to Roosevelt, and in a very different vein, was the poem Edith wrote within days of the former President's death in January 1919, less than two months after the armistice. It was called "Within the Tide": a slow-circling, brooding, sixty-line blank-verse poem, written, as Edith told Roosevelt's sister Mrs. Corinne Robinson, "out of a heart-wrenching sorrow, sorrow for the lost friend and for the great leader gone when he was most needed."

She thought of another great American leader, Lincoln, struck down in his prime, and of the poem Walt Whitman had written about him, "When Lilacs Last in the Dooryard Bloom'd." "But there is no Whitman singing in this generation," she admitted sadly. She cast the work in terms of a tribal legend she had read about in *The Golden Bough*—according to which, when a man dies, his dead friends come at twilight to the shore and escort him by boat to the lands of the blessed.

Never had so vast a throng assembled, Edith Wharton's poem goes on to say, as did on that winter evening, within the tide on Long Island—a throng that included Roosevelt's son Quentin, killed in battle ("There's no use of my writing about Quentin," Roosevelt had told Mrs. Wharton; "for I should break down if I tried"), others close to the "great American," and all those countless ones

> that have loved right more than ease,
> And honour more than honours. . . .

The poem, which was quickly and frequently reprinted, moves quietly between the personally reminiscent and the legendary. Edith Wharton's own grief was palpable: "No one will ever know what his example and his influence were to me."

4

In the winter of 1917, Edith's spirits sank to the lowest pitch of the entire war: a gloom which partook of the atmosphere of near despair that seized most of France as the war entered its fourth calendar year. There seemed, for the moment, a real chance that Great Britain would be forced to sue for peace, and France left to carry on alone. In another attempt to win the war by a single vast effort, the Germans, at the start of the year, instituted unrestricted submarine warfare on all vessels, Allied or neutral, encountered in the waters around the British Isles, off the coast of France, and in the Mediterranean. Within three months more than 1,000 English ships were sunk and the monthly loss of tonnage had risen to 880,000. Lloyd George, who had replaced Asquith as Prime Minister the previous December, gradually bullied the Admiralty into organizing a convoy system, and the danger was averted. But if the fear of actual defeat was thus overcome, there was a dreary apprehension in France that the war might simply go on forever. Mutinies broke out in the French forward divisions, and it would not be long before various French political figures—Joseph Caillaux among them —were sent to jail for the treasonous act of urging a settlement with Germany.

Physical conditions that icy winter were terrible. There was a severe shortage of coal, and electricity had been cut by fifty percent. Edith Wharton celebrated her fifty-fifth birthday on January 24, 1917, with frozen pipes and candlelight. Berry, Bourget, and du Bos joined her, all of them, Edith wrote Berenson, "licking our chilly chops" over Berenson's essay on Leonardo da Vinci and its critical demolition of "The Last Supper." "Ever since I first saw it (at 17)," Edith said violently, "I've wanted to bash that picture's face in."

In fact, of course, the German U-boat campaign had historically the opposite effect to the one intended. It failed to bring England to her knees, and it brought the United States into the war. On February 3, Wilson answered the threat to American shipping by breaking diplomatic relations with Germany and ordering American vessels to make armed defense of themselves. Edith Wharton had spoken of Wilson's "asphyxiating exhalations," which seemed to her to hang over everything like a fog at sea; but the February declaration buoyed her considerably. "It's good to feel one's self part of civilization again," she wrote Max Farrand; she had clung to her American identity despite a mixture of anger and shame over the national policy, but now Americans had the right to take their place in the center of things. On April 2 the United States Senate approved Wilson's declaration of war by eighty-two to six. From that moment to the armistice, Edith Wharton's spirit rarely flagged, however battered her body might often feel to her.

One of the fascinating themes in literary history is the impact of a great war upon the creative imagination—its capacity to galvanize or to crush, and the oddly varying pace at which either process works; all this dependent to some extent upon the writer's actual involvement in the conflict. In the case of Edith Wharton, as in that of many others, the long-range effect of the war was to create the sense of a huge disruption of historical continuity: something that expressed itself in much of her best work after the war. But the immediate consequence was a temporary cessation of fiction writing and a stint of journalism. She sent an occasional melancholy message to Charles Scribner to say that her novel "Literature" was not progressing.

For a long period, indeed, Edith had been too busy, tired, and distraught even to read very much. But rather suddenly, toward the end of January 1917—as though aroused by the recent meeting of the French Academy, its first since the outbreak of the war—she fell to reading with the old voracity; by Easter Sunday she could tell Berenson that she was now reading "libraries." She devoured Traubel's gossipy account of Walt Whitman's last days in Camden, and read with admiration Edgar Lee Masters' Whitmanesque *Spoon River Anthology* (1915) with its monologues about life in rustic midwestern America. She enjoyed some essays by George Santayana and others by Berenson; she explored the work of Ernest Renan. The latter led her back to the New Testament, which, she said, had never greatly struck her before. Her sporadic religious ruminations had not drawn her to the life of Christ or of the disciples, although she had taken several titles—including *The Valley of Decision* and *The House of Mirth*—from the Old Testament. Now she found a number of "good bits" in the Acts of the Apostles and the Epistles of St. Paul. "How kind of me!" she added hastily.

She was also immersing herself in German writing. She would never be reconciled to modern Germany, nor ever bring herself to visit the country again; but she was ready to reaffirm her loyalty to the older German literature and the German language. The correspondence between Goethe and Schiller absorbed her: "Goethe always schillered when he wrote to Schiller, didn't he?" she observed to Berenson. She went back to the German chansons de geste and the thirteenth-century Old Norse Edda: both her addiction to the prehistoric and her growing sense that the present historical moment had a certain mythic grandeur to it were gratified by the *Volüspa*, with its prophetic vision of the creation and destruction of the earth and the fate of the old gods; the *Song of Thrym*, and its tale of the deeds of warlike divinities; and "the splendid ruffianly *Hübarlied*," from which she translated for Berenson's benefit a sonorous passage about the dread power at nighttime of the ghosts of dead heroes.

These diversified stimuli only made the more acute her feeling of intellectual loneliness. Geoffrey Scott was long since back at Settignano. "Oh, to be in Tatti now that Geoffrey's there," she wrote wistfully. Her attempt to interest a young Frenchman at Rosa de Fitz-James's in the old heroic sagas elicited the bemused response: *"Oui, c'est curieux, en effet."*

Gradually she was able to pick up her own work. *Xingu and Other Stories* had appeared in October 1916, but, as Edith acknowledged, there was almost nothing new in it—the only entry written since the war began was the one called "Coming Home." It was singled out by reviewers as the best tale in the volume, no doubt because of its topicality: a young Frenchwoman saves the home of her fiancé's family by becoming the mistress of the German officer commanding the occupation troops. *Xingu* contains several stories that are far superior, including "The Long Run," "Autres Temps . . .," and "The Choice." There is also the quietly savage ghost story, "Kerfol," about an American tourist in Brittany who in the courtyard of an old château is confronted by a pack of (so he later discovers) spectral dogs. They had been the pets of the lady of the château some three centuries before and had been strangled by the lady's suspicious, vengeful husband; their ghosts had thereafter attacked and killed the husband. It is one of Edith Wharton's finest exercises in the imagination of violence, terror, and the erotic.

Best of all, perhaps, is the title story, which so delighted the Roosevelt family. Written in Edith Wharton's masculine vein of satiric humor, it tells of a Mrs. Roby and the culture-seeking Lunch Club which she throws into a state of awed bewilderment by holding forth mysteriously about something called Xingu. The latter appears to be a species of occult and possibly disgraceful philosophy—deep, long, hard to penetrate, and with many branches. Xingu is belatedly revealed as a river in Brazil which, fed by many branches, flows a thousand miles into the mouth of the Amazon. The meeting breaks up in disorder.

From Hyères in the spring of 1916, Mrs. Wharton wrote Charles Scribner that, though she still expected to finish "Literature" someday, it would probably not be until after the war. But she had made a start on another novel called *The Glimpses of the Moon* and asked if Scribner wanted it "for the magazine." The publisher scarcely had time to consider the possibility before Edith began to speak about still another book:

> I am taking a few weeks' rest at Fontainebleau and am making use of my leisure to write a "long short" story, of the dimensions of *Ethan Frome.* It deals with the same kind of life in a midsummer landscape, and is a thing I have had in mind for several years. I expect to finish it in a few weeks and I imagine it will reach a length of about 30,000 words. I should like to know if you would like this for the magazine, for, as you know, I always offer everything first to Scribner's.

Since Scribner had already agreed to fall magazine publication of *Bunner Sisters*, the extended tale Edith Wharton had written almost twenty-five years earlier, he cabled back that he could not "see place for new short novel."

It was an unlucky communication, and there followed a long and increasingly depressing exchange of letters over the next eighteen months, with little inexactitudes and forgetfulnesses accumulating on both sides. When Scribner asked if he might publish the book version of *Summer*—the new companion piece to *Ethan Frome*—Mrs. Wharton replied that she had already accepted an offer from Appleton which combined serialization *and* book publication "on terms so advantageous that, in view of your refusal, I should not have felt justified in rejecting." Scribner, as he said, was "a little disheartened by this transfer," but he took the blame for any misunderstanding, and added: "I do appreciate the support you have given the magazine and the house." After an interval he inquired cautiously as to when—since "Literature" was not after all to be forthcoming—Mrs. Wharton might give them some other novel. At this point Edith revealed that she had contracted with Appleton not only for *Summer* but also for *The Glimpses of the Moon;* even so, "Whenever you want a novel for Scribner's I shall be glad to give it to you."

By "Scribner's," she meant *Scribner's* magazine, and Scribner himself perfectly perceived Mrs. Wharton's position: "Unless we can use the serial, you will prefer another publisher. Is not this treating us with less consideration than our previous relations entitle us to expect?" He confessed that he had not "the heart to re-read the old letters but you certainly interpreted them to mean something never intended by me." And he went on:

> I think it would be generally regarded that we have managed your books fairly well and they certainly have had our best attention. But I do not make any personal appeal. You know that we will gladly welcome any opportunity to publish for you. Meanwhile I am glad to know that your interest in the magazine still continues.

The last sentence reflected a rather bitter, if concealed, irony on the part of the unflaggingly courteous and proudly sensitive publisher. The unhappy fact was that *Scribner's* could not compete financially with the popular journals—*McClure's* and the others—to which Edith Wharton was beginning to turn.

As for Edith, she was faced with more than one dilemma touching these transactions. The war had had a wrenching effect upon her relation to the kind of contemporary materials she customarily dealt with; she felt she had rather lost her way among them. She had put aside *The Glimpses of the Moon* because its subject—an impecunious young American couple living by their wits in high society—eluded her imagination. Even more so did "Literature," which was to trace the education of an American writer in the prewar period. She was now doubting that she ever would finish this novel, and could not commit herself to the future. "These four years"—it was now May 1918—"have so much changed the whole aspect of life that it is not easy to say now what one's literary tendencies will be when the war is over."

She could also write in all fairness about the heavy financial drain upon her in the past few years. Her literary earnings had been minimal since 1913—at just the time when the American government instituted a federal income tax—and her contributions to the refugee organizations had been immense. She could no longer afford to refuse offers of fifteen thousand dollars for serial rights and an equal amount in advance royalties on the subsequent book. But she proclaimed her "old affection for Scribner," and told her long-standing friend Brownell that she could "never get used to any other origin, and always sit down and weep under the willow tree when I remember Jerusalem."

Scribners would publish only one other work of fiction by Edith Wharton during her lifetime, *A Son at the Front* in 1923. Charles Scribner was to call the departure of Edith Wharton from their list, after twenty-five years and nineteen titles, "the greatest blow ever given to my pride as a publisher."

For *Summer* the editor at *McClure's*, saying that he had never in his life been so happy to get hold of a serial, paid seven thousand dollars, and raised the price of the magazine to fifteen cents. The episode of the publication of *Summer* was a turning point no less fateful for Edith Wharton than for Scribners. It marked the opening of a long period during which she would take in ever larger amounts of money, chiefly for serial rights in widely selling "picture magazines." But the world of big earnings, as she would discover, contained qualities by no means the most beneficial for the free imagination.

Summer, Edith wrote Gaillard Lapsley, "is known to its author and her familiars as the Hot Ethan." It is set in the same Berkshires region as its predecessor, and there is even mention of Starkfield, where the Frome household might be imagined miserably living on. Nettleton, where the two young people go to watch the Fourth of July fireworks, was, Edith told Lapsley, the Pittsfield they had once visited together for the same purpose. But though the story begins in June and most of it takes place during hot summer days, as against the wintry setting of *Ethan Frome*, it comes to its climax in an atmosphere of varied and almost palpable chill and ends (in its closing sentence) with a drive through "the cold autumn moonlight."

The central incident is almost a deliberate stereotype. In the small isolated New England hamlet of North Dormer, Charity Royall, a passionate and untutored girl who works in the village library, is seduced and left pregnant by an artistically minded young man from the city, Lucius Harney. She has some dealings with a scoundrelly abortionist, but she is finally rescued by her guardian, Lawyer Royall, who quietly marries her and makes it clear that he will do nothing but surround her with benevolent protection.

Aspects of the early Edith Wharton—shy, intense, proud, lonely, fearful, stubborn—reappear in a different coloration in the handsome Charity Royall, whose first spoken words are: "How I hate everything!" As to Lucius Harney, he is another of his creator's attractive and ineffectual males: charming, eloquent, and undependable. But the center of attention is Lawyer Royall. He is craggy and flawed, sometimes drunken and abusive; once, out of desperate loneliness and wayward desire, he tries to force himself upon his ward. But he is an essentially decent person, a kindly wreck of a man and still the most imposing figure in North Dormer; a sort of degraded god, and a masterly characterization. When Berenson singled out Royall for special admiration, Edith exclaimed delightedly: "Of course *he's* the book."

But though it is rooted in actualities and is controlled by Edith Wharton's usual keenness of psychological perception, *Summer* also gives off intimations of something darker, stranger, more ominous—a domain of experience she normally approached only in her ghost stories. It is represented by the Mountain, which looms portentously over the little village: the home of illiterate outlaws, a scene of chilly squalor, violence of speech and gesture, and probably incestuous passions. Here is Edith Wharton's only direct confrontation of the most furious and lawless impulses that lie buried in human nature; and it is by artful contrast with the Mountainfolk that Lawyer Royall appears so basically humane.

The Mountain, Edith told Brownell, "is Bear Mountain, about fifteen miles from Lee." The story, she said, had its origins in the haunting account of a "mountain burial" which the rector of the church at Lenox, who had officiated at it, once described to her. The funeral service for Charity's mother—in an ice-cold room by the light of a single candle, while the minister's sublime words echo against the drunken cursing of crowded shadowy figures squabbling over who owns the unlit stove—is the best scene in the book, and one of the most powerful Edith Wharton ever wrote. It may be, too, that this phase of the novella sprang from Edith's sense of what, in the same letter to Brownell, she called "the convulsed world" of violent disorder that surrounded her.

But it sprang even more from that part of Edith Wharton that regularly responded to the appeal of the unexplored, the precivilized, and the dangerous

—to Nietzsche and *The Rite of Spring,* to Conrad's *The Heart of Darkness* and *The Secret Sharer.* Conrad in fact, writing from his home near Ashford in reply to a presentation copy and a comforting letter (his son had just departed for the front), was full of praise for *Summer.* Everywhere, he said, the book "presents itself *en beauté—toujours en beauté,"* and he had special admiration for Mrs. Wharton's prose style. "I've always loved your rhythms, so very fine, distinct and subtle. On opening the book I let myself be carried away by them. . . . Truly it was a great delight."

Such comments were the more welcome, Edith remarked, after "the shy and frightened letters I've been getting from a few old friends in Boston to whom I felt bound, in friendliness, to send a copy." Sara Norton, for example, had "sternly reproved" Edith for writing *Summer.* Howard Sturgis, however, thought the tale a "little gem and wonder," and that Edith really was "a very great artist." He and Lubbock were agreed in finding parts of *Summer* as good as anything in *Madame Bovary,* and he concluded: "Polished and rotund and complete and compact this great little book affects me as being." These carefully chosen words stand up well many decades later.

Some of the book's reviewers shared Sara Norton's puritanical recoil: a portion of the American literary press continued to bewail the fact, year after year, that one of the country's most highly regarded writers (and a well-bred woman at that) persistently delved into subjects that gave offense to the genteel. The Boston *Transcript* felt obliged to warn its readers that the story "will have reverberations both loud and long." But it was widely observed that, despite the sordidness of the tale, simple goodness did after all win out in the end (so the denouement was misread). And there was no questioning of Mrs. Wharton's position as one of the finest stylists and craftsmen of her time. Like *Ethan Frome, Summer* made a sizable critical dent, but failed to recoup for its publishers the seven-thousand-dollar advance against royalties.

5

Edith Wharton's French agency and publisher, the Plon Nourrit, had approached her in the fall of 1916 about a translation of *Summer,* and she had turned to André Gide. "Can you imagine it?" she wrote him, addressing Gide as always in French (highly idiomatic, with an occasional trifling mistake). "I have had the audacity to ask myself if you would accept the translation."

The inquiry was perhaps not as audacious as Edith made out. She and Gide were fairly good friends by this time, and in one of their not infrequent conversations Gide had confessed to wishing that it had been he, rather than Charles du Bos, who had translated *Ethan Frome.* He was also at this time performing some literary errand for Mme. Wharton (probably refugee correspondence). "I realise the indiscretion of my question," she said, "especially at the moment when you are busy with the translation of 'my letters.' But there it is! I long for it too much not to raise the question."

She pressed a little: she had never written anything with more joy—"or, perhaps one should say, with less anguish"; it had saved her from falling ill out of sheer grief over the war; it was "a simple tale," and he could do the job quickly. Gide hesitated, and then declined; Edith pronounced herself "desolated." Charles du Bos was again called upon, and after many sessions produced what Edith described as a "lamentable" translation—though Gide was not to say so.

André Gide in 1916 was forty-seven years old: tall and slender, with a long and extremely sensitive face, and a certain intensity as well as fragility of manner. His unconsummated marriage with his first cousin, Madeleine Rondeaux, had endured for two decades, while Gide experimented rather earnestly in other modes of sexual gratification. He had drawn upon his experiences, as well as his vast learning, in a number of writings which had established him as a major new force in French literature, among them the books known in English as *The Immoralist*, *Strait Is the Gate*, and *Lafcadio's Adventures*. With Jacques Copeau and Jean Schlumberger, he had founded the *Nouvelle revue française* in 1908; among the younger men, there was no more commanding or beguiling presence on the local literary scene.

Edith Wharton and André Gide had met in the early days of the American Hostels, and for a year or more their exchanges had largely to do with refugee work. The relationship deepened somewhat in the late fall of 1915, when the two of them spent several days together in and around Hyères. (About an earlier planned trip to England, where Henry James and Arnold Bennett were expecting them, Gide had written: "It would have amused me to travel with [Mrs. Wharton]. But this was not the moment.") They explored Toulon and had lunch in an odd little restaurant; they drove along the sea and took a picnic basket up into the hills. Gide accompanied Edith to Les Plantiers for a visit with Paul Bourget, with whom Gide had not been previously much acquainted.

While Edith was out of the room, commiserating with the ailing Minnie Bourget, Gide and Bourget began to talk about homosexuality, Bourget asking whether the main figure in *The Immoralist* was a pederast. They discussed the matter, and Gide was about to learn whether in Bourget's opinion a homosexual should be considered under the head of sadism or masochism, when Mrs. Wharton came back. The conversation turned to other subjects, and Gide regretted not hearing "Mrs. Wharton's opinion, if she had one." Bourget then read aloud from his own work, so moved by it that he nearly wept. From Gide's journal:

> Out of the corner of our eyes, Mrs. Wharton and I glance at each other, not knowing which deserves more wonder, Paul Bourget's emotion or the mediocrity of those pages.

Gide further endeared himself to Edith Wharton after the death of Henry James, in the winter of 1916. The French writer had grave reservations about James as a novelist (his characters, Gide felt, were lifeless), but he knew of Mrs. Wharton's devotion to her fellow American and wrote her several letters by which she declared herself "profoundly touched." He managed to intuit and to formulate her state of affliction—of feeling surrounded by a darkness ever colder and thicker. "The sentiment you speak of," she wrote him, ". . . has haunted me for a long time, and with the extinction of the great ray of light that was the soul of Henry James, it only becomes doubly tragic."

Edith Wharton took to calling Gide *"Cher Monsieur et ami"* and to making literary suggestions. On her advice Gide read and admired *Spoon River Anthology*, and he and his wife read aloud together Richard Henry Dana's *Two Years Before the Mast*—about which Gide exclaimed to a friend: *"Un peu special— mais passionant!"* Edith groped her way, with cautious enjoyment, into the exotic world of André Gide's writings, spending "an exquisite evening" with his volume *Prétextes:* "What you have written about the *Thousand and One Nights,* among so many other things which have enchanted me, gave me a very lively and particular pleasure." Gide solicited from Mrs. Wharton letters of introduction for Jacques Copeau, who, as founder of the Théâtre du Vieux-Colombier in Paris, was planning a trip to America to look into theater conditions there. Edith complied, though disavowing her usefulness: "I have never mixed in the world of the New York theater, and I haven't been there for ten years."

There were discussions of other possible collaborations. Gide had written a little study of Conrad which Dorothy Bussy was translating; when her brother Lytton Strachey declined to write a preface, Gide—no doubt aware of her addiction to Conrad—asked Mrs. Wharton if she might be induced to do it. Nothing came of this, but there was more protracted talk about the translation of *The Custom of the Country,* of which Robert d'Humières had completed about a third at the time of his death. Edith finally decided to leave things as they were. Mme. d'Humieres was insisting that every correction in the text of the sixteen chapters done by her husband should be indicated by a footnote. "That is absurd and impossible," Edith Wharton told Gide. "My advice is, in short, not to publish the translation. Should I write to M. Proust? Would you let me know?"

There was, Gide replied, no need to write Marcel Proust: "He was waiting word from you to take action." Gide agreed that the translation should be abandoned. But the reference suggests that Proust must have shown some interest in taking over the French version of *The Custom of the Country.* It is unthinkable that he should have actually done the work: he was wholly occupied with the steadily expanding portions of *Remembrance of Things Past* which were to follow *Swann's Way* (the latter having appeared in 1913). But he seems at least to have discussed the possibility with Gide. Proust would have been attracted by the novel itself, with its American perspective on the Faubourg St. Germain and its portrait of contrasting American social manners historically observed. He is likely, too, to have felt a double piety toward his old friend Robert d'Humières, as a fellow writer and as one afflicted by what Proust regarded as the "disease" of homosexuality. In any event, the project was called off by Edith Wharton even before Proust needed to bow out.

It is an irony that both Marcel Proust and Edith Wharton could have savored that, for all the many things they had in common and despite geographical proximity for some sixteen years, their paths never actually crossed. In the high reaches of Parisian social life, they missed each other as though by divine planning. Proust entered the Faubourg world in 1894, at the age of twenty-three. After becoming the familiar of the *ducs* and *duchesses*, the *comtes* and *comtesses* he would draw upon, splice, and reshape for his epic novel, he withdrew abruptly following the second trial of Alfred Dreyfus in 1899. (Proust was the staunchest of Dreyfusards, and pilloried Schlumberger for his rumbling anti-Dreyfus position.) By the time, in 1906, that Edith Wharton was introduced to the aristocratic milieu, Proust had been absent from it for some years. The war and a need for broader human contact lured Proust back into the world, in particular to the center of social gravity at the Ritz Hotel. But at this stage it was Edith Wharton who had largely retired from the scene—racking personal problems had already caused her to curtail her social involvements, and her refugee work reduced them even more drastically. In addition, of course, the Ritz represented what she most detested in the changing city.

Even so, the range of friends they had in common makes it more than surprising that the two never met. There was Jacques Emile Blanche, who had done a telling pencil sketch of Proust as early as 1891, and Anna de Noailles, whose effervescent personality and fitful love life intrigued and exasperated Proust. There was Abbé Mugnier, with whom, as it happened, Edith Wharton was on affectionate terms for some years before he and Proust got beyond a certain wariness with each other. The names accumulate: Robert d'Humières; Rosa de Fitz-James; Cocteau and Gide; the d'Haussonvilles; Charles du Bos; the young writer Jean Louis Vaudroyer, who came to Edith Wharton's rescue at Châlons; Louis Ganderax, the hard-driving editor; in the latter part of the war, even Bernard Berenson, whom Proust much respected.

Above all, there was Walter Berry, who by the summer of 1917 was consuming oysters and champagne with Marcel Proust at the Ritz once or twice a week. The year before, Berry, prowling the bookshops of the Left Bank, had come upon an early eighteenth-century volume bearing the arms of the Guermantes family. Berry and Edith had been equally enthralled by *Swann's Way*, and the names of the aristocratic Guermantes' had become part of their conversational vocabulary. Berry took pleasure in sending the volume to Proust, and was soon being entertained in Proust's rooms at 102 Boulevarde Haussmann.

As a dapper, cultivated, French-speaking American, with a tart tongue and a cosmopolitan outlook, Walter Berry was a new phenomenon for Proust—who agreed with his friend, and Edith's, Paul Morand that Berry resembled an American in a novel by Henry James. Proust in turn was not only a dazzling conversationalist, with rabid enthusiasms and intense hatreds; he was also the social historian of the regime to which Berry's *snobisme* drew him like a magnet. Berry quickly became a figure in what Proust's biographer George D. Painter calls "the new dynasty of friends" that was forming about the recognizedly great writer; Proust even confided to Berry something of an unhappy homosexual love affair.

The war solidified the friendship. Proust, already convinced that only the entrance of America could save the Allied cause, was further convinced that Walter Berry's speeches were chiefly responsible for that historic act. A year after the armistice, Proust published a collection of pieces called *Pastiches et mélanges* and dedicated it to Berry. "Why Berry?" someone asked. "Because he won the war!" Proust replied.

It is hard to believe that Berry made no effort to arrange a meeting between his old and his new friend, but there is no record of any such endeavor. Nor was there ever a direct communication between the Boulevarde Haussmann and the Rue de Varenne. Edith Wharton later regretted she had not followed her impulse and written Proust a word of warm praise for *Swann's Way* when that novel was meeting with such little success. She also said that what she had heard about Proust, particularly his predeliction for dukes and duchesses, diminished any desire she might have to know him. Had they met, there would have been much to talk about, presumably after an interlude of mutual intimidation—from French social history to the art of fiction to asthma, from which both suffered for comparable though by no means identical psychosomatic reasons. There once floated a rumor that Proust invited Mme. Wharton to meet him at the Café Royale a little after midnight one evening, and that Mme. Wharton indignantly declined: a later portion, obviously, of the developing comic image of both of them.

Of all the novelists, European or American, whose lives overlapped her own, Marcel Proust was the one that Edith Wharton by background and training was best equipped to appreciate. The analyst of the ebbing New York society recognized on sight the genius of the writer exploring its immensely more complex French counterpart. She sent a copy of *Swann's Way* to Henry James within two months of its publication; James held back a little, but eventually, according to Edith Wharton's memory, he "devoured it in a passion of curiosity and admiration," discerning in it "a new master" and "a new vision."

Edith would feel a slight falling off with each of the succeeding volumes, but she attributed it to Proust's worsening ill health, and then to the early death (at fifty-one) which denied him the opportunity to revise. In an essay on Proust in the 1920s, her praise was nearly unbounded. "His endowment as a novelist," she said, ". . . has probably never been surpassed"; she ranked him with the Tolstoy of *War and Peace* and the Shakespeare of *King Lear.* Nor did she shrink from even the most scabrous of the Sodom and Gomorrah scenes: Proust was unmatched, she claimed, in portraying "the viler aspects of the human medley."

Halfway through *Time Recaptured,* the last part of *Remembrance of Things Past,* there appears what may be Proust's only reference to Mrs. Wharton. The narrator, coming back to Paris after the war, goes to the Rue de Varenne to look for the Prince de Guermantes' *hôtel,* only to discover that the prince has moved to the Bois de Boulogne and that his *hôtel* was now the setting for "the *soirées* of an American woman in whom I had no interest." This may have been a bit of sly fun—Edith Wharton was the only American woman on the block at the time. Yet one wonders what she would have made of it, had she accepted the invitation, many years later, to complete the translation of *Remembrance of Things Past,* left unfinished at Scott Moncrieff's death, by doing *Time Recaptured.* But though greatly flattered, she declared that she was too old and too easily tired to take on the task. So in the matter of translations of each other's work, as in their personal lives, the paths of Edith Wharton and Marcel Proust managed by a kind of fatality never to connect.

21. The Bells of Ste. Clothilde

As the summer of 1917 waned, Edith Wharton prepared for a visit to Morocco. "What do you think of the idea of undertaking such a trip at a time like this?" she asked Gide. "Do you think I am absolutely crazy?" It was not, in fact, an unsuitable moment for the venture. On the western front, things were relatively quiet. The French had again suffered heavy casualties along the Somme in an attack that gained about six hundred yards the first day; but General Henri Philippe Pétain, the most realistic of the French commanders, had taken charge with the calm announcement that he would hold the line and wait for the Americans and the tanks. It was a moment of pause in Edith Wharton's life as well. The Red Cross was on the verge of taking over some of her charities, and the hostels seemed to be running themselves. She wrote Berenson that she was looking forward to " 'living like a lady again.' "

There was also the recurring appeal of the African desert. Gide had sent Mme. Wharton a copy of his novel *The Immoralist*, a key episode of which takes place in Tunis. Having read it avidly, she remarked: "Your beautiful evocation of the desert I have so loved, far from awakening my nostalgia, gives me a taste in advance of what is awaiting me there." And finally, there was Edith's great admiration for General Hubert Lyautey, resident general of French Morocco.

She had encountered Lyautey a few times in Paris and had studied his career. He was in her view a genuine modern hero, and later historians have only confirmed this judgment. Tall, slim, erect, and still youthful at sixty-three, Lyautey was the rarest kind of soldier-statesman. Less flamboyant and romantic than Lawrence of Arabia, he was also perhaps wiser and more effective. In 1912 he had rescued the Sultan of Morocco from a huge Berber uprising and had seen to the establishment of a French protectorate. Since then, he had instituted a vast program of modernization in the country, but had also been careful to protect the integrity of the old Arab cities and to honor the Moslem religious traditions. The occasion for Edith Wharton's visit in September 1917 was another instance of Lyautey's policy: an annual fair in the coastal town of Rabat which exhibited age-old artisan skills alongside new industrial products.

With Walter Berry, Edith crossed from Algeciras to Tangier and made her way down in a military car, over spine-jarring roads, into French Morocco and over to Rabat. Edith faithfully attended the fair, but found more to interest her in the Casbah, in a gory ritual known as the Sacrifice of the Sheep, and in a visit to the sultan's harem. Later, in the fanatically religious hill town of Moully-Idriss, she and Berry witnessed a singularly gruesome ritual dance in which the howling participants hacked at their skulls and breasts with hatchets until blood flowed freely onto their garments and shoes and formed little pools among the stones. The dance, Edith learned, commemorated the death of a seventeenth-century saint and symbolically reenacted the subsequent suicide of his faithful slave.

Storing up this "bestial" but oddly stirring image of raw violence, Edith and Berry moved on in early October to Fez and the former summer palace of the sultan's wives, which was now the residence of the hospitable General Lyautey. With the others she explored the far-spreading city, with its atmosphere of heavy overripeness, riding on a pink-saddled mule down covered streets like tunnels, into squares crowded with Jewish marriage processions, past bazaars oddly lacking in the sprawling vivacity Edith remembered from Tunis. In the harem of a local dignitary, surrounded by his wife, daughters, and concubines, she similarly noted an air of "somewhat melancholy respectability." She knew about the precocious sexual education prevalent throughout the society: girls married by the age of nine, boys given their first black woman upon reaching puberty; but she had the impression that "both sexes live till old age in an atmosphere of sensuality without seduction."

She thought of young girls brought down willy-nilly from the mountains or snatched from a garden near the sea by a fat merchant and imprisoned for life in his dimly lit harem. Studying the passive faces of the concubines, Edith felt all her feminism rising up in futile anger and helpless compassion. The Eastern world had again laid its magic upon her, but she had never been more conscious of the irreplaceable Western value of personal freedom.

2

At the same time, events were conspiring to strengthen, and clarify, her sense of herself as an American. Although American fighting troops would not reach France in any significant numbers until nearly Christmas of 1917, the first regiment had arrived in Paris in time to take part in a Fourth of July procession —an affair that culminated, amid roars from the French crowd, with the presentation of the American flag to General John Joseph Pershing at the Invalides. Edith Wharton thought it all "really splendid," and that the troops and the hordes of advance personnel were the very best of their American kind; how, she wondered sardonically, could they have emerged from the Wilson Administration?

Her response to the military differed sharply from that to the representatives of what she called that "blatant scourge," the Red Cross. During negotiations with this organization in the spring, tempers became so frayed that there was the closest thing yet to a genuine falling-out between Edith and Elisina Tyler. Mrs. Tyler was under the impression that she was about to be shifted, without consultation, to a subordinate position in a new outfit run by inexperienced strangers, and, as she wrote her husband, all her "smoldering rebellion has been fanned into flame." Edith quickly wrote her a reassuring and heartwarming letter, and Elisina realized again that "she is sound all through."

> Really, when one thinks her over she is a perfectly splendid person. One must give her rope because she is a full rigged vessel and can't manoeuvre in a toilet basin, but if I have the courage and speed to keep up with her, I believe she will always make for port in the end.

Through the winter and spring of 1918 the Red Cross officials continued their effort to gain control not only of Edith Wharton's tubercular homes, but of the American Hostels as well; the latters' financial resources were running out. Walter Berry raised a large sum from a new entity called the Lafayette Fund, and the worst threat was averted. But Edith's brush with the bureaucrats persuaded her that, while some of them were no doubt well intentioned, all were ignorant of French ways of doing things and of the French language, and she even dropped a hint that a few were speculating in charities.

The contrast between her attitude to the American fighting men and to the civilian administrative types was characteristic. The fact is that never at any time was Edith Wharton anything *but* an American: which is to say, as an English friend remarked, never anything but herself. Unlike many of her fellow expatriates, and especially the female ones who married into the British or French aristocracy, Edith Wharton never took on the manners and speech habits, the critical posture and, as it were, the pseudo-identity of the re-created European. She remained quintessentially American in her way of conducting herself—and never more so than when she was virulently criticizing certain aspects of America as against its superior manifestations. In later years those manifestations appeared to her as phenomena of a world long vanished; but there was some real justification for Bernard Berenson's remark to a French associate that the four most authentic Americans in his generation were Edith Wharton, Henry James, Henry Adams, and himself.

Berenson was installed at the Ritz when Edith came back from Morocco; with several interludes, Paris would be his home for many months to come. He had been looking for an official job, suited to his special abilities, with the newly arrived American forces, and at dinner in the Rue de Varenne in early December Royall Tyler (himself now a uniformed member of American intelligence) told him a position awaited him as adviser to the General Staff. His assignment was internal developments in Italy and Germany, and his rank was interpreter first class. Hearing this, Edith remarked that he had been given his proper title at last.

Upon Edith's reappearance Berenson pronounced her "very, very dear" and vowed he would see her daily. As to women friends in Paris, Berenson divided his time judiciously between four of them: Edith Wharton; the always stimulating Charlotte de Cossé-Brissac; Natalie Barney, the highly cultivated Ohio-born woman who presided over a cult of Lesbos and a high-powered literary *salon* in the Rue Jacob; and Linda Thomas, the internationally famous beauty and exceedingly womanly woman who would marry Cole Porter. Berenson took great if differing pleasure from his hours with each, but, as Mary wrote him, "Edith seems to emerge as the realest of all thy friends." Berenson agreed.

With Berenson in local residence, Edith's social and artistic life quickened. She had him to dinner to meet André Gide, he in turn escorted her to a gathering at Linda Thomas', and after he took an apartment on the Avenue du Trocadéro, Edith was a regular guest at meals, along with members of the Paris art world she would not otherwise have met. On Christmas Day 1917, while snow fell heavily outside and the Eiffel Tower loomed ghostlike in the obscurity, Berenson dined on turkey and plum pudding at the Rue de Varenne, with Rosa de Fitz-James, Royall and Elisina Tyler, and Edith's second cousins Le Roy and Freddy King.

There were the inevitable moments when Berenson thought Edith insensitive or thoughtless and wounding to his vanity, and he lamented her frequent preference for jokes and gossip rather than the sustained exploration of some single serious topic, selected by himself. In this regard, he told his wife (contradicting himself about Edith, as he often did), Edith was as bad as she was. But far more customary were Berenson's references to her as "lovable," "devoted," "dearer than ever," and the like.

To Berenson in these days Edith revealed aspects of herself she had not hitherto shown. Driving to St. Cloud one drizzly afternoon, she spoke—in Berenson's paraphrase—of her "cheerless, loveless" childhood and adolescence, with parents and relatives who "meant nothing to her," and guided by "standards of heartless correctness." Over a lunch tête-à-tête she confided that although she enjoyed brilliance in another person, all she really expected from her friends was that they spend time with her and love her. Alluding to the most recent of Walter Berry's favorites (a young lady from Cleveland), Edith broke out into "a despairing diatribe" over Berry's social frivolity.

These reports were filtered through Berenson's somewhat self-engrossed vision, but some of them suggest that Edith was passing through a mood of tired loneliness; the busiest American woman in Paris, and the one perhaps most surrounded by comfort and attention, still felt, occasionally, the old mortal solitude. Once when Berenson admitted having spoken harshly to Mary, Edith cried: "If only I had somebody who would scold me and quarrel with me!" She had already declaimed upon "the never-get-anywhereness of most human intercourse," and she was now saying disconsolately that she had not made a single real friend in all her years in Paris; if she were to die today there would be a pompous and well-attended funeral, after which everyone would go out to dinner. About this, Mary Berenson observed that Edith's way of counting friends was "as the Buddha used to say, 'not the way the question should be put.' " Edith was presumably referring only to the French people she had come to know, but it was a surprising remark considering persons like du Bos, Abbé Mugnier, St. André, Charlotte de Cossé (who admired her war work extravagantly and vocally), and Bélogou.

In fact and as always, she was renewing old friendships and making new ones; the war put no end to her thickening republic of the spirit. With Berenson and others she helped found the Tuesday Lunch Club, where the talk ranged from the jailing of the peace-advocating Joseph Caillaux to recent works of scholarship and literature. Maurice Paléologue, the learned French ambassador to Russia, showed up at the meetings, and William Archer, the English critic and dramatist with whom, long before, Edith had discussed a possible production of one of her plays. Royall Tyler came regularly, as did Carlo Placci, Berenson's garrulous Tuscan friend. The most faithful participant was Jeanne de Margeries, Edmond Rostand's sister and the wife of another eminent diplomat; Edith until now had known her only slightly. Berenson passed on the contention that during the previous winter all of Paris thought that Edith Wharton "was dying of a broken heart because of the way W[alter] carried on with Mme. de Margeries." Showing no signs of such affliction, Edith felt nothing but increasing warmth for the French woman.

But the prize figure in the group was Eric Maclagan, currently head of the British Ministry of Information bureau in Paris. Fifteen years younger than Edith Wharton, Maclagan was a tall, spare man with a thick head of hair, an expressive face, and teeth that gleamed prominently when he smiled. He was the son of the former Archbishop of York, William Maclagan, who had been called in to assist the aging and arthritic Archbishop of Canterbury at the coronation of King Edward VII and Queen Alexandra. Eric Maclagan had joined the staff of the Victoria and Albert Museum in his mid-twenties and had become assistant keeper of architecture and sculpture.

He was a person of quick vitality, flashing intelligence, and great warmth of spirit. He was also an authentic gourmet, with a highly trained palate and a flair for discovering excellent but little-known Paris restaurants. On these expeditions he was regularly accompanied by St. André and Royall Tyler, the three gourmet-musketeers, as they thought of themselves; the number increased to four during the frequent visits to the city of John Hugh Smith. Maclagan, in addition, was a skilled raconteur of bawdy stories—he had, as Berenson said, "a pretty nose for entertaining indecencies." For this and other reasons Edith Wharton, upon meeting him, declared him *"délicieux"*; no new friendship in this period ripened more rapidly or endured more firmly.

Other relationships deepened steadily. In Elisina Tyler's prolonged absence at Genay, Edith made the most of Royall Tyler's bachelor company. Tyler had better access than most to war news, and Edith cherished his "good-communiqué smile," when he would slip in during a dinner party and whisper the latest encouraging report in her ear.

Periodically, she reached out for those separated from her by war or circumstance. After Berenson left for London in June 1918, she wrote: "You have been so dear and kind and faithful to me all these months I want to tell you again how much it has mattered to me, and how *désemparée* your going has left me." In London, Berenson met Robert Norton for the first time: "a very dear creature," Edith said, "and such a tender friend—and tenderness is the thing I've had least of in my supposedly so *comblée* existence, and touches me more than many shining qualities." She was especially grateful for an affectionate letter from Gaillard Lapsley: "I know that affection burns on steadily through any length of silence."

Edith was stunned in February 1918 by the news that Geoffrey Scott was about to marry Lady Sybil Cutting. Bayard Cutting, Jr., had fulfilled the sad expectancies by dying of consumption in 1910, scarcely into his thirties. In a memoir of him Edith Wharton spoke of Cutting's unceasing yet orderly passion for life even during his last and obviously numbered days. "The most distinctive thing about him," she said, ". . . was that his tastes were so inwoven with his personality," and he had above all "a receptiveness of mind and a tolerance of heart."

Lady Sybil had settled, with her young daughter Iris, in the Villa Medici, a handsome place at the end of a long drive on the Fiesole slope: a healthy walk, but not too strenuous a one, from the Villa I Tatti. There was a liaison of sorts with Bernard Berenson, before he succumbed to the more elusive attractions of Belle Greene and in 1915 there had been surmise about a marriage to Percy Lubbock. From Sybil, Edith had heard repeatedly the story of Lubbock's fishing his cigarette from the back of Sybil's dress and of her fainting romantically into his arms. Lubbock fought shy for the time being, and it was Geoffrey Scott who, in late April, became Sybil Cutting's second husband.

All concerned were more than a little nervous about Edith's reaction, and none wanted to be the first to tell her. About Scott, Edith felt that "some subtle link of understanding on most subjects bound us together with hooks of steel"; but she had turned gradually away from Lady Sybil. When Mary Berenson wrote her apprehensively about the wedding, Edith was "reduced to a squeak."

I have been *practicing liking it* for 24 hours and am obliged to own that the results are not promising. . . . Never again to see him except encircled by that well-meaning waste of unintelligence: oh, dear—*enfin. "C'est la guerre."*

A friend in later life remarked that Edith Wharton almost never engaged in personal criticism—that is, "where she really loved. My word," the friend continued, "she did it all right otherwise." Probably none of Edith's acquaintances came in for more sheer venom than Lady Sybil Scott. But at fifty-six, as Edith put it to Berenson, she was feeling herself a "poor elderly feminine female." She had a distinct touch "of the greedy *amante* in my affection for all of the happy few I care for at all." Lady Sybil was to outrage that quality in her yet again before this chapter of Edith's life was over.

3

The year 1917 ended with the Italian rout at Caporetto and the British disaster at Passchendaele in Flanders—perhaps the war's ultimate horror, with well over 300,000 men killed floundering in the sea of mud caused by the heavy November rains. In March 1918 the Germans launched their mightiest offensive in France, sixty-two divisions along a forty-seven-mile front. Air raids sent Edith Wharton and her household nightly down into the basement of 53 Rue de Varenne, and by day there was the constant boom of the long-range German guns known, after the wife of their inventor, as Big Berthas. Turning into her street one afternoon, Edith heard the familiar crash near at hand; luckily, she said, Big Bertha had made a mistake "and dropped in at my *old* number (58) where she sat down in the court with a dull thud." She spoke lightly, but had to admit that such moments kept her nerves "jigging and sarabanding."

Edith was experiencing an unaccustomed surge of patriotism. "Our troops cover themselves daily with fresh glory," she wrote Minnie Jones; "the whole of France rings with their praises—praise of their skill as well as their pluck." To half a dozen correspondents she quoted with delight the statement attributed to General Gouraud that the Americans were as good as the best of the *poilus*. She was even induced to give a lecture on America—her first and last appearance on a platform—before a French audience curious about their new allies; the talk was "clear and crisp and brief," Berenson reported, "and yet containing it all."

On July 4, from the high terrace of the Hotel Crillon, Edith watched the grand parade down the Champs Elysées to the Tuileries, where fifty thousand Parisians were massed in waiting. There came first the Garde Nationale,

and then our wonderful, incredible troops, every man the same height, and marching with long rhythmical stride that filled the French with admiration and wonder. Two regiments from camps, and then the infantry and marines from Chateau Thierry in their trench helmets [at this a great shout arose from the French]; then some poilus from the same sector, and then the American Red Cross nurses, who scored the biggest hit of all!

Her historical imagination, Edith declared, "fairly burst in the struggle to deal with all the associations and analogies which the scene evoked." She was, of course, thinking of her great progenitor, General Ebenezer Stevens, fighting side by side at Yorktown with the Marquis de Lafayette, and of the scenes of combat and triumph her parents had witnessed in 1848 in almost the identical spot Edith was now overlooking. In that moment history coalesced for her, and she was one with her own ancestry.

On an evening in early August, Edith was sitting in her drawing room with Royall Tyler, talking as usual about the war: perhaps about the successful resistance to General Erich Ludendorff's campaign and the belated but crucial appointment of Marshal Ferdinand Foch as head of the newly created Supreme Allied War Council. Their talk was suddenly interrupted by the reverberating sound of distant guns. They stared at each other, then rushed to the balcony. They stood there, she would recall, listening to the far-off noise—"relentless, unbroken, portentous." Finally Tyler turned to Edith, his face alight with excitement: it was, he said, the opening of Foch's long-awaited offensive.

During the previous year and a half Edith had been seeing a good deal of a young American named Ronald Simmons. A graduate of Yale, Simmons had managed to escape the solid family business he had been expected to enter and had turned to the study of art history and an attempted career as a painter. It was to these ends that he had settled in Paris soon after the outbreak of the war. Edith came to know him in the spring of 1917, when he became secretary of the committee for the tubercular military.

Simmons was a short, fat, shyly good-natured person in his early thirties, with weak eyes that missed nothing and dark hair that curled tightly over a wide forehead. He seemed to know everyone in Paris and, partly due to a talent for listening, he was universally liked. In conversation, Edith wrote, everything about him listened: his wrinkled forehead, his screwed-up eyes, his lips twitching thoughtfully beneath his closely clipped moustache. Edith, as she put it, "instantly read, through his jolly fatness, all the fine things vibrating in his heart and mind."

She took him into her deepest affections. To Berenson—who also found Simmons delightful and refreshing and whom the younger art student approached with a sort of lively reverence—Edith spoke of Simmons' "younger brotherly" feeling for her, and elsewhere she indicated a maternal devotion to him. But Lapsley, looking back, thought that on Edith's side there had been something of an Indian-summer romance. Lapsley was normally the least trustworthy witness to Edith Wharton's emotional life; in this instance, however, his intuitions may have been sound. Certainly about no other of her male friends in 1917 and 1918 did Edith speak with so warmly intimate a tone.

The moment America entered the war Simmons presented himself at the Paris recruiting office; he was commissioned a captain in intelligence and assigned to the Marseilles area. Edith remembered him as looking rather like an amiable teddy bear in his rumpled uniform. From Marseilles he wrote her long cheerful letters, and they had an engagement to dine in Paris in mid-August. On August 12 he died very suddenly of double pneumonia in the English hospital at Marseilles.

"So much of me is dead," Edith had written Berenson a month earlier. "My sorrows are real and substantial, and I lunch and dine with them daily." The new blow was almost more than she could bear. "This breaks me down to the depths," she said; "this news has paralysed me." Days later she was still speaking of "the dreadful shock of Simmons's death," and saying that no one but his own mother would feel it as keenly as she. "And then," she added piteously, "he never had a show—and he did so want it and hope for it!" She began at once to memorialize him: in an obituary poem "for R.S." in *Scribner's* and as the character called Boylston in *A Son at the Front*, a novel dedicated (as was *The Marne*, a shorter work of 1918) to Ronald Simmons.

Bernard Berenson, who was back in Paris in early October after an absence of several months, told his wife that during a lunch with Edith they had "wept together over Simmons." If the report is accurate, it is the only recorded moment when Edith Wharton shed tears in the presence of another person (Lapsley declared flatly that he had never seen her cry). She was adamantly opposed to any public display of feeling, and sternly demanded that others keep as firm a rein on their emotions as she did.

Grief must be contained. In the same way, physical illness was not to be catered to. The previous May, Edith had undergone a mildly serious "cardiac crisis" and was declared to be suffering from anemia. It was no doubt the onset of this trouble that explained her curious performance over lunch with Elisina Tyler on the Quai Bourbon when she repeatedly scolded Bertha, the maid, for her failings, complained about the bread, and smashed an elegant water glass (according to Elisina) by flinging it to the floor. When Mary Berenson heard of the anemic condition, she flew into a panic: "Does thee know that pernicious anemia is *fatal?*" she wrote her husband. She would pray, if there were anyone to pray to: "We *can't* lose her, the best of friends." Edith, on the contrary, wrote gaily enough about her symptoms, and assured everyone that Dr. Isch Wall said there was no cause for alarm.

Soon after her recovery Edith learned of the death of her brother Freddy Jones, in Paris, at the age of seventy-two. In reply to a sympathetic letter from Elizabeth Cameron, Edith said she felt sad only because her other brother, Harry, had not taken the occasion to communicate with her. She went on resolutely: "Besides, the real things nowadays concern the real people, and not the poor phantoms who have voluntarily ceased to live so long ago. Minnie and Trix made up to me for my wretched family, and all my thoughts and interests are with them." She had nothing but praise for Minnie Jones, who had had "a lot of hard knocks lately" (mostly financial ones) and who was behaving so bravely and gallantly through it all.

Edith was in no mood to be unduly indulgent toward Mary Berenson when, during the summer, Mary underwent a nervous collapse, caused largely by nearly intolerable pain in her bladder and the frightening necessity of a major operation. Edith expressed sympathy, but urged Mary to resign herself "to a summer of immobility, fresh air, boredom—and *counting your mercies.*" She offered a personal credo which rang with the conviction of experience:

I believe I know the only cure, which is to make one's centre of life inside of one's self, not selfishly or excludingly, but with a kind of unassailable serenity—to decorate one's inner house so richly that one is content there, glad to welcome any one who wants to come and stay, but happy all the same in the hours when one is inevitably alone.

She teased herself a little for such solemn counsel, but then returned to the serious vein. No one but Mary could really help "to gather up the fragments. And life is worth it—just being alive and looking on is a magnificent adventure."

To B.B., meanwhile, and in an unconscious echo of Mary's observations on Edith five years before, she declared that Mary was simply a spoiled child who had had too happy a life. Very likely, she thought, the English specialist whom Berenson was consulting would insist that the two separate. In this, the greedy *amante's* prediction was not borne out.

If anything, Edith was more severe about Elizabeth Cameron, who collapsed emotionally after suffering three blows in succession. On March 28, Henry Adams had died at eighty; soon afterward her daughter and only child, Martha (who had become Mrs. Ronald Lindsay), died after a long illness; and her husband, former Senator Cameron, succumbed. Mrs. Cameron retreated into the unrelieved gloom of her English home, Stapleton House, in Dorset, which she turned into what Mary Berenson called a "tomb cult"—Martha was buried on the premises—and issued only an occasional letter of helpless, almost suicidal grief to Berenson. Edith, to whom the missives were forwarded, found them unutterably dismal reading and voiced impatience over Elizabeth's "evil lethargy." "Oh, B.B.," she cried, "*nothing* matters in times like these but the sense of being the captain of one's soul."

Months later Edith was still severely critical of Elizabeth Cameron; her behavior, she told Mary Berenson, made her wonder "when our sex is coming out of the kindergarten." The "real unpardonable sin," she argued, was the denial of life: "There is no end to it in its mercy as in its pain, but the mercies are more wonderful and immeasurable than the pain." Mary meditated what she called Edith's statement of "her inextinguishable confidence in life," and hoped that Edith would never experience, as she had just done, nine months of "restless physical agony" from cystitis and of shuddering uncontrollably in "nervous illness." She was herself staying with Elizabeth Cameron at Stapleton House at the time, and thought Edith ought to know that her hostess was creating for herself "a dignified, moderately beneficent and contented existence."

Yet no more than others in France was Edith Wharton spared loss and grief down to the last moment of the war. Among the "relatives in khaki" who had been showing up was young Newbold ("Bo") Rhinelander, the son of her first cousin Tom Rhinelander. With a number of adventurous Americans, Bo, barely twenty-one, had come to France in 1916 to join the American Ambulance Corps. After a year with that unit he enlisted in the Army Air Corps and was assigned to a squadron forming at Clermont-Ferrand.

During stretches of leave in Paris, Bo dropped by to see his second cousin. Edith was delighted with him, and his zest to "have a crack at Archie," and looked on fondly while he scuffled with eight-year-old Bill Tyler on her drawing-room carpet or played ragtime tunes on his mandolin. She tried, without success, to arrange a meeting between Bo and the Paul Bourgets, who were staying near Clermont-Ferrand: "I know he would charm them . . . and Bourget's talk would stimulate and interest him." Edith had it clear in her mind, and not without reason, that aerial warfare and the cultivated conversation of Paul Bourget were indissolubly linked phases of the same grand enterprise.

On September 26, wearing his high English riding boots and a fuzzy brown short coat, Bo took off with his squadron on a raid deep inside German territory. On the way back they were surrounded and attacked by a swarm of German planes, and when the party returned to base Bo Rhinelander's plane was not with them. For days Edith sought vainly—through the Red Cross, the American Embassy, the French and American high commands—to get information. Soon after the armistice she learned definitely that Bo was dead, and arranged a burial in the cemetery of the quiet French village near which he had crashed.

4

At almost the same time that Newbold Rhinelander was shot down, General Pershing succeeded in encircling St. Mihiel, on the Meuse River south of Verdun. It was the first great feat of American arms as an independent force, and as a sign of new and increasing Allied strength it helped precipitate the final events. Hindendorf appealed to Wilson for peace; Ludendorff resigned; Germany became a republic.

On a hushed November day Edith Wharton, at work in her apartment, heard at an entirely unusual hour the bells ringing in nearby Ste. Clothilde, where Abbé Mugnier had ministered for so many years. They were responded to by the bells of St. Thomas d'Aquin, St. Louis des Invalides, and other churches in the Faubourg. Nôtre Dame joined in, and the Sacré-Cœur. Edith, Gross, Elise, and the rest crowded onto the balcony, almost unwilling to believe the message in that "gathering rush of sound and speed."

We had fared so long on the thin diet of hope deferred that for a moment or two our hearts wavered and doubted. Then, like the bells, they swelled to bursting, and we knew that the war was over.

At five o'clock that morning the German delegates had signed the terms of the armistice in Marshal Foch's railway carriage in the forest of Compiègne.

The Possessive Years: 1919-1937

PART SIX

22. The Age of Innocence

With the war's end Edith Wharton grew more conscious than ever how drastically she had been cut off not only from the nourishing members of her "Happy Few," but from her own past, from the worlds—seen now across the abyss of the four-year holocaust—in which she had grown up and passed most of her adult life. She was aware of a need to restore both continuity and rootedness to her existence. Toward that end, and with a determined clarity of impulse, she took steps at once practical and imaginative. The practical measure was to establish herself in the first home of her own possession since The Mount; to this was soon added another home in the southerly part of France; and in both domiciles, she quickly gathered around herself her long-absent friends. The fruit of her imaginative quest was *The Age of Innocence*. Within a year of the armistice she could look upon herself, in her own words, as a person who had come back to life, on the alert for fresh experiences, relationships, and literary endeavors.

As early as 1917, in fact, she had begun to search for a home outside Paris, and her choice fell upon a small estate named Jean-Marie, whose high blank wall fronted a cobbled street in the quiet village of St. Brice-sous-Forêt, a dozen miles north of Paris. Elisina Tyler had come upon it during a visit to the nearby convalescent homes at Groslay and Montsoult. Like many other properties in the northern suburbs, it had been abandoned during the German threat to Paris in September 1914 and was now in squalid condition. Edith's knowing eye saw the promise of the long low house and the extensive gardens; the absentee owner, a Mme. Binet, whom Edith found otherwise annoyingly uncooperative, was willing to let it go for a modest sum. Negotiations went forward for almost a year, but meanwhile, teams of carpenters, painters, plumbers, and gardeners were hired, and the immense creative task of preparing a new home got under way.

Edith was feeling another surge of desire for a place in the country, where there would be fruit trees to plant and flowerbeds to lay out, and the sense of growth and blossoming around her. She had had no such environment since the sale of The Mount in 1911. And Paris, into which she had sunk with euphoria a decade before, was becoming hateful to her, especially after the peace conference began there in January 1919. The city, she wrote Berenson, "is simply awful —a kind of continuous earthquake of motors, busses, trams, lorries, taxis and other howling and swooping and colliding engines, with hundreds of thousands of U.S. citizens rushing about in them and tumbling out at one's door." Even the Rue de Varenne apartment failed any longer to charm; it seemed to her empty and echoing.

A further attraction of Jean-Marie was its history. It had originally been called Pavillon Colombe, after two sisters who had been installed there by their lovers around the middle of the eighteenth century. These Venetian-born young ladies had come to France with their father, a wandering musician, and had taken the name Colombe as their stage name when they joined the Comédie Italienne. The older one, a tall, queenly person with a classical Venetian countenance and a compliant disposition, was a brilliant success, one of her most popular roles being that of Sophia Western in a comic opera based on Fielding's *Tom Jones,* and she so inflamed an English milord that he bought her from her father for one hundred louis d'or. Her younger sister, Adeline, was less skillful as an actress and a singer, though the great Italian comic playwright Goldoni had spoken of her favorably. Her energies and talents lay elsewhere; a high-ranking French officer was said to have died as the result of excesses committed with her, and it appears to have been to Adeline that the word *cocotte,* literally a small kettle, was first applied in its modern meaning of courtesan.

Edith Wharton was entranced by this connection with French social and erotic folkways. She declared grandly that her presence would purify the estate of its delightfully corrupt associations, but one of the first things she did was to change the name back to Pavillon Colombe. It would be her summer and autumn home for the next eighteen years.

While work was going forward at St. Brice, Edith, just before her fifty-seventh birthday, fled Paris, the peace conference, her intrusive compatriots, and very bad weather for a four months' stay at the Hotel du Parc in Hyères. Robert Norton, released from the British Admiralty, was with her, and Edith agreed with the opinion of John Hugh Smith that the war had given him "just the maturity and judgment he lacked, or was perhaps too shy to express." It was at Hyères, in the winter and spring of 1919, that Edith and the tall, quietly good-looking "Beau Norts" became the deeply affectionate friends they would thereafter remain. Berenson, who came down for a fortnight toward the end of March, observed that Norton, gentle and impersonal in manner, made "neither effort nor demand," and he understood why masterful women like Edith Wharton so much enjoyed him.

A kind of exultant vitality flowed back into Edith's being as the days passed. She felt, as she put it to Berenson, that she had almost literally died in Paris and had come back to life "in some warm peaceful temperate heaven of the Greeks, chock-ful of asphodel and amaranth." She found herself ravished by "views of land and sea such as never were before, because no previous eyes ever saw them after a war like that." Of a morning Norton vanished for several hours of sketching, while Edith lay abed with her writing board. They met at noon and, with a lunch basket prepared by Gross, went off with Cook for a picnic by the sea or in the hills. There followed a long, rambling walk, and they returned to the hotel "deliciously air and sun-drunk." After a rest they dined together, and later there was leisurely talk about books, reading aloud, and thoughts for the future. Many plans, she remarked, "curl up from our after-dinner cigarettes" and were lazily abandoned.

One plan which, far from being given up, only grew firmer over the months had to do with a curious piece of property in the old part of Hyères, high up above the modern town. Though it looked like a ruined fortress, it had in fact been a convent for "Clarisses"—nuns of the order of St. Claire—built within the walls of an old château; its proper name was Ste. Claire du Vieux Château. Edith and Norton climbed up several times to inspect it, and in her present state of intoxication with Hyères, she determined to get hold of it on a long lease, as a winter residence.

The location was splendid, with a view down over the rooftops of Hyères to the Mediterannean and the thin strip of land that curved out to the wooded rise of the Giens peninsula; to the left and right, like blurred dots in the distance, were the Isles of Gold; farther away still loomed the Maritime Alps. The entire area was a still relatively undiscovered stretch of the French Riviera. Hyères had achieved a certain fame decades earlier when Queen Victoria and her entourage stayed there, but the wealthy and highborn English who hastened to the Riviera each year the moment their native skies assumed a fixed overcast look tended to cluster a good many miles to the east, in the section between St. Raphael and Monte Carlo. Already, within months of the armistice, Edith Wharton was visualizing a life divided between the temperate climate of the southern coast from December to June and the peaceful village at just the right distance from Paris for the rest of the year.

Edith had no competitors for the purchase of Ste. Claire, but there was an enormous amount of repair, refurbishing, and landscaping to be done. An intelligent American friend, an architect named Charles Knight, made a careful examination of the near-wreckage and pronounced that it could be put in shape at manageable cost. "I am thrilled to the spine," Edith wrote Royall Tyler. "*Il y va de mon avenir;* and I feel as if I were going to get married—to the right man at last!"

2

The acquisition of the Pavillon Colombe and the lease of Ste. Claire, with the huge improvements required for both places, were decidedly expensive undertakings. Edith told Berenson during his visit to Hyères that her personal income had been "reduced by half," because of the federal income tax and the decline of New York real estate values. This was almost certainly an exaggeration (the income from her various trusts seems never to have fallen much below twenty-five thousand dollars a year), but in any case the larger funds needed could only come from her writing.

During the first three years of the war her literary earnings were virtually nil. *Summer*, in 1917, brought her fourteen thousand dollars, and the following year she took in that much and more from a number of items. These included a flimsy tale called "Writing a War Story," and the more substantial and amusing "The Refugees," for which the *Saturday Evening Post* paid fifteen hundred dollars. For several thousand dollars, and several different magazines, Edith Wharton wrote a group of articles—"a series of disjointed notes," as she not inaccurately called them—which were collected in 1919 as *French Ways and Their Meaning*. It is a hurried, rambling book, though not lacking in the usual perceptive and delicate observations of the French reverence for life.

The unifying theme, if the book has one, is that of individual freedom: something the author declared the typical German to be indifferent to ("so long as he is well-fed, well amused and making money"), but which the Americans and the French equally esteem. The French woman, however, as against her American counterpart, is regarded as a truly free spirit who stands beside her husband or lover in his work as in his idle hours, while the American woman disappears from sight upon marriage and withers away in the company of her children and the wives of other men. Nor, the analysis continues with an air of personal knowledge, does the Anglo-Saxon character understand love as the French do. For the former, love is divided between the two unrelated elements of sentimentality and sex ("one half, all purity and poetry, the other all pruriency and prose"); only the French are capable of the ideal combination.

The balance of Edith Wharton's income for 1918 came from the serial rights and advance royalties for a short novel called *The Marne*. Rutger B. Jewett, her engaging and dedicated editor at Appleton, found it "the most poignant story of the war which I have read," and, writing in August 1918, he may have been right. But this tale of young Troy Balknap, who visits the forward area in France with his mother after the first battle of the Marne and who returns later as an ambulance driver and is wounded during the second Marne engagement, has little staying power. The best of it, and this must have soon seemed dated, evoked Edith's contempt for the imperturbable blindness of Americans back home during the war and the self-inflation of those who had glimpsed the devastated areas through the windows of a chauffeur-driven car. " 'The tragedy of it—the tragedy—no one can tell who hasn't seen it, and been through it,' Mrs. Balknap would begin, looking down her long dinner table between the orchids and the candelabra."

Edith Wharton's career as one of the leading money-makers among the writers of her time may be said to have begun in April 1919, near the end of her stay at the Hotel du Parc in Hyères, when the editor of *Pictorial Review* conveyed via Jewett an offer of eighteen thousand dollars for the serialization of her next novel. For Edith, gazing up acquisitively at the old ruined convent above the town, this was timely news; but there was some uncertainty as to which of her several works-in-progress would in fact constitute her next novel. *The Glimpses of the Moon*, contracted for with Appleton two years earlier, remained at a standstill. Mrs. Wharton offered in its stead *A Son at the Front*, a large-scale portrait of Americans in Paris during the war, which had occupied her chief attention for the previous six months. Contractual negotiations were begun, only to have both Vance, at the *Pictorial Review*, and Jewett smitten with misgivings. Was not the war old hat? Did anybody really want to hear or read about it any longer? The poor response to *The Marne* seemed an answer to the questions.

Edith Wharton set aside the manuscript of *A Son at the Front* next to that of *The Glimpses of the Moon*, and after an interval came up with the scenario of still another novel. It bore the working title "Old New York" and the scene was laid in 1875. The two main characters, Langdon Archer and Clementine Olenska, are both unhappily married. Falling in love, they "go off secretly," Edith explained, "and meet in Florida where they spend a few mad weeks" before Langdon returns to his pretty, conventional wife in New York, and Clementine to an existence, separated from her brutish husband, in Paris.

The New York editors leaped at the proposal. The *Pictorial Review* duly paid eighteen thousand dollars for the serial, and to this Appleton added fifteen thousand as an advance against royalties. All told, Edith Wharton's literary income skyrocketed in 1919 to almost forty thousand dollars, more than she had earned in a single year since 1906. And to an appreciable extent, *The Age of Innocence* (as the book was shortly renamed) came into being as the result of a shrewd estimate of the literary market by both the editor of a slick picture magazine and the representative of an up-and-coming firm of publishers.

There were, of course, other and more significant sources. The enduring effect of the war upon Edith Wharton (as upon countless other sensitive and thoughtful persons) was to give her an entirely new consciousness of history— as a writer, as an American, and as an individual human being. She had re-marked to Jewett that "the face of the world is changing so rapidly that the poor novelist is left breathless and mute, unless like Mr. Wells, he can treat things 'topically,' which I never could." With *The Age of Innocence* under way, and with a clearer sense of her own creative situation, she held forth to Berenson on the relation between the Great War and the writing of fiction, saying (in Berenson's paraphrase):

Before the war you could write fiction without indicating the period, the present being assumed. The war has put an end to that for a long time, and everything will soon have to be timed with reference to it. In other words, the historical novel with all its vices will be the only possible form for fiction.

She was, in addition, revolted by what she could see of postwar America, and the impression grew in her that something crucially valuable had been lost. The spurt of patriotic emotion aroused by American troops marching down the Champs Elysées had quite subsided, and if she had turned against Paris, it was in good part, as we have noticed, because of the hordes of Americans darkening the scene by their noisy persistent presence. She was becoming acquainted, she told Elisina Tyler, with "the new American cad," and discoursed scathingly about two visiting members of a New York refugee committee, each in her view a worse bounder than the other. Her country's retreat into isolationism was a further cause of disgust.

> I say nothing about what you say of public affairs [she wrote the equally horrified Sally Norton] except that I agree with you on every point, and am humiliated to the soul at being what is now known as an "American." All that I thought American in a true sense is gone, and I see nothing but vain-glory, crassness, and total ignorance—which of course is the core of the whole evil.

Impelled by such angry and despairing sentiments, Edith Wharton went in search, imaginatively, of the America that was gone. Looking across the vast abyss of the war, she located the lost America in the New York of her girlhood: the New York she had come back to in 1872, after six years in Europe; the world in which she had passed her adolescence and the first years of her womanhood —a safe, narrow, unintellectual, and hidebound world, but from the tremendous distance of time and history, an endearing and an honorable one. It was there that she set the main action of *The Age of Innocence.*

The identification was meaningful, of course, to Edith Wharton personally. "I am steeping myself in the nineteenth century," she informed Sara Norton on another occasion, "which is such a blessed refuge from the turmoil and mediocrity of today—like taking sanctuary in a mighty temple." But the writing of *The Age of Innocence* was much more than the act of a historical imagination alienated from the present hour, and Edith Wharton was by no means simply fleeing from an unattractive present to a well-protected past. Certain urgent and personal needs in her nature were being responded to.

Amid the bewildering scenes of the postwar world, and cut off by the war from the conditions of life which had gone into the making of her, Edith Wharton at some level of her psyche felt a strong imperative to get back in touch once more with the self she had been. *"Je me cherche, et je ne me retrouve pas,"* she had remarked sadly to Berenson in the last days of the war; the doors of memory, imagination, and creativity seemed locked to her. She needed almost desperately, as a literary artist and as a woman, to rediscover in herself the vital continuity she looked for in vain in the world around her. Two decades before, after she had to a considerable degree broken free from her American past and her inherited social milieu, she had attempted to realign herself with that past through a series of stories and a long novel, each taking as its theme the linking up of past and present. Now, in 1919 and 1920, after an incomparably greater cleavage from everything she had known and been, she summoned her energies to a far greater act of reconciliation. In *The Age of Innocence*, Edith Wharton sought to come back to herself—though in what terms, and with what success, it remains to be seen.

3

It was a time of severance and a time of reuniting. Another way in which Edith set about reconstructing her life was what is known in the Hebrew tradition as the process of "ingathering"—the bringing together again of dearest friends whom she had seen only intermittently or not at all for the better part of five years. Busy as she was with the multitudinous work of repairing and planting, she took time to importune those absent and separated to join her at St. Brice as soon as it was ready. Her society of friends, in the spring of 1919, had assumed for her an almost historical importance. "We've got such long arrears to make up for," she wrote Gaillard Lapsley, "and we're dancing on such a tight-rope and volcano kind of world that the Happy Few must 'get together" whenever they can—and never let go again."

Her Paris regulars were in attendance when she returned from Hyères in mid-April: the Bourgets, the du Bos', St. André, Rosa de Fitz-James. Berenson, who spent the better part of the year in the city as an observer at the peace conference, should also be reckoned among them, and also, to Edith's pleasure, Eric Maclagan, attached to the British peace delegation and, on the side, working on a translation of Machiavelli. Percy Lubbock, similarly on hand for the moment, thought Edith seemed harried by the Paris hurly-burly—"as well she might be," he told Lapsley—but felt sure she would calm down once she was settled in "her pretty little old white house and green garden at St. Brice (I saw them —they are charming, charming)." He only hoped she would not drive back into Paris "uncontrollably every day." Berenson, however, worried that Edith would be cut off at the Pavillon Colombe from the centers of activity and stimulus; but as to that, Edith, to paraphrase a saying of Emerson's, was determined now to plant herself in her own domain and let the wide world come around to her.

Another matter of communal intercourse arose in connection with the letters of Henry James. It was originally proposed that James's family should handle an edition of his correspondence (and that this would be "all that is wanted in the way of a Biography"); but Edith Wharton felt strongly that someone was needed to decipher the vast number of letters to her and the other members of the old

Queen's Acre constituency—"someone," as she wrote Edmund Gosse, asking him to intercede in the case, "familiar with the atmosphere in which Henry and our small group communed together." Her candidate was Percy Lubbock, because of his "extraordinary literary sense," and also, she suggested to Margaret James, because of his "almost magical insight into your uncle's point of view." The issue was complicated by Mrs. William James's unrelenting hostility toward Edith Wharton—she had it fixed in her mind that Mrs. Wharton was a woman of immoral imagination, if not character, and blamed her exclusively for the birthday-gift affair of 1913. Lubbock was eventually invited to edit the letters, but only after being warned to guard himself against "a certain influence" (i.e., Mrs. Wharton), and he in turn voiced indignation that a literary treasure of this kind should be dependent upon the conflicting whims of "two *women.*"

While lingering in town Edith and her household, from the balcony of a friend's house on the Champs Elysées, watched the *rentré des troupes*, the grand victory parade on Bastille Day, July 14. For Edith it was all a spectacular blur of surging crowds and massed flags, of generals riding by and regiments wheeling, of sunlight on rifles and helmets, cannons and tanks. That celebrational display, which brought to a splendid climax Edith's twelve-year residence in Paris, was followed by a more private ceremony: what she called the ritual opening of the Pavillon Colombe on August 7.

Berenson took part in the occasion. Lubbock and Lapsley came for a fortnight's stay, and Edith kept them up late discussing "Henry questions." Abbé Mugnier spent a day at the Pavillon, holding forth amusingly on the inveterate French distrust of foreigners; John Hugh Smith arrived, and the Bourgets; the Walter Gays drove up from Le Bréau, and Charles du Bos from St. Cloud. "Somebody has bobbed in for every meal," Edith remarked with satisfaction. The new home was alive, her society of friends was reestablished, and she was able to turn back, after a long interruption, to her novel.

One of the Happy Few was conspicuously and sadly missing. Howard Sturgis, at sixty-four, had entered his last illness—something brought on, perhaps, by the personal agony of a war that his tender nature was not equipped to endure. He died peacefully in his sleep soon after the turn of the year 1920. "There was none like him," Percy Lubbock wrote in an obituary letter to the London *Times:*

. . . so rich, so various, so loveable, so inexhaustibly engaging and amusing a nature . . . Endlessly soft-hearted, yet with a hard unsentimental veracity that often took people by surprise; wilful and whimsical, yet with an intellectual sanity, an abiding sense of proportion that nothing could tamper with; quick as a flash in wit and ironic intelligence, patient and scrupulous in kindness.

4

The Age of Innocence was half finished when, at the end of November 1919 and in unusually tempestuous weather, Edith moved back to 53 Rue de Varenne for her last stay there of any length. It was a dispiriting moment. "To be back in this huge apartment, with no heart to fill it with people, and to tramp about in daily deluge, and crawl home to—nothing in particular." It took her two months to choose which of the furniture so lovingly selected for the Rue de Varenne should be taken out to St. Brice, which shipped down to Hyeres, which stored in a warehouse. Before January 1920 was out, she was again at Hyères, where she rented a pleasant villa called Le Bocage from an English baronet, at a cost of sixteen hundred dollars for four months. Edith was, for the moment, involved with four different places of residence, just as four different novels were either moving forward or awaiting their turn. ("I have never been able to write one novel without having another one going on at the same time," she explained to the somewhat dazed Rutger Jewett. The immediate reference was to a work called "The Necklace," begun the previous October and never completed.) Nor could it be said that Edith Wharton was a passive observer of the large labors at Ste. Claire and the Pavillon Colombe.

During the winter of 1920 she saw to the purchase of an insurance policy for the Pavillon; arranged a loan of twenty thousand dollars from the Lincoln Trust Company to help pay for the work at both villas; bought herself a Louis XV bed in Toulon for seven hundred dollars and a mantelpiece from Marseilles for two hundred dollars; and had her cousin Herman Edgar sell one of her New York properties, at 739 Broadway. (Edgar would shortly resign as her trustee, and there was a flurry of legal documents to be signed, notarized, and returned.) Having supervised the September planting at Ste. Claire, she exchanged long letters with Charles Knight about the Pavillon Colombe gardens, and went into detail about the separate little houses being constructed on the grounds for Arthur White and Charles Cook. "Every domestic detail," she wrote Berenson, "has become a kind of Matterhorn, over which one has to be roped and hooked and hoisted, with every chance of perishing in an avalanche or down a precipice on the way."

Edith, as always, took special care in the matter of household staffing. The long-standing group was intact, and for some years had included an extremely competent housemaid, an Englishwoman named Louisa Butler. There were now added a new major-domo, Favre (Arthur White had been elevated to Mrs. Wharton's "general agent"), a dark-haired, white-coated youngish man; and Roger, an amiable youth with a shuffling gait who had been taken on as a kitchen boy before the war and now returned to be Mme. Wharton's cook for more than a decade.

There were vexing little troubles with some of the lesser members. Alice, a chambermaid, was sent on her way: she had threatened to quit several times, but when her fiancé jilted her she asked to be kept on; Mme. Wharton assented, only to discover that Alice was advertising in the newspapers for another position as *femme de chambre*, signing herself "Alice, 53 de Varenne." Among those Edith tried out as a successor was a highly recommended young woman who arrived in a sleeveless dress which barely reached her knees. When Louisa handed her a cap and apron, she said scornfully: *"Moi—mette cela? J'aime mieux m'en aller."* "Which she did by the next train," Edith informed Elisina Tyler, "though she had changed her mind by that time." Edith Wharton was perhaps unusually good with those who worked for her, but she sometimes felt that if she ever lost her faith in human nature, it would be due to the carryings-on of French servants.

Her most valuable acquisition was a new secretary, Jeanne Duprat, a short, slight, dark-haired woman of early middle age, who came to the household in the last year of the war. Self-effacing and efficient, Mlle. Duprat could take dictation in French. Edith Wharton wrote her English-language letters by hand, as she did her fiction, Mlle. Duprat then transcribing those—the innumerable business letters—of which there was to be a copy.

Still further items claimed Edith's attention. There were her increasing private charities, including the quarterly checks to Minnie Jones, and the establishment of a trust fund for three Belgian children whom Edith had taken on as her personal "cases." She faithfully paid her French income tax, about twenty-two hundred dollars for the year, and exchanged letters and telegrams about a French translation of *The Age of Innocence* and a Danish version of *The Reef*. And a task close to her heart was the creation of a new grave for Ronald Simmons in the Cimetière St. Pierre in Marseilles; Edith advanced twelve hundred dollars, commissioned a marble worker to build a vault, and with Mrs. Simmons' grateful approval saw to the transfer of the body from its ugly original grave.

It was in the midst of these assorted preoccupations and distractions that Edith Wharton continued to work against the inexorable deadline on *The Age of Innocence*. On April 5 she could report that the novel was finished. "You are a wonder," Jewett said to her. "Do you marvel that I bow low before such energy?"

5

The Age of Innocence began to appear in the monthly *Pictorial Review*, flanked by advertisements for soap flakes and "Sani-flush" for cleaning toilet bowls, in July 1920. Even as she was depositing the final payment (of sixty-five hundred dollars) from the magazine, Edith had her first taste of procedures in the world of mass publication, as against those in a firm with the high literary standards of Charles Scribner's Sons. She was notified casually that the *Review* proposed cutting some of the installments, since the space was needed for illustrations and other displays. Edith, outraged, reminded Jewett that she had set aside *A Son at the Front* upon urgings from New York and had met the deadline for a novel of quite another order. She had in fact "done really a superhuman piece of work in writing within the year the best part of two long novels, entirely different in subject and treatment." In view of all this, "I cannot consent to have my work treated as prose by the yard."

Appleton was more knowingly respectful than the magazine. The novel was published on October 20 to the accompaniment of lavish advertising which pronounced her the greatest woman novelist in America. There was a swelling chorus of praise from the reviewers. Henry Seidel Canby, in the New York *Evening Post,* said the book did honor to American literature, and against some carpings that Edith Wharton's scope was a narrow one, he replied that indeed it was—like that of Jane Austen and Guy de Maupassant, who chose to study human nature in its articulate rather than its broad-ranging manifestations. A reviewer in *The Nation* observed tellingly that Mrs. Wharton had described the rites and habits of old New York "as familiarly as if she loved them and as lucidly as if she hated them." Elsewhere, the book was found to be packed with unsparing perception, hypnotically readable, and, in the words of one admirer, the perfect fruit of an austere and disciplined talent.

These comments were undoubtedly deserved. Both in its shapeliness and its richness of human feeling, *The Age of Innocence* is a minor masterpiece, one of Edith Wharton's three or four most elegant novels. But there was at least one demurrer: Vernon L. Parrington, at work upon his monumental study *Main Currents in American Thought,* in which artistic considerations were subordinated to liberal political doctrine, referred to Edith Wharton as "our literary aristocrat" and implied that for all its craftsmanship her book was irrelevant to the more pressing issues of the day. But Professor William Lyon Phelps of Yale wrote excitedly in *The New York Times* that Mrs. Wharton was a writer who brought glory to her country and that some of the scenes in this, her best book, were worthy of Conrad or Henry James. If the latter remark gave Edith a familiar twinge, she could be assuaged by another contention that, much more than the leading product of "the James School," she was an originator of her own.

Within a few months *The Age of Innocence*, aided by this volley of enthusiasm, earned back more than the $15,000 advance. By April 1921, 66,000 copies had been sold, and the figure eventually reached about 115,000 in the United States, Canada, and England. In the latter country, it may be added, the reception was generally good. Katharine Mansfield, in the *Atheneum,* found the temperature of the novel a bit cool for her taste, but praised its construction; the *Times Literary Supplement,* along with other periodicals, regarded it as Edith Wharton's finest composition to date. The book was still selling steadily at the end of 1922. Over a two-year period *The Age of Innocence* netted its author nearly $70,000—a figure which included $15,000 from Warner Brothers for the film rights.

One or two reviewers alluded, somewhat pretentiously and without specification, to various anachronisms and other mistakes in the novel. In fact, the only real embarrassment, hastily removed in the second printing, had the clergyman who was performing the marriage of Newland Archer and May Welland invoke the opening words of the burial service: "Forasmuch as it has pleased Almighty God . . ." The former member of Calvary Church heard about this from several readers, including an admiring and amused cleric, and put on metaphorical sackcloth in her replies. Otherwise, Edith Wharton had done her homework most thoroughly, drawing on her remarkable memory and with immense help from Minnie Jones. At Edith's request Minnie had put in hours of research in New York and at Yale, pinning down the exact dates when Mme. Christine Nilsson sang *Faust* at the old Academy of Music, when Delmonico's moved north to Twenty-sixth Street, and the times of the first Patriarchs' Balls, the Assemblies, the Friday Evening Dancing Classes.

The result is a warmly accurate portrait of a vanished physical and social scene. Here is Edith Jones's New York of the brownstone era, with its rival opera houses, its Gramercy Park and Washington Square and Central Park, its new Metropolitan Museum, its "Pennsylvania terminus" (located in New Jersey and reached by ferry)—that "big reverberating station" seen on a somber, snowy afternoon, lit by gas lamps. Here too is Newport in the 1870s: still innocent, unencumbered as yet by the gigantic "cottages"; Bellevue Avenue and Ocean Drive, along which the victorias and barouches paraded daily; the archery contests and horse shows and tennis parties.

The story has chiefly to do with the thwarted love for each other of Newland Archer and Countess Ellen Olenska, the former Ellen Mingott of New York— thwarted in particular, in two successive and parallel episodes, by Ellen's lovely, conventional, and calculating young cousin, May Welland, first as Archer's fiancée and later as his wife. Around these three central figures there hovers a large cast of characters, expertly delineated and delicately distinguished. In portraying them Edith Wharton was not only remembering the numerous individuals who thronged her parents' drawing room or whom she encountered at dinner parties and the great balls, but she was also bringing them back to life and into her own life. *The Age of Innocence* in this regard is a strenuous act of revivification. In no other of Edith Wharton's novels were the names of the characters so audibly close to those of their originals.

There is, in short, a procession of lively and recognizable ghosts. The Reverend Dr. Washburn of Calvary, the father of Pussy Jones's friend Emelyn (still briskly alive, incidentally, in New York), walks again in the briefly seen clergyman the Reverend Dr. Ashmore. Egerton Winthrop reappears in the gossipy, snobbish, and intelligent Sillerton Jackson, as does William Travers, the entertaining socialite father of Matilda Gay. Lucretia Jones peers out at us from behind the "firm placid features" of Archer's mother-in-law, Mrs. Welland.

Edith Wharton was slyly evasive about one or two of these identifications. When Minnie Jones thought to detect the Jewish-born millionaire August Belmont in the name and figure of the mysterious immigrant financier Julius Beaufort, Edith was quick to deny it—no doubt because Beaufort also incarnated a portion of her reprehensible cousin George Alfred Jones, who had, like Beaufort, embezzled money to support his mistress. But there could be no denying Mrs. Mason Jones—Edith's formidable, benevolent Aunt Mary—in her guise as the lordly and obese Mrs. Manson Mingott, established in the bulging home she had built on upper Fifth Avenue, surrounded by quarries, saloons, wooden greenhouses, and goats grazing in rocky fields.

There are times when Mrs. Paran Stevens assumes control of Mrs. Mingott's personality: manipulating to get her hands on her late husband's fortune, marrying her children into the European aristocracy (Lady Paget, the former Mary Stevens, could still be encountered at London gatherings), hobnobbing with ambassadors and sponsoring opera singers, serving food at her lavish dinners that was as bad as William Travers proclaimed it to be. Mrs. Stevens' son Harry, Edith's fiancé for the season of 1882, comes back as young Carfry, whom the Archers meet in England and who is heading for Switzerland, seeking a cure for his consumption, and afterward to Oxford. And in Carfry's tutor, it has been suggested, we have the only known portrait of the able young man whom some alleged to be Edith's father. (See Appendix A.)

It is from the vital context of these re-creations that the two central characters draw their fullness of being. For in *The Age of Innocence*, Edith Wharton divided her own past self between Newland Archer and Ellen Olenska. In Archer, she brought back the restive and groping member of the old society she had once been, and as she traced Archer's career she suggested how sedate and yet how unfulfilled she might have become had she failed to break free of that curiously attractive social prison. It may even be that she changed Archer's first name, just before publication, from Langdon to Newland to bring it closer to her own middle name, Newbold. In Countess Olenska, Edith Wharton offered a partial sketch of the intense and nonconformist self, "the young hawk" as someone had called her, that had escaped—though only into a miserably unhappy marriage (the coarsely unfaithful Baron Olenski, from what little we know of him, is poor Teddy Wharton stripped of all his redeeming features). In the scenes between Newland and the countess, Edith Wharton was performing, as it were, a retrospective act of self-confrontation.

The most vivid and also the most richly significant scene in this regard is the penultimate one, the dinner party given by Archer's wife, May, on the occasion of Ellen Olenska's departure for Europe. The patrician van der Luydens are there and Sillerton Jackson, and representatives of the Welland and Mingott clans. It is all an elaborate ritual, masking what is in effect the ejection of the disturbing Ellen Olenska from New York society: "the tribal rally," Archer suddenly realizes, "around a kinswoman about to be eliminated from the tribe."

Edith Wharton, always addicted to anthropology (one may recall the ritualistic poem on the death of Theodore Roosevelt), was here making most skillful use of her readings in *The Golden Bough* and other works. In doing so, she was not only appraising her former New York world in tribal terms, but was also dramatizing her own gradual alienation and withdrawal from that world as an act of casting off by a society that could neither understand nor contain her. Archer, surveying the placid, well-fed guests bent over their canvasback ducks, sees them suddenly as "a band of dumb conspirators, and himself and the pale woman on his right as the center of their conspiracy." Continuing in her own voice, Edith Wharton remarks:

> It was the old New York way of taking life "without effusion of blood": the way of people who dreaded scandal more than disease, who placed decency above courage, and who considered that nothing was more ill-bred than "scenes," except the behavior of those who gave rise to them.

In the epilogue, via Ellen Olenska's later life, Edith Wharton described what had in fact become of herself: permanently expatriated and living in the Faubourg St. Germain section of Paris; separated once and for all from her husband; making the rounds of theaters and galleries; consorting with the aristocracy in the old *hôtels*.

And in that ending, the various times link up with one another. Following the main action set in the late 1870s, near the time of Edith's social debut, the epilogue takes place thirty years later, in 1907: that is, the moment when Edith first settled in Paris. Archer, musing on a bench outside Ellen's Paris building and gazing up at the windows of her apartment, reminds himself (Edith Wharton is careful to note) that he is only fifty-seven years old—Edith Wharton's exact age in 1919 when she wrote the larger part of the novel.

Archer and Olenska, their relationship broken by the bland, implacable force of New York society, will never see each other again. But in the world of her imaginings, Edith Wharton, by the act of writing the novel in just the way she did write it, brought together the phases of her life and her nature. Her successive New York and Europeanized selves—*their* relation, as she had felt, sundered by the Great War—were, for an indeterminate moment in 1919 and 1920, in harmony.

6

In May 1921, *The Age of Innocence* was awarded the Pulitzer Prize—the first time a woman, and only the third time any individual, had been so honored. The award, sponsored by Columbia University, was given annually "for the American novel which shall best present the wholesome atmosphere of American life and the highest standard of American manners and manhood." Edith Wharton, though pleased by the distinction and not less so by the prize money (one thousand dollars, which went at once into her gardens), was taken aback when she discovered the flatulent terms in which she had been honored. A further discovery disconcerted her even more.

The jury (Robert Morss Lovett, Stuart Sherman, and a reluctant Hamlin Garland) had actually chosen another novel, *Main Street* by Sinclair Lewis, but the trustees of the university rejected that recommendation on the grounds that *Main Street* had given offense in certain quarters and took it upon themselves to select *The Age of Innocence*. In a characteristically sportsmanlike gesture, Lewis wrote Edith Wharton, congratulating her on the award and expressing his deep admiration for her work. Edith replied from St. Brice in August:

What you say is so kind, so generous, and so unexpected, that I don't know where to begin to answer. It is the first sign I have ever had—literally—that *"les Jeunes"* at home had ever read a word of me. I had long since resigned myself to the idea that I was regarded by you all as the—say the Mrs. Humphry Ward of the Western Hemisphere; though at times I wondered why. Your book and *Susan Lenox* (unexpurgated) have been the only things out of America that have made me cease to despair of the republic—of letters; so you can imagine what a pleasure it is to know that you have read *me*, and cared, and understood. It gives me a *"Nunc Dimittis"* feeling—or would, if I hadn't still about a hundred subjects to deal with!

As for the Columbia Prize, the kind Appletons have smothered me in newspaper commentary; and when I discovered that I was being rewarded—by one of our leading universities—for uplifting American morals, I confess I *did* despair.

Subsequently, when I found the prize should really have been yours, but was withdrawn because your book (I quote from memory) had "offended a number of prominent persons in the Middle West," disgust was added to despair.—Hope returns to me, however, with your letter, and with the enclosed article, just received.—Some sort of standard *is* emerging from the welter of cant and sentimentality, and if two or three of us are gathered together, I believe we can still save Fiction in America.

The letter ended with a warm invitation to St. Brice. Two months later Sinclair and Grace Hegger Lewis came out from their Paris hotel for lunch at the Pavillon. Though Lewis and Edith Wharton were not to become especially close friends, they made a point of seeing each other intermittently over the next years. There were further visits to St. Brice and meetings for lunch or tea in Paris; the Lewises came down for a short stay in Hyères; Edith drove down to the sumptuous country home near Fontainebleau which the Lewises had rented for the summer of 1923, bringing with her John Hugh Smith and Gaillard Lapsley —"two delightful men," Lewis thought.

In the tall, gangling, copper-haired, and fast-talking Sinclair Lewis, Edith

Wharton found much to stimulate and divert her. Thirty-six at the time of the Pulitzer Prize affair, Lewis could certainly be counted among *"les Jeunes"* in American fiction. He had just entered the decade of his most notable literary achievement—*Main Street* would be followed in impressive succession by *Babbitt, Arrowsmith, Elmer Gantry,* and *Dodsworth*—which would culminate with the Nobel Prize in 1930. Lewis' genuine respect for Edith Wharton can be traced to his undergraduate days at Yale in the early 1900s, when he read and studied her short stories. Her name appeared regularly thereafter on the little lists he used to compile of those whom he regarded as the most accomplished, and hence the most competitive, living American writers. Lewis seems even to have spoken of Edith Wharton's influence on him, and though this is far from evident in the tone and texture of his characteristic work, Lewis could find in Edith Wharton's novels—preeminently in *The Age of Innocence*—the mixture of derision and affection toward old New York that he sought to display toward Gopher Prairie, Minnesota, and Zenith, Ohio.

Soon after their first encounter at St. Brice, Lewis wrote Mrs. Wharton to ask if he might dedicate *Babbitt* to her. "I'm a little dizzy!" was Edith's immediate reply. "No one has ever wanted to dedicate a book to me before—and I'm so particularly glad that now it's happened, the suggestion comes from the author of *Main Street. Yes*—of course!" (She had forgotten at least one other dedication, that of Eliot Gregory's collection of articles in 1900, *The Ways of Men.* Edith Wharton, it might be added, took the occasion to have Lewis sent a copy of Percy Lubbock's *The Craft of Fiction*—"full of interesting and suggestive things for people of our trade"—but it is improbable that Lewis took much to heart this resolutely Jamesian discussion of its subject. He did, however, urge his publisher's attention onto Marcel Proust, in the wake of Mrs. Wharton's expressed enthusiasm.)

Something in the younger writer's appreciation of her drew from Edith Wharton discourse about the profession of fiction such as she rarely indulged in, in her private correspondence. When *Babbitt* appeared in the fall of 1922 she wrote Lewis another long literary letter of both a particular and a general kind.

There is so much to say about *Babbitt* that I don't know where to begin—unless at the dedication, which gives me an ever warmer glow of satisfaction, now that I've read what follows, than when you first announced it to me!—If I've waited as long as this to have a book dedicated to me, Providence was evidently waiting to find just the Right Book. All my thanks for it.

And what next? Oh, do jump on a steamer, and come over and have a talk about it! It kept me reading til one a.m. the other night, and started me again at 5—and at every page I found something to delight in, and something to talk about.—The prevailing impression, when one has finished, is of an extraordinary vitality and vivacity, an ever-bubbling spring of visual and moral sensibility—and this kind of "liveness" is one of the most important qualities in any work of fiction—or of any other art—

I don't think *Babbitt* as good a novel, in the all-round sense, as *Main Street*, because in the latter you produce a sense of unity and depth by reflecting Main Street in the consciousness of a woman who suffered from it because she had points of comparison, and was detached enough to situate it in the universe—whereas Babbitt is in and of Zenith up to his chin and over, and Sinclair Lewis is obliged to do the seeing and comparing for him. But then there is much more life and glow and abundance in the new book; you must have felt a stronger hold on it and a richer flow. I wonder how much of it the American public, to whom irony seems to have become as unintelligible as Chinese, will even remotely feel? To do anything worthwhile, one must resolutely close one's ears and eyes to their conception of the novel; and I admire nothing more in your work than your steady balancing on your tight-rope over the sloppy abyss of sentimentality.

I've only begun to say what I wanted; but the rest must be talk—except for one suggestion, which I venture to make now, that is, that in your next book, you should use slang in dialogue more sparingly. I believe the real art in this respect is to use just enough to *colour* your dialogue, not so much that in a few years it will be almost incomprehensible. It gives more relief to your characters, I'm sure, than to take down their jargon word by word.

Thank you again for associating my name with a book I so warmly admire and applaud, and believe me, with kindest remembrances to Mrs. Lewis,

Your most sincerely,
E. Wharton

Edith Wharton's regard for Lewis' writing was unfeigned. "He really *is* an artist," she said to Hugh Smith; in her view, "the average modern novelist" could live for a year on Sinclair Lewis' leavings. On another occasion, after mentioning several contemporary American writers, she declared with unusual bluntness that Lewis was the only one in the lot "with any guts."

Another consequence of the Pulitzer award gave peculiar relish to Edith Wharton's ironic soul. Early in 1921 she had begun to contemplate further fictional explorations of old New York, reaching back to earlier moments in the nineteenth century. Her thought was to put together two novellas in a volume to be called "Among the Mingotts," and she soon completed the first of them, a story called *The Old Maid*, set in the New York of the 1850s.

It was a poignant tale of illegitimacy. Charlotte Lovell, a niece of Mrs. Manson Mingott, has a brief affair with an impoverished young man and gives birth in secret to a baby girl. The child is absorbed into the household of Charlotte's cousin Delia after the latter's marriage, and grows up calling Delia "Mamma." Her "Aunt Charlotte," meanwhile, becomes to all outward appearances the stereotype old maid, a figure of thoughtless fun to her own daughter; but Charlotte, though at considerable personal sacrifice, agrees to the end that the truth must never be disclosed to the girl.

The story was turned down by one magazine after the other. "It is a bit too vigorous for us," said the editor of the *Ladies' Home Journal;* it was powerful, no doubt, said another, but it was simply too unpleasant. Though she had suffered from this sort of puritanical philistinism for more than fifteen years, Edith Wharton managed to be dumfounded by the new expression of it. Had the readers of those magazines never read such tales of illegitimacy as *The Scarlet Letter* or *Adam Bede?* "And how about my own *Summer?*" Then came the front-page news that *The Age of Innocence* had been selected as the novel of the year which best presented the wholesome atmosphere of American life and the highest standards of American morals. An award of wholesomeness thus coincided with a rejection on the grounds of distasteful sexuality; but the publicity attending the prize encouraged *Redbook* to buy *The Old Maid* for $2,250. The novella turned into one of Edith Wharton's most durably popular and profit-making stories, with a dramatic version having a good run on Broadway in the mid-1930s and a film rendition co-starring Bette Davis and Miriam Hopkins in the first of their series of tear-inducing melodramas.

7

It was just before Christmas 1920 that Edith Wharton was finally installed in Ste. Claire, the entrance there being delayed by heavy gales that ripped off tiles, ruined wallpaper, and sprang leaks all over the château. But Christmas morning found her basking in the sunlight on the terrace, reading a letter from Berenson, and looking down on the Porquerolles and the other Isles of Gold, "floating on a silver sea just below me." She had never before felt so intimately connected with the physical universe, she wrote Berenson: "The communion with sun and moon risings and settings, and the wheeling of the great winter constellations [are] so far beyond what any of us had imagined that we are still in the period of ecstatic ejaculations."

The establishment of her second European household in less than two years represented a further stage in her withdrawal from contemporary America, even as she was imaginatively repossessing herself of the America that had vanished. She rarely missed an opportunity to deprecate her country's most visible qualities, but she was conscious, too, that her last valued associations with it were slipping away. Just after New Year's 1921, Barrett Wendell fell gravely ill; he had written her "a perfectly charming letter" in full appreciation of *The Age of Innocence*, and when Wendell should go, Edith remarked, "the last of the tradition we care for will disappear." By mid-February, Wendell was dead.

Walter Berry, at the same time, was busy moving his books and furniture from 14 Rue St. Guillaume to 53 Rue de Varenne, where he had taken over Edith Wharton's lease. "53 hasn't the charm of 14," he wrote Berenson, but he had a great deal more space to move about in. At sixty-two Berry was white-haired and white-moustached, tall and slightly stooping, with the aura of an elder statesman much used to imposing public appearances. He hoped, he added on a postcard to Berenson, to stay in the Rue de Varenne apartment "till I go out feet first": a hope that would be quite precisely fulfilled.

In later years there spread one of the more foolish of the legends that have clustered around Edith Wharton. This was given currency in *The Passionate Years* by Caresse Crosby, the wife of Berry's cousin Harry Crosby. In it, a secret stairway in 53 Rue de Varenne connected the apartments of Edith Wharton and Walter Berry, presumably used by them to creep up and down to illicit assignations. The image is not without its attraction, but the fact is that at no moment were Edith and Berry simultaneously apartment dwellers at No. 53, or anywhere else. Berry had been Edith's houseguest for a few months while he was looking about for a place of his own, and the back entrance to the guest suite from the courtyard may have confusingly given rise to the legend. Berry, otherwise, was no more than Edith's successor in the apartment where she had lived since the start of 1910.

Before her first season at Ste. Claire was over, Edith Wharton had settled into the endlessly gratifying routine of life which would be the pattern of her winters and springs for years to come. Work in her bedroom in the morning, with the watchful assistance of Jeanne Duprat; at noon, given half decent weather, the inevitable picnic, followed by a two-hour walk. Often Edith and her guests would go to the Tour Fondue, a picturesque ruin of a tower at the tip of the Hyères peninsula, from which one could make—as Edith frequently did—the short trip across the water to the Porquerolles. Or they might go to Les Sablettes, on another tiny spit of land below Toulon, or into the hills and the tree-shaded meadows farther inland. Occasionally they drove as far west as Marseilles, for purchases and a visit to the grave of Ronald Simmons. At other times a meal would be spread out on the big smooth rocks crowding the shoreline at Le Levandou, or the party would venture eastward through Cannes to Grasse and back along the Grand Corniche, which Edith had traveled with Teddy in their first automobile.

Berenson paid his first visit to the château in April, and after experiencing "the softness of the April air, the incense-like fragrance of the pines and cypresses," and "the artistic beauty of the rocks" above the "opalescent sea," pronounced it all to be "sheer paradise."

Hyères offered only sparse possibilities for the community-seeking chatelaine of Ste. Claire, and houseguests were the most important. Lady Adela Essex had recently bought a house not too far away, and Sir Alan and Lady Johnstone were about to do the same. At Lady Ian Hamilton's winter home Edith pleasurably came upon some of her prewar English friends. The person Edith saw most of was her associate from the refugee days and sometime hostess, Martine de Béarn —henceforth to be known as Mme. de Béhague; her husband at the time of the divorce demanded she cease using his family name and take back her own. The relationship between these two cultivated, wealthy, and forceful women was never an easy one. Edith was wont to describe Mme. de Béhague as a spoiled child in a tantrum, but she herself displayed resentment when Martine periodically carried off Robert Norton to her yacht or local residence. Yet, socially and intellectually, in the thin Riviera society neither could quite do without the other.

It was during this first season at Hyères that Edith came to know the person who in the latter years became the most treasured new recruit for her republic of the spirit. This was Philomène de Lévis-Mirepoix, from one of the leading ducal families in France. A glowingly lovely young woman in her early thirties, Philomène had lived with her family next door to Edith Wharton in the Rue de Varenne before the war, and once or twice had had the rare experience of dining alone with Edith at No. 53. In 1912 she had caused a mild flutter in the Faubourg by bringing out a piece of lyrical autobiographical fiction called *Cité des lampes,* an appealing mixture of religious sensibility and delicate sensuality.

Not long afterward, Philomène went through what the kindly Abbé Mugnier retrospectively described as her "period of moral anguish." She disappeared from France for a number of years. In 1920 she turned up at Hyères with her five-year-old daughter, Florence, living with her widowed mother, the dowager duchess —an old woman of grand eccentricity and formidable piety, in Edith Wharton's view—shrinking from all human intercourse save the bevy of "tuppenny abbés" with whom her mother filled the life-diminishing household.

At once increasingly enchanted and perplexed by her new friend, Edith set herself to bring Philomène de Lévis-Mirepoix back into the living social world. Philomène was beautiful and charming, she had at times a delicious sense of humor and every generosity of spirit; but to Edith's concerned gaze, she also seemed capriciously resistant to the process of her social regeneration. The trouble was, Edith thought, that Philomène was an easy prey to all kinds of intellectual nonsense. Writing to Berenson, whom Philomène was about to visit, Edith begged him "not to befuddle her with Freudianism and all its jargon. She'd take to it like a duck to—sewerage." Setting aside her own flirtations with Freud and the unconscious, Edith asserted in her most eighteenth-century manner that what Philomene really needed was "to develop the *conscious,* and not grub after the sub-conscious. She wants to be taught first to see, to attend, to reflect."

Edith only imperfectly guessed at the inward bleakness beneath the winning exterior of the young woman who could say to Berenson that she was bringing him nothing but an empty head, a heart full of affliction, and an erratic soul. Even so, Edith kept at it, taking her for walks and drives with her houseguests and to call on the Bourgets, and enlisting the immediate and powerful support of Martine de Béhague in the rescue operation. It was Berenson, meanwhile, who most encouraged Philomène to return to writing; eventually, under the pen name Claude Sylve, she became one of the better-known writers and journalists in France.

For all Philomène's refusal to act in exactly Edith's decisive and rational way, Edith grew to love and rejoice in her more all the time. The day would come when Edith spoke of her as one of the two most "radioactive" women she knew, the other being the Princess de Poix, the mother of the young Vicomte de Noailles.

8

At St. Brice during the summer of 1921, Edith was busy with *The Glimpses of the Moon*, which had come to life again, and with an unbroken flow of old and newer friends. Lubbock and Hugh Smith, on arrival, struck her as in the best of fettle and downright huggable; but Geoffrey Scott was in more questionable condition. He was in the throes of a trial separation from Lady Sybil, having fallen more or less in love with Nicky Mariano, the attractive young woman who had recently joined I Tatti as Bernard Berenson's librarian. Mrs. Scott had agreed to the arrangement—Geoffrey had taken a position at the British Embassy in Rome —even though she felt that "marriage is a constructive thing, and no good can come of these separations." (Lady Sybil had difficulty with her consonants, and Edith was given to unkindly imitations of her: "Mawwidge is a constwuctive thing.") Scott showed more mental energy than Edith expected, but she wished he could have more time for his literary work.

At the literary *salon* in Versailles of Prince and Princesse Bassiano—who also appeared regularly in Mme. Wharton's guestbook—Edith reencountered André Gide. Sometime later Gide sent her his superlative little book on Dostoyevsky with a cordial inscription, and Edith told him that the book had "clarified the labyrinth" for her and gave her a sense of arriving at last at the "mysterious, terrible and disturbing man himself." (To others Edith Wharton said that, as between the two giants of nineteenth-century Russia, she always felt much more at home with Tolstoy.) It was at the Bassianos', too, that she first met Paul Valéry, stocky and soft-voiced and just emerging, at fifty, from more than two decades of self-imposed literary silence, much of it given to the study of mathematics and to odd jobs, including that of librarian for Martine de Béhague. Valéry had returned to the remarkable, if somewhat esoteric, prose and poetry that revealed genuine literary genius and were the basis of a growing cult. Edith found his work hard to penetrate, but she greatly enjoyed his company, periodically, both at St. Brice and Ste. Claire.

Edouard Vuillard, a painter who had done a portrait of Walter Berry, was occasionally in view. He was an artist of about the same gifts and the same aesthetic predelictions as Jacques Emile Blanche—both belonged to what might be called the conservative modernist group, a group that had looked upon Matisse, Picasso, Bracque, Dérain, and the other Post-Impressionists and Cubists as *les fauves* (the name was coined after the Paris exhibition in 1905), or wild beasts.

It has often been observed that Edith Wharton had no contact with these painters, that she never penetrated the circle that formed itself amid the crowded canvases at 27 Rue de Fleurus, near the Luxembourg Gardens, the prewar home of Gertrude Stein and her brother, Leo, and after 1909, of Gertrude and Alice B. Toklas. The point may be made differently. Neither Gertrude Stein nor her brother nor her companion ever came to know Edith Wharton, or to be a member of the international assortment of poets and novelists, painters, playwrights, and socialites that flowed through 53 Rue de Varenne. The two rich human and artistic Paris worlds of these two expatriate American writers astonishingly failed to overlap to any real extent. So it continued through the 1920s and into the 1930s. While Gertrude Stein was offering counsel to James Joyce, Ernest Hemingway, Sherwood Anderson, and many others, Edith Wharton was playing hostess to Paul Valéry, André Gide, Sinclair Lewis, Aldous Huxley, and Kenneth Clark. A meditative essay on differing tastes and temperaments could be written about this phenomenon.

The Glimpses of the Moon was finished in mid-September. Edith uttered a loud "Ouf!" of relief, told Berenson that "for the first time in three years I've stopped working," and departed for England—a fortnight's visit there had become part of the autumn routine. She put in some days at Lamb House, where Robert Norton was now the resident and custodian. For Edith it was more than poignant to enter the familiar doorway with no arms outspread to greet her; yet, as she wrote Lapsley:

> It is a singular joy to see the house so happily and reverently lived in, with a continued sense of the Master, and with the gayety, life, activity, one sometimes longed for in the old days.

At Lapsley's rooms at Trinity College, Cambridge, Edith spent the evening in the company of A. E. Housman, the elderly and reserved professor of Latin at the university, who was prouder of his volumes on the obscure classical writer Manilius than of his famous poetry. It was a rare moment for Edith Wharton, who had extravagantly admired Housman's book of poems, *A Shropshire Lad*, since Elisina gave her a copy of it in 1913. When Lapsley gave her Housman's second collection, inaccurately named *Last Poems*, Edith reported herself gulping it down "in my coarse carnivorous way." If it lacked the "continuous excitement" of the earlier verses, it reflected "that great gift of experience, the only one we can count on between the cradle and the grave (and that only if we're capable of receiving it); the gift that modern art affects to spurn, but will have to go back to."

With Queen's Acre in other hands after the death of Howard Sturgis, Edith Wharton felt strongly the need for another English center where she could mingle with her Happy Few, and for a half dozen years Mary Hunter's Hill Hall served this purpose. Edith concluded this English visit by driving there with John Hugh Smith. It was a place to delight in, but Edith regarded the level of cultivation as almost comically below that of Queen's Acre—as evidenced by a contretemps with Stephen McKenna, a precocious minor novelist of delicate health, who informed her thoughtfully that "trying to read James makes me blind with rage." There were other acquisitions, transitory or permanent, as the autumn passed.

But the sense of loss continued to balance the sense of gain in Edith Wharton's consciousness. On All Souls' night, in November, after placing flowers from her garden on the soldiers' grave in the St. Brice cemetery, Edith sat alone into the late hours, listening to the church bells and remembering "All my dead: my darling old Doyley, Egerton, Eliot, Bob Minturn, Henry, Ronald, Anna, Renée Landormy, Howard, Edith Fairchild."

23. A Rooted Possessive Person

As the decade of the 1920s went forward, one of the major phenomena Edith Wharton had to take stock of was the new literary age presided over in good part by James Joyce and T. S. Eliot. To do so was to measure herself against it, to reappraise herself and her reputation as a writer.

In September 1922 she struggled her way through Joyce's *Ulysses*, and told Berenson that she had indignantly cast it from her. "It's a welter of pornography (the rudest school-boy kind), and unformed and unimportant drivel." She was by no means alone in this reaction; Berenson, when he got around to it, was wittily derisive about *Ulysses* and influential readers in England found it chaotic and perverse. But perhaps the key phrase in Edith Wharton's indictment was "rudest schoolboy kind." What she resented was not so much the "pornography"—particularly in Molly Bloom's monologue—as its adolescent male tone that she seemed to hear echoing crudely. Still Edith was uneasily aware of the book's immense *succès d'estime*—this kind of thing, she confided to a new acquaintance, was making her "accustomed to being regarded as a deplorable example of what people used to read in the Dark Ages before the *'tranche de vie'* had been rediscovered."

She rendered an equally negative verdict on one of the other major literary products of the year, T. S. Eliot's *The Waste Land*. During the war Mrs. Perry Belmont had sent her Eliot's *The Love Song of J. Alfred Prufrock*, along with a volume called *Spectra*, a book for some time taken to be an important example of contemporary experimental poetry, but which turned out to be a clever satire by Witter Bynner and A. D. Ficke. Edith Wharton found both books extremely "amusing," as she wrote Mrs. Belmont, but relatively insignificant and interesting mainly as revealing the influence of Whitman (a surprising judgment, till one thinks about the rhythms in the two volumes). Whitman, she thought, "is rather a big meal for such small digestions, and the result is not particularly striking. But I am glad to know what the new American songsters are doing." *The Waste Land*, five years later, seemed to her to lack even the enlivening presence of Walt Whitman; it was a poem, like Joyce's novel, ridden by theory rather than warmed by life. To this she added plaintively in a letter to Lapsley: "I *know* it's not because I'm getting old that I'm unresponsive."

When Proust's *Cities of the Plain* appeared in the same year, 1922, with its account of the secret life of Baron de Charlus and its discourse on the causes and varieties of homosexuality, Edith Wharton could only exclaim, "Alas, alas!" Nonetheless, each of the successive volumes of *Remembrance of Things Past* fascinated her as much as they disturbed her, and she never questioned her belief in Proust's creative genius. She grew caustic when A. B. Walkley, the English critic, scolded Proust for his erotic subject matter. Walkley, she said, had "crowned a long career of asininity" with this article, and had joined "Quiller-Couch under the sofa where that master of aesthetic takes refuge whenever A-d–lt–ry is mentioned." She regarded Proust's death in November as an unmitigated calamity, particularly since he had not lived to put the final touches to the last volumes.

As to more conventional fiction, Edith wrote the ailing Sara Norton (who had asked for some worthwhile titles) that "I am so bored by all novels except the superlatives that I seldom read one unless sure of my ground." In fact, Edith Wharton was prone to give new fiction a passing chance, though she also tended to discard the books or pass them on to others. She faithfully read each new book by Sinclair Lewis and had noticed the first writings of F. Scott Fitzgerald. A novel called *Futility* by an unknown writer named William Gerhardi impressed her greatly; Edna Ferber's immensely popular *So Big* struck her as "thin and inconclusive."

Walter Berry remarked zestfully that *Cities of the Plain* was "terrific" and that there was "nothing like it outside of Kraft-Ebbing." He fancied that Proust would next examine the sexual aberrations of "the ladies." Edith Wharton had something of the same premonition. The publication of the novel coincided with a letter from an American admirer, possessed of a photograph of Edith, "who finds my face 'irasistable,' and wants to 'kiss my eyes into smiles, and draw some of the sadness from my mouth.' As the writer is a lady," Edith went on, "it seemed to me singularly fitting that this frank expression of good will should coincide with the new Gomorrhas."

Edith Wharton's attitude toward homosexuality showed a sort of predictable inconsistency. Upon male homosexuals, whom she referred to collectively as "The Brotherhood," she cast a generally knowing and tolerant eye. About a new friend she made at this time, she remarked to Hugh Smith that he looked rather like "a homo"—he was "certainly swamped in sex, and will probably *untergehen* to that"; the possibility did not deter her from reveling in the man's company. André Gide's proclivities had no effect upon their relationship, nor did those of Cocteau; and there had been Robert d'Humières and others whom she liked and admired.

She was less discerning and less tolerant of the Sisterhood. Looking back, she suspected her girlhood friend Emelyn Washburn of what she called "degeneracy," but at least in the early days she failed to intuit the latent tendencies of the mannish Vernon Lee. The habit of several well-born Parisian ladies, like Anna de Noailles, of experimenting sexually in both directions also seems to have escaped her—or perhaps simply not to have interested her. When Radclyffe Hall's autobiographical novel about lesbian experience, *The Well of Loneliness*, was published in France—after being banned in England and fiercely condemned in America—Edith Wharton dismissed it as "dull twaddle."

Edith Wharton made a point of steering clear of Natalie Clifford Barney, the golden-haired widow from Dayton whose shrine in the Rue Jacob has already been mentioned. To her friend Blandine de Prévaux, Edith said imperiously that she didn't care whatever else she might do, "but you must never go near Mrs. Barney." Mme. de Prévaux would remember that Edith looked upon Mrs. Barney as "something—appalling."

If the quotation is accurate, it is to be regretted. Natalie Barney was a remarkable, kindly, and gifted woman. Though she appeared as a lesbian figure in a number of writings (for example, in Liane de Pougy's *Idylles sapphiques*); an array of uncommonly talented male writers regularly participated in her *salon*. Among these were Rilke, T. S. Eliot, Ezra Pound, Bernard Berenson, and Paul Valéry. Indeed, Natalie Barney's *salon* had long been a formidable rival to that of Mrs. Wharton, and one suspects that it was this, as much as moral disapproval, that aroused Edith's hostility. In the fall of 1926, Edith Wharton found herself at lunch in an American gathering, in Walter Berry's apartment, that included Natalie Barney and Berry's cousin Harry Crosby and his wife, Caresse: for Edith, perhaps, one of the less gratifying social occasions of the period.

2

The Glimpses of the Moon, having run its course in the *Pictorial Review*, was published by Appleton in August 1922, just as Edith Wharton was completing its successor, *A Son at the Front*. The new novel was a runaway best seller, the bookstores in America and England disposing of more than 100,000 copies in the first six months. To the $17,000 for the serialization, Appleton added another $28,000 in royalties, and the film rights went for $13,500 more. Before a year was out, Edith Wharton earned nearly $60,000 from *The Glimpses of the Moon* and some $10,000 from several short stories and the novella *False Dawn*, which the *Ladies' Home Journal* took for $5,500.

The film version, with dialogue by F. Scott Fitzgerald, opened to glowing reviews in Washington the following April. Bebe Daniels was said to be splendid as "the impulsive heroine whose high ideals and extravagant taste fight for primacy"; Nita Naldi was sinuously attractive as the "super-vamp" married to a millionaire, and Maurice Costello returned to the screen, impressively, as her doting husband. One paper observed that the jazz accompaniment to the film provided by the theater's pianist was also much appreciated.

Despite the financial success of *The Glimpses of the Moon*, not all the portents were encouraging. Edith Wharton had described the novel to Berenson as "the adventures of a young couple who believe themselves to be completely *affranchies* and up-to-date, but are continually tripped up by obsolete sensibilities and discarded ideals." The young couple in question, Nick and Susy Lansing, equally penniless, marry each other with the thought of having a gay year or so cadging off their wealthy friends, and with the understanding that should either one capture the affections of some rich person, he or she will be free to dissolve the match. Put to the test, they cannot finally go through with the proposition.

"I'm so glad you like *The Glimpses*," Edith wrote Berenson, who added in the margin of the letter: "n.b. I didn't." Nor did a good many of the critics, a number of whom found the book sentimental and conventional. Heywood Broun, in the New York *World*, said that "even Edith Wharton cannot make so dowdy a cast of characters enthralling," and Gilbert Seldes wrote more harshly that for once he felt cheated by Mrs. Wharton's work. In England, J. Middleton Murry described the novel as unpersuasive and Nick Lansing as a young fool; Rebecca West remarked with bite that *The Glimpses of the Moon* was a dead thing which made her understand the despair of those who believed the novel had had its day.

With an eye on the mounting sales, Rutger Jewett observed to Edith that "the Young Intellectuals . . . like young terriers worrying a muff, have lashed themselves into idle rage over your novel." There was, meanwhile, a sufficient amount of praise. Probably the most influential review, that in *The New York Times*, was written by Katharine Fullerton Gerould, for whom the novel was superior to anything written in years. Edith was much moved by Mrs. Gerould's remarks and told Jewett that "she is a cousin of my old friend Morton Fullerton, and it was I who sent her first ms. to Mr. Scribner, and called his attention to the literary promise which she already gave. So you see I deserve a good word from her." She wrote a word of thanks to Mrs. Gerould in Princeton, and Morton's cousin and one-time fiancée thereafter composed a review of Edith Wharton's fiction, laudatory in the extreme but by no means without discernment in the context of a general essay on fiction. Appleton put it out as a little brochure. Edith, writing in for more copies, called it "an admirable piece of literary criticism" and suggested that Katharine Gerould include it in a volume of essays.

The Glimpses of the Moon has its characteristically entertaining moments, and there are nicely done sketches of Venice, the Italian lakes, Paris, and Fontainebleau; but it is not very readable today. The novel, in fact, represented no one of the several fruitful directions in which Edith Wharton's imagination was moving or about to move, while it did represent certain weaknesses and dangerous temptations by which she was beginning to be beset.

Edith Wharton's most compelling work in the two decades after the Great War was of several kinds. Most obviously, there was the fiction that harked back to various moments in the nineteenth century: *The Age of Innocence, Old New York*, the posthumously published *The Buccaneers*, and short stories like "After Holbein" and "Roman Fever." In these she was, among other things and with greater or lesser intensity of effort, carrying forward a major creative enterprise in this period: forging a continuity between a re-created past and the living present. But among the fiction set in the present time, the best of it arises from a vital new concern of Edith Wharton's, almost a new compulsion: what might be called the maternal imagination. Novels and tales like *The Mother's Recompense, The Children,* "Her Son," and again (for the modes inevitably overlap) *The Old Maid* and "Roman Fever," reflect Edith Wharton's shifting attempt to contrive a vision of experience and human character from the perspective of a mature and motherly figure—or that of conspicuously motherless children. On this, there will be more to say.

Another vein which Edith Wharton would eventually mine effectively was that of partly disguised or explicit autobiography: *Hudson River Bracketed* and *A Backward Glance.* And the point is that *The Glimpses of the Moon*, with its contemporary portrait of a young couple confusedly on the make, could draw on none of the creative energies summoned up by the three categories described.

One must also notice failings or limitations that *The Glimpses of the Moon* shared with some of the much more vigorous work. There was, for one thing, Edith Wharton's loosening grip upon the American idiom. A brilliant young critic who signed himself Edmund Wilson, Jr., even while speaking appreciatively of *The Age of Innocence,* had written that her style seemed a bit awkward in places. Impressed by his other insights, Edith Wharton wondered whether "Mr. Wilson, Jr.," might not be right "when he says I can't write English any more? I shall take up my pen with a distrustful hand tomorrow at 8 A.M." It should be said that any American who lives abroad for a period and deals to any extent in the language of the country of residence soon discovers himself groping for the most commonplace English phrases; and Edith Wharton by 1922 had been living in Europe uninterruptedly for more than a decade, speaking French daily, when she was not speaking Italian. The wonder is that her command of English held as firm as it did.

It remains true that there are odd blemishes to the style of *The Glimpses of the Moon,* some of the dialogue is implausible, and even the portrait of American manners in unsure. Dimly aware of this, Edith told Jewett that "I ought to go back to America, at any rate for a month or two," to refresh her knowledge of the native scene and of American speech. That accomplished, she planned to write a sequel to *The Glimpses of the Moon*—the further adventures of Nick and Susy Lansing, to be called "Love Among the Ruins." This work her creative instinct soon persuaded her to abandon.

There was also the matter of writing for magazines with mass circulation. "You are the only author in the magazine field," Jewett remarked, "who is writing literature and at the same time being paid the high figure which is usually the reward of tosh"—Vance, at the *Pictorial Review,* had just beaten out a rival editor by offering twenty-seven thousand dollars for Edith Wharton's next serial. It might have been more accurate to say that Edith Wharton at times allowed herself to write, not the best and most demanding fiction of which she was capable, but only the best fiction acceptable to popular-magazine editors and tolerable to magazine readers. She never consciously "wrote down," but she drove herself to write too fast and perhaps too much, because of financial need; not only to meet the huge and steady expenses of her two estates, but also the ever pressing list of her private charities. There were, nevertheless, important occasions until the year of her death when her imagination was wholly absorbed by the work in hand, with no slightest regard for the limiting responsiveness of editors or readers.

3

Sara Norton, who was thought to be convalescing satisfactorily after having a tumor removed, suffered a relapse and died in the summer of 1922. Soon afterward Edith learned of the death of her brother, Harry Jones, at Fontainebleau. She described her feelings to Berenson, laying all the blame for the long estrangement on Harry's wife, Tecla:

My poor brother Harry died ten days ago. It is no present loss, since he had not been allowed by his wife to see me for nearly ten years, and the only two occasions on which I succeeded in breaking through the barriers produced only a tragic impression of some one enslaved and silenced.

But he was the dearest of brothers to all my youth, and as our separation was produced by no quarrel, and no ill-will of any sort on my part, but only a kind of mute subterranean determination (apparently) to separate himself from all his family, my feeling is one of sadness at the years of lost affection and companionship, and all the reawakened memories of youth.

She attended the funeral service and gave a withering report of it to Minnie Jones; it culminated with the widow's invitation to a gathering after the ceremony, to which Edith replied, *"Merci, non!"* as she swept out of the church. She had her less attractive moments.

Edith Wharton would begin *A Backward Glance* with the comment she had originally written to Elizabeth Cameron: "There is no such thing as growing old. There is only sadness"—the recurring sadness, for the aging survivor, of the loss of friends. A few months after Harry Jones's death, Rosa de Fitz-James was operated on for cancer; she clung grimly to life for a while, but by the end of the following summer she was dead. "Poor, lonely unhappy woman," Edith said of her to Minnie Jones; unhappy during the long years of marriage in name only, and lonely because she had outlived the *salon* world at the center of which she had flourished for so many seasons. Her death, Edith felt, was "really the end of pre-war Paris for me."

But postwar Paris also had its attractions. Of her old group Edith was still seeing a great deal of the engaging Blanche and the endearing Abbé Mugnier, of the Bourgets and the du Bos'. But she was also in the company of much younger people, like Blandine de Prévaux, a great-granddaughter of Franz Liszt and his mistress Comtesse Dacou, and the witty and attractive Marquise Berthe de Ganay (Martine de Béhague's sister). The liveliest member of the new group, and for Edith the most gratifying company, was Vicomte Charles de Noailles, a trim, sturdy young man in his late twenties, with a handsome face and a small black moustache; he was a remote relative by marriage of Anna de Noailles. Charles shared with Edith a passion for gardening ("She was a great gardener," he said, "and very serious technically"; he rivaled her on both counts), and the friendship first arose among the plants, shrubbery, and fruit trees of Ste. Claire.

The *vicomte* also had certain literary and artistic leanings—it was he who put up the money for his friend Jean Cocteau's superb surrealist film *The Blood of a Poet.* This part of his nature was enhanced by his marriage in 1923 to the young heiress Marie-Laure Bischoffsheim, the unconventionally beautiful granddaughter of Laure de Sade (herself a descendant of the notorious marquis, and, as the Comtesse de Chevigné, the original of Proust's Duchesse de Guermantes). The young couple moved into St. Bernard, adjoining Ste. Claire. Edith Wharton, predictably, did not get along with Marie-Laure, who was far more in touch with the avant-garde sets and movements than she, and not infrequently Charles strolled over to call by himself.

For these French friends, Edith Wharton had an air of great elegance and distinction, but she sometimes gave them the impression of living in another, much earlier epoch. Speaking with some of them today, one finds them united in their admiration for Edith's compassionate friendliness with Philomène. "Mrs. Wharton appeared so severe," Mme. de Prévaux has said, "but with Philomène she was *exquisite,* tremendously so." But they also could find her intimidating; in a characteristic image, she is seen sitting so stiffly upright in her chair that she looked (says one of them, drawing on a French idiom) as if she had swallowed an umbrella.

Speaking of Edith Wharton, Philomène de Lévis-Mirepoix once remarked upon the phenomenon of so enormously well known a woman being so little known to her associates. Philomène meant Edith's French associates—among whom she herself penetrated more deeply into Edith's nature than most. Others, like Madeline Saint-Renée Taillandier, confessed themselves baffled. Mme. Taillandier, the sister of Edith's old friend André Chevrillon and the wife of a diplomat, had been beguiled by Edith Wharton into translating *The Age of Innocence* into French—the result, *Au Temps de l'innocence,* was a most satisfactory rendering—and she spent many days and evenings at the Pavillon Colombe. Then and later, she found some unsurpassable barrier in Edith Wharton, something unknowable about her.

There was, Mme. Taillandier said in a sensitive portrait, a deeper reserve in Edith Wharton than she had known in any other woman. She never heard her confess to a feeling of sadness, nor did she ever hear her laugh—the Frenchwoman missed the two qualities which most struck Edith's American and English friends. When Edith came downstairs at twelve thirty after the morning's work, she became—so Mme. Taillandier remembered—the complete hostess and encouraged no reference to her writing, her achievements, her successes. Yet Mme. Taillandier suspected that it was shyness that led to such reticence, and she was sometimes conscious of a strong "interior resonance," of an element of passion behind the calm reserve and the even voice.

There was no language barrier: Edith spoke French perfectly, according to Mme. Taillandier (and others). But there were, evidently, whole worlds of experience and discourse, of comedy and recollection, which Edith could not share with the natives of her adopted country. If she could be stiff in her outward manner, it was probably due neither to austerity nor shyness. She was preparing herself to be courteously bored.

4

In reply to a query from Berenson, who had inherited Henry James's habit of looking askance at Edith's extravagant way of life, she had tried to explain why she had "two houses and gardens and a motor." It was, she said, because she was "a rooted possessive person, and I always shall be." Her establishments, with her large staffs of servants and gardeners, gave her what her bountiful nature desired: an ordered life, a carefully tended beauty of surroundings, and above all, total privacy.

By the winter of 1923 some important changes had occurred in her central staff. Charles Cook had been forced to leave. The formerly lean and wiry chauffeur from Lee, Massachusetts, had grown corpulent and cosmopolitan with the years and was beginning to resemble a somewhat overfed diplomat. Just when Edith was beginning the autumn move to Ste. Claire, he suffered a slight stroke, and although his recovery was certain, he could never again drive a car. "Materially, I can look after poor Cook for all his days," Edith wrote; but thinking back on "our epic *randonées*" (circuits), the countless motor trips across New England, Italy, France, Germany, England, Spain, and North Africa, Edith felt sadly bereft. A little before Christmas, Cook and his Swedish wife took ship for America and vanished from Edith's sight—though, since she pensioned him handsomely, not from her life. Edith was soon describing Cook's successor, an Englishman named Franklin, as "perfect, beyond my wildest dreams." The new head gardener at Ste. Claire, Simon, appeared promising. And there was a new footman, an eccentric and gaily attractive Italian named Romano, married to a girl in Hyères who was, Edith suspected, no better than she should be.

Rooted and possessive though she was, shut up each morning with her work (a series of rather macabre short stories at the moment) and with her visitors and social engagements later in the day, Edith Wharton was even so not immune to the occasional impingement of the outside world. A month after the inaccurately called "march on Rome" of Benito Mussolini's supporters in October 1922, Edith was remarking casually that *"Fascisto* Italy is evidently to differ in no important regard from the other"*: cables to Berenson at Settignano went as grotesquely astray—one ended up in California—as they always had. Edith, in her French habitat, was slow to grasp the meaning of Fascism. The Berensons, however, understood at once the probable evil consequences of the seizure of power and began to discriminate sharply between their pro-Mussolini and anti-Mussolini friends in Tuscany.

Edith had not gotten over the detestation of contemporary Germany (as against the older German literary culture) aroused in her at the outset of the war, and she voiced eager approval of the Allied occupation of the Ruhr basin in January 1923 after Germany had defaulted on its war debts. And when, some time later, the ashes of Jean Jaurès were transferred to a place of honor in the Panthéon, Edith thought it a "revolting spectacle." Still belligerent, Edith found it disgraceful that a spokesman for peace, and a socialist, should be treated as a national hero.

As always, the combination of violence and sexual passion arrested her attention. In April a pair of young lovers killed themselves near the cross at the top of the hill behind Ste. Claire. This was perhaps too close to home, but Edith was quite relishing the tale that began to emerge from New Brunswick, New Jersey, where, the previous September, the murdered bodies of the Reverend Edward W. Hall and Mrs. Eleanor Mills, the choir leader in his church, were found under a crabapple tree on a derelict farm. Edith followed the sensational case with the liveliest interest, through the trial of the clergyman's wife and her two brothers, and the astonishing testimony of the so-called pig woman. She sent clippings about it all to Lapsley, underlining in red pencil passages from the love letters between the victims.

Another segment of the outside world reached over to touch Edith Wharton directly in that winter of 1923. The president of Yale wrote to say that the university would like to bestow upon her the honorary degree of Doctor of Letters at the graduation ceremonies in June, if Mrs. Wharton could arrange to be present in person. Her immediate instinct was to refuse, and she did so as gracefully as possible. She explained her feelings to Lapsley, in a letter of mid-April:

America? No—I'm *afraid*. I'd love the two voyages with you; enough, almost to risk the rest! But when I think of publishers, relations, friends, invitations—and see how little I can do, without great intervals of rest and monotony—I quail at the thought. I wish I didn't.

She was also, obviously, quailing at the mere thought of confronting the native country she had not set foot in for a decade, and with a great war intervening. She passed on to Lapsley a long letter from Walter Maynard which gave a frightened picture of the changes wrought in New York—700,000 Russian-Jewish refugees in the city, and all of them sick.

Yet the thought recurred to her that perhaps she ought to have a look at "the new U.S.": "I badly need to if I'm going to go on writing about it." It was put to her earnestly by Yale, meanwhile, that it was a duty for her to come, since this would be the first time in the history of the university that a woman had been so honored. Edith yielded, though she grumbled in an aside to Elisina that it meant changes in her European travel plans and an interruption of her work. Somewhat fearfully, she started her preparations, and on June 9 she sailed on the *Mauretania* from Cherbourg for New York.

"Same old Atlantic" was all she could muster herself to say—along with the notation that there was no one she knew on board—on her first crossing since she had gone to Beatrix Jones's wedding in 1913. Minnie Jones and Trix and Max Farrand were waiting on the dock when the ship reached New York on the fifteenth, and they escorted her to the St. Regis Hotel, all dining together in Edith's rooms there.

The next day was a busy one. Edith hurried around to the Cunard and White Star office to arrange for her return passage. She lunched with Trix, and afterward Minnie took her to call on Edward Sheldon at his apartment. Edith must have been dreading the visit, but almost the moment she sat down in the aquarium room next to Sheldon, who was stretched out on the sofa, she said to herself, and so told Sheldon when she wrote him later from St. Brice, "Why this is a live human being at last."

It was a singularly felicitous phrase. Edward Sheldon, thirty-seven years old at the time, had leaped to fame in the New York theater in 1908, only one year out of Harvard, with the play *Salvation Nell*, starring Minnie Maddern Fiske. It was followed by a series of other successes. But as early as 1915, Sheldon, the brightest name in the America theater, began to be conscious of a certain stiffness in his knees; by 1917 he was bedridden with what was described as progressive arthritis. By 1921 he was virtually paralyzed, lying motionless on his back in his colorfully decorated apartment.

Ned Sheldon displayed an extraordinary mental fortitude, something beyond courage, which lent him a resilience, a warmth, and at times a positive gaiety of spirit. It was just his glow of life that Edith so quickly responded to in the stiffly immobile figure near her in the apartment that June afternoon. She recognized an "instant sympathy" between them, a sympathy based on a common interest in books, the theater, people, and stories of crime. Later they sent each other volumes of true-crime stories (Edith would tell Sheldon that the Lizzie Borden ax-murder case was an especially choice vintage, and she would base a story on it), and Edith declared that one of her most gruesome products of 1923 had been written especially for Sheldon.

That same afternoon Minnie and Edith drove out to Westbrook, the Cuttings' meandering and beautiful estate on Long Island. Olivia Cutting, the sister of Edith's friend Bayard, now long deceased, was there, and Bayard's daughter Iris, a lovely young woman of twenty-one, with a deep quiet intelligence and a love both of literature and of the men and women who made it. She would write with delicate acuteness about Leopardi, about Shelley and his mistress, about Byron's doomed little daughter Allegra.

Iris Cutting provided a charming account of the evening at Westbrook. The company wanted Edith to talk about Paris and Anna de Noailles, about visitors like Carlo Placci and the events taking place there, but Edith kept returning insistently to the New York scene, to the friends of former years and the milieu of her young womanhood.

The W's house on 11th Street, had it really been pulled down? Did her hostess remember the night they had dined there before the Colony Club ball? The X's daughter, the fair one, had she married her young Bostonian? Had Z indeed lost all his money? For the whole evening this mood continued. At one moment only—as the last guest had gone, she turned half-way up the stairs to wave good night—I caught a glimpse of the other Edith, elegant, formidable, as hard and dry as porcelain. Then, as she looked down on her old friends, the face softened, even the erectness of her spine relaxed a little. She was no longer the trim, hard European hostess, but a nice old American lady. Edith had come home.

After two more days at Westbrook and a visit with Eunice and Walter Maynard nearby, Edith and Minnie drove up to New Haven, arriving in time for Edith to dress for dinner in the home of Yale president James Rowland Angell. Next morning, June 20, Max Farrand picked her up and took her to the Corporation Room in Woodbridge Hall, where the other "honoraries" were assembling and donning their robes. Garbed in cap and gown, Edith joined the slow, stately procession—which for her possessed an unexpectedly impressive medieval flavor—around the campus and back to the big hall, where a crowd of graduating seniors and aspirants for higher degrees were waiting.

The Yale College class of 1923 contained a number of young men, all finishing up with high honors, who would become distinguished in the academic and literary worlds. Among them were F. O. Matthiessen, the author of *American Renaissance* and various studies of Henry James; Walter Blair, a notable student of American literary humor; and Max Lerner, the cultivated and influential liberal journalist. Several members of the class would enjoy eminence on the Yale faculty: Gordon Haight, who would write the definitive biography of George Eliot; William Dunham, a specialist in English medieval history; Joseph Curtiss, an expert in English literature and history; and Lewis Curtis, another English historian.

Before the ceremonies were over, Edith Wharton had received the first Doctor of Letters degree ever bestowed upon a woman by Yale, and the first and only academic degree of her life. The citation read:

> She holds a universally recognized place in the front ranks of the world's living novelists. She has elevated the level of American literature. We are proud that she is an American, and especially proud to enroll her among the daughters of Yale.

The American visit—as it turned out, the last Edith Wharton was to make —covered only eleven days. On the morning of June 26, in scorching heat, she was seen off on the *Berengaria* by Minnie and Trix. "Same old Atlantic," she observed on the six-day voyage back to Cherbourg. "So glad to be back," she added on July 2, safely reinstalled in the Pavillon Colombe.

The hurried days in New York, Long Island, and New Haven did not arouse in her any new affection for her native country. Horton's vanilla ice cream, which she consumed in quantities during the hot days and looked back upon wistfully from St. Brice, seems to have been one of the few items she regarded with respect. In August she sent Lapsley, about to leave for America, a clipping which described the country as it appeared to English eyes which knew it only from the movies. "A rich and strange life," mused the reporter; flunkies abounding, no books, no music on the piano; the only occupation of the householders—invariably rich and often living in ranch houses—being the writing of checks or notes of marital farewell.

"We cannot wonder," the writer ended solemnly, "that immigrants come by myriads to share it." But Edith, on the basis of her tour, said: "Little does the 'English writer' know how much this film resembles reality."

5

A visitor to the Pavillon Colombe in the summer of 1923, if he came from outside Paris, would be met at the Gare du Nord by Franklin and driven the forty-odd minutes to St. Brice. Passing through high doors set in the wall on the village street, the new arrival found himself in a place of ineffable tranquility. There were subdued sounds from without—voices, a passing car, church bells—but inside, one seemed to have stepped back two hundred years into a realm of profound peace and beauty, quite removed from the contemporary world.

While Edith passed her morning at work, the visitor, occupying one of several guest rooms, was encouraged to indulge himself. He was likely to be awakened by the singing of a hundred birds, and before breakfast came there was time to throw open the blinds, let the sunlight flood in, and gaze down on the lawns and flowerbeds immediately below, so close below that one felt a curious refreshing intimacy with them. Beyond lay a variety of artfully related gardens and an orchard; to the right were two trim cottages, the homes of Arthur White and of Franklin.

Breakfast arrived: an inviting tray crowned with peaches, apricots, and a dish of strawberries with rich cream. Presently the guest would go downstairs, out onto the terrace and into the gardens, to move trancelike (so several visitors felt) past sweet-smelling formal box hedges and down paths bordered by banks of nasturtiums which had been allowed to spill over. He could pause beside the stone pond in the shadow of the trees, with water lilies and the reflection of rose petals, and a little moss-covered statue of Pan with a water jet in his hand. Edith might appear at her window to call down something—her voice carrying against the mild clatter of a woodpecker tapping his beak on a willow tree—perhaps a question about the later plans of the day: Paris, as it might be, an exhibition of Cézanne. But she could often be prevailed upon to forgo any such excursion and allow her guest to luxuriate further in what Mme. Taillandier declared to be a very paradise.

Edith would appear about noon, elegantly dressed, with gloves and parasol and her face half hidden beneath a straw hat, taking her position on a crumbling stone seat while the guest, under her watchful eye, applied scissors to the rosebushes. Then it was time to feed the enormous old goldfish, said to have been put in the pond originally by one of the kings of France. Edith, taking crumbs from an embroidered bag, would bend over the pond calling down to them, *"Poisse, poisse!"* One visitor had the temerity to point out that fish cannot hear, but only feel vibrations. Edith paused, as though arrested by this scientific contention; but she decided not to believe it, and again began to cry softly, *"Poisse, poisse!"* the bloated fish, indeed, gliding hungrily to the surface.

The six rooms on the ground floor, from the library to the dining room, opened one into the other, and each opened onto the narrow walk running along the south side. It was almost exactly like The Mount, though the order of the rooms was reversed, and it revealed again Edith Wharton's basic principle in the arrangement of house interiors. Each room was distinctly itself; one never had the impression (as Edith remembered having in her parents' New York home) of being half in one room and half in another; yet the several rooms flowed together to create an atmosphere of unity and quiet harmony.

"Here," one English visitor wrote, "was such a high goal of perfection in food and wine, in talk, books, old furniture, pictures and the art of living, that to savour it truly exerted one's highest mental faculties." Another visitor, a Frenchwoman, thought the décor *too* perfect, and felt the lack of those comfortable signs, so familiar in a French household, of a mother-in-law's bad taste—an ugly clock, a too heavily tapestried chair. Percy Lubbock, editing the reminiscence just quoted, underscored the word "wine" and wrote in the margin: "No." Despite the best efforts of connoisseurs like Royall Tyler and Eric Maclagan, Edith never did gain expertise in wine. But one could expect a lavish midday meal, even on a warm summer day: lobster a l'Americaine (so ran one menu), followed by a tender roast chicken with peas; next, filets of sole, and finally "a very creamy and delicious strawberry dish."

After lunch Edith and her guest would make their way to the library, through the long drawing room with its Italianate mirrors and the sitting room, through the tiny boudoir with plaster doves above the curtained bed to commemorate the Colombe sisters, past another small room and into the library, behind which lay an old eighteenth-century water closet with a gleaming wooden bath and brass taps shaped like swans' heads. The ritual passage required the guest, whom Edith always had precede her, to open five successive doors.

Later there would be intervals of rest and of sociable communion. Edith liked to dress for dinner, if only out of respect for the dinner in store. The latter was likely to be the product of the French, as against the American, cuisine: petite marmite (on one occasion), truite meunière, poularde au riz, an ice, and coffee followed by a fine cognac. Thereafter the company moved back to the gray-walled library, its low tables covered with new books, the door open onto the garden, from which there drifted the scent of jasmin. Edith would glance briefly at the English, French, and American newspapers, as though to remind herself that a world still existed outside the high walls of the Pavillon Colombe.

There would be talk: gossip, jokes, reminiscences; the taking down of books from the shelves and readings from Montaigne or Browning, from Hardy or Shelley or A. E. Housman. Edith took particular pleasure in "poetry evenings," and made leisurely plans for an anthology of love poems to be edited with Robert Norton (*Eternal Passion in English Poetry*, published finally in 1939). Eventually, it came time for Favre to fasten the little coats around the snoozing Pekinese and take them for their evening walk. And then, rarely later than ten thirty, it was time for bed.

It was to these enchanted surroundings, to this generally relaxed but well-ordered and well-supplied daily pattern, that guests came for a night or two, and visitors from Paris for lunch, tea, or dinner. And from these surroundings Edith drove in to the city several times a week, to dine with Berry at Laurent's, just off the Champs Elysées, to visit an exhibition, to have lunch with the seventy-year-old and grandly aristocratic Duchesse de Rohan.

There were more purely literary encounters. The Sinclair Lewises were much in evidence that summer. On a little motor trip with Berry that carried them down to Nohant, Edith found herself, over lunch at Pontigny, in the company of André Gide, du Bos, Schlumberger, André Maurois, and Lytton Strachey. They spent the time talking about the difficult art of translation: an exchange one wishes had been transcribed. Edith Wharton had met Strachey the year before in London, and knew of him through Mary Berenson, whose daughter Ray Costelloe was married to Lytton's brother Oliver. Strachey's recently published biography of Queen Victoria seemed to Edith a masterpiece, and she was highly amused, too, by Strachey's flashing wit and little squeals of laughter. He embodied, she decided later, as much as anyone she knew, "the old English culture" represented by the men of letters.

About André Maurois, Edith was notably less perceptive. Even a few years after this meeting, and after seeing him frequently, she was speaking of Maurois to Lapsley as "a friendly and 'very bright' little Jew" who was discovering English literature but was quite unequipped to teach it. Maurois, thirty-eight years old in 1923, would win Edith's esteem with his biography of her old friend and his own, General Lyautey, and he had by that time sufficiently refuted Edith Wharton's opinion by writing exemplary lives of Shelley, Byron, and Disraeli.

6

A Son at the Front was published by Scribners in early September 1923. While reading the proofs and making last-minute corrections, Edith Wharton had kept herself busy with other professional chores. She wrote a queer, longish tale called "The Young Gentleman"; finished with some difficulty *The Spark*, the third of the novellas she now conceived of as constituting a volume to be called *Old New York;* did a Christmas article for the *Delineator;* and pressed ahead sporadically with her next novel, *The Mother's Recompense.*

She was writing so much and so variously that she periodically lost track and had to confess to Jewett, who was her agent as well as her editor, complete forgetfulness about a story promised or written or even published. The letters between Edith Wharton and Jewett were now systematically divided into different categories, a dozen or more per letter, most of them bearing the titles of works-in-progress. The other day, she told Jewett casually in one report, she had written a short story, "Miss Mary Pask," while recovering from the grippe. Nothing could be more casual or offhand than that story, in which a visitor to a house in Brittany is erroneously led to believe that his tremulous hostess is in fact a dead person. The admiring Vance paid eighteen hundred dollars to run it in the *Pictorial Review.*

Jewett described *A Son at the Front* to Edith Wharton as "the best novel written by you or anyone else for years," which was generous of him, since the novel had for a while been committed to Appleton. Its actual publisher, Charles Scribner, had been even more generous in accepting the wartime novel as the substitute a decade late for the novel promised him by Edith Wharton after *The*

Custom of the Country in 1913—and after patiently watching *Summer, The Age of Innocence,* and *The Glimpses of the Moon* appear successively under a rival imprint and, in the latter two cases, bring in large sums of money for their fortunate publisher.

The depiction of wartime Paris and the forward areas in *A Son at the Front* is done with a sure hand, and gives those memorable scenes a kind of permanence. The novel contains, too, the attractive portrait of Ronald Simmons, in the guise of the eager young Boylston; Edith told Elisina Tyler that the book was intended as another wreath on Simmons' grave, and added that the central figure, John Crampton, an expatriate gentleman-painter, was based in part on Elisina's husband. The main theme is Crampton's stubborn, unsuccessful efforts to prevent his son from being sent to the battle area. In the author's view, Crampton was evidently intended to stand for the kind of American who remained selfishly insensitive to the crisis of civilization building about him; but that phenomenon had little urgency five years after the armistice, and the book has an air of refined pugnacity over an issue long decided.

From a later vantage point, a different and more enduring theme can be seen emerging: that of the willful and significantly wrong exertion of parental authority. Edith Wharton in her early sixties was moving away from what had been the almost exclusive preoccupation of her previous seven novels and five novellas, and the great majority of her short stories. In those she had concentrated primarily on courtship, youthful love affairs, marital relations and disillusionment, adultery. They had been mainly stirred into being by the single most consequential event of her life: her marriage to Teddy Wharton. With that behind her, and the war a thing of the past, Edith Wharton's vision was beginning to make out the next and perhaps the last crucial area of human experience, both in the developing life of a human being and the developing career of the literary imagination. This was the varieties of relationship—nourishing or suppressive, loving or self-centered—between the generations, between older and younger people, between parents and children. Picking up the topic touched on briefly in a few earlier writings, *A Son at the Front* was Edith Wharton's first large-scale attempt, though an unfocused one, to grapple with this enormous human reality.

The new novel aroused much more intense and contrary reactions than its predecessor. Raymond Mortimer in the *New Statesman* dismissed it as the most distasteful war story that anyone could have the misfortune to read; the ever dependable William Lyon Phelps saw in it extraordinary power and beauty, and all the dignity of Greek tragedy; and so it went. *Scribner's* had paid fifteen thousand dollars for the serial, but the book version seems not to have earned half that much in royalties.

A Son at the Front was the last of Edith Wharton's books published in England by Macmillian. That venerable firm had brought out all of her titles since *The House of Mirth.* But in 1921 Edith Wharton's American publisher, Appleton, set up shop in London and took over the English editions of her work.

Though it continued to cast an enormous shadow over life in Europe, the war had receded into history, and to some extent *A Son at the Front* was—in the sense in which Edith had spoken of such things to Berenson—a historical novel. In the four novellas she wrote during the period of the novel's composition, she journeyed much more successfully into a more remote past, in an act of imaginative piety.

The subtitles of the stories in *Old New York* locate them in time: "The 'Forties' " *(False Dawn);* "The 'Fifties' " *(The Old Maid);* "The 'Sixties' " *(The Spark);* "The 'Seventies' " *(New Year's Day).* In *False Dawn,* Edith Wharton wove an account of her parents' courtship, with details of life on the Edward Renshaw Jones country estate, adding what she remembered of an anecdote once told her by Charles Eliot Norton about his meeting in Switzerland with John Ruskin. Into *The Old Maid,* she may have put something of her feeling upon hearing the rumor, years before, that she might have been an illegitimate child; but the emphasis is all upon the feelings of Charlotte Lovell, the psychically deprived unmarried mother.

The Spark is a story about a New York socialite who, as a wounded soldier in the Civil War, had been tended by a kindly bearded figure, and who is dismayed to discover later that his hospital friend, whose name was Walt Whitman, had written some rubbishy verse. Here Edith Wharton was combining the war-infested atmosphere of her infancy and her lifelong affection for Whitman with her own Whitmanesque attentions to the homeless, the wounded, and the tubercular in the more recent war. *New Year's Day,* which begins in a house on West Twenty-third Street very much like the Joneses' and with the uncomprehending observations of a child exactly Edith's age in the mid-1870s, draws upon a domestic scandal which had rocked the Jones family and their friends in its time.

The facts of New York social history intrigued her more and more. The famous Fifth Avenue Hotel (of which Paran Stevens had been part owner) had long since burned down; given this, Edith told Jewett, she felt no compunction about using it as the scene of the illicit affair in *New Year's Day.* When Loring Schuyler at the *Ladies' Home Journal* ventured that she had been mistaken in one of the stories to have the young people playing poker—surely a more modern game—rather than whist, Edith Wharton brought him up short: "When I was a young married woman in the nineties, the 'smart set' in New York left whist to the old people and always played poker or baccara." These flights of memory led her as early as the winter of 1923 to contemplate writing her memoirs—"to avoid having it inaccurately done," she remarked, "by someone else after my death, should it turn out that my books survive me long enough to make it worth while to write my biography."

Jewett thought this an excellent idea, and pointed out that *The Social Ladder*, readable and gossipy reminiscences of Edith Wharton's New York by Mrs. John King Van Rensselaer, a kin by marriage of Walter Berry, was causing a certain stir. What she had in mind, Edith explained, was simply a record of the years 1865 to 1890; nothing intimate, but a picture of growing up in that vanished society and of the first faltering steps in a career of writing. She would not, however, complete her autobiography for another decade.

Old New York was published in May 1924 in four volumes, boxed, with graceful illustrations in the end papers by Edward Caswell. Appleton came in for widespread praise for this inventive act of book-making, in the planning of which many hours had been spent. The reviewers, who had scarcely sent in their comments on *A Son at the Front*, sounded a trifle jaded, but most of them joined in a chorus of muffled applause. Against some complaints that the locales were too narrow or that the fictional tapestry seemed worn, the more general note was that the stories collectively had to be reckoned among Edith Wharton's best work (which they were), and there was growing recognition of the fact that she had become the ablest living social historian in fiction. Lloyd Morris wrote in *The New York Times*, out of his own extensive knowledge of nineteenth-century New York, that all the tales deserved broad popularity, and that *The Old Maid* deserved enduring fame as one of the most beautiful stories in the whole range of American literature.

The Old Maid was selected by many reviewers for special admiration, and that melancholy drama sold three times more than any of the other individual volumes. Of the boxed sets, 26,000 were sold in the first six months and about 3,000 single volumes. Edith Wharton's royalties were close to $15,000.

Her reputation and her literary income continued to inflate, and there seemed to be nothing that could seriously reduce either. Vance paid her $27,000 for the serial rights to *The Mother's Recompense*, and when Edith Wharton gallantly complied with his sudden call for help by delivering the manuscript some months ahead of schedule, he gave her a bonus of $5,000. One cannot easily determine her literary earnings in these years; the money was coming in so fast and in such large sums that in the fall of 1924, fearful of the tax rates, Edith implored Jewett not to send her any more for the time being. Over the period from 1920 through 1924, it would be a fair estimate that her work brought in about $250,000. This was on top of an average annual private income of some $30,000.

It says something about her literary reputation that, for a series in *The Bookman* on the most accomplished and best-known contemporary novelists, Wilbur Cross, himself a figure of distinction in the world of letters, chose to write about Rudyard Kipling and Edith Wharton. (Edith would find his essay "very kindly meant but not nearly as good as Mrs. Gerould's.") In September 1924, Brand Whitlock, the Ohio-born author of a series of reform-minded novels about social evils in the Midwest, wrote Robert Underwood Johnson, president of the American Academy of Arts and Letters, about that entity's alleged regulation against female membership. He was eager to nominate Edith Wharton; but as a woman she was ineligible, he said, and this was absurd. Women were now able to vote and to run for office; in fact, they were running the country. And Edith Wharton was "without any doubt the most distinguished of American novelists, and it is a glaring anomaly, and a reproach to our Company, that she is not in the Academy."

There had, in fact, been one woman, the aged Julia Ward Howe, in the American Academy, that most honorific of assemblies of creative artists and intellectuals. But the bylaws of the academy, as drawn up in 1904, while not ruling against women, stipulated that its fifty members be drawn exclusively from the 250 persons already members of the parent company, the National Institute of Arts and Letters.

Whitlock's communication had its effect. Soon afterward Edith Wharton was awarded the institute's Gold Medal, given annually for "distinguished services to art or letters in the creation of original work." William Dean Howells, in 1915, had been the only other novelist so honored; Eugene O'Neill was given the medal in 1921—a figure Edith Wharton, who regarded O'Neill as the only American playwright worth the name, could be flattered to follow. In her message of acceptance Edith declared that she was especially gratified by the reference to service: this, she said, had always been her aim as a writer. Two years later, in 1926, she was elected to the National Institute. In 1929 she received the academy's fourth Gold Medal (her only female predecessor was Mrs. Van Rensselaer) "for special distinction in literature," and in 1930 she entered the academy.

While recognition and acclaim were thus increasing in high literary places, Edith Wharton's personal and domestic life continued along familiar lines. The year's routine now included a fortnight in a suite on the top floor of the Hotel Crillon, while the staff was closing the Pavillon Colombe and journeying south to shake out the carpets at Ste. Claire. En route to Hyères in 1923, Edith made a detour to Settignano.

It was on this occasion that Edith began to become acquainted with Nicky Mariano (she never used her baptismal name, Elizabeth), the half Neopolitan and half Balkan aristocrat who had joined the staff at I Tatti as librarian in 1918 and who had gradually been induced to take general charge of Berenson's affairs. Miss Mariano was a slender dark-haired woman in her mid-thirties, with a winning smile, an open countenance, and an endearing manner. The two had met in London a few months earlier, but Edith had not addressed a word to her, and

Nicky stored up the impression of a conventionally dressed woman, awkward in her movements and nervous, with an ugly mouth "shaped like a savings box," though with fine eyes and a clear engaging laugh.

They got on better at I Tatti, where Edith begged Miss Mariano to lead the way in shopping tours among the antique shops in Florence, and Nicky learned to put up with Mrs. Wharton's habit of lingering with fastidious dissatisfaction over item after item. Genuine friendship, however, had to wait another two or three years until one day in Naples when Nicky happened to ask after Edith's maid, Elise. It was the way to Edith's heart; her eyes lit up, and in an instant her manner changed once and for all to one of warmth and intimacy. It is difficult, perhaps impossible, to find anyone today who knew Nicky Mariano during her forty years with Berenson and later who does not remember her with a rush of affection. Edith Wharton was soon referring to her, even in the privacy of her diary, in terms she reserved for the much-loved few.

"I return each time to my little houses (each one) with such a frenzy of affection and zeal for improvement," Edith wrote Elisina Tyler, soon after making her reentry at Ste. Claire in a deluge of winter rain. Norton was already there, and Lapsley arrived shortly. Early in the new year (1924), young Henry Cabot Lodge came for a visit. Edith had not seen him since the summer of 1914, when Cabot, who had spent two years in the Paris school that Edith had recommended to Bessie Lodge, was taken back to the Lodge home near Boston. Cabot had Brahmin good looks and was of such a height that he always seemed to be stooping slightly to make himself heard; he was two years out of Harvard and making a career of journalism, with a special concern for public affairs. Edith, who thought he had developed beautifully, took a great fancy to him. Cabot stood somewhat in awe of Mrs. Wharton, and was the more touched and surprised when she reached up to kiss him good-bye at the Toulon station.

Nothing in the winter of 1924 provided Edith Wharton with more pleasure and amusement than a visit from the writer William Gerhardi. Fifteen months before, she had written Gerhardi, out of the blue, a letter of robust praise for his novel *Futility*, declaring it the best novel about Russia that she had read since *Oblomov*.

Over the year following, the two writers exchanged a series of letters. Edith Wharton agreed to having her first communication used in English advertisements for *Futility*, though it was much against her custom, and she prodded the New York firm of Duffield and Company—whose editor was a friend of Minnie Jones's—into bringing out an American edition. For the latter she wrote a strong preface, saying among other things: "One wonders at the firmness of hand which has held together all the fun, pathos and irony of the thronged sprawling tale." In his excitement Gerhardi asked if he might dedicate his next novel, *The Polyglots*, to Mrs. Wharton.

He was, meanwhile, at work upon what turned out to be a first-class study of Anton Chekov—some of whose stories Edith Wharton admitted to liking, though she could only read him in bits, being unable to stand the "English-of-all-work in which the hapless foreigner is always offered to us." There was also comment about the work of Katharine Mansfield, who, though dying of consumption in Switzerland, had launched *Futility* by finding an English publisher for it. Edith had not been impressed by such of Katharine Mansfield's stories she had encountered. At Gerhardi's urging she now read "Bliss," "The Garden Party," and other tales. Miss Mansfield had undoubtedly, she thought, the temperament of a writer, but the stories were "all just *beginnings*, full of happy bits, but with all the difficulties shirked."

William Gerhardi—or Gerhardie (with a soft *g*), as he later spelled it—had been born in Petrograd of a Russian father and an English mother. During the war he joined the British army and later made his way circuitously to England. He studied for three years at Oxford, and it was there, as an undergraduate, that he wrote *Futility*. After an interval of silence the novel was publicly declared a work of genius by H. G. Wells, Rebecca West, and other influential spokesmen. At twenty-six Gerhardi was suddenly a literary lion, though a most unlikely one: tall, with a pale oval face, a red mouth, and a taut manner; accustomed to living on two shillings and sixpence a day, and habitually dressed in unpressed trousers and an ill-fitting tweed coat; a brilliant if unsettling conversationalist.

He came down from his temporary residence in Innsbruck to Ste. Claire in early January 1924. He arrived late at night, carrying in his bag several large chunks of buttered bread, and these he secretly flushed down the toilet. Next morning White, with a stern look but naming no names, reported that the entire plumbing system in the château was out of order because someone had put bread in the lavatory. Edith later spread the story that Gerhardi understood her to be an elderly woman of limited means and, recalling his own hungry days in Siberia, had brought food for the household only to discover it was a palace of luxury, and took calamitous means to conceal his mistake. Gerhardi allowed this version of things to travel.

Edith, who thought Gerhardi more like a troll than a human being, rejoiced in the unpremeditated quality of his talk. He understood the butler, Favre, to be called "Father," and so addressed him in his slightly lisping manner, confiding to Mrs. Wharton that Favre seemed "pessimistic." At dinner the first evening, during a pause following the soup course, he turned to the woman next to him and said: "But where is Mrs. Wharton?" indicating surprise that they had begun without their hostess.

> She looked at me with sad, inquiring thoughtfulness [Gerhardi recalled] and said: "I am Mrs. Wharton."
> "Oh," I said, "are you Mrs. Wharton?"

She looked at me as if she thought I couldn't be all there. "Of course I am," she said. "Oh . . . good evening," I said.

Edith's sad thoughtfulness was due to the fact that she and Gerhardi had spent most of the day together in the gardens. But it seems that her large hat had so hidden her features that her guest never had a glimpse of her face.

So winter drifted into spring, a succession of glittering mornings and glowing afternoons, of uninterrupted labor on the novel, of picnics and long walks, visits made and received, and poetry in the evenings. Edith bought a small, fast eighteen-horsepower Peugot, and it was with this *"torpédo de Dion"* that Franklin met Daisy Chanler at Toulon. For a rarity Daisy was accompanied by her husband, Winthrop, who normally preferred Edith Wharton's books to her person and who was heard to remark that the only time Edith had looked pretty was once when she was being kissed under a palm tree. Elisina came with Gioia, and Percy Lubbock, looking "as radiant as a new bridegroom," an ambiguous compliment since Percy arrived with a rather agreeable young man. "The stream of visitors ceases not," Edith wrote happily. "Even Christopher La Farge [Florence's older son] and the pretty bride turn up soon for a night."

The Mother's Recompense was already running in the *Pictorial Review* when Edith returned to St. Brice; about a third of it remained to be done, but, remembering the similar experience with *The House of Mirth*, Edith refused to worry. Her tight schedule still allowed time to take part in social gatherings, one of which, at her old apartment in the Rue de Varenne, included Linda Thomas, now Mrs. Cole Porter. At another, she took lunch with Lady "Emerald" Cunard and Lady Sybil Colefax, the two leading hostesses in London during the 1920s. With the former, Edith never hit it off very well, but with Sybil Colefax, an effervescent woman who shared Edith's affection for Bernard Berenson, she formed a long, if guarded, friendship. Paul Valéry came often to the Pavillon Colombe that summer; a young man who was present at some of these occasions remembers sitting enthralled by the swift brilliance of the verbal play.

In September, during the regular fortnight in England, Edith passed a number of days at Hill Hall. Geoffrey Scott, Percy Lubbock, Gaillard Lapsley, and Robert Norton joined her there, and for a moment Mary Hunter's home was perfectly fulfilling its function as the successor to Queen's Acre. It was an ideal visit—and a last visit. Before another reunion of the Happy Few could be arranged, Charles Hunter had died. His widow put Hill Hall on the market and with a cheerful air set about doing up her London home. Other members of the family rushed to seize or sell everything they could, and, hearing of this, Edith reflected broodingly, as though issuing a final verdict on mankind: "Humanity is becoming one-dimensional. There is no substance, no depth left."

24. The Last Days of Walter Berry

With *The Mother's Recompense*, which appeared in April 1925, Edith Wharton finally took possession of the literary ground she had been moving toward ever since completing *The Age of Innocence* five years earlier. It was the most finely wrought of a series of dramas about parents and children. As such, it also reflected Edith's clarifying sense of herself as a woman and a writer of a certain age, testing out her relationship to those much younger than she.

Kate Clephane, a woman in her early forties, has abandoned her impossibly pompous husband and baby daughter twenty years before, to go off for a brief fling with a wealthy lover. She settles thereafter into a somewhat dingy expatriate set on the Riviera, an empty, card-playing manner of life interrupted only by an intense little affair with a younger man, Chris Fenno. As the novel opens, Kate is summoned home by her daughter, now just turning twenty-one, and returns to America and the big old Clephane house on Fifth Avenue. Kate and her daughter, Anne, establish a warm relationship until Fenno reappears, falls in love with Anne, and becomes engaged to her. After a long and agonizing hesitation, and after agitated scenes successively with Fenno and Anne, Kate decides she cannot bring herself to tell her daughter the truth. She allows the marriage to go through, turns down a compassionate proposal by a faithful friend, and goes back to an adequately endowed but lonely life in southern France.

There is the familiar image of marital distress and of extramarital sexual fulfillment. But this is subordinated to the potent issue of the parent-child relationship. The transformation of Kate Clephane over the chapters from a formerly unfaithful wife to a dedicated mother is done with a sure hand—to the point where her identity is fixed in references to her simply as "the mother." "To play the part of Anne's mother," she tells herself, ". . . was what she wanted with all her starved and world-worn soul."

To play that role requires her, for a while, to attempt in secret to block the marriage between Anne and Fenno. But if the reader is tempted to question Kate's motive in doing so—to question whether she is acting as a concerned mother or as Fenno's vindictive abandoned mistress—he soon discovers that Kate questions herself in the most candid terms:

> Jealous? Was she jealous of her daughter? Was she physically jealous? Was that the
> real secret of her repugnance, her instinctive revulsion? Was that why she had felt from

the first as if some incestuous horror hung between them?

She did not know—it was impossible to analyze her anguish.

And in the principle on which Kate bases her final decision—that of the futility and utter wrongness of inflicting "sterile pain" on anyone—Edith summed up a lifetime of personal suffering.

The Mother's Recompense tells us a good deal about the course of Edith Wharton's imagination in these years. The fact is that when Edith Wharton in the 1920s talked about the relation between generations, more often than not she meant *literary* generations—more particularly, her own relation, as a woman in her sixties who had come to literary fruition twenty years before, with the younger writers who were appearing on the postwar scene to varying acclaim. Writing to the twenty-six-year-old William Gerhardi, the twenty-nine-year-old Scott Fitzgerald, the thirty-five-year-old Sinclair Lewis, what she stressed in each case was her assumption of an unbridgeable gap between herself and them and her joy at discovering that the distance could be overcome.

Add to this that, like Kate Clephane, she had been separated geographically as well as chronologically from her country during a long expatriation, and we realize that one layer of *The Mother's Recompense* expresses Edith Wharton's desire to establish some sort of contact with the American authors of the new generation and their new ways of doing things—as well as the difficulties, perhaps the near impossibility, of the effort. Her feelings in this regard would deepen into a sense of injury at being sometimes treated, critically, as out of date—this would be especially apparent in *Hudson River Bracketed* four years later. But if the part of her that wrote *The Age of Innocence* strove after a continuity with attractive moments in time past, another part of Edith Wharton sought a meaningful connection with the youthful heralds of the future. Her identity as a human being and a writer could only be forged, and reforged, by effecting ties in both directions.

Some of the reviewers, including one or two who badly misread the denouement, were hard on *The Mother's Recompense,* and Edith confessed herself more bothered by adverse or unintelligent criticism than usual. "As my work reaches its close," she remarked to Minnie Jones, "I feel so sure that it is either nothing, or far more than they know. And I wonder, a little desolately, which?" It was at this moment that she began the little diary, mentioned earlier in the preface, in which she hoped to render a truer account of her inner nature than that in reviews and published comments about her.

Even the expressions of praise she received without much pleasure, observing dryly that one commentator said the new novel made her the equal of Galsworthy, and another that of Scott Fitzgerald. The latter reference was to a review by Louis Bromfield, whose first novel, *The Green Bay Tree,* had been published the year before. Bromfield found the writing hypnotic and the narrative "handled with a technical skill approached by only one other book we have read this year,

The Great Gatsby. " This was a large claim in a season that, in addition to Scott Fitzgerald's small masterpiece, had ushered in Sinclair Lewis' *Arrowsmith,* John Dos Passos' *Manhattan Transfer,* Willa Cather's *The Professor's House,* Sherwood Anderson's *Dark Laughter,* and Ernest Hemingway's *In Our Time.* But similar praise echoed in the remarks of those who rated *The Mother's Recompense* Mrs. Wharton's best work since *The House of Mirth,* or even, like John Farrar in *The Bookman,* the best of all her novels.

The commercial success of this emotionally harrowing tale was surprising. Within weeks of its April appearance, Edith, who had already banked more than fifty-five thousand dollars in the first few months of the year, was instructing Jewett in a panic of affluence to send her no more money until the spring of 1926.

2

Edith Wharton was altogether averse to either Ste. Claire or the Pavillon Colombe being treated as a shrine to which pilgrims might freely come to pay homage to the Great Lady. They were her personal homes, central elements in the configuration of her ongoing and rigorously private life. When she received a letter from a young woman addressed to her at Ste. Claire and asking for full particulars of herself and her literary career, she remonstrated with Jewett for giving out her whereabouts. "My friends all know where I live," she said, "and that is all I care about." Jewett made haste to assure her that he never did supply her address but simply explained to inquirers that Mrs. Wharton was "traveling in Europe" and that he would be glad to forward letters to her. Given the amount of fan mail thus forwarded, some of it funny, some touching, begging for autographs, photographs, literary advice, and personal messages, and declaring her to be the favorite novelist of an individual, a class, an entire school, a book-reading club, Edith's policy had everything to recommend it.

She did allow her homes to be photographed for English-language magazines (*Country Home and Garden* among them), and was more than gracious when groups of local schoolchildren came by bus to explore the grounds. A visitor to St. Brice might, on Corpus Christi day, witness the religious procession through the Pavillon gardens: the priests bearing the canopy, the young girls veiled in white, the young boys and the nuns, the little children carrying baskets of roses which they sprinkled before the advancing canopy. Otherwise, Edith Wharton kept the barriers up.

The occasional fellow American writer, however, was encouraged to call. The year before, after a flurry of letters and telegrams, Hamlin Garland had spent a July afternoon at the Pavillon. Garland, still best known for his sketches of Dakota farmland life in *Main-Traveled Roads* (1891), had more recently published his autobiographical *A Son of the Middle Border.*

Sinclair Lewis continued to be visible, showing up at Hyères in March 1925 with the resplendent sales figures of *Arrowsmith* at his fingertips. In July of the same year, a month after Edith had made the spiraling trip north with Robert Norton, Teddy Chanler came to call with Scott Fitzgerald. Edith felt a proprietary affection for her friend Daisy's twenty-two-year-old son, having attended his baptism at Newport in 1902, the occasion enlivened by the heavily protected presence of the child's godfather, Theodore Roosevelt. Teddy, besides, was a sensitive youth with a keen developing interest in music, and was one of the members of his generation with whom Edith felt most in accord.

Upon her arrival at the Pavillon, Edith had found a copy of Fitzgerald's *The Great Gatsby* with "a friendly dedication," and she wrote the author at once:

I am touched at your sending me a copy, for I feel that to your generation, which has taken such a flying leap into the future, I must represent the literary equivalent of tufted furniture and gas chandeliers. So you will understand that it is in a spirit of sincere deprecation that I shall venture, in a few days, to offer you in return the last product of my manufactury.

Meanwhile, let me say how much I like Gatsby, or rather His Book, and how great a leap I think you have taken this time—in advance of your previous work. My present quarrel with you is only this: that to make Gatsby really Great, you ought to have given us his early career (not from the cradle—but from his visit to the yacht, if not before) instead of a short summary of it. That would have situated him, and made his final tragedy a tragedy instead of a *"fait divers"* for the morning papers.

Fitzgerald was to say that Mrs. Wharton's letter contained one of the two pieces of intelligible criticism his book had received, referring perhaps to what Edith Wharton went on to observe:

But you'll tell me that's the old way, and consequently not *your* way; and meanwhile, it's enough to make the reader happy to have met your *perfect* Jew, and the limp Wilson, and assisted at that seedy orgy in the Buchanan flat, with the dazed puppy looking on. Every bit of that is masterly—but the lunch with Hildesheim, and his every appearance afterward, make me augur still greater things.

In a postscript, she asked "if you and Mrs. Fitzgerald won't come to lunch or tea some day this week. Do call me up." Zelda Fitzgerald stayed behind in their walk-up apartment near the Place de l'Etoile, but Fitzgerald asked Teddy Chanler to come along and lend moral support. Fitzgerald revered Edith Wharton even more than did Sinclair Lewis; and testimony to his feeling was Fitzgerald's need, on the drive to St. Brice with young Chanler, to fortify himself with a series of drinks. He took them, his biographer has said, like pills to ease a nervous stomach.

Gaillard Lapsley was the only other guest at the Pavillon. Conversation was slow and awkward, and finally Fitzgerald, swaying a little against the mantelpiece, proposed telling "a couple of—er—rather rough stories." Rather rough stories, within the limits of genuine humor, were what Edith Wharton relished, and she smiled her approval. Fitzgerald thereupon got entangled in an anecdote about an American couple who by mistake spent a night in a Paris bordello. His hostess, listening attentively, commented at last that the story "lacks data"—the kind of rounded realistic information and description that the flustered Fitzgerald was unable to provide.

After the other two guests had departed, Edith remarked to Lapsley that "there must be something peculiar about that young man." Lapsley observed that Fitzgerald had obviously been drinking. Edith Wharton's record of the occasion consists entirely of a diary notation: "To tea, Teddy Chanler and Scott Fitzgerald, the novelist (awful)." Fitzgerald's reaction to the meeting was implicit in his remark to Maxwell Perkins some months later that *The Mother's Recompense* was "just *lousy.*"

A high point for Edith Wharton in the winter of 1926 was reading *Gentlemen Prefer Blondes* by Anita Loos, "which the literary committee of Ste. Claire (R. Norton, G. Lapsley and EW) unhesitatingly pronounce the greatest novel since *Manon Lescaut.*" Edith was only slightly exaggerating her response to this popular gem of American literary humor. In the same letter, to Hugh Smith, she spoke deprecatingly of Proust's recent *Albertine disparue:* "Walter calls it 'Proust *disparu,*' and he's nearly right." She allowed herself to be quoted as saying that Miss Loos's book "is *the* great American novel." This unmodified comment was flanked in advertisements by James Joyce's remark that he was putting *Gentlemen Prefer Blondes* "in place of honor" and George Santayana's solemn contention that it was unquestionably "the best book on philosophy written by an American."

Gentlemen Prefer Blondes consists of the diary ruminations of Lorelei Lee, a cheerfully amoral and dim-witted young woman from Little Rock, who, after shooting her employer for trying to entice her into a nasty situation, beats her way across the Atlantic and across England and the continent, engaging in a series of dalliances and intrigues. Edith probably saw in the novel a deft satirical twist on her own satirical comedies of manners, as Lorelei, moving from one Ritz Hotel to another, mixes with American tourists, British baronets, and French solicitors and makes vague stabs at improving her mind by reading Conrad and Benvenuto Cellini. The heroine's rushingly incoherent speech and phonetic spelling also attracted her. The characterization of Undine Spragg in *The Custom of the Country*, Edith thought, was now vindicated.

She wrote Frank Crowninshield, at *Vanity Fair*, a word of praise for the novel, and Crowninshield passed it on to Anita Loos, at the same time sending Edith a picture of the author—perhaps the smallest, and certainly one of the prettiest women on earth, he said. Some months later Edith overcame her dislike of the Ritz in Paris to take part in a lunch in honor of Miss Loos and her husband, John Emerson, president of Actors' Equity. The occasion was arranged by Berry, who had known Miss Loos a little in New York, and Geoffrey Scott was among the guests.

A cruise through the Aegean was scheduled for the end of March, something Edith had been dreaming about for a long time. Her previous Aegean trip, with Teddy Wharton and James Van Alen in 1888, had been, she said, "the crowning wonder of my life, and yet how ignorant I was." Recalling the expense of that adventure, she calculated that a cruise of half the length would now cost one-third more, about twenty-eight thousand dollars, and of this she was prepared to put up more than half.

She had chartered the *Osprey*, a 360-ton steam yacht from England, carrying five "master cabins" and two cabins for servants. Daisy Chanler and Robert Norton gladly agreed to come along; Berenson fended off an invitation, but made the welcome suggestion that Logan Pearsall Smith be asked.

On March 16 the *Osprey* sailed into the harbor at Hyères for an overnight stay, and Edith hurried down to meet its skipper and inspect the yacht. She took with her Beatrix and Max Farrand, who had paused on their way to Belgrade, where Max was to inaugurate a new annual chair in American history; he had left Yale and was now heading up a Harkness fund for postgraduate traveling fellowships. Pearsall Smith and Daisy Chanler arrived on the thirtieth. The next afternoon Edith and the others went on board at Les Sablettes, a few miles west of Hyères, and, with the entire Ste. Claire household lined up on the dock and waving vigorously, the *Osprey* pulled out into the Mediterranean.

The cruise lasted for ten idyllic weeks—an experience, Edith told Berenson, that belonged "to a quite other-dimensional world." The *Osprey* passed through the Strait of Messina and crossed the Ionian Sea to Cephalonia and Zacynthus. There were late evenings on deck under the stars, afternoons of sun and sea spray, explorations of island coasts, and bumpy drives through the hills. The yacht turned northward and sailed along the Gulf of Corinth. At Delphi they lunched on a ham-and-veal pie prepared by their accomplished cook, consuming it under trees of hoar olives, just below the Castalian Spring. From Itea they could see snow far away on the slopes of Mount Parnassus. Years later Edith would vividly recall gazing up at that spectacle and saying to herself: "Old girl, this is one of the pinnacles."

By the end of the month the *Osprey* finally entered the Aegean, making its way with studied leisure among the islands: to Delos, and a climb to the top of Mount Kynthos; to Patmos, and a donkey ride to a fortified monastery; to Rhodes, and a guided tour through the old part of the capital city, and down to Lindos, which Edith thought quite unchanged since she had seen it almost forty years before.

The seas were unexpectedly rough on the passage to Cyprus, but further enchantment awaited them on the island. Edith and Daisy made the long and arduous ascent to the twelfth-century castle which the Crusaders had renamed Dieu d'Amour—not for the Christian god of love, but after the pagan god Eros, son of Aphrodite, who in pre-Christian times had been the "liege lady" of Cyprus. It was "the most fantastic fairy castle imaginable," Margaret Chanler would say, "built on a high rocky peak . . . two thousand feet above sea level, and surrounded by sheer precipices." Resting on board next day, Edith began to write a story called "Dieu d'Amour"; it was another of her medieval-legend tales like "The Hermit and the Wild Woman," and it dealt—as that story and several of her poems to and about Morton Fullerton had done—with the conflict between sacred and profane love. This time, sacred love won a somewhat melancholy triumph. At the same moment, relaxing meditatively in his stateroom below, Logan Pearsall Smith was writing the first pages of his reminscences, *Unforgotten Years.*

As the weather turned sultry, the *Osprey* crept through the smaller islands —to Santorini and Melos, and across to Cynthia on the southern coast of Sparta. Of an evening Robert Norton enthralled the others by reading from the volume Edith had brought with her on the earlier trip, Butcher and Lang's translation of the *Odyssey.* By May 30 the yacht had anchored at Syracuse, in Sicily, where Daisy Chanler went off to Mass and the others to inspect the Greek theater. At Naples there were two days with the Berensons; B.B. broke his self-imposed rule and consented to escort Edith through the museums. In early June the party was back at Ste. Claire.

3

For Edith Wharton, the *Osprey* cruise was a planned return to scenes recollected from one of the happiest moments of her earlier life. The following September a similar impulse took her, with Walter Berry, to the Bergamasque in northern Italy and the lakes she had visited with Teddy and the Bourgets in 1899. Berry, who had resigned from the American Chamber of Commerce in Paris a few years before, had evidently been unavailable for the Aegean trip, but during the summer of 1926 he was regularly on hand, taking Edith to dinner at Laurent's and La Perouse, inviting her to lunch with Ava Ribbesdale, and introducing her to young David Bruce, Andrew Mellon's son-in-law, who was in the earliest stage of one of the most fruitful diplomatic careers of the century.

In Bergamo they made the winding drive up to the old walled city, looming above the sprawling modern one below. Here they lingered in the extraordinary Piazza Vecchia, a combination of treasures more picturesque, if less awesome, than those in the "Square of Miracles" in Pisa. Thereafter Edith and Berry descended from Bergamo to the Po Valley and drove across to Venice, where they walked to the Accadèmia to see the Veroneses, went out to the Lido for lunch, and dined on the Grand Canal with the Duke of Marlborough and his bride of several years, the sprightly Gladys Deacon. Edith then had her first view of the South Tyrol: Belluno, Cortina d'Ampezzo (which she particularly liked), Riva at the head of Lake Garda. They journeyed west through Bergamo again to Aosta, near Mont Blanc and the Swiss border; here by prearrangement they met Berenson and Nicky Mariano.

Edith would have reason for remembering every detail of this motor trip. Six weeks after her return to St. Brice, on November 14, Berry underwent an emergency operation for appendicitis. Edith had begun her pre–Ste. Claire fortnight at the Crillon ("a severe discipline," she said, "and I endure it only by living on my roof top and thanking heaven I'm not at the Ritz"); she now put off the move south for a little. She went to the hospital daily, taking on her shoulders responsibility for a number of decisions. The extremely pretty eighteen-year-old French nurse drove Berry almost frantic with her ministrations, until he burst forth in a speech Edith never thought to hear him make: "Oh, for God's sake get me one who's old and ugly." She found him a stolid middle-aged Englishwoman.

Berry, recuperating slowly through December, was convinced that the operation had been unnecessary. He was well enough by the twenty-first to come down on the Blue Train to Hyères, to spend Christmas there with Edith, Norton, and Lapsley. He returned to Paris on New Year's Day, and ten days later Edith had a telegram from Jules, Berry's manservant, that Berry had suffered a stroke.

Edith at once assumed the worst, and while waiting bleakly for the night to pass—the last train from Toulon had left before the telegram arrived—she wrote Hugh Smith: "I hope with all my soul it will be short and fatal. Anything else for him won't bear thinking of." But when she reached Paris next day and hurried around to the Rue de Varenne, she found Berry not as stricken as she had feared. He had had "a slight embolism of the brain," and his speech was impaired, but he seemed otherwise not seriously affected. He could move about cautiously, he could read (though only detective stories) and write, and his mind seemed as clear as ever. Within a week he was able to go out for a drive each day; there was slow but marked daily improvement.

But Berry was unutterably depressed, and especially by the prospect of the months of convalescence that lay ahead. Edith was soon at her wit's end, and desperately uncertain whether to stay on while Berry grew steadily and vocally exasperated by her "hovering about," or whether she could with any assurance leave him to the doctors and nurses. Berry made it clear that he wanted minimum medical attention. Her best advice was a long period of rest and fresh air: in short, a sojourn at Hyères; this Berry rejected violently.

Edith finally went back to Ste. Claire at the end of January 1927, to be greeted by a furious telegram from Berry; his sister, Mrs. Nathalie Alden, was rushing over from America despite his strict instructions that she was not to be notified, and it was all Edith's fault. Nonetheless, a few weeks later Berry did install himself at Ste. Claire, and began, as Edith put it, to crawl "through his desolate days of convalescence." Margaret Chanler was also there, laid up with water on the knee, and she took away with her an image of Edith Wharton pathetically eager to be of comfort and considerate in all ways, and Berry complaining grumpily about the lack of heat in his room and the position of the pillow behind his back.

Edith stuck to it, though she found Berry's perpetual sadness "so profound, and so penetrating, that I was benumbed by it." Berry, who returned to Paris in late March and departed almost immediately to consult a specialist in Bern, was belatedly remorseful. "I'm missing Ste. Claire dreadfully," he wrote from Switzerland, "—though what it must have been for you, dear, I can't think: tied down to a stuttering paralytic." The doctor in Bern seemed to Berry to confirm his suspicion about the appendectomy, and he began to feel a stir of wary optimism.

4

While tending to the despondent Walter Berry, Edith had been busy with her own practical affairs, impelled by a sudden need to increase her income. The rooted possessive person was anxious to sink her roots more deeply and to enlarge her possessions. She had recently laid out several hundred thousand francs for a small property across the street from the Pavillon Colombe, which she used chiefly as a vegetable garden; and during the winter of 1927, with the help of Boccon-Gibbod, she negotiated for the outright purchase of Ste. Claire le Château, which she had originally taken on a long lease. As the latter transaction drew to its close, Edith took thought as to how she might find the roughly forty thousand dollars needed for the purchase.

She had just completed a novel called *Twilight Sleep*, destined for Vance at the *Pictorial Review*. The editor of the *Delineator* offered forty-two thousand dollars for her next novel, a work to be called *The Children;* Vance's offer for this book had gone up to thirty-five thousand dollars, but no contract had been signed, and Edith was inclined to accept the larger figure. Jewett was skeptical, on the grounds that the *Delineator* was even less worthy of Edith Wharton's fiction than its rival. "Work of high literary quality," he wrote, "is not so good for these popular magazines as the typical lowbrow serial publication. Mary Roberts Rinehart and Kathleen Norris grind out ideal stuff—for serialization. You write novels without a thought for the magazine." Edith responded to this doubtful premise by deciding in favor of the high-paying Palmer at the *Delineator*, promising that the novel to follow *The Children* would go to Vance in the spring of 1929. Vance took this amiss, feeling, Jewett reported, that "he has always played the game to the top of his bent with you."

The discussion grew farcically confused. Edith suggested that if Vance were to have *The Children*, which was progressing nicely, Palmer could be given a choice of not one but two novels—both of which were tentatively called "The

Keys of Heaven." Palmer gracefully relinquished *The Children,* and chose the second of the two scenarios of its successor. Edith was not yet satisfied. Was Vance going to hold to the thirty-five thousand dollars he had first proposed? She had quite been counting on the additional seven thousand dollars: "It was with this expectation that I ventured to buy Ste. Claire, as I owe all such luxuries to my literary industry." As a sporting gesture, Vance raised the fee to forty thousand dollars.

In an attempt to set things straight, and feeling, so he said, as if he were filling out Edith Wharton's dance card at a ball, Jewett summarized the situation in June:

Vance at the *Pictorial Review* would pay $40,000 for *The Children.*
Palmer at the *Delineator* would pay $42,000 for *The Keys of Heaven.*
Palmer offered $50,000 for the novel after that, and Vance and another editor begged to remain in contention.

Edith Wharton had begun work on the longer and more interesting version of "The Keys of Heaven" soon after the war, but the novel was never completed. This might seem an occasion for regret, since the material appeared perfectly suited to her interests, talent, and personal knowledge. It concerned the real-life story of Henriette Desportes, who, in the Paris of the 1840s, became governess to the children of the Duc and Duchesse de Praslin, and who so aroused the Duke's passions that, in one of the most brutal murders in French history, he hacked his beautiful but insanely jealous wife to death. The story then moved from the Paris Edith's parents had known to the New York of the 1850s, the time of *The Old Maid.* There was a period in the Berkshires, where Henriette lived with her husband, the minister Henry Field. The tale then carried forward through the New York of Edith's own childhood, to a narrow brownstone house on East Eighteenth Street, a few blocks from the Joneses'.

Edith Wharton's outline followed the original story closely up to the point where her heroine, renamed Laure de Lassy, marries the Reverend Henry Shreve of Stockbridge, Massachusetts. But the ingredients failed to unite in the kind of moral action that Edith Wharton's imagination required at this stage in her career; perhaps she might have written the book fifteen years earlier. It fell to Rachel Field, a direct descendant of Henriette Desportes Field, to make a quite absorbing novel from the historical events, *All This, and Heaven Too,* in 1939.

Twilight Sleep was published in mid-June 1927, and by early August it had replaced Sinclair Lewis' *Elmer Gantry* at the top of the best-seller list. Edith Wharton was not displeased by this, since she had been put out by Lewis' forceful portrait of a scoundrel and his satire on the corruptions of American religious life. *Elmer Gantry,* she told Lapsley,

is a pitiful production. America *is* like that, no doubt, but not all and only like that. As I said to Walter the other day, the trouble with them all is that they don't know what a gentleman is, and after all it was a useful standard to get one's perspective by.

Twilight Sleep (a title referring to the comatose condition in which most American women of gentle birth, according to the author, pass their adult life) is the most overplotted of Edith Wharton's novels. It concludes with the young heroine being accidentally wounded by her mother's first husband, who had gone gunning for someone else—a melodramatic way of suggesting that young people in American society had become the victims of their elders. Such was the turn that Edith Wharton's continuing drama of generations was now taking. Issues of genuine moral gravity are, in fact, at stake in the novel, but they remain blurred amid the comings and goings. Edmund Wilson, nonetheless, called *Twilight Sleep* an acute and entertaining piece of social criticism, and most other reviewers approached Mrs. Wharton's seventh volume of fiction in as many years with respect. Only Dorothy Gilman, in the Boston *Evening Transcript*, was uncompromisingly harsh. The novel, she said, seemed of a deliberately commonplace nature designed for readers of serials and, artistically speaking, it was not only painful but disastrous.

The career of *Twilight Sleep* was a predictably brief one, but before it disappeared from view it brought Edith Wharton some twenty-one thousand dollars in royalties from Appleton, in addition to the thirty thousand for the serial. Edith acknowledged her gratification, but wished the sales in England had not been so laggard and Appleton's advertising there so skimpy. To this Jewett responded by sending on the English book-trade report that showed *Twilight Sleep* just behind Arnold Bennett's collection of stories, *The Woman Who Stole Everything*, high on the best-seller list, and well ahead of Sir Arthur Conan Doyle's *The Casebook of Sherlock Holmes*.

5

The oppressive atmosphere at Ste. Claire in the late winter of 1927 was considerably lightened by the arrival of Geoffrey Scott, who came at the beginning of March and stayed for two months. Edith had thought he looked distraught and unwell when he stopped at the Pavillon Colombe the previous summer, but now he was better in every way and was "gloriously good company." His manner was gentle, his conversation brilliant, his thick dark hair as untidy as ever.

Scott had passed through a difficult time. There had been an affair with Victoria Sackville-West before he was replaced in her affections by Virginia Woolf. He and Lady Sybil were divorced, and Sybil married Percy Lubbock in December 1926. Edith was outraged by this last development. "This is the third of my friends she has annexed," she told Lapsley. She was genuinely indignant, but she could also make caustic fun about the matter. "I see you and Robert going next, and then B.B., and finally even Walter—kicking and screaming!" She warned Hugh Smith that she feared for his safety as well, and added, *"This thing has got to stop."*

About Lubbock's behavior she confessed to "a predominating sense of disgust," and because of her continuingly intractable attitude, the breach not only with Sybil but with Lubbock too was a final one—the only episode of its kind in Edith Wharton's history. She tended, as we have seen, not to be at her best with the wives and women friends of her men friends, but never had she broken with a man who had been as close to her, as much admired and loved by her, as Percy Lubbock, one of the last survivors of the old "inner circle" which went back twenty years.

Not long after Geoffrey Scott returned to London in the spring of 1927, there occurred a remarkable turn in both his material and literary fortunes. An extraordinary discovery had been made in Malahide Castle in Ireland, where, in what became a world-famous ebony cabinet (something like a tallboy) and in nooks and attics of the castle, there had been turned up a mass of papers by or relating to James Boswell—including leaves from his *Life of Johnson*, a great many letters, and a series of private journals. It was undoubtedly one of the most dramatic literary finds ever made. Lieutenant Colonel Ralph Heyward Isham, an American who had served with distinction in the British army during the war and who was known as a collector of Johnson materials and a daring and energetic man, had negotiated for the purchase of the documents at enormous prices. Casting about for an editor of the Boswell papers, Isham, after being turned down by his friend T. E. Lawrence (whose translation of the *Odyssey* he had helped to fund), was advised to consider Geoffrey Scott. In his *Portrait of Zélide* (1925), a beautifully written account of the witty and cultivated Dutch woman Belle de Zuylen, Scott had shown an excellent knowledge of the character and career of his heroine's friend Jemmy Boswell. In the wake of that achievement he had been commissioned to write a life of Boswell for the British Men of Letters series.

In September, Scott was invited to dine with Isham at the latter's suite in Claridge's Hotel to discuss the undertaking. He arrived trembling with excitement, spent forty-eight hours without leaving the suite, and was signed on to edit the immense treasure at a very substantial sum. For Edith Wharton, who regularly placed *The Life of Johnson* on the list of her favorite books, it was one of the happiest conjunctions of her life. She described herself as grinning all over at Geoffrey's "Boswell haul." (Further Boswell papers were periodically discovered at Malahide Castle over the next twenty-five years, and another hoard in closets, bean sacks, and bundles at Fettercairn House, near Aberdeen, in Scotland. When Isham's fortune began to be exhausted by the purchases, there came to his aid Edith Wharton's old friend and fellow traveler in the Aegean, James Van Alen, who put up $124,000. The entire editorial enterprise was eventually taken over by Yale University, whose Professor Chauncy B. Tinker had been responsible for the initial discovery of the papers.)

In June, a few weeks after getting back to St. Brice, Edith had noted in her diary: "Work and gardening. Happy solitude." The latter phrase was hardly an apt one for those typically busy summer days. Eric Maclagan appeared. He was now the director of the Victoria and Albert Museum in London, and was on his way to America to deliver the Charles Eliot Norton lectures for 1927–28 at Harvard. Among the several French museum directors Edith invited to meet him was her cherished new friend Louis Metman, head of the Musée des Arts Décoratifs in Paris, an uncommonly good-looking and civilized person, a scholar, and an amusing man of the world.

A friendship was also ripening with Louis Gillet, curator of a museum at Chaalis, near Senlis, and a literary critic and art historian. Gillet was robust and severely handsome, with an aggressive, thrusting black beard and a disconcerting habit of rolling his eyes up in his head when struck by a new thought. Gillet's steady stream of learned studies and translations were substantial enough to earn him a seat eventually in the Académie Française, though he had not, perhaps, a mind of the very highest order. But Edith Wharton was startled and gratified when so eminent a man offered to translate *The Mother's Recompense*. It appeared under the title *Le Bilan* ("The Balance Sheet"): a good job of work which led Schlumberger, blind now and having to be read to aloud, to exclaim with enthusiasm: "How marvelously Mme. Wharton writes French."

Paul Valéry remained faithful. In July the wedding of Philomène de Lévis-Mirepoix and Comte Jules de la Forest-Divonne was announced. The count was a graceful and calm-natured young naval officer; in fact, he was a good deal younger than Philomène, but Philomène was so eternally youthful in looks and manner, as someone remarked, that the difference in age was of no importance. Edith rejoiced that her friend's long period of loneliness and anxiety was over.

6

The American Legion invaded Paris in mid-September 1927, a huge, roaring, clamoring crowd of war veterans. Edith hid out fearfully behind the high walls of the Pavillon Colombe, but Walter Berry, widely regarded as the first American citizen in Paris, had to submit to an endless series of banquets, cocktail parties, and speech-making affairs.

The result was perhaps inevitable. On the morning of October 2, Jules telephoned Mme. Wharton to say that Berry had suffered another stroke during the night. Berry had previously given his manservant careful instructions that should he again be stricken, no one was to be told, not even his doctor, not even Mme. Wharton. Edith moved in at once to a suite at the Crillon and met Jules at Les Invalides, where Jules explained his dilemma. She then visited her own doctor, who consulted with Berry's physician, and by a complicated process Jules reported his observations of Berry while the latter slept and advice was filtered back to Jules as to what little could be done.

For a week Berry lay totally paralyzed in the Rue de Varenne apartment, finally unable even to take food. On October 9, Jules noticed his eyes flickering toward the telephone, and when he asked "Mme. Wharton?" Berry blinked his assent. Edith came at once, and for three days was able to be with him for half an hour at a time each morning and afternoon. On the eleventh she sat by him for long minutes, holding him in her arms and murmuring about old times together. Berry pressed her hand faintly at each memory. Early next morning Jules called to say that Berry seemed much weaker. Edith reached the Rue de Varenne by eight thirty, but Berry had died twenty minutes before.

The funeral, on October 17, was of a splendor almost unknown even in Paris. The specially constructed hearse, with plumes and silver insignia, drawn by four black horses with handsome dark coverings and white reins, led a great procession along the Avenue George V to the American Pro-Cathedral. These were representatives of the President of the French Republic and other high dignitaries. The ceremony took on an air of a national occasion, for in addition to the representation of power, wealth, and art, there were wreaths from the *mutilés* with whom Berry had worked during the war, from French nurses, from outlying French villages. The mayor of Belleau was present to speak for the community near which Berry had arranged for the purchase of Belleau Wood as a national memorial to three American infantry divisions.

But that colorful moment of tribute to one of France's most valuable American friends was almost forgotten in the bickering that followed between relatives and legatees. There were "ghastly hours" at the Rue de Varenne with the Marquise de Polignac, the former Nina Crosby and one of Berry's favorites, who was bequeathed a fine painting Edith had understood was to go to her. Harry Crosby, Berry's younger cousin and an able and wealthy dilettante of arts and letters, was Berry's executor and much in the middle of things with his strong-minded wife, Caresse. Berry's will left all his books to Edith Wharton, but Crosby was determined that some at least would make their way into his own library in the Rue de Lille. As discussions went forward Edith, who had begun by regarding Crosby as "inexperienced and unmanageable," ended by regarding him as "a half-crazy cad." Crosby, after agreeing that Mrs. Wharton had every right to the books, moved on to the opinion that in claiming the whole collection, her behavior was disgraceful and "she should be damned well ashamed of herself." Eventually, it seems, there was a satisfactory division of the spoils.

Edith found these visits to her old apartment almost too painful to endure. "I think of that apartment, and what I have lived through of joy and sorrow," she wrote Lapsley, "[and] my soul recoils from the idea of ever crossing its threshold again." Even so, she spent an afternoon there with Nathalie Alden, Berry's invalided sister, going through Berry's letters and retrieving all that Berry had kept from those Edith had written him over forty-four years. She made a ritual burning of the lot.

Berry's body had been cremated and the ashes brought by Harry Crosby to the Pavillon Colombe, where Edith had established a temporary altar for a Requiem Mass. There was then further dispute among the several women about the disposition of the ashes. The urn was finally buried in the Cimetière des Gonards at Versailles on October 29, with only Edith and the family in attendance on the grassy cemetery slope. "The stone closed over all my life," Edith said in her diary.

During those last days, Edith wrote Hugh Smith, Berry "had wanted me so close and held me so fast, that all the old flame and glory came back, in the cold shadow of death and parting." "What agony," she told her diary, and several times she was so distraught with grief that she could not remember at the end of the day what she had done, where she had been. Slowly she began to assess what the loss meant to her. "Through all the comings and goings in his eager ambitious life"—this also to Hugh Smith—"I was there, in the place he put me in so many years ago—of perfect understanding." And to Lapsley she wrote:

No words can tell of my desolation. He had been to me in turn all that one being can be to another, in love, in friendship, in understanding, and I could give thanks and warm my heart at the memory of it, but for the slow agony of the last year, and the terrible last days alone with him. All my friends are dearer to me than ever.

One difficulty in trying to define Berry's role in Edith Wharton's life is the spate of contradictory images that has come down to us. In Edith Wharton's view he was the wisest, kindest, and essentially the *dearest* man she had ever known, indispensably encouraging and astute during her literary apprenticeship and her years of illness (which he certainly was), and in later times the one person she could invariably turn to for understanding and counsel. Berry penetrated more deeply than Edith Wharton, and perhaps than any other American, into the world of French modernist art and letters, and his French friends admired and were amused by him. But Edith's English-speaking friends disliked or detested Walter Berry almost to a man, an exception being made for Henry James. Berenson had turned vehemently against him, finding him—perhaps out of deepening resentment at Edith's subservience to Berry—cold, self-centered, and irrelevantly clever. If the French thought there was something scandalous in Berry's failure to marry Edith after her divorce, the English and Americans were merely astonished and irritated that anyone would even broach the possibility.

Margaret Chanler once spoke of Berry as "the dominant seventh chord" in Edith Wharton's life. Dominion Berry unquestionably exercised, though not until a later date than had been supposed—not really until about 1910; and it was far more of an intellectual, one might almost say spiritual, than of a physical kind. Affinities of this sort are often mysterious; one rarely has a sufficient record of verbal exchanges, moments of emotional and sensual harmony, a companionable sharing of tastes and interests. What seems clear is Berry's ability to impose his authority over a woman who increasingly felt the need of masculine authority (who wanted, as she told Berenson, someone to scold her), just as she sometimes wished she could be like the empty-headed pretty women Berry usually preferred.

25. Letters and Shadows

By the end of October 1927, Edith Wharton had wearily but staunchly taken up work on *The Children.* Two days later the Berensons and Nicky Mariano came to her succor. She had written Berenson, in a "passion of loneliness," that she felt utterly lost and without direction, and Berenson cabled that they would come at once. "What friends you are—what friends!" Edith cried. "Since your telegram yesterday I have felt alive again."

The Berensons were still in Paris when Edith left on the Blue Train for Hyères, and they followed her south within a fortnight. Royall Tyler was in from Budapest; Lapsley and Norton made their annual appearance; children from the local school serenaded the household from the terrace; and there were readings in the evening—Jane Austen, and the stories of Hans Christian Andersen, which Nicky brought as a present. The 1927 Christmas party at Ste. Claire went some way toward soothing Edith's agony of spirit, and when it was over Berenson wrote Mary (who had returned to I Tatti ahead of him):

> I shall be awfully sorry to leave Edith. I have never admired, esteemed and loved her as during this visit. She seems fine, happy almost, and in full possession of all her gifts, thoroughly enjoying life. Let us do likewise. We have much to live for.

When Mary wrote Edith to praise her courage and resilience, Edith, thanking her, said that she tried "to accept sorrows and renunciations, and to *build* with them, instead of letting them tear me down."

In the midst of her deep but contained grief over Berry, Edith felt little beyond a certain sad irony and a quiet flow of memory when she learned by cable from Susie (Mrs. William) Wharton that Teddy Wharton had died on February 7, 1928, at the age of seventy-nine. Edith had heard next to nothing from or about him for more than a decade. When his sister, Nancy, had died some years earlier, Edith had written him and had received no response. Word reached her that Teddy was heard to say occasionally, with pathetic incomprehension about the divorce, "Puss shouldn't have done that to me." Billy Wharton was gone too, and Edith could only imagine how lonely her former husband must have been.

"I am thankful to think of him at peace after all the weary agitated years," Edith wrote Robert Grant. "You will go back to the far-off past of our youth together, as I do tonight." Teddy, she said, had been "the kindest of companions till that dreadful blighting illness came upon him." And to Lapsley, evoking an image that might have been drawn from *Ethan Frome* or the story "The Long Run," she said: "It is a happy release, for the real Teddy went years ago, and these survivals of the body are ghastly beyond expression."

Teddy Wharton left an estate of $56,685 to Pearl Leota Barrett, the trained nurse who took care of him after Nancy's death. Two of his nephews and a niece contested the will, arguing that Teddy had already given Miss Barrett gifts of money in the amount of $65,000. The challenge was disallowed.

The Nobel Prize awards in December 1927 were watched with special interest by Edith Wharton and her friends. More than a year before, a movement had been started to gain the prize in literature for her. More accurately, since no prize had been given in 1926, one of the two awards expected for the current year was hoped for. The prime movers were Robert Bliss, the American ambassador to Sweden, and his wife, Mildred, whose attitude toward Edith had considerably mellowed with the passage of time.

They first approached Arthur Hadley, president emeritus of Yale, with the thought that, since the university had given Mrs. Wharton the honorary doctorate a few years earlier, Hadley might nominate her in the university's name. Hadley replied that it would be improper for him to speak for Yale, but he consulted with William Lyon Phelps, and in mid-January 1927, Phelps drew up a statement for the Nobel Committee nominating Edith Wharton as "the foremost living creative literary artist of America," whose award of the Nobel Prize in literature "would cause great rejoicing among American and Continental critics." It was signed by six other eminent professors of English at Yale.

Robert Bliss knew the chances were problematical. The annual nomination of Thomas Hardy was beaten back by committee members who regarded his work in fiction as immoral, and there were several octogenarian members who were totally out of touch with modern writing. But Bliss and his wife bestirred themselves to elicit letters of support from distinguished sources. From Washington, Chief Justice Howard Taft (who as a member of the Yale Corporation had joined in the selection of Mrs. Wharton for the degree) wrote that Edith Wharton "has reached and sustained a higher level of distinction [in fiction] than that of any other contemporary in her own country." The aging Elihu Root—formerly Secretary of War and then of State, United States Senator, presidential representative at a series of historic conferences, and himself a winner of the Nobel Peace Prize —described Edith Wharton's work as "distinguished by most skillful and sympathetic delineation of character and by a deep understanding of the truths of life."

From his home in Pall Mall, Lord Balfour, after remarking to Bliss about his very high opinion "of my friend, Mrs. Wharton," told the Stockholm committee that "Mrs. Wharton . . . is known wherever the English language is spoken and wherever she is known she is admired," and alluded to her great powers of imagination and penetrating insight into human nature. Paul Bourget took time out at Costebelle to identify Mrs. Edward Wharton, not unpredictably, as presenting *"un example bien remarquable de ce que le génie Américan peut ajouter à la culture Européenne en se l'assimilant."* Jules Cambon, one-time ambassador both to Washington and London, added vigorous words about Mme. Wharton's elegant style and about the justice and force of her observations of society.

Edith Wharton seems honestly not to have set her hopes on the award. "I have never for a moment imagined that the Nobel Prize Committee would cast a favourable eye in my direction," she told Robert Bliss in February 1927, "and shall experience no shock of disappointment when I am told that someone else has been chosen." Her only action was to have all her writings forwarded to Stockholm. The awards did finally go elsewhere. One was given to Grazia Deledda, for her ritualistic accounts of the passions and perversities of Sardinian provincial life. The other recipient was Henri Bergson, the great French philosopher.

Edith Wharton had no quarrel with the choice of Bergson, whom Bourget had taken her to call upon once or twice. But she felt strongly that if it was indeed Italy's turn to be honored, the prize should have gone to Gabriele D'Annunzio. As for herself, since Henry James had been passed over for the Nobel, despite her own efforts, it might even have been a little embarrassing for her to have been selected. But she was obviously touched to the core by the efforts and interventions of her friends and by the praise for her years of creativity.

Edith finished *The Children* ("Thank heaven!") before the end of January 1928 and turned without interruption to her next and more ambitious novel, *Hudson River Bracketed*—it was this, rather than the abandoned "Keys of Heaven," that was to go to the *Delineator*. Afternoons and evenings were given to the customary Riviera outings and entertainments, including a dinner party for the King and Queen of Denmark, and the usual run of visitors from Paris, London, and New York.

As the Georgian age assumed its own social and intellectual identity, Edith Wharton was becoming the familiar of a number of its representatives. Some of these new friends she encountered during a summer fortnight in England. Among them was the hospitable and gossipy Sir Philip Sassoon, an uncle of the poet Siegfried Sassoon, a long-time member of Parliament, an enormously wealthy and charming man of Bombay Jewish stock (in India, a Jew is known as "Sassoon-man"), and a famous patron of the arts. Sir Arthur Salter (later Lord Salter), some eighteen years younger than Edith, came to her as an old friend of the Tylers. Edith was not initially impressed: "a sort of 'roll-top desk' person," she said, and a mere "statistician." She soon corrected this misjudgment and came to value the attractive and imposing qualities by virtue of which Sir Arthur became economic adviser to several Prime Ministers. But she instantly took the measure of the much younger Steven Runciman, a Scotsman who first turned up at Ste. Claire with a letter from Gaillard Lapsley: a nice-looking youth with rumpled hair and drooping socks, and already exhibiting the brilliance and erudition he would display as the most distinguished Byzantine historian of his generation.

Edith was never cordial to the Bloomsbury group as such, though she relished her rare meetings with Lytton Strachey. She was on her guard against Virginia Woolf, especially after an article by the latter which seemed to argue that American writers should cultivate their native idiom and not, like Henry James and Edith Wharton, strive after the king's English. In the fall of 1928, Mary Berenson urged Edith to read *Orlando*, Virginia Woolf's fictional fantasy about sexual change over the centuries, and a novelistic portrait of Vita Sackville-West. Edith replied that the photographs of the author in the advertisements "made me quite ill. I can't believe that where there is exhibitionism of that order there can be any real creative gift."

According to Berenson, Edith admired none of Virginia Woolf's novels, though recognizing that she had "prodigious gifts in other directions." A high-born English lady once remarked to Edith that Virginia Woolf had the most avid curiosity she had ever known. Mrs. Wharton, the lady recalled, "didn't quite like that. Had Virginia really a great curiosity? she queried; certainly Virginia had a very imaginative mind, perhaps a very poetic mind, but was she fundamentally endowed with *true* curiosity?" The lady in question, Lady Aberconway, told herself afterward that Mrs. Wharton's "curiosity about things and people exceeds even Virginia's. She stimulated everyone. I want her for my friend."

When she met Arthur Waley, Edith made much of the fact that he had nothing to do with Bloomsbury. At thirty-nine, Waley had ten volumes of translation and commentary on Oriental literature behind him, and was bringing out one by one the six volumes of his famous rendering of the medieval Japanese *Tale of Genji*. "I had my usual panic, which I always have when I am going to meet anyone I have admired for a long time," Edith wrote. She might well have found alarming Waley's habit of dropping in an instant from rapid-fire conversation into chilling silence. But she found Waley quickly responsive, and they had a good deal in common: a conviction about the great importance of friends, rarefied beliefs about human conduct, a delicacy of literary perception.

Edith's English fortnight in 1928 took her first to Robert Norton at Lamb House. At Sandgate, on the coast near Folkstone, she was introduced to a young writer of promise, Evelyn Waugh; two years later she would be laughing out loud at Waugh's novel *Vile Bodies*. In the busy London *salon* of Lady Colefax, Edith was fairly swathed in titled and important personages. But she was wearied by such large batches of distinction, and went back thankfully to relax in the garden at Lamb House. Four days later she drove over through Exeter to Tintagel, on the west coast of Cornwall. Fog enveloped King Arthur's castle, and Edith felt that she was "fulfilling an old dream in coming to this legendary headland which is as wild and haunted as its name." The name would reverberate in that of the Duke of Tintagel, one of the central characters in Edith Wharton's last and unfinished novel, *The Buccaneers.*

2

The Children was the September 1928 Book-of-the-Month Club selection, and it rapidly climbed to the top of the best-seller list. By November it had brought her more money than any novel she had ever written. When Edith wrote Jewett in early November asking if he could send her $2,000 to cover expenses on the new library at Ste. Claire, Jewett gave her a careful accounting: during the current year and before she had asked him to stop, he had deposited about $39,000 in her account; since then over $41,000 had accrued, with some $15,000 yet to come. The figures included $25,000 from the Paramount Famous Lasky Corporation for the film rights to *The Children*. The novel earned its author upwards of $95,000 from all sources, and her other writings in 1928 brought her several thousand more. Her expenses kept pace.

While these sums were being bandied about, during a visit to Hyères of Rutger Jewett, Edith asked him why picture magazines paid so much for novels by what she liked to regard as "serious writers." She could not delude herself that magazine readers were really interested in such work. It was not the readers who kept the prices up, Jewett surprised her by saying; it was the advertisers. "They won't pay top-notch rates," Edith quoted him as saying, to Berenson, "unless they're *enclosed in an Edith Wharton or a Galsworthy story!!!* Now beat that."

It was, however, exactly as a species of magazine-serial fiction that a number of critics were hard on *The Children*. Gorham Munson wrote in *The Bookman* that Mrs. Wharton had written a model serial for a certain rather low-grade audience, with sufficient doses of spice and sentiment, and a kindly bachelor figure to add tone. This competent book, he said flatly, was simply not written by the author of *Ethan Frome*. There were the familiar voices of approval, especially for the air of good humor that brightens many of the novel's pages. But a larger percentage of commentators than before found the story thin and artificial, and there were allusions to Mrs. Wharton's declining powers.

The Children is undoubtedly a novel of surfaces, though not unengaging ones. Geographically, they are limited mainly to Venice and the South Tyrol, places Edith had visited with Walter Berry less than two years earlier, and which she here invoked with all her old assurance and vitality of detail. More important, and as its title suggests, the novel represents a further stage in Edith Wharton's survey of the relations in her time between parents and children. One has the sense, however, that in this novel she was *observing* these phenomena from a certain distance, rather than (as in *The Mother's Recompense*) writing out of her own "maternal" consciousness.

"The children" are seven in all, ranging from the fifteen-year-old Judith to the infant Chipstone, and they are the products of a variety of couples— of the rich, rudderless Wheaters' two marriages to each other and their marriages to different spouses in between. Edith Wharton derives genuine comedy from the effort of the forty-six-year-old bachelor Martin Boyne, who encounters the brood in Algiers, to sort out which is the offspring of whom. The movement of the novel is, indeed, a steady drift of the comic toward the poignant: for the heart of the action is the finally unsuccessful effort of the young people, aided by Boyne, to cling together as a unit in the face of their parents' (and one counts seven of the latter, as well) passing through an endless series of couplings and uncouplings. Edith Wharton's indictment of the nearly grotesque irresponsibility of the parental generation reaches an extreme in this otherwise good-natured novel.

At the same time, the novel reflected Edith Wharton's growing fascination with persons fifty and sixty years younger than she. She was taking special pleasure now in visits not only with the Charley du Bos' but with their daughter Primrose, with the Boccon-Gibbods and their two infants, with the daughters of Louis Gillet. One of the latter, Louisette, translated a novella of Mme. Wharton's, and Gillet himself translated *The Children* (as *Leurs Enfants*), stumbling only over the queer word "steps," which the youngsters use casually to designate their assorted stepbrothers and stepsisters. Edith was developing an almost sociological interest in the phenomenon of children, a consciousness of a significant new breed of humanity with whom it behooved her to come to grips. The same Englishwoman who spoke to her about Virginia Woolf recalled Mrs. Wharton asking intently about her own children: what was it like to *talk* to a child, to talk to a really *young* child every day?

3

It was in late August, not long after Edith's return from England, that Logan Pearsall Smith brought out to St. Brice Desmond MacCarthy, whom she instantly pronounced delightful. MacCarthy's beaklike nose, voluble tongue, and wholly engaging manner had earned him the name "Affable Hawk." His voice was warm and friendly. He was infectiously lazy and socially quite undependable; no one ever minded in the least. Though Virginia Woolf would say that "Desmond was the most gifted of us all," he never produced the great work that was expected of him. But his literary perceptions, particularly in dramatic criticism, were of the finest, and his periodical writings, mostly during his editorship of *The New Statesman and Nation* and the *Sunday Times* (where he succeeded Edmund Gosse), have been collected into six still eminently readable and profitable volumes. He was one of the most humane men of his time, and Edith Wharton, who simply prized him, later saw as much of him as possible. On his side MacCarthy thought his hostess displayed "an admirably furnished, clear strong mind," but that she perhaps stood too much in need of luxury and of agreeable and undemanding companions.

Peering out from the serene privacy of the Pavillon Colombe, Edith took occasional stock of the changing world. Mary Berenson sent her *The Cause* by her daughter Ray Strachey, about the role and status of women in contemporary society. Thanking her, Edith observed that for her part she believed "women were made for pleasure and procreation." As on other occasions, and considering especially her own role in life, one cannot be entirely sure of the *tone* of a remark like that. All things considered, it probably represented less a divergence from her former sympathy with independent-minded women than an acknowledgment of a somewhat bitter fact of life. As early as *The House of Mirth* she had recognized that, in American society at least, women were regarded by men as no more than momentary ornaments. Little in her experience since then had led her to revise this recognition.

After the American election in November, Edith studied a photograph of the oval-headed President-elect, Herbert Hoover, and concluded that the "mug" that stuck out above his stiff high white collar was "a perfect example of standardisation." Political affairs were no more gratifying in France, where the fall of Poincaré led her to exclaim "What a country!"—Poincaré was the French statesman whom she had most admired. Political developments in both hemispheres, however, seemed too lackluster for the moment to occupy her mind as she moved into the Crillon. "I am taking my usual intensive course in Paris," she wrote Berenson, "administered by the usual group—Béhague, Paléo, Philomène, Abbé, Mildred Bliss, Tylers, Noailles, Poix etc. etc. All very pleasant, but making me feel daily more and more how completely I was made for country solitude and early hours." A session with Philomène, she added, was better than a violet-ray treatment.

After considerable remodeling at Ste. Claire there were now four guest bedrooms and a good-sized new library, with a brownish brick floor half covered with rugs and a bellpull presented by Elisina Tyler. Simon, the head gardener, had been dismissed for dishonesty and neglect; Edith's secretary, Jeanne Duprat, had in a rather short period become the wife and then the widow of a M. Féderich.

Robert Norton, for a rarity, was not on hand for Christmas. He was overseeing his first one-man show in Bond Street, and though the serious illness of King George V was having a dampening effect on most activities in London, twenty of his watercolors sold within two weeks. Sir Louis Mallet made a seasonal visit: an agreeable and "conversable" diplomat who had rounded out a notable career as ambassador to Turkey and was now living in retirement in the south of France. There was constant movement back and forth between Ste. Claire and St. Bernard, and between Edith Wharton's household and the estate called Polynésie in Hyères which Martine de Béhague had acquired a few years before, and where she had built a massive villa hanging above the sea, with parks sweeping upward to rolling green hills.

A final Christmas greeting for 1928 was a message from New York that the stage version of *The Age of Innocence* was a distinct success. Pleased but skeptical, Edith wrote Lapsley that "no one knows how long a play without murderers or niggers will be able to hold the public." The abrasive reference was probably to *The Emperor Jones* and *All God's Chillun,* two popular plays dealing variously with murder and black people by Eugene O'Neill, always greatly esteemed by Edith Wharton. The excellent script of her own play was by Margaret Ayer Barnes, the prize-winning Chicago novelist. With Katharine Cornell beautiful and authoritative in the role of Ellen Olenska, the play ran until the end of the theatrical season in mid-June 1929. The following fall it was taken on the road for four months, playing nine cities between Baltimore and Chicago. From this, her first venture onto the stage since the unlucky production of *The House of Mirth,* Edith Wharton drew up to $750 a week; $23,500 in all.

4

Edith Wharton was in the habit of remarking in her diary several times a year that it was the worst February or the worst August, the coldest winter or the hottest summer in twenty years or even in history. But the weather in January and February 1929 really was atrocious by Riviera standards. The temperature dropped below freezing and stayed there; winds raged about the high-perched château; Edith celebrated her sixty-seventh birthday in a blinding snowstorm that left the roads almost impassable. The pipes froze in the house, and the water in the pigeons' bath outside. Everyone caught cold, including Cabot Lodge and his wife of two years, the former Emily Sears, who came for a few days in January. Lodge was on a short leave from his duties covering Congress for the New York *Herald-Tribune.*

What truly afflicted Edith was the devastation of her gardens. The howling gales began by destroying two splendid evergreens, the pride of Ste. Claire. Trees and shrubs were then smashed and torn up everywhere, and others were killed by the grinding cold; of rare plants not a trace remained. By the middle of February, Edith had to acknowledge that her so lovingly planned gardens had been all but wiped out. In her diary, using much the same language she had for the death of Walter Berry, she spoke of the "torture" she was feeling for her "dead garden." To Lapsley she exclaimed despairingly: "Oh, Gaillard, that my old fibres should have been so closely interwoven with all these roots and tendrils."

But interwoven they were: here as elsewhere, Edith Wharton's gardens were a projection of her own nature. The destruction of the gardens at Ste. Claire in the winter of 1929 was a personal disaster of the worst sort.

The shock to her mental system was followed by, and related to, a comparable shock to her physical system. The weather turned unseasonably mild, and Edith surveyed the wreckage between visits with Louis Metman, the Paris museum director, and sunlit drives into the hills. Coming back from Cannes on March 4, she caught a severe chill. The infection spread; the next day she suffered a violent and protracted fit of nausea. The high fever that set in and lingered for days caused heart palpitations—of such a kind that Robert Norton and Elisina Tyler (the latter had rushed down from Antigny at word from Norton) thought, wrongly, that Edith had actually suffered a heart attack. When the fever finally subsided, around March 15, Edith was predictably in a state of total exhaustion. The local doctor's chief prescription was absolute rest. There was no questioning the fact that she had nearly died.

Her several plans and projects were thrown into disrepair almost equal to that of the gardens. She had learned to her consternation a fortnight before the attack that the senior editor at the *Delineator*, without so much as a word to either Jewett or herself, had begun to run *Hudson River Bracketed* the previous September, six months ahead of the agreed-upon schedule. "I cannot tell you the harm Mr. Graeve's inexcusable action has done to me, and, I fear, to my novel," she wrote Jewett. The sudden need for haste at that otherwise shattering time made her so nervous that in fact it slowed work down. Now, of course, she was forbidden even to think of work for an indefinite period.

For many months she had been talking with Berenson about a trip to Syria, a country unknown to her. Daisy Chanler and Norton were to be in the party, and a certain Mr. de Lorey. The report that Sybil Lubbock had enjoyed Syria did nothing to deter Edith. "As a fainting-field she no doubt found it unrivalled," she remarked to Berenson with customary malice, "and if Mary and I are took the same way, we shall have you and Mr. de Lorey to 'fall back upon' (hence the expression)." There followed the kind of on-again off-again planning and counter-planning that so unsettled Berenson. But in March, Berenson understood from Mme. Féderich's letter that there could be no Syria for Mme. Wharton that year.

Edith had also decided to go back to America during the spring. Nicholas Murray Butler, the president of Columbia University, had written that the university wished to give her the honorary degree of Doctor of Letters in June. The thought of seeing *The Age of Innocence* on Broadway also attracted her, and she longed to get away from the daily view of her dismal surroundings. She accepted the invitation on February 15 and booked passage for herself and Daisy Chanler on the *Minnewaska* for May 25. It fell to her secretary to cancel the sailing.

Not till the end of April did Edith begin, in her diary phrase, to crawl back to life. Elisina left—"I can never tell you what Elisina has done for me," Edith wrote Mary Berenson. Margaret Chanler took over. In early May, Edith was working *"doucement"* on her manuscript, so Mme. Féderich said, and late in the month her doctor approved her traveling north to Paris, after being made to grasp the fact that there were such things as sleeping cars and that some people even bought berths in them.

A long succession of quiet days at Versailles and St. Brice further reduced her sense of fatigue. At the end of July she felt able to board the Golden Arrow for Calais and Dover. In London she made a brief trial of her strength in the *haut monde*. Surviving this, she passed a number of hours with Geoffrey Scott, sauntering through the National Gallery. She had never seen Scott in better form, full of excited confidence about the huge Boswell enterprise and about to go to America to closet himself again in Colonel Isham's home on Long Island.

After a number of days amid Lawrence Johnston's tormentingly perfect gardens at Hidcote, Edith went back to Lamb House, and from there she drove with Norton the few miles to Bodiam, where, she recalled, "over twenty years ago I went with H. James and M.F." The next day, August 15, as she was preparing to go to lunch at nearby Lympne with Mrs. Winston Churchill, her daughter Sarah, and Sir Louis Mallet, Norton came in with the London *Times*, which carried the story of Geoffrey Scott's death in New York, at the age of forty-six. He had died suddenly, in a hotel, of pneumonia.

Dazed and heartbroken, in her diary words, Edith could scarcely bring herself to accept this new loss. She had come genuinely to love Scott, and the cruelty of his dying at the moment he was coming so splendidly into his own was hardly to be borne.

Oh, Gaillard [she wrote], what a mockery it all is! He had got on his feet, he had pulled himself out of all the sloughs, he was happy, ambitious, hard at work, full of courage and enthusiasm. The Furies had been letting him simmer.

Scott had lived to add six exemplary volumes of James Boswell's papers to his own otherwise few but enduringly brilliant writings. There remained the bitter sense of greater promise unfulfilled, and a friend lost.

5

Edith Wharton's fortitude was never more apparent than in the latter months of 1929, when she set about the two major tasks of reclamation that confronted her: the re-creation of the gardens at Ste. Claire and the completion of *Hudson River Bracketed*. In early October she went down to Hyères, found a gardener named Joseph—he would be the ablest of her Riviera gardeners—and took him around the devastated grounds. They visited nurseries in the area, consulted with horticulturists, brought in an expert on rock gardening. Systematic planting began at once. Edith's Christmas guests were astonished to find the Ste. Claire terraces largely restored within less than a year of the catastrophe.

She forged ahead doggedly on *Hudson River Bracketed,* meeting magazine deadline after deadline, at times working, against her habit, until late in the afternoon at a desk set up in the Pavillon Colombe garden. At one moment she wondered if she might not cut the narrative short, in the interests of keeping to schedule. It was already clear in her mind that there would be a sequel, and perhaps the present novel could break off at an earlier point. Oscar Graeve at the *Delineator* vetoed the suggestion, commenting that "with so much that is already unsatisfactory, a special ending to lop it off would indeed be the last straw." It was a churlish remark, given the magazine's editorial malfeasance and Edith Wharton's nearly fatal illness. She was deeply offended. "I will never again willingly give a line of mine to the *Delineator,*" she informed Jewett. She had still not fully taken the measure of the publishing world she had surrendered to.

She finished the novel on October 22. It was a work of over five hundred pages, Edith Wharton's longest since *The Valley of Decision,* and had been written in the space of twenty-one months, during four of which she was unable to write a line. "I am sure it is my best book," she confided to Jewett, who was now editor in chief at Appleton, "but I have little hope that the public will think so." She would put it and its sequel, *The Gods Arrive,* on the list of her five personal favorites among her fiction—the others were *The Custom of the Country, Summer,* and *The Children*—but her prophecy about its reception was accurate. A common note in the reviews, indeed, was exactly that it did *not* rank with her best work; it would not stand foremost, Percy Hutchinson said typically in *The New York Times,* nor would it rank last. Only Mary Ross in the *Herald-Tribune* was unreserved in her admiration: *Hudson River Bracketed,* she said, invoking a curious but possibly apt adjective, was the most "generous" book Edith Wharton had ever written. Sales fell below those of *The Children* by about one-third, but even so, the novel added another sixty thousand dollars to Edith Wharton's income.

It is easy to see why she had a special tenderness for the novel. On New Year's Day, 1930, she set forth some of her reasons in a letter to Elisina Tyler, who had praised the book to the skies.

I am overwhelmed by what you say of *Hudson Riv.* After allowing for all the indulgence of your affection, there seems so much more praise than the book deserves—yet I would rather hear it of this than of any other book I have written. It is a theme that I have carried in my mind for years, and that Walter was always urging me to use; indeed I had begun it before the war, but in our own milieu, and the setting of my youth. After the war it took me long to re-think it and transpose it into the crude terms of modern America; and I am happy to think I have succeeded.

The work "begun . . . before the war" was "Literature," the first notation for which was made in Dresden in August 1913, on the German tour with Berenson. "Literature" was to deal, as *Hudson River Bracketed* deals, with the unsteady development of the literary artist under the circumstances of American life. In fact, not much of the older effort was transposed into the later completed novel.

Edith Wharton wrote about eighty pages of "Literature," in typescript and manuscript, before abandoning it at the outset of the war. The story is set in the time and place of Edith's childhood and youth; the finished portion, which traces the early years of a boy named Dicky Thaxter, is crowded with precise personal reminiscences, from a nurse named Hannah to the kindly deaf grandmother who allows the child to shout poetry into her ear trumpet. Thereafter, according to the elaborate scenario, the narrative was to follow Thaxter's career through college, several liaisons and marriage, wanderings in Europe, and the completion —at the time of his early death—of most of a fictional trilogy, which we are intended to believe was a major literary achievement.

"Literature" was conceived in part, one gathers, as a portrait of the American literary situation at the time of its composition. Edith Wharton modeled Thaxter's personal and creative career fairly closely on that of the once enormously admired poet and playwright William Vaughan Moody, who similarly died at an early age, leaving behind the better part of a philosophically ambitious verse-drama trilogy. Nor did Edith Wharton scruple to give the name Carmen Bliss to Thaxter's mistress in Europe, thus juggling with the spelling and the sex of the prolific Canadian-born poet Bliss Carman. Other aspects of the contemporary literary scene were, evidently, to be dwelt upon.

The literary scene in the late 1920s was, correspondingly, a major element in *Hudson River Bracketed.* But the emphases had markedly changed since those of "Literature." The challenges that stirred or beset the sixty-seven-year-old Edith Wharton were significantly different from those of 1913.

Hudson River Bracketed—the title refers to an early nineteenth-century style of American architecture—gives us about five years in the life of Vance Weston, a young man who has grown up in the go-getting, forward-looking atmosphere of midwestern towns with names like Euphoria, Hallelujah, Pruneville, and Advance (the birthplace which supplied Weston with his first name). Following a traumatic experience of sexual disillusionment, Vance comes east to Paul's Landing, on the Hudson, where he boards with a cousin of his mother. He falls in love with and eventually marries Laura Lou Tracy, the frail and ignorant but physically enticing daughter of his landlady; but he also comes somewhat under the spell of Halo (née Héloïse) Spear, who lives on a neighboring estate and soon herself makes a loveless match, for complex financial reasons, with the clever, insubstantial Lewis Tarrant.

Vance is peculiarly drawn to an unoccupied but perfectly preserved nearby house called The Willows. Built in 1830 and a fine example of Hudson River Bracketed style, it becomes for him an imperfectly perceived symbol of the rich American past which he now confusedly longs to attach himself to. In the library of The Willows he discovers poetry—Coleridge, Marlowe, Marvell, Goethe—

and the revelations of poetic beauty spur him to seek out a literary career of his own. He writes a short story which causes wide reverberations and almost wins the much-sought-after Pulsifer Prize, carrying a cash award of two thousand dollars. But his main energies are given to the writing of *Instead,* a short novel intended to enshrine The Willows and the character of its last inhabitant, a woman who flourished in the later nineteenth century. It is a grand success, but Vance is advised to direct his attention to the postwar world about him, and he makes a start on a novel about contemporary New York. By this time he has confessed to himself and to Halo Tarrant that he is hopelessly in love with her, and that she is the inspiration of his best work. Laura Lou fortuitously dies, and Halo appears with the news that she has left her husband. Vance and Halo are drawing closer together as the narrative ends.

Hudson River Bracketed is much too long. The pressure under which Edith Wharton had to meet the *Delineator's* deadline caused her, in a familiar way, to write many more pages than her story required. One consequence is that its most suggestive themes are stretched thin, and often lost sight of, over large distances of narrative.

The confinements of marriage and the lure of extramarital love for a person of greater sensitiveness and largeness of spirit than the partner's are present, as almost always. But more compelling, via the career of Vance Weston, is Edith Wharton's sense of her relation as a writer to the newly fashionable breed of younger novelists and, partly as a result of that, her recurring need to relate her postwar self to the more serene, elegant, and cultivated America of half a century before.

Edith Wharton states her case through Halo Tarrant's urgings that Vance write "something quiet, logical, Jane–Austen-y," something content with the old conventional way of beginning and developing a story, and the opposite of what all the "on-the-spot editors" were looking for. And Vance feels himself estranged from the bright new authors whose novels and stories make such a hit: "These brilliant verbal gymnastics—or the staccato enumeration of a series of physical aspects and sensations—they all left him with the sense of an immense emptiness underneath." Edith Wharton is unrestrainedly satiric about the popular literary modes of the moment, but there is no missing a certain defensiveness of tone —and more, her sense of deepening hurt at being critically underrated or disregarded in favor of younger writers, even while she remained one of the best-selling novelists in the country.

Vance, meanwhile, also bespeaks Edith Wharton's impulse, no doubt prodded by her literary situation, to attach herself to the former age. It is, again, a pressing question of personal identity: it is out of his effort to locate his "primordial personality," his "indestructible inmost self," that Vance studies The Willows and its human history so closely. He wants, he says, to live into the minds of the people who lived there, "to try and see what we came out of," to get "that sense of continuity that we folks have missed out of our lives—out where I live."

In *The Age of Innocence* and *Old New York*, Edith Wharton had sought to achieve such continuity through the setting, stresses, and texture of her narratives. *Hudson River Bracketed* is a novel *about* a literary figure who consciously sets out to do the same thing. At the same time, it is about a writer who begins with something like a historical novel, as Edith Wharton did in *The Valley of Decision*, and then turns to explore his contemporary New York, as she had also done in *The House of Mirth*. It cannot be said, however, that these various parallels and recurrences combine to make *Hudson River Bracketed* a superior work of fiction. It has fascinations and attractions, and it represents a telling moment in the life story of Edith Wharton, but it is, finally, laborious and unsure.

6

If Edith Wharton was increasingly disturbed by her status vis-à-vis younger or avant-garde literary types, her interest in young *people* as such continued to grow, and it was gratified during a week's visit by Bill Tyler, who arrived from Antigny two days after Edith completed *Hudson River Bracketed*. Slight of stature, immaculate, his features combining his mother's delicate grace and his father's masculine strength, Bill Tyler at eighteen had already developed the ingratiating charm of speech and manner and the steady sly humor which made him the young person to whom "Edoo" was most devoted. He had taken leave from Harrow, where he was preparing for Oxford, because a spot had been discovered on his lung; it turned out not to be a serious affliction, but rest, fresh air, and quantities of good food had been prescribed. Edith and he spent a lazy and companionable week basking on the terrace and puttering in the garden.

Edith had invited a few persons of interest to meet her engaging young friend, and Royall Tyler came out to dine at the Pavillon. While Edith wrote Elisina about her delight in Bill and his visit, she could hear father and son shouting with laughter in the next room. Two months later Bill happened to write Edoo about a recent pleasant evening of music. "What a darling Bill is," Edith wrote his mother, "to think of me when he enjoys things," adding, in one of her most percipient remarks about friendship: "It is the most delightful way of living in the minds of one's friends."

A little contretemps disturbed the otherwise gay 1929 Christmas party. Bernard Berenson—who had come with Nicky Mariano to join the faithful Lapsley, Norton, and Hugh Smith—returned from lunch at St. Bernard one day visibly shaken. The de Noailles' had hung a painting said to be by Picasso in their sitting room, and Jean Cocteau pronounced it as complete and satisfactory a work of art as anything by Raphael. Berenson, who could see nothing in it but a small isolated circle, a column of small newsprint, and a piece of brown sacking, attempted to argue that the work had no artistic value at all. Cocteau burst into a torrent of aesthetic verbiage, and Marie-Laure grew so agitated that she could only keep powdering her cheeks and rouging her lips. Back at Ste. Claire, Berenson declared that he had never felt such an outsider. No one in the Ste. Claire household ever discovered that the entire affair was a hoax perpetrated by Cocteau, who had himself put together the absurd montage as a device for attacking Berenson's hostility to modern painting.

The summer of 1930 saw Edith Wharton's household visited by a series of grotesque accidents. The previous months had been calm ones. There had been a few weeks in Spain with Daisy Chanler, Edith's third view of that country in five years; the hotels were mostly described as unspeakable, and about the accommodations at Ubeda, Edith permitted herself to adopt the tag line of a bawdy joke—"Christ, what a night!" Returning to St. Brice, she found a cable from New York inviting her to take over the unfinished portion of Scott Moncrieff's translation of *Remembrance of Things Past* by doing *Le Temps retrouvé*. "It is out of the question, of course," she wrote Berenson, "but I am gratified at having been asked to succeed so really great a translation and should perhaps say yes if I were forty or fifty years younger." She was moving steadily ahead on *The Gods Arrive*.

Then, on July 1, Edith's cook Roger died as the result of a motorcycle crash. He had been with Edith on and off for eighteen years; he was only thirty-five and was married, with a small boy. On the day Roger died, a member of the Hyères staff, the footman Edith referred to as "poor crazy sympathetic Romano," was shot and killed by his wife, whom Edith alleged to be a town prostitute. Four weeks later, with a houseful of guests at the Pavillon awaiting their dinner, Roger's elderly successor was found lying senseless on the kitchen floor covered with blood. He had suffered a hemorrhage caused by the bursting of an abscess in his liver. By the end of the month he was dead.

Preparing to go to Salsomaggiore in September, Edith rehearsed these developments to Gaillard Lapsley, concluding: "Cook No. 2 died last week—Louisa has the shingles—and the half-hour hurricane last week wrecked my two cut-leaf maples next the house and wiped out all flowers and vegetables." To this hyperbolic résumé, she added that Cook No. 3 was insipid and would not be kept long.

7

The shadow of death again lay around her: now, of course, mainly the inevitable accompaniment of advancing years. Walter Maynard had died of pernicious anemia at the age of fifty-four. To Eunice Maynard, Edith wrote with characteristic stress: "I loved Walter dearly—I always felt happy, *at my ease and understood,* when I was with him"; she could still see his eyes shining with anticipation of jokes about to come. But to Lapsley she confessed that her heartache was also due to the sense that Maynard had never quite lived, had always seemed on the verge of living. She saw him from afar as a type of the finest and most touching of the New Yorkers she had known—like Newland Archer, a person to whom nothing, finally, was permitted to happen. "How little they got out of it all."

Rhinelander and Newbold cousins died, leaving her, she seems to have felt, the last survivor of the family she had been born into. But for Edith Wharton, as the year 1930 drew to its close, perhaps the most distressing loss of all was the death of her little dog Choumal. The Pekinese caught an infection which left her reduced to "dreadful gaspings," and had to be put away.

Edith herself was in quite good health, though Berenson observed that her activities were diminished and that "she no longer outstrides and out-lives me" —a fact which made her, Berenson thought, a better companion than ever. But her consciousness of death was such that at times there was almost something inviting, something sweetly tempting, in the contemplation of it. "I have known that long shadowy tunnel," she wrote Mary Berenson after an illness that had nearly cost Mary her life, "and how it lures one on." At the end of the year she was writing a story called "Pomegranate Seed," about a widower who, after he remarries, receives a number of mysterious letters addressed in a hand so faint as to be illegible. When he disappears, his wife and mother realize with dawning horror that the letters have been peremptory summonses from his dead wife, and that he has obeyed them.

This first-class ghost story was in part a modern revision of the legend—a lifelong obsession with Edith Wharton—of Persephone and her sojourn in the underworld. But if, as she approached seventy, Edith Wharton could appreciate the appeal of those dark regions, it only intensified her awareness of what the land of the living might yet hold in store for her.

26. A World Grown Somber

The autumn of 1930 found Edith Wharton still virtually unaware of the cata-
clysm that had occurred in the New York stock market the year before or of the
political storm signals that could be heard from several sections of Europe. Her
luxurious, carefully and even ritualistically designed existence went forward,
seemingly never to change. There was *The Gods Arrive,* the sequel to *Hudson
River Bracketed,* to write; but to her conscious mind, it was not to involve any
departure from her recent fiction and its recurring emphases. In fact, however,
the vein represented by novels like *The Mother's Recompense* and *Hudson River
Bracketed*—the drama of generations and the search for continuity—was almost
exhausted. And as the clamor of outside events gradually reached her ears over
the next four or five years, it brought about yet another and final transformation
of her relation to herself and a condition of psychic liberation such as she had
never fully known before. But before that moment there was a severely difficult
time to get through.

Her openness to new friendships and new experiences, meanwhile, continued
unabated, and she was constantly exhilarated by fresh appearances in her life and
momentarily arresting encounters. In the autumn of 1930, at I Tatti, she had seen
something of Berenson's neighbor Ugo Ojetti, the enormously influential director
of the newspaper *Corrière della Sera,* an authoritative if conservative art critic,
and a garden lover. During the same visit, at the home of another neighbor, Edith
was at last introduced to George Santayana. In the presence of the man whose
philosophical writings she had long revered more than anything else in English,
she was seized with a peculiarly severe fit of shyness.

Later, cruising south through Tuscany with Berenson and Nicky Mariano, she
paid a visit to La Foce, the magnificent estate which Iris Cutting and her husband
of some years, Antonio Origo, were carving out of a desolate, stony stretch of land
below Siena, and which would eventually resemble the beautifully receding landscape of a fifteenth-century Sienese painting. Driving on into the hills to Cortona,
Edith ran into other friends of Berenson's, including Count Umberto Morra, the
young novelist Alberto Moravia, and Kenneth Clark, sometime protégé of Berenson and an art critic and historian of extraordinary promise.

Like everyone else, Edith immediately warmed to Morra, an infinitely kind and courteous man, the treasured friend and helper of writers, artists, and scholars up and down the Italian peninsula. She was prepared to enjoy Moravia too, for she had found his first novel, *Gli indifferenti*—a deftly composed account of lackluster adultery and intrigue—a masterful work. Moravia was a stocky young man, a trifle lame, with a handsome, scowling face and given to little bursts of salacious and improbable comment. The latter gave Signora Wharton no offense, but Moravia seemed to her too self-preoccupied for good conversation. Within a matter of months Kenneth Clark would become one of the most valued friends of her remaining years.

To Ste. Claire, just before Christmas 1930, there came Aldous Huxley and his wife, Maria, bringing with them Cyril and Jean Connolly. Edith thought Connolly, who was earning himself an excellent reputation by his literary articles in the *New Statesman*, extremely intelligent and with a commendable sense of fun, though perhaps a somewhat "lesser number" than Huxley. But she described his wife as "an awful lump," according to a report from Nicky Mariano. This was hardly a reference to Jean Connolly's physical contours: she was a slender and lovely nineteen-year-old girl from Baltimore. It had to do rather with her inability to join the talk. Things were not helped by an undercurrent of strain between the Connollys and the Huxleys, but on this occasion it was Edith Wharton who was the source of another's frozen shyness—receiving Mrs. Connolly's conversational efforts in a silence that reduced the young woman to staring wordlessly at her plate.

Aldous Huxley, who had taken a villa for the winter at nearby Sanary, was a decided acquisition to the little Riviera community, Edith wrote; he was "human, conversable, full of fun, and extremely social." He was another member of the Thomas Arnold clan, being the son of Mrs. Humphry Ward's younger sister Julia—as well as the grandson of T. H. Huxley, from whose biological writings Edith Wharton had drawn much mental sustenance. At thirty-six, Aldous Huxley was a tall, slender man with somewhat defective vision and of uncertain health. Edith had felt admiringly in tune with his earlier novels: *Antic Hay, Those Barren Leaves,* and other works of social satire and endlessly witty talk in one of the great English literary traditions. When his futuristic *Brave New World* appeared in 1932, Edith—just then beginning to take in the cataclysmic historical changes occurring around her—declared it to be "really great" and a masterpiece not about possible horrors to come but about the horrors already upon the Western world.

Edith would exchange half a dozen visits with the Huxleys each winter for the next years, and her delight in them only grew with every season. In the proffered opinion of Lady Ottoline Morell, Aldous Huxley liked Ste. Claire only because of its Victorian milieu; but he was temperamentally disposed to appreciate the graces of life at the château. He also enjoyed the company of Mrs. Wharton, whom he sometimes treated with a sort of elegant informality. Once when she arrived unannounced at the villa in Sanary, Huxley escorted her into the drawing room by pressing gently against her behind with his cupped hand. The other guests were struck dumb by the performance, but Edith, glancing back at her host, gave him a quick sweet smile.

Huxley enlarged Edith Wharton's horizon by bringing in other persons of interest. It was at the Huxleys' villa that Edith first met Bronislaw Malinowski, the Polish-born scholar who exerted the greatest influence in his generation upon British anthropological studies. He was best known for his epochal and beautifully written book on the natives of the Trobriand Islands off New Guinea. Edith Wharton could sate some of her long-standing intellectual passion for anthropology during many hours with the blond, good-looking scholar. She found him as informative as he was charming. He also seemed to her "wistful, wise and sad" —the latter, apparently, because his wife was cruelly crippled by arthritis, though for all that she was a gay and nimble-witted creature.

In March 1931, Kenneth and Jane Clark paid their first visit to Ste. Claire. "They are really rewarding, both of them," Edith wrote Berenson, adding further words of enthusiasm. Clark, the scion of a family whose large income came from cotton thread, and already regarded as something of a genius in his undergraduate days at Oxford, came to Settignano in 1927 to pursue art history under Berenson's direction. He brought with him as his bride a young woman of Irish origin, also a former student at Oxford, with a luminous mind and a deeply engaging manner, and for several years the Clarks occupied a remodeled villa close to I Tatti. Clark's apprenticeship having been concluded, they were now living in England. In the spring of 1931, at scarcely twenty-eight, Clark was appointed keeper of the Ashmolean Museum in Oxford, which housed the richest small collection of art in the country.

Edith Wharton's attention had originally been drawn to Clark through his book on Gothic architecture. But the relationship with both Kenneth and Jane rapidly developed beyond a sharing of views on art and literature and mutual friends into a kind of domestic intimacy. They exchanged useful little gifts, worried about one another's health, ran errands for each other, asked advice about practical matters. In October 1932, Jane Clark, already the mother of one son, gave birth to twins, Colin and Colette, and the Clarks asked Edith to be godmother to the boy and Nicky Mariano to the girl. Edith's pleasure was boundless, and she promised to practice "god-motherly attitudes," in the hope that the period until the actual christening could be "tided over without too much risk to their souls." As a present for the occasion, she gave Colin the christening mug which her mother, Lucretia Jones, had provided for her own baptism seventy years before.

The friendship with Kenneth Clark was another element in the unfolding pattern of Edith Wharton's relations in old age with much younger persons. For her, Kenneth was a quite dazzling young man, with every beauty of mind and body, supremely gifted for his vocation, and with the world opening all before him. Though he was literally young enough to be her grandchild, Edith remained somewhat in awe of the prodigy and kept reminding herself, in letters to Kenneth, that he was a busy and important official and she only a "lazy old lady." But Clark's pungent personality and offhand vigor of judgment made him easy company. Clark had, as well, immense and outspoken respect for Edith Wharton's work; Lord Clark is on record as saying that the strongest influences upon him were Edith Wharton and Bernard Berenson. As his admiration ripened into manifest affection for her personally, Edith began to feel fully relaxed in Clark's presence.

More so, indeed, than she sometimes did in Berenson's. Once, when a winter holiday party at Ste. Claire was breaking up, Clark walked out with Berenson to B.B.'s car. Sitting back in the "panting Lancia," Berenson uttered a sigh of relief and observed that he felt exactly as though he had just been let out of school. The car drove off, and Clark made his way back to the terrace, where Edith stood waving good-bye. "Now," she remarked, turning to the house, "I can take off my stays."

2

One of the first things Edith did on crossing to England in July 1931 was to drive out to Richmond for lunch with Kenneth and Jane Clark. The festive three weeks that followed included attendance at *The Barretts of Wimpole Street*, Edith recording her annoyance that the incestuous aspect of the story had been deleted. Moving from one social center to another, she encountered a flock of her newer English friends: Desmond MacCarthy, Arthur Waley, Sacheverell Sitwell (Edith found "Sachie" helpful in making travel plans), Harold Nicholson, and Lord David Cecil, MacCarthy's son-in-law and a young literary scholar of lustrous ancestry.

But older ones were as much in evidence as ever: at a big house party at Taplow, on the Thames, there was Eddy Marsh, being witty and attentive, and Sir James Barrie, being "voluble, cheeky and extremely funny," Edith wrote Lapsley. She was several times in the Hyde Park Gardens home of General Sir Ian and Lady Hamilton, the former still rather tragically under the shadow of the Gallipoli disaster, but no less mentally vibrant than she had known him. She sat at lunch next to H. G. Wells, whom she always regarded as an attractive bounder and an erratic but remarkable writer.

Wells brought back memories of the old prewar days at Stanway, and a special gratification of this visit was the strong renewal of friendship with Mary, Countess of Wemyss, whom Edith had first known at Stanway as Lady Elcho. Edith had caught only passing glimpses of her old friend in the years since her husband had been elevated to the earldom of Wemyss, but from this moment forward the two aging women grew very close to each other. Although Lady Wemyss now had to support herself with two canes, she remained in youthful spirits, impulsive and charmingly scatterbrained.

Edith Wharton's reconnections with her personal past took two other and quite different forms at this time. One was a quickening of the relationship with Morton Fullerton. She had kept in touch with Fullerton sporadically after the war, in letters that normally began *"Cher Ami,"* though once she addressed him as "Dear W. Morton Fullerton," after he had so signed himself. A jocular trace of the old intimacy endured. When Fullerton sent her a French novel which, he said in the inscription, they had once read aloud together, she replied tartly: "I was *not* the lady you read the book with years ago." Writing from Hyères, she added that the place was "the very *'cielo della quieta'* that Dante (whom we did read together) found."

For a period in the 1920s, Fullerton had been the European agent for Appleton, but he and Edith were only rarely in each other's company. She was taken aback when, sending a word of praise for *Hudson River Bracketed*, Fullerton let slip that he had not been reading her work in recent years. "It is a shock," she said, "to find that your avoidance of my presence for so many years extended to my books! I had flattered myself that though you felt only indifference for the old friend, you still followed her through her books." Fullerton hastened to atone, and suggested dining together. *"Cher Ami,"* Edith replied warmly, "—of course I want to see you—always!"

Early in 1931, Edith asked and quickly received Fullerton's assistance for one of her charities. Thanking him, Edith remarked with a rush of affection: "I have had many dear friends—and only two in whose case I wanted the friendship to be total. You see how I lean on one of them now that the age of good works has come." She followed with an eloquent invitation to Hyères, and though he was unable to come down, he began later to appear more regularly at the Pavillon Colombe.

Looking ahead: Morton Fullerton outlived Edith Wharton by fifteen years, dying at the age of eighty-six in 1952. In the years before the war he held several journalistic positions, chief among them that of American correspondent for *Figaro*. He stayed on in Paris during the occupation, living in a little apartment in the Boulevard des Batignolles and looked after by a Mme. Pouget; he also kept an office, which he visited daily, in Rue Mont Tabor, near the Place Vendôme. Fullerton received financial help from Washington, via the Swiss government, and Edward Tuck bequeathed him thirty thousand dollars. He was unmolested by the German authorities despite his outspoken views, and his French friends rejoiced in doing good turns for the aging but, as one associate has remembered him, still sprightly and dreamy-natured journalist.

After the liberation his younger cousin Hugh Fullerton, then in the American foreign service, came to Paris, immediately looked up his relative, and arranged for the sale of Morton's letters from Henry James, George Meredith, George Santayana, and others to Harvard University for eighteen hundred dollars. Lewis Douglas, the American ambassador to the Court of St. James's, also gave generous assistance (Fullerton had counted Douglas' father among his vast set of distinguished friends) and paid the hospital expenses during Fullerton's last illness and those of the funeral. He was buried in the Cimetière des Batignolles.

The other person with whom Edith had "wanted the friendship to be total" was, of course, Walter Berry, and Berry, four years after his death, was the source of a flurry that came to a head in the summer of 1931. From Berry's sister, Nathalie Alden, Edith had heard that a man named Leon Edel proposed writing Berry's biography, on the grounds that he had been the friend of three great novelists: Marcel Proust, Henry James, and Edith Wharton. Edith flew into a panic, and wrote Gaillard Lapsley, with whom Edel seemed to be acquainted, asking how the enterprise might be stopped. Few of Berry's papers were extant, she said, and in any case she would have no part in what she was sure would be a piece of gossipy hack work.

The affair, in fact, was a modest attempt at honorable literary conspiracy. The twenty-three-year-old Leon Edel, who was at the Sorbonne writing a dissertation on Henry James, had undertaken to assist a friend in the latter's own academic labors. The friend was eager to get hold of Edith Wharton's letters to Walter Berry, which Caresse Crosby teasingly (and falsely) claimed to possess but would not release. It was in pursuit of those letters that Edel devised the ingenious letter to Berry's sister. Lapsley, meanwhile, replied soothingly to Edith that Edel was an accredited scholar and a young man of integrity. At the end of June 1931, Edel went out by invitation to St. Brice and made a quiet show of abandoning the Berry project. He and Edith hit it off well and saw each other again; a few years later, with Percy Lubbock, she wrote a strong recommendation of Edel for a Guggenheim grant, on the basis of which he finished his study of James's plays. He began, as well, his meditations on what turned out, some thirty-five years later, to be probably the finest literary biography ever written by an American, his five-volume life of Henry James. The latter phase of it reflected some of the leisurely reminiscences by Lapsley and Edith Wharton that Edel had listened to on a summer afternoon.

3

Edith Wharton completed *The Gods Arrive* at Ste. Claire in January 1932. A sequel to *Hudson River Bracketed*, the novel tells of the further vicissitudes in the life of Vance Weston, his discovery of Europe, the shifting about of his creative ambitions, and, centrally, his extramarital affair with Halo Tarrant—an affair interrupted for a long period by Vance's irrational infatuation with Floss Delaney, a highly sexed vamp from Euphoria, Illinois. Vance and Halo are not unmovingly reunited at the end, to the great relief of Robert Norton when Edith read him the last chapters over Christmas. Admitting he was a sentimentalist, Norton had feared that Edith would follow her more characteristic habit of consigning her main figures "to irrevocable separation and unhappiness."

New York magazine editors were leery of the illicit liaison which occupied so much of the book, and which led to Halo's out-of-wedlock pregnancy; the actual or implied "not nice" dogged the elderly novelist as it had perturbed the growing child. The *Saturday Evening Post,* which had counted on taking the novel, said that though it was splendidly written (a verdict which would raise an argument today), "the central idea . . . puts it quite out of the question for us." *Liberty* and *Collier's,* after expressing interest, shied off. Edith Wharton was forced to swallow her pride and come to terms with Oscar Graeve at the *Delineator,* for all her resentment of his treatment of the book's predecessor. Graeve observed blandly that "the situation, that of a man and woman unmarried and living together, is a little startling for magazine publication," but the *Delineator* was liberal, Edith Wharton was eminent, and he was prepared to ride out the protests he expected from some readers. He set about arranging four quarterly payments amounting in all to fifty thousand dollars.

The Gods Arrive had a very good press, though its sales were the poorest of any novel Edith Wharton had written in years—the royalties from Appleton came to less than eighty-five hundred dollars. Even reviewers who judged it second rate by Edith Wharton's standards were quick to say that her second best was superior to practically anything else being written in America. The fact was that Edith Wharton seemed to have become something of an institution, and one so firmly and justly established that the annual publishing ritual was virtually immune to critical attack. Not that the usual carpers were lacking—particularly among those who, in the third year of the Depression, were looking for fiction more socially and politically minded in nature.

The best thing about the book, one is tempted to say, is its title, from a poem by Emerson: "When half gods go / The gods arrive." It is a crisp formula for the replacement of false or partial values by genuine ones. This process is enacted in the novel when Vance Weston breaks free from Floss Delaney, goes for a lonely rugged period to a camp in Wisconsin, there has something of a religious experience through reading St. Augustine's *Confessions,* and returns to Paul's Landing and the maternal sanity of the pregnant Halo Tarrant. His false starts, his wrongheaded literary efforts, and his emotional and moral waywardness are now perhaps behind him, and he may be ready for creative work drawn from the depths of himself and for a fulfilling life with Halo.

In the handling of these matters Edith Wharton's last completed novel is a curious and mixed performance. Personal memories, both older and more recent ones, play the expected part: Paris, Senlis, Chartres; London high society (a Lady Guy Plunder appears to be a combination of Lady Colefax and Lady Cunard); the Riviera. Edith's sense of the genuine creative process and her defensive disdain for fashionable new writing once more gain expression; the novel takes what was becoming an annual swipe at *Ulysses*. One aspect of Edith Wharton's literary personality is given its clearest formulation: "As for Vance, though he had to the full the artist's quivering sensitiveness to praise, and anguished shrinking from adverse criticism, he felt neither praise nor blame unless it implied recognition of what he had been striving for."

But one gathers the odd impression that Edith Wharton is frequently drawing not directly upon memories, but upon her previous literary treatment or transcription of memories. As the pages turn, one is reminded less of some particular moment in Edith's past than of a story closely or remotely based upon that moment. Halo's disillusionment with Vance, for example, carries us back not to Edith and Teddy some years after their marriage, but to "The Lamp of Psyche," which grew out of their dwindling relationship. Elsewhere, we hear clear echoes of "Souls Belated," *The House of Mirth*, and later works.

Edith Wharton had long enjoyed making secretive use of her own previous writings in new compositions, and her instinct to do so more extensively than ever in the present instance was probably a sound one. As has been suggested, her deepest life—that is, her deepest feelings—existed more and more in her writings, rather than in the externals of experience from which they had sprung. In *The Gods Arrive* she was, in a not entirely well-focused way, surveying some of the products of her literary career and writing an odd, disguised form of autobiography.

Before the magazine proofs of *The Gods Arrive* reached her desk, Edith Wharton was hard at work on her authentic autobiography. She had begun the book which would finally be called *A Backward Glance*, after Walt Whitman's reminiscences, and was scouring up memories and family gossip that took her back to her early years and behind them, to her eighteenth-century forebears, the courtship of her mother and father, and their adventurous tour of Europe in 1847–48. She was engaged, in short, in her most strenuous and straightforward act of relating her present self to the furthest reaches of her past.

Like many older people (she was seventy in January 1932), Edith Wharton could recall with great clarity the events of her childhood and adolescence, but her memory grew progressively less dependable as she approached the later periods. She sometimes grew forgetful of what had happened only a few days before; in a letter to Lapsley she expressed fear that she might be repeating everything she had said a week earlier, adding that she resembled "the pathetic case of the old lady confessing over and over again her one adultery." As she moved ahead with the memoirs, she turned regularly to Lapsley for confirmation of facts.

Her questions to him mostly concerned Henry James. When did he die? Before the end of the war, of course, but exactly when? With regard to what interminable work of fiction did James make the priceless remark: "Yes, I have trifled with the exordia"? In what context did he say something about Edith's having tasted blood? James's "great apostrophe to death" was consulted over. Edith had heard that at the moment of his last stroke James had murmured: "So it's you at last, august stranger." Others remembered it as: "So here it is at last, the distinguished thing"—and as such it has gone into the record.

4

For all her backward glancing, Edith Wharton was more alert than ever to the changing world around her, and the major dramas of the day. She had made no mention of Charles Lindbergh's epochal flight from New York to Paris in May 1927, but she shared Jewett's excitement over Admiral Byrd's aerial discovery of the South Pole in December 1929, and made an exultant entry in her diary in September 1930 when Costes and Bellonets made the first successful flight from Paris to New York. The kidnaping of the Lindbergh baby in the spring of 1932 filled her with horror, and she passed on to Lapsley a letter from Mildred Bliss in New York which spoke of the heartfelt sympathy on all sides "for those agonising young parents whose lives are ruined whether they get back their child or not." On May 15, Edith wrote in her diary: "I am haunted by murder of Lindbergh baby. What a sad Whitsunday."

She contemplated the American national election in November ("our damned election") with mixed feelings, but clung to the hope that the next President, whoever he was, might help repair the country's economic wreckage and bolster the morale of her compatriots. She was comforted by some articles of Walter Lippman, whom she had met once or twice and whom she was reading with mounting admiration, which contended that the election was at the least sure to lead to the end of Prohibition and of war reparations. But though Franklin Delano Roosevelt would be credited by several of Edith's friends with accomplishing much of what she had wanted, his New Deal looked to her too much like outright socialism.

A few years before, Upton Sinclair had written asking for her support with regard to his novel *Oil*, which had been declared obscene. The charge, Edith Wharton wrote, was absurd; "I shall be glad if my name is of any use to you in freeing the novel from this unjust and ignorant aspersion." *Oil* concludes with the hero, after experiencing the depredations of the American oil monopoly, embracing the tenets of socialism. Mrs. Wharton criticized the book for turning into a political pamphlet and remarked: "I make this critique without regard to the views which you teach, and which are detestable to me."

She yearned for the other Roosevelt, though a year after the election she was grudgingly admitting that "even those least in sympathy with the Roosevelt experience" were acknowledging that things were better in America, that business had improved and people were once again making purchases.

Still, she tended to identify Roosevelt as the instigator of a pernicious form of government, only somewhat less venal, though far more pacific, than the modes of totalitarianism presided over by Hitler, Mussolini, and Stalin. She reserved her harshest words for Hitler, whose "propaganda on the wireless" she said was "all angry screams and accusations of cowardice against any one who loves peace and beauty better than a general massacre." But all the countries of Europe which she knew best and had loved the longest were falling prey to political evil, and she saw little difference to draw between Facism and Communism. Spain had "gone red," she wrote Lapsley, explaining why she would never again visit that country, and under the Berensons' political tutoring she had grown sufficiently informed about Mussolini's oppressions to wonder if she could even return to Italy.

As to France, she was convinced that her adopted country was drifting irreversibly toward bolshevism. Her worst fears appeared to be fulfilled by the general strike—rather aimless, as it turned out—and the six days of bloody rioting in Paris in February 1934. She remained glued to the radio, sure she was listening to a historical tragedy, and despairingly rereading letters from Boccon-Gibbod which told of the numbers of persons killed in the street fighting.

Year by year the march of events in France made her grimmer. "We are on the edge of bolshevism here," she said to Lapsley in June 1936, "and I don't think most people realize it. They will soon." She had barely settled into the Crillon that month when strikers took possession of the hotel and she was forced to move out to St. Brice. This undignified experience caused her to conclude that "we are hanging over the brink of a precipice, and I suppose the next convulsive jerk will send us toppling." A month later, in England, she let her travel plans hang on the possibility of large-scale mob activities on Bastille Day.

Her historical vision turned apocalyptic. As early as December 1931 she had been speaking to Berenson about "this angry sombre world." Two years later it had become "a raving chaos," of a sort to make her feel unable any longer "to tell my feeble tales (designed for a quieter universe)"; perhaps she should limit herself to travel. She took to citing the story of a French abbess who, when faced with certain disaster and asked what she would do, replied that she would take a lover for the night.

More than ever—the image had been growing in her mind for more than a decade—she saw her small circle of friends, devoted to the arts, to beauty, to good conversation and the graces of life, as a last stronghold in a collapsing civilization. Reflecting on "all the shattering, crashing, smashing that has gone on in the world," she suggested to Berenson that they should all "go up on the Consuma Hill"—the Berensons' summer home—"like Boccaccio's set, and try to forget all about it."

5

The fall of the New York stock market in October 1929 had made little immediate impression. Like certain other Americans of considerable means living abroad, Edith Wharton was only imperfectly aware of the great economic depression for more than two years after it had so spectacularly begun. A letter from Mildred Bliss in March 1932, after the Blisses had made a tour of the United States and had heard many "panicky tales of economic distress," opened her eyes somewhat to the worsening situation. The same month she received an instructive jolt when the *Pictorial Review* offered her the relative pittance of $750 for a story called "Joy in the House"—about one-quarter her usual rate. Her new friend and Senlis neighbor, the young novelist Louis Bromfield, declared $750 "a ridiculously low price for an Edith Wharton story"; Edith held out, in vain, for $1,000.

Everybody in Paris was poor and frightened about the future, she wrote Mary Berenson in June. She herself was feeling the pinch to the extent of having to reduce the two garden staffs at Ste. Claire and the Pavillon Colombe. The ninety-one-year-old Edward Tuck, that most dependable of philanthropists, reduced his annual subscription to Edith's convalescent program by two-thirds. The Crillon cut its room rates drastically. During the first part of 1932, Bernard Berenson, reporting that his income was down almost seventy percent, voiced genuine concern that he might have to sell I Tatti; by midsummer he announced that the worst had not happened and that they could hang on to the villa. "We shall have to be careful, but not mean." The Charles de Noailles' were said to have lost millions, though they were alleged to possess millions more in far-flung real estate.

Edith Wharton's personal income was suffering visibly because of the stagnant condition of New York real estate. But her manner of living had for a long time been supported largely by her literary earnings, and by the summer of 1932 it was clear that these were seriously threatened. This was not only due to the "parlous times for the magazines as for all the publishers" of which Rutger Jewett spoke, alluding to the great decrease in advertising; an equally important element in Edith Wharton's case was the tone and nature of her best work.

"Joy in the House" was turned down by a series of editors, because, as one of them explained, readers would be offended by the ugliness of its theme. It is in fact one of Edith Wharton's better and more bitterly ironic tales—the story of a married woman who returns to her husband and child after a six-month affair with a gifted but unstable painter to learn, within days of her arrival, that her lover has committed suicide, that the great display of roses spelling out "Joy in the House" which had greeted her had represented her husband's smug satisfaction with that event, and that she had walked back into a lifelong imprisonment.

Readers of mass magazines, she realized, were in no mood for such harsh realities, and wanted nothing but bland nonsense that "would distract the mind from world affairs." America had entered its long moment of self-induced stupefaction, when, in the midst of misery and fear, only the most luxuriously fantastic flights from reality were assured of success in literature or on the screen. Edith Wharton agreed reluctantly to publish in Hearst magazines, since her literary income was crucial both for her and those dependent on her; but she ruled out any publication which reflected Hearst's own political views.

By January 1933 the chatelaine of Ste. Claire was bickering with Ellery Sedgwick at the *Atlantic Monthly* over a sum of $50—the difference between the $300 offered and the $350 demanded—for an article called "Confessions of a Novelist." A few months later she engaged in an acrimonious quarrel with Loring Schuyler of the *Ladies' Home Journal* about the fee for her memoirs. The figure of $25,000 had originally been settled on, but Schuyler pointed out that this was several years before and that prices had gone down markedly in the past twenty-four months. The memoirs, besides, were too long for the magazine, but if she would cut them by 40,000 words they would pay her $20,000.

"Absolutely decline reducing price," Edith cabled Jewett, "and will sue him unless agreement kept." To Jewett's conciliatory reminder that the *Ladies' Home Journal* had been losing a good deal of money, Edith turned an unsympathetic ear. "I will neither take back the manuscript nor accept a lower price for it," she wrote. "No doubt the *Ladies' Home Journal* is hard up, but so am I, and I imagine that they have larger funds to draw upon than I have." Schuyler eventually yielded, with reasonably good grace, and the $25,000 was duly paid.

Eyeing the public as shrewdly as she could, Edith wrote several light-fingered tales, and they were accepted at once. A Venetian frolic called "A Glimpse" brought in $2,000, and Hearst's *Cosmopolitan* paid the large sum of $5,000 for a trifle called "Bread Upon the Water" (later "Charm Incorporated," the phrase Edith had invented for Robert Norton). She was unhappy about such *jeux d'esprit*, but when she returned to her more customary vein she ran into attitudes so cavalier that they left her shaken. "Duration," a stiff little anecdote about two aged folk, was taken by the *Woman's Home Companion* for a good fee after Edith Wharton had carefully revised the ending at the editor's request. But the latter then decided not to publish it and asked Jewett to try to place it elsewhere. "When I think of my position as a writer, I am really staggered by the insolence of the letter," Edith wrote Jewett. "I am afraid that I cannot write down to the present standards of the American picture magazines."

The literary institution she had seemed to embody was no longer receiving the deference it had grown used to. Immediately after completing her memoirs Edith Wharton began a novel called *The Buccaneers*, and Jewett started dickering for serial rights. Vance was no longer at the *Pictorial Review,* and the magazine declined to honor the informal offer of $50,000 which he had once made for any novel by Edith Wharton. *Cosmopolitan* was approached, and its tough-minded editor, expressing modified interest, suggested she send in an outline of the story, and proposed paying her $1,000 for an option on it. "I have never before been treated like a beginner, and do not like it," Edith said to Jewett. And again: "I have never before been treated so casually."

She was both hurt and extremely worried, and her first reaction was to look for another New York agent. "You do not need an agent any more than a duck needs rubbers," remarked Jewett, who had acted in this capacity for a dozen years without accepting any commission. He arranged the sale of her excellent story "Roman Fever" to *Liberty* for $3,000, but Mrs. Wharton nevertheless shifted over to James Pinker, the son of Henry James's former agent.

The gesture was accompanied by a strongly worded letter which complained that Appleton, in addition to failing as her representative, never advertised her work sufficiently and had been unsatisfactory in general in its promotion. This elicited a long response from D. W. Hilman, chairman of the Appleton board. "Your letter of July 11 [1934] is so manifestly unfair and unjust," he began, that he thought a résumé was in order of the relation between Appleton and Edith Wharton. In the past twenty years Appleton had put into her hands some $580,000 in royalties and various serial, movie, and dramatic rights they had negotiated for her, and on which she had saved $58,000 in commissions. Most of this had in fact come since *The Age of Innocence* only thirteen years before.

Hilman also informed Mrs. Wharton that Rutger Jewett, driven by extreme overwork and anxiety, had suffered a total breakdown. He rallied during the fall, but suffered a relapse and died just before Christmas.

Edith explained to Lapsley that she *had* to keep on with her writing: "If I don't, Minnie will have no motor—nor I either, much longer." The well-being of her sister-in-law, now nearly penniless at eighty, weighed heavily on Edith's mind, and she said as much to Vernon Lee one November evening as she was leaving Villa Palmerino, after her old friend had taxed her with producing so vast a quantity of work so much below her best level. Next morning Vernon Lee sent a letter around to I Tatti by hand:

> What you told me yesterday at the gate, about having to make money for your sister-in-law, has left me bitterly ashamed of the unjustifiable words I had just said. Please forget them. And remember only the very real admiration I have for so much of your work; and my gratitude for so much kindness.

Minnie Jones was only the most important on Edith Wharton's list of continuing and even expanding private charities. Mary Hunter who had been a recipient was no longer one: broken in spirit by the appalling changes in her fortunes, the former mistress of Hill Hall had died, apparently of heartsickness, in January 1933. But there remained an array of "lame ducks" in Paris and southern France, in England and the United States; and no matter how diminished her income, Edith never failed to remember them and to ask assistance from others.

Abbé Mugnier had gradually lost his sight, and Edith gladly subscribed to a Faubourg fund to pay for the daily taxi which took him out to dine. In the summer of 1933 the fund was enlarged to cover an operation on his eyes. It was more successful than had been hoped. The abbé could see again a little, Edith wrote Berenson; he looked twenty years younger, and his voice was like the chime of bells.

6

It was during a two-week stay in Rome in May 1932 that Edith Wharton made her diary entry about the Lindbergh tragedy. She had rediscovered the ancient city the year before, after seventeen years' absence from it, and all her old feelings welled up. Why live anywhere else? she asked Berenson with a kind of jubilation. She had brought Nicky Mariano with her, and together they made the rounds of the Rome that Edith had first come to know forty years before.

There was a perceptible change in Edith Wharton's involvement with Rome on this visit and the one that followed. She wandered the immensities of St. Peter's, as before, drove out along the Via Appia to see the chapels of the San Sebastiano catacombs, climbed heights from which to view the city, and went through the richly ornate Borgia rooms, with their gilded ceilings and Pinturicchio frescoes, in the Vatican. She looked again at the Roman villas and their gardens, called on old friends, and dined with Umberto Morra and Alberto Moravia, Luigi Pirandello being observed at the next table. But she also attended Pontifical High Mass in the enormous and echoing San Paolo Fuore le Mure, and a Requiem Mass at Santa Maria sopra Minerva.

Returning to Rome six months later with Nicky and Berenson, she stepped up her attendance at religious services: Whitsunday Mass at St. Peter's; High Mass on Trinity Sunday at Santa Trinità dei Monti; vespers at Santa Agnese. She arrived early for a Pontifical High Mass at San Anselmo and was much moved by the long procession through the cloister. She was, in short, beginning to interest herself strongly in the rituals and ceremonies, in the liturgical experience of the Christian religion, and in the meanings they exemplified.

It is impossible to date the quickening of Edith Wharton's concern with the forms and substance of Christianity—as against Christian architecture, history, and spectacle. Perhaps it can be traced to the death of Walter Berry in 1927 and her own near death two years later. These events, while deepening her sense of physical mortality, seem to have enlarged her awareness of the life of the spirit, and thence of the rituals by which that life might be exercised and enriched. But there was, of course, more to the matter than that.

Edith Wharton's childhood passion for reading sermons and her stray wonderings about the vagaries of religious doctrine had been smothered by the tutelage of Egerton Winthrop in late nineteenth-century scientific rationalism. The effect of this body of thought upon her intellectual ruminations was an imposing one during her many agnostic years. But rationalism in turn had been modified by her developing consciousness—stirred at Amiens, Chartres, Beauvais —of the aesthetic and historical importance of Christianity over the centuries of European civilization. Even so, her occasionally flaring religious impulse—during the affair with Fullerton, for example—had been limited to the area of private morality and personal relations, and of the alleged "split" between soul and body; and there was an intense, much-brooded-over, and ongoing conflict (as she had once poetically described it) between the nun and the wild woodland woman in her, between her Christian and her Nietzschean side.

It was not until her late sixties that she began to take a genuine interest in the *church*—that is, in the life, the teachings, and the practices of the Church of Rome. The change, in Gaillard Lapsley's opinion, was due to a growing realization that the rationalistic system was simply insufficient to explain "what life and reflection had taught her." In France and Italy she could watch at close quarters the very different "system" of Roman Catholicism.

In the personal dimension there was another factor: the rather rare kind of full human maturity she had reached in her sixties, something expressed elsewhere in her novels on the parental theme. Maturity and the religious sensibility were becoming related in her mind. It is unclear, and in fact it is doubtful, whether Edith Wharton ever underwent anything like the moment in *The Gods Arrive* when Vance Weston, in the wilds of Wisconsin, reads St. Augustine's *Confessions* and comes to an overwhelming insight. But the nature of that insight is unmistakable, and its importance for Edith Wharton can be judged from the stress laid upon it in the novel. The passage from St. Augustine which kindles Weston's dragging spirit is this:

> And Thou didst beat back my weak sight, dazzling me with Thy splendour, and I perceived that I was far from Thee, in the land of unlikeness, and I heard Thy voice crying to me: "I am the Food of the full-grown. Become a man and thou shalt feed on me."

"The food of the full-grown—of the full-grown!" Vance repeats to himself, and he quotes the phrase again to Halo in the ending.

She began to read histories of the religious orders and lives of the saints. Kenneth Clark, who inherited much of her library, observed that it contained "a higher proportion of books on religion . . . than on anything else." One of the late entries in her commonplace book said: "I don't believe in God but I do believe in His saints—and then?" There was always the irresistible influence of Abbé Mugnier, who once remarked to her that he loved God so much he wished there were several of Him. She was also greatly impressed by the curé of St. Brice, a cultivated and devoted young man with a sense of humor and what Lapsley described as an "abundance of inner fire."

Of her intellectual and imaginative absorption in religious questions during these years, there is no doubting. When Kenneth Clark gratified her by saying that she was the only person he knew who understood equally well the Protestant and the Catholic mentality, she confided "that it had always been her greatest ambition to write a novel the center of which should be the conflict of these two impulses." In the course of a drive to Beauvais, she was even able to outline to Clark the detailed plot of this never-to-be-written work.

Items like that led her intimate friends to speculate how far Edith Wharton was drifting toward actually joining the Church of Rome. There was a certain psychological basis for such speculation. Taking note of her recurring fits of restlessness and contrasting them with her watchful stillness in one or another of the Roman cathedrals, Nicky Mariano and Berenson wondered whether Edith "might find her peace in the Roman Church." Going to Mass with Edith at San Paolo, Nicky was astonished and moved to find herself in the presence

not as I had feared of an impatient and rather spoilt woman, easily bored and anxious to move on, but of someone quite close to me, carried away with me and like me into another sphere, with no stiffness or impatience left in her, no thought of the passing hour and of other plans.

It might also have been that in San Paolo, Edith could find an at least temporary peacefulness from which the ugly sounds of the "angry sombre world" were shut away.

If Edith Wharton never did join the church, it may have been, as Lapsley believed, because she was still, after all, too much of an "intellectual rationalist" to accept its transrational doctrines. Nor could she be easily imagined subduing her strong-willed self to the rigors of church discipline. "There was at the center of her," Lapsley wrote, "a tough and unreduced *ego* that would have made any submission impossible for her." That is perhaps a different way of saying what someone once remarked to Nicky Mariano: "If Edith should be converted to Catholicism, my heart would go out to her confessor."

Such formulae and witticisms, however, do scant justice to Edith Wharton's fundamental nature, however intellectualized a part of it may have been. In the usually unspoken depths of herself there remained, there grew, an immense wonder about the real order of the universe and the progress through it of the human spirit. During one of the slow, murmuring conversations with Elisina Tyler in her last days, she touched on these mysteries. Mrs. Tyler recorded the words in her diary:

"We can have no certainty for what is beyond the world," she said.
"No proven certainty," I replied. "But there is a deep truth in the saying, '*La Pensée ne meurt pas.*' " She smiled at the quotation (from Teilhard de Chardin).

"Religious thought is certainly a great power. The greatest of all. It embraces everything. And now science has moved so far away from the standpoint of the materialistic school that perhaps we are on the very edge of a great discovery."

"The great discovery?" I said.

"The limitless spaces," she replied softly.

27. The Life-Wonderer

"Why do I have these fits of sudden fatigue?" Edith Wharton asked herself in her diary in early January 1934. It was in some ways an extraordinary question for her to raise. She was seventy-two; she had just launched onto a most demanding new novel, *The Buccaneers;* she was reading proof on *A Backward Glance,* had recently seen to the publication of *Certain People,* her eighth volume of short stories, and was completing several of the tales in the collection to come. Her personal and business correspondence was enormous, and she was busy replying to offers to dramatize or film a number of her works. Her public and private charities were time-consuming. The deluge of Christmas cards and cables needed to be acknowledged.

Over the holiday season she had entertained Hugh Smith, Lapsley, Norton, and young Steven Runciman, and the Berensons and others were expected shortly. On her seventy-second birthday Edith declared that she felt "exactly as I did forty years ago," and White, driving Berenson over from Toulon, told him earnestly: "If you saw her from the back, sir, you'd think she was thirty." But a few days later, after a lunch gathering with six guests, she confessed to being very tired. "I enjoy seeing people," she wrote, "but it uses me up."

She was feeling the aftermath of a difficult year. The previous spring disaster had struck her household twice in quick succession. Edith's personal maid, the skilled and devoted Elise, suffered what was called a nervous collapse and was then diagnosed as pernicious anemia; she was sent to a nearby hospital. On April 14 the faithful and benign Gross was seized, in Edith's words, with "senile dementia and suicidal mania."

The eighty-year-old Alsatian had been failing for two years, and in recent months there had been a nun from the local convent in constant attendance. She passed most of her time sitting in the sun, but her mind remained clear, and she was as interested as ever in the smallest household details. Now, in the space of an afternoon, she was transformed into "a wild, frightened and obstinate stranger." She evinced a violent hatred for everyone around her, most of all for her friend and employer of nearly five decades. "To see those little suspicious eyes peering at me," Edith wrote, "where I have found for forty-five years an open tender gaze of faithful devotion is rather beyond endurance." Edith agreed reluctantly that Gross should be taken to the convent at Esperance.

Elise was brought back in early May, but Edith told Lapsley that there was "just *no* hope." "All my life goes with those two dying women," she wrote in her diary. Elise died on May 29, and Edith buried her, after a Requiem Mass, in the English part of the cemetery at Hyères. Gross, at the convent, sank into unconsciousness, and Louisa Butler, the third member of the central trio of women servants, broke down completely over these events and went back to her family in England for a stay.

Edith went north to Paris in June feeling "tired and bewildered." She crossed to England for several weeks, and though the thought of poor Gross tugged at her heart, her spirit was brightened a little by a visit with Robert Norton to Lady Wemyss at Stanway, where they had first met twenty-five years before. There was a pleasant little tour of Wales with Gaillard Lapsley, and a call upon the Clarks in Oxford.

In October, Edith recorded the fact that "Darling Gross died peacefully this morning. With me 1884–1933." Gross was buried next to Elise in Hyères.

Edith was again smitten by a sense of desolating solitude. "Since Walter's death I've been incurably lonely *inside,*" she wrote Berenson, "and these two faithful women kept the heartfire burning." She had no lack of interior resources, she said, and she had her work: "But this long vigil alone with all my past, wears the nerves thin." Yet she managed, as so frequently and in her own special way, to derive emotional gain out of emotional loss and to find the peculiar gratifications that experience provided for her stage and condition of life. Even in the summer after Elise's death, she was commenting to Berenson:

> Never having suffered from accedia, and feeling more and more, the older and more solitary I become, the pregnant, piercing, beauty of mere being-aliveness, I find it difficult to enter into the other state of mind.

Three years later, she was able to speak in the same vein:

> I wish I knew what people meant when they say they find "emptiness" in this wonderful adventure of living, which seems to me to pile up its glories like an horizon-wide sunset as the light declines. I'm afraid I'm an incorrigible life-lover, life-wonderer and adventurer.

It was as a "life-wonderer" that Edith Wharton, despite the occasional physical setback, passed her sunset years—years of increasing serenity and of a display of creative power almost disconcerting in its special nature and high accomplishment.

2

With the drastic change in her personal life, Edith Wharton felt the need for at least a temporary change of scene, and she had the intuition that she should make haste. "I am possessed of a strange fever to fill up some of the numerous lacunae in my world map before the curtain falls." That to Berenson, and to Lapsley she confessed a "restless desire to tick off as many places as possible before the crash." A little glimpse of Wales satisfied a part of that desire, and in late August 1933 she accepted an invitation to the summer music festival in Salzburg.

On the day of her arrival Edith ran into Percy Lubbock in the lobby of her hotel. He had never looked better, younger, or thinner, in her opinion. She asked if she might call on Lady Sybil and was told "tomorrow"; next day Percy explained that his wife had passed a bad night and was confined to her hotel room, though later Edith observed her driving about town and sitting nearby in the afternoon chill of the Domplatz. The week passed without the two women exchanging a word.

Two months later, when Edith was staying at I Tatti, efforts were made by both Lubbocks to induce her to come over to the Villa Medici. Edith's response was to send Percy, by the hand of Gaillard Lapsley, a cool but not wholly uncompromising note in which she suggested she might be willing to overlook "the past"—that is, Percy's marriage to the former Mrs. Cutting and Mrs. Scott.

Percy wrote back in considerable anguish:

O Edith—you see *I* felt, seven years ago, as I still feel, that *you* might have thought you owed it to our old friendship and our many ties—not to say your still older and apparently friendly acquaintance with Sybil—to make sure you rightly and fairly understood what had happened—if there was anything in it that seemed wrong to you. And you wouldn't even try. You only made it clear that Sybil was under your disapproval—and there you left her all these years. And now you are ready to "forget" the past—as if a word to me, when at last we met by chance, should be enough to make Sybil do so too, you imply. Well, she was willing to let it be enough. Salzburg was impossible; she could only do what she did by staying in bed all the rest of the time—and finally we had to fly from the racket of that hotel sooner than we had intended (as I wrote at the time to you). On the next opportunity, when you were again within reach, she wrote, and asked you to come and see her. Have you or has she, on the whole, shown more generosity?

As for your suggestion that I must, all things considered, dissociate myself from Sybil in this matter—I don't think I need say more.

I still hope for happier times.

Such happier times were not to be. Edith dismissed this cry for understanding as "a haughty letter" and said to Lapsley, who remained on excellent terms with Lubbock, that "I suppose you are more Christian-minded than I am."

Given all these circumstances, it is profoundly puzzling that Gaillard Lapsley, as her executor, should have invited Percy Lubbock to write the memoir of Edith Wharton after her death, and that the choice should have been applauded by Berenson and Hugh Smith, who were equally privy to the finality of the breach. Even more disconcerting was the warm approval voiced by Edith's old friends when *Portrait of Edith Wharton* appeared in 1946. Literarily, it is undoubtedly a work of art, written with all the stylistic grace at Lubbock's command, witty and ingratiating by turns. But the book's most striking characteristic to the thoughtful reader is the subtly distributed malice toward its subject, a careful, muted downgrading of Edith Wharton as a human being and a writer. The picture that emerges is surreptitiously false in many places.

Lubbock appears to have been unconscious of the effects he had wrought. When an intelligent younger friend, after reading the *Portrait*, remarked to him that it had the air of having been written by someone who loathed Edith Wharton, Lubbock struck his forehead with both hands and exclaimed, "But I *adored* her!"

3

Neighbors and visitors at Ste. Claire in the winter of 1934 helped alleviate Edith's solitude even as they contributed to her fits of fatigue. There was Louis Bromfield, whose numerous volumes now included the Pulitzer Prize–winning novel *Early Autumn*: "a charming boy," Edith said to Louis Gillet about her thirty-eight-year-old compatriot. Bromfield was another ardent gardener, and he and Edith exchanged as many opinions about roses and dahlias as they did about literary matters. H. G. Wells was occupying a farmhouse near Grasse. Edith would have liked to see more of him than she did, but she regarded Wells's mistress of the moment—a liberated spirit named Odette Keun—as "a bad example of her kind," and a woman who tended to dominate all conversation.

Beatrix Farrand stopped by for a few days. The tall, reserved, sixty-one-year-old landscape architect was, in her aunt's report, feeling pleased about her recent work of remodeling and planting the grounds at Dartington Hall in South Devon, the home of Leonard Elmhirst and his wealthy American wife. Trix, Edith remarked to Berenson, "must be the only person in the world with a big new job, and Mrs. E. the only person who can pay for it." Mrs. Farrand's most remarkable accomplishment, now nearly finished after ten years of intermittent labor, was the creation of the vast and varied gardens at Dumbarton Oaks in Washington, the estate which Robert and Mildred Bliss had acquired in 1923 and where they had now settled after Bliss's retirement from the diplomatic service.

Trix could stay only briefly at Ste. Claire, for she had to hurry back to Yale, where she had been commissioned to design the courtyards of the eight new residential colleges established there by her old client Edward Harkness. The assignment delighted Edith Wharton, whose ties with Yale had been further strengthened by an agreeable afternoon with Richard Purdy, a young instructor in English at Yale. Edith was pleased too by the appointment of Arnold Whitridge as master of Yale's newly built Calhoun College; the son of Lucy Arnold Whitridge, Arnold was a sensitive literary scholar at whose wedding in Paris, years before, Edith had served as a witness.

There were inevitable changes in the "regulars" at Ste. Claire. John Hugh Smith had grown quite deaf; plucking at his lip, he would roar down the dinner table asking that some remark or other be repeated to him. His cultivated and active involvement with art and literature had not in the slightest diminished. Robert Norton's hair had turned white. Berenson thought it unbecoming, but for others it made the English watercolorist more nobly good-looking than ever. As for Lapsley, he had taken on a good deal of pomposity over the years and had become intolerant of any subject or person that lay outside his rather confined universe. Only "Angry-Saxons," to borrow Berenson's phrase, were admitted as worthy of consideration, as the last repositories of decency and right thinking. But even Berenson allowed that Lapsley was uncommonly well informed about English literature, especially the Victorian novel.

These same regulars were observing comparable changes in their hostess. She had, in the view of some of them, become at times irritatingly fidgety and restless, leaping up from her straight-backed chair to set a book right on the shelf or push a chair into place, making a small scene over a discovered stain on a piece of furniture, interrupting conversation to make sure that every guest at tea was supplied with a little table for his cup and plate. "For God's sake, Edith, sit still!" Norton would exclaim, and would then take Berenson for a walk to ask why Edith was so endlessly fussy.

Lapsley dated this development to Edith's serious illness in 1929; but not all the watchers of Edith Wharton detected any excessive restiveness. Berenson periodically reported to Mary that Edith was "less fussed than I have ever known her," and that she was "angelic." Philomène sometimes found Edith astonishingly tranquil. It might also be said that Edith made so little of her daily creative labors that few of her well-cosseted guests reflected that after a morning's concentrated work she might well be permitted a temporary edginess—especially since it relaxed so quickly into an affectionate supervision of her companions' comfort.

The inescapable picnic had become a somewhat nerve-racking ritual. There was the busy preparation, the seeing to it that the hampers, the book box and maps, the sticks and umbrellas, capes and rugs were assembled, the circling back to the house for some forgotten item (Had she remembered the anklets to protect against shark bites? someone would ask solicitously). But the picnic itself was always worth it—chicken and ham, eggs and olives and cheese, salads, chocolates and oranges. And as to Edith Wharton's personality, the regulars agreed to an individual that, as Norton once put it, the "little weaknesses" were "obliterated by the big qualities of which one was always conscious"—her generosity, her compassion, her loyalty.

4

A tour of Scotland in September 1934 completed the present stage of Edith Wharton's leaf-by-leaf consumption of her European world, which had also included several "shimmering days" in Amsterdam and views of the "splendid Gaugins" and the "great Van Gogh collection." In London she was guided about the National Gallery by Kenneth Clark, who pointed out some of the rehangings he had supervised and the new acquisitions. The summer before, Clark, at the age of thirty, had accepted the invitation of the Prime Minister to become director of the gallery. "It would have been the act of a mugwump to refuse," he told Berenson, even though it meant a serious interruption in his studies. Clark had consulted with Edith Wharton over the appointment, and Edith had warmly approved.

There was also a ceremonial gathering in the Clarks' London house, in which William Royall Tyler was a key figure. Bill had completed his years at Balliol, and though his natural disposition was toward art history, he had, for lack of better, taken a job in a New York bank. Edith regretted the decision, even if she did not share the hostility current in the American 1930s toward the entire breed of bankers. This attitude was reflected in a joke by Louis Bromfield, which Edith passed on to Bill's father: "There was a terrible scandal in Connecticut last week. A white girl married a banker." As to that, Edith felt,

... there is much sour grapes ... in the present American attitude. The time to denounce the bankers was when we were all feeding off their gold plate; not now. At present they have not only my sympathy but my preference. They are the last representatives of our native industries.

Still, if Bill Tyler had to work in a bank, she wished he might do so in some European branch. She read with astonishment his letters from New York describing both the "endless resources" and the "inhuman desolation" of the city, commenting that "neither attribute belonged to it 50 years ago, or even twenty-five, but I am afraid it has sold its soul now past redemption."

When Bill did come over, in the summer of 1933, it was to settle his engagement to Bettine Fisher-Rowe, the daughter of a British naval officer and the descendant via her mother (Eve Digby) of a Dorset family par excellence of landed gentry. Expressing impatience to meet the young lady, "Edoo" wrote: "Meanwhile please tell her that she is the luckiest damsel on our planet, and that if I were half a century younger she wouldn't have a look-in!" The couple were married in London at the end of August 1934, and in early September Edith had them to a gay toast-drinking lunch at Kenneth and Jane Clark's house on Portland Place.

5

Edith was possessed of considerable physical toughness, but she was subject in these years not only to fits of tiredness but to graver illnesses. She controlled the exhaustion by periods of puttering and idling and by taking to her bed at the end of the afternoon: something necessitated as well by a series of colds and bouts of influenza. In May 1934 she had an alarming attack of the grippe. She had driven from Rapallo south along the new Autostrada above the cliffs, and thence inland to Florence, and had continued to Rome with Nicky Mariano and Berenson. She had scarcely arrived at the Hotel de Ville before she came down with chills and fevers, and lay half unconscious in her hotel room for the entire two-week duration of her stay.

Edith spent a quiet, fairly healthy, and productive summer and fall at St. Brice, with the trip to England and Scotland, already mentioned, tucked in between. The peaceful atmosphere was momentarily disturbed by news of the assassination of Engelbert Dollfuss, the Austrian Prime Minister, in July. Looking out at a world which gave signs of imminent disaster, Edith remarked to Lapsley, reversing the saying of Wordsworth, "Bliss is it to be old." She saw something of the Walter Lippmans in the fall—Lippman's personality as well as his profoundly rational political philosophy appealed to her. She made the annual transition south, by way of I Tatti, and passed the winter and early spring at Ste. Claire, with the usual Christmas household and exchanges of visits with the Huxleys and the de Noailles'. The Clarks came to stay, and Lady Wemyss. Then, on April 11, 1935, Edith was stricken with another attack.

It seems to have been a mild stroke, not perhaps as severe as the attack that had felled her six years before, but the more disturbing for being the second of its kind. For a time she lost the sight of her left eye. Elisina Tyler, the only person notified, at Edith's request, came down after a few weeks. By the end of May, Edith was walking and motoring, though, as she told Kenneth Clark, she had lost her "usual rather pedantic and precise relation to Time," and was confused about the dates of things immediately past or to come. In early June she drove back with Elisina to Paris in easy stages.

A most obedient patient, Edith limited her summer activities very strictly, almost the only outing being to a private showing of Italian paintings at the Petit Palais, arranged for her by Ugo Ojetti. This was a tremendous experience—"a great tidal wave of beauty"—and one sympathizes with Edith's need to sit down and rest for an hour after emerging from the gallery. Ojetti then went out to the Pavillon Colombe and, in Berenson's words, "was enchanted with the garden, the house, and above all the ritual of life of which he talked as if it were a revelation. So it is," Berenson went on, "this discovery of a more refined and a more exquisite order of daily life. It is indeed one of the highest achievements of humanisation."

Minnie Jones, who came for a short stay, seemed to Edith brisker than ever in her early eighties. But in late September, just as Edith was beginning to feel herself again, she had word that Minnie had died suddenly in a London hotel. By an unhappy coincidence, Beatrix Farrand was simultaneously ill in New York, and her husband—now director of the Huntington Library in San Marino, California—was too remote to be of help. Edith rallied her forces to make the journey to England, departing in such haste that a British consul had to meet her at Dover with a visa. The funeral was in Hertfordshire, and Minnie was buried beside Mrs. Humphry Ward. It was Edith who saw to the burial and the disposition of Minnie's effects, and who wrote her niece a full accounting.

Coming back wearily to St. Brice, Edith felt that she had lost two months of progress toward health. But she was soon capable of a five-hour picnic with Norton. And she was again hard at work: on *The Buccaneers*, a variety of short stories, and a proposed sequel to *A Backward Glance*.

6

In her early seventies Edith Wharton entered into a new mood of sensuality, as women of that age are said not uncommonly to do; and one sign of it was the way her opinion of contemporary writing was sometimes guided by the degree and kind of sexuality in it. She looked upon the prolific and brilliant French novelist Colette as "one of the greatest writers of our time," a woman who could communicate directly to her about the infinitely subtle nature of female passion and about "the tears in sensual things." She identified a recent novel by Colette, cheerfully enough, as "pornography *à la vente,*" and went on to praise its "last wonderful pages on jealousy." The erotic element in *Ulysses*, on the other hand, still struck her as "silly," though she was now willing to agree that the early work of James Joyce had considerable merit.

After reading an erotic English novel sent her by Mary Berenson, she remarked that her chief reaction was laughter—in the way she and Lapsley "used to rock with laughter over chosen extracts from the *Journal of Abnormal Psychology.*" (She once suggested that Lapsley send Norton, as a Christmas present, a book she had seen advertised: "La nouvelle *Initiation Sexuelle . . .* Le plus complet dans le genre, le *plus liberé*"—underlinings by Edith—"illustrations dans le texte.") These unimaginative and learned writers, she continued, "take that glorious and ignoble, that magical and mysterious Ark, the human body, and scramble over it with their goggles and their geological hammers," as boring and irrelevant as an academic commentator on *Faust*.

The diversity of Edith Wharton's literary taste was indicated by the two American novels to which she accorded the highest praise in these years. One was Theodore Dreiser's *An American Tragedy*, which she read belatedly in 1933, and by comparison with which, she said to Berenson, the work of Sinclair Lewis seemed reduced to mere newspaper reports. Dreiser's sometimes fumbling style must have dismayed her, but something in his compassionate vision of the human being trapped and doomed to disaster by the very nature of things evidently seized her imagination.

The other was George Santayana's one venture into fiction, *The Last Puritan*, which came into her hands in late 1935. She was enraptured by it, and thought that its immense sales were the most encouraging sign of American literary maturity she had yet seen. "It's *exactly* my old 1885 Boston," she exulted in a letter to Lapsley, and she reveled in the novel's stately, ironic prose.

Edith Wharton continued to read new writing of merit—for example, the work of her somewhat remote Riviera neighbor Somerset Maugham, whom she never encountered but for whose story about puritanical righteousness and lust, "Rain," she had a particular fondness. But her strongest allegiances remained with the great masters of the nineteenth century, English, French, and Russian.

These were the writers she had examined with a kind of loving shrewdness in the five essays she had collected in 1925 under the title *The Writing of Fiction.* The art of narrative, she told Robert Grant at the time, was being threatened by the new generation of scribblers; and in the essays she pointed to the current lack of restraint and the interest in "dirt-for-dirt's sake," to the self-defeating lust for originality, and to the forgoing of the discipline of technique. The moment had come, she thought, to get back to first principles and great exemplars.

The Writing of Fiction is a modest little book that, following its author's belief, does not strain after any startling theoretical originality. But it is steadily sane and judicious, and it displays an easy command of the history of narrative —Edith Wharton identified Diderot's "appalling 'Neveu de Rameu' " as "the first great figure in modern fiction" some thirty years before that notion made its way into Anglo-American criticism. As she considers central questions about her subject, she returns time and again to the same cluster of names: Balzac and Stendhal; Jane Austen, Trollope, Thackeray, George Eliot, and Meredith; Tolstoy, and though less often, Dostoyevsky. Among later writers Hardy and Conrad are glanced at with reserved friendliness.

The book has surprisingly little to say about Flaubert, though what it does say is respectful. A scene in *The Golden Bowl* is singled out for special praise, but the comments on Henry James are otherwise sparing. Edith Wharton, in fact, was turning away somewhat from what she now regarded as too carefully wrought fiction, of the sort represented by Flaubert and James. It was this mode of narrative that Percy Lubbock had taken as his model in *The Craft of Fiction;* and while Edith had admired that treatise when it appeared in 1921, her opinion of it evidently declined as the personal relationship with Lubbock deteriorated. She may even have intended her own critical volume to be a response, a counterargument, to Lubbock's.

Americans other than James were skimped or neglected entirely. *The Scarlet Letter* is mentioned as one of the few "great novels written in English" that is a story of "pure situation." Melville is listed along with Dumas and Stevenson as an enjoyable concocter of "gallant yarns" of adventure. Dreiser is not named.

One senses a certain hedging in the references to Sir Walter Scott and Charles Dickens. In fact, Edith Wharton could make little of either, and continually reread them in an effort to discover why others admired them so much. But she came late in life, as have other discerning readers of fiction, to a juster appreciation of Anthony Trollope than she had previously had. "Trollope seems to me to have got nearer the eternal verities than Thackeray," she wrote Berenson. "He's more grown up, and belongs rather with Tolstoy and Balzac."

Meanwhile, the old favorites stayed with her. "Ah, Jane, you sorceress," she exclaimed, after listening to Norton read aloud from *Sense and Sensibility* over a series of January evenings in 1934. In the course of a rereading of George Eliot's *Middlemarch*, she fell to debating with Berenson and the other guests whether Casaubon was impotent and whether his marriage with Dorothea Brooke was ever consummated.

7

Some of her own most assured writing in her last years similarly reached back to the nineteenth century and the European scene before the war. In *A Backward Glance*, published in 1934, she accomplished one of her finest literary feats as she brought back to life her ancestors and her parents and beautifully evoked old New York and Newport, Paris and the Fauborg during *la belle époque*, Edwardian London during the season. It is reticent enough personally, in all truth, and yet it is also deeply revealing. Any number of persons in the large cast—Howard Sturgis, Rosa de Fitz-James, Minnie Bourget, George Meredith—spring into existence in a sentence or a short paragraph, and the pages contain the most attractive and persuasive sketch of Henry James ever recorded.

"Roman Fever," the one happy aftereffect of the sickness that ruined Edith Wharton's visit to Rome in 1934, is another instance of backward glancing. The dialogue of the tale takes place in the mid-1920s on the Janiculum Hill above Rome. But the minds of the "two American ladies of ripe but well-cared for middle age" drift back to the turn of the century—to old New York and to an erotic intrigue in Rome that had an astonishing consequence concealed until the present moment and the last sentence of the story.

It is a brilliant piece of short fiction, and the newly formed *Liberty* was glad to pay three thousand dollars for it. Some of Edith Wharton's short stories in the 1930s were, indeed, as good as any she ever wrote. The collection called *Here and Beyond* (1926) was perhaps her only volume of tales that has virtually nothing in it to commend; but the three gatherings she brought out between 1930 and 1936—*Certain People, Human Nature*, and *The World Over*—contain a dozen items that must be ranked with her best. There are such splendid ghostly tales as "Pomegranate Seed" and "Mr. Jones," a story of indescribable cruelty, imprisonment, and violence set in the 1820s; and a brooding murder mystery called "A Bottle of Perrier," which, to Berenson's consternation, Edith Wharton wrote in a single day.

"Her Son," which is really a novella, is an addition to Edith Wharton's fictional studies of illegitimacy and the parent-child relation, and a work of considerable power. "After Holbein" enacts a remorseless dance of death in which, around the turn of the century, a once regal New York hostess (she is modeled, apparently, on Mrs. Astor) continues in her senility to receive nonexistent guests at her Fifth Avenue mansion, wearing her jewels and a purple wig. An elderly inveterate diner-outer wanders into her house by mistake and, his mind failing, joins in the illusory ceremony before he is felled by a stroke. Among several stories of infidelity, "The Day of the Funeral" gives us Edith Wharton's briskest opening gambit: "His wife had said: 'If you don't give her up I'll throw myself from the roof.' He had not given her up, and his wife had thrown herself from the roof."

Edith Wharton's last completed story, "All Souls," was sent to her agent in February 1937 and was published posthumously. It is a ghost story of sorts, set in some indeterminate past in a remote country home in Connecticut. It tells of the mounting terror of the normally level-headed Mrs. Clayburn, who awakes on All Souls' Day to find that her entire staff of servants has disappeared and that she is temporarily crippled by a badly sprained ankle. Through the endless November day she hobbles in pain and fright through the empty house, wondering if her wits are turning and unable to summon help. Next day the servants are in their regular places, and Mrs. Clayburn learns later that they had been summoned, either by a ghostly apparition or "more probably, and more alarmingly, a living woman inhabited by a witch," to attend an orgiastic coven in the Connecticut hills. It was at once fitting and revealing that Edith Wharton's last short story, and a highly superior one, should draw together just that set of human and supernatural, domestic and erotic ingredients.

One turns from one of these tales to another filled with a kind of wonder—as to why Edith Wharton had permitted herself such relatively slack work in the 1920s. It may well be that she regarded these short items as rather trifling sources of subsidiary income, while her chief energies went into a series of novels—an attitude reflected in the more negligible items, of which there are still too many, even in the 1930s.

But with the larger efforts, too, we confront something of a problem. Edith Wharton's novels after *The Age of Innocence* have usually been treated with undue critical severity. In fact, *The Mother's Recompense* is very handsomely done and comprises a searching and subtle portrayal of several acute human issues; *The Children*, if lighter in tone and texture, fleshes out its important theme in a witty, touching, and eminently readable manner. It remains true that *Twilight Sleep* and the two works devoted to Vance Weston are seriously and variously marred, though the pattern of Edith Wharton's accomplishment in fiction would be much the poorer without them. The problem, however, really arises with *The Buccaneers*, the novel Edith Wharton left unfinished at the time of her death, and which is unmistakably superior to anything she wrote after 1920.

What characterizes *The Buccaneers*, as it does "Roman Fever" and one or two other stories in *The World Over* of 1936, is a serenity that pervades the narrative in a long atmospheric glow. It is not quite a matter, apparently, of some miraculous recovery of power in the twilight of a long life, though a fresh kind of power can be felt welling up. It is rather, one speculates, that Edith Wharton in her last years moved gradually into a new state of being.

It was as though she had abandoned the attempt to find continuity between the present historical moment—the "angry sombre world"—and a more peaceful earlier period. *The Buccaneers* is set mostly in the England of the 1870s, and when she was sketching out the book she wrote Jewett: "Every year that passes makes that distant period of the 'seventies' seem more like a fairy tale." It is precisely an air of fairy-tale enchantment that breathes through the pages of *The Buccaneers*, while there is a firmness of outline, a psychological and moral clarity, and an aesthetic control that had been partially lacking in Edith Wharton's novels for a number of years.

At the same time, she had entered into almost total possession of her *personal* past, an event no doubt much aided by the writing of *A Backward Glance*. She had arrived at a deep harmony with her own life history and was able, unperturbed, to confront the whole truth about herself. Two radically different documents testify to this condition.

The first is the manuscript fragment of a short story or novella called "Beatrice Palmato." It reflects the mood of renewed sensuality already referred to, and is the most startling piece of fiction Edith Wharton ever wrote. In the summer of 1935 she commented to Berenson on a story by Moravia that in her view contained an inadequate treatment of the always interesting theme of incest. "Faulkner and Céline did it *first,*" she remarked, "and did it *nastier.*" She added that she herself had "an incest *donnée* up my sleeve that would make them all look like nursery rhymes," but that business was too poor and attitudes too prudish for her to risk trying to sell it. The *donnée* referred to, in all probability, was "Beatrice Palmato." (See Appendix C.)

The story tells of an ongoing incestuous relationship between a wealthy, handsome, silver-haired gentleman of artistic and literary leanings, a resident of London, and his daughter Beatrice, the issue of which is a baby girl. The fragment that Edith Wharton actually wrote describes the final full consummation of the relationship, some little time after Beatrice's marriage to a simple-minded country squire. But it is made clear that father and daughter have been exchanging the most ardent and intimate caresses for a number of years, to the point where their love-making has taken on a well-rehearsed ritualistic quality.

The outline Edith Wharton also left behind reveals with a sort of brilliant deviousness (the way the story was intended to reveal) that Palmato, the father, had previously made sexual advances to his older daughter, and that she had killed herself after being seduced by him. These events brought the unfortunate mother to a nervous breakdown; and when, later, Palmato initiates the affair with Beatrice (aged twelve), the mother goes insane, tries to murder her husband, and dies soon afterward in a lunatic asylum. "Beatrice Palmato," as conceived and as partially written, does indeed make the treatment of incest by Moravia and the others seem tame.

Even the names were chosen to add, subtly, to the sense of perversity and eroticism. "Beatrice," pronounced in the Italian manner, derives from Beatrice Cenci, the tragic heroine of a real-life drama of incest and murder in sixteenth-century Rome; Shelley, who held that incest was the most poetic of motifs, based a verse play upon the story. "Palmato" is related to the Italian words for "muscle" and "hand," and constitutes a discreet pun upon the male member, as metaphorically described in the fragment.

Only a trained psychologist might say with any assurance why Edith Wharton wrote just this story—just this *portion* of this story—at just this time, and why, having written it, she did not destroy it. She had, to be sure, evinced a steadily developing interest in the theme of incest. It had been dimly adumbrated in *Summer* and touched upon in *The Mother's Recompense* (when Kate Clephane felt that "some incestuous horror hung between" herself and her daughter). Edith, it will be recalled, had lamented the deletion of the incest motif from *The Barretts of Wimpole Street*, and she had been planning a narrative based upon the story of Lizzie Borden, with such a motif added and writ large.

In a broader context, "Beatrice Palmato" can be seen as the climax, unexpected and yet perhaps inevitable, of the parents-children theme that Edith Wharton had dealt with so often in the 1920s. The little fragment is, of course, pure and utter fantasy. But one guess is that her real and her creative life had led Edith Wharton to the point where she could finally acknowledge and give fantasy form to the strong physical attraction she had once felt for her own father, the consciousness of which she had buried deep for many decades. This was one part of the truth about herself that she could now confront, and even take a singular pleasure in.

An overwhelming intensity of pleasure is, indeed, experienced by young Beatrice. The sexual detail of the fragment is extraordinarily explicit: so much so that on the first reading one scarcely notices the exquisite artistry with which the experience is presented. More than likely, Edith Wharton had resolved to demonstrate that she could do much better than James Joyce at this kind of writing, and that, as against Joyce, Lawrence, and other male observers of female sensuality, she could give a truly accurate portrayal of a woman's sexual response. At the same time, she wanted to show that *she* could do it: that she could write elegant pornography as well as her usual fiction of manners, implication, and insinuation. If these were her ambitions, she fulfilled them.

"Beatrice Palmato" must be ranked as pornography—if that word can ever be associated with a work of art; for it is, quite simply, a beautiful composition.

It has the unmuffled verbal resonance, the nearly flawless rhetorical coherence, of "Roman Fever," "All Souls," *The Buccaneers,* and other achievements of this remarkable final creative period. Like those writings, "Beatrice Palmato" suggests that Edith Wharton at this stage was not only in tune with her past, but that she had unimpeded access to her imagination.

Nor can it be doubted that vividly remembered personal experience controls the account of erotic play. As it does so, we can see Edith Wharton looking back, in a refreshed perspective, upon yet another phase of her history. She was recapturing her first enjoyment of the varieties of sexual love in the relationship with Morton Fullerton, discovering again a beauty and a fulfillment she had denied in the wake of Teddy Wharton's revealed misconduct. By making the sexual relationship an incestuous one, moreover, she seems to have been investing her memory of the affair with a dark romantic *frisson,* as a violation not only of propriety but of the ultimate taboo; "Beatrice Palmato" was planned as the first story in a volume to be called "The Powers of Darkness," a title under which "All Souls," with its occult orgies, might also have been listed. Edith may equally have been implying a belated understanding of the strange appeal to Fullerton of the involvement with his sister-cousin Katharine.

A more ambiguous understanding of Teddy is likewise hinted at in the story. Beatrice Palmato is conscious, as Edith had once been, of "the dull misery of her marriage," and the moment of her deflowering (a week before the completed scene opens) was no less cruel a shock than the occasion had been for Edith. But among the emotions with which Beatrice faces her husband at their last encounter is a "remorseful tenderness." There had been guilt on her side, too, Edith could now freely acknowledge. A certain tender remorse for Teddy would be evident in Edith's remarks about him in her own final days.

Edith Wharton was a woman who gave the impression of firmly withholding aspects of herself from the public gaze, even while wanting those aspects to be eventually known. She retained the fragment and outline of "Beatrice Palmato," it may be supposed, for the same reason that she refrained from destroying the 1908 journal addressed to Fullerton, kept the autobiographical fragment "Life and I," and made up a packet of letters conspicuously labeled "For My Biographer." Properly discreet and evasive in her lifetime, she took determined steps to see that later generations would know her as she truly was.

Nothing more different from "Beatrice Palmato" can be imagined than the gently lyrical account by Philomène de la Forest-Divonne of an autumn afternoon visit to the Pavillon Colombe in 1935 or 1936. Yet Philomène's sketch, in its own way, gives a comparable portrait of an elderly woman in serene and clear-eyed harmony with her past.

Writing as Claude Sylve, Philomène had earned an excellent name for herself in the field of letters, both as a journalist and as the author of an exotic prize-winning novel, *Benediction*, which Robert Norton translated for Edith Wharton's American publishers, with an introduction by Mrs. Wharton. On the afternoon in question, according to Philomène's sensitive description, a psychological transformation took place before her eyes.

There are certain mysterious moments when affinities suddenly become more visible, moments favorable to the conjunction of friendships. Among so many passed with Edith, one day remains marked among all others.

I had gone to see her at St. Brice and I found her alone. I had the impression this time of approaching her without her "armour," without the stiff envelope of things to be done, of domestic regulations, of secretaries and guests. I had arrived after lunch; it was raining and it was full autumn. One felt that leisurely pause between seasons when nature itself seems arrested; a day deliciously empty, when there was nothing to *do*, and one must be content simply to *be* . . . And simply, and together, we *were*. All the little cares seemed to have disappeared; and it is never the big ones that disturb the true exchange between human beings.

The dear hostess's face had a relaxed air, as by a rare tranquility. The rapid blinking of her eyelids, the sign of a restless desire for perfection, slowed down. It was no more, as one looked, than a palpitation of thought, a stirring of light within. Her gaze no longer searched for a flower to set straight, the table to be shifted, the cushion to offer you.

And then, into the salon where the fire gleamed equally with the last roses, Edith brought the past. She brought it in the form of an album where there were carefully pasted (amid a number of rare photographs) clippings of critical articles about her first writings. I would sacrifice several visits, a trip, many walks with her than have this day lost to me! . . . It is one of my precious memories; on that afternoon I felt what Edith *could have been for the children she never had.*

While showing me these newspaper extracts that her old governess had formerly assembled—before they became too numerous—she accepted her literary glory, without vanity, without false modesty, as one accepts something ineluctable, as one accepts the blood of one's race.

"I was writing little stories when I was four," she said to me, not at all boasting about her gift, but also not seeking to deny it. This detachment, this tranquility in the face of her success had a great deal of nobility. Capable of lyricism, but without any romanticism, she never sought for "the sombre pleasure of a melancholy heart" and I was struck that day by the real gayety with which she evoked the mood of "never again."

With how much delicious affection she made me a participant in her earliest memories. And how certain I was that day (I have remained so ever since) of all the warmth hidden beneath the snow . . .

The Buccaneers, with "Roman Fever" and the others, was written out of an imagination stirred by what Philomène called a "light within" and undistracted by the details of housekeeping—undistracted, as well, by the radio reports from Paris, Berlin, and Rome suggesting daily that some terrible revolution was at hand.

The novel runs to some 355 pages in book form, apparently about three-fifths of the work as planned. It begins on the terrace of the old Grand Union Hotel in Saratoga, during the races, and then, after a dip into the New York of the Assembly Balls and the Thursday evening dances, it moves on, in Edith Wharton's words, to "aristocratic London in the season, and life in the great English country-houses as they were sixty years ago." It follows the early social missteps of the spirited Nan (Annabel) St. George, who, joining the then current invasion of the British aristocracy by young American heiresses, marries the kind but deadly dull Duke of Tintagel, but after a few years abandons him for the man she really loves, an impoverished former Guards officer.

Edith Wharton's ability to make settings palpable was never more evident. The "fog-swept ruins of Tintagel" which had so enthralled her in the summer of 1928 here become part of the book's emotional as well as physical scenery. It is on the ramparts of the Arthurian castle that Nan first meets the duke, and in marrying him later she feels obscurely that she is relating herself to the "rich low murmur of the past" that she hears emanating from the Cornish headlands. Honourslove, the estate of Nan's lover on the edge of the Cotswolds in Gloucestershire, seems based on Lady Elcho's Stanway; and the cottage on the Thames near Runnymede, where she spends a summer, is brought vividly into being.

Amid the "band of marauders," Nan St. George is flanked by other lively American girls, who also make questionable English matches—most conspicuously the green-eyed Conchita Santos-Dios, who combines features of the Minnie Stevens who became Lady Paget and of Edith's friend the former Consuelo Yznaga. But the most memorable character in the long fragment is none of these. It is rather Nan's "little brown governess," Laura Testvalley, a descendant of a *risorgimento* hero and a cousin of Dante Gabriel Rossetti's. The middle-aged and adventurous Laura is in fact so richly complex a person, and is endowed with so much humanity, that she threatens to run away with the narrative. Out of her desire to see "love, deep and abiding love, triumph for the first time in her career," as Edith Wharton put it, Laura becomes Nan's co-conspirator in the escape from Tintagel, and for this is denied her own single possibility of a comfortable and affection-surrounded old age.

The Buccaneers was published in 1938, with Edith Wharton's outline of the entire story and with an intelligent afterword by Gaillard Lapsley, who discussed the three most effective scenes in the novel. Lapsley made a judgment in favor of publication on the grounds that, though it was unfinished and contained passages the author would not have allowed to stand, the script "comprises some work as good as any she had ever done," some work indeed "too good to hold back." He was right, and one can only be grateful.

8

As the year 1936 opened, Edith Wharton, in her own phrase, was "blazing along several White Ways at a time." *The Old Maid,* very well dramatized by Zoë

Akins and with Helen Menken and Judith Anderson in the leading roles, had opened at the Empire Theater a year before and was a stunning success. In May 1935 it won the Pulitzer Prize for drama; audiences increased in numbers, and it was decided to continue it through the summer. It then took to the road, where, two years after its debut, it was still being performed. By the start of 1936 an English company was touring the provinces.

Ethan Frome, in a dramatization by Owen and Donald Davis, and staged by Guthrie McClintic, opened in Philadelphia in the first week of January 1936. Raymond Massey was reported to be extremely powerful in the role of Ethan; Pauline Lord was effective, if a touch too attractive, as Zeena; and Ruth Gordon was superb as Mattie Silver. Opening night was an unqualified success, with comments ranging from "singularly good" to "magnificent." The play moved on to a run of more than four months at the National Theatre in New York, and an even longer career on the road. *Ethan Frome* was one of the more successful productions in a theatrical season which also included Robert Sherwood's *Idiot's Delight*, Sidney Kingsley's *Dead End*, and Bella and Samuel Spewack's *Boy Meets Girl*.

It was from the two plays that Edith Wharton reaped her best financial rewards in her last three years. The year 1934 had been a relatively low point, with literary earnings of scarcely twenty thousand dollars, and most of that being from Hollywood options or purchases of her stories for films. There were moments when Edith was genuinely fearful about her financial condition—as much, it would seem, for those dependent on her, including her servants in a time of shrunken employment, as for herself. But from early 1935 onward, she had little to worry about. Records of her income from plays are only partially obtainable, but it appears to have been not less than $130,000.

In the summer of 1936, Edith made the trip to England and went to the festival at Glyndebourne (where the gardens had been designed by Beatrix Farrand) to see *Don Giovanni*. The fall passed quietly, though Edith was much annoyed by the reelection in November of Franklin Roosevelt—despite Zoë Akin's efforts to reassure her, citing the opinion of informed friends that Roosevelt was a dedicated and honorable man and decidedly superior to Alfred Landon, the Republican candidate. Edith reached Ste. Claire in early December, after a fortnight at I Tatti, and the start of the year 1937 found her in excellent form. Her handwriting—always a dependable index of her health—was clear and vigorous. Norton and Lapsley were on hand for the holiday; the Huxleys drove down periodically; Charles de Noailles came to dine and kept the company laughing until late in the evening. On January 24 she passed her seventy-fifth birthday. Some time later, upon being told that the goldfish at the Pavillon Colombe might be as much as seventy-five years old, Bill Tyler exclaimed at the thought of any living thing reaching such an age. "Well," Edith remarked to him, "it feels pretty good when you get to it."

Guests passed in and out of Ste. Claire: Norton, Mary Wemyss, looking worn and nervous, Jane Clark. Bill and Betsy Tyler arrived toward the end of March with their newborn child, Royall; the doting Edith promptly renamed him Hercules, which she then foreshortened to Herc. Charlotte de Cossé-Brissac visited, and Paléologue, Carlo Placci, and Florence de la Forest-Divonne: a typical winter and spring.

Most of the time Edith felt extremely well. She was working steadily on several literary enterprises, including "A Little Girl's Old New York," a postscript to *A Backward Glance*. But there were intermittent attacks of giddiness, and she wrote in her diary a month after her birthday: "Tired of these sudden collapses." Personal losses also affected her more deeply than usual. In mid-April she was grief-stricken by the death of Linky, the little Pekinese who had been with her for eleven years. "Oh, my little dog . . ." she wrote shakily in her diary, before it fell blank. The death of Mary Wemyss in an English nursing home a month later left her even more distraught.

With Marie, the personal maid who had replaced Elise, and Smith, the new English chauffeur, she started on the slow journey back to St. Brice at the end of May. She broke the trip at Ogden Codman's Château de Grégy, south of Paris, and here, on about the first of June, she had another stroke. On June 3, at the insistence of the local doctor, she was transported by ambulance to the Pavillon Colombe. Elisina Tyler, advised by telegram, arrived from Rome the next day.

9

Edith Wharton lingered on for two more months, and there was a short period toward the end of July when it even seemed that she might miraculously recover her health. She had moved to a chaise longue in her bedroom near the window, had taken a few steps, and had finally been carried downstairs to be pushed about the garden in a wheelchair. Her pleasure at the sight of friends who came to see her—Kenneth and Jane Clark, Hugh Smith and Royall Tyler, Norton and the Bill Tylers—gave her such momentary vitality that she seemed to some of them better than she was. But to Elisina Tyler the doctor held out little hope, and Edith herself seemed to have made her mind up.

"I think," she said one day, "that Shakespeare never wrote a more beautiful line than: 'I am dying, Egypt, dying.' " Elisina told her gently that she must think only about getting well. "I don't think I shall ever be well again," Edith replied matter-of-factly, and went on to talk about her belongings. "Please remember I want Nicky Mariano to have all my dresses. She hasn't much money to buy dresses . . . And I ought to make a present to the commune of St. Brice."

While Elisina sat next to her, Edith would doze for a time, then, without opening her eyes, begin to talk in a soft voice as if picking up an interrupted conversation. "Once we crossed the Stelvio pass, and sent a postcard to Henry James with the words: *from a summit to a summité* [prominent person]. How he laughed . . ." Within her dying body, her mind raced from subject to subject. She murmured on about literature, about Flaubert and Balzac. Balzac's novels were not well written, Elisina protested, and Edith retorted: "Well, you might as well say that there are cobblestones in the street." She talked about Ronald Simmons and Walter Berry: "Walter loved life so . . ." and then, musingly, "If he made friends of women much younger than himself, it was because youth and the joy of life go together."

She often spoke of Teddy Wharton. "He enjoyed life so. He was always so kind to animals, and they always approached him without fear. Dogs, and children, and all natural things know their friends by instinct." After a pause, she continued: "Those who love life too eagerly make the mistakes the world condemns." She asked Elisina to look through all the letters from Teddy, somewhere in the Pavillon, and burn those she thought best to burn; Elisina apparently destroyed them all. Another time, reverting to Teddy, Edith said: "I had to choose. Our staying together would have increased his disgrace. It was always the plea for 'one more chance,' that plea of the weak." And later: "There was no cruelty and no unkindness in him. Yet he was cruel and unkind through weakness."

James, Simmons, Teddy, Walter Berry: they had all become characters, now, in the long novel of her life. She spoke of them as she did of figures in a story by Balzac or one of her own tales. Though Edith Wharton had not been denied her passionate interlude, though she had loved and suffered, had been exalted by events and almost inconsolably grieved by them, her most intense feelings had for many years been reserved for her writings. It was, finally, her writings that constituted the life she had most truly and deeply lived. At the same time, the actualities of her experience, the men and women she had loved, seemed to her increasingly to be creatures of fiction, parts of some other narrative she had yet to compose. In one of her last remarks to Elisina, Edith recalled acquiring the habit of "making up" in her childhood, even before she was able to read. In the reminiscences of the closing hours, she was still making up.

The last days were serene ones. The loveliest of St. Brice summers drifted by, and Edith drifted with the days, gazing out at the garden from the chaise longue or moving slowly about it in the wheelchair, dozing, remembering, planning small bequests. On August 4 she wrote a line to Matilda Gay at Le Bréau: "I am just sending you this line by Elisina, to tell you how sorry I am not to be able to go with her to see you this afternoon. I should have been quite willing to go, but Elisina and my maid behaved so awfully about it that I had no alternative but to go on dozing on the sofa."

It was a last little flash of the old spirit, but the handwriting was tremulous and ran all over the page. Edith Wharton died a week later, just before six on the evening of Wednesday, August 11.

All next day and the day after, she lay behind the closed blinds of her bedroom while a steady procession of friends drove out from Paris to pay their last respects. Louis Gillet came for a lonely farewell look at the Pavillon Colombe gardens; some subtle essence, he thought, had disappeared from them. Robert Norton, thinking back on their times together at the Pavillon, wrote Lapsley: "What a great personality emerges from them all." From his cottage on the grounds Arthur White wrote forlornly to Berenson: "I feel out of place here now and would like to vanish."

On the morning of August 14 a guard of honor formed in the courtyard, composed of war veterans and others Edith Wharton had so long befriended in the village of St. Brice. As the coffin was brought out, flags were lowered and a bugle call was sounded. The coffin was transported to the Cimetière des Gonards in Versailles, where another deputation of veterans led it to the grave.

Some twenty-five old friends, Kenneth Clark and Louis Metman among them, attended the simple funeral service Edith had outlined a few years before. The dean of the American Cathedral in Paris read a few prayers, and the body was lowered into the double plot Edith had bought near the grave of Walter Berry. On the gravestone was inscribed:

> Edith Wharton
> Née Edith Newbold Jones
> January 24, 1862–August 11, 1937

and the Latin phrase she had selected:

> *Ave Crux Spes Unica.*

Appendixes

Appendix A

THE QUESTION OF EDITH WHARTON'S PATERNITY

At some still undetermined moment in Edith Wharton's life, a rumor arose that she was not in fact the daughter of George Frederic Jones, but the daughter of the young man she identifies very briefly in her memoirs as the "extremely cultivated English tutor" of her two brothers. A rumor of this kind is always, needless to say, exceedingly difficult to prove or disprove with any finality, and in the present case the nature of such evidence as there is makes any firm conclusion impossible.

For example, Matilda Gay—a daughter of the popular and witty New York broker and man about town William R. Travers—is quoted by a second person as having said: "It could not be doubted. She was the image of him." Mrs. Gay was a few years older than Edith Wharton, and her father, an inveterate gossip, was privy to every secret whispered in and about New York society. Unfortunately, Matilda Gay is herself on record as never having laid eyes on Edith until the latter was eleven years old—some years after the English tutor may be presumed to have left the Joneses' service (he did so, it is safe to guess, when they went to Europe in late 1866—Freddy having finished his schooling by this time, while Harry was heading for Cambridge, England). To detect a similarity at seven years' remove is not unthinkable, but it must be suspect.

Nor is it even clear that Matilda Gay was quoted accurately. A quotation from another source is still more puzzling. Margaret Terry Chanler, in her old age, is responsible for the following story. Once she and Edith were driving across England and as they passed through a little village, Edith remarked: "My father was born here." To this, Mrs. Chanler, who was well aware of the rumor, asked curiously: "Are you sure?" Edith replied: "No, I am not sure, and I don't care." The language and tone sound authentic; the trouble is that never on any occasion did Margaret Chanler and Edith Wharton drive in England together. They enjoyed each other's company in France and Spain, in the Aegean islands, and even in Newport, but never in England.

Margaret Chanler's role in the history and diffusion of the rumor is an important one. She used to tell her daughter Hester Pickman that during her anti-American moods in the 1920s and 1930s, Edith would express pleasure at the thought that her father was an Englishman. Mrs. Chanler was perhaps Edith Wharton's most intimate woman friend in their shared maturity, and she was a highly intelligent, thoroughly honorable, and deeply religious person. If she really believed the English tutor to have been Edith Wharton's father, she must have had fairly strong reasons. There can be no doubting that she did so believe. It was Edith's paternity, she wrote Percy Lubbock, that accounted for the shadow that lay so mysteriously over her friend's life.

The source and timing of the rumor are equally beclouded. Matilda Gay, again, has been quoted as insisting that Edith Wharton's English paternity was "a fact well known in New York to the close social world into which Edith was born." That is a vague enough statement, and at Elisina Tyler's request the New York architect Frederic King—Edith Wharton's second cousin, and a good friend and frequent visitor in her late years—made inquiries. Matilda Gay had spoken to him about it too, he acknowledged, but no one in the immediate family knew of it, and "no one who remembers Edith in the early Newport days—the very few left—heard of it at the time." His guess was that the rumor started sometime in the 1920s.

On the other hand, two ancient ladies, the Beekman sisters, once surprised each other and a third person by admitting that they had, each of them, secretly looked askance at Edith Jones at the time of her social debut in 1879, on the grounds of her allegedly irregular birth. This anecdote has been filtered through the memory of the third person, now dead, as reported to and then recounted by still a fourth person. Even so, it has, somehow, a faint ring of truth.

It is almost entirely unlikely that Edith Wharton was herself the source of the rumor. The childhood fantasy of the girl who imagines that she is a changeling, or that her real father is some romantic foreigner rather than the man the world accepts—these are familiar phenomena, but they do not fit with Edith Wharton's filial attitudes. She was obviously devoted to George Frederic Jones and proud to be his daughter, while from adolescence onward her relations with her mother were cool and distant. Indeed, Edith Wharton's posture with regard to her two parents was one of the most conventional ones she ever adopted.

She may have first heard the story around 1909. It was at that time, anyhow, that she wrote an amusing tale, "His Father's Son," about a young man who deludes himself into the conviction that his father is not the prosaic manufacturer of suspender buckles who married his mother, but a great Polish musician who had toured America during the year of his conception. Some of the aspects of this story suggest that Edith Wharton was playing with the ingredients of the rumor as they had been conveyed to her, and was treating it all, precisely, as a case of immature fantasizing.

For the rest, her personal reaction seems to have been compounded of interest and skepticism. Both Frederic King and Mrs. Chanler were of the opinion that Edith Wharton actually believed the rumor, and Mrs. Chanler added that her friend had once made an effort to track the tutor down—in England, presumably—only to discover that he was dead.

Here we may comment upon another phase of the problem. Edith Wharton, in her thirties, suffered more than once what psychologists of a later generation would call an "identity crisis"; but these troubled moments had to do with her *role* rather than her *origins*. She underwent periods of debilitating uncertainty about her position as a woman and a wife and about the strength of her commitment to a literary career. Later there was a developing conflict of sorts between her sense of herself as an American and her alienation from her native land, especially after the war. But she remained unmistakably American to the end of her life; and at no time does she strike one as in the least troubled about the very sources of her existence.

The story, on the face of it, is not as implausible as it first might seem. It is not altogether inconceivable, to put it flatly, that Lucretia Jones might have carried on an adulterous affair with a young Englishman under her own roof, the offspring of which was baptized Edith Jones. Lovers and mistresses, to be sure, were far less common among the older families to which the Jones–Rhinelander set belonged than among the social element known in the 1860s and 1870s as "the new breed," and for this very reason, the young rakes in the New York clubs enjoyed shocking their elders by charging the most proper of the long-established families with every kind of misconduct. But in one case quite close to home, the charge was true.

At almost precisely the same time that Lucretia Jones was by later rumor alleged to be carrying on an illicit affair in her own home, her first cousin Mary Stevens Strong was doing just that. The former Miss Stevens had borne her husband, Peter Strong (a nephew of the diarist), two children by the time her widowed brother-in-law moved in with them. She and her brother-in-law—a man, it was said, "of religious inclinations"—lived together in secret for several years before, in a fit of conscience, she confessed everything to Peter Strong. A sensational trial followed, during which some members of the Strong family began to side with the much-abused Mary.

Equally close to home was the debacle of George Frederic's cousin George Alfred Jones. Edith Wharton would remember her second cousin's name being whispered by her mother in a sort of scandalized hiss, but when she asked what he had done, Lucretia would only mutter, "Some *woman!*" George Alfred, married to the former Harriet Coster (a "bilious brunette," according to the unsympathetic George Templeton Strong), had absconded with a great deal of money in order to support his attractive mistress in high style. When his financial depredations came to light, George Alfred along with his wretched wife were required to repay the entire amount of money. They retired to the country and a small business making dolls. Society trembled with horror and excitement over the episode.

Whether Lucretia Jones was capable of a secret erotic passion like her cousin and her in-law is perhaps another matter. She gives the impression of having been a woman of few and limited emotions, and one concerned primarily with correctness in the externals of life. Yet "worldly" was the word most often pronounced about her; though it no doubt referred essentially to her Parisian wardrobe, her low-cut gowns, and the style of living she conspicuously displayed, the quality observed may have been associated with different and hidden urgings. One also recalls the dimly, almost resentfully romantic girl of sixteen, and one wonders what she had become in her late thirties.

On its more serious side, of course, the rumor of Edith Wharton's paternity grew out of the great disparity between her own literary and intellectual gifts and those of any known member of her crowded ancestry over half a dozen generations. As to this, too little is known about heredity and creative talent to make much of a judgment. One returns, besides, to the enormous and varied energy of her great-grandfather Ebenezer Stevens; to adapt one of the wiser sayings of Sherlock Holmes, energy in the blood is liable to take the most unexpected forms.

More immediately, the rumor must in part have expressed the old society's astonishment, and indeed its dismay, at one of its daughters turning out to be a writer of near genius. For much of that society there was something positively *wrong* about a well-bred woman writing fiction—it would be a very long time before Edith Wharton herself overcame this feeling. It may not be too subtle to suppose that the wrongness was transferred to a questionable paternity.

On the other hand, George Frederic Jones is not unimaginable in the role of a writer's father. He was an incessant reader, if an undiscriminating one, with an interest in history; and his diary shows him to have been intermittently adept in the handling of words. Edith Wharton found nothing surprising in the fact that his daughter should become a writer of novels. In the wake of the great success of *The House of Mirth* in 1905, she told an older friend that "I often think of Papa . . . and wish he could have been here to encourage me with my work."

Edith Wharton's stories of illegitimacy, finally, do not shed much light on the case. After "His Father's Son," she touched on the theme five more times. Dealing for so long, as she did, almost exclusively with the vicissitudes of marriage, she would have been bound to do so. A review of these instances suggests that though she regarded the matter with increasing seriousness, her main interest was not how it felt to be an illegitimate child, but how it felt to be the mother of one.

As for the "extremely cultivated tutor," his name has not survived, and Edith Wharton made no other explicit reference to him. But there is some evidence that the figure of M. Rivière in *The Age of Innocence* is based upon him. Rivière is the young Frenchman whom Newland Archer and his bride encounter in

London, where he is acting as the tutor of a consumptive English lad.

He is about thirty, with a thin, ugly face "to which the play of ideas gave an intense expression." His father had died young after a modest career in diplomacy, and the son had gone into journalism and had tried his hand as an author, without much luck. He made a living by tutoring English boys, but he had a mother and an unmarried sister to support and he was desperately poor. He is, even so, content enough with the life of the mind and of letters, and in Paris had conversed with eminent literary personages. Good conversation is meat and drink to him; and he is anxious (to Archer's consternation) to look for more of it in New York City.

This, certainly, is the profile one would put together of Edith Wharton's father; a person of a certain intellectuality and journalistic skill but something less than creative capacity. But as Rivière disappears from *The Age of Innocence*, so the English tutor vanished from history. The family folklore has him going west in the United States after the Joneses went to Europe, and one strain of it has him being killed in the battle of Little Big Horn.

On balance: there was definitely a rumor about Edith Wharton's illegitimacy, and it was a fairly tenacious one; but it did not originate with her or with anyone close to her in her childhood. It attracted Edith Wharton's attention during the first decade of the century, and she was sufficiently stirred to make some attempt at validating it. It had no visible psychological effect upon her. The rest lies in the domain of contradictory surmise and undependable memory. And though the testimony of Margaret Chanler, however garbled, must give one pause, my own guess is that the rumor is false.

Appendix B

THE FULLERTON PAPERS

The most notable event during the years this book was in the making was the discovery and acquisition of a sizable batch of papers relating to William Morton Fullerton. It was the end of a long process—and, as it has turned out, the beginning of another.

The first day I actually started work on the life of Edith Wharton, I came on the track of Morton Fullerton, a name I had never heard before. It was in The Hague, in January 1967, at the home of Ambassador and Mrs. William Royall Tyler. I had flown in that morning from New York, and by nine thirty I was sorting through the numerous boxes of materials in the little study the Tylers had kindly set aside for me. Examining some papers in what was described in the inventory as a "brown leather case," I found myself reading several letters to Mr. Tyler's mother, signed by one Fullerton, alluding in the most outspoken (and for me, at this stage, implausible) way to Edith Wharton's recklessly passionate nature. At the time of these letters, Elisina Tyler—who as Mrs. Wharton's legatee had inherited a great many documents as well as the Riviera property— was planning a biography of her friend of twenty-five years. "Please seize the event, however delicate the problem," Fullerton told her, "to dispel the myth of your heroine's frigidity."

Who on earth, I asked over lunch, is Morton Fullerton? Not without a little sigh, Ambassador Tyler identified him for me: an American journalist who had spent most of his adult life in Paris and who had undoubtedly at one time had some sort of affair with Edith Wharton. Mr. Tyler added that Fullerton's much younger cousin was director of the American Hospital in Neuilly, just outside Paris, and that he could supply me with a good deal more information.

A few days later I was in the Neuilly office of Hugh Fullerton: a tall, courteous gentleman, with a vigorous personality and a ready smile. He was not at first very happy to learn that someone was inquiring into Cousin Morton's liaison with Mrs. Wharton, but he set himself out to be as helpful as possible. In the course of our talk Morton Fullerton began to take shape: his looks and bearing, his journalistic career, his private life. Hugh Fullerton turned over to me a few postcards from Edith Wharton to his cousin and the pocket diary in which Morton had made jottings—including the erotic dream quoted in Chapter Eleven—in the 1890s.

Edith Wharton had once written a poem, Hugh Fullerton said musingly, describing in a well-nigh scandalous manner a night she had spent in a London hotel with Morton. Morton had passed the poem along to Hugh. The latter led me to believe that he had burned it.

There matters stood for more than a year. In the summer of 1968, I was fortunate enough to engage the services of Miss Marion Mainwaring, a gifted scholar (Ph.D., Radcliffe), the author of several books, and now a free-lance writer living in Paris. Miss Mainwaring agreed to explore as fully as possible the Parisian phase of Edith Wharton's life; in particular, the matter of Morton Fullerton.

Over the next two years Miss Mainwaring pursued her task with unflagging zest and brilliance. She put together a composite picture of the Faubourg St. Germain before the First World War; uncovered the exotic background of the Pavillon Colombe in St. Brice; identified scores of individuals whose names appeared with frequency in Edith Wharton's diaries, and held long conversations with a number of the survivors among them.

But it was to the figure of Morton Fullerton that she especially addressed herself. Hearing from Hugh Fullerton, with whom she regularly consulted, that Cousin Morton had been married briefly early in the century, she battled the Paris bureaucracy with adroit patience until it released to her the curious divorce decree mentioned in Chapter Eleven. Following the trail of Fullerton's wife, Camille Chabert, Miss Mainwaring eventually had in hand a fairly complete chronology of her life, to be placed alongside a similar chronology of the life of M.F. Further hard research disclosed the fact that the woman who had been blackmailing Fullerton—the "obscure and vindictive old woman" referred to by Henry James—was probably a certain Henrietta Mirecourt.

Out of these various extended inquiries, there arose the challenging possibility that Morton Fullerton, upon his death in 1952, had left behind in his Rue Mont-Thabor office a large number of letters and other papers. These became the prime target of Marion Mainwaring's investigations. One trail led—via newspaper advertisements and letters to a good many *hôtels de ville*—to a country inn in central France, and disappeared there.

Then, suddenly, Miss Mainwaring discovered the location of Camille Chabert's last place of residence; it was a nursing home for the elderly and infirm. Calling there, Miss Mainwaring was given the address where Mme. Fullerton had spent most of her later years. This was on the Champs Elysées. Miss Mainwaring betook herself promptly to the address—and there were the papers.

Camille had swept them up in the wake of her former husband's death and carried them off to her own home (she was, obviously, obsessed by Fullerton to the end of her days). When she herself died in the mid-1960s the papers were lying about in her rooms in total disorder. By this time an Englishman, a Mr. George Nolan, the Paris representative of a British industrial company, had rented office space on the ground floor of Camille Chabert's home. They had become friends; Camille talked at length about her husband and showed Mr. Nolan the papers. After her death, since no one else showed up to claim them, the Englishman bundled them together and brought them down to his office.

Marion Mainwaring made a rapid inventory, and there followed several transatlantic phone calls. In the fall of 1970 the Beinecke Library at Yale purchased the entire collection for a reasonable sum. At Christmas, Miss Mainwaring brought them from Paris to her home outside Boston. I retrieved them and delivered them to the library.

The product of this feat of detective work is a massive one. There are numerous letters from the Ranee of Sarawak to Fullerton, and a few from him to the ranee. There are about forty letters from Katharine Fullerton to Morton, her cousin and one-time fiancé. From these I have quoted in Chapters Eleven and Fourteen, with the most gracious acquiescence of Katharine Fullerton's daughter, Mrs. Sylvia Loughnan, and her son Christopher Gerould. The collection includes a series of missives from Fullerton's parents and letters to them from Camille Chabert, as well as several letters from Camille to her former husband; and there are some ardent letters from other young women variously infatuated with Fullerton. Beyond all these, there is a batch of letters from a now obscure English literary friend. From Henry James, only one or two not very significant communications—James's other letters having been sold by Fullerton to the Houghton Library at Harvard.

From Edith Wharton, nothing. The Houghton Library acquired twenty-two letters to Fullerton, written between 1916 and 1932, and these are the ones I have quoted from. As to the others—for example, the daily letters Edith Wharton seems to have written in the spring of 1908—either she had Fullerton return them and then destroyed them; or, as appears equally unlikely, Fullerton himself did away with them; or—and this is the best bet—they remain hidden somewhere, awaiting Marion Mainwaring's next pursuit.

From her Paris base, Miss Mainwaring is now launched upon a biography of Morton Fullerton. It is to be hoped that the volume will include her own first-hand account of the search after the Fullerton papers.

While this scholarly drama was unfolding, I had of course kept in close touch with the participants. In the fall of 1971, after considerable brooding, I wrote Hugh Fullerton a letter. It was about the love poem by Edith Wharton that he had allowed me to think he had destroyed. The passage of time had convinced me that no one as devoted to the literary arts as Hugh Fullerton could have brought himself to burn a poem by Edith Wharton, even one as unconventional (so it seemed) as the one written after the London experience with M.F. On this assumption, I wrote to ask if Hugh would consider selling the work to Yale. His rueful smile was almost visible in his reply. Yes, he had the poem, and would be glad for Yale to acquire it. By mid-January 1972 the poem "Terminus" was in the safe at Beinecke.

Having yielded with extraordinary grace on this matter, Hugh Fullerton then unearthed the poem "Colophon to The Mortal Lease," inscribed in Edith Wharton's hand to M.F., along with another minor verse, and made a personal gift of them to me. He also composed and sent on a careful account of Morton Fullerton's last years, during and after the Second World War. The importance to my narrative of these generous actions will have been apparent.

To round things out: there are twelve letters from Henry James to Fullerton (mostly about the blackmailing affair, in 1907) and three from James to Katharine Fullerton in the Firestone Library at Princeton. There are also three letters from Fullerton to Theodore Roosevelt, written between 1911 and 1914, in the Library of Congress, and a number of letters to Frederick Macmillan in the British Museum in London; these several documents were transcribed by Miss Mary Pitlick. The other letters to Fullerton I have made use of (for example, the two from Oscar Wilde) are in the Houghton Library. The William Royall Tyler collection includes two unpublished poems by Edith Wharton addressed to Fullerton, as well as Fullerton's letters to Elisina Tyler.

Appendix C

"BEATRICE PALMATO"

The outline and the brief fragment of the story "Beatrice Palmato," here presented, are in the Beinecke Library of Yale University, along with a mass of other unfinished stories and novels. They seem to have been written sometime in 1935. The name "Beatrice Palmato" appears in a notebook as early as about 1920, but it stands alone on an otherwise blank page, between fairly detailed outlines of novels (including *The Age of Innocence*) that Edith Wharton did in fact write and stories she did not go on to compose. It may well be that the ingredients of "Beatrice Palmato"—including those that went into that choice of name, as I have suggested in Chapter Twenty-seven—were in Edith Wharton's mind by 1920. But it remains probable that she was not ready to write it for another fifteen years. The manuscripts show that she revised as meticulously and felicitously in these cases as in all others.

She could not conceivably have intended the fragment to be part of "Beatrice Palmato," had the story ever been sent to press. It does not really accord with the outline (which planned to *conceal* the incest until the last page), and in any event, no respectable magazine in the world would have published it. This makes it only the more intriguing that the fragment got written. Cynthia Griffin Wolff —a psychologist and a professor of literature who is well launched on a psychologically oriented study of Edith Wharton's fiction—has speculated persuasively, in conversation, about the matter. She suggests that Edith Wharton wrote the fragment in order to articulate fully to herself the precise nature, feeling, and history of the incestuous experience which was to lie behind and to color the actual narrative. Mrs. Wolff remarks that it was as though Joseph Conrad had written out a private account, for his own imaginative purposes, of "the horror," that unspecified phenomenon that overwhelms Kurtz in *The Heart of Darkness*.

One possible literary source of the fragment is Alfred de Musset's classic work of pornography, *Gamiani*, written in the early nineteenth century. There is a likelihood that Edith Wharton knew this novel, which was circulated in a private edition in 1926. Its central figure was based at a certain remove upon her lifelong favorite, Musset's mistress George Sand. Morton Fullerton, it may be recalled, meant it as a high compliment when he said that Edith Wharton in love displayed the reckless ardor of a George Sand.

Outline of "Beatrice Palmato"

Beatrice Palmato is the daughter of a rich half-Levantine, half-Portuguese banker living in London, and of his English wife. Palmato, who is very handsome, cultivated and accomplished, has inherited his father's banking and brokering business, but, while leaving his fortune in the business, leads the life of a rich and cultivated man of leisure. He has an agreeable artistic-literary house in London, and a place near Brighton. The wife is handsome, shy, silent, but agreeable. There are two daughters and a son, the youngest. The eldest, Isa, who looks like her mother, commits suicide in mysterious circumstances at seventeen, a few months after returning from the French convent in which she has been educated. The mother has a bad nervous break-down, and is ordered away by the doctors, who forbid her to take little Beatrice (aged 12) with her. After a vain struggle, she leaves the child in the country with an old governess who has brought her up, and whom she can completely trust. The governess is ill, and is obliged to leave, and Beatrice remains in the country with her father. He looks for another governess, but cannot find one to suit him, and during a whole winter takes charge of Beatrice's education. She is a musical and artistic child, full of intellectual curiosity, and at the same time very tender and emotional: a combination of both parents. The boy, whom Mrs. Palmato adores, and whom her husband has never cared for, is a sturdy sensitive English lad. He is at school, and spends his holidays with his tutor. Mrs. Palmato is still abroad, in a sanitorium. The following autumn (after a year's absence) she comes home. At first she seems better, and they return to London, and see a few friends. Beatrice remains with them, as neither parent can bear to be separated from her. They find a charming young governess, and all seems well.

Then suddenly Mrs. Palmato has another nervous break-down, and grows quite mad. She tries to kill her husband, has to be shut up, and dies in an insane asylum a few months later. The boy is left at school, and Mr. Palmato, utterly shattered, leaves on a long journey with Beatrice and a new maid, whom he engages for her in Paris. After six months he returns, and re-engages the same governess. Eighteen months after his wife's death he marries the governess, who is a young girl of good family, good-looking and agreeable, and to whom Beatrice is devoted.

The intimacy between father and daughter continues to be very close, but at 18 Beatrice meets a young man of good family, a good-looking rather simple-minded country squire with a large property and no artistic or intellectual tastes, who falls deeply in love with her.

She marries him, to every one's surprise, and they live entirely in the country. For some time she does not see her father or the latter's wife; then she and her husband go up to town to stay for a fortnight with the Palmatos, and after that they see each other, though at rather long intervals. Beatrice seems to her friends changed, depressed, overclouded. Her animation and brilliancy have vanished, and she gives up all her artistic interests, and appears to absorb herself in her husband's country tastes. The Palmato group of friends all deplore her having married such a dull man, but admit that he is very kind to her and that she seems happy. Once her father takes her with him on a short trip to Paris, where he goes to buy a picture or some tapestries for his collection, and she comes back brilliant, febrile and restless; but soon settles down again. After 2 1/2 years of marriage she has a boy, and the year after a little girl; and with the birth of her children her attachment to her husband increases, and she seems to her friends perfectly happy. About the time of the birth of the second child, Palmato dies suddenly.

The boy is like his father, the little girl exquisite, gay, original, brilliant, like her mother. The father loves both children, but adores the little girl; and as the latter grows to be five or six years old Beatrice begins to manifest a morbid jealousy of her husband's affection for this child. The household has been so harmonious hitherto that the husband himself cannot understand this state of mind; but he humours his wife, tries to conceal his fondness for his little daughter, and wonders whether his wife is growing "queer" like her mother.

One day the husband has been away for a week. He returns sooner than was expected, comes in and finds the little girl alone in the drawing-room. She utters a cry of joy, and he clasps her in his arms and kisses her. She has put her little arms around his neck, and is hugging him tightly when Beatrice comes in. She stops on the threshold, screams out: "Don't kiss my child. Put her down! How dare you kiss her?" and snatches the little girl from his arms.

Husband and wife stand staring at each other. As the husband looks at her, many mysterious things in their married life—the sense of some hidden power controlling her, and perpetually coming between them, and of some strange initiation, some profound moral perversion of which he had always been afraid to face the thought—all these things become suddenly clear to him, lit up in a glare of horror.

He looks at her with his honest eyes, and says: "Why shouldn't I kiss my child?" and she gives him back a look in which terror, humiliation, remorseful tenderness, and the awful realization of what she has unwittingly betrayed, mingle in one supreme appeal and avowal.

She puts the little girl down, flies from the room, and hurries upstairs. When he follows her, he hears a pistol-shot and finds her lying dead on the floor of her bedroom.

People say: "Her mother was insane, her sister tried to kill herself; it was a very unfortunate marriage."

But the brother, Jack Palmato, who has become a wise, level-headed young man, a great friend of Beatrice's husband, comes down on hearing of his sister's death, and he and the husband have a long talk together—about Mr. Palmato.

The End

Fragment of "Beatrice Palmato"

"I have been, you see," he added gently, "so perfectly patient—"

The room was warm, and softly lit by one or two pink-shaded lamps. A little fire sparkled on the hearth, and a lustrous black bear-skin rug, on which a few purple velvet cushions had been flung, was spread out before it.

"And now, darling," Mr. Palmato said, drawing her to the deep divan, "let me show you what only you and I have the right to show each other." He caught her wrists as he spoke, and looking straight into her eyes, repeated in a penetrating whisper: "Only you and I." But his touch had never been tenderer. Already she felt every fibre vibrating under it, as of old, only now with the more passionate eagerness bred of privation, and of the dull misery of her marriage. She let herself sink backward among the pillows, and already Mr. Palmato was on his knees at her side, his face close to hers. Again her burning lips were parted by his tongue, and she felt it insinuate itself between her teeth, and plunge into the depths of her mouth in a long searching caress, while at the same moment his hands softly parted the thin folds of her wrapper.

One by one they gained her bosom, and she felt her two breasts pointing up to them, the nipples as hard as coral, but sensitive as lips to his approaching touch. And now his warm palms were holding each breast as in a cup, clasping it, modelling it, softly kneading it, as he whispered to her, "like the bread of the angels."

An instant more, and his tongue had left her fainting mouth, and was twisting like a soft pink snake about each breast in turn, passing from one to the other till his lips closed hard on the nipples, sucking them with a tender gluttony.

Then suddenly he drew back her wrapper entirely, whispered: "I want you all, so that my eyes can see all that my lips can't cover," and in a moment she was free, lying before him in her fresh young nakedness, and feeling that indeed his eyes were covering it with fiery kisses. But Mr. Palmato was never idle, and while this sensation flashed through her one of his arms had slipped under her back and wound itself around her so that his hand again enclosed her left breast. At the same moment the other hand softly separated her legs, and began to slip up the old path it had so often travelled in darkness. But now it was light, she was uncovered, and looking downward, beyond his dark silver-sprinkled head, she could see her own parted knees and outstretched ankles and feet. Suddenly she remembered Austin's rough advances, and shuddered.

The mounting hand paused, the dark head was instantly raised. "What is it, my own?"

"I was—remembering—last week—" she faltered, below her breath.

"Yes, darling. That experience is a cruel one—but it has to come once in all women's lives. Now we shall reap its fruit."

But she hardly heard him, for the old swooning sweetness was creeping over her. As his hand stole higher she felt the secret bud of her body swelling, yearning, quivering hotly to burst into bloom. Ah, here was his subtle fore-finger pressing it, forcing its tight petals softly apart, and laying on their sensitive edges a circular touch so soft and yet so fiery that already lightnings of heat shot from that palpitating centre all over her surrendered body, to the tips of her fingers, and the ends of her loosened hair.

The sensation was so exquisite that she could have asked to have it indefinitely prolonged; but suddenly his head bent lower, and with a deeper thrill she felt his lips pressed upon that quivering invisible bud, and then the delicate firm thrust of his tongue, so full and yet so infinitely subtle, pressing apart the close petals, and forcing itself in deeper and deeper through the passage that glowed and seemed to become illuminated at its approach . . .

"Ah—" she gasped, pressing her hands against her sharp nipples, and flinging her legs apart.

Instantly one of her hands was caught, and while Mr. Palmato, rising, bent over her, his lips on hers again, she felt his firm fingers pressing into her hand that strong fiery muscle that they used, in their old joke, to call his third hand.

"My little girl," he breathed, sinking down beside her, his muscular trunk bare, and the third hand quivering and thrusting upward between them, a drop of moisture pearling at its tip.

She instantly understood the reminder that his words conveyed, letting herself downward along the divan till her head was in a line with his middle she flung herself upon the swelling member, and began to caress it insinuatingly with her tongue. It was the first time she had ever seen it actually exposed to her eyes, and her heart swelled excitedly: to have her touch confirmed by sight enriched the sensation that was communicating itself through her ardent twisting tongue. With panting breath she wound her caress deeper and deeper into the thick firm folds, till at length the member, thrusting her lips open, held her gasping, as if at its mercy; then, in a trice, it was withdrawn, her knees were pressed apart, and she saw it before her, above her, like a crimson flash, and at last, sinking backward into new abysses of bliss, felt it descend on her, press open the secret gates, and plunge into the deepest depths of her thirsting body . . .

"Was it . . . like this . . . last week?" he whispered.

Major Sources and Acknowledgments

I. Major Collections of Edith Wharton Papers

Code letters for these collections are given in parentheses. Particulars of individual correspondences may be found in II, following.

Beinecke Library, Yale University *(BL)*

Here there may be as many as 50,000 items relating to Edith Wharton. Partly out of her gratitude to Yale for awarding her an honorary degree in 1923, and because of her growing association with the university, Edith Wharton asked Gaillard Lapsley, who was to be her literary executor, to offer her "literary correspondence" to Yale.

When Lapsley delivered the documents in the summer of 1938, they consisted primarily of letters *to* Mrs. Wharton—"incoming mail." Some 162 letters from Henry James, between 1900 and 1914, comprise the most important element. To the incoming mail over the years were added letters *from* Edith Wharton, contributed by the recipients or their heirs—letters, in particular, to Gaillard Lapsley, Sara Norton, Mary Cadwalader Jones, Margaret Terry Chanler, and John Hugh Smith.

The original donation also included among other valuable materials: diaries for 1905, 1906 and 1924–34; an early *"donnee* book" (notes for stories and novels); notebooks and account books; literary contracts. There are well over 100 manuscripts of uncompleted stories and novels, some not more than a page in length, others running to 75 pages. Twelve boxes (upwards of 50 thick folders) of business correspondence, mostly with Appleton & Company from 1919 onward, help swell the total number of items in the Beinecke archives.

My debt to Donald Gallup, curator of American archives, and to the staff of the Beinecke Library is an enormous one. All have been unfailingly helpful, considerate, and efficient.

William Royall Tyler Collection, Dumbarton Oaks, Washington, D.C. *(WRT)*

Upon Edith Wharton's death Elisina Tyler, as her residuary legatee, inherited a great many letters and papers, as well as real estate and personal belongings. The Wharton papers eventually descended to Mrs. Tyler's son, now director of the Center for the Study of Byzantine Art at Dumbarton Oaks.

The letters include almost 400 from Edith Wharton to members of the Tyler family. Among the voluminous incoming mail are 100 letters from Bernard Berenson.

Of inestimable value in this collection are the two overlapping diaries of 1908 and the "line-a-day" diaries from late 1920 to 1937. The European journal kept by George Frederic Jones in 1847–48 is also in *WRT*, as are piles of photographs, newspaper clippings, fan mail, recipes, stray poems, literary notebooks, and her "common place" book.

My gratitude to William and Bettine Tyler is recorded in VI, below.

Villa I Tatti, Settignano, Italy *(VT)*

In the former home of Bernard Berenson outside Florence (now the Harvard Center for the Study of Renaissance Art) are more than 600 letters from Edith Wharton to Bernard Berenson and Mary Berenson, from 1909 to 1937.

A meticulous inventory of the rich Berenson archives was compiled by Nicky Mariano and distributed by the Harvard University Press in 1965. The archives contain several thousand letters of value to the biographer of Edith Wharton, beyond those written by and to her. Most important are the letters between Bernard and Mary Berenson after Edith Wharton had come to know them. But there are also untold numbers of letters addressed to the Berensons by individuals who were friends of Mrs. Wharton's and who reported or commented on her.

To Professor Myron Gilmore, former director of I Tatti, and Mrs. Sheila White-head Gilmore; to Signora Fiorella Superbi and the library staff at I Tatti, I express enduring gratitude. Perhaps the happiest hours I spent in the preparation of this book were those in the library or on the terrace or strolling through the gardens of the Berenson villa—more than once, as may be imagined, feeling palpable presences about me.

Firestone Library, Princeton University *(FL)*

Here, included in the huge gift of literary correspondence by Charles Scribner to Princeton some years ago, are several thousand items between Edith Wharton and various members of the Scribners publishing firm and *Scribner's* magazine. They begin in 1891 and continue for more than forty years.

My gratitude is very large to Alexander Clark and the staff of Firestone for their most thoughtful cooperation.

Houghton Library, Harvard University *(HL)*

Houghton Library houses scores of letters from Edith Wharton to Sara Norton (beginning in 1901), Elizabeth Norton, Mrs. Corinne Roosevelt Robinson, and others. Even more valuable for my purposes are the innumerable letters from Henry James to various correspondents, among them Howard Sturgis, Gaillard Lapsley, William Morton Fullerton, and Mary Cadwalader Jones.

Quotations from the Henry James letters and one or two Edith Wharton letters in the Houghton Library are made with the permission of the Harvard College Library. I am most grateful to William Bond and Miss Carolyn Jakeman for courteous assistance over a number of years.

Percy Lubbock Memoirs *(PL)*

When Percy Lubbock began to write *Portrait of Edith Wharton* in the late 1930s, he solicited memoirs from some four dozen persons who had known her. Twenty-six of them responded: some with little sketches of two or three pages; some with recollections running to fifteen or twenty pages; Gaillard Lapsley with a forty-eight-page memoir.

Lubbock had these reminiscences bound in two volumes, with an additional folder containing notes and short letters. In his *Portrait* he made skillful but sparing use of the materials; the greater percentage was not drawn upon.

Marchesa Iris Origo, as the daughter of the former Lady Sybil Cutting and hence later the stepdaughter of Percy Lubbock, inherited this collection. In the spring of 1969 I called upon Marchesa Origo in her beautiful villa on the Via di Monte Savello in Rome, and after a long and fascinating conversation came away with literally a suitcase full of material. My gratitude for the Marchesa's act of generosity and for other help is expressed in II, below.

Louis Auchincloss Collection *(LA)*

As a fellow novelist of manners and as a devotee of the writings of Edith Wharton, Louis Auchincloss began collecting letters from Mrs. Wharton and letters relating to her soon after graduating from Yale. He now has six stout portfolios of papers, from 1893 onward. Many of these are to Walter and Eunice Maynard, the parents-in-law of Mr. Auchincloss's brother. But there are many others of value, including some to Mary Cadwalader Jones and to Mildred Bliss.

Louis Auchincloss's sizable contribution to this book is properly acknowledged in VI, below.

II. Individual Correspondences, Memoirs, Biographies

With a few exceptions, only actual correspondences are listed—that is, cases where at least two or three letters were written on both sides. Single letters of praise for some particular writing of Edith Wharton's, or some special achievement, or letters written in connection with an individual venture (*The Book of the Homeless*, for example) are mostly —though not entirely—excluded. Almost all letters of these several kinds cited or quoted in the text may be found in *BL*.

Aberconway, Lady (Christabel). Short, valuable memoir in *PL*.

Adams, Henry. *The Letters of Henry Adams*, edited in two volumes by Worthington Chauncey Ford (1930, 1938), will soon be replaced by the much more complete edition of Adams' correspondence edited by Charles R. Vandersee in collaboration with Ernest Samuels.

Thirty-seven letters (1909–15) from Adams to Berenson, with periodic reference to E.W., in *VT*. Ernest Samuels, in *Henry Adams: The Major Phase* (1964), has deftly traced the relationship with E.W.

Akins, Zoë. Two 1936 letters to E.W. in *WRT*. There are four letters from E.W., also in 1936, in the Huntington Library, San Marino, California; my thanks are due to Alan Jutz, Assistant Curator.

Allhusen, Dorothy. Thirty-nine letters from E.W. (1920–37) in *BL*.

Appleton and Company. Scattered letters from E.W. to Joseph A. Sears (1917–18) in *BL*. For later letters to Appleton, see Rutger B. Jewett.

Austin, Alfred. Twelve letters from E.W. (1903–15, some undated) in *FL*.

Bahlmann, Anna. Scattered through the correspondence between E.W. and the Scribners editors in *FL* are a number of letters in Anna Bahlmann's hand. Most of these were dictated and signed by E.W., but a few were written by Miss Bahlmann herself and contain personal comments.

Bell, Marion (Mrs. Gordon). Mrs. Bell's little memoir in *PL* is the source of several observations about The Mount and E.W.'s declared attitude toward her fictional characters.

Belmont, Mrs. Perry. There are 4 letters a from E.W. (1914–18) in the Columbia University Library. I am indebted to Kenneth A. Lohf, Librarian for Rare Books, for these letters, especially the one of December, 1918, about T. S. Eliot and others.

Berenson, Bernard. *VT* contains 447 letters (1909–37) from E.W. to Berenson and copies of 34 letters (1910–37) from Berenson to E.W. Of the 3,258 letters from B.B. to his wife at *VT*, several hundred after 1909 refer—sometimes at length—to E.W. Of the 155 letters from B.B. to Louis Gillet (1909–43) in the same archives, a number likewise speak of E.W., as do several of the 41 letters to Henry Adams (1907–16). There are 100 letters (1928–36) from B.B. to E.W. in *WRT;* 31 (1910–37) in *BL*. A few letters from B.B. to Elisina Tyler in *WRT*.

See also Bernard Berenson, *Sketch for a Self-Portrait* (1949) and *Sunset and Twilight* (1963); Nicky Mariano's admirable *Forty Years with Berenson* (1966); and Sylvia Sprigge's limited and unsatisfactory *Berenson* (1960). A full-scale life of Berenson, in two volumes, is being prepared by Ernest Samuels. Professor Samuels and Mrs. Jayne Samuels (see VI, below) are also the sources, in conversation, of much indispensable information about the Berensons and their associates.

Quotations from the Berensons' letters are made with the kind permission of Dr. Cecil Anrep, representative of the Berenson estate.

Berenson, Mary. There are 179 letters (1909–36) from E.W. in *VT*. Of 3,440 letters from M.B. to B.B. at *VT*, about 100 allude to E.W.

From M.B.'s diaries and letters to other persons in *VT*, Jayne Samuels thoughtfully extracted for me certain early scoffing references to E.W., and the report to Geoffrey Scott about E.W.'s behavior in New York in 1913.

Berry, Walter Van Rensselaer. Within days of Walter Berry's death in October 1927, Edith Wharton went around to his Paris apartment, retrieved all the available letters she had written Berry over the years, and apparently destroyed them all. (This is the only considerable instance of Edith Wharton making away with anything she had written.) Dr. Harrison Wood came into possession of one or two stray letters from E.W. to Berry and kindly made them available to me.

BL contains 95 letters from Berry to E.W. (1899–1904). William Royall Tyler turned up, among his parents' papers, half a dozen letters from Berry to E.W., including the 1923 reminiscence of the days together in Bar Harbor in 1883. The postcards to Henry James, co-signed by Berry, are in *BL*.

In *VT* are 65 letters (1910–26, many undated) from Berry to Bernard Berenson. Cards to Berry co-signed by E.W. and Henry James were found by Mary Pitlick in the University of Southern Illinois library in the Walter Berry archives. Some letters from Berry to Mrs. Bliss were lent me by Louis Auchincloss.

The Harvard Alumni archives contain several useful reports by Berry to his 1880 class secretary. See also Caresse Crosby's entertaining but error-ridden *The Passionate Years* (1953). Geoffrey Wolff's forthcoming life of Harry Crosby will set the record straight in a number of ways. The best account of Berry's relationship with Proust is in George D. Painter's *Marcel Proust: The Later Years* (1964). Berry's funeral is described in Janet Flanner's *Paris Was Yesterday* (1972), as well as in letters from E.W. and from various other persons to Elisina Tyler in *WRT*.

Bigelow, W. Sturgis. Two important letters to E.W. in *BL*. The Harvard Alumni archives contain a general account of Bigelow's career. For much further and more personal information, I am indebted to John W. Crowley's unpublished life of George Cabot Lodge. See also Mr. Crowley's "Eden off Nantucket: W. S. Bigelow and 'Tuckanuck,' " in *Essex Historical Collections*, Vol. 109, No. 1 (January 1973).

Binswanger, Dr. J. Six medical reports (June–July 1910) to E.W. about her husband in *BL*.

Blanche, Jacques Emile. Particularly valuable memoir of E.W. in *PL*. A good account of Blanche's personality and career in George D. Painter's *Marcel Proust* (1959 and 1964).

Bliss, Mildred and Robert. A number of letters from E.W. to Mildred Bliss (1913–28) in *LA*. A few letters from Mildred Bliss to E.W. in *BL*, filed under Gaillard Lapsley, to whom E.W. forwarded them. Letters from both Robert and Mildred Bliss to various persons in 1926 about the possible award of the Nobel Prize to Edith Wharton (see Nobel Letters).

On Mildred and Robert Bliss, see Walter Muir Whitehill, *Dumbarton Oaks* (1967). There are also glimpses of Mildred Bliss in Elisina Tyler's letters to Royall Tyler during the war, culled and sent on by William Royall Tyler.

Boccon-Gibbod, André. Memoir of E.W. in *PL*.

Bourget, Paul. Half a dozen letters to Henry James (1893–1911) in *HL* provide useful general information. The letter of May 30, 1899, recounts the northern Italian trip with the Whartons. One letter to E.W. in *WRT*.

Bourget's account of his visit to Newport in 1893 is in *Outre-Mer* (French and American editions, 1895).

The best brief memoir of Bourget is Edith Wharton's obituary article in French, "Bourget d'Outre-Mer," published in the *Revue hebdomadaire*, June 1936. The manuscript of the article is in *BL*. Albert Feuillerat's biography of Bourget (1937) is too congested to be usable.

Many interesting sidelights on Bourget during the war years are in letters from Berenson to his wife in *VT.*

Bromfield, Louis. A number of letters from E.W. (1932–36), mostly about gardening, in the Smith College library.

Brooke, Margaret, Ranee of Sarawak. See especially her second memoir, *Good Morning & Good Night* (1934). On her letters to Morton Fullerton, see Appendix B.

Brownell, William Crary. The correspondence between Brownell and E.W. is one of the major items in the Scribners archives in *FL.* The first extant letter from E.W. is dated August 26, 1893; that from Brownell, July 5, 1897.

Brownell presided over the publication of E.W.'s books from *The Decoration of Houses* (1897) through *Artemis to Actaeon* (1909). Most of the time thereafter, E.W. dealt directly with Charles Scribner. Almost all the letters from E.W. to Brownell from late 1908 onward—since they did not bear upon publishing matters—were donated by Brownell to his alma mater, Amherst College, to whose librarian I owe many thanks. They are the source of many of the literary opinions of E.W., cited in the text.

On Brownell's life, see *William Crary Brownell: An Anthology of His Writings, Together with Biographical Notes and Impressions of the Later Years*, by Gertrude Hall Brownell (1933). See also *Of Making Many Books*, by Roger Burlingame (1946). E.W.'s obituary article on Brownell appeared in the November 1928 issue of *Scribner's.*

Three letters from Brownell to E.W. (1909–13) in *BL.*

Buckler, William Hepburn. A charming letter in *PL* provides the glimpse of Edith Jones at the Patriarchs' Ball in the winter of 1883. A letter to Gaillard Lapsley in *LA* gives further information. A six-page memoir of E.W. to Buckler was kindly given to my associate Miss Mary Pitlick by Miss Charlotte Wrinch, Buckler's great-granddaughter. It describes the carriage drive from Rome to Siena and visits to The Mount and E.W.'s postwar French homes.

Burlingame, Edward L. Scores of letters to and from E.W. (mostly between 1889 and 1907) in *FL.* See also *Of Making Many Books*, by Roger Burlingame (1946).

Cameron, Elizabeth. About 75 letters from E.W. (1903–19) in the National Gallery, Washington, D.C.; courteously supplied by Jerome Edelstein, Librarian. There are 11 letters from Mrs. Cameron to Berenson (1919–36) in *VT*, and recurring glimpses of Mrs. Cameron in letters between Berenson and his wife.

On Elizabeth Cameron, see especially Ernest Samuels, *Henry Adams: The Middle Years* (1958) and *Henry Adams: The Major Phase* (1964).

Chanler, Margaret Terry. There are 97 letters from E.W. (1902–33) in *BL* and 4 letters from E.W. (1926–32) in *HL.* Several letters from Mrs. Chanler to Theodore Roosevelt are in the Library of Congress. Two short memoirs of E.W. in *DL.*

Mrs. Chanler's two volumes of memoirs, *Roman Spring* (1934) and *Autumn in the Valley* (1936), contain views of E.W. from her appearance at a Newport gathering in 1880 to the Aegean cruise in 1926.

Two of Mrs. Chanler's daughters have been especially helpful to me, both in conversation and in writing. Mrs. Hester Pickman provided fascinating reminiscences of her mother and E.W. and of the attitude of each of her parents toward E.W. She also, most kindly, gave me several volumes, published by Mrs. Chanler, of memoirs and letters. Mrs. Laura White had recollections in particular of E.W. during the prewar Paris days, and graciously gave me a memoir of E.W.'s niece, Beatrix Farrand, inscribed by Mildred Bliss.

Chanler, Winthrop. An important source is *Winthrop Chanler's Letters, Collected by His Wife* (1951), ed. by Margaret Terry Chanler (among the books given me by Mrs. Pickman). Chanler's letter about *The House of Mirth* was uncovered by Mary Pitlick among the Margaret Terry Chanler papers in *HL*.

Clark, Kenneth and Jane. About 120 letters and postcards from E.W. to Kenneth and Jane Clark (1931–36) are in the Clarks' possession, and very kindly lent to me by them. There are 7 letters from Kenneth Clark to E.W. (mid-1930s) in *WRT*, and 4 letters from Jane Clark to E.W. (1937) and 3 from Kenneth Clark (1936–37) in *BL*. A letter of 1938 from Kenneth Clark to Percy Lubbock, in *PL*, is revealing about E.W.'s late religious interests. Among the 150 letters from Clark to the Berensons (1928–59), some of the early ones refer to E.W.

I am immensely beholden to Lord and Lady Clark for several very rewarding visits, both in Saltwood Castle, Kent, and in London. Some of the wisest—as well as the most affectionate and admiring—insights into Edith Wharton's character and writings derived from these visits. In addition, the exceedingly hospitable Clarks supplied fresh perspectives on E.W.'s closest associates and were helpful in identifying some of her friends in the art world. They also passed on several amusing and revealing anecdotes. I count the hours with Kenneth and Jane Clark among the high points of the past seven years.

Cocteau, Jean. Francis Steegmuller's massive *Jean Cocteau* (1970) is the best and most useful of several biographies, and offers excellent sketches of Anna de Noailles and other figures on the Paris scene from about 1910 to 1930.

Codman, Ogden. A large collection of letters from Codman to members of his family (1920s and later) was made available by the Atheneum in Boston to Mary Pitlick, through the kindness of David McKibbin, the curator. Many of these reminisce about E.W. Miss Pitlick also taped a long and informative conversation with Mr. McKibbin, touching on the Ralph Curtises, E.W.'s alleged illegitimacy, and other matters.

Colefax, Lady Sybil. Almost 400 letters to Bernard Berenson (1918–50) in *VT*. A number of these delightful if not always decipherable letters (which were examined for me by Nancy L. Lewis) give news of E.W.

On Lady Colefax, see Harold Acton, *More Memoirs of an Aesthete* (1972).

Conrad, Joseph. Two letters to E.W. (1913, 1917) in *BL*.

Cortissoz, Royal. There are 24 letters from E.W. (1915–37) in *BL*. Royal Cortissoz, for many years the highly conservative art critic of the New York *Herald Tribune*. This correspondence adds curiously little to our knowledge of E.W. Two letters to E.W. in *WRT* about the death of Walter Berry.

Cossé-Brissac, Comtesse Charlotte de. There are 105 letters to Berenson (1909–52) in *VT*. Many of these, especially during the war, speak of E.W.

Crawshay, Mary. There are 98 letters to Berenson (1904–30) in *VT*. Several refer to E.W., and a few were written from Ste. Claire.

Crosby, Caresse. On her memoir *The Passionate Years* (1953), see comment under Walter Berry, above.

Curtis, Ralph. Of 386 letters to Berenson in *VT* (1909–22), nearly 50 talk about E.W. and her work.

Cutting, Bayard Jr. See Iris Origo, *Images and Shadows* (1970). Marchesa Origo thoughtfully provided me with the full text of E.W.'s memoir of Cutting quoted in Chapter Three of that book.

Cutting, Lady Sybil. See Lubbock, Lady Sybil.

Deacon, Gladys (Duchess of Marlborough). There are 25 entertaining letters to Berenson (undated, but apparently around 1900) in *VT*.

Du Bos, Charles. Indispensable memoir of E.W. in *PL*, reproduced with some deletions in Percy Lubbock's *Portrait of Edith Wharton*. In *VT*: 27 letters from du Bos to Berenson (1909–36) and 29 from Berenson to du Bos (1906–33), some of which make reference to E.W.

Du Bos, Zezette. *VT* contains 50 letters to Berenson (1929–52), with references to E.W. in some of the earlier of these. Mme. du Bos kindly shared with me her recollections of E.W. and Walter Berry during a conversation in her Paris home in 1967.

Farrand, Beatrix Jones. There are 98 letters from E.W. (1930–37) in *BL*. One letter from E.W. (1935) and several from Mrs. Farrand to E.W. in *WRT*. One important letter from E.W. in *LA*. Two letters to Elisina Tyler (1937) and one letter to Wayne Andrews (protesting his account of her aunt in his introduction to *Selected Short Stories of Edith Wharton* in 1958) in *WRT*.

See also *Beatrix Jones Farrand: An Appreciation of a Great Landscape Gardener*, compiled by Mildred Bliss (privately printed, 1960).

Farrand, Max. There are 22 letters from E.W. (1914–37) in *BL*.

Fitch, Clyde. There is one letter (1907) in *BL*.

Fitzgerald, F. Scott. The June 1920 letter from E.W. is quoted in Andrew Turnbull, *Scott Fitzgerald* (1962). Turnbull is also the most dependable source for the meeting between Fitzgerald and E.W. and for Fitzgerald's reaction to *The Mother's Recompense*. It was Professor Matthew Bruccoli who informed me about Fitzgerald's involvement with the screen version of *The Glimpses of the Moon*.

Forest-Divonne, Comtesse Philomène de la. Beautifully written memoir of E.W. in *PL*, and a tender obituary notice of E.W. in *WRT*. The 117 letters to Bernard Berenson (1921–37) and the 8 letters to Mary Berenson (mostly undated) in *VT* comprise a key source of information about E.W. from 1921 until her death.

This gracious and zestful person invited my wife and me to call upon her and her family in their Neuilly home on two occasions in 1973. (The comtesse had previously given a productive interview to Miss Marion Mainwaring.) Present on both occasions were the comtesse's courtly husband, Conte Jules de la Forest-Divonne, and their daughter and granddaughter. The visits provided a range of information about E.W. and about her relations with her friends. I retain a deep personal and familial gratitude, and a sizable biographical debt.

Fullerton, Katharine (Mrs. Gordon Gerould). See Appendix B.

Fullerton, W. Morton. See Appendix B.

Gardner, Isabella Stewart. See *Mrs. Jack* (1965), by Louise Hall Tharp. Mrs. Tharp was kind enough to give me additional information about Isabella Gardner.

Garland, Hamlin. There are 9 letters (1906 and 1919–24) in the University of Southern California Library.

Gay, Matilda and Walter. Much of my information about the Gays came from William R. Tyler, who supplied full personal portraits. The August 4, 1937, letter from E.W. to Matilda Gay is in *WRT.*

Gerhardi (later Gerhardie), William. About 20 letters from E.W. (1921–30) are in the University of Texas library, and 21 letters from Gerhardi to E.W. (1922–31) in *WRT.*

   Gerhardi's *Memoirs of a Polyglot* (1931) describes his arrival at Ste. Claire in 1922. "William Gerhardie," in Michael Holroyd's *Unreceived Opinions* (1974), is an excellent survey of the writer's life and work.

Gide, André. Fifteen letters from E.W. (1915–23) are in the Bibliothèque Doucet at the Sorbonne. I am indebted to Professor Jacques Cotman, a Gide expert at York University, Ontario, who transcribed these letters and passed them along to my associate Miss Mainwaring. One letter from Gide (March 1916), in *BL*, speaks of Proust and the translation of *The Custom of the Country*. See also Gide's *Journals, 1914–1927*, Vol. II (1948).

Gilder, Robert W. There are 6 letters from E. W. (1906–09) in *BL.*

Gillet, Louis. There are 59 letters from E.W. (1923–36) in *BL*. *VT* contains 181 letters from Gillet to Berenson (1903–43); many of these in the 1920s and later refer to E.W.

   Gillet wrote an attractive obituary article on E.W. for *Figaro* in August 1937.

Goschen, Vivienne. Her fine memoir in *PL* is a main source for my description of a characteristic visit to the Pavillon Colombe.

Gosse, Edmond. There are 2 letters from E.W. (1916) and 3 letters to her in *BL*. One letter from E.W. to Gosse (June 1916, about the Henry James letters) is filed under Gaillard Lapsley in *BL.*

Grant, Robert. There are 47 letters from E.W. (1900–36) and 3 letters from Grant to E.W. (1907–13) in *BL*. *HL* contains 7 letters from E.W. Grant's 15-page memoir of E.W. in *PL* is especially valuable.

Hiltman, D. W. His letter of July 1934 about E.W.'s total earnings from Appleton and Company is in *BL.*

Howells, William Dean. There are 4 letters to E.W. (1900–19) in *BL.*

   Kenneth S. Lynn's *William Dean Howells: An American Life* (1971) gives a full-scale account of Howells' life up to about 1900.

Huxley, Aldous. A few rather trifling letters to E.W. (early 1930s) in *WRT.* Sybille Bedford's fine biography, *Aldous Huxley* (1974) provided valuable information and anecdotes.

James, Henry. There are 162 letters to E.W. (1900–15) in *BL* and 12 letters from E.W. to James (1908–15).

In *HL:* 77 letters to Morton Fullerton (1890–1902); 142 letters to Howard Sturgis (1905–11); 77 letters to Gaillard Lapsley (1897–1913); 30 letters to Mary Cadwalader Jones (1902–15); and pocket diaries (1909–15).

In *FL:* 12 letters to Morton Fullerton (1899–1907), the last six dealing with Fullerton's harassment by his landlady, and 3 letters to Katharine Fullerton (1905–08).

In the British Museum are 2 letters to Frederick Macmillan (1909) about the proposed "secret" advance to Fullerton.

Sixteen letters to Walter Berry (1905–11), were published by the Black Sun Press (1928).

Leon Edel's multivolume *Henry James* (1953–72) is incomparably the richest source for James's life and career, and one of the most distinguished literary biographies of our time. Volume V, 1901–1916, was especially valuable for me. Quotations from James's letters other than those listed above are taken, gratefully, from this volume.

Millicent Bell's *Edith Wharton and Henry James: The Story of Their Friendship* (1965) provides a suggestive account of its subject, though it is inevitably marred in a few places because of the unavailability of certain materials. I am also grateful to Mrs. Bell for providing other information and suggesting leads.

H. Montgomery Hyde's *Henry James at Home* (1969) is a beguiling portrait. In the winter of 1970, Mr. Hyde was good enough to escort me to Lamb House, a National Trust property then occupied by the hospitable Rumor Godden and her husband.

The pages on James in Edith Wharton's *A Backward Glance* offer perhaps the best brief sketch of Henry James the man.

James, Margaret. Copy of a letter from E.W. (June 1916) filed under Gaillard Lapsley in *BL.*

James, William. Two letters (1911) to E.W. in *BL.* Gay Wilson Allen's *William James* (1967) is the definitive biography, and the source for James's 1910 visit to E.W.

Jewett, Rutger B. About 350 letters between Jewett and E.W. (1917–34) in *BL.*

Johnson, Robert Underwood. Thirteen letters from E.W. (1900–11) in *BL.*

Jones, Edward (E.W.'s uncle). There are vivid periodic glimpses of Edward Jones in the four volumes of George Templeton Strong's diaries (1952).

Jones, George Frederic. His diary of the European tour in 1847–48 is in *WRT.* A letter of 1856 to Daniel Webster, applying for a passport, is in the Library of Congress. There are occasional references to George Frederic Jones in George Templeton Strong's diaries.

Jones, Lucretia Rhinelander. The 1882 letter from Lucretia Jones to her brother Frederic Rhinelander, about Edith's engagement, was kindly lent me by the late Frederic R. King.

Jones, Mary Cadwalader. *BL* contains 270 letters from E.W. (1903–37); there are obviously a great many missing from the period 1904–14. Two letters from E.W. (1914, 1921) in *LA*. One letter (1904) to Theodore Roosevelt in the Library of Congress.

Mrs. Jones's *Lantern Slides* (1937) gives the story of her life up to her marriage to Frederic R. Jones in 1870.

Kinnicutt, Francis L. Eight letters to E.W. (1909–12) in *BL*. I am most grateful to Mrs. Henry Parish II for much information about Dr. Kinnicutt and his family.

Kipling, Rudyard. Two letters (1923) to E.W. in *BL*.

Lapsley, Gaillard. There are 363 letters from E.W. (1904–37) in *BL*. Lapsley's long memoir of E.W. in *PL* is in some ways the most valuable item in that collection. Forty letters from Lapsley to Bernard and Mary Berenson (1931–46) in *VI.* contain numerous references to E.W., even some years after her death.

Millicent Bell, in *Edith Wharton and Henry James* (1965), traces Lapsley's early career. Professor William Dunham of Yale gave me a helpful appraisal of Lapsley's reputation as a medieval scholar.

Lee, Vernon (Violet Paget). Four letters from Vernon Lee to E.W. (1928–37) are in *WRT*. There are 2 interesting letters (1903 and 1907) from E.W. in the Colby College Library; I owe thanks to the librarian, Richard Cary. In *VT* there are 23 letters from Vernon Lee to Bernard and Mary Berenson (1894–1929); several in the late 1920s refer to E.W.

Peter Gunn's *Vernon Lee* (1964) is the fullest account of her life. Other interesting information was kindly given me by Signora Flavia Farinacini, at one time a friend and neighbor of Vernon Lee's.

Lewis, Grace Hegger. Four letters from E.W. (1926–32) in University of Texas library.

Lewis, Rosa. Her memoir *The Queen of Cooks—and Some Kings* (1925) was "recorded" by Mary Lawton.

Lewis, Sinclair. Two long letters from E.W. (1920, 1922) are quoted in their entirety by Mark Schorer in *Sinclair Lewis* (1963). Schorer's definitive biography is the source for my brief tracing of Lewis' career. There is one especially interesting letter from Lewis to E.W. (1930) in *WRT*, giving his opinion of his American literary contemporaries. On Faulkner: "Mostly, I don't know what he is talking about. . . . I too am becoming a conservative."

Lodge, Elizabeth Davis. See following item.

Lodge, George Cabot ("Bay"). Ten letters from E.W. to Bay and Elizabeth Lodge (1902–11) are in the possession of his son, former Ambassador Henry Cabot Lodge, who kindly allowed my associate Miss Pitlick to make copies of them. Two letters from E.W. (1907–08) are in the Massachusetts Historical Society (one alluding to Walter Berry's unseemly behavior on a transatlantic crossing).

During a long conversation in the American Embassy in Paris in the winter of 1969, Ambassador Lodge gave me much valuable information about his father and about Sturgis Bigelow and others.

Henry Adams' *The Life of George Cabot Lodge* (1911) has been superseded—

biographically, if not stylistically—by John N. Crowley's unpublished biography, to which I am much indebted.

Lodge, Henry Cabot (the elder). Two letters (1909, 1910) to E.W. in *BL*.

Lodge, Henry Cabot (the younger). Ambassador Lodge's autobiography, *The Storm Has Many Eyes* (1973), is a main source for his visits to Ste. Claire.

Lubbock, Percy. Two letters to E.W. (1925, 1933) in *BL* and 260 letters to Gaillard Lapsley (1908–34), the latter carefully examined for me by Miss Kathy Wirkus. The letter to E.W. in November 1933, pleading for a reconciliation, is in *WRT*. Lubbock's diaries for 1919–25 and a few letters to the then Lady Sybil Scott were made available to me by Georgette Lubbock (Percy's niece by marriage). There are 16 letters to Bernard and Mary Berenson (1920–49) in *VT* and 2 letters to Lapsley after E.W.'s death in *LA*. Other letters to Lapsley, about Lubbock's *Portrait of Edith Wharton*, were retrieved by Louis Auchincloss from the Appleton archives.

On Lubbock's *Portrait*, see Preface and pp. 515–16.

Lubbock, Lady Sybil. Lady Sybil's memoir of visits with E.W. in New York, Florence, and Salsomaggiore is in *PL*. There are 99 letters to Bernard and Mary Berenson (1909–40) in *VT*, a number of which make passing reference to E.W. See also the autobiography of Lady Sybil's daughter Iris Origo, *Images and Shadows* (1970).

Lyautey, General Herbert. E.W. devoted a section of *In Morocco* (1920) to the life and achievements of General Lyautey. André Maurois' *Lyautey* (1931) is the standard biography.

McAllister, Ward. His *Society as I Have Found It* (1890) contains a partial listing of the original "400."

MacCarthy, Sir Desmond. One letter to E.W. (1931) in *WRT*. Among 5 letters to Mary Berenson (1932–39) in *VT*, that of July 11, 1932, gives MacCarthy's reaction to the style of life and conversation at Ste. Claire.

The posthumous collection of literary essays and articles by MacCarthy called *Memories* (1953) has two brief but telling sketches of him by Raymond Mortimer and Cyril Connolly. MacCarthy also figures prominently in Quentin Bell's *Virginia Woolf* (1972).

Maclagan, Eric. There are numerous interesting references to E.W. among the 76 letters from Maclagan to Bernard and Mary Berenson (1910–50) in *VT*. There is one letter to E.W. (1932) in *WRT*.

A detailed memoir of Eric Maclagan was given me by his son Michael, who had drawn it up. He also put at my disposal his father's diary during the Paris peace conference in 1919.

I owe a special debt of gratitude to Michael Maclagan, professor of Byzantine history at Trinity College, Oxford. He is a sort of walking *Burke's Peerage*, with an encyclopedic knowledge as well of persons unmentioned in that compilation. I enjoyed two visits, in 1973, to the Maclagans' hospitable home in Oxford, arriving the second time with some three dozen queries in my notebook. Most of these Michael Maclagan answered out of his head. He provided me with thumbnail sketches of two score individuals, including a number of Edwardian figures, drew up genealogical charts, lent me source books to peruse, and added numerous other bits of information. This learned and courteous man was especially helpful about his father's close friends John Hugh Smith, Royall Tyler, and Alfred St. André.

Macmillan, Sir Frederick. There are 30 letters from E.W. (1905–28) in *BL;* also statements of financial earnings (1907–25) and signed contracts for E.W.'s books from *The House of Mirth* through *In Morocco.*

The Macmillan archives in the British Museum contain 200 letters from and to E.W. (1901–1930), including those about the commissioning of Morton Fullerton to write a book on Paris.

Simon Nowell-Smith, who was largely responsible for preserving the Macmillan archives intact and for cataloging them, has provided a sampling of these rich materials in *Letters to Macmillan* (1967; I owe thanks to Arthur Crook for my copy). In the winter of 1970 I spent a pleasurable and informative evening with Mr. Nowell-Smith discussing various literary friends of Edith Wharton and Henry James.

Marbury, Elizabeth. Her memoir *My Crystal Ball* (1923) contains some interesting references to E.W.

Margeries, Jeanne de. Six letters from E.W. (1918–25) were kindly lent me by Roland de Margeries via Marion Mainwaring.

Mariano, Nicky. Among the 450 letters to Bernard and Mary Berenson (1922–52) in *VT*, a goodly number speak of E.W., with accounts of visits to Ste. Claire and exploring the cathedrals of Rome with E.W. *VT* contains 6 letters from E.W. to Nicky Mariano, but there are no extant letters from Miss Mariano to E.W.

Nicky Mariano's *Forty Years with Berenson* (1966) offers a picture of E.W. that, according to Kenneth Clark in the Foreword, is "of more value to future historians of American literature than many doctoral theses."

Marsh, Sir Edward. Christopher Vernon Hassal's *A Biography of Edward Marsh* (1959) is the indispensable source for Marsh, and a valuable guide to a number of Edwardian and Georgian figures. It also contains an attractive little passage about E.W.

Maynard, Walter and Eunice (Ives). There are 36 letters from E.W. (c. 1901–33) in *LA*. Mr. Auchincloss has had this informative collection printed privately, with helpful explanatory comment by himself. The volume also contains Eunice Maynard's brief memoir of E.W., the original of which is in *PL*.

Mitchell, Dr. S. Weir. Two letters from E.W. (1902, 1905) in *BL* and one letter (1905) from Mitchell to E.W. in praise of *The House of Mirth.*

On Dr. Mitchell's career and his invention of the rest cure, Mary Pitlick put together a folder of materials, including: Dr. Mitchell's *Lectures on Diseases of the Nervous System, Especially in Women* (1885) and *Doctor and Patient* (1888); *S. Weir Mitchell, Novelist and Physician,* by E. P. Earnest (1950); and *S. Weir Mitchell, M.D., Neurologist: A Medical Biography,* by Richard D. Walter, M.D. (1970).

Mugnier, Abbé Arthur. Four letters to E.W. (1932–36) in *WRT*, and 36 letters to Bernard Berenson (1919–39) in *VT*, some of which allude to E.W.

A good account of Abbé Mugnier is given by George D. Painter in *Marcel Proust: The Later Years* (1964). Further sidelights were provided by Lord Clark.

Nicholson, Molly (Mrs. Reginald). Mrs. Nicholson's memoir of E.W. in *PL* has some choice remarks about E.W.'s way with people she did not like. Of 35 letters to Berenson (1937–58) in *VT*, only the first refers to E.W.

Noailles, Comtesse Anna de. One letter to E.W. (1916), congratulating her on the Legion d'Honneur award, in *BL*.

Excellent portraits of Anna de Noailles are found in Francis Steegmuller, *Jean Cocteau* (1970), and George D. Painter, *Marcel Proust: The Early Years* (1959). See also *Anna de Noailles*, by Louis Perche, in the *Poètes d'aujourd'hui* series (1964).

Noailles, Vicomte Charles de. In February 1973 my wife and I spent an unforgettable day with the Vicomte de Noailles. It began with an elegant lunch in his Paris apartment in the Place des Etats-Unis and continued with a drive down to Fontainebleau and a visit to the Hôtel Pompidour, one of the vicomte's country homes. As it happens, Edith Wharton's brother Harry Jones had occupied in turn both the Paris and Fontainebleau residences.

In the course of six hours of conversation with the wise, witty, and courtly Vicomte de Noailles—and in the wake of a long interview with him by Marion Mainwaring— we covered a great deal of territory, including the passion for gardening that the vicomte shared with Mrs. Wharton.

In the Hôtel Pompidour he pointed out (not with much pleasure) the montage that had been put together by Cocteau and attributed, as a work of genius, to Picasso in order to play a hoax on Bernard Berenson.

Nobel Prize letters. All the materials relating to the 1926–27 effort to win the prize for E.W. were supplied by Louis Auchincloss.

Norton, Charles Eliot. There are 18 letters from E.W. (1901–08) in *HL*. One letter to E.W. (1907) in *BL*, and one letter to E.W. (1901) in *WRT*. Part of another letter (1902) to E.W., copied by Sara Norton, is among the letters from Miss Norton to E.W. in *BL*.

Kermit Vanderbilt's *Charles Eliot Norton* (1957) is the standard biography, though it contains a number of lacunae. *The Letters of Charles Eliot Norton*, edited by Sara Norton (1913), while otherwise engrossing, has little of relevance for my enterprise.

Norton, Elizabeth Gaskell (Lily). There are 95 letters from E.W. (c. 1901–22) in *HL*, and a not altogether sympathetic memoir of E.W. in *PL*.

Norton, Robert. Norton's 25-page memoir in *PL* is one of the most valuable documents for E.W.'s biographer.

The letter from Norton to Lapsley (1929) about E.W.'s physical collapse is also in *BL*, among the Lapsley papers. There are 8 letters to Berenson (mid-1930s, mostly undated) in *VT*, and 3 letters to Lapsley, after E.W.'s death, in *LA*.

Norton, Sara. There are 217 letters from E.W. (1899–1922) in *BL* and 2 letters to E.W.

(1902, 1913). *HL* contains 19 letters from E.W. (1900–14). Several letters from E.W. (1902–03) were most kindly lent me by Marchesa Iris Origo.

Miss Norton's touching, illuminating "Notes About E.W.'s Early Life: Things She Has Told Me" is in *BL*.

Origo, Iris. One letter to Louis Auchincloss (1965) about E.W., in *LA*. One letter from E.W. (1936) supplied by Marchesa Origo. Her *Images and Shadows* (1970) contains a number of fine insights into E.W.

My gratitude to Marchesa Origo for several kinds of help, and for exquisite hospitality, over the past six years is boundless. She not only turned over to me the entire collection listed here as *PL*, along with 39 letters from E.W. to various persons, but she also brought her wisdom and experience to bear on a number of questions concerning E.W., including her relations with Walter Berry. Coming to know Marchesa Origo and her remarkably charming husband Marchese Antonio Origo has been one of the finest rewards of this work.

Perry, Bliss. Five letters from E.W. (1905–07) in *HL*. One letter from E.W. (1906), about Walt Whitman, in the Overbury Collection at Barnard College; for this letter, my thanks are due to Mrs. Patricia K. Ballou, curator of the collection.

Placci, Carlo. About 15 letters from E.W. (1913–30) are in the Biblioteca Nazionale in Florence, discovered and copied by Mary Pitlick.

Proust, Marcel. I have depended largely on George D. Painter's masterful two volumes: *Marcel Proust: The Early Years* (1959) and *Marcel Proust: The Later Years* (1964). In *A Backward Glance*, Edith Wharton devotes several perceptive pages to Proust, and in *The Writing of Fiction* a chapter to him.

In 1970 and again in 1973, I had the privilege of long conversations with George Painter, at his desk in the British Museum. Mr. Painter is as knowledgeable about Paris during *la belle époque* as Michael Maclagan (see above) is of Edwardian England. We went through a large list of characters, mostly members of the Faubourg nobility, who used to call on E.W. regularly, and Mr. Painter identified and commented on each of them almost without hesitation.

Mr. Painter also gave me of his wisdom about the literary life, and the role not only played by but assigned to literary artists within their society.

Rhinelander, Newbold ("Bo"). Copies of Bo Rhinelander's last letters to his family in September 1918 and of two letters from a fellow airman to Tom Rhinelander were given me by Louis Auchincloss.

Rhinelander, Tom. There are 10 letters from E.W. (1916–28) in *LA*, and one letter to E.W. in *WRT*.

Richardson, William K. Interesting, anecdotal memoir of E.W. in *PL*.

Robinson, Corinne Roosevelt. There are 23 letters from E.W. (1904–31) in *HL*.

Roosevelt, Theodore. Three letters to E.W. (1911–15) in *BL*. Three letters to E.W. (1897–1915) and 4 from E.W. (1911–15) in the Library of Congress, transcribed by Mary Pitlick. One letter to and one from Walter Berry (1915), also in the Library of Congress.

Rutherford, Louisa ("Poodle"), and family. Mary Pitlick transcribed a batch of letters from Louisa Rutherford to her sister Margaret and other family letters (the 1880s) in the Library of Congress. George Templeton Strong's diaries contain a good portrait of Professor Lewis Rutherford over a number of years.

St. Helier, Lady (Mary Jeune). Her *Memories of Fifty Years* (1909) gives a charming, rambling account of her life up to about 1900. I am indebted to Professor Richard Purdy of Yale for much other information about Lady St. Helier and her family.

Sargent, John Singer. Four letters to E.W. (1912 and 1915) in *BL*.

Scott, Geoffrey. Though Scott was an important figure in E.W.'s life from 1911 until his death in 1929, the only relevant extant first-hand documents are one letter to E.W. (1916) in *WRT* and two letters to Berenson (1911, and undated) in *VT*.

Nicky Mariano's *Forty Years with Berenson* (1966) offers a useful, if discreet, picture of Scott. Nigel Nicolson, in *Portrait of a Marriage* (1973), was the first to disclose Scott's short-lived affair with Vita Sackville-West. Scott, surprisingly, seems never to have appeared in any British reference book.

It is to Professor Frederick W. Hilles of Yale that I owe the larger part of my knowledge of Scott (apart from references to him in letters from E.W. and Berenson). Professor Hilles put together a massive folder of documents relating to the discovery and publication of the Boswell papers, and these included a helpful account of Scott as their first editor. Among these documents were: Frederick A. Pottle's "The History of the Boswell Papers," which served as the Introduction to *Boswell's London Journal* (1951), and Christopher Morley's Preface in the same volume. Even more valuable for my purposes was a 25-page section on Scott from a then unpublished full-scale history of the Boswell papers by David Buchanan, a young Scottish lawyer. My thanks are due to Mr. Buchanan as well as to my old friend and chairman, Professor Hilles.

Scribner, Charles. There are many hundreds of letters between Charles Scribner and E.W. (1905–35) in *FL*, and a few letters to E.W. (1905–13) in *BL*, including the one of April 1913 about the secret gift to Henry James. See also *Of Making Many Books*, by Roger Burlingame (1946).

My great gratitude to the present Scribners staff is recorded in VI below.

Sheldon, Edward. Six letters to E.W. (1933–36) were provided by William Royall Tyler. See also the life of Sheldon, *The Man Who Lived Twice*, by Eric Wollencott Barnes (1954).

Simmons, Ronald. There are 2 letters (1918) to E.W. in *BL*. A short, factual sketch of Simmons is found in George Henry Nettleton's *Yale in the World War* (1925).

Sinclair, Upton. A copy of the 1927 letter from E.W. about the banning of Sinclair's novel is in *WRT*.

Smith, A. John Hugh. Two letters to E.W. (1908) and 142 letters from E.W. (1908–37) are in *BL*. A few letters from Hugh Smith to Percy Lubbock, after E.W.'s death, were passed along by Louis Auchincloss.

Hugh Smith's illuminating little memoir of E.W., in *PL*, is the source, among other matters, of the "Bective" anecdote in Chapter Thirteen.

Smith, Logan Pearsall. Three letters to E.W. (1926–33) in *WRT*, and 6 letters—for me, not important—to the Berensons (1908–28) in *VT*.

Pearsall Smith's memoirs, *Unforgotten Years* (1938), open with amiable allusions to E.W. as his hostess aboard the *Osprey*. Desmond MacCarthy's sketch of Pearsall Smith in *Memoirs* (1953) is useful, and there is further information in Nicky Mariano's *Forty Years with Berenson* (1966).

Stevens, Ebenezer. A copy of the letter from Lafayette to E.W.'s "great progenitor" in *WRT* (the original was given by Mrs. Frederica Rhinelander Landon to the New-York Historical Society), with letters from James Madison and others. Also in *WRT* is a biographical sketch of Stevens by his son John Austin Stevens.

Stevens, Henry Leyden. Apart from the letters of Louisa Rutherford, most of the information about E.W.'s one-time fiancé comes from *Town Topics*, newspaper articles, letters from Emelyn Washburn to Elisina Tyler, and the family lore mentioned below.

Stevens, Mrs. Paran. There is a good deal about Mrs. Stevens in the social histories of Dixon Wecheter, Cleveland Amory, and others (see IV, below). More is provided by stories in *The New York Times* and the obituaries in the *Times* and the New York *Herald*. Dr. Harrison Wood, who was in touch with a descendant of Mrs. Stevens, added further bits of family lore.

Strong, George Templeton. His diaries, 1835–75, edited in four volumes by Allan Nevins (1952), are a magnificent source for New York society during the years covered, and the finest example of the art of diary writing in American literary history.

Sturgis, Howard. Twelve letters to E.W. (1904–17) in *BL*. One important letter of 1905 to E.W., in praise of *The House of Mirth*, in *WRT*. An attractive sketch of Howard Sturgis is in Percy Lubbock's *Mary Cholmondely* (1928). E.W.'s *A Backward Glance* contains the fullest portrait.

Taillandier, Madeleine Saint-René. Her 20-page memoir of E.W., partly reverential and partly questioning, is among the most valuable entries in *PL*.

Trevelyan, Sir George Otto. Three letters to E.W. (1912–23) in *BL*.

Tyler, Elisina Royall. About 375 letters from E.W. to Mrs. Tyler (1913–36) are in *WRT*. Also in *WRT*: letters to Mrs. Tyler (mostly in 1938; see Appendix A) about E.W.'s alleged illegitimacy; Mrs. Tyler's own notations on this matter; Mrs. Tyler's diary account of E.W.'s last days. There are 8 letters from Elisina Tyler to Berenson (1934–37) in *VT*, all referring to E.W.

William Royall Tyler gallantly transcribed passages touching on E.W. from several hundred letters between Elisina and Royall Tyler during the war years. With no less generosity, Mr. Tyler also transcribed passages from scores of letters (in the 1920s and 1930s) from his mother to Hayforth Peirce, an associate of Royall Tyler during the war, and a competent, self-taught Byzantine scholar. He showed me other documents of his mother's, as shedding further light on her personality, lent me a number of photographs, and added reminiscences and views of his own.

Tyler, Royall. About 70 letters from E.W. (1919–35) in *WRT*. Most of my knowledge of Royall Tyler comes from conversations with William Tyler and letters from him.

Royall Tyler also figures in Walter Muir Whitehill's *Dumbarton Oaks* (1967); and Michael Maclagan (see above) added valuable observations about his father's old friend.

Tyler, William Royall. A dozen letters from E.W. (1916–34) in *WRT*. About 80 letters from William Tyler to me (1967–74).

Updike, Berkeley. A very valuable memoir of E.W. in *PL*, mostly about the early years at Land's End and The Mount. One letter to E.W. (1913), about the divorce, in *BL*.

Leonard Baskin supplied me with a characterization of Berkeley Updike, and his own expert's appraisal of Updike's accomplishments in the art of printing.

Vanderbilt, Consuelo (Duchess of Marlborough; later, Mme. Jacques Balsan). Her memoir *The Glitter and the Gold* (1952) contains interesting glimpses of E.W.

Ward, Mary Augusta (Mrs. Humphry). Enid Huws Jones's recent biography, *Mrs. Humphry Ward* (1973), is a clear and compact account of her subject's life and career, and contains a genealogical chart of the descendants of Thomas Arnold of Rugby. It replaces the older biography by Janet Penrose Trevelyan.

Washburn, Emelyn. Two letters to E.W. (1934–35) in *WRT*, and 4 long and very important letters to Elisina Tyler (1938) in *WRT*, give bountiful information about E.W. from her adolescent years through her engagement to Harry Stevens and marriage to Teddy Wharton.

Wemyss, Lady Mary (formerly Lady Elcho). One letter to E.W. (1933) in *WRT*. Lady Wemyss's *A Family Record* (privately printed, 1932; no author given on title page) gives a moving account of the Elcho family life at Stanway in the Edwardian days.

Wendell, Barrett. Two letters to E.W. (1899, 1913) in *BL* and one to Morton Fullerton (1911). One letter to Lapsley (1913) and one letter to E.W. (1913), filed under Lapsley and touching on the attempted birthday gift to Henry James, in *BL*. One letter to Edward R. Wharton (1899), in praise of *The Greater Inclination*, in *BL*. There are 41 letters to Berenson (1901–20) in *VT*, with periodic references to E.W.

The standard life is *Barrett Wendell and His Letters*, by M. A. De Wolfe Howe (1924).

Wharton, Edward Robbins. One newsy letter of 1884 to his aunt, Mrs. Cleveland, in the Berg Collection of the New York Public Library, transcribed by Mary Pitlick. One equally informative letter of 1907 to Sara Norton, telling of the Whartons' arrival in Paris, in *BL*. Several letters to E.W. in 1910, from the sanatorium in Switzerland. The latter, on deposit in the Smith College library, exist in the German translations made by Dr. Binswanger or a member of his staff.

Four letters from E.W. (1911–12) in *BL*. These letters, mostly written at The Mount and delivered by hand to Teddy Wharton, exist in Anna Bahlmann's transcriptions. There is one not unimportant postcard about the state of his health to Mrs. William Vaughan (1909) in *LA*.

Medical letters relating to Edward R. Wharton's illnesses. In addition to 6 letters from Dr. Binswanger (see above), there are 3 letters (1910) from specialists in Paris and Switzerland in *BL*.

Wharton, Nancy. Five letters to E.W. (1909–10) in *BL*. One letter from E.W. (1910), in Anna Bahlmann's transcription, in *BL*.

Wharton, William Fisher. One letter from E.W. in Anna Bahlmann's transcription and the draft of another letter in E.W.'s hand (both 1911) in *BL*. William Wharton's public career can be traced in the Harvard Alumni archives.

White, Arthur. One letter to Berenson (1937), after E.W.'s death, in *VT*.

Whitlock, Brand. One letter to Robert Underwood Johnson (1924), urging the election of E.W. to the American Academy of Arts and Letters, in the Academy archives.

Winthrop, Egerton. Four letters to E.W. (1913), supporting her divorce proceedings, in *BL*.

III. Other Unpublished Sources

1. WILLS

The wills of George Frederic Jones and Lucretia Rhinelander Jones were procured by Mary Pitlick from the Probate Court records in New York, and those of William Fisher Wharton and Nancy Spring Wharton from the Probate Court records in Boston.

Edith Wharton's American and French wills are in *WRT*.

2. PROPERTIES

I had a variety of expert assistance in this area of investigation. Documents relating to the purchase of Land's End were procured in Newport by Paul Andrews. Those pertaining to the purchase, rental, and sale of the twin houses at 882 and 884 Park Avenue were acquired by Mary Pitlick, who also dug up details on Teddy Wharton's purchase of the Mountfort Street property in Boston in 1909. Information about the acquisition of the Lenox–Lee property on which The Mount was built was furnished by Kathy Wirkus, with the kindly help of the staff of the Lenox library. A description of the interior of The Mount, provided by Edward R. Foster, helped to clarify my own first-hand impressions.

To all these individuals, my warm appreciation. My thanks are also due to the staff of the Fox Hollow School in Lenox (to which The Mount currently belongs) for showing me blueprints for The Mount and garden plans.

I am extremely grateful to Sheila Vigano for permitting me to explore the Pavillon Colombe at my leisure.

3. PASSPORTS

Passport applications by Edith Wharton, Edward R. Wharton, Walter Berry, and W Morton Fullerton were courteously transmitted by the State Department archivist.

4. WAR ACTIVITIES

All the unpublished materials on Edith Wharton's refugee aid and other war work are in *BL*.

5. HONORS

Documents relating to the award to Edith Wharton of the Legion d'Honneur, including the citation and letters of congratulations, and to the Belgian decorations are in *BL*.

I am indebted to Mrs. Eloise Segal for making available documents concerning the awards to Edith Wharton by the National Institute of Arts and Letters and the American Academy of Arts and Letters, and Mrs. Wharton's election to those two bodies.

6. FINANCES

The 1888 bequest from Joshua Jones, with an analysis of his complicated will, was kindly given by Dr. Harrison Wood.

The firm of White and Case, in New York, courteously supplied (via Mary Pitlick) a mass of materials relating to the trust fund established for Edith Wharton under her mother's will and to the various transactions involving her New York properties.

Edith Wharton's literary earnings for the years 1904–14, meticulously inscribed by herself, are in an account book in *BL*. Her earnings from Appleton and Company between 1912 and 1934 may be calculated from her editors' letters to her during those years; they are also listed in toto by D. W. Hiltman, chairman of the Appleton board, in a letter to E.W. of July 25, 1934. Other information appears in letters from editors, American, British, and French, and her several translators *(FL* and *BL)*.

An account book of 1921, in *BL*, gives an indication of characteristic month-by-month household expenses.

IV. Other (Selected) Published Sources

A. EDITH WHARTON

Her discreetly revealing memoir of 1934, *A Backward Glance*, is of course the source from which the biographer begins. In addition, *BL* contains a 50-page fragment called "Life and I," which was intended to be the first section of *A Backward Glance*. Mrs. Wharton evidently decided it was too outspoken about her early development and deleted it. Among other matters, it includes the frustrating discussion with her mother just before her marriage.

Edith Wharton's *A Motor-Flight Through France* (1909), *Fighting France* (1915) and *In Morocco* (1920) are further important portions of autobiography. "A Little Girl's Old New York" describing the days of childhood and adolescence, and life in the Jones family household, appeared in the August 1938 issue of *Harper's*.

Comment on Percy Lubbock's *Portrait of Edith Wharton* (1947) may be found in my Preface and Chapter Twenty-seven, and comment on Millicent Bell's *Edith Wharton and Henry James* (1965) under Henry James in II, above. Grace Kellogg's *The Two Lives of Edith Wharton* (1965) is a dedicated work, based, however, on an insufficiency of materials.

Blake Nevius' *Edith Wharton: A Study of Her Fiction* (1961) remains the most cogent work of its kind, though it will soon be challenged by Cynthia Griffin Woolff's more psychologically oriented study. I have learned a good deal from Mr. Nevius' book, even if I have also learned, in the course of time, to disagree with parts of it. I am grateful to Mr. Nevius, in addition, for bits of biographical information in conversation and letters.

Louis Auchincloss's abundantly illustrated *Edith Wharton: A Woman in Her Time* (1971) crowds a good deal of information and wise commentary into a relatively short space. Mr. Auchincloss has also written several cogent and sympathetic essays on Edith Wharton.

It was Edmund Wilson's essay "Justice to Edith Wharton," in *The Wound and the Bow* (1941), that restimulated interest in her life. Wilson followed with an important and questioning review of Percy Lubbock's *Portrait* in 1947.

Anyone familiar with the writings of Erik Erikson, particularly *Identity: Youth and Crisis* (1968), will recognize their pervasive influence upon my account of the first four decades of Edith Wharton's life.

B. OLD NEW YORK

The titles under this heading, and the five headings that follow, are *in addition* to those mentioned in II, above.

Charles H. Crandall, ed., *The Season: 1882–1883*

Clarence Gohdes, "Driving a Drag in Old New York," *Bulletin of the New York Public Library*, Vol. 66, June 1962

Lloyd Morris, *Incredible New York* (1951)

Gustavus Meyers, *A History of the Great American Fortunes* (1904)

Samuel L. Shoemaker, *Calvary Church Yesterday and Today* (1936)

Nathan Silver, *Lost New York* (1971)

William Rhinelander Stewart, *Grace Church and Old New York* (1924)

Mrs. John King Van Rensselaer, *The Social Ladder* (1924)

Dixon Wecheter, *The Saga of American Society* (1937)

L. H. Weeks, ed., *Prominent Families of New York* (undated but 1901)

I am grateful to the always helpful and friendly staff of the New-York Historical Society, which, in addition to some of the titles above, contains the valuable Appleton's *Dictionaries of New York and Vicinity* for the 1870s and 1880s; early New York telephone directories; and many other useful memoirs, pamphlets, and historical studies. I am grateful as well to the New York Public Library, particularly its genealogical archives; and to the New York Society Library and the Frick Art Reference Library, both of which contain portraits of members of the Jones clan. My thanks are likewise due to the staff of the Americana section of the Columbia University library, for information about such graduates of Columbia as George Frederic Jones.

Dr. Harrison Wood, formerly of the Yale Medical School and an addict both of old New York and Edith Wharton, assembled for me a packet of relevant materials, including selections from *The Vanderbilt Legend*, by Wayne Andrews (1941); the *Diary of Philip Hone* (1828–51); and a history of the Chemical Bank of New York. Dr. Wood also supplied numerous bits of special information and suggestions. For all of this, I am deeply indebted.

C. NEWPORT, BAR HARBOR, AND LENOX

Cleveland Amory, *The Last Resorts* (1952) and *Who Killed Society?* (1960)
Maude Howe Elliot, *This Was My Newport* (1944)
George C. Mason, *Newport and Its Cottages* (1875)
Nancy Sirkis, *Pleasures and Palaces* (1963, with an Introduction by Louis Auchincloss)
Mrs. John King Van Rensselaer, *Newport: Our Social Capital* (1905)
David H. Wood, *Lenox: Massachusetts Shire Town* (1969)

I recall with much pleasure the gracious hospitality of Mr. and Mrs. Edward N. Foster in Newport in the summer of 1968, and the educational guided tour of the island they gave me.

I am grateful to the staff of the Redwood Library in Newport for pointing me to old Newport directories, early issues of *Town Topics*, the Newport *News*, and the Newport *Journal*, and other important sources. I record again my thanks to the staff of the Lenox library. Thanks also to Robert Wilhelm for putting me on the track of further information about old Bar Harbor.

D. PREWAR FRANCE

Jean d'Agrève, *La Societé parisienne de nos jours* (1908)
Alamanach de Gotha for 1908
Duc de Brissac, *En d'Autres Temps: 1900–1939* (1972)
René Escaich, ed., *La France politique et sociale de la "Belle Epoque," 1900–1914* (Les Cahiers d'Histoire, Jan.–Feb. 1969)
André de Fouquières, *Cinquante ans de panache* (1953) and *Mon Paris et ses parisiens* (1953)
James R. Mellow, *Charmed Circle: Gertrude Stein & Company* (1974)
Marquis de Rochegude, *Promenades dans toutes les rues de Paris par arrondissements* (1910)
Roger Shattuck, *The Banquet Years* (1958)
Barbara Tuchman, *The Proud Tower* (1966)

E. PREWAR ENGLAND

Samuel Hynes, *The Edwardian Turn of Mind* (1968)
Anita Leslie, *Edwardians in Love* (1972)
Robert Martin, *Jennie: The Life of Lady Randolph Churchill*, Vol. I (1969), Vol. II (1971)
J. B. Priestley, *The Edwardians* (1968)
Barbara Tuchman, *The Proud Tower* (1966)

F. THE WAR YEARS

In addition to standard historical overviews of the Great War, special mention should be made of Barbara Tuchman's remarkable account of military developments during the summer of 1914, *The Guns of August* (1962). Edith Wharton's *Fighting France* is the best English-language picture of Paris during the war.

G. THE LATER YEARS AND MISCELLANEOUS SOURCES

Frederick W. Allen, *Only Yesterday* (1931)
John Malcolm Brinnin, *The Sway of the Grand Saloon: A Social History of the North Atlantic* (1971)
Sylvia Brooke (Ranee of Sarawak), *Queen of the Headhunters* (1970)
Martin Green, *The Von Richthofen Sisters* (1974)
Lucy Kavalier, *The Astors* (1968)
Norman and Jeanne Mackenzie, *H. G. Wells* (1973)
Edmée de la Rochefoucauld, *Paul Valéry* (1954)

Let me also record my thanks to the staffs of the Harvard Alumni archives and the Massachusetts Historical Society.

V. Other Personal Acknowledgments

During the years of work on this book, I have incurred more debts than I can any longer be sure of remembering. But in addition to those persons mentioned in II and III above, I know my thanks are due, for particular information, to:

Harold Acton; Rolando Anzilotti; Simon Michael Bessie; John Morton Blum; Victor Brombert; Matthew J. Bruccoli; Reverend Albert B. Buchanan; Cora Champney; Colin Clark; Peter J. Conn; Daniel Corey; Arthur Crook; Ian Greenlies; Hugh Honour; Nelson Dean Jay; Grace Kellogg; Mrs. Marion King; Henry Adams La Farge; Mrs. Fredericka Rhinelander Landon; Richard H. Lawson; Claire Leighton; Walter Lippmann; Glenn Loney; Georgette Lubbock; Joseph P. McDermott; Mrs. Langdon Marvin; Jo Mielziner; Reverend Benjamin Minifie; Brother Patrick More; Umberto Morra; Elting Morrison; Richard Purdy; Henry Hope Reed; Charles Seymour Jr., Reverend Victor Stanley; Mrs. Katharine Warren; Arnold Whitridge; Edmund Wilson; Geoffrey Woolf.

In the Paris area, and beyond those referred to in II above, the following have granted informative interviews to Marion Mainwaring and me, or have kindly answered written inquiries: Duc de Brissac; Mme. Coderoy de Tiers; Mme. Beatrice Cuirot; Marquis de Ganay; Mary McCarthy; Roland de Margeries; Mme. Blandine de Prévaux.

VI. Special Acknowledgments

1. This book would not have been possible without the generous support of the John Simon Guggenheim Foundation in 1968–69 and of the National Endowment for the Humanities in 1972–73.

2. During the early stages of the work, I benefited enormously from long conversations with William Goodman. The late David Segal, my first editor, contributed much to the opening chapters. No thanks would be sufficient to my present editor, Marion N. Wyeth, for his tireless labors and key suggestions. I am scarcely less beholden to Armitage Watkins

for advice and encouragement. Herbert Fierst, counselor to the Edith Wharton estate, has been steadfast in his help.

3. Burroughs Mitchell gave me free access to the Scribners archives and library in New York, supplied a copy of *Fighting France,* and produced needed information on the sales of Edith Wharton's books and related matters.

4. Another attraction of the Villa I Tatti in 1972–73 was the almost daily presence of Ernest and Jayne Samuels, at work in tandem on the definitive biography of Bernard Berenson. Both gave me not only precious items culled from the Berenson papers, but highly suggestive insights into the characters we were mutually concerned with.

5. Among the early readers of my manuscript, Daniel Aaron, Judith Lindau McConnell, and Robert Penn Warren offered indispensable advice, as well as encouragement. I benefited particularly from conversations with Mr. Warren and his shrewd suggestions about my final section.

Norman Holmes Pearson, one of the ablest manuscript editors of our time, went through the work with devoted thoroughness. It has been immeasurably improved by his comments. Professor Pearson's knowledge of American social and literary history also proved invaluable.

To Louis Auchincloss, who also read the manuscript carefully and made detailed suggestions and corrections, I owe more than I can easily say. He began by lending me the portfolios identified earlier as *LA.* Since then our correspondence on E.W. matters has filled two thick folders. But Mr. Auchincloss's contribution goes beyond these important particulars to a steady and enthusiastic interest in the work, expressed in a stream of letters, telephone calls, and lengthy visits.

6. From the outset of this undertaking, Leon Edel has been unflaggingly helpful. With characteristic generosity and promptness, Professor Edel has answered a long series of inquiries over several years, has written in detail about several episodes or speculative matters, and has met with me for consultations about the Henry James–Edith Wharton era.

7. It will be evident from notations earlier in this bibliographical essay that I was privileged to be aided not only by "research assistants," but in certain cases by something closer to collaborators.

The extraordinarily productive work in France by Marion Mainwaring has been described in Appendix B. That description, however, does insufficient justice to Miss Mainwaring's painstaking research into many members of the Faubourg St. Germain before the First World War or to the skillful interviews mentioned in II, above. Miss Mainwaring also collected relevant books, documents, maps, photographs, and other important materials.

The contributions of Mary Pitlick, relating to the American phases of Edith Wharton's life, have been listed in earlier sections. But, again, that listing scarcely reflects the range of Miss Pitlick's participation in the work, which began in 1966. In 1969–70 a grant to her from the National Endowment for the Humanities—for which I was and am immensely grateful—made it possible for Miss Pitlick to devote full time to her collaborative task. Our frequent consultations have been extremely rewarding for me; and it was Miss Pitlick who periodically put my ever-expanding files in order. She is now preparing an edition of Edith Wharton's letters, a number of which she herself uncovered in various collections.

David Milch has been another *sine qua non* of this book. His practical assistance has been in the way of checking facts, procuring books, and Xeroxing materials. As grateful as I am for all that, I owe Mr. Milch even more for the wealth of suggestions he made out of his extensive literary, psychological, medical, and legal knowledge.

Professor Herwig Friedl, of the University of Heidelberg, during a year in the United States in 1973–74, dug up and made available to me a great many Edith Wharton letters from libraries other than those listed under "Major Collections" above. This erudite young man, who is writing his own book about Edith Wharton and American culture, also sharpened my understanding of a number of critical points.

The latter sections of my book owe a great deal to intensive conversations with Cynthia Griffin Wolf, of the University of Massachusetts in Amherst. Mrs. Wolff, as was mentioned earlier, is well launched on a psychologically oriented study of Edith Wharton's fiction, and I am bound to confess that my treatment of the later novels derives in good part from her perceptions. It was Cynthia Wolf who, to our shared incredulity, discovered the outline and fragment of "Beatrice Palmato," presented in Appendix C.

8. I would like to pay tribute to my mother, Beatrix Baldwin Lewis, whose powerful and accurate memory reaches back to the turn of the century, and to individuals in the New York and London societies among which Edith Wharton once moved.

9. My largest debt, and the one I am happiest to acknowledge, is to William Royall Tyler, owner of the Edith Wharton estate, and Bettine Tyler. Hints of Mr. Tyler's strenuous efforts on behalf of the enterprise have been given earlier; they have been far beyond any call of duty. On a number of occasions, at the Tylers' ambassadorial home in The Hague and at Dumbarton Oaks, Mr. and Mrs. Tyler have provided memorable hospitality. It should be stressed that at no time and in no way did Mr. Tyler seek to influence the biography. But his deeply interested and acute inquiries often led me to reconsider and sometimes revise certain narrative lines. To come to know Bill and Betsy Tyler has been an honor.

Index

Jewett *(cont'd):*
458–9, 466, 472, 474, 484, 488, 490, 504, 506–8, 524
Jewett, Sarah Orne, 81, 150
Joffre, Gen. J. J. C., 367, 379
Johnson, Robert Underwood, 269
Johnston, Lawrence, 489
Johnstone, Sir Alan, 437
Johnstone, Lady Nettie, 379, 437
Jones, Beatrix, *see* Farrand, Beatrix Jones
Jones, Colford, 21–2
Jones, Edward, 14
Jones, Edward Renshaw, 14
Jones, Frederic Rhinelander (Freddy), 5, 12, 17, 21, 26, 47, 51, 55, 58, 79, 332
death, 412
inheritances, 47, 59, 101
marriage, 46–7
Jones, George Frederic, 11–13, 15, 22–5, 458
attitude of Edith to, 24
Europe, 14–15, 17–19, 42–3
illness and death, 42–4
library, 28–9
marriage, 12
will, 47–8, 59
Jones, Henry Edward (Harry), 5, 15, 17, 21, 26, 36, 38, 50, 58, 136, 330–2
break with, 331–2, 355, 412
death, 447
engagement, 20–1
inheritances, 47, 59, 101
Paris, 46, 79, 165, 168, 191, 208, 258, 282
return to U.S., 210
trustee of Edith's estate, 273
Jones kin, 12–14
Jones, Joshua, 59
Jones, Lucretia Rhinelander (Mrs. George Frederic), 9, 10–11, 16, 22–4, 49
anti-intellectualism, 29
attitude of Edith to, 24
baptism of children, 5–6
death, 100–1
debut, 11
debut, Edith's, 33
distancing from, Edith's, 67–8
engagement of Edith to Stevens, 44–5
Europe, 14–15, 17–19, 43, 46, 79
marriage, 12
marriage of Edith to Wharton, 51, 53, 55
reaction to first story by Edith, 30
reflected in fiction, 24, 78–9, 326, 431, 458
sex and, 25, 50, 53–4
social life, 36–7
verses of Edith privately published by, 31
Jones, Mary Cadwalader (Minnie) (Mrs. Frederic R.), 5, 26–7, 39, 59, 82, 112–13, 173, 290, 356, 412, 431, 461, 522
aide to Edith, 300, 366, 371, 430
comment to on writing, 465
death, 519–20
financial aid to, 388, 428, 508

Jones, Mary *(cont'd):*
James, 146, 128, 144, 146, 166, 177, 314, 323, 340
Paris, 282
Roosevelt, Theodore, 391
visit to U.S., Edith's, 451–3
World War I, 366, 371, 384, 410
Jones, Mary Mason (Mrs. Isaac), 13, 21–2, 37, 431
Jones, Tecla (Mrs. Henry E.), 331, 447
journal ("Life Apart"), 184, 203–5, 207–8, 219, 224, 227–9, 235, 308, 526
journalism, World War I, 376, 378
Fighting France (Wharton), 376, 386
"Look of Paris," 378
Joyce, James, 8, 442, 468, 520, 525
Jusserand, J. J., 387, 390

Keun, Odette, 516
Kimball, Alonso, 182
King, Archibald Gracie, 33
King, Miss C., 5
King, Freddy, 407
King, John, 23
King, Le Roy, 197–8, 208, 227, 407
Kinnicutt, Dr. Francis P., 94, 267–8, 273–4, 292, 310, 316
Kipling, Rudyard, 241, 243, 299, 380, 382, 459
Knickerbocker Club, 36
Knight, Charles, 421, 427

Ladies' Home Journal, 435–6, 444, 458, 507
La Farge, Bancel, 291
La Farge, Christopher, 463
La Farge, Florence (Mrs. Grant), 170
La Farge, Henry, 291
Lafayette Fund, 406
Landormy, Renée, 368, 441
Land's End, *see* Newport
Lane, John, 89
Lapsley, Gaillard, 126, 137, 146, 317, 334, 360, 409, 433, 483, 517, 532
Berry biography, Edel's proposed, 501
on *Buccaneers*, 529
comments to on: America, 451, 453; authors and works, 331, 442, 456; deaths, 478, 481, 489, 494–5; destruction of garden, 487; family, 356; finances, 508; friends, various, 334, 425, 474, 499, 514; Hyères, 494; James, 382–3; memory lapses, 503–4; politics and state of world, 369, 374, 505, 519; return to U.S., 450; theater, 487; travels, 239, 515; writing, 332, 396
eroticism, 520
humor, sense of, Edith's, 324
James, death of, 382, 504
Hyères (Ste. Claire), 5, 461, 480, 493, 517, 529
James, gift for, 339–41
Lenox, 137, 312
Lubbock memoir of Edith, 515

Schopenhauer, 139
Schuyler, Loring, 458, 507
science and technology, interest and responsiveness to, 6–7, 56–7, 97, 108, 128, 182, 214, 228–30, 271–2, 504
Scotland, 517
Scott, Geoffrey, 345, 356, 381, 394, 463, 469, 474, 489
  Boswell papers, 475, 489
  death, 489
  marriage to Lady Sybil, 409–10, 439, 474
  North Africa, 357
  St. Brice (Pavillon Colombe), 439
  secretary to Edith, 379, 386
Scott, Lady Sybil, *see* Lubbock, Lady Sybil
Scott, Sir Walter, 28, 521
Scribner, Charles [*see also* Scribners (Charles Scribner's Sons); *Scribner's* (magazine)], 209, 214, 340, 445
  James advance, Edith and, 342–3
  Wharton works, 77, 113, 159, 180, 236, 311, 345–6, 393–6, 456–7
Scribners (Charles Scribner's Sons), 379
  James's publisher, 342–3
  Fullerton book, 346
  Gerould publisher, 250
  Sturgis novel rejected by, 141–2
  Wharton works, 78–9, 82, 87–8, 95, 98, 123, 180, 311–12, 456–7
  see also Brownell, William Crary; Scribner, Charles
Scribner's (magazine), 60–1, 65–6, 70–4, 81, 91, 95, 114, 123, 140, 218, 224, 253, 280, 297, 346, 395–6, 412
  serializations, 95, 144, 151, 164, 170, 181, 209, 308, 331, 457
  travel sketches, 107
  war article, 378
  see also Burlingame, Edward L.; Scribner, Charles
Sedgwick, Ellery, 507
Selders, Gilbert, 445
self-deprecation, 3–4, 31, 70–2, 74, 114, 297–8, 325
self-image (*see also* Temperament), 88, 93, 109, 134, 166–7, 192, 349–50
  fiction and, 104, 155, 164, 181–2, 424–5, 431–2, 464, 492–3, 524–6
Seneca, 236
Serristori, Countess, 374
sex, *see* Eroticism
Shaw, George Bernard, 241
Sheldon, Edward, 451–2
Sherman, Stuart, 433
Simmons, Ronald, 384, 411–12, 531
  death and memorialization of, 412, 428, 437, 441, 457
Sinclair, Upton, 151, 312, 504–5
Sitwell, Sacheverell, 499
Sketch for a Self-Portrait (Berenson), 268
Smalley, G. Co., 89

Smith, John Hugh, *see* Hugh Smith, John
Smith, Logan Pearsall, 269, 315–16, 329, 469–70, 485
snobbery, 53, 212
Snyder, Carl, 231
social awareness, 28, 58, 66–7, 104, 107
social life
  1870's, 20, 22–4, 29, 33–7
  1880's, 38, 40–2, 44, 47, 51–2, 54
  1890's, 68
  attitude toward, Edith's, 66–7, 84
  reflected in writing, 35, 42, 47, 431–2
  see also England; Paris; names of persons and places
Spain, 17, 318, 362, 494, 505
Spanish-American War, 6, 81, 139
Spencer, Herbert, 56–7
Spoon River Anthology (Masters), 393, 400
star-charting, 182
Stein, Gertrude, 440
Stendhal, 86, 90, 103–4, 106, 208, 230, 236, 521
Stephens, Leslie, 108
Stevens, Ebenezer, 8–10
Stevens, Henry Leyden (Harry), 37–40, 42–4, 52
  engagement to Edith, 44–7
Stevens, Marietta Reed (Mrs Paran), 36–7, 40–2, 51
  in *Age of Innocence*, 431
  engagement of son to Edith, 44–6
Stevens, Mary Fisk (Minnie), 37, 40
Stevens, Paran, 40, 45
Stevenson, Robert Louis, 54, 85
stories (*see also* Fiction writing), 13, 74, 95, 224, 310, 522
  "After Holbein," 13, 446, 523
  "Afterward," 296
  "All Souls," 523, 526
  "Angel at the Grave," 99
  "April Showers," 30, 71
  "Autres Temps . . . ," 333–4, 394
  Berry as literary counselor and critic, 85, 98–9
  "Best Man," 146
  "Blonde Beast," 296
  "Bolted Door," 237, 253
  "Bottle of Perrier," 522
  "Bread upon the Water," 507
  Certain People, 513, 522
  "Charm Incorporated," 407
  childhood "making up," 17–19, 531
  "Choice," 228, 233, 309, 394
  collections (*see also* titles), 87, 98, 131, 233, 296, 394, 513, 522
  "Coming Home," 394
  "Confessional," 98, 212
  "Coward," 81
  criticism, *see* Fiction writing, criticism; titles
  Crucial Instances, 98–9, 109–10
  "Cup of Cold Water," 81
  "Day of the Funeral," 522
  "Debt," 296
  Descent of Man, 123, 131–4